MISTRESS TO AN AGE

A LIFE OF MADAME DE STÄEL

BY

J. CHRISTOPHER HEROLD

Illustrated

HAMISH HAMILTON
LONDON

First published in Great Britain, 1959
by Hamish Hamilton Ltd
90 *Great Russell Street, London WC*1
© 1958 *by J. Christopher Herold*

PRINTED IN GREAT BRITAIN BY
WESTERN PRINTING SERVICES LTD BRISTOL

PREFACE

THIS work is not offered as a 'definitive biography'. In the first place, despite the impressive literature and documentation already published on Madame de Staël and her friends, a still larger mass of material remains unknown; in the second place, definitive biographies can be written only about people who are quite dead. Sometimes, to be sure, they still show some feeble signs of life, but the definitive biographer gives them the *coup de grâce*.

At the end of the last century, Lady Charlotte Blennerhassett wrote a splendid three-volume work on Madame de Staël which almost might have been definitive. It is an impressive work, and still a very useful one. It almost buried Madame de Staël. Madame de Staël's mother, who had an obsession about 'precipitate inhumations', hoped to escape that fate by having herself preserved in a basin of alcohol and visited daily by her husband; Madame de Staël herself, who observed on that occasion that this was not the way in which *she* proposed to be remembered, was much too alive to stay buried after Lady Blennerhassett had embalmed her. She never ceased to protest her untimely burial: long-hidden documents turned up, and still are turning up, still-living witnesses to her passions and to the passions she inspired; scholars re-read her works with a fresh eye for the vigour and originality of her intelligence; others, studying the lives of her great contemporaries who also were her friends and enemies—a Napoleon, a Byron, a Talleyrand, a Goethe, a Chateaubriand—constantly found her on their path and often enough let her divert them from it. Thus a new Staëlian literature sprang up, investigating special aspects and relationships and making public a number of revealing documents: letters, diaries, manuscripts, police reports, and the like. These aspects and relationships were, however, as manifold as the documentation was overwhelming, encompassing not only Madame de Staël's labyrinthine and astonishing love life but also the political and intellectual history of Europe from the eve of the French Revolution to the first years of the Bourbon Restoration, not to mention the literatures of several nations. Those who wrote on

Madame de Staël, if they wrote at all seriously, limited themselves to some specific aspect or relationship. When I began this work, enough had been published to convince me that a new synthesis was not only possible but also desirable; I therefore made it my task to write a general biography—not a definitive biography, which merely would bury Madame de Staël once again, and unsuccessfully at that, but a fully rounded one, which would restore her to life in the public mind.

To this conviction there soon was added another: to write an exhaustive account of Madame de Staël's life not only would exhaust the biographer's own life but also would require a kind of mind and temperament that had no affinity whatsoever with the type of intellect that was Madame de Staël's. Writing the present work was an exhausting enough task: but throughout it I felt sustained by an intellectual sympathy and a similarity of interests with the 'subject' of the biography. In my attempt to unravel and understand the life of her passions, I remained a fascinated spectator, always trying to understand yet refusing to be swept along; but in discovering her thought, I found myself an active partner in a conversation, a conversation in which I became aware, almost at first hand, of her supreme powers in that art, and in which she often helped me to find my own convictions, for which I had long been groping. Decidedly, Madame de Staël is not dead.

In my labours, a number of persons have assisted and obliged me—though not nearly as many, I regret to say, as I had hoped. Some of the persons who assisted me most were dead long before I was born—among them Mme Necker de Saussure, M. Sainte-Beuve, and others whose writings are listed in my bibliography. I am particularly indebted to them for the easy grace with which they put their materials and knowledge at my disposal.

Among the living, I am indebted first of all to the Comtesse de Pange, Madame de Staël's great-great-granddaughter, for the encouragement she gave me when I began my project, an encouragement without which I might never have pushed it very far; I am equally indebted to her, as are all Staëlian scholars, for her profound researches and for her liberality in making family documents available: no person has done more than she for the revival of Staëlian studies. I also wish to extend my most heartfelt thanks to Professor Donald M. Frame of Columbia University, who carried out a difficult mission at the New York Public Library with immense sagacity and precision; to Dr. John D. Gordan, of the New York Public Library, for giving me permission to use

Madame de Staël's unpublished letters at the Henry W. and Albert A. Berg Collection; to Professor Bengt Hasselrot of Uppsala, for his kind and warm encouragement and for producing, with miraculous speed and at a critical moment, a portrait of Eric Magnus Staël von Holstein; to Mr. Daniel Eaves, for drawing my attention to a virtually unknown portrait of Madame de Staël at the M. H. de Young Memorial Museum in San Francisco; to Mrs. Florence Yao Chu, of the Library of Stanford University, for her patient and efficient magic in obtaining books from libraries all over the world; to my wife Barbara, for putting up with Madame de Staël for five years and for typing five thousand pages; and to Mr. Stephen Zoll, my patient editor.

The late Professor Pierre Kohler of Berne, at the outset of my labours, gave me advice which proved extremely wise and helpful.

I feel an immeasurable debt of gratitude to the authors and editors of the following works, as well as to their publishers: E. Beau de Loménie, ed., *Lettres de Madame de Staël à Madame Récamier* (Paris: Domat, 1952); Georges Bonnard, ed., *Le Journal de Gibbon à Lausanne* (Lausanne: F. Rouge & Cie., 1945); Paul Gautier, *Madame de Staël et Napoléon* (Paris: Plon, 1903); Othenin, Comte d'Haussonville, *Le Salon de Madame Necker* (Paris: Calmann-Lévy, 1882) and *Madame de Staël et Monsieur Necker* (Paris: Calmann-Lévy, 1925); R. L. Hawkins, *Madame de Staël and the United States* (Cambridge: Harvard University Press, 1930); Pierre Kohler, *Madame de Staël et la Suisse* (Lausanne and Paris: Payot, 1916); E. Lavaquery, *Necker, fourrier de la Révolution* (Paris: Plon, 1933); Maurice Levaillant, *Une Amitié amoureuse: Madame de Staël et Madame Récamier* (Paris: Hachette, 1956); Jean Mistler, *Madame de Staël et Maurice O'Donnell* (Paris: Calmann-Lévy, 1926); Jean Mistler, ed., *Lettres à un ami* (Neuchâtel: A la Baconnière, 1949); J. E. Norton, ed., *The Letters of Edward Gibbon* (3 vols.; London: Cassell, 1956); Comtesse Jean de Pange, *Madame de Staël et François de Pange* (Paris: Plon, 1925), *Monsieur de Staël* (Paris: Editions des Portiques, 1931), and *A.-G. Schlegel et Mme de Staël* (Paris: Albert, 1938); Alfred Roth and Charles Roulin, eds., *Journaux intimes de Benjamin Constant* (Paris: Gallimard, 1952).

M. Georges Solovieff, in order to facilitate my work, has had the kindness to bring to my attention the existence of 150 hitherto unpublished letters of Madame de Staël to Narbonne, of which he is preparing a critical edition.

The present edition of this work contains a number of corrections. I am particularly grateful to Mr. Jesse G. Bell, Jr., for pointing out to me my many sins against the English language; to Professors Albert Guérard and Peter Gay, for protesting about several errors of fact or interpretation; and to Messrs. Hamish Hamilton and Roger Machell, for introducing further improvements. Any inaccuracies which may be left are due solely to my negligence or stubbornness.

J. Christopher Herold

December 9, 1958

CONTENTS

PART ONE

The Neckers

1. The Obscure Years of Monsieur Necker   3
2. The Romance of Suzanne Curchod   10
3. Madame Necker's Drawing Room   22
4. The Trinity and the Triangle   32

PART TWO

Love and Politics

5. Marriage and Emancipation   55
6. Revolution and Intoxication   76
7. Love and Politics   89
8. The Heartbreak and the Terror   116
9. Benjamin   132
10. 'This Miserable Gypsy Life'   147

PART THREE

Two Tyrants

11. Ideology   187
12. The Ideophobe Defied   212
13. Weimar, Berlin, and Fate   251
14. The Isle of Calypso   272
15. Corinne and Adolphe   299
16. Farce, Tragedy, and Histrionics   337
17. The Sword Beats the Spirit   376

PART FOUR

The Vanity of Human Wishes

18. Caliban   395
19. Defeat in Victory   410
20. Not the Port but the Grave   438

    Epilogue   461

    Bibliographic Notes   465

    Index   475

ILLUSTRATIONS

Madame de Staël and Benjamin Constant at Chaumont	*frontispiece*
	acing page
Jacques Necker	32
Suzanne Necker	33
Germaine Necker aged thirteen	64
Germaine Necker aged nineteen	64
Eric Magnus Staël von Holstein	65
Louis de Narbonne-Lara	65
Talleyrand	128
Mathieu de Montmorency	128
Benjamin Constant	129
Madame de Staël	160
Madame de Staël as Corinne	161
The Château of Coppet	288
Albert de Staël	289
Albertine de Staël	289
Auguste de Staël	289
Madame Récamier	320
Château of Coppet, grand salon	321
Château of Coppet, Madame de Staël's bedroom	321
Sismondi	416
Madame de Krüdener	416
Zacharias Werner	416
Louis Alphonse Rocca	417
John Rocca	417

Part One

THE NECKERS

That family of Madame de Staël's certainly is a strange one—father, mother, and daughter all kneeling before one another in perpetual adoration, smoking one another out with reciprocal incense for the edification and mystification of the public.

NAPOLEON

B

THE OBSCURE YEARS OF MONSIEUR NECKER

—————————

GERMAINE DE STAËL was the daughter of Jacques Necker. This was the salient fact of her life—from the day of her birth, which she credited almost exclusively to her father, to the day in 1817 when the Duc de Broglie deposited her body at the feet of her parents who were confidently awaiting the Day of Judgment lying side by side in a basin filled with alcohol. Above the portal leading into the monument Madame de Staël had placed, nine years before her death, an allegorical bas-relief. 'My mother takes my father by the hand,' she explained, 'to lead him to Heaven, and he looks down with kindness upon a kneeling figure shrouded in a veil.'

The veiled, kneeling figure is Germaine herself. Rarely was a life spent more publicly or proudly; yet even the proudest will cover their nakedness and bend their knee to worship at the altar. To Madame de Staël the distinction between her earthly and her heavenly father lacked definition.

Had she been told that, a century and a half after her father's death, it would seem advisable to explain to the reading public who Jacques Necker was, she would have been incredulous. She had spent her first twenty-five years hearing her father extolled by a continuous and near-universal chorus of hosannas; she had witnessed a nation rising in arms, tearing down a Bastille, and humbling a king, ostensibly for the sake of that father; quite understandably she entertained exaggerated notions of his greatness.

Idols are worshipped for their supposed magical powers. When they are no longer worshipped, it becomes apparent that they are puppets. Thus it happened with Jacques Necker. However, though no exception to that general rule, he holds in the history of idols a unique distinction: of all the men who achieved unlimited popularity, he was the only banker.

His origin was modest enough. Generations of obscure Neckers, most of them Lutheran pastors, had lived, bred, and died in Brandenburg and Pomerania. To be born into a Brandenburgian or Pomeranian pastor's family was not a key to wealth and honours, but it offered certain possibilities, provided some talent was present. A survey of the class origins of North German intellectuals in the eighteenth century would probably reveal a preponderance of pastors and pastors' sons. The career of Karl Friedrich Necker, Jacques Necker's father, followed a familiar pattern: a modest boyhood at Cüstrin; legal studies; a stroke of luck in the shape of an appointment as tutor and travelling companion to Count Bernstorff, son of the chief minister to the Elector of Hanover; some more good luck when the Elector ascended the English throne as George I; a gratuity of £200 per annum voted by Parliament, in return for which he was to direct a boarding school for young Englishmen in Geneva; appointment as professor of public law at the Academy of Geneva—in a word, glory.

Ever since the age of Calvin the tiny republic of Geneva has wielded an influence entirely out of proportion to its size. Yet, despite its cosmopolitanism, its society was tightly closed and by the eighteenth century its government had fallen into the hands of a jealous oligarchy. At the top of its rigid class system stood those who enjoyed full rights of citizenship; next came the 'burghers', whose children might aspire to citizenship. For a foreigner to purchase burgher's rights cost up to 21,000 florins: Karl Friedrich Necker obtained them gratis. The free gift was granted him in 1726 in recognition of his merits as a professor, but one suspects that his marriage in the same year to Jeanne Gautier, daughter of the First Syndic of the Republic, was not unrelated to the honour. Charles Frédéric Necker, as he now signed himself, became an accepted member of the Genevese élite.

He had two sons, Louis and Jacques. Louis, the elder, seemed at first destined to play a more brilliant part than his plodding brother. As a student he showed a decided bent for the sciences; upon graduation he followed in his father's footsteps, tutoring a number of German, Dutch, and English noblemen and travelling with them across Europe. Back in Geneva, he applied for the chair of mathematics at the Academy. Love won him the professorship; love was to make him lose it. 'All I wanted,' he wrote in comment upon his marriage, 'was to obtain the chair I had come to apply for, but others gave me to understand that a wife would be suitable for me. I approved of this idea; Mademoiselle André pleased me; she also pleased my parents;

we asked for her hand; I was fortunate enough to obtain it. . . . This young lady is pretty and has an amiable character and a very handsome fortune.'

She continued to please him for several years but died in 1759, leaving Louis Necker bereft of legal marital solace. The pastor Vernes, a man of worldly tendencies and a friend of Voltaire, had a brother who on the subject of sexual morality entertained outdated notions. In 1760 Louis was consoling himself for his widowerhood with the wife of the pastor's brother, when her husband surprised them and, with evangelical zeal, emptied his pistol into the mathematician. The affair created some stir: Louis had to make amends on his knees before the assembled Consistory and lost his professorship.

To sleep with a Calvinist pastor's sister-in-law and to be shot at by her husband was enough to make a man a hero and a martyr. Louis's interrupted adultery won him the immortality of a laudatory mention in the letters of Voltaire, who was gleefully watching the proceedings in Geneva from neighbouring Ferney. Packed off to Paris to join his brother Jacques, Louis thus arrived in the capital with the best recommendations; as a compatriot of Rousseau, a man of science and of sensibility, and a victim of fanaticism, he was assured of a respected place among the philosophic coterie. Instead, however, he followed his brother's advice, went to Marseilles, and shortly afterwards became a millionaire. A few years later, having purchased the estate of Germagny or Germany, near Lausanne, Louis Necker styled himself Monsieur de Germany, presided over the banking house of Germany & Girardot, and married off his son into one of the most distinguished families of Geneva, the de Saussures.

What was the secret of this miraculous rise?

If one muses over the business mores of eighteenth-century France, one cannot escape the impression that in order to make a million or two a man merely had to give himself the trouble of picking them up. The ethics of finance were so far removed from all pettiness and triviality that even a man of the strictest principles could operate quite freely within their bounds, and the opportunities were virtually unlimited. Speculation—on government papers, on grain prices, even on royal lottery tickets—presented so little risk, thanks to the abundance of tips, leaks, indiscretions, and other means of correcting chance—that it hardly deserved the name. A treasury that was chronically on the brink of bankruptcy, combined with a disarmingly corrupt administration, allowed the widest latitude to anyone who could lend capital, float loans, or create credit. On the agony of the public treasury private finance grew healthy and fat.

Side by side with unbridled greed in all classes there persisted, by sheer inertia, a medieval prejudice against treating money as a commodity: the taking of interest, though always practised on a small scale, still fell under the ban of the Church, and as a result France had no banking system of its own. It was with the Paris branches of the Protestant banking houses that modern French finance originated. Among these houses, the Dutch and Genevese were foremost. Given the opportunities of the time, every shaveling errand-boy in a Genevese bank was a potential Rothschild.

Jacques Necker left school at the age of fifteen to enter the bank of Isaac Vernet as a clerk. His services were satisfactory; after two years his modest salary was doubled and he was transferred to the bank's Paris branch. To be eighteen and freshly arrived in Paris—especially the Paris of Louis XV—is a combination of circumstances that offers many temptations; but Jacques Necker's temperament was not of a sort to make him waste the best years of his life in enjoying them. The gaming tables, the actresses' dressing rooms, the Palais-Royal, and the other places of perilous delight failed to attract him; nor did his thoughts turn towards love or marriage; he even renounced whatever feeble literary ambitions he may have had; instead, he devoted himself to the task of making himself indispensable to Monsieur Vernet. Whether or not his singular devotion to the manipulation of credit and securities represented a great sacrifice is a matter of conjecture. In later years, when he reached glory, he affected disdainful boredom towards the lowly activities of the counting house; the fact remains that for a quarter of a century he imposed upon himself the rigorous discipline of mere money-making.

The peace negotiations of 1762–3, which ended the Seven Years' War, gave Necker the opportunity to lay the foundations of his fortune. A mystery shrouds the operation by which, through a judicious purchase and sale of French and English treasury bonds, Necker made his first millions; certain it is that his partner in the operation, a highly placed official in the French foreign office who had supplied him with the political intelligence needed to make the speculation successful, subsequently spread the rumour throughout Paris that Necker had hoodwinked him and pocketed the entire profit—a small matter of 1,800,000 livres. However, it would be a mistake to apply twentieth-century business ethics to eighteenth-century practices. Except for a few eloquent dissenters, subsequent historians agreed that, no matter what qualities Necker may have lacked, honesty was his outstanding virtue.

Once in the current, Necker was to drift fast from million to million. The wheat famine of 1764 and the liquidation of French holdings in Canada were golden opportunities in this best of all possible worlds. The latter transaction, which is said to have netted him a 30 per cent profit, found some critics, yet even the most virulent was constrained to admit that the operation was not an outright swindle.

Isaac Vernet had retired in 1762; his nephew and successor, Thélusson, gave Necker a 25 per cent interest in the firm; three years later, Necker assumed the sole direction of the bank, while Thélusson took over the London branch. Necker was thirty-two years old. He could look back with some satisfaction on his achievement, but his ambition was not satisfied; nor did he aim, as would a lesser man, at a mere doubling or tripling of his millions. He wanted glory. To this, financial power was an indispensable means, but by itself it was not enough—not, at any rate, in the France of the 1760's. If he wanted to exercise his genius in broader and nobler fields, he had to enlist two forces—society and public opinion. These were ruled by women. Like his brother Louis, who had to marry in order to obtain a professorship, Jacques Necker realized that 'a wife would be suitable' for him.

Necker by 1764 had won a respectable position in the world of finance, but he was little known outside banking circles, the treasury, and the Swiss colony in Paris. The man who was to govern France in her most fateful crisis was still a social nonentity, an unostentatious millionaire who lived and dressed modestly, kept no mistress, wrote no books, was never seen in any important salon, consorted mostly with fellow Genevese, and showed no resentment when the Controller General of Finance, the abbé Terray, addressed him with familiar cynicism as 'my dear usurer'. His genius, as yet undiscovered by the *philosophes*, *littérateurs*, and journalists, was only beginning to be discovered by himself. One suspects that the following portrait, written by his wife shortly after their marriage, was only partly meant in jest:

> Picture to yourself the most humourless fellow in the whole world, so completely persuaded of his own superiority that he does not even see mine; so convinced of his own powers of penetration that he is ever being cajoled; so certain that he possesses every talent in the highest degree of perfection that he does not look elsewhere for instruction; never astonished at the littleness of others, because he is always enveloped in his own greatness; ever comparing himself to those about him

so that he may have the pleasure of seeing that no comparison is possible;
confounding men of parts with the ignorant because he thinks himself to
be placed upon a mountain, and that all creatures inferior to himself
must be on the same level below him; preferring fools also because he
thinks they make a more striking contrast with his own sublime genius;
and with all this as capricious as a pretty woman.

Vanity was Necker's outstanding defect. Nowhere is it more pitilessly
portrayed than in the bust Houdon made of him at the apogee of his
career: the haughty angle of the nose, the half-closed eyes whose gaze
seems to brush past the top of an imaginary interlocutor's head in order
to contemplate some profundity midway up in the air; and the com-
placently ironic smile that turns the lips up in what is almost a smirk.
Withal, a slightly grotesque appearance: enormous chin, forehead receding at an angle of forty-five degrees, and a pyramidal way of doing
his hair that was the astonishment of his younger contemporaries. His
conversation consisted for the most part of a profound and absent-
minded silence; his writings betray a lack of education and a certain
inarticulateness which has been unjustly blamed on his native Genevese
idiom. But Necker's career reached its flowering in an age when men
had become tired of quick-wittedness, which had come to seem an almost banal quality, and when it began to be assumed that slowness and
inarticulateness were the symptoms of a deliberate, profound mind.
Hence the great reputation of the English. Lack of education could be a
positive asset, particularly in a man who was qualified to speak on
economics by his practical experience in money-making. And eccentrici-
ties in behaviour and coiffure merely confirmed a man's emancipation
from an artificial conformity. However, since he lived in an age when
the silence of genius might easily pass unnoticed amid the fireworks of
conversational virtuosity, it was indispensable that someone less restrained should draw attention to his qualities.

Perhaps these considerations held some place in Necker's mind when,
in the summer of 1764, he cast himself in the unfamiliar role of a lover.
The first object of his attentions was a young Protestant lady, the
beautiful Germaine de Vermenoux. The widow of a Swiss officer and a
relation, by marriage, of Necker's partner Thélusson, Madame de
Vermenoux possessed wit, charm, money, and social connections.
It was in vain, however, that Necker sought to conquer her heart.
Madame de Vermenoux had no desire to sacrifice her independence,
especially to Necker, who made her yawn. Thus it happened that she
frequently excused herself on some pretext and left Necker alone with

the governess of her young son, a Swiss girl of twenty-seven, Suzanne Curchod.

There is no record of what was said in the tête-à-têtes between Monsieur Necker and Mademoiselle Curchod. Undoubtedly their conversation always remained on a chaste and elevated plane. After some prodding, Necker declared that his happiness depended on her. In December they were married, and only after the ceremony was over did the young couple break the news to Madame de Vermenoux. Madame de Vermenoux had lost a suitor and a governess, but she was not inconsolable: 'They will bore each other to death,' she commented succinctly; 'at least, it will give them something to do.'

2

THE ROMANCE OF SUZANNE CURCHOD

'WHEN God had finished creating Madame Necker, he stiffened her with starch inside and out.' This pronouncement by one of Madame Necker's contemporaries even her most devoted admirers could not entirely deny. One may say that Suzanne Necker made of her virtue a necessity for others. But to conclude from her cold and affected rigidity that hers was not a passionate soul would be a serious error. From her idyllic girlhood in the Jura mountains to her bizarre entombment by the shores of Lake Geneva, her life was spent in a state of sustained emotional hypertension. Madame de Staël, who at the bottom of her heart detested her mother, took after her in this and other ways.

Suzanne Curchod was born in 1737 at the parsonage of Crassier, a village in the foothills of the Jura in what is now the canton of Vaud. Like Necker, she came from a family of pastors; like Necker, who in the middle of his life discovered ancestors in Irish royalty, she claimed a noble descent. Her ancestors were French Huguenots; her family undoubtedly had ties with the petty nobility. Still, even at the height of her power, when the Court of Versailles humbly paid court to her, her persistent attempts to secure legal recognition of her noble status remained frustrated. Noble or not, the Curchod family was beyond all dispute poor. Suzanne was brought up at home. Her father, who must have had a dash of that eccentricity so common in his age, gave her an education suited for a Leonardo da Vinci. At sixteen, Suzanne was a fluent Latinist, knew some Greek, was well-versed in mathematics and the natural sciences; played the harpsichord and the violin; and painted. She was, moreover, a beauty, and by no means unaware of it.

Understandably enough, the parsonage of Crassier became a popular gathering place for young ministers of the Gospel. They practised their sermons before the father and their compliments before the daughter.

The poems they addressed to her make one suspect that even then Suzanne was as receptive to bold suggestions as she was reluctant to satisfy them. One swain, after commenting appreciatively on her eyes, breasts, features, and complexion—which to him 'announced yet other charms'—concludes his stanza with the lines:

> But your ceaseless moralizing
> Which forever is my bane
> Spoils all the joys I am devising—

a complaint her admirers were to repeat for forty years.

The attentions of amorous Calvinists may have been flattering, but Suzanne regarded them as mere rehearsals for a vaster stage. 'As you sat upon a chair,' one of them reminisced, 'you leaned forward with a condescending air, which showed plainly enough how poorly you thought of their conversation, and that you were yourself thinking of something much more interesting.' Something more interesting turned up in 1757, when she was twenty.

Suzanne at that time had begun to make frequent trips to Lausanne. Apart from being the nearest city, Lausanne presented a unique blend of attractions, not only to daughters of country parsons but also to a cosmopolitan *élite* which was making it a favourite meeting place. Perched on its hills above the serene expanse of the Lake of Geneva, surrounded by vineyards and facing the snow-clad peaks of Savoy, Lausanne combined cosmopolitanism with small-town sociability. Its eight thousand inhabitants were ruled with a firm but paternal hand by the bailiff representing Their Excellencies, the councillors of the Republic of Berne; under his watchful eye, each man was free to express the most liberal opinions, provided he entertained no idea of acting on them. Though it had eclipsed Geneva as a fountain-head of Protestant theology, Lausanne lacked the constricting rigour of Calvin's city, and its pastors were ready to reconcile dogma with the enlightened temper of their time—which is to say that they gave up dogma altogether. Lausanne society, drawn largely from the gentry and nobility of Vaud, had an easy-going bonhomie all its own, a slightly mocking playfulness and dash that gave it character and style.

Among the remarkable features of Lausannois social life was the freedom and simplicity of the relations between young people of both sexes. Forming associations with such poetic names as 'Academy of the Waters' and 'Society of Spring', the young people would meet, without chaperones, for the purpose of such amusements as dancing, flirting, and the discussion of interesting topics: 'Is love really made sweeter to us by reason of its mystery?' 'Can the same kind of friendship exist between a man and a woman as between two men, or two women?' 'Which of all the pleasures is the most delicate?' Innocent pastimes, one might surmise—and, on the whole, be right. Yet among the childhood reminiscences of some who grew up in Lausanne about that period there are also memories of stupendous laxity in sexual matters. Suzanne's chastity cannot be suspected, but there hovered above the Academy of the Waters a certain erotic ambiguity.

Suzanne Curchod not only frequented the Academy of the Waters; she also became its president under the name of Thémire. It was no doubt during that period that she perfected the stiff and precious artificiality that marked her conversation and correspondence ever after; but she had not yet lost the gaiety which must have made these qualities endurable or even attractive. And yet, at twenty, she was still unmarried. Surely there was no lack of suitors, even though she had no money: but Suzanne Curchod had set her aim high. At last, in June 1757, she met a young man who seemed worthy of her. 'He has nice hair,' she wrote of him, 'a pretty hand, and the appearance of a man of good birth. His expression is so singular and so intelligent that I do not know anyone who is like him. . . . The variety of his mental acquirements is prodigious.'

The young man thus described was known in Lausanne as Edouard de Guibon; it was thus he affected to sign his name, but he is better known under a different spelling as the author of the *Decline and Fall of the Roman Empire*. It was, indeed, difficult to meet anyone quite like him.

Of the same age as Suzanne, young Gibbon had been packed off to Lausanne in 1753, after his escapade into Roman Catholicism. Two years later, he could write to his aunt, 'Dear Madam, I have at length great news to tell you; I am now a good protestant & am extremely glad of it', but in fact he had effectually rid himself of all religion and was dividing his time between prodigious studies and the pleasures of society. French had become his second language, and Lausanne had won his heart: he was to spend a large part of his life there.

Gibbon had heard a great deal of Suzanne Curchod before he met her. 'The wit, the beauty, and erudition of Mademoiselle Curchod were the theme of universal applause,' he recalled in his memoirs. 'The report of such a prodigy awakened my curiosity; I saw and loved.' In his diary, he noted, under the date of June 1757: 'I saw Mademoiselle Curchod, *omnia vincit amor et nos cedamus amori.*' He permitted himself 'to make two or three visits to her father's house' and 'passed some happy days there, in the mountains of Burgundy, and her parents honourably encouraged the connection'.

Suzanne reciprocated his feeling. Not that she experienced any tempestuous passion; it would be unusual for an unmarried girl of twenty to fall in love entirely without practical objectives, and an English gentleman of birth and means was a desirable choice even without prodigious mental acquirements. Physically, no one would seem more ill-cast in a romantic role than Edward Gibbon, but at twenty he had not yet grown grotesque. A miniature portrait made of him at that age does, it is true, show a younger edition of the triple-chinned and jowly baby face that Sir Joshua Reynolds immortalized twenty-two years later; however, the nose is still clearly discernible, and his phenomenal cheeks have not yet reached the rotundity of later years. Nor had he acquired that legendary corpulence which on one occasion, when he had fallen on his knees to woo a lady, was to prevent him from rising up again, so that a servant had to be summoned to his aid. Still, even at twenty, his pudgy cheeks, his tiny mouth, and the bags under his eyes were not made to inspire passion. To Suzanne Curchod, this made hardly any difference; love to her was a purely intellectual activity. Gibbon's gentle manners, lively spirits, dazzling conversation, and formidable intellect, joined to the advantages of his birth, made him a partner worthy of the president of the Academy of the Waters and presaged a brilliant career in whatever field he chose.

There could, of course, be no formal engagement without the consent of Gibbon's father, whom Gibbon failed to inform of his marriage plans. In April 1758, Gibbon *père* ordered his son back to England. It was, presumably, only in August that the subject of Mademoiselle Curchod was raised by the son. On August 24, Gibbon wrote to Suzanne the letter which has become famous in the annals of male priggishness: 'I cannot begin! And yet I must. I take up my pen, I put it down, I take it up again. You perceive at once what I am going to say. Spare me the rest.' Yet he does not spare her the rest, proceeding instead, for several pages, to turn the knife in the wound. His father had made it plain to him that if he wished to marry 'his foreigner', he was free to do so on his income of £300 per annum, but that by so doing he would put his father into the grave prematurely and trample underfoot his duties as an Englishman. 'I withdrew to my room, I stayed there for two hours. . . . I went out to tell my father that I would sacrifice all the happiness of my life to him.'[1]

In one of his autobiographic fragments Gibbon recalled his decision with these well-known words: 'The romantic hopes of youth and passion were crushed . . . by the prejudice or prudence of an English parent. I sighed as a lover, I obeyed as a son.' His studies, he noted elsewhere, were sometimes interrupted by a sigh breathed towards Lausanne, but 'the pleasures of town life, the daily round from the tavern to the play, from the play to the Coffee-house, from the Coffee-house to the Bagnio,' did much to console him. When it came to his equanimity in supporting losses, Gibbon was indeed engagingly frank. 'Some natural tears were soon wiped,' was his comment on his mother's death; and on his father's timely passing: 'The tears of a son are seldom lasting.' And, again, of Suzanne Curchod: 'The remedies of absence and time were at length effectual.'

Two more opposed temperaments than those of Gibbon and of Suzanne Curchod could be imagined with difficulty only. 'The first indispensable requisite for happiness,' Gibbon wrote towards the end of his life, 'is a clear conscience, unsullied by reproach or remembrance of an unworthy action. . . . I am endowed with a chearful temper, a moderate sensibility, and a natural disposition towards repose.' No one had a less moderate sensibility than Suzanne Curchod, nor was anyone less inclined towards repose. Her reply to Gibbon's extraordinary letter runs to about eight hundred words with practically no punctuation; it is a desperate, chaotic, pathetic document. Still, through the genuine accents of an almost crazed soul, there pierces some calculation, too: '. . . now I wish to have some news from you sometimes, the interest I shall take—but above all I ask you for a prompt reply to this letter, you will find an address in the envelope, the Geneva post office will perhaps make me languish less long'—and thus indeed a short-lived

---

[1] J. E. Norton, ed., *The Letters of Edward Gibbon*, I, 106. The letter is dated from Beriton, August 24, 1758. An unknown hand changed '1758' to '1762'. Until recently the later date was generally accepted as the correct one by Gibbon's biographers, and Count Haussonville, in *Le Salon de Madame Necker*, even assumes that this was the only letter Gibbon wrote to Suzanne during his absence from Lausanne in 1758-63 (he wrote at least five). It would indeed have been inexcusable for Gibbon to wait for four years to write to his fiancée and then to announce that he could not marry her. The actual course of events was definitely established by Miss Norton in her monumental edition of Gibbon's *Letters* (1956), I, 391-401. See also Georges Bonnard, ed., *Le Journal de Gibbon à Lausanne* (1945), pp. 281-304. All earlier accounts are based on a misreading of the date and hence unfair to Gibbon.

correspondence developed which may have given her some justification in hoping that Gibbon's decision was not final.

Gibbon returned to Lausanne on May 25, 1763, almost six years later, and immediately threw himself into a whirl of activities—dances, cards, theatrical performances, courting a married lady referred to in his journal as 'the little woman', riotous parties with fellow Englishmen, and—one wonders when—his usual prodigious studies and readings. He had been in Lausanne for less than a week when a letter from Suzanne reached him:

> Sir:
>
> I blush at the step I am taking, I would like to hide it from you, I would like to hide it from myself. Is it possible, great God! that an innocent heart should abase itself to this point? . . . No matter—I am carried away against my will. I owe this effort to my peace of mind; if I do not seize the opportunity that presents itself, there will be no more peace for me. Could I taste this peace, if my heart, so inventive at self-torture, convinced itself that your apparent coldness merely proved your delicacy? . . . I beg you on my knees to release my crazed heart from its doubts. Sign the complete admission of your indifference, and my soul will become reconciled to its fate. Certainty will give me the repose for which I long. You would be the most contemptible of men if you refused this act of frankness, and the God who can look into my heart, and who loves me no doubt, although he makes me pass through the most painful ordeals—this God, I say, will punish you despite my prayers if there is the least dissimulation in your answer, or if by your silence you toy with my peace.
>
> If ever you betray the secret of my unworthy demand to anyone, even to your dearest friend, the horror of my punishment shall be the measure of my fault: I shall regard myself as guilty of a dreadful crime of whose atrocity I had not been aware. Already I begin to feel that I am committing an ignoble action which outrages my modesty, my past conduct, and my present feelings.
>
> Geneva, this 30th of May

Suzanne's letter could figure very plausibly in one of her daughter's novels.

Gibbon set her mind at rest. His reply is lost, but its content can be guessed from Suzanne's rejoinder, dated June 4, and from a remark he made in later years: 'A matrimonial alliance has ever been the object of my terror rather than my wishes.' However, he offered Suzanne his friendship, and she accepted it.

It was only in this second letter, of June 4, that Suzanne mentioned her parents' death to Gibbon. No doubt he had been informed by others of this circumstance, and he must have known under what difficulties she was earning a living. After her father's death in 1760, she and her mother had moved to Geneva, where she supported herself by giving private lessons to children; by the standards of the time, this was heroic conduct for a young girl of good looks and good family. Her obligation to work for a living was regarded as a misfortune rather than a disgrace; she was received in the best houses and much sought after; she still might have found a husband without difficulty. However, Suzanne had kept her suitors in suspense, still waiting for something better to turn up, perhaps still waiting for Gibbon to return, and venting her growing bitterness and frustration on her ailing mother; the domestic life of the two women must have borne a close resemblance to hell. In January 1763, four months before Gibbon's return, Madame Curchod died, leaving Suzanne penniless and in a paroxysm of self-reproach that marked her character for the rest of her life.

Suzanne was in a state of nervous prostration when one of the former divinity students who had studied Suzanne's divinity at Crassier came to her rescue. He was the pastor Moultou, of Geneva, whose children she was teaching, and who took her into his house when her mother died. Moultou became her trusted friend and protector. He also happened to be well acquainted with Voltaire (he used to take Suzanne to visit the Patriarch of Ferney every Saturday), and he was one of the few intimate friends of Rousseau; all in all, a pastor of liberal tendencies, more *philosophe* than clergyman. It so happened that Moultou was visiting Rousseau at Môtiers, near Neuchâtel, when Rousseau showed him a letter announcing the possible visit of a young Englishman named Gibbon. Moultou told Rousseau the sad story of Suzanne and asked him to intervene with Gibbon on her behalf, which Rousseau promised to do. On May 31 Moultou returned to Geneva. On June 4 Suzanne wrote to Gibbon: she accepted his offer of friendship, agreed that 'there should be no more mention of this old story', and concluded by offering Gibbon a personal introduction to Rousseau.

Perhaps Gibbon smelled a rat; at any rate, he did not go to Môtiers. Even if he had gone, it would have done Suzanne little good, for on the very day she was writing to Gibbon, Rousseau wrote to Moultou: 'Mr. Gibbon is not my man; I cannot believe that he is Mademoiselle Curchod's. A man who cannot sense her worth is unworthy of her; but a man who has been able to sense it and then detaches himself from her deserves contempt. She does not know what she wants; that man serves her interests better than does her own heart.'[1]

If Moultou showed Rousseau's pronouncement to Suzanne, it had no effect on her. Nor had Gibbon's reply of June 23: 'Mademoiselle, must you still now offer me a happiness which reason forces me to forgo? I have lost your love; your friendship remains mine, I cannot hesitate in accepting such an honour. . . . But this correspondence, Mademoiselle—I appreciate all its agreeable qualities, but at the same time I sense all its danger. . . . Allow me to avoid it through silence.' If Gibbon intended this to be the last letter that was to pass between him and Suzanne, fate and Suzanne decided otherwise.

On the evening of August 4 or 5 well over a hundred guests were assembled in Voltaire's private theatre at Ferney to watch the sixty-nine-year-old sage impersonate Genghiz Khan in his *Orphelin de la Chine*. Both Gibbon and Suzanne happened to be in the audience. The final curtain came down at half-past eleven. Then, says Gibbon, 'the whole company was asked to stay and sat down about twelve to a very elegant supper of a hundred covers. The supper ended about two; the company danced till four, when we broke up, got into our coaches, and came back to Geneva just as the gates were opened.' It was the first time Gibbon had come face to face with Suzanne since he had left her in 1758. What passed between them (at the supper table? or during the dance?) may be gathered from a letter Suzanne wrote to him on September 21, after letting her fury rankle for six weeks. 'I was so intimidated and crushed at Ferney by your continuous display of false gaiety and by the harshness of your replies that my trembling lips absolutely refused to serve me.' With playful indifference, he had accused her of duplicity, of flirting with other men while writing heartbroken letters to him. 'You said, though in different words, that you blushed for me because of the part I was playing. . . . Allow me to retrace my conduct.' This Suzanne does over several pages, bitterly, pathetically, and sarcastically in turns. She ends up by thanking God for preserving her from marrying such a monster:

> Yes, I begin to believe it: you would have resented my existence; it might have interfered with your ambition for wealth or fame, and your ill-disguised regrets would have led me through despair to the grave.

---

[1] When Gibbon read this letter a quarter of a century later in Rousseau's published correspondence, he was understandably upset. 'That extraordinary man,' he wrote in 1789, 'whom I admire and pity, should have been less precipitate in condemning the moral character and conduct of a stranger.'

Should I blush at having written to you, you hard-souled man whom once I thought so tender? . . . My conduct, you say, contradicts my words. And how, if you please? I acted toward you as one would act toward any gentleman—a man who is incapable of breaking a promise, of seducing or betraying—and you in return have been pleased to tear my heart to pieces by the most nicely contrived and most admirably executed tortures. I shall therefore no longer threaten you with celestial punishment—an expression that once escaped me on the impulse of the moment—but I can assure you now, without having a gift for prophecy, that you will one day regret your irreparable loss in discarding forever the too loving and too open heart of

S.C.

To female self-righteousness Gibbon opposed male self-righteousness:

I have received a most unexpected letter [he wrote in his diary on September 22]. It is from Miss C. A dangerous and disingenuous woman! With this air of candour that reigns in your letter, those honest and tender feelings you parade, I felt some regret and almost remorse. . . . She was amusing herself at Lausanne without forming any attachments. So be it. But these amusements nevertheless convict her of the most odious dissimulation, and while infidelity may at times be mere weakness, duplicity is always a vice. It was in July 1758 that she wrote to me from Crassier this strange letter, full of love and despair, her eyes filled with tears, her health weakened by sorrow. In the same month of July she was in Lausanne full of health and charm . . . tasting of all the pleasures, founding academies, distributing prizes, composing literary works, and playing at love if she was not making it. . . . This singular affair has, in all respects, been very useful to me. It has opened my eyes to the character of women, and it will serve me for a long time as preservative against the seductions of love.

Gibbon returned to his studies and amusements, but in mid-February of 1764 his peace was disturbed by the arrival in Lausanne of Mademoiselle Curchod. She stayed until April 5, and Gibbon met her almost daily—at suppers, parties, theatricals, and even tête-à-tête. As he noted in his diary, she 'gave herself over furiously to her taste for pleasure'. They talked 'with all the freedom of casual acquaintances'; they 'jested quite freely about [their] past affections'; but at times they felt disturbing flutterings: 'It's all the pure love of angels with her, but my senses were stirred, and hers too were not entirely at rest.' At a performance of Voltaire's *Zaïre*, Gibbon observed her sobbing ostentatiously; 'however, when she removed her handkerchief, all that could be seen was a fresh and rosy face, without a trace of tears. . . . How that girl plays at sensibility!' On the eve of her return to Geneva, he called on her: 'We chatted in a jesting tone, which I redoubled without difficulty in order to make her feel that I looked on her departure with indifference. This sentiment is not feigned. Time, absence, and above all my knowledge of the false, affected character of that girl have extinguished the last sparks of my passion.'

It may seem strange to find Suzanne flitting from party to party, from play to play, for weeks on end, during a period in her life when, according to her letters and reminiscences, she was earning a living as a governess, abandoned by her lover, bereft of her mother, and brokenhearted on account of both. A man of moderate sensibility like Gibbon could draw only one conclusion: Suzanne Curchod was insincere. Yet this ambiguity was to run through her entire life—was, in fact, to run through the life of her daughter, or it would not be worth noting here. It was not so much insincerity as self-dramatization. And self-dramatization is the mechanism by which a hypersensitive temperament can develop a toughness that is denied to more thick-skinned souls. It is the mechanism which allowed Suzanne to spend thirty years by the edge of her private abyss without ever falling into it, steeling herself in an interminable succession of nervous crises that never prevented her from pursuing her social obligations and ambitions. Just so Germaine de Staël would be able to indulge in paroxysms of grief over the loss of one lover at the same time as she energetically pursued another, spent nights discussing philosophy, brought up her children, kept a sharp eye on her business transactions, meddled in politics, and produced book after book. Such a diversity of simultaneous absorptions, passionate, intellectual, domestic, and financial, is possible only to the most rugged constitutions and can be kept up only at the expense of the nerves of others, who lack the actor's talent of slipping in and out of roles at will. To the Gibbons of this world such souls are dissembling, and their sufferings are not to be believed. That Suzanne Curchod could, within the same day, touch the bottom of despair and shine in society without doing herself any violence seemed to Gibbon impossible, and yet there can be no doubt that this was so.

Though still under the impact of her mother's death and her lover's treason, Suzanne had by no means given up the world. Much in demand in society, she had formed friendships far above her rank, notably with the Duchesse d'Enville, and such friendships made it difficult for her to accept her station. As in the days at Crassier, she still was waiting

for 'something more interesting'. As in the days of Crassier, there was
no lack of marriage offers. The most serious candidate was a Monsieur
Correvon, a lawyer in Yverdon, with whom she corresponded for several
years. She never exactly turned him down, for, after all, the 'something
more interesting' might never turn up, and Monsieur Correvon had to
be kept on ice for such an eventuality; but she succeeded in prolonging
the negotiations by stipulating rather extraordinary conditions—e.g.,
that she should not be obliged to live at Yverdon with her husband for
more than four months of the year. These negotiations were still in
progress when Suzanne received an interesting offer of another sort.

Madame de Vermenoux had come to Geneva to consult the most
fashionable medical man of the time, Dr. Tronchin. She was pretty, a
widow, young, and delicately ailing, and it thus seems entirely fitting
that she should have taken lodgings with the susceptible pastor Moultou. Shortly after Suzanne's return from Lausanne, Madame de Vermenoux announced her intention of going back to Paris; she needed a
tutor for her eight-year-old son and a companion for herself; would
Suzanne accept the position at 400 francs a year? Moultou encouraged
her to accept; in June 1764, Madame de Vermenoux and Suzanne left
for Paris.

After two weeks in Paris, Suzanne had spent some 240 francs for
'dresses, bonnets, etc.' 'I am in the greatest embarrassment,' she reported to Moultou. 'I cannot, as you very truly say, leave Madame de
Vermenoux without acquitting all my obligations to her; and to do that
I must marry in spite of myself and against all my inclinations. I cannot
bear to think of it, and yet I would sooner do this than continue to play
my present part, for I am being ruined for things which are pitiful to
think of.'

To get married—but with whom? She had not a penny, she did not
know Paris, she was twenty-seven years old, and—as Gibbon had
already noted—she was apt to antagonize the women and to frighten
the men. The Duchesse d'Enville, on hearing of her impending move
to Paris, had written to Moultou: 'I am glad that Mademoiselle Curchod
has found a position, but I doubt she will be as happy here as she was in
Geneva. Simplify her if you want her to succeed! She won't get anywhere either with her metaphysics or with her coiffure: for God's sake,
simplify her!' But to simplify Suzanne Curchod was beyond human
power. For a marriage, this was hardly a promising combination of
circumstances. Small wonder that, when Jacques Necker appeared, it
was love at first sight.

Still, Monsieur Necker was not a man to commit himself without making thorough inquiry; in this particular case, he even made a trip to Switzerland to obtain first-hand reports on his beloved's reputation. Suzanne trembled. 'Without a miracle,' she wrote to Moultou, 'I give up all hope of success.' She was prepared for the worst: 'If our castle in the air should tumble down, I shall marry Correvon next summer.'

In December Suzanne had her man. It was only then she informed Correvon. 'I see very clearly,' the disappointed suitor wrote by way of felicitation, 'that you looked upon me as a miserable makeshift.' Nevertheless, he forgave her for marrying a man with an income of 35,000 livres a year. 'With that, you will no longer need help from anybody.'

On the evening before the marriage ceremony, Suzanne sat down and wrote a *billet-doux* to her bridegroom: 'Oh my Jacques, my dear Jacques, never ask me to express my feelings, let me enjoy my happiness without thinking,' she began, then proceeded to expound her feelings and to think over several pages. 'When I contemplate my bliss, I fear that it may escape me, and I cannot think of the sweetness of life without foreseeing the moment when it must end. The anguish of my heart and the funereal images by which it is agitated might prevent me from satisfying you.' Strange language for a bride! Her words are the first signs of Madame Necker's incessant preoccupation with her own death, of the necrophilia that thirty years later was to lead her into her vinous tomb. The rest of the letter is no less remarkable: 'Yes, my friend, you are the chain that unites me with the universe. . . . My dear friend, you must never tire of a feeling which my heart makes inexhaustible. Let the instant of my death be the supreme moment of your love, and it will be the most beautiful day of my life.'

Thus began the marriage that all Europe was to admire as a model of marital virtue and bliss.

3

MADAME NECKER'S DRAWING ROOM

ADAME DE STAËL, the only fruit of this marriage, had on the subject of paternity some singular ideas. Writing of her father after his death, she expressed regret at not having met him long before she was born, because in marrying him she would have found happiness. This was by no means the only arresting thought Madame de Staël expressed on her father. On another occasion, when both her parents were still alive—in the summer of 1790—Edward Gibbon was the Neckers' guest in Switzerland. Gibbon had but recently and vicariously seen the declining Roman Empire come to its final fall, and Necker had still more recently presided in person over the liquidation of the French monarchy. Comparing the historian's awesome mind and jowl with the fallen minister's phenomenal wattles and virtue, she could not help speculating. 'He was in love with my mother once and wished to marry her. When I look at him, I ask myself if I could have been his daughter, and I answer, no. Only my own father could have brought me into the world.'

In reality, it was Madame Necker who gave birth to Madame de Staël, and a rude shock it was to her. The event took place on April 22, 1766, in the midst of one of Madame Necker's severe, prolonged, and frequent nervous prostrations. Like her wedding, her pregnancy turned her thoughts to her favourite topic, death, and filled her with terror. Her father, the good pastor of Crassier, had given her a very complete education, but a discussion of obstetrics was not a part of the curriculum; nor had the Academy of Waters, when analysing the more refined aspects of love, gone into the sordid details to which this noble passion so often serves as prelude. Reporting on her ordeal, Madame Necker gave vent to her indignant surprise:

> I confess that my terrified imagination fell far short of the truth. For three days and nights I suffered the tortures of the damned, and Death was at my bedside, accompanied by his satellites in the shape of a species

of men who are still more terrible than the Furies, and who have been invented for the sole purpose of horrifying modesty and scandalizing nature. The word *accoucheur* still makes me shudder. . . . The revolting details of childbirth had been hidden from me with such care that I was as surprised as I was horrified, and I cannot help thinking that the vows most women are made to take are very foolhardy. I doubt whether they would willingly go to the altar to swear that they will allow themselves to be broken on the wheel every nine months.

Madame Necker never allowed herself to be broken on the wheel again. But the tortures of childbirth were only the beginning of her maternal tribulations. By ill luck, Anne Louise Germaine Necker happened to be born four years after the publication of Rousseau's *Emile*, and her mother resolved to bring her up according to his teachings. The first item in the programme was breast feeding, a pastime that had become very fashionable in the highest society. Madame Necker heroically offered her celebrated bosom to her daughter, but after 'withstanding all the pains and tortures of that condition for nearly four months', she was informed that Germaine was starving, and 'with bitter regret' she desisted. A big Flemish girl took over. 'I do not leave her out of my sight,' reported Madame Necker. 'She is very pretty and loves to chatter.'

In fact, Madame Necker never trusted anyone to bring up her daughter. 'Governesses,' she noted, 'have always one great disadvantage; if they are qualified for their calling, they intercept the child's affection for its mother. What I should like is a simple Protestant chamber-maid, gentle, pliable, and educated, who can read with perfection and who is well-versed in her religion.' Despite her numerous inquiries, this pearl could never be found. To be sure, a nursemaid was hired, 'excellent as far as physical care is concerned, reliable, gentle, and virtuous—but stupid, Catholic, uneducated, and clumsy.' The really unforgivable sin was to be Catholic, an affliction which, through the fault of Louis XIV, was the lot of the overwhelming majority of French nursemaids. Madame Necker put up with it so long as she felt that Germaine's intelligence was immune to the corruptions of Popish superstition, but when Germaine was two years and five months old the time was ripe for a change.

With the same heroism with which she had addressed herself to breast feeding, Madame Necker resolved to undertake her daughter's education singlehanded. It had taken only four months of breast feeding before the doctors had warned her that Germaine was starving to death; it was to take thirteen years of selfless devotion to her daughter's mental and spiritual welfare before the doctors announced that Germaine had suffered a nervous and physical breakdown and had to be taken away from her.

Germaine was twenty-nine months old when Madame Necker, who had *Emile* but not the Bible in her library, ordered a copy of the latter treatise, along with a catechism and other 'books of devotion that I might need for the instruction of my little one, who is beginning to speak and to understand'. It was about the same time that the family gave up their spacious but unfashionable house in the Marais, which was contiguous to Necker's offices, and moved into a sumptuous *hôtel* in the rue de Cléry. The move was symbolic of an entirely new direction in the Neckers' life.

To Germaine the first steps in Necker's ascent could hardly have been significant. Her parents' trip, in 1767, to Lausanne and Geneva merely meant that she was left alone with her Flemish nurse. To Necker it meant his appointment, a few months later, as minister of the Republic of Geneva to the Court of Versailles—a modest enough diplomatic post, but a decisive step towards his transformation into a statesman. Necker's appointment in 1769 to the directorship of the French India Company established his reputation as a financial administrator and gave him vast scope to exercise patronage; but to his daughter it merely meant that her father became less visible than ever and that he was preoccupied, tired, and important. When she entered her fifth year, there could be no more question that her father was the best and greatest man in the world.

The central plant where Monsieur Necker's reputation was manufactured was situated in Madame Necker's drawing room, and in this drawing room Germaine grew up. Until her twelfth year she never had a playmate, but she was on familiar terms with Diderot, D'Alembert, Gibbon, and Buffon. Madame Necker had laboured for four years to make her salon supreme in Paris, and by 1770 her victory was complete. Her earliest recruits were in the second rank of fame, but they were well chosen: Suard, whose influence as a publicist and critic was beginning to make itself felt; Marmontel, the abbés Raynal, Galiani, and Morellet, all zealous missionaries of the philosophic creed; Grimm, whose *Correspondance littéraire*, subscribed to by the monarchs of Germany, Scandinavia, and Russia, was the most exclusive and distinguished literary news-letter in history; and the poet Thomas, now forgotten but then held to be the equal of Young and Thomson, now also forgotten. It took Madame Necker four years to capture her biggest prize. In 1765 Diderot wrote to his mistress, Sophie Volland: 'There is a Madame Necker here . . . who raves about me. She is subjecting me to a regular persecution to lure me to her house.' By 1769 he succumbed. Still, the final sanction was wanting: Madame Necker had not yet succeeded in getting Voltaire to correspond with her. To be truly admitted into the Church, such a correspondence was *de rigueur*.

On April 17, 1770, Madame Necker achieved, by one brilliant stroke, her victory over Voltaire. Grimm reported the event to his subscribers: 'On the seventeenth of the month past there has been held at Madame Necker's an assembly of seventeen venerable philosophers; in the course of which, after having made the prescribed invocations to the Holy Ghost and eaten a copious dinner, and talked nonsense on a number of subjects, it was resolved by unanimous vote to erect a statue in the honour of Monsieur de Voltaire.'

Madame Necker, included in the count of the 'seventeen venerable philosophers', was the prime mover of this project and acted as secretary to the subscription committee. The well-known statue by Pigalle was the result. How could Voltaire resist? He addressed verses to her, christened her Hypatia, and corresponded with her regularly for the eight years that remained to him. His praises, however, usually contained a grain of irony, and his comment on his sittings for Pigalle lacks reverence: 'When the people in my village saw Pigalle unpacking the instruments of his trade, "Hey, look at this," they said, "he's going to be dissected; it will be fun." '

Madame Necker decided to have her day of the week, as did the other queens of the salons, but she avoided competition. A *philosophe* never had to eat at home except on Fridays and Saturdays; he could go to Madame Geoffrin's on Mondays and Wednesdays, to Helvétius' on Tuesdays and Thursdays, and to Baron Holbach's on Sundays. In January 1770, Grimm announced that 'Sister Necker wishes it to be known that she gives a dinner every Friday. The Church will accept, because it thinks very highly of her, and also of her husband. It were to be wished it thought equally well of her cook.' The Church, it may be added, was pleased also at the prospect of eating their Friday dinners at a Protestant household, where the fast was not observed.

It was a strange choice Madame Necker had made in playing hostess to the philosophic party—a notably irreligious, blasphemous, and libertine assembly. But though her choice was contrary to her high moral and religious principles, it was perfectly natural in every other respect. The *philosophes* constituted the best-organized and most eloquent publicity agency that Providence ever put at the disposal of an ambitious politician. They were the press, they were public opinion, they were the teachers of kings; no single group of intellectuals ever held such power before or since.

Madame Necker saw to it that strict decorum was maintained. Since (as the abbé Morellet noted disapprovingly) the mistress of the house was 'averse to licence in religious opinions', the subject was generally avoided. At times it happened that somebody forgot himself, and Madame Necker would burst into tears. As a result, the gatherings at the Neckers' lacked the freedom and ease that could be found at the house of Baron Holbach. Even Galiani, who carried on a rather bold flirtation with her, speaks of 'the sublimity of your too glorious transcendentalism'. It was the diminutive and irrepressible abbé Galiani who one evening stated, with disarming cynicism, the real reason for the success of the Neckers' salon: 'I recollected,' he wrote to Madame Necker in 1771, 'that fearful and ever memorable evening when I was declared a monster because I dared say what everybody else thought. I said that I liked men only for their money, and Monsieur Necker is rich; I said that I liked women only for their beauty, and you are pretty.'

Virtuous though she was by common consent, Madame Necker did not renounce flirtation. The flutterings Gibbon had mentioned began to stir anew each time they met; Galiani and Buffon were permitted to risk some daring compliments; and Thomas adored her jealously, silently, and romantically.

Of all the descriptions of the Neckers' Fridays, Galiani's is perhaps the liveliest:

> A Friday does not pass [he writes to Suzanne from Naples] but I go to you in spirit. I arrive, and I find you one minute adjusting your dress; the next minute you are lying on the *duchesse*. I seat myself at your feet. Thomas groans to himself silently; Morellet storms with passion; Grimm and Suard laugh heartily; and my dear friend Creutz [the Swedish ambassador] notices nothing. . . . Dinner is announced. We go out; the others eat meat; I abstain. But while I am admiring the ardour with which the abbé Morellet cuts up the turkey, I eat so much of that Scotch green codfish . . . that I get a fit of indigestion. We rise from the table and drink our coffee, everyone speaking at the same time. The abbé Raynal agrees with me that Boston and English America are forever separated from England; and at the same time Creutz and Marmontel

agree that Grétry is the Pergolese of France. Monsieur Necker thinks it is all very well; he inclines his head and goes away.

The account agrees with Madame Necker's own observation on her Fridays: 'As for me, I always listen, but I am nearly the only one who does. Monsieur Necker neither talks nor listens, but he amuses himself by sucking his thumbs.'

Monsieur Necker's silent thumb-sucking, as well as his absentminded entrances and exits, were generally regarded as symptoms of profound and intensive preoccupation with affairs of state. No man was pronounced a genius by the sharpest of minds of his time with less effort on his part.

If there was anyone besides Madame Necker who listened rather than talked, it was her daughter. Every Friday, Germaine took her place beside her mother's chair, sitting very straight on a small wooden stool, her large eyes fixed on the speakers. 'It was something to see how Mademoiselle Necker listened,' a witness reminisced years later. 'Her eyes followed the movements of those who were speaking, and they seemed to anticipate their ideas. She did not open her mouth and yet she seemed to take her turn in the conversation, so much expression was there in her mobile features.'

Germaine was six years old when her father ceased to be a banker and became an economist, author, and philanthropist. The step consisted in selling his interest in his bank to his brother Monsieur de Germany and in proclaiming that henceforth only the public wealth was to occupy his thoughts. According to Madame Necker, he left the management of his entire fortune to her. Needless to say, she was well advised, and Monsieur Necker lost nothing by it. Thanks to his publicity organization and to his own well-timed writings (of which more in a later place), his name was on everyone's lips when, in 1776, Turgot was forced to resign as Controller General of Finance. A trip to London, which Necker made in the company of his wife and daughter in the spring of that year, may or may not have had the purpose of winning financial support from the English banks; certainly, one month after his return there poured into France the copies of a newly founded newspaper, the *Courrier de l'Europe*, published in London, which savagely attacked Turgot and, in later years, sedulously praised Necker.

The publicity bore fruit: Louis XVI appointed Necker Assistant Controller General in 1776 and, in the following year, placed him at the head of the country's financial administration. Since foreigners could not sit in the council of ministers, and since to be naturalized Necker would have had to abjure his Protestant faith, he was given the title Director General of Finance, with direct access to the King but without membership in the cabinet. This anomalous position in fact strengthened his power since he had the King's private ear while the other ministers could work with the King only in council. The Controller General's office corresponded not only to the ministry of finance but also, to a large degree, the ministry of the interior. Since it was generally recognized that only financial and administrative reform could save France from ruin, it clearly fell on Necker to perform this miracle. This he boldly promised to do, and France was at his feet.

On her wooden footstool, Germaine sat in the navel of the universe and gazed upon her father's halo.

The Neckers had moved into the residence of the Controller General, but except for this Germaine's life was unchanged. Madame Necker, though the wife of a minister, was still her daughter's governess. Despite the demands of her salon, her charities, her household, and her precarious health, she could not abandon her daughter's education to a stranger; only a Necker possessed the necessary virtues to bring up a Necker.

Madame Necker, by some astounding feat of self-delusion, imagined that she was bringing up her daughter according to the teachings of Rousseau—'like Emile', she wrote. A greater contrast than the education Rousseau prescribed for Emile and the education Germaine received from her mother would be difficult to imagine.

Rousseau, it may be recalled, had Emile brought up in the country, isolated from the corrupting influences of society. Germaine spent her childhood in a drawing room in the middle of Paris. Emile's tutor avoided any kind of formal instruction, seeking instead to let his pupil learn only through direct experience and guiding him in the spontaneous development of his natural gifts. 'For Madame Necker, all education consisted in instruction,' we are told. 'She taught Mademoiselle Necker Latin and English, and she made her copy long extracts from books; but she never spent one hour alone with her in familiar conversation.'

Emile had not yet learned to read when Germaine had read a whole library. Emile's tutor reserved the idea of God for the end of his pupil's education; Germaine learned her catechism before she was three. Emile did not know of the existence of women until he was an adolescent; Germaine had listened to discussions of love from infancy on.

Emile's body was made strong and healthy by open air and exercise; knowledge and love of nature were the only discipline in his curriculum; and nature was his only textbook. 'The education of Mademoiselle Necker,' a childhood friend reminisced, 'was directed entirely towards the development of the mind. Exercise, walks, everything that pleases and fortifies children did not in the least enter into Madame Necker's plans. And so her daughter knew how to dance, but not how to run. She recited Thomson's *Seasons* but could not tell a hyacinth from a tuberose.'

There is one more striking contrast between Germaine's education and Emile's. Rousseau had Emile brought up not merely in solitude but away from his parents. 'Oh, Emile hadn't any father,' he said to Boswell. 'He didn't exist.' He knew, of course, that Emile's education was an ideal model rather than a practical possibility; but surely there is a middle ground between being brought up without parents and being, in a sense, married to them, as Germaine was. Her emotional involvement with her mother and father was the most decisive factor in her formation.

That Germaine was starving for affection was only too obvious. 'Madame Necker loved her daughter tenderly,' says the witness already quoted. 'I had a thousand proofs of it. But she made no serious attempt at getting to know her. Duty was for her a religion which interfered with all her feelings; her maternal love was righteous rather than spontaneous.'

Germaine herself, in her novel *Corinne*, drew a ferocious caricature of her mother, whose least pleasant traits she transferred to her fictional Lady Edgermond:

> She liked to make others' lives as drab as possible, perhaps so as not to feel too much regret at the dissolution of her own. But since nobody admits the personal motives of his opinions, she founded hers on the general principles of an exaggerated morality. She never tired of taking all joy out of life by making the least pleasure a subject of reproach and by prescribing some duty to make up for every hour employed in any activity that differed from the day's routine.

Duty and sacrifice were the great words in Madame Necker's vocabulary. So was love. But one suspects that to her the three words were synonymous. As a result, her manifestations of maternal affection were indistinguishable from icy showers. She restrained not only her own affection for her daughter but also—and this was worse—her daughter's affection for her.

It was bad enough to be brought up with Calvinist strictness at the headquarters of the *philosophes*; it was perhaps still more confusing to be denied love while love was in everybody's mouth. Love was analysed at Madame Necker's gatherings. Love was the subject matter of the novels Germaine was beginning to read in her early teens. ('The elopement of Clarissa,' she writes, 'was one of the events of my childhood.') And not only of novels. At eleven Germaine was already a regular theatregoer. Racine, Richardson, Rousseau were the three *R*'s of her sentimental education.

Sensibility ruled the age. Germaine was violently stirred by the intense, the almost neurotic cult of emotion that was in the air—all the more so perhaps since she knew nothing of sexual love until her marriage. Madame Necker hoped to cultivate her daughter's sensibilities—but genteelly, and the emotional intensity that Germaine's affection both gave and demanded must have frightened her. At any rate, she slapped it down.

When Germaine was thirteen, she wrote to her mother, during one of her absences:

> My dear Mama, I want to write to you. My heart is drawn tight; I am sad; and in this large house, which only a few days ago contained everything that was dear to me, in which my whole world and my future were confined, I see now only a desert. I see now, for the first time, that this great space is too large for me, and I run into my little room, so that I need not see the void that surrounds me. This short absence makes me tremble for my destiny.

Madame Necker reacted thus:

> Your style is rather high-flown. Do not go so much beyond yourself to praise and caress me. This shows a want of taste, common enough at your age. When one has lived longer one sees that the true way to please and to interest people is to describe one's thought exactly, without affectation, and without display. . . . Your letter to your father was simple and nicely written.

No doubt Madame Necker was right—the style was high-flown—but it sat ill on her to make this reproach, her own epistolary style being as twisted and affected as any. If she suspected that Germaine's feelings for her father were more genuine than for herself, she was right, too: indeed, the fact was becoming embarrassingly obvious. But Germaine's desperate attempts to break through her mother's starch were genuine enough, even if her methods were disingenuous. 'I have discovered,' Madame Necker wrote to her husband, 'that she used to feign coughing fits, to which she was subject, that she might enjoy better the warm affection I showed her.' Now it is true that later in her life Germaine resorted to fainting fits, threats of suicide, and other spectacular devices in order to achieve much the same purpose, though not with her mother. The victims of these demonstrations did not take to them more kindly than Madame Necker had. Perhaps they would have been right if they had blamed Madame Necker for them.

The coughing fits were Germaine's last attempt in a desperate cause: indeed, it was at that time that Germaine's mind and body rebelled against her mother's regime. She fell seriously ill, in fact showed signs of a manic-depressive state—periods of languor alternating with nervous excitement. Dr. Tronchin, who had settled in Paris, was called in. His verdict: complete rest, no mental effort whatever, complete freedom, residence in the country. Madame Necker, though deeply shocked to be rewarded with such ingratitude after thirteen years of unstinting sacrifice and devotion, complied. Her part in Germaine's education was ended. Henceforth, their relationship was not that of mother and daughter but of two rivals, and in the bitter, secret struggle it was the younger and more vigorous who triumphed.

Madame Necker's education stamped her daughter for life, but not in the manner she had intended. Years later, when Germaine had for some time been outshining her mother, her admirers thought they were paying Madame Necker a compliment when they gave her credit for her daughter's accomplishments. 'It is nothing,' Madame Necker sadly replied, 'absolutely nothing beside what I had hoped to make of her.'

4

THE TRINITY AND THE TRIANGLE

GERMAINE NECKER was in her twelfth year when her mother decided that she needed a companion. The attributes required for the honour of playing with Mademoiselle Necker were so many that no girl answering the description could be found in all Paris. In fact, the entire French nation seems to have been regarded by Madame Necker as untrustworthy—excelling, no doubt, in all those activities that should be ruled by taste, wit, and manners, but wanting in seriousness, a sense of duty, and, above all, moral elevation, which cannot be attained outside the Reformed Church. France was a country that must be loved; but in all serious matters such as morals and finance it should be ruled by Genevese. From Necker's nomination as Director General of Finance in 1777 to the outbreak of the Revolution twelve years later, a remarkable influx of Genevese and Lausannois could be observed in Paris. Most of them found their way to the Neckers' house, and although Germaine spent her entire childhood in France, she never was allowed to forget that she was apart from the society she lived in: Protestant, republican, and heir to the sober virtues of Geneva.

Among the Genevese who flocked to Paris in 1777 were Madame Huber, a girlhood friend of Madame Necker's, and her thirteen-year-old daughter Catherine. Madame Necker, satisfied that Catherine 'had received an austere education in the bosom of a family whose strictness of principles was well known to her', decided that she was worthy of becoming Germaine's playmate. Catherine left an account of their first meeting:

> She [Germaine] was small for her age; her complexion was swarthy; her huge eyes dominated and illuminated her face. Her long chestnut hair[1] was gathered under a small bonnet; she was laced in whalebone and wore a very simple dark dress.

[1] Her hair later turned black.

JACQUES NECKER
After a portrait by Joseph Sifrède Duplessis

SUZANNE NECKER
From an engraving at the Musée Carnavalet

When she saw me, her face lit up, her eyes sparkled. The pleasure of seeing a companion of about her age filled her with a joy she could scarcely contain, and when her mother said to her, 'Minette, here is the friend I am giving you,' she kissed her hands and looked at me ecstatically. . . . All confused, and blushing crimson, I lowered my head. Madame Necker gently lifted it by the chin, kissed me on the forehead, and said to me, 'Go, my dear girl, and become acquainted with my daughter in the garden.'

Mademoiselle Necker took hold of my hand, and no sooner had we passed the threshold than she flung her arms around me and told me that she had been waiting for me for a long time, that she was sure that she would love me until she died. . . .

In the garden Germaine asked Catherine at once what she was studying, what foreign languages she knew, whether she often went to the theatre. When Catherine said she had been to the theatre three times in her entire life, Germaine was amazed. She promised that they would go often; after each play they would write down what they remembered and what had impressed them most: her mother insisted on it. Catherine was delighted. 'It will be just like when I come home from church.'—'It's curious how similar it is!' exclaimed Germaine. 'I too make summaries of the sermons I hear. Oh, what fun we shall have! How happy we shall be! We must write to each other every morning.'

These effusions were interrupted by dinner. 'No sooner had Germaine taken her accustomed seat than four or five old gentlemen approached her and spoke to her with the most solicitous interest. One of them wore a little round wig; he took her hands into his, kept them for a long time, and began conversing with her as if she were twenty-five years old. That man was the abbé Raynal.' More guests came after dinner, and Catherine was astonished to see that each new arrival in the drawing room, after greeting the hostess, paid his compliments to the daughter or jested with her, 'depending on the degree of intimacy on which he was with Monsieur and Madame Necker'. Germaine answered them with the utmost poise. 'Often, while her mother led the general conversation, Mademoiselle Necker presided over her own particular one. The guests delighted in attacking her and embarrassing her with questions above her age. . . . Madame Necker, so severe in other respects, approved of their interest in her daughter. . . . She looked upon this as on a sort of intellectual gymnastics.'

But when, on the following morning, Catherine's mother offered to

c

take Germaine and Catherine for a drive in the Bois de Boulogne, Madame Necker was struck dumb at the boldness of such a proposition. Germaine, in her twelfth year, had never gone out of the house without her mother. 'Her maids, her secretary, who were present, stared in surprise. Madame Necker debated the matter in her mind, in utter silence, while her poor child trembled in fear and hope. . . . At last, after a moment of general consternation, the great favour was granted.' Madame Huber promised to return at six in the evening, and Germaine, excited by the prospect of this high adventure—or rather of the first moment of freedom in her life—spent the afternoon at the window overlooking the courtyard and refused to eat her dinner. When, at last, Madame Huber returned, Germaine, with pounding heart, had to endure a long admonitory lecture by her mother on the subject of carriage doors, the safest way of stepping down from a carriage, and the dangers of traffic in the Bois de Boulogne, before she could race down the stairs and throw herself into the perilous vehicle. 'She could not speak, so intense was her emotion, and she kept kissing my mother's hands and throwing her arms around my neck,' Catherine recollected. 'Little by little she calmed down, but she looked neither at the road, nor at the trees, nor at the carriages, nor at the people. . . . She saw only her happiness and was completely absorbed in it.' If Catherine recalled these details so vividly long after Germaine was dead, it was because throughout the forty years their friendship lasted Germaine seemed to be driving through the Bois de Boulogne, seeing neither the roads nor the trees, completely absorbed in her happiness—or unhappiness.

Every afternoon at three o'clock Catherine Huber was driven to the Contrôle Général, where she stayed with Germaine until ten in the evening. They did their lessons together; sometimes they went to the theatre or opera; but their favourite pastime was to act out tragedies—'especially the dénouements'. Seated amid a mound of books in Madame Necker's library, they would select a play in the evening, learn their parts the following morning, and declaim in the afternoon. Germaine's passion for play acting lasted through her life, and the dividing line between drama on and drama off the stage lacked precision with her. In her later teens she took lessons in elocution from one of the greatest actresses of her century, Mademoiselle Clairon, who still later was to play a bizarre role in Germaine's domestic life.

The great classical tragedies—Racine above all—were her favourite fare. For opera she showed less understanding. Although in later years she professed enthusiasm for music (she also played the piano and sang creditably), it is perfectly clear that music affected her only superficially —therapeutically, one might say, for it calmed her nerves. She was too intellectual to understand the emotional, too emotional to understand the intellectual meaning of music. For a disciple of Rousseau and the future propagandist of German Romanticism, this was as singular a trait as was her indifference to nature.

Starved for affection, torn between constant emotional tension and intellectual activity, between worldly glitter and Calvinist severity, over-stimulated and over-restrained, precocious and ignorant, Germaine entered puberty. The demonstrative intensity with which she manifested her emotional needs met a cold reception from her mother and, it may be surmised, a not entirely satisfactory one from her companion. It was thanks to her illness that she discovered the object of her life's first passionate love: her father.

Dr. Tronchin had prescribed the countryside for a cure. The Neckers owned a country residence at Saint-Ouen, near Paris. There Germaine was packed off; no more books, no more *philosophes*, no more salon. Dr. Tronchin also had prescribed the company of Mademoiselle Huber, who spent every week-end from Friday through Monday at Saint-Ouen, and he laid down the law on the girl's dress: whalebones, bonnets, everything constricting was outlawed. Germaine followed the doctor's prescriptions punctiliously as to her toilet but not as to abstinence from intellectual pursuits. Her outdoor amusements in the château's vast park were romanesque and literary rather than relaxed and natural. She would await her friend's arrival crowned with a wreath of fresh roses, surprise her with tender notes placed in little baskets made of twigs, which she suspended from trees, and carve her own and Catherine's names, accompanied by suitable verses, on innumerable tree trunks. Thus transformed into a Forest of Arden, the park also served as outdoor stage for a new variety of theatrical performance. Since they knew of no plays whose cast was limited to two female performers, they decided to compose their own comedies, first agreeing on a plot and then improvising their lines, in the manner of the Italian comedians.

Even physical exercise required literary inspiration. Germaine had either seen, or read, or heard of a new ballet, based on *Télémaque*. The scene opened on the island of Calypso, with lightly clad nymphs prancing about the stage and shooting off arrows as they went. Germaine developed a sudden passion for archery, and Madame Huber was

prevailed upon to procure the indispensable equipment from the ware-
house of the Opéra: bows, arrows, quivers, and two complete outfits
for the hunting nymphs. Clad in gauze, the two nymphs practised target
shooting for several weeks: the only sport Madame de Staël ever was
to master.

Germaine spent the entire summer of 1779 at Saint-Ouen. She grew
taller, gained weight, improved her complexion, and completely recovered her physical health. But her nerves remained hypersensitive.
To burst into tears, as she did, at the slightest provocation—a word of
reproach, a sign of affection, an indelicate jest, a moving line of poetry
—was of course the fashion of the time; but not everybody responded
to the fashion so spontaneously as did Germaine Necker. Nor was
everybody able, as she later proved she was, to carry a hyperacute
sensibility into the most robust passions.

That summer Germaine fell in love with her father. Necker often
came to Saint-Ouen to relax from the demands of his office. Sometimes
he brought company—his wife, a few favoured familiars. Thus one of
the girls' theatrical performances, for which the servants' talents had
also been enlisted, was applauded by an audience including Monsieur
and Madame Necker, the abbé Raynal, Marmontel, and Buffon—an
august and forbidding assembly, considering the occasion. More often,
however, Necker came alone. 'To see his daughter,' says Madame
Rilliet-Huber (the former Catherine Huber), 'was his only and dearest
relaxation. He never criticized her, let her talk freely, enjoyed the wit
she displayed, applauded her enthusiastically, caressed her, and left her
content and with refreshed spirits.' Indulgent and amused, reluctant
to take any part in his daughter's education, he basked in her adoration
and returned it to her. 'Madame Necker,' he often remarked with a
smile, 'has taken care of the more serious part of my daughter's education, and I am teaching her a sense of humour.'

The intimate understanding that sprang up between father and
daughter soon took on an air of complicity.

In the eyes of the scoffers, the Necker trinity offered a ludicrous
spectacle indeed: father, mother, and daughter in a hypostatic union,
at the same time idols and worshippers, sacrificing and burning incense
to one another, in perpetual mutual adoration, while a chorus of priests,
acolytes and muezzins proclaimed their praises and a vast orchestra
and choir joined in, punctuating their ecstatic hymns with clashes of
cymbals and the thunder of tympani. Such is the picture Napoleon on

Saint Helena drew of them, and there was a good deal of truth in it. But it is a composite and impressionistic picture, and it explains nothing. The truth is that the Neckers' mutual adoration seems unreserved only in retrospect. Madame Necker in her diaries complained bitterly of her husband and daughter at the same time as she proclaimed his divine genius to the public. Monsieur Necker became his daughter's accomplice in undermining his wife's authority, and even her social pre-eminence. It was only after her death, partly from a feeling of guilt, partly from mere habit of obeying his wife's instructions, that he devoted himself exclusively to her cult. Mademoiselle Necker hated her mother; and while it was impossible to love one's father more, her devotion to him was not as boundless as her public utterances may lead one to believe. When, during the Reign of Terror, she was obliged to stay at her father's estate in Switzerland for longer than she wished, she heaved a sigh: 'I adore my father. It is a cult. But people do yawn at church.'

It was not a trinity that the Neckers formed but rather a triangle.

When Madame Necker entered marriage, she had already laid down a complete plan or scenario of what that marriage was to be: Necker would be her link with the universe; their life would be spent in unreserved mutual devotion; the day of her death was to be, thanks to his love, the most beautiful day of her life. This was the outline she had drawn in her wedding-eve letter, and any departure from it in real life distressed her. It was her whim to re-enact the idyll of Philemon and Baucis; but Philemon never floated international loans, Baucis never gave Friday suppers, and neither wrote books. It was not long after their marriage that Madame Necker began to realize, to her dismay, that her husband continued to devote himself to his career; at the same time, Monsieur Necker began to object to his wife's literary ambitions. Her diary contains many communications with God, some of which are less than enthusiastic reflections on her husband. 'Thou knowest,' she writes, 'if I have loved, and if I still love, the husband Thou hast given me; but his character, in spite of its great virtues, obliges him to seek happiness away from me.' And another day: 'Rash woman that I have been! I have sacrificed everything to my illusion; I have brought all my strength to bear on an object that now fails me, and I am falling into an abyss.' When Necker reproached her with spending too much time reading and writing, she wrote to him (all the Neckers were addicted to writing letters to one another from room to room) that

she would make a bargain: the moment he resigned from the India
Company she would 'lay aside Fénelon and never take up a pen upon
any other subject'. If Madame Necker devoted so much energy to
founding a salon and to acting as her husband's publicity chief, it was
not exclusively because she had been born a blue-stocking and ambitious. No doubt she realized only too clearly that, on the one hand,
Necker could not fill her life and, on the other hand, his ambition was
unbounded; combining the agreeable with the useful, her salon filled
her void while satisfying the vanity of both.

Outwardly the happiness of their union could not be publicized
enough; it entered into Madame Necker's conviction of what ought to
be, and moreover it furthered Necker's reputation as a paragon of civic
virtue. (In some cases, as when she flaunted her connubial bliss at the
rather vexed Gibbon, it also satisfied her own vanity and a natural
enough urge for revenge.) But when alone, Madame Necker poured out
her heart to God. The mere disenchantment of her first years of marriage was to change into torture when her daughter reached her middle
teens. What Necker no longer gave her, he gave Germaine. With
Germaine his taciturnity changed into almost adolescent exuberance;
she cajoled him, flattered him, entered into his preoccupations, discussed politics and economics, and no doubt gave him a sense of youth-
fulness and freedom that no longer emanated from his wife. In return
he gave her his indulgence. When Madame Necker criticized her
daughter, he came to her defence; and when a visitor remarked to
Germaine somewhat tactlessly, 'Your father appears to love you more
than your mother,' Germaine retorted, not without presence of mind,
'My father thinks more of my present happiness, my mother of my
happiness in the future.' But to Germaine the future had no concrete
meaning. 'I never was able to believe in the existence of next year
except as in a metaphysical notion,' she once remarked.

Germaine was conscious of the rivalry. When, in the fashion of the
time, mother and daughter had composed literary portraits of their
idol and showed him their respective efforts, Germaine noted in her
diary: 'He admires Mama's portrait very much, but mine flatters him
the most.'

Nor could the conspiratorial nature of Necker's and Germaine's
intimacy escape Madame Necker. One morning, when the family and
a guest were sitting at breakfast, Madame Necker was called outside
on some business. The minute she had disappeared, Germaine tossed
her napkin at her father. The Director General of Finance wound the

napkin around his wig, turban-fashion, and father and daughter began to dance around the table in silent pantomime until Madame Necker's steps could be heard approaching. Necker removed his turban; both resumed their seats, still without a word, and breakfast proceeded in utter silence.

A grim struggle was secretly taking place in that idyllic family. In impotent self-defence, the older woman allowed her failing health, her nervous crises, her increasingly morbid obsession with death to poison her husband's and daughter's happiness. A living reproach, a constant inspiration to remorse, she found solace in their tears. Necker himself, while fleeing to his daughter from the pall his wife cast on her surroundings, had become absolutely dependent on his wife in all the small matters of living, and his infidelity filled him with a permanent feeling of guilt. The only thing he might reproach her with, he once remarked after her death, was that she had never given him an opportunity to forgive her anything. This was meant as a tribute. Forgiveness, indeed, was Madame Necker's exclusive prerogative; she enjoyed that pleasure, which she withheld from her family, with increasing frequency.

The secret struggle inside the Necker household was paralleled, on a vaster stage, by a struggle that was to shake the French monarchy, and Monsieur Necker was at its centre. To understand the complex ties that bound the father and the daughter, it is necessary to picture not only the microcosm of the Necker family but also the extraordinary position which Necker held in the eyes of the nation. For, to Germaine, Necker was more than the ideal companion: he was a hero with divine attributes.

'Monsieur Necker loves virtue as a man loves his wife, and glory as he loves his mistress,' said Madame de Marchais, who knew him well.

'I always lacked a strong urge to acquire either money or celebrity or power,' Madame de Staël quotes her father as saying. For a man who spent the first twenty years of his adult life making millions and the following thirteen years seeking to govern the largest nation of Europe, this was an odd view to hold of himself. His daughter endorsed it, however. 'My father,' she wrote after his death, 'always had that elevation of the soul, that sensibility which rules out any consuming ambition for the goods of this world: his only passionate love was the love of glory.'

This sharp distinction between love of glory and ambition may be valid in theory (love of glory seeks the common good: ambition is

selfish), but it is difficult to draw the line in practice. To many contemporaries and to a sizeable group of historians Necker was inordi-
nately vain, ambitious, arrogant, fatuous, and incompetent; to others
he was a genius, a prophet, a saviour, and a victim of his integrity and
kindness. In the adulatory portrait Madame Necker wrote of him and
which he was not afraid of publishing in his lifetime, she made the
curious remark that her husband's only talent was to possess genius.
And Necker himself never ceased to advertise the fact that in all worldly
matters he was the most helpless of men. A banker who did not care for
money; a man who employed several newspapers and a stable of propa-
gandists but who did not seek celebrity; a man who craved office but
who was not interested in power; an unworldly minister of finance; a
genius without talent—what manner of man was Monsieur Necker?

He had prepared his way to power by acting as financial agent to
the French government and by sitting on the board of the India Company. But it was no longer enough to be a financier: the wealth of
nations had become a province for the investigation of philosophers;
political economy was the youngest science. The cry of *laissez-faire* had
been taken up by the Physiocrats; Turgot was becoming the favourite
candidate of the *philosophes* for the office of Controller General; the
government experimentally abolished internal trade barriers in the
commerce of grains. Thanks to the greed of speculators, among them
the Necker brothers, the experiment failed disastrously. Necker, who
had no taste for the dogmatic metaphysics of the economists, saw his
opportunity in opposing *laissez-faire*. In 1770 Diderot, the most prominent regular of the Neckers' Friday evenings, published the *Dialogues
on the Commerce of Grains*, by another regular, the abbé Galiani. One of
the most entertaining works on economics ever written, the *Dialogues*
struck a smart blow at the *laissez-faire* school. 'No one,' remarked
Voltaire, 'has ever written more amusingly on famine.'

To push his advantage, Necker soon turned author himself. In 1773
he published his *Éloge de Colbert*. Madame Necker's salon had become
a meeting place for a quorum of the French Academy. The French
Academy crowned Necker's book with its first prize. Nevertheless, his
rival Turgot still held the allegiance of the leaders of the philosophic
party; for all the love letters Voltaire and Diderot wrote to their
Hypatia, Turgot was still their man when Louis XVI appointed him in
1774 to repair the disasters wrought by the abbé Terray's administration. The hosannas with which even his intimates greeted Turgot's
accession irked Monsieur Necker. Before long Turgot's attempted

reforms, which might have saved the monarchy, were systematically sabotaged by the speculators, the Parlement, and an irresistible combination of special interests. Turgot's attempt to restore free trade inside France unhappily coincided with a bad harvest year, and the resulting famine was blamed on him. Necker knew better; nevertheless, in 1775, at a time when Turgot stood most in need of support, Necker chose to publish his book *On Legislation and the Commerce of Grains*, which was nothing short of stabbing Turgot in the back. In 1776 Marie Antoinette obtained Turgot's dismissal, and after a brief interval Necker succeeded to his rival's functions if not his title.

It was Necker's theory—a seductive one—that France was, fundamentally, economically sound; all that was needed was to restore confidence and credit. If order could be brought into the chaos which had prevailed, except for brief intervals, in the administration of public finances; if economies could be made by reforming waste and abuse; and if the public regained enough confidence to subscribe to government loans, then the budget could be balanced *without levying a single new tax*. These were magic words. Magic, of course, was all that was needed. Loans were oversubscribed (their terms were very generous), and foreign capital poured in.

Despite the huge expenses of the American war (which Necker strenuously opposed, to the point of being suspected of connivance with England), no new tax was levied. On the other hand, the public debt rose alarmingly. Turgot's persistent mutterings of 'charlatan' from the sidelines did not keep the whole philosophic party, even (with some reluctance) Voltaire, from giving their full support to Necker. The abbé Raynal, known as the chief tympanist of Necker's band, aided by the other old retainers—Suard, who published the *Journal de Paris*, Henri Meister, who had succeeded Grimm as editor of the *Correspondance Littéraire*, the abbé Morellet, an indefatigable legman, and a host of lesser lights—persuaded France that her salvation rested exclusively in Necker's hands. Necker drank in the tribute with a humble consciousness of his worth. To be called a guardian angel by an archbishop did not strike him as extravagant. He delivered daily lectures to the King, united more and more powers under his control, and wrote interminable preambles to the reform edicts which, in the name of the King, heaped abuse on the King's predecessors.

In 1781 Necker overreached himself. In order to acquaint the public with the flourishing condition of the kingdom, he secured from Louis XVI the permission to publish his famous *Compte rendu au Roi*—

c*

purportedly a candid report on the financial situation of France but in fact a rosy account of his own administration. It even contains a glowing tribute to his domestic bliss and to Madame Necker. The book could not be reprinted as fast as it sold. 'This unprecedented and ever memorable composition,' Buffon wrote to Madame Necker, 'will do more good and redound more to the honour of our century than all our books put together in a heap.' The bishop of Mirepoix reported that 'the archbishop of Toulouse cried over it, so strongly did it affect him'. Among the numerous allegorical prints celebrating Necker's book was one entitled 'Triumph of Monsieur Necker over Envy'. Its legend explained the allegory:

> On a cloud, the bust of this wise minister can be seen being carried by genii in the direction of the Temple of Memory. One of the genii holds a copy of the *Compte rendu* and illuminates it with the torch of Truth, proclaimed by the voice of the Nations; Fame places the civic crown on the Bust; in the foreground Wise Government checks (with the aegis) the audacity of Envy, which, lifting its mask and advancing (its mouth filled with snakes), seems to be about to clip (with scissors) the wings of Fame, who has already risen far above her.

Necker's contention that an account should be given the nation on the state of its finances will find few critics today. His *Compte rendu* would have been an admirable innovation but for the fact that his figures were patently incomplete, unrealistic, and dressed up. Despite the paeans, there also were eloquent critics. For a while Necker held his own against them, but the row which was raised perturbed the King. Necker's colleagues—old Maurepas, the chief minister, and Vergennes, the foreign secretary—at long last saw an opportunity to rid themselves of their rival. Necker himself furnished the occasion when, although a foreigner, he demanded full membership in the council of ministers. Maurepas and Vergennes threatened the King with their resignation if he gave in, and Louis, ignoring the pleas of Marie Antoinette, who spent the entire day weeping for Monsieur Necker, invited Necker to resign.

That evening, on May 19, the Neckers left their official residence and moved to Saint-Ouen. The shock was rude, but balm was soon forthcoming. The news of Necker's dismissal was received with general consternation. From every corner of France letters poured into the Neckers' château, bewailing this ungrateful treatment and the loss it meant to the nation: among the writers were princes, bishops, peasants, soldiers, even priests and nuns. The Court itself, led by the weeping Queen, openly sympathized with the fallen minister; princes of the blood, marshals of France, and cardinals paid their respects at Saint-Ouen. For the next seven years, until his fateful recall in 1788, Necker remained an almost official power and regarded himself as leader of the opposition. 'He is a man,' wrote Catherine the Great, 'whom Heaven has destined beyond all contradiction to occupy the most glorious position in Europe. He must live; he must survive one or two of his contemporaries, and then his star will shine with incomparable brightness, and his contemporaries will be left far behind him.' With this the Neckers agreed.

To regard Necker as a charlatan or to attribute sinister designs to him would be unfair. Many of his reforms were sound, and his intentions were excellent. But, as Napoleon was to observe acutely, Necker overestimated his powers, and 'there is no greater crime than to take on a ob one does not know'. Gouverneur Morris, a frequent guest at Necker's house, observed that Necker was mediocre, ignorant, and lacking in understanding of economics and politics. In the circumstances this was indeed a crime. Yet those who knew him well, including Morris, gradually came to esteem him more highly and to discount his vanity.[1]

He was by no means a fool, and in some ways he was ahead of his times. His realization that France was rich, that only the government was poor, and that credit was the heart of prosperity—these certainly are ideas that have gained some currency in our times; but his lucidity was balanced by his blindness to the need of taxation, without which the credit was bound to collapse—as indeed it did, burying Europe in its ruins. His opposition to the *laissez-faire* doctrine, to Turgot's Panglossian notion that 'the general well-being is the result of the efforts of each individual to further his own interests', was based not on a study of economics, of which he knew little, but on considerations of social justice. Government regulation, he insisted, was necessary to protect the people against lawless exploitation, and in the conclusion to his book on the *Commerce of Grains* he echoed Rousseau's *Second Discourse*:

> It seems that a small number of men, after dividing up the earth among themselves, have created laws for their common protection against the masses. . . . And yet, it must be said that after the establishment of laws

[1] Morris, who in 1789 succeeded Jefferson as minister of the United States to France, also acted as Necker's business adviser when Necker became interested in buying American real estate.

to safeguard property, justice, and liberty, almost nothing has been done as yet for the most numerous class of citizens. 'What do the laws of property mean to us?' they well might ask. 'We own nothing. Your justice? We have nothing to defend. Your liberty? If we do not work tomorrow, we die.'

Though by no means so revolutionary as his rhetoric makes him sound, Necker was genuinely concerned with the fate of the proletariat, as most of the more radical revolutionists were not. Undoubtedly his craving for popularity was partly the cause of this concern; but anyone who has taken the trouble to read his writings must sense the genuine kindness of the man, which especially in his later years transcended his vanity. When his ability was put to the test in 1789, his lack of statesmanship became evident: he had no programme, except to maintain himself in power and to alleviate the suffering of the masses by temporary expedients.

Necker's daughter saw in him the embodiment of kindness, but she never shared his sympathy for the toiling masses. After Robespierre's overthrow, when 'the most numerous class of citizens' stood in breadlines before empty bakeries, she could write that the non-propertied classes must not be allowed a voice in government; 'they have greatly contributed to the Revolution, but then they too will reap its chief benefits: civil liberty, which is the right and prerogative shared by all. Is this nothing? All true goods are included in that liberty.' Before the Revolution the Princesse de Lamballe had asked, 'Why don't they eat cake?' After the Revolution Germaine asked, 'Why don't they eat liberty?' Whatever his shortcomings, Necker knew that liberty is inedible.

Except for love of glory and mutual indulgence, there was little that father and daughter had in common. Germaine resembled her mother much more; she was, in fact, Madame Necker without the starch. What is more, she would have liked to *be* Madame Necker. She regretted not having married her father, whom she addressed, even in her late thirties, in terms usually reserved for lovers, and she taught her own children to call Necker their father.

Still more remarkable (though rarely remarked upon) was Necker's conduct with his daughter. Germaine's superlatives lose much of their significance when it is realized that she addressed all her friends in almost identical terms—a habit which makes it difficult to determine the actual degree of intimacy she reached with them; but Necker never wrote to anyone, not even to his wife, as tenderly as to his daughter. When Monsieur de Staël, her future husband, dances with her, Necker objects to his lack of ardour; he cuts in on the dance: 'There, sir, I shall show you how one dances with a girl when one is in love with her.' He gives his demonstration, and Germaine is so overwhelmed by the contrast between her father and her fiancé that she tears herself loose and runs to her room to cry.

The diary in which this episode is recorded was kept by Germaine in 1785, when she was nineteen. On its first page, Germaine wrote: 'Turn the leaf, Papa, if you dare, after reading this epigraph. Ah! I have placed you so close to my heart that you must not begrudge me this small area of intimacy which I shall share only with myself.' If Necker, encouraged by this prohibition, did turn the leaves, he could read this:

[July] 31 [1785]

I did not write yesterday. I was still in bed when my father came to see me, and I gave him the hour I reserve for my diary. . . . We spoke of nothing in particular, but every instant was filled with gaiety and sensibility. What grace, what charm he can display when he wants to! . . . I shall try one day to write his portrait, but in order to do this successfully one would require all the qualities one wishes to describe—that is to say, a sort of universality. . . . Yet how is it possible that we are not always in harmony, that sometimes there is passion, sometimes a chill? Why is it that sometimes I discover faults in his character which are harmful to the gentle intimacy of our lives? It is because he wants me to love him like a lover while he speaks to me like a father; because I want him to be jealous of me like a lover while I act like a daughter. It is the struggle between my passion for him and the inclinations natural enough to my age, which he wants me to sacrifice completely, that makes me unhappy. To watch the protracted length of this very struggle makes him impatient; we do not love each other to the point of excess, and nevertheless we come so close to it that I cannot bear the idea of anything reminding me that we have not reached it yet. Of all the men in the world it is he whom I would have wished for a lover.

In a letter Germaine wrote in 1792 to another lover, she reported on her father's sentiments for her eldest son (whose paternity she credited to the lover): 'My father, who for many years has used me as a plaything, is pleased with this substitute. Sentiments that require a basis of equality are not necessary to him: friends are less congenial to him than the mass of mankind or children. This is how he is made;

an angel like you cannot be found twice in a lifetime.'[1] To those who believed that Germaine blindly worshipped her father, such clear-sighted strictures may be disturbing. The truth is that her unqualified idolatry of Necker came only after his death, just as Necker's unqualified idolatry of his wife came only after Madame Necker's death. The 'protracted struggle' that took place in Germaine at nineteen, between her passion for her father and her natural inclinations, still was consuming her at thirty-eight.

If Necker was her god, she worshipped him like a pious sinner—adoring and transgressing. As soon as she reached independence, her conduct seemed almost calculated to earn his disapproval. But Necker was an indulgent divinity, and Germaine was his plaything; she appreciated and took advantage of his mercy, yet the kind of love he gave her could not satisfy her needs. His condescending indulgence was no less frustrating than Madame Necker's starched intolerance. She rebelled against him no less than against her mother. The many men she was to love all seem to have been chosen for the contrast they offered to her father's image, and the love she exacted from them required an absolute basis of equality. Strait-laced virtue would not dictate her conduct, nor would she be anyone's plaything.

If she instead of her mother had married Necker, things might have been different. In her diary Germaine wrote:

> If in the middle of his career a loving woman had opened her arms to him and cried, 'Stop and go no further! Let me replace the goal you are seeking, rest on my bosom, find your glory in my admiration, your happiness in my passion! . . .'—oh, I believe, I am certain, that he would have thrown himself into these arms forever.

Although Germaine thought that she might have been that woman, it is extremely doubtful if she would have wished to stop him on his path to glory any more than her mother did. If she worshipped him, it was as an ideal object, as a hero. She exulted in his power, his popularity, his genius, and her entire life was spent in celebrating him. When, in 1783, her mother wanted her to marry William Pitt, she refused. 'I have a different destiny,' she wrote in her diary. 'I am the daughter of Monsieur Necker.' It was a prouder distinction than to be the daughter of a king. Being Necker's daughter set her above the jurisdiction of mere men. For Necker was a being apart, legally a citizen of Geneva and spiritually a citizen of Heaven. He served his King by an act of kindly

---

[1] To Louis de Narbonne, 12 November 1792; unpublished at the time of this writing. Quoted with the permission of the Berg Collection of the New York Public Library.

condescension: as a Protestant and citizen of a republic, he could speak to Louis XVI like a teacher to a pupil; as a millionaire he was conscious of his independence. This circumstance was not without an effect on his daughter's conduct: she talked as to equals to those sovereigns who paid their court to her; and to the one sovereign who did not, she spoke with definite arrogance, though kingdoms trembled at his name. Father worship was, in her, indistinguishable from self-exaltation and self-indulgence.

In 1783 Germaine was seventeen and it was time to think of marriage. One of the richest heiresses in Europe, she would have had no difficulty in finding a husband but for the fact that her parents narrowed down the choice to Protestant noblemen. Among the several candidates, Baron Eric Magnus Staël von Holstein, secretary of the Swedish embassy in Paris, had waged a campaign for Germaine's hand ever since Germaine had turned twelve; the prospect of Necker's millions gave him a constancy of purpose which he lacked in all other enterprises. With the help of Marie Antoinette, Gustavus III of Sweden, and several ambassadors and duchesses, he eventually was to see his patience rewarded, but in 1783 a formidable rival appeared in France. He was William Pitt, a child prodigy who at the age of twenty-three had just resigned as Chancellor of the Exchequer. It is not certain whether Pitt knew, at the time, what projects Madame Necker had for him.

Madame Necker did not lack imagination. The following facts struck her: Pitt and Necker were both geniuses; they had been 'opposite numbers' in England and in France; they both had resigned their exalted posts and were waiting to be recalled to even more exalted ones. France and England had just made peace; what could be more appropriate than that their future harmony should be sealed by the marriage of England's most promising statesman with the daughter of France's tutelary genius, herself already celebrated for her brilliant endowments? The idea of a dynastic alliance between ex-ministers of finance was a novel one, but once it had been conceived of, the project seemed virtually pre-ordained. The son of Lord Chatham and the daughter of Necker united in the bond of marriage conjured up idyllic images of peace, prosperity, and unity between Europe's mightiest rivals. That Pitt might think differently does not seem to have occurred to the Neckers; his flattered acceptance was a foregone conclusion. One may imagine Madame Necker's consternation when the project foundered on her own daughter's obstinate refusal.

Germaine remained adamant in the face of her mother's pleas and tears: if she married Pitt, she would have to live in England, and this was a terrible fate, for it meant living away from her father. If Pitt had known that he was the cause of hysterical scenes in the Necker household, he could have stopped them simply by pointing out their altogether academic nature. But he did not know, and Madame Necker, though she had to yield, never forgave her daughter. 'Why is it,' Germaine asked in her diary two years later, 'why is it that this wretched England had to bring out in Maman the inflexible coldness she displays towards me?' Indeed, Madame Necker never recovered from the blow of her daughter's ingratitude and disobedience, and life under the parental roof became infernal.

When, in 1785, Baron de Staël intensified his offensive, Germaine was ready to accept him. Her father had acquired the barony and castle of Coppet, on the Lake of Geneva, and was toying with the thought of withdrawing to its proud isolation. 'May he forgive me,' wrote his daughter, 'but I have not yet collected enough memories to live on them for the rest of my days. . . . My heart, though it adores him, would take fright if the door should close forever on us three.' Nothing could be clearer: marriage was the road to freedom and life. Monsieur de Staël 'is a man whose conduct is perfectly correct, incapable of saying or doing anything stupid, but sterile and inert; he will not make me unhappy, for the simple reason that he cannot contribute to my happiness, and not because he could trouble it. . . . Monsieur de Staël is the only convenient choice for me.' Such were the reflections with which the disciple of Rousseau, the worshipper of passion, the prophetess of romantic love and marriage, went to the altar.

Germaine at nineteen had as yet no concrete idea of what kind of freedom it was that French women obtained through marriage. She had grown up amid talk of love in an age of moral dissolution, surrounded by the most enlightened and emancipated minds of her time—and yet, thanks to Madame Necker's heroic efforts, she was absolutely innocent of the facts of life.

> I do not know yet what this sin is that a woman can commit, but surely it will be explained to me before I take my solemn vows. I should look upon myself with horror, I should horrify nature, if the daughter of Monsieur and Madame Necker made in the presence of God an oath that she did not keep. Enough on this horrible subject; to suppose the possibility of a crime is to give it a degree of plausibility!

Right down to the style, it is Madame Necker pure and simple who is speaking here. Unlike Madame Necker, of course, Germaine was to break her vows with spectacular frequency.

The general similarity between the diaries of mother and daughter is so striking that it is difficult to understand Madame de Staël's assertion that she resembled her father more than her mother. The similarity extends even to their common preoccupation with death. 'The sweet thought of my own death makes the death of the person that is dear to me less horrible,' Germaine wrote in her diary. 'And yet, when the time of parting comes, let me expire first.' Such was also Madame Necker's recurrent prayer. But whereas Germaine escaped her morbid obsession by throwing herself into activity and diversion, Suzanne Necker made no effort to resist its fascination. She caressed the thought of death, and she prepared herself for it so meticulously that dying became her exclusive activity and concern.

Madame Necker's illness took a severe turn after Germaine had so stubbornly refused to marry Pitt. Fondly imagining herself on the point of death, she seized the opportunity to heap reproaches on her daughter under the pretext of forgiving her. In the customary Necker fashion, she did this in writing:

> Pay attention, my child, to the last wishes and orders of your mother.
> . . . You may perhaps reproach yourself for certain instances in your conduct toward me if you compare them with the pleasure you might have given me; but if I now awaken in your heart any feelings of remorse, I would also tell you how you may appease it. . . . I leave to your father all those claims that I had upon your affection. . . . Wherever he wishes to go, follow him. Live in his house. . . . Leave this world that you have but ill known, and live for God, for your father. . . .

Such, for the nine years that remained to her, was Madame Necker's tone in her more amiable moments. She carried it even into her dress. 'A woman whose head was covered by a very thick black veil that fell below her chin,' thus Madame de Charrière describes her in 1784. The following summer her premonitions were intensified. Germaine, seized by remorse, fell on her knees by her mother's bedside: 'Stifling with tears, I was about to faint. "Ah!" cried my mother, "you have made me happy for a long time." '

When not exclusively preoccupied with her own mortality, Madame Necker found a worthy occupation in the conversion of dying old Buffon. To convert that obdurate materialist, she sent him a copy of her husband's book *On the Importance of Religious Ideas*, and poor

Buffon spent his last hours having Monsieur Necker's pieties read aloud to him. She installed herself by his bedside, watched him agonize for five days, and had the satisfaction of hearing him declare that he died in the religion in which he had been born. This was the man who had said of nature: 'Time, space, and matter are its means, the universe its object, movement and life itself its aim and end.' What a triumph for Madame Necker!

That life itself should be the aim and end of nature—she would not have it! The idea of a universe without Madame Necker was too unbearable. As early as 1777 she began to plan elaborate measures by which, in some vague way, she hoped that communication between her own departed spirit and her husband might be facilitated. In addition, she lived in a permanent fear of being buried alive. This fear had its origin in her acquaintance with certain practices in hospitals. Some years earlier Louis XVI had put her in charge of a hospital which still bears her name, and she had noticed that in their haste to clear the beds for new patients, the attendants occasionally buried an old patient before he was quite dead. She did her best to put a stop to such negligent conduct and even wrote a treatise *On Precipitate Inhumations*, but the fear that the same fate might befall her became an *idée fixe*. In her successive last wills she prescribed in ever more minute detail how she was to be embalmed before her burial. 'I beseech you not to neglect these details,' she begged her husband in 1777. 'Do exactly as I tell you. It may be that my soul will wander round about you. It may be that I shall taste the delight of seeing you perform with exactness all the desires of her who loves you so fondly.' Poor Monsieur Necker!

After Necker's downfall in 1790 and his retirement to Switzerland, Madame Necker once more had to revise her instructions. She conferred at length with doctors and architects and resolved on the following: a mausoleum for herself and her husband was to be constructed on their estate of Coppet; there she was to be preserved in a stone basin filled with alcohol, large enough to accommodate both her and her husband in a similarly pickled state. Necker was to have the key to the tomb and visit her regularly. After his death the tomb was to be walled up.

Madame Necker died in 1794. Her husband followed her instructions punctiliously, and while the mausoleum was building he kept her corpse for three months under his roof—three summer months.

Madame de Staël, who showed little emotion at her mother's death, commented almost sarcastically on her burial. 'Perhaps you do not know,' she wrote to Meister, 'that my mother has given such singular, such extraordinary orders concerning the various methods of embalming her, preserving her, placing her under glass and in spirits of wine, that if, as she thought, her features had been perfectly preserved, my unhappy father would have spent his life in contemplating her. It is not thus that I understand the urge to be remembered.'

Such were the last years of Madame Necker. They were fateful years indeed not only for the Neckers but for Europe. At the time when Germaine was married in 1786, France knew still, in Talleyrand's words, 'the sweetness of living'. When Madame Necker was buried, France was under the Reign of Terror. Throughout these years Germaine was at the centre of events.

She entered marriage and life most inadequately prepared. She was wealthy, the daughter of a famous man, acclaimed for the liveliness and brilliance of her conversation and intelligence; she had begun to write and, though as yet unpublished, had been praised by the most influential critics. On the other hand, she was not pretty (some said ugly); she possessed little solid learning, despite all her mother's lessons; she knew life mainly through literature; and she had no manners whatsoever. Between Rousseau and her mother she had received a singular education and grown up a savage in a drawing room. Scarcely released from her mother's oppressive domination, she was to throw herself into everything she undertook with a domineering impetuousness that astonished the world. Life had to be lived with ever-burning intensity, and the 'proud and noble passions' (a recurring phrase in her writings) were to be her supreme law. Restraint and moderation she scorned; nor did she display the least selfconsciousness. 'Altogether a most embarrassing person,' Madame de Genlis said of her in 1782. 'About eighteen, wild, vain, but good-natured and with a much larger provision of wit than beauty' was Gibbon's verdict two years later.

But the men were attracted to her. The Comte de Guibert, a genius of amatory as well as military strategy, composed a word portrait of her under the name of Zulmé:

Zulmé is only twenty years old and she is a priestess of Apollo! . . . Her great dark eyes are alight with genius. Her hair, black as ebony, falls around her shoulders in wavy locks. Her features are marked rather than delicate. . . . She has that which is more than beauty. What variety and expression in her face! What delicate modulations in her voice! What perfect harmony between thought and its utterance!

And so forth. Pure flattery, one would say, if it were not for the fact
that other men, who became her slaves, succumbed to precisely those
charms. Germaine remembered this portrait when, in 1793, she wrote
Zulma, a short novel of which she said that more than anything else
she had written 'it belonged to her soul'. And what is the central theme
of *Zulma*? 'Love is above the laws, above the opinion of men; it is the
truth, the flame, the pure element, the primary idea of the moral
world.'

That she was not beautiful, either then or later, is generally agreed
upon. Of medium height, she was, at twenty, still thin; later, stocky
and ample. Her complexion was swarthy; her lips thick, almost negroid;
her nose both prominent and upturned; her dresses always in bad taste.
Her hair, later arranged in black ringlets protruding from an ever-
present turban, she still wore long and powdered. The one feature on
whose extraordinary beauty everyone agreed was her eyes. They were
huge, magnificent, luminous. Although often described as black, they
are shown light and greenish in her portraits. Proud of her arms and
bosom, she wore décolleté dresses no matter what the time of day. The
general effect of her appearance varied widely, perhaps according to the
temperament of the beholder. Guibert saw in her the portrait of the
Muse of Poetry. Gouverneur Morris said, 'She looks like a chambermaid.' Madame de Charrière, like most women, described her as ugly.
Ugly or not, there can be no doubt that she was attractive, and that
after five minutes of conversation the question of physical beauty became irrelevant. She seduced, not the senses, but the sensibilities of
men: no one who came in touch with her could entirely escape that
fascination.

Since circumstances had placed her at the very centre of the European
stage, at the summit of the political and intellectual *élite*, her powers of
fascination could not fail to manifest themselves on a spectacular scale.

Part Two

LOVE AND POLITICS

> *The pursuit of politics is*
> *religion, morality, and*
> *poetry all in one.*
> MADAME DE STAËL

> *Love, supreme power of the*
> *heart, mysterious enthusiasm*
> *combining poetry, heroism*
> *and religion!*
> MADAME DE STAËL
> (*Corinne*, XIII.i)

5

MARRIAGE AND EMANCIPATION

O N August 19, 1772, at Stockholm, Gustavus III, King of the Goths and the Vandals, friend and admirer of Rousseau and Voltaire, overthrew, by a military *coup d'état*, the constitution of his country and became an absolute monarch. There was no resistance; all was over in twenty minutes. Among the noblemen who distinguished themselves on that occasion, the young King noticed an ensign of the guard whose excellent timing, vocal expression, and lung power in shouting 'All goes well! Long live the King!' had the most salutary effect on the success of his enterprise. Ensign Eric Magnus Staël von Holstein was commissioned a lieutenant the following day.

Born twenty-three years earlier in a castle in Ostergotland, the eighth child of a cavalry captain, young Staël had grown up in the rough and rustic style characteristic of impoverished branches of noble houses: a father who divided his time between hunting and breeding; a mother who, widowed after a life spent in bearing and burying children, had sold her estate so that her sons might follow a career; military service beginning at the age of thirteen. While his fellow nobles bought themselves commissions and freely engaged in such dissipations as became their station, Staël knew the humiliations of poverty; but he had certain assets that distinguished him from the common run of squires. Though scarcely educated, he possessed the kind of intelligence and adaptability that is needed to make one's way into the highest social spheres: ambition, cunning, persuasive charm, and a handsome, winning appearance —fair hair, finely chiselled features, an elegant figure, and hands too refined for a subaltern in the Ostergotland Regiment.

King Gustavus, who had formed his tastes in France, had a liking for handsome young men as well as for French countesses. In his 'dear Staël' he discerned a mixture of ambition, frivolity, and cleverness which he jovially encouraged in the expectation of putting it to good use.

After a two-year leave spent travelling and acquiring worldly polish, Staël returned to Sweden and was appointed chamberlain to the Queen. But Stockholm soon wearied the young man, who dreamed of a vaster stage. In March 1776 Staël requested to be promoted to captain and to be given leave to enter the service of King George III, who was then preparing to send an expeditionary force to the American Colonies. Gustavus granted the request on March 14; on April 1 dear Staël was in Paris. He had not been able, he explained to his King, to obtain a suitable position in the British service. Gustavus, amused by the escapade, put a good face on it and appointed him attaché to the Swedish ambassador, Count Creutz.

Creutz took the young man under his wing; within a few weeks Staël had conquered Paris and Versailles. The ladies were charmed by 'Little Staël'; so was the Queen, who was developing a fondness for Swedes in general and for Count Fersen in particular. Unlike 'Big Axel' Fersen, 'Little Staël' had no money, but his mentor Count Creutz soon taught him the art of borrowing without repaying. Who would refuse credit to a man who had private entrée with the Queen? 'Monsieur de Staël leads a very busy life,' Creutz wrote to Gustavus. 'He is very well received at Court, and all the young women of France would tear out my eyes if I did not promote his career. Madame de La Marck and Madame de Luxembourg would exterminate me. . . . Comtesse Jules de Polignac feels a tender friendship for him. . . . Madame de Boufflers loves him like a son.'

The Comtesse de Boufflers, a beauty then in her sixties, was, like Count Creutz, one of the intimates of Madame Necker's salon; she also had developed a warm friendship for King Gustavus when, as Crown Prince, he had conquered the hearts of Paris, and she had kept up an intimate correspondence with him. That Little Staël had succeeded in being loved by her like a son was proof of his diplomatic and strategic talent.

By dint of reckless spending, Baron de Staël (he had in the meantime assimilated the title of baron, held by another branch of his family) manœuvred himself into a position which forced all his protectors to do something more for him than love him. He was, as Creutz reported to Gustavus in 1778, 'at the end of his resources and without a penny': something must be done for him, lest one of the most promising talents be wasted. Baron de Staël knew exactly what. There was only one way out—to marry a rich heiress. To marry into the high French nobility was out of the question, but fortunately the richest heiress available happened to be the daughter of a Genevese commoner, Mademoiselle Necker. She was only twelve years old, to be sure, but marriage negotiations took time, and besides it was not unusual for girls to be married at fourteen or fifteen. The chief difficulty was, as Madame Necker pointed out to Madame de Boufflers when the latter put the proposal before her, that Monsieur de Staël was nothing and that Mademoiselle Necker had no compelling reason to marry a nobody. This difficulty had been foreseen. Of course Mademoiselle Necker was not expected to marry a nobody; but if Monsieur de Staël had the prospect of marrying Mademoiselle Necker, the King of Sweden would be able to do justice to Monsieur de Staël's talents and appoint him to succeed Count Creutz as ambassador. Count Creutz, Madame de Boufflers, Marie Antoinette herself would employ their influence with the King of Sweden to bring about this result. Madame Necker replied noncommittally that if Staël became ambassador, there might be a chance.

At Drottningholm Castle, in May 1778, Staël extracted a vague promise of help from his King. Gustavus' position was clear: Staël could not become ambassador unless he married Mademoiselle Necker. The Neckers' position was equally clear: Staël could not marry Mademoiselle Necker unless he was ambassador. A less tenacious man might have flinched in the face of such an impasse; but Staël was fighting for his life, and the obsessive thought of Necker's millions sustained his strength through eight years of agonizing suspense. The vague assurances held out by Gustavus in his replies to Creutz's and Madame de Boufflers' pleas justified his hopes, but by 1783 nothing had happened yet, and there was talk that Mademoiselle Necker, now seventeen, would marry Mr. Pitt. Staël's frenzy changed into consternation when, in the same year, it was announced that Creutz had been appointed foreign minister and that the successor nominated by Gustavus was not Little Staël but Baron Taube. 'I am in a desperate situation,' Staël appealed to his sovereign, 'and nothing can save me from the abyss unless Your Majesty consents to revoke the order that causes my misfortune.' Creutz, for his part, pointed out to Gustavus that the traditional Franco-Swedish alliance would collapse if Staël was not nominated: 'He has, with the King's consent, the right to be received in private audience by the Queen—a right which I, though ambassador, am unable to obtain.'

As if this were not enough, Marie Antoinette herself sent a personal message to Gustavus, hinting that nothing was better suited to promote friendship between the courts of France and Sweden than the nomination of Monsieur de Staël as ambassador. Gustavus, who desperately needed French subsidies, saw the point. Still, he felt, he might as well make the most out of the bargain. If Staël wanted to be ambassador, he would have to earn his post; if Marie Antoinette wanted him in Paris, she would have to pay for the privilege. Gustavus nominated Staël as chargé d'affaires in the absence of Count Creutz and sent him the following instructions:

> It is up to you to justify the favour of the French Court and to make yourself worthy of mine. . . . Take advantage of the kindnesses of the Queen of France and turn them to the profit of the fatherland: this is the finest and noblest means of deserving the ambassadorship you desire. . . . The first negotiation I entrust to you is the acquisition of an island in America, an acquisition on which I have set my heart: it is Tobago I want. If you succeed by clever means and by stimulating in the Queen of France a desire to see her recommendation justified by the successful outcome of so important a negotiation, you will be my ambassador. But if you do not obtain Tobago (for it is Tobago I want), I must tell you in all sincerity that you will have to be satisfied with the title of minister plenipotentiary and give up the ambassadorship.

To marry Mademoiselle Necker one had to deal in West Indian islands. Monsieur de Staël felt that the demand was cruel. There was no reason why Sweden should ask for Tobago, except that islands were being generally traded at the peace conference then taking place in Paris. In vain did the chargé d'affaires implore the Queen and Vergennes to take pity on his plight; what was a little island in the Antilles to France, compared to what being ambassador and marrying Mademoiselle Necker meant to him! Tobago was out of the question. However, one could not turn Little Staël down altogether; the French government offered, instead of Tobago, the tiny island of Saint-Barthélemy. Gustavus declared himself satisfied, and in 1784 Little Staël was made ambassador extraordinary to His Most Christian Majesty.

The way to Mademoiselle Necker's hand seemed clear. 'You will be the richest nobleman of Sweden,' Gustavus wrote to Staël; and, since he was at the time travelling in Italy, he even promised to come to Paris to sign his ambassador's marriage contract. But when the King came to Paris in May 1784, there still was no marriage contract; on the other hand, entertaining his sovereign cost Staël 200,000 livres. If ever a man was trapped, it was Baron de Staël, or so at least it seemed. A desperate appeal was made to Madame de Boufflers, who acted as the ambassador's ambassadress to Monsieur and Madame Necker.

On May 21, 1784, the Neckers stated their conditions: (1) the ambassadorship must be guaranteed to Monsieur de Staël for life; (2) if any unforeseen circumstances should terminate his ambassadorship, he was to receive a pension of 20,000 livres per annum; (3) Staël had to be raised to the rank of count; (4) Staël had to give the solemn promise never to force his wife to reside in Sweden; (5) Gustavus had to confer upon Staël the Order of the Polar Star; (6) the marriage contract had to be approved and signed by Marie Antoinette. For the daughter of a former governess and a former bank clerk, these were surprising conditions.

After another year spent in negotiations, a compromise was reached: Gustavus balked at the Polar Star and the title of count; to the other conditions he substantially agreed. In July 1785 the happy suitor was introduced to his prospective bride. Germaine's first impression of him has already been recorded: correct, sterile, inert. Staël's first impression of Germaine is not known; it is doubtful whether, after bending all his efforts for eight years to the single purpose of marrying her, he was capable of seeing in her anything but the personification of 650,000 livres, her dowry.

On January 14, 1786, in the Lutheran chapel of the Swedish embassy, Germaine Necker became the wife of His Excellency, Eric Magnus, Baron Staël de Holstein. Among the witnesses was Count Fersen. The marriage contract had been signed, on the eve, by the King and Queen of France and by all the princes of the blood. One might have said that the Neckers had done well by their daughter, yet the Empress Catherine II commented, 'Everybody thinks Mademoiselle Necker has made a very disadvantageous marriage.' Madame de Boufflers, the chief architect of the marriage, wrote to Gustavus that she had little hope it would be a happy one.

> There is no doubt that she has absolutely no idea of social behaviour and conventions, and she is so spoiled by admiration for her wit that it will be hard to make her realize her shortcomings. She is imperious and strong-willed to excess, and she has a self-assurance that I have never seen matched by any person of her age, no matter of what rank.

Since Jacob grazed his uncle Laban's sheep, few men had laboured as doggedly to obtain a girl's hand as had Baron de Staël. But Jacob, after twenty years' service under his uncle and father-in-law, could return to his home wealthy and honoured. Monsieur de Staël's term of servitude had merely begun.

.   .   .

According to the French custom of the time, the young couple spent the first few days after their wedding at the house of the bride's parents. On the Thursday of the week following, Germaine moved into the Swedish embassy, rue du Bac. Faithful to the Curchod-Necker tradition, she took her leave in writing and on a tragic note: 'At this moment, as at the moment of death . . .' It was the style of her mother, to whom the letter was addressed. 'Happiness,' Germaine concluded, 'will come later; will come at intervals; may come never.'

Germaine's diary of 1785 shows that she entered marriage ignorant but without illusions. 'He will not make me unhappy, for the simple reason that he cannot contribute to my happiness.' It almost seems as if she was determined not to give her husband a chance. It is true that Monsieur de Staël had married her solely because of her money: the purity of his motive was absolute. But this was no reason not to love his wife once he had married her, and in fact he did love her. 'I am convinced,' wrote a secretary of the embassy in 1787, 'that she loves him and esteems his character, but he loves her more.'

That Germaine loved and esteemed her husband seems a strange assertion in view of the expressions of loathing and contempt with which she wrote of him and of her marriage in later years. She would rather kill herself than spend two months with her husband, she declared in 1792; and in *Delphine*, ten years later, she wrote that 'if there is any circumstance that could justify us in raising a complaint against our Creator,' that circumstance was an unhappy marriage. 'Woe to the woman who is obliged to take her life into her own hands, to cover up the defects and pettiness of her husband, to free herself from him and to bear all alone the burden of existence!'

It is true, however, that during the first two or three years of their marriage, the Staël *ménage* appeared, outwardly at least, harmonious and united. Germaine had not expected to find a Saint-Preux in her husband. Her marriage, she knew, partook more of the nature of an international treaty of friendship and commerce than of a private arrangement, and her principal object in entering it was to emancipate herself from her mother. It was, perhaps, the fact that Monsieur de Staël insisted on loving her more than she loved him that made the marriage intolerable for her. Germaine wrote many times—in her letters, in her books—that happiness in marriage was the greatest bliss attainable to woman, and that she had been deprived of it. So eloquent and insistent was she on this subject that she convinced most of her readers. It is surprising, therefore, to come on Monsieur de Staël writing to her, in 1798, that the greatest misfortune he ever experienced was to have been 'obliged to renounce the only happiness a rational being and a sensible heart can desire—the happiness that can be found only in a tender and intimate marriage'. There can be little doubt that it was Germaine, and not her husband, who refused tenderness and intimacy.

Having reached port after eight years of travail, Monsieur de Staël took it into his head that Germaine should be not only his salvation from insolvency but also his wife in every sense of the term. He understood that being her husband gave him rights over her, while she understood that being a wife gave her freedom. There is no reason to believe that she refused to perform the duties of the marriage bed, or that these duties were, in the first months of her marriage, distasteful to her. It is true that not only her books but even her most passionate love letters are singularly reticent about the physical side of passion; unquestionably, physical love was, for her, never more than a natural part of integral love—not the most important part, by any means, but in no way to be shunned. What she craved above all was love or, nearly indistinguishable from it, friendship; the sexual act might be indulged in or renounced in the interest of either. But she was incapable of either love or friendship without intellectual and nervous exaltation, and for such exaltation Monsieur de Staël was not a fit object. He meant to be loved; he courted his own wife, pleaded for her love—but always on the inadequate ground that he was her husband. Since their paths seldom crossed, most of his pleading was by letter, and one of his complaints was that he rarely enjoyed her company. 'I tell you once again,' she replied to one of his notes, 'that if I am necessary to your happiness, you must give some happiness to me, so that I may give you some in return. I, by myself, shall manage as best I can.'

Since she repeated these words to various lovers in later years, it is possible to form an idea of what she understood by giving her some happiness. To give her happiness, it was necessary to accept as a favour whatever she gave of herself and to give whatever she asked as a duty. The worst offence was to be jealous. If, for her happiness, it was necessary to lead her own life, with her own friends, it was Monsieur de Staël's duty to indulge her; to assert his rights as a husband was to forfeit them, and to claim for himself liberties that he refused to her was altogether intolerable. 'By the way,' she wrote to him after a tiff, 'there is much talk of your keeping a mistress, and the hours you keep make me inclined to believe it. I warn you that I find this every bit as wicked as to have a lover.'

If the Staëls seemed a united couple, the reason was that, in one respect at least, there was a complete community of interests between them. The Swedish ambassador had hitched his political fate to Necker's, and to promote the cause of his father-in-law was, for the first four years of his marriage, his principal care. This established between him and Germaine a certain conspiratorial intelligence and comradeship. Having served notice on her husband that he had no rights on her, she treated him with the affectionate cordiality one reserves for old business associates, showing her claws only on the rare occasions when Eric Magnus proved recalcitrant. This was all the easier because she still held the purse strings. Thus Germaine, freed of her mother's domination, victorious over her husband in defending her independence, and taking the fullest advantage of her ambassadorial rank, emancipated herself and asserted, imperiously, her right to seek happiness. As for her husband, he could write, five years after his marriage, to his most intimate friend: 'I am as unhappy as a rational man can be.'

In view of Monsieur de Staël's inadequacy, it was merely a matter of time before Germaine found a worthier object of her emotions. Unfortunately for herself and for her lovers, what she asked for was the impossible. On the one hand, the father image continued to dominate her: 'There can be no passion in a woman's heart unless she feels for the object of her love an admiring respect not unmixed with fear, and a deference bordering on submissiveness,' she declared in the preface to *Delphine*. On the other hand, she sought out men of refined sensibilities: imaginative, creative, alert to nuances, intellectually agile, and submissive like troubadours or Arthurian knights—in other words, men who had a decided feminine admixture in their character. Admiration, respect, fear, deference, submissiveness are what she received rather than what she gave: in all her relationships with men she was condemned to be the stronger, the dominating partner. The men, too weak to dominate, unwilling to be dominated, took to flight.

Before she was able to give herself over to her passions, she had to exorcise the spectre of incest. For a girl who had no concrete notion of the physiological side of love, and who had written in her diary that of all men she would prefer her father as a lover, the discovery of what love involved must have been a shock. But Germaine's robust nature asserted itself; not for her the complications of Freudian novels. The means of exorcism was the same as she was always to use: public confession—or, perhaps more accurately, public profession; for she purged herself by affirming her rights rather than by acknowledging her wrongs. The first of the literary works in which she represented her most personal experiences in the thinnest of disguises was a three-act drama, *Sophie; or, The Secret Sentiments*, written in the first year of her marriage (1786–7) and published in 1790. Unlike Rousseau's *Nouvelle Héloïse* or Goethe's *Werther*, which set the still current fashion of self-cure by way of art, *Sophie* possesses no literary merit whatsoever; it has the distinction of containing some of the most inept verses ever penned by a major French writer. The main thing, to her, was to get her message across to a handful of people who also figured in various disguises in her fiction.

The setting of *Sophie* is duly romantic: 'The stage represents an English garden. On one side, an urn surrounded by cypresses; on the other, a closed pavilion. . . .' The heroine, Miss Sophie Mortimer, is Germaine at seventeen in English disguise; she has been adopted by a Frenchman, the Comte de Sainville, clearly recognizable as Necker. The marriage between the Count and the Countess is shown as a loveless one, but of the Countess's identity with Madame Necker no doubt is possible. The fourth important character, Lord Bedford, may safely be identified as William Pitt, although in a sense he is imaginary since Germaine never met Pitt. Sophie is sought in marriage by Lord Bedford, but she refuses him, being in love with her guardian without realizing it. The Count, in turn, is secretly in love with his ward, whose bust he worships in the mysterious closed pavilion. The Countess, trying to persuade Sophie to marry Lord Bedford, opens her eyes both to the true nature and the hopelessness of her feelings for the Count. Sophie is filled with horror at the realization of her sinful passion, and filled with mixed horror and joy when she discovers that she herself is the object of the Count's secret flame. The lovers have barely made their embarrassing discovery when the Countess arrives, perceives Sophie's bust, which the Count has crowned with a flower wreath, and, with the words, 'Heavens! Ah wretched me! Her bust! I die!' faints on the steps leading into the pavilion. The Countess's recovery is followed by a four-cornered contest of generosity among the Count, the Countess, Sophie, and Lord Bedford. Lord Bedford departs unwed, and Sophie is allowed to remain with her guardian, the assumption being that time and virtue would transform passion into friendship.

Since the play could not have fulfilled its cathartic function if the principal dramatis personae had not been acquainted with it, Germaine

unabashedly read it to her parents. Madame Necker was shocked, as
well she might have been.

How Necker reacted is not known. Surely he cannot have missed
the allegory; but the half-amused, half-critical attitude which he assumed towards women's writings in general may have relieved him of
the necessity of giving his opinion on this one in particular. As soon
as Necker had perceived his daughter's propensity for scribbling, when
she was seventeen, he had nicknamed her Monsieur de Saint-Écritoire,
and his slightly heavy irony towards her literary activities continued
until his death. The *saint écritoire* referred to was a portable hinged
desk set, which Germaine carried about with her and which could be
opened so that she might place it on her knees: she did not dare to
ask for a writing table of her own when she stayed at her father's
house. One of the first things she did after Necker's death was to put
a desk into her room at Coppet; but the portable *écritoire* continued
to accompany her on her walks and travels and became almost as indispensable as the twig or the bit of paper which she kept twisting between
thumb and forefinger, to the exasperation of nearly everyone who knew
her. It is probable, then, that Necker ignored the message of *Sophie*
and indulged his daughter's passion for both literature and himself with
a tolerant smile.

Writing *Sophie* had a result which Germaine had not, perhaps, consciously intended. It liberated her from her bonds with her father.
This contention may seem novel or even absurd: yet there are certain
concrete indications that would appear to back it up. Germaine had
resigned herself to the nature-given fact that her father could never
satisfy the needs of love as she now understood it: marriage had opened
her eyes to what love could be, to what her husband was not, and to
what her father should never be. She was free to turn elsewhere. To
be sure, she continued to regret that she had not been born into Necker's
generation and married him, but it was merely a regret. Her love for
her father remained undiminished, but it was a different kind of love, a
love which did not keep her from pursuing a political line on which he
frowned, from having lovers of whom he disapproved, or from being
bored in his company. 'My father is kind, very kind,' she once wrote to
a friend, 'but one can never get inside him. Every sentence starts a new
conversation and makes one worry about finding a topic for the next.'

In *Delphine*, Germaine represented herself in at least two characters:
the heroine, Delphine, and a secondary character, Madame de Cerlebe,
who had turned away from an unfeeling and mediocre husband to

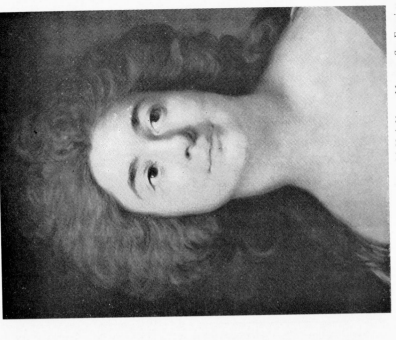

GERMAINE NECKER
Age about 19, from a portrait by Joseph Sifrède Duplessis

GERMAINE NECKER
Age about 13, from a drawing by Carmontelle

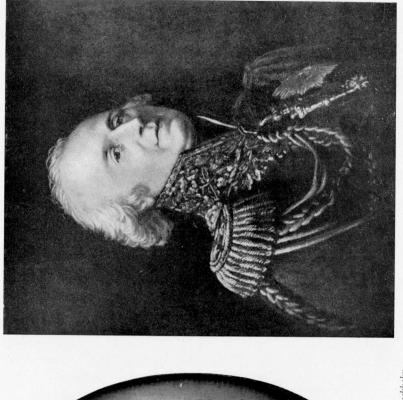

LOUIS DE NARBONNE-LARA
From a contemporary portrait

Nationalmuseum, Stockholm

ERIC MAGNUS STAËL VON HOLSTEIN
From a portrait by Ulrica Pasch at Gripsholm Castle, Sweden

devote herself to her aged father. 'Men often assure us of their love,' Madame de Cerlebe declares, 'but the truth is, perhaps, that a woman is necessary only to her father.' Germaine wanted to be necessary to someone, for not to be necessary is not to be loved: but, significantly, Madame de Cerlebe appears only as a commentator, and it is Delphine who is the heroine—Delphine who wants to be loved by, and to be necessary to, a man who is not her father. The fact is that after the Revolution forced Monsieur Necker to leave Paris, in 1790, Germaine spent not one more day with him than circumstances and her conscience demanded.

If she could not have happiness in love, which was life itself, she needed noise, activity, movement. 'What I love about noise is that it camouflages life,' she wrote to her husband from Coppet. During the first two years of her marriage Germaine threw herself into the noise with reckless abandon; she could not have found a better place and time to suit her temperament than Paris in the last years of the old régime.

It was on January 31, 1786, two weeks after her wedding, that Madame de Staël made her official entry into society. Her presentation, at Versailles, to the King and Queen did not pass without a mishap. The dress she wore for the occasion was the masterpiece of Mademoiselle Bertin, the celebrated couturière, who, in the words of the Duchesse d'Enville, had sought 'to translate into satin and lace the genius of the father, the virtues of the mother, and the candour of the daughter'. Germaine, who was both impetuous and gauche, had arrived late and, in jumping from the carriage, had weakened the seams of Mademoiselle Bertin's delicate construction. Presented to Marie Antoinette, she performed the three traditional low curtsies; at the third curtsy, when custom prescribed that she pretend to take hold of the hem of the Queen's dress and to kiss it, the trimmings of Germaine's train got caught and parted company with her.

The King, seeing her embarrassment, remarked with a smile, 'If you cannot feel at ease with us, you will never feel at ease anywhere.' The Queen took her into her boudoir and engaged her in conversation until a chambermaid had repaired the damage, for the presentation was to be followed by an official dinner for eighty-four guests. Before the day was out, the episode had made the rounds of Paris; admirers composed quatrains on Germaine's graceful modesty, and enemies made epigrams on her clumsiness.

D

The malevolence with which Madame de Staël was received by her contemporaries, especially the women, almost as soon as she made her début in society, was a remarkable phenomenon. Undoubtedly the attacks had largely political motives and were aimed at the Necker family in general; the product of such touted virtues was bound to be scrutinized with invidious intent, and weaknesses that might have been overlooked in the daughter of a less self-righteous couple were pitilessly criticized in the daughter of Monsieur and Madame Necker. The reaction astonished Germaine. 'How convinced I was,' she has Delphine say, 'that it was enough to be kind and good in order to open up all hearts as soon as I appeared, and that all social relationships were a continuous interchange of gratitude and affection!' Instead, she found herself criticized, ridiculed, and hated: she talked incessantly; she had more wit than either tact or sense; she ignored social conventions; she was a stiff and prudish Calvinist; she was irresponsible, ambitious, scheming, arrogant, shameless; she was ugly and dressed without taste. Some conceded her genius; and a handful of friends, women as well as men, fell under her spell and admired her with more or less reluctant devotion. Indeed, it became apparent from the outset that whatever love and glory she was to obtain she would have to conquer inch by inch, by every means or weapon at her disposal. That all the charges levelled at her had some foundation cannot be denied. Indeed, it is easier, at the distance of a century and a half, to understand the critics and the scoffers than the devotees. But if one would see the real person rather than a caricature, one must keep in mind that the true cause of the enmities she drew upon herself did not lie in any of the defects that were blamed in her; these were as visible to her most devoted friends and lovers as they were to her enemies. Her unforgivable sins were her independence, her defiance of public opinion, her ruthless pursuit of happiness, and her conscious superiority. In a woman these were sins only exceptional minds could forgive.

With the sublime self-righteousness of a true Necker, Germaine was able to walk through life, leaving in her wake a host of exasperated lovers, of ruined causes, of disastrous intrigues, and a crowd of onlookers who gaped or laughed at her, depending on their temperaments, without ever reproaching herself with any faults save those of having loved too generously, though, too idealistically, and acted too enthusiastically —and these, of course, were not faults but virtues. The vices were on the side of the others: cynicism, selfishness, petty feelings, calculation, the tyranny of convention. That the world did not want as much of

Madame de Staël as Madame de Staël was eager to give of herself was the world's fault, not Madame de Staël's. Exaltation was always pure, derision always corrupt: such was the basis of Germaine's beliefs, and on it she constructed and acted out her theory of freedom—in love, in politics, in literature. It is firmly laid down in her first important piece of writing, the *Letters on Jean-Jacques Rousseau* (1788), and it supports, with unsagging consistency, every sentence she wrote in her life.

Love, politics, literature—Germaine never acknowledged any boundaries between these, nor between private and public life. But love came first and led to the others. It was in love that she first discovered the dualism of exaltation and cynicism, of fire and ice, and that she resolutely placed herself on the side of the principle of heat and life against the Mephistophelian sneer, the triumphant grin of those who know that everything warm must grow cold in the end. The discovery came with the brutal change from girlhood in the Necker household to womanhood in the society of the Paris of 1786.

> Young girls never depend on themselves. Everything around them conspires to shield their hearts from the impression of the senses. The virtuousness—and often also the ambition—of their parents keeps watch over them. Even the men, with their bizarre principles, wait until a woman is married before they speak to her of love. At that point, everything changes: one no longer seeks to exalt their minds with romantic notions but to soil their hearts with cold jests on everything they have been taught to respect.

Thus she wrote shortly after her marriage, in the *Letters on Jean-Jacques Rousseau*. A less robust temperament might have drawn back in resignation, accepted the coarseness of men as irremediable, and suffered a life of submissive frigidity. But Germaine's sensibility was not genteel but tempestuous; not ladylike but rugged. She was determined to know love, in the teeth of the cynicism and prudishness of society. Love was not immoral: society was. It did not take Germaine long to make the transition from the shock she expressed in the *Letters* to the protest she registered in *Delphine*: 'In our century,' she said in the preface, 'it is not love that corrupts morality, but the contempt of all principles which has its cause in the contempt of all feelings.' In the novel itself the defence of the rights of love is more specific: 'Between God and love, I recognize no mediator but my conscience. . . . Egoism is permissible to a feeling heart; whoever centres his existence in love may, without remorse, detach himself from the rest of the world.' Against love marriage has no validity; there is no binding power in

'duties which are the result of fortuitous circumstances, which depend
on the whims of laws or on the sanctions of priests, and which subject
man's conscience to the decisions of other men.'

These sentiments were not, perhaps, original; but original was the
way she chose to inspire love. It was through conversation.

No sooner had Germaine assumed the status of a married woman
and ambassadress than she took over, for all practical purposes, her
mother's salon. Voltaire, Rousseau, Diderot, D'Alembert were dead,
and with them the era of the *philosophes*. The era of the politician was
beginning. The tone and the topics of conversation had undergone a
corresponding change: on the eve of the French Revolution Madame
Necker's Academy of the Waters seemed to lie in the mists of a golden
past. Madame Necker was lost in the new kind of talk, but her daughter,
who one day was to inform the Duke of Wellington that talking politics
was her whole life, felt completely in her element. The deficit, the
budget, taxation, reforms—these were delightful topics: all the more
delightful since their acute timeliness presaged Necker's recall to the
ministry. By making Madame Necker's salon her own forum, Germaine
soon placed herself at the very centre of political life.

She also formed her own circle at the Swedish embassy in the rue
du Bac, which she transformed into a subsidiary of the Necker machine.
Here, however, life had more of a mundane glitter, and conversation
was not always as intensely intellectual as one might expect. On
December 5, 1786, Charles de Constant, cousin of the man who was
to become Germaine's chief victim and torturer, attended a gathering
at the Swedish embassy. Freshly arrived from Geneva for the express
purpose of speculating on the Paris Bourse, Charles had, despite his
youth, been to China twice, and obviously took himself to be a very
interesting personage. But the crowd he met at Madame de Staël's
was not curious about China; 'Two or three fine gentlemen approached
me and asked me, "So you have been in China, sir?", and without
waiting for an answer, they pirouetted on their heels and went on to
talk about the theatre, about news from Court. All these conversations
are about trifles, and a man who does not know the names of the writers
and the important people, and what they have been doing in the past
week, is looked upon as a stupid animal and nobody says a word to him.'
The conversation of which Charles the Chinaman spoke so contemp-
tuously was a sport that only a well-trained team could play, whose
rules were difficult to understand, since they forbade competition.

For Germaine, conversation was, next to love, the principal *raison d'être*. In her book on Germany she devoted an entire chapter to the subject of conversation, and it belongs to the best of her writings. In France, she explains:

> words are not merely, as they are in all other countries, a means to communicate ideas, feelings, and needs, but an instrument one likes to play and which revives the spirit, just as does music in some nations, and strong liquors in others. [It is] a certain way in which people act upon one another, a quick give-and-take of pleasure, a way of speaking as soon as one thinks, of rejoicing in oneself in the immediate present, of being applauded without making an effort, of displaying one's intelligence by every nuance of intonation, gesture, and look—in short, the ability to produce at will a kind of electricity which, emitting a shower of sparks, relieves the excess of liveliness in some and rouses others from their painful apathy.

The art of conversation had reached its perfection in France in the years preceding the Revolution, and although Germaine was critical of the conventionality, the 'pedantry of frivolousness', which resulted from its rules, she needed it as much as the air she breathed. She was by all accounts the most brilliant talker of her time, but it was not in large assemblies, such as the one described by Charles Constant, that she revealed her powers. The smaller the circle, the more inspired her conversation, and those who knew her best were agreed that she reached her highest flights in the intimacy of a tête-à-tête. She could be witty, and she could sustain a conversation on court, theatre, and social gossip more entertainingly than most; hence those who met her only at large gatherings thought her disappointingly superficial and frivolous. Perhaps none of her writings reflects this kind of conversation more faithfully and amusingly than do the news-letters she addressed, in the late 1780s, to King Gustavus of Sweden. But this was not what made her conversation unique and completely different from the verbal ballets of eighteenth-century salons. She was at her best when she spoke on those subjects which filled her with passion. Her emotional intensity and intellectual grasp, the improvisatory yet sure-footed rush of her eloquence, the electrifying enthusiasm she communicated for her ideals, produced on her audience an effect that can be compared only to a rare musical experience. Hers was an 'intellectual melody', as she says of her heroine Corinne. When she had her inspired moments, which could last for nearly an hour, her listeners were absolutely under her spell, sometimes even reacting physically, so tense was the excitement she generated.

And yet she conversed; she did not orate. Contrary to the testimony of ill-wishers, she was not an incessant talker. It is true that she talked a great deal, and even when not talking she tended to leave her mouth slightly open; but her most remarkable talent consisted not so much in communicating her own ideas as in inspiring and helping others to formulate theirs. It was in this, rather than in her inspired flights, that her power resided, and she used it to its fullest extent. As a prettier woman would put her physical charms to their best advantage, so Germaine inflamed men by the mere power of words. As her contemporary Charles de Lacretelle remarked, she thus obtained by dint of the most formidable verbal exertions what a pretty woman would have got with a mere smile. Once she had discovered a vulnerable spot in a man's sensibility, she played upon it with such consummate skill that her victim was bewitched into seeing and sensing in her the promise of fulfilment of all his desires; his most secret longings were aroused; and, since her choice fell invariably on men of extreme sensitivity, their sexual passion was stimulated by the mental processes of the imagination to a pitch they could never have attained through their senses alone. When this point was reached, they were doomed.

Germaine took conversation as a means to seduction so much for granted that she endowed her heroine, Delphine, with that power, even though she credits Delphine with physical charms that would have been sufficient by themselves. Describing a brilliant gathering at which her lover was present, Delphine writes: 'For a long time I made conversation with him, in front of him, for him.' And her lover reports on the occasion thus: 'I saw, I heard a woman such as there never was. She is an inspired being.' In *Corinne* Germaine was to transfigure inspired conversation into poetry.

It is not surprising, then, that Madame de Staël, within a year of her marriage, held court among her admirers like a queen. She was not averse to displaying those physical advantages which she undeniably had: her voluptuous arms, which she always left bare; a generous bosom, which she did not cover even when travelling; and a pair of legs whose substantial proportions seemed to assert the presence of the flesh, lest anyone should suspect her of being pure intellect. As was the fashion in pre-Revolutionary France, she received her morning calls in bed or while being dressed, with only a token tribute paid to modesty. A Swedish diplomat who called on her one morning found her in the process of having her hair powdered by one chambermaid, her hands manicured by another, and raising one leg to be taken care of by a third;

the only way she was able to acknowledge his presence was by an infinitesimal nod of the head. She was to cling to this good old custom of the *ancien régime* through the rest of her life, receiving visitors in bed and hiding little of what they might see—a habit which scandalized the younger generation.

Monsieur Necker's long duel with Calonne, who had become chief minister in 1785, had begun with the publication, in that year, of Necker's three-volume treatise on *The Administration of Finance*. The work is said to have sold 80,000 copies within a year. But while the Necker propaganda machine was playing crescendo, the enemy forces were not idle, and their number included such formidable though ill-assorted champions as Calonne, Condorcet, and Mirabeau. In February 1787 Calonne, addressing the Assembly of Notables which he had convened in the hope of reforming the fiscal structure of France, threw a bombshell into Necker's camp by claiming that Necker's *Compte rendu* of 1781, which had shown a surplus of 10,000,000 livres, should, if honest, have shown a deficit of 46,000,000. Outraged, Necker wrote to the King to obtain his permission to answer Calonne's libel.

The King, for once, was seriously annoyed. 'I do not intend,' he declared, 'to make of my kingdom a republic of vociferating amateur statesmen, like the city of Geneva.' He refused Necker permission to reply to Calonne and soon afterwards peremptorily dismissed Calonne: a plague on both your houses. Necker, triumphant over Calonne's dismissal, published his reply without royal sanction and held himself in readiness for a call from the Court to resume the direction of affairs.

On April 13 an emissary from Louis XVI, the Baron de Breteuil, did in fact call on Necker and handed him a letter from the King; but the letter was a *lettre de cachet*, ordering Necker to leave Paris within twenty-four hours and to stay at a distance of at least forty leagues. 'It appeared to me,' wrote Madame de Staël, 'to be an act of unexampled despotism.' To be sure, the unexampled despot relented within a few hours and permitted Necker to stay at his estate at Marolles, near Fontainebleau, a short distance from Paris. The indignant Monsieur Necker, accompanied by his ailing wife and his pregnant daughter, moved into his bitter exile at Marolles, a delightful place where he was in the habit of spending a part of the summer months. Since the Court was, at that time, at Fontainebleau, Necker had actually moved closer to it instead of farther away.

Germaine had been pregnant for several months, a condition to which she responded, according to her cousin, Madame Necker de Saussure, with a marked distaste. She had spent the autumn of 1786 with the Court at Fontainebleau, where the King was either hunting or hearing Mass. (When he was doing neither, the court bulletin announced laconically, 'Today His Majesty is doing nothing,' which meant, Madame de Staël pointed out in a letter to Gustavus III, that the King was working with his ministers.) Her life had been a succession of dinners and suppers: three times a week one supped with the Princesse de Polignac, Germaine reported to Gustavus; three times a week with the Princesse de Lamballe; once a week with the Queen, who usually made her appearance at eleven o'clock to play a game of billiards. If it were not for games, nothing would happen at all: a hostess's principal care was to lure her guests to a trictrac table as quickly as possible. Though sharply critical of the emptiness of this life, Germaine missed its noise in the solitude of Marolles. Above all she missed the Comte de Guibert.

Hippolyte de Guibert, if not Germaine's first lover (the honour probably belongs to a more celebrated contemporary), was, at any rate, the first among her friends to make Monsieur de Staël seriously jealous. He had known Germaine from childhood and had written her flattering portrait as Zulmé when she was twenty. At forty-four, after a life of frustrated literary and military ambitions, he was posing as a misunderstood and persecuted genius. He shared the fate of great military writers after him: his most important innovation, the organization of armies into self-sufficient divisions, was adopted only after his death in 1790. Germaine, who wrote his eulogy in that year, saw in Guibert certain similarities with her father, and in his exaggerated sensitivity, his ambition—his love of glory as she preferred to call it—he possessed all the qualities she sought in a man. Whatever the degree of their intimacy, there is reason to believe that Monsieur de Staël was justified in thinking it too great. (In 1809 Guibert's widow created a literary sensation by publishing the now classical love letters addressed to him by Julie de Lespinasse and announced her intention to publish other letters by other women: it was one of the rare occasions when a husband had provided for his widow's material comforts by being unfaithful to her. Madame de Staël, terrified by this rumour, dispatched her son Auguste to Paris, who apparently succeeded in buying the letters back, thus avoiding a scandal.[1]) Monsieur de Staël's reproaches drew from Germaine an instantaneous and devastating reply. Monsieur de Staël

[1] See Jean Mistler, ed., *Lettres à un ami* (1949), Benjamin Constant to Claude Hochet, 6 September 1809, p. 164.

wished to see her letters to Guibert? Well, she would show them to him. Monsieur de Staël read the letter his wife chose to produce: it was an elaborate reproach to Guibert for having advised her, four years earlier, against marrying William Pitt. Pitt had in the meantime become Prime Minister to George III, and if Germaine were Mrs. Pitt instead of the Baroness de Staël, Louis XVI would never have dared to subject her father to the indignity of exile.

Monsieur de Staël capitulated: to prove his devotion to Monsieur Necker, he filled his dispatches to Stockholm with glowing praise and optimistic predictions for his father-in-law; in fact the style of his communication became suspiciously similar to Madame de Staël's. What is more, he accepted the role of the Neckers' ambassador to Louis XVI. The order of exile against Necker was revoked after two months, and Marie Antoinette made it a point to announce the news personally to the Swedish ambassador. But Germaine was not easily reconciled; the Queen must be punished for serving Monsieur Necker so ill as to allow the *lettre de cachet* to be issued in the first place, and Monsieur de Staël received detailed instructions from his wife on the manner in which he was to mark the Neckers' displeasure: 'I think it is now more necessary than ever that you keep yourself in the background. But if the Queen asks to see you, speak to her, as we have already agreed, showing a great nobility of sentiment for my father and letting her perceive that the termination of his exile is more important to the Queen and to the King than it is to my father.'

It is scarcely necessary to dwell on the peculiarity of a situation in which the ambassador of Sweden to France is instructed by his wife on how to cold-shoulder the Queen of France and to promote the recall of his father-in-law to the direction of the French government. The oddity of this did not escape the King of Sweden, but for the moment he was merely amused.

On July 31, 1787, Germaine gave birth to her first child, a girl. She was christened Edwige-Gustavine, after her godfather, Gustavus III, with Count Fersen representing the King at the baptism. Unlike Germaine's succeeding children, none of whom was sired by Monsieur de Staël, Edwige-Gustavine appears to have been legitimately conceived. Her father, at any rate, was touchingly devoted to the weak and skinny child, who lingered in this world for only a year and eight months. Despite all the 'scraped boiled beef' her parents tried to feed her, she died on April 8, 1789. What were Germaine's impressions of motherhood,

D*

what her reactions to the child's death? There is so little direct testimony that several of Madame de Staël's biographers seem unaware of the child's existence. Gustavine's death undoubtedly affected her more deeply than appears on the surface; there are traces in her writings, especially in *Delphine*, which discreetly recall the experience. But such losses were accepted philosophically in her time, and it is only too obvious that other happenings held a larger place in Germaine's thoughts. The only being whose death she dreaded, and whose death made her lose her self-control, was her father; but Monsieur Necker was then very much alive. He was reaching the apogee of his career.

These were the steps that led to Necker's recall: the failure of the Assembly of Notables to implement Calonne's proposals; Calonne's dismissal; the brief administration of Loménie de Brienne (the same archbishop of Toulouse who had wept so copiously over Necker's *Compte rendu* in 1781); Brienne's decision, in August 1788, to call the States-General, which had not met for almost two centuries; and his resignation a few days later. Necker's hour had come. The state was on the verge of bankruptcy, the provinces in turmoil, tax collection at a virtual standstill, and the monarchy on the way to spontaneous disintegration. It was a time for miracle workers. Necker was offered the Controller Generalship with the powers of a prime minister (the civil disabilities of Protestants had, in the meantime, been abolished). Although aware of the thanklessness of his task and lacking any concrete plan to meet its challenge, he eagerly accepted the post for which he had been pining for seven years.

'The public joy on this change of administration was very great indeed,' wrote the American minister in Paris, Thomas Jefferson, to John Jay. After relating how the people of Paris 'were amusing themselves with trying and burning the Archbishop in effigy', and how about eight to ten people were killed in the ensuing riots, Jefferson added: 'The public stocks rose 10 per cent on the day of Mr. Neckar's [sic] appointment.'

Necker had been recalled merely to stop the gap in the Treasury; the States-General had been called merely to vote new taxes: yet France suddenly was swept by the almost universal conviction that, in actual fact, a new era was dawning, that France was to be given a new constitution—that, in the full meaning of the modern phrase, a New Deal would be made. Almost overnight the country was deluged with tracts and pamphlets, and constitution making became the universal parlour game of the King's twenty million subjects.

Well might the minister of the United States observe that 'the French ladies miscalculate much their own happiness when they wander from the true field of their influence into that of politicks'; the ambassadress of Sweden was not to be deterred from taking her position at the very centre of the excitement. But her exultation was not unmixed with fear. 'If the circumstances were different,' she wrote to Gustavus III, 'I would have taken pleasure in announcing my father's nomination to Your Majesty. But the ship has been placed under his command at so desperate a moment that all the admiration I have for him is barely enough to inspire me with confidence.'

The winter of 1788-9, following a crop failure, was the coldest for eighty years. Forty thousand workers were unemployed in Normandy alone, says Jefferson; thousands streamed into Paris in search of free bread, and at the street corners braziers were lighted where they could warm themselves and eat their soup.

Necker took no small credit for feeding the famished. His gesture of declining a salary of 220,000 francs was well advertised, as was the fact that he had put more than two million francs of his personal fortune at the government's disposal for the purchase of wheat—at 5 per cent interest, to be sure. Arthur Young noted in his journal (June 10, 1789) that, according to some well-informed Frenchmen, Necker had deliberately exaggerated the gravity of the famine for the sake of increasing his popularity; whether or not this was his sole objective, he did at any rate attain it.

By the spring of 1789, on the eve of the meeting of the States-General, Necker appeared to have worked another miracle: he had tided the nation over the winter and raised enough loans to keep the administration going. Even those among the leaders of the coming Revolution who intended to get rid of Monsieur Necker at the first opportunity realized that, for the time being, their best course was to join in singing the great man's praises. Necker, for his part, did everything in his power to ensure the victory of the Third Estate at the impending meeting. At no time had his popularity been greater.

How hollow that popularity was, no one could have foreseen. Intoxicated with the delirious optimism of the day, Germaine had forgotten her earlier apprehensions. The moment no longer seemed desperate but pregnant with the fulfilment of all of man's hopes. And her father was to be the instrument.

6

REVOLUTION AND INTOXICATION

ON May 4, 1789, from a window at Versailles, the Swedish ambassadress watched an imposing procession. The twelve hundred elected deputies of the French nation were on their way to church, to hear the Mass on the eve of the opening of the States-General. The crowd looked on in silence as the three hundred prelates and priests in their robes, the three hundred nobles with plumes and swords, marched by. Then, in simple black cloaks, the Third Estate. Of their six hundred deputies, Robespierre among them, only one enjoyed fame, or rather notoriety—the Comte de Mirabeau, deputy of Aix-en-Provence. Madame de Staël took a close look at the ugly, ravaged, pockmarked features of the man who passed for vice incarnate, a desperado and a traitor to his class:

> It was difficult not to take a long look at him, once one had noticed him. His huge head of hair distinguished him from all the others. It was as if his strength derived from it, like Samson's. His face gained in expressiveness from his very ugliness, and his whole person suggested a strange power.

Standing beside Madame de Montmorin, the wife of the foreign minister, Germaine gave expression to her elation 'at seeing, for the first time in France, the representatives of the nation'.—'You make a mistake in rejoicing,' said Madame de Montmorin in a cutting tone of voice. 'Great disasters will come of this, both for France and for us.' After recalling these words twenty-seven years later, Madame de Staël added:

> This unfortunate woman perished under the guillotine with one of her sons; the other son drowned himself; her husband was torn to pieces in the September massacres; her oldest daughter died in a prison hospital; her younger daughter . . . succumbed to the weight of her losses before she was thirty years old.

On May 5, in an improvised structure erected over the great avenue at Versailles, the King and Queen, from their dais, solemnly opened the meeting of the estates. At the sight of the weakness of the King's features, and the visible emotion of the Queen, whose face was deathly pale, Germaine admits that she experienced a moment of fear. This was dispelled by the ovation Monsieur Necker received as he prepared to address the assembly.

Great things had been expected from Necker's speech. The occasion was to inaugurate a new era, and Necker was to sound its keynote. Growing dismay could be observed in the faces of the deputies and the audience when Necker droned on, citing figures and statistics, on the exclusive topic of the public debt and taxation. After half an hour, his voice gave out; the rest of the speech, which lasted two and a half hours more, was read for him. In the face of an assembly that included some of the most powerful orators of modern times, this was an inauspicious beginning. To be sure, the solution of the financial crisis was the purpose for which the States-General had been called, but this was not what they wanted to hear and especially not at such length. The only thing the deputies seemed to listen to with pleasure was Necker's assurance that if the proper measures were taken, no new taxes would be needed. The only thing Necker refrained from mentioning was that the treasury was empty.

With his disappointing performance, Necker missed his only chance of gaining leadership instead of mere popularity. The lesson was not lost on the deputies; from that day on, Necker was, for all practical purposes, ignored by the national assembly.

The burning question during the weeks that followed concerned a procedural matter: should the three orders—clergy, nobility, and Third Estate—vote separately, the majority of each order constituting one vote; or should the votes be counted by heads? In the former case, the two privileged orders were assured of a permanent majority of two to one; in the latter case, with a substantial minority of the clergy and the nobles voting with the six hundred deputies of the Third Estate, the reverse was equally certain. Necker, in his opening speech, had favoured the vote by orders; but in the face of majority opposition, he soon abandoned this stand, suggesting instead a complicated compromise which was promptly rejected by the Third Estate under Mirabeau's and Siéyès's leadership. That he was resigned to a victory of the Third Estate is clear from the letters his daughter addressed to her husband during these fateful weeks. To mitigate this victory, both father and daughter pinned their hopes on persuading the Third Estate to propose, and the King to accept, a bicameral constitution modelled on the English system. There can be no question of the wisdom of such a compromise, but the Neckers were operating in disregard of political realities: a constitutional monarchy *à l'anglaise* found no favour with the royal family, and Necker had no influence with the deputies of the Third Estate.

It was clear to all but the Neckers that the ministry could not steer a middle course between reaction and revolution unless an alliance could be established between Necker and the moderate leaders of the Third Estate. Malouet, who shared Necker's British constitutional views, happened to meet Mirabeau at the house of a common friend late in May. A heart-to-heart talk revealed that Mirabeau, despite his low estimate of Necker's abilities, was willing to establish such an alliance in order to prevent 'the impending invasion of democracy'. Backed by Montmorin, Malouet thereupon called on Necker and proposed a meeting between him and Mirabeau. Necker, Malouet recalls, stared at the ceiling. After a while, he agreed to meet the man whose morality fell so deplorably short of Madame Necker's standards; he would at least listen to what the tribune had to say.

The meeting was arranged; Mirabeau came into the great man's presence. Necker assumed his noblest and chilliest air: 'Well, sir, Monsieur Malouet tells me that you have some propositions to make. What are they?'

Looking the minister over from head to foot, 'My proposition, sir, is to wish you a good day,' said Mirabeau, turned on his heel, and stalked out of the room. Back at the meeting hall of the Third Estate, he stepped across several benches in his haste to reach Malouet. 'Your man is a fool,' he said. 'He'll have news from me.'

He did have news indeed. On June 17 the Third Estate, joined by a number of deputies of the clergy and the nobility, proclaimed itself the National Assembly; on June 20 the Oath of the Tennis Court was sworn.

Necker's self-righteous arrogance sealed the fate of the monarchy as well as his own. It was on his popularity he based all his illusions. After rejecting Mirabeau's offer of alliance, he promptly proceeded to alienate whatever confidence he still enjoyed at Court. There was no salvation, he advised Louis XVI, but in respecting the sanctity of public opinion, and public opinion was overwhelmingly in favour of the Third Estate. Force was out of the question, for the troops were disaffected and unreliable. Louis XVI vacillated; but the Queen and the Comte d'Artois

(Louis's youngest brother and the future Charles X) were beginning to regard Necker as a traitor. At the cabinet meetings of June 19–22 Necker ran into severe opposition. The Comte d'Artois, meeting him as he was about to enter the council chamber, gave vent to his pent-up hate. 'Where do you think you are going, you miserable foreigner?' he cried, shaking his fist at the guardian angel. 'What business have you in the council, you upstart? Go back at once to the village you came from, or I shall make an end of you.'

When, at the council, Necker's plea for compromise failed, the minister handed in his resignation. 'No, sir,' exclaimed the Comte d'Artois, 'we shall keep you here as a hostage, and we shall make you responsible for whatever happens.' Necker gave in to the extent of approving the draft of the royal declaration, to be read on June 23, by which the King enjoined the States-General to meet separately by orders and to cease questioning the historic prerogatives of the privileged orders. At the same time the declaration abolished all class privileges in the matter of taxation and made other concessions to the bourgeoisie.

In the night of June 22 Necker changed his mind and decided to dissociate himself from the royal declaration. His supporters, his wife and his daughter above all, had besought him not to 'tarnish his glory' by seeming to approve the declaration, and when the States-General met the following day to hear the King's speech, Necker's seat was empty. That, by his absence, he signified his opposition to the King and encouraged the assembly to revolt surely must have been clear to him. The King, having made his speech amid an icy silence, departed. The deputies of the Third Estate and their allies from the other two orders remained in their seats. Then came the well-known scene: Dreux-Brézé, the King's master of ceremonies, delivering Louis's injunction to disperse, and Mirabeau thundering in reply, 'Go tell your master that we are here by the will of the people and shall not yield except to the force of bayonets!'[1]

No bayonets appeared, and the deputies in a body, accompanied by a frenzied crowd of spectators, proceeded to Necker's quarters. 'Long live Monsieur Necker! Stay with us! Be our guide and our father!' Thus, according to the *Gazette de Leyde*, was the guardian angel hailed by the deputation.

---

[1] In her account of these events, written at the end of her life, Madame de Staël does not mention Mirabeau's theatrical apostrophe, which, indeed, may belong to legend rather than history.

Amid the noise of the demonstration, an emissary of the Queen arrived, asking Monsieur Necker to the palace. There the royal couple begged him to remain at his post; Necker graciously agreed. He returned to his house carried on the shoulders of the crowd. As he was ascending the stairs, a lady pressed him in her arms. 'Since I am treated in such a way,' he said, 'I have no choice but to stay and die at my post.' In his drawing room, he was greeted by more ovations and speeches; again he affirmed his resolution to die at his post.

Madame de Staël, lost in the thick crowd, was ecstatic. 'The intense enthusiasm is still present in my memory,' she wrote about 1816, 'and revives the emotion it stirred up in me in those happy days of youth and hope. All those voices repeating the name of my father seemed to belong to a crowd of friends who shared my respectful love.'

On June 27 the King, on Necker's pressure, gave his no longer needed sanction to the events of June 23 and commanded the three estates to meet jointly as the National Assembly. Yet at the same time the well-founded rumour spread that his secret advisers had persuaded him to order a general troop movement from the frontiers; Paris and Versailles were surrounded by 20,000 men. On July 10, replying to Mirabeau's protest, Louis declared that he had no designs against the Assembly but merely wished to maintain public order. The next day, a Friday, at three o'clock in the afternoon, Necker was about to begin dinner with his family and several friends, when Monsieur de La Luzerne, minister of marine, had himself announced and handed him a letter. Necker read it and, without a word, put it in his pocket. The letter, from the King, notified Necker of his dismissal and ordered him to leave the country immediately and *sans bruit*—in secret. Apart from squeezing his daughter's hand several times during the dinner, he gave no sign of emotion. When the party rose from the table, he drew his wife aside and spoke to her briefly. He then retired to write a few hasty notes —among them one to his daughter, who in the meantime had returned to Paris, still unaware of what had happened—and called for the carriage in which he always took his evening drive. Madame Necker, still in her dinner dress, joined him. A day later, they arrived at Brussels.

It was only on the morning of July 12 that Germaine received her father's message, which advised her to go to his estate at Saint-Ouen so that she might avoid becoming the object of a popular demonstration. The news had, however, already become public. To the Swedish embassy there flocked 'deputations from all the city's quarters', she recalled in 1804, 'and they addressed me in the most exalted language on the subject of Monsieur Necker's departure, and on what I should do to force his return. I do not know what my youth and my enthusiasm might have led me to do, but I obeyed my father's wishes.'

At Saint-Ouen, Germaine found a second message from her father, informing her of the route he had taken. On July 13, having summoned her husband to her side, she left for Brussels, where she arrived the next day. Reaching her father's hotel after this exhausting journey, she found her parents in the same clothes in which they had risen from the dinner table at Versailles—still covered with the dust of the road, she recalled, perhaps with a little exaggeration, for surely Monsieur Necker had had ample time to have his coat brushed. In her emotion she threw herself at his feet.

While at Brussels Necker recalled that a few days before his dismissal he had been asked by Messrs Hope, bankers at Amsterdam, to guarantee payment for a shipment of wheat which was on its way to Paris. Necker had agreed to make the two million francs he had deposited with the royal treasury the surety required by the bankers. Afraid that his dismissal might frighten the Amsterdam bankers, he dispatched from Brussels a letter to Messrs Hope, renewing the guarantee. These famous two million francs, which were confiscated after Necker was put on the list of *émigrés* in 1793, were to haunt Madame de Staël's life; Necker never recovered them, and she herself claimed them unsuccessfully until one year before her death. History records no other example of an ousted finance minister leaving a major part of his fortune in the treasury of the country from which he is running away; the opposite, to be sure, happens often enough.

Exactly what occurred at the council of war held at Brussels among Necker, his wife, his daughter, and his son-in-law, remains a mystery. The upshot was that Necker, accompanied by Monsieur de Staël, proceeded post-haste to Basel; his wife and daughter were to follow by slower stages. Monsieur de Staël's role, it may be noted in passing, was peculiar; it is unusual for an ambassador to leave his post at a moment of historic crisis in order to serve as escort to a minister ousted by the government to which he is accredited.

Madame Necker and Germaine had halted at Frankfurt, on their way to Basel, when a courier from Paris reached them with momentous news: the people of Paris, incensed by Necker's dismissal, had risen in arms on July 14; the troops had joined the rebellion; the Bastille had fallen; and the King had recalled Monsieur Necker to the ministry for the third time.

Necker had taken lodging at the hotel 'The Three Kings' at Basel on July 20; his wife and daughter joined him on July 23. According to Madame de Staël, they found him undecided whether or not to accept the ministry. Madame Necker, she recalled, 'was far from dazzled by all these successes and had no desire for my father to accept his recall. . . . He allowed me to listen to the motives of his decision, and I bear witness that it was with the saddest misgivings that he resolved upon returning.' One may surmise that Germaine made no effort to assist her mother in keeping Monsieur Necker from reaping the fruits of his victory. On July 24, just before leaving Basel, Necker wrote to his brother that it seemed to him as if he were drawn into an abyss. Still, the attractions of power were irresistible.

> What a blissful moment [Madame de Staël recalled in 1804] was that journey from Basel to Paris! . . . I believe that nothing like it ever happened to a man who was not the sovereign of his country. . . . The most enthusiastic acclaim accompanied his every step: the women who were working in the fields fell on their knees as his carriage passed by; the principal citizens of the localities through which we passed acted as postilions to lead our horses; and in the cities, the inhabitants unhitched the horses to pull the carriage themselves. . . . Alas! It was I above all who rejoiced in his popularity, it was I who was intoxicated by it.

In Paris, as they drove to the city hall, the entire population was lining the streets, windows, and rooftops. Their ovations reached a climax in the square facing the Hôtel de Ville, where an immense crowd converged upon 'a single man—and that man was my father'. Recalling the scene shortly before her death, Germaine acknowledged it the strongest impression and the last happy day of her life. The 'inconceivable electricity' of that ecstatic moment made her soul 'succumb to emotions that exceeded its strength. When I recovered consciousness, I sensed that I had touched the extreme limits of happiness.'

While Germaine was swooning on the balcony of the city hall, Necker by a magnificent gesture of ineptitude was forfeiting the last trump that remained in his hands: his popularity.

To reinstate Monsieur Necker, to make his daughter touch the extreme limits of happiness, it had been necessary to plunge a kingdom into chaos and to massacre several of the invalid veterans who formed the garrison of the Bastille—among them its governor, the Marquis de Launay, one of the gentlest souls in France, whose head had been paraded through the streets at the end of a pike. The total count of the inmates freed was seven: four counterfeiters, one sex offender, and two madmen, whom the crowd had carried in triumph from the prison to the insane asylum.

This was grotesque enough; Necker's first official action upon his return bordered on the fantastic. France was in anarchy, her government impotent, her army in the process of dissolution, her coffers empty, her people risen in arms, demanding a new order. One might think that Necker, convinced of his unique ability to set things right, would have started out by calling a meeting of the cabinet, the party leaders, and the military command, in order to agree with them on a firm course of action. But the experience of his journey had confirmed him in his fixed idea that he needed no one's advice, that between him and the masses no one was to intervene. He had not yet reached Paris when the news reached him that Baron de Besenval, commander of the army which had been concentrated around Paris two weeks earlier, had been arrested by the revolutionists and was in danger of his life. Necker's first official act was to dispatch a note to Paris asking for the immediate release of Besenval; when he addressed the crowd at the Hôtel de Ville his speech consisted entirely of a plea for Besenval's life. Since the crowd had come to cheer Necker, which was a way of cheering themselves, they cheered; but Necker's strange concern over the fate of the unpalatable Besenval created a poor impression.

Besenval, then in his sixty-eighth year, was a Swiss who had spent his life in the French service; though he had distinguished himself on the battlefield, his reputation rested chiefly on his innumerable amorous conquests. He had been popular in the entourage of Marie Antoinette, a circumstance which had not endeared him to the masses. On April 28, a week before the opening of the States-General, he had ordered his troops to fire on a crowd of demonstrating factory workers, and 'to kill every last one of them'. This, too, did not make him popular. But a few weeks later a mysterious intelligence seems to have sprung up between Besenval and his compatriot, the chief minister, and during the tumultuous days of July 12–14, Besenval, despite higher orders, kept his troops outside Paris, standing by idly while the revolution was being accomplished.

Royalist historians have hinted strongly at some connivance between Besenval and Necker. Necker's exclusive preoccupation with Besenval's fate at a time when the destiny of France was at stake quite understandably made him suspect to extremists on both sides. Whether he acted from the fear that Besenval might make embarrassing revelations or from a more generous though impolitic impulse, his action cost him the support of the masses—in other words, his only asset. Besenval's release was countermanded by the National Assembly, which thus signified its contempt for the government; the gallant baron was allowed to return to his homeland only after lengthy and complicated procedures. Thus, at the very moment when his outward power stood at its zenith, Necker's impotence was made manifest by his inability to secure the one trivial demand he chose to make.

The miracle was that Necker succeeded in hanging on for thirteen more months. Without allies, with his popularity waning every day, he was allowed to continue a shadow existence so long as his inertia did not interfere with the dynamic forces at play. Ignored by the Assembly, distrusted by the Queen and her party, Necker in his splendid isolation became estranged from reality.

While, at Versailles, the Assembly was working out a constitution and the Declaration of the Rights of Man without benefit of Monsieur Necker's advice, the royal couple fell increasingly under the influence of unofficial and reactionary advisers. Incapable of following a firm line of action, Louis XVI was ill-served by a chief minister who suffered from the same weakness. On the one hand, he deferred to Necker's opinion and refused to move the Court and the Assembly farther away from Paris; on the other hand, he periodically attempted, in the manner characteristic of weak men, a limited and ineffectual show of strength. By the end of September 1789 he had refused to accept the Declaration of the Rights of Man without a complementary Declaration of Duties, and he had called the Regiment of Flanders to Versailles. This was hardly enough to control the situation, but it was exactly what was needed to cause an explosion.

On the morning of October 5, under a steady downpour of rain, a strange procession was making its way from Paris to Versailles. In the van marched five or six thousand women and children; they were going to ask their King to give them bread. Indeed, the food supply of Paris was thoroughly disorganized, and another winter of famine was threatening. Among them there was, however, a more than generous sprinkling of prostitutes, whom the organizers of the march had drummed up for the purpose of swelling the ranks and enlivening the morale; thanks to them the column took on the aspect of an army of maenads rather than of worried mothers. On their heels came, on horseback, the commander of the National Guard, General La Fayette, propelled ahead, rather than followed, by his troops, and dazed in bewilderment that he was there at all. Behind the National Guards an even more picturesque column brought up the rear, armed with pikes, sticks, knives, ropes, and other assorted instruments. Together with the prostitutes, these men, recruited from the underworld of Paris, constituted the private army of His Royal Highness the Duke of Orléans. Disorderly though it looked, it was a well-organized host.

The King, that day, was not doing nothing: he was out hunting.

Madame de Staël was at the Swedish embassy when word reached her that a mob was marching on Versailles. Without wasting a moment she ordered her carriage and, by taking various secondary roads, succeeded in reaching the palace before the slow-moving host. She found the Court huddled in the antechambers, in terror for their lives, while the King, who had at last been found and brought back, was closeted with his ministers.

One of the ministers, Saint-Priest, proposed to move the government to Rambouillet; the King, at the head of his guards, was to fight his way through if necessary. 'If you follow this advice,' Necker is said to have told the King, 'it will cost you your head.' There was no reason to be over-alarmed, he pointed out. The King decided to await events.

It was night when the first marchers, soaked to the skin, arrived at Versailles. Some of the women made their way into the Assembly hall, where in the presence of the deputies they took off their clothes to dry. Others congregated before the palace gates, which had been locked; the prostitutes prepared for a busy night with the guards. About midnight the National Guards arrived. La Fayette presented himself to the King, radiating confidence and reassurance. His troops were loyal, the demonstrators had dispersed, everything was under control, and everybody could go to sleep. Setting an example, the general went to bed. It was the night that La Fayette 'lay down against his King'.

The Neckers, with their daughter, also retired. Their apartments were connected with the palace by a long corridor.

At dawn Germaine was awakened when a lady, totally unknown to her, burst into her room to report that a mob had penetrated into the Queen's antechamber and massacred the guards posted at her door; the Queen had barely had time to flee into the King's apartment through a secret passage. Necker, it turned out, had already gone to the palace to join the King: Madame Necker and her daughter hastened after him. Hurrying through the connecting corridor, they heard musket shots from the courtyards; on reaching the gallery they saw pools of blood on the parquet; in the next room the royal bodyguards and the National Guards were embracing one another in an effusion fo fraternity, shouting, 'Vive La Fayette!' Germaine and her mother ran on into the grand salon, into which the Court was crowded. Below, in the courtyard, the mob was screaming for the King and Queen to come to Paris; the shots, it turned out, had been fired out of sheer exuberance and fun: there was no fighting.

At that moment Marie Antoinette entered the salon, self-possessed but tense—as, indeed, she had every reason to be: the bed from which she had fled but a few minutes earlier had been slashed to pieces by the knives and pikes of her callers, who thought she was hiding under the covers. Now a shout came from the courtyard, asking for the Queen. Fully expecting to be torn to pieces, Marie Antoinette took her two children by the hand and calmly went out on the balcony. The roar continued: 'No children!' Marie Antoinette took the children back and went out alone. Her courage seemed to appease the crowd. The threats gave way to acclamations, followed by the resumption of the chorus, 'The King to Paris!'

On leaving the balcony, Marie Antoinette turned to Madame Necker and, convulsively suppressing her sobs, remarked, 'They will force us, the King and me, to go to Paris, with the heads of our bodyguards carried before us on the points of their pikes.'[1]

The Queen's prophecy did not turn out to be literally true: the heads were kept out of her sight while she, the King, the government, and the Assembly were being brought to Paris that day. The Neckers chose to travel separately, by way of the Bois de Boulogne. The rains of the preceding day had cleared the atmosphere. 'The weather,' Germaine recalled years later, 'was exceptionally splendid. The air barely stirred the trees, and the sun's radiance dispelled all darkness from the landscape. Not a single external object corresponded with our sadness.'

It was a peculiarity with Germaine, whom nature usually left indifferent, that she responded with the greatest sensitivity to landscape and weather at moments of crisis.

Under the cloudless autumn sky, swaying atop the pikes, the guardsmen's heads made their way to Paris. Still Monsieur Necker did not resign.

---

[1] This narrative follows the account given by Madame de Staël in her *Reflections on the Trial of the Queen* and *Considerations on . . . the French Revolution*. In neither work is there any mention of the famous episode of La Fayette accompanying the Queen to the balcony and kissing her hand.

With the transfer of the government and of the Assembly to Paris, the actual authority was passing to the political clubs and to the revolutionary 'sections' of the capital. Their power, however, was only beginning to make itself felt. On the surface, the government remained in control, and the Assembly continued to draft a limited monarchic constitution. The King had accepted the Declaration of the Rights of Man and the articles of the Constitution thus far worked out; Germaine and her political friends still saw a chance of consolidating what the Revolution had accomplished and of arresting its further progress.

Necker's part in the events of October 5 and 6 had been negligible. The new hero of the day was La Fayette, whose political ineptitude, egregious self-reliance, craving for popularity, saviour complex, and incapacity to control events made him a worthy successor to the 'guardian angel'. Even within his specific sphere, finances, Necker's activities looked more and more like the antics of a shadow-boxer practising his art in a sealed vacuum. While his policy was degenerating into a frenzied solicitation of short-term loans, at increasing interest rates, for ever smaller amounts—by which Necker expected to keep France going from week to week—the Assembly under Mirabeau's guidance changed the entire face of the French economy by nationalizing the property of the Church and the *émigrés* and issuing paper money in the form of *assignats* on the confiscated property. Though Necker predicted rather accurately what would come of this, still he did not resign. Nor did he resign when the Assembly refused to vote the loans he demanded. Finally, after the Assembly had cornered him with its insistent demands for a full accounting, he published, on July 21, 1790, a report on his financial administration. The nation gasped at his figures: they showed a surplus of 99 millions.

The patent absurdity of Necker's accounting methods was greeted by an outburst of invective in the Assembly, in the daily press, and in broad-sheets. 'Resign and go die in peace,' was the friendly advice Brissot gave him, and it was taken up in unanimous chorus by all the parties. The severe reprisals taken at Nancy against a mutinous Swiss regiment served as further pretext for anti-Neckerian propaganda. On September 2 a mob marched on Necker's offices, with shouts that suggested it would be fun to burn them down. Although the rioters were in a holiday mood, intending no real harm, the occasion presented a fine opportunity for La Fayette to get rid of his rival. This he accomplished by dispatching an aide to Monsieur and Madame Necker, by whom he assured them that he had six hundred men ready to defend their lives. Necker, protesting that he wished above all to avoid blood-shed, accepted with alacrity the offer of a carriage which La Fayette had sent him with unusual foresight.

Without waiting to see the turn of developments, at nine o'clock in the evening, the Neckers slipped out of Paris, to Saint-Ouen. From there, on September 4, Necker sent his resignation to the National Assembly, which received it with profound indifference. On September 8 he and his wife left for Switzerland.

Germaine remained behind. On August 31 she had given birth to her eldest son, Auguste. She also had a lover.

7

LOVE AND POLITICS

————————

THE man who, by Madame de Staël's own testimony, fathered her eldest son was not her first lover. The distinction of being first belonged in all likelihood to the abbé de Talleyrand, who also was the only one among her lovers to turn his back on her. Talleyrand was undoubtedly one of the most intelligent men of his age; he also was one of its most enigmatic. Born in 1754 into one of the oldest noble families of France, he was crippled in his legs by a childhood accident. Since this made him unfit for a military career, he forfeited his right of primogeniture and was destined to the Church, a calling for which he had the greatest aversion. It was he who once remarked that only those who had lived before 1789 could know the sweetness of living: he tasted that sweetness to the full, and his refined libertinism scandalized even a society which took a lenient view of sinful clerics. When he was named bishop of Autun in 1788, it was over the protests of his own pious mother.

In the mind of posterity the name of Talleyrand stands for immorality, cynicism, duplicity, corruption, greed, calculation, opportunism; those who have studied his career will also concede him an immense inner strength of character, wisdom, and an unfailing sense of responsibility as a European. Few men have so fully succeeded in placing their private immorality at the service of their public conscience, and none disdained more haughtily any attempt to justify his conduct to his contemporaries or to history. His imperturbable calm, his drawling indolence, his utter indifference to abuse and humiliation, his incapacity to betray emotion, hid an over-refined sensitiveness and pride.

One of Germaine's later friends, the Duke of Argyll, who saw Talleyrand in 1803, described him thus in his diary:

> Monsieur Talleyrand is the most disgusting-looking individual I ever saw. His complexion is that of a corpse considerably advanced in corruption. His feet are distorted in every possible direction. His having

learned to walk steadily with such wretched materials is proof that he is a man of considerable abilities.

Benjamin Constant, who knew him as well as any man, says cruelly, 'Monsieur Talleyrand's character has been determined by his feet.' When Germaine met that strange ecclesiastic in the late 1780s, his physiognomy had not yet taken on its bloated, corpse-like complexion, and despite his hobbling gait he had no difficulty in conquering women. There was in his manner, in his conversation, an insinuating sweetness and a delicate charm that combined feminine sensibility with virile intelligence and strength. Still unaware of his abysmal selfishness, which subordinated all considerations to his interests and security, Germaine was seduced by this combination of qualities.

There is no indication that there was much passion in their love. What she craved in him was 'the most intimate qualities of the soul'; they alone could inspire the 'perfection of delicacy' that made everything he said so seductive. 'The sweetness and, as it were, softness' of his conversation made Germaine's troubles vanish in his presence. Even after losing him as a lover she continued to depend on his company for her happiness, defended his qualities against his detractors, launched him on his great career, and turned against him only after he had shattered her last illusion of friendship.

When, in *Delphine*, Madame de Staël took her revenge on Talleyrand and portrayed him in the character of Madame de Vernon, Talleyrand remarked, 'I understand that Madame de Staël, in her novel, has disguised both herself and me as women.' None of the men whom she loved could regard her entirely as a woman, and Talleyrand, who was attracted by her intellectual rather than by her feminine qualities, soon came to look upon her as a political ally rather than a mistress. At the time Germaine met him, he was under vows not only to the Church but also to the Comtesse de Flahaut, who had borne him a son.[1] Germaine was not averse to sharing her lover with Madame de Flahaut—she usually was liberal-minded in this respect—but clearly such an arrangement could not have satisfied her thirst for love and glory. Shortly before the outbreak of the Revolution—late in 1788 or early in 1789—she met the man who became the first of her grand passions. Probably it was Talleyrand who introduced him to her.

Louis, Vicomte de Narbonne-Lara, was thirty-three years old when

---

[1] That son, the Comte de Flahaut, continued the tradition and sired the illegitimate half-brother of Napoleon III, the Duc de Morny. Talleyrand perhaps was also the real father of the painter Delacroix.

Germaine met him. He was not only handsome, intelligent, sensitive, and a notorious conqueror of hearts: he was also cloaked in mystery.

Born in Italy, in a castle belonging to the Duke of Parma, he was the son of—but who knows? Perhaps of Louis XV and the Comtesse de Narbonne-Lara; or even, as rumour had it, of Louis XV and his daughter, Madame Adélaïde. He was baptized at Versailles, with Madame Adélaïde as godmother, the future Louis XVI as godfather, and the Comte de Narbonne-Lara conspicuously absent. Brought up like a prince of the blood, he spent, in quick succession, the fortunes of the Comtesse de Narbonne, of Madame Adélaïde, and of his wife, whom he married in 1782. With the powerful protection he enjoyed, he was assured of a brilliant military career, and there was no need for him to give himself the trouble of serving in the American war, as so many of his fellow officers did; by 1786 he commanded a regiment without ever having fought a battle except on sofas and beds. Louis XVI, his cousin once or twice removed, as the case may be, on numerous occasions exiled the spirited young man to various remote garrison towns, but each time Madame Adélaïde intervened. At the time he met Germaine, all he had to show for the first thirty-three years of his life was a host of mistresses, at least two illegitimate children, and an incalculable accumulation of debts. But he possessed the same indefinable charm, the same refined simplicity of manners as Talleyrand, and added to these both physical beauty and a certain nobility and idealism.

Germaine's salon in the rue du Bac had become a political meeting place for the liberal aristocracy which soon was to carry out the first phase of the Revolution. Gouverneur Morris, a frequent guest, described Germaine to George Washington as 'a woman of wonderful wit, and above prejudices of every kind', and her house as a Temple of Apollo. (To his diary he admitted, 'I feel very stupid in this group.') Narbonne, both by temperament and by education, was not sympathetic to the libertarian tone that prevailed at the rue du Bac, but Germaine's exalted eloquence carried him away and awakened in him the ambition of fulfilling his gifts in the cause of freedom and progress. For three years he abandoned himself to the prevailing euphoria and allowed Germaine to guide him towards glory. 'The moment he saw me,' she confided to his friend the Comte de Clermont-Tonnerre (who was also talking love to her), 'he changed his destiny for my sake. He broke his attachments and consecrated his life to me. In a word, he convinced me that he could love me well enough, and that he would consider himself happy to possess my heart, but that if he lost it irremediably, he could not survive.'

By July 1789 Gouverneur Morris had guessed the degree of Germaine's intimacy with Narbonne; towards the end of the year it had become a matter of public knowledge. The publicity of the liaison was more than Monsieur de Staël could endure, and when he discovered that his wife had spent twelve hours tête-à-tête with Narbonne, he tried to forbid him his house. Germaine was outraged. That she had spent twelve hours with her friend was pure calumny: the correct number, she informed her husband in a note, was six. Moreover, since Monsieur de Staël had not been present, he had no right to make insinuations. The purity of her sentiments gave her the strength and the courage to insist on receiving Monsieur de Narbonne. 'I have a great deal of friendship for Monsieur de N., but nothing of what you write to me about him is true.'

There is a strong ring of truth in these words: Germaine lied with sincerity and conviction. In December 1789 she was pregnant by Narbonne. Monsieur de Staël flattered himself that the was he father—a fact which proves that, at least at strategic intervals, Germaine fulfilled her marital obligations to him—and there seemed to be no reason to doubt his paternity until the recent discovery of Germaine's letters to Narbonne. Thus, on October 2, 1792, she wrote that all her blood rebelled at the idea of Monsieur de Staël calling Auguste his son in her presence, and in November she informed her lover that little Auguste's character already seemed to show some traits of her 'divine friend'.[1] Friendship, in Germaine's vocabulary, could go a very long way.

Monsieur de Staël's suspicions, then, were well founded. Germaine's rebuke to him had, however, the desired effect of making him mind his own business, which in her eyes consisted principally in serving Monsieur Necker. The fact that the Swedish ambassador had, in July 1789, abandoned his post in order to serve his exiled father-in-law as postilion had caused King Gustavus to raise his eyebrows, but Germaine, in a long letter to that monarch, had taken all the blame on herself. The latter, dated September 4, 1789, after a glowing account of the events of July 14, concludes as follows:

[1] Unpublished letter owned by the Berg Collection of the New York Public Library. While these allusions are not conclusive proof, Germaine's letters leave absolutely no doubt of Narbonne's having sired Germaine's younger son, Albert, born late in 1792.

It remains for me to give Your Majesty an account of my personal conduct. I have obtained, I have exacted, from Monsieur de Staël that he absent himself for ten days in order to accompany my father at a moment when his life and liberty were, at the very least, exposed to danger. . . . I dared to be certain that Your Majesty would approve of my action. It is with respect but without apprehension that I give Your Majesty this account of Monsieur de Staël's conduct.

That the daughter of a Genevese upstart should presume to make decisions in his name for his ambassador was a little too much for even the most benevolent of despots. But then as always Germaine was blissfully unaware of other people's real thoughts. Gustavus had admired Rousseau; Gustavus was enlightened, a champion of liberty and philosophy; Gustavus had throughout his reign made a show of opposing the nobility and of relying on popular support. What was more natural, Germaine reasoned, than that Gustavus should welcome the birth of liberty in France? In her own letters and in her husband's official dispatches, she never seemed to doubt that the King sympathized with the Revolution. Louis XVI, so Gustavus was informed, was 'a nonentity'; Marie Antoinette 'has just received such a lesson that it is believed she will no longer meddle with anything'.

Now kings tend to be sensitive to slurs on the royal dignity, and none was more sensitive than Gustavus III. At the very time when Madame de Staël was extolling to him the glory of the Fourteenth of July, he was beginning to dream of himself in the role he actually assumed two years later as leader of Europe's princes against the Revolution. One may imagine with what emotions he looked on his ambassador's reports. Soon enough, his increasing displeasure with his ambassador made itself manifest in the instructions Staël received from Stockholm. By that time, however, the luckless diplomat was too far committed to his pro-revolutionary policy. Besides, he had become a desperate man.

As soon as Germaine was able to travel after giving birth to Auguste, she followed her father to Coppet, where he was licking his wounds. Monsieur de Staël, left behind, was not allowed to enjoy his freedom. In letter after letter, Germaine continued to instruct him in his duties, and since she held the purse strings, her messages carried more authority than those of the King of Sweden. Staël felt suicidal. 'My wife causes me every possible trouble,' he wrote to his friend, Nils von Rosenstein. 'My parents-in-law are of no help whatever. Although they are aware that my conduct towards their daughter goes far beyond what might reasonably be expected of me, they do nothing to compensate me.' To ask for the least sum of money, he added, would be folly: 'Knowing their disposition, I would be sure to be placed under my wife's guardianship forever.'

An abysmal thought. But he needed money. He had, indeed, committed an incredible folly: he had fallen in love with a woman approaching her seventies, the former actress Mademoiselle Clairon, who had coached Germaine so well in the vanished days of the Neckers' salon. Playing on this pity, on his despair, on his pathetic need to be understood, forgiven, and mothered, she had caught the ageing boudoir hero in an inescapable net—inescapable not because his passion was permanent, or because he felt bound by oaths, but because his engagement was duly signed, notarized, and stamped: he had made over to Mademoiselle Clairon a life pension of 5,000 francs per annum. 'You are bringing me back,' wrote *la* Clairon, 'to the sweet and innocent illusions of my youth. I shall owe you the happiness of loving until my last breath.' A few years later she sued him for breach of contract.

Reviving Clairon's sweet and innocent illusions was not the only manner in which King Gustavus's ambassador manifested his increasing eccentricity. He also had turned to the Swedenborgian sect, was deeply involved in the mysticism of the Illuminati, and indulged in conjuring spirits.

As early as the eleventh century, the chronicler Adalbert of Bremen remarked upon the adeptness of the Swedes for sorcery. In the Age of Reason, and at the court of the enlightened despot Gustavus, two opposed schools of socrerers and soothsayers were engaged in secret and mortal combat. King Gustavus's clairvoyant, Miss Arfwedsson, whose oracle he consulted on every important occasion, was all-powerful, but she was decidedly outnumbered by the soothsayers who surrounded the King's brother, Duke Charles of Sudermania, for whom they predicted a glorious future. Most influential among them was the Duke's friend, Baron Reuterholm, who, before witnesses, had put the Duke into a hypnotic trance to make him prophesy the role he was to play in the regeneration of mankind. Reuterholm came to France at the outbreak of the Revolution to visit the various lodges of Free Masons and Illuminati. In the Swedish ambassador he found a most receptive pupil and friend. Baron de Staël already had attached to his embassy a Swedenborgian named Halldin, whose speciality it was to make spirits appear in mirrors (he thus produced John the Baptist) and to read the future in books stained with blood. Under Reuterholm's influence these innocent pastimes took a more serious turn.

At one of the séances held in 1790 in Staël's presence, a medium revealed that Duke Charles was 'in possession of Truth itself' and that Reuterholm must be his only instrument. Reporting these prophecies to Reuterholm, Staël continued: 'Mention of the King was also made; what has been said concerning His Majesty is of great interest but of such a nature that I dare not trust it to my pen.' In view of what happened to the King two years later, these words have a sinister sound.

The programme of the sect probably was not fully known to Duke Charles. One of its spokesmen formulated it thus:

> The edifice of the universal republic to be established has, as its ultimate aim, the happiness of mankind. Intelligence and virtuous endeavour must serve as its bases. Those who excel by their intelligence must govern the world. . . . We must set fire to the cities and destroy them, for they are schools of tyranny, corruption, and misery. . . . By a spontaneous return to nature, free societies will then form on the model of the Golden Age. . . . It is the French Revolution which will accomplish all these marvels; the Revolution is the divine deed *par excellence*, the most solemn deed ever witnessed on earth since the Deluge; it is nothing less than the Day of Judgment for the tyrants.

Gustavus III had a remarkable ambassador in Monsieur de Staël. Though unaware of Staël's involvement with his future assassins, he had grown distrustful enough to dispatch Baron Taube to Aachen late in 1789, with the mission of acting as his unofficial ambassador to Louis XVI. Count Fersen, Gustavus's agent at Versailles, instructed Taube as follows:

> The King commands me to let you know that all of Staël's dispatches are prejudiced in favour of the Revolution; he will pretend to pay attention to what Staël reports to him, but only in order to penetrate more deeply into the revolutionists' projects and ideas. The King orders you to explain this to the King and Queen [of France], so that they may not be deceived by it.

Staël's mystical exaltation, while it led him into dangerous political waters, did nothing to extricate him from his private difficulties. On the contrary, in addition to everything else the thought of his sinfulness began to torture him. 'My fate would be more tolerable,' he wrote to Reuterholm, 'if I could bear my cross, if the old Adam in me were less alive, if I frankly resigned myself into the hands of God. . . . Pray for me, my friend, so that my weak faith may be strengthened. My tender friend, my heart is oppressed; I am flooded with tears. Pray, ah!

pray—' and so forth for several pages. He even asked him to pray for
Madame de Staël.

Her husband's mystico-political exaltation was altogether alien to
Germaine's spirit. She ignored it. His conflict between 'the old Adam'
and his idealist aspirations she would have found equally incomprehensible had she taken the trouble to find out its existence. Soul searching
was the one activity she never indulged in. Endowed with an intelligence that was brilliantly suited for analysis, classification, and generali-
zation, she brought it to bear almost exclusively on society, rarely on
individuals, never on herself. Finding her existence only in total, global
commitment, she might as well have ceased existing as attempted to
separate the elements that made up her life—personal relationships and
politics, for instance, or love and friendship. They all existed simultaneously, not side by side, but merged into one single stream of
experience. This superb emotional muddle, combined with an utterly
rational and analytical intelligence, produced paradoxical results.

Her love-and-politics complex was one of these paradoxes. Politics
with her was always intensely personal, 'a matter of proper names', as
she put it. Exaltation for such abstract causes as freedom, justice, or
virtue required a hero who personified them or, at the least, friends
with whom the exaltation could be shared. And yet, with all her
enthusiastic raptures in which political ideals, hero worship, and sexual
love became fused into a seemingly irrational tangle, her political aims
remained invariably prosaic, moderate, practical. The metaphysical
ravings of the Illuminati were not for her, nor were the fanaticism
of either Jacobins or royalists, nor even the abstract rigidity of Rousseau's disciples. The aim towards which all her delirium tended was
simply a bicameral constitution, a representative government based on
property qualifications, and a guarantee of civil liberties. Rarely was so
much emotion placed at the service of so rational an aim.

Another paradox was her lack of exclusiveness in love. On the one
hand, she made love an absolute condition, a matter of total involvement; on the other hand, no one could have been more matter-of-fact,
more reasonable, in accepting imperfections in that relationship. Faithfulness in the narrow sense (as opposed to loyalty) is possible only to
those who seek an attainable goal in love; no one who spends his life in
quest of the ideal of absolute love can afford to be faithful, unless by
some miracle he chances to stumble on the desired object from the very
start. Germaine had no such luck, and she had no illusions except the

ultimate one. There was no reason why she should renounce her quest for the sake of being faithful to a man who had been found wanting; at the same time, there was no reason why she should turn from a man merely because he fell a little short of the ideal. Infidelities on either part were of little account, and the boundaries between love and friendship were indistinct. In this, she was the child of her century: the sexual act was not, as it has since become, a touchstone, and loyalty in friendship was placed above sexual fidelity. Germaine, however, carried the blurring of the boundaries a little further than most. Incapable of letting an old lover go, no matter what compromises, pressures, and ruses were needed to prevent his emancipation, she herself was compelled to resume her own quest whenever a new potential lover appeared. This incapacity and this compulsion created a general impression of promiscuity—an unjust estimate of her character.

When Narbonne had 'changed his destiny' in order to fly to glory on the wings of Germaine's love, he had been obliged to sacrifice his acknowledged mistress, the Comtesse de Laval, a woman considerably older than he. But Germaine was not content with snatching away the Countess's lover; she also fell in love with her son, Mathieu de Montmorency-Laval.

Born in 1767 into one of the greatest houses of France, Mathieu had been brought up with the manners of an aristocrat and the convictions of a liberal. He had served in the American campaign and greeted the French Revolution with enthusiasm. As a deputy for the nobles in the States-General, he stood considerably to the left of Necker and opposed the minister's pet scheme for a bicameral legislature; a House of Lords, he warned, would serve as a bastion of privilege and lead to the restoration of tyranny. It was he who led the nobility in stripping itself of all privileges in that strange orgy of self-sacrifice that took place on the night of August 4.

At the time when Germaine met him (the date is not certain), Mathieu de Montmorency must have appeared to her as the synthesis of all that was noble, good, and beautiful, both in the past and in the future society. Tall, slender, very blond, refined and elegant in his manners, burning with the most disinterested idealism, incapable of a vulgar thought or action, he embodied the most precious qualities of the aristocracy and placed them at the service of the cause of justice and equality for all mankind. There was about Mathieu something otherworldly and almost angelic that caused his mother to remark, 'Poor Mathieu! He is a dupe, a dupe!' But to be the dupe of one's

E

generous emotions was, for Germaine, far preferable to its opposite, and when later tragic events made Mathieu expiate his revolutionary past in the service of altar and throne, she bore with the reformed sinner as patiently as he bore with her, the unreformed one.

When, in the morning of July 14, 1817, Mathieu received a message informing him that Germaine had just died, he noted the date: 'Fatal day!' The allusion was not only to the fall of the Bastille; even the first anniversary of the day of Necker's triumph had brought tragedy into Mathieu's life. Unhappily married, he had given his heart, long before he met Germaine, to Pauline de Laval, the wife of one of his cousins, who shared his revolutionary fervour. On July 14, 1790, the new constitution was to be solemnly sworn to, on the Champ de Mars, by the King, by 60,000 deputies of the *départements*, and by the armed forces. Pauline de Laval, in company with other fashionable enthusiasts, spent the entire night of July 13–14 carting dirt in a wheelbarrow on the Champ de Mars, which had to be graded for the occasion. She caught a chill and died of pneumonia, victim of an excess of patriotic zeal.

For Germaine, who never pushed her convictions to the point of pushing wheelbarrows, the Feast of the Federation (as the celebration of July 14, 1790, was called) might well have seemed a personal triumph in love and politics. As, from the diplomatic box, she watched her lover Talleyrand, bishop of Autun, celebrating High Mass at the altar raised on the field, in the presence of the King and Queen, before a crowd of hundreds of thousands assembled on the anniversary of her father's triumph, which was to become the national holiday of France, in order to solemnize a constitution which she had helped to shape, a constitution under which she expected her lover Narbonne to play a brilliant role—she could not help being carried away by the illusion that in her hands were the reins of power and of love.

It was shortly after this celebration, it seems, that Germaine fell in love with the quasi-widowed Mathieu. Sainte-Beuve, invoking the testimony of Madame Récamier, asserts that the love between Germaine and Mathieu was always platonic. It is true that Germaine was with child until August 31 and that she was absent from Paris from October 1790 to January 1791. But it is also true that she once mentioned Mathieu among the three men she had most loved in her life, and that the other two—Talleyrand and Narbonne—had undoubtedly been her lovers. Whether then or at a later date, it is most probable that, at least briefly, the relationship was more than platonic: with no one was it easier to blur the line between friendship and love than with the angelic but seductive Mathieu.

Whatever the nature of her relationship with Mathieu, it is clear that Germaine's love for Narbonne became, if anything, more passionate in the following years—perhaps because Narbonne tended to slip away from her while Mathieu remained faithful. In the curious sentimental pentagon formed by Germaine, Talleyrand, Narbonne, Mathieu, and Mathieu's mother, Madame de Laval, all except Madame de Laval were satisfied with the imprecise *status quo*. To define it would have meant its destruction.

Germaine's bliss at the Feast of the Federation was mixed with apprehension. 'At the very moment when his [Necker's] triumph appeared to be celebrated,' she recalled, 'he felt perhaps that there no longer was any hope.' Indeed, six weeks later Necker was fleeing to Switzerland. The crowds no longer pulled his carriage; in Vesoul they even stoned it. But Necker's fall was not so heavy a blow to Germaine as might have been expected. She had Narbonne; she had Talleyrand and Mathieu; she had the whole Constitutional party. Through them she would complete, consolidate, and contain the Revolution. History would vindicate her father, and she would make history. It was with great reluctance that, in October 1790, she left Paris with her new-born son to join her parents at Coppet, where she could neither make history nor enjoy the company of friends and lovers.

Necker had bought the castle and barony of Coppet in 1784. Situated on the shore of the Lake of Geneva, about ten miles from Geneva, in what is now the canton of Vaud and what was then Bernese territory, the castle dated from 1457 but had been rebuilt, except for one of its towers, after a fire in the sixteenth century. Necker in acquiring it became the Baron of Coppet. On the night of August 4, 1789, the nobility of France had, at Versailles, renounced all its feudal rights and revenues; but Necker, the presiding genius in this act of generosity, continued to draw his feudal dues from his estate, since it was safely outside France.

He had bought Coppet both as a retreat and a source of income. Its somewhat dilapidated condition required a good many repairs. Neither he nor his daughter had ever intended to make it a permanent residence; even after Coppet, much against their will, became just that, they were in the habit of renting an apartment in Geneva for the winter months. The château, an imposing, handsome edifice, is hidden from the lake

front by the tall trees of its park. Only the upper windows offer a view
on the lake and on the snow-capped mountains of Savoy; built in an
age when beauty was seen in restful greenery and gentle, harmonious
lines rather than in the wild majesty of desolate peaks, the house is
oriented towards the land and the Jura, not the lake and the Alps.

Madame de Staël had no eye for either. When years later, Chateaubriand, her guest, envied her for the splendours of her exile, she simply
sighed, 'Ah! The gutter of the rue du Bac!' Her letters from Coppet and
Geneva in the winter of 1790–1 set the tone for the years to come. 'This
country does not please me at all,' she wrote to Gibbon. 'I have a strong
desire to return to Paris and, above all, to make sure that my father will
return there.'

But Necker knew well that a return was impossible, and Madame
Necker, dividing her time between opium and neurasthenia, was absolutely opposed. Not that Necker had resigned himself to his fate. After
spending four days at Coppet, Gibbon wrote to Lord Sheffield, 'I . . .
could have wished to have shewn him as a warning to any aspiring youth
possessed with the Demon of ambition. With all the means of private
happiness in his power he is the most miserable of human beings: the
past, the present and the future are equally odious to him.'

While Necker brooded over the fickleness of nations and the ingratitude of kings, Lausanne and its environs were filling up with refugees
from the Revolution; for the most part, they held him responsible for
all their ills and spoke of him as the devil incarnate. 'One must pretend
to be very aristocratic here,' Germaine wrote to her husband from
Geneva. 'The Genevese, the Bernese, the French refugees are incredibly
fanatic in this respect. I believe that I might almost become a Jacobin
again—if it were possible to forget the Jacobins' disgraceful conduct
towards my father.'

The Genevese, who had for many years watched Necker's career
with envy and derision, were not at all displeased at his discomfiture.
The Neckers had given themselves airs, and giving oneself airs has at
all times been the most unforgivable crime in Geneva. Madame de
Staël, in addition to the airs she gave herself, had flown in the face of
everything that Calvin's city stood for. 'If you promise me the most
absolute secrecy,' she wrote her husband, 'I shall confess to you that
the society of the Genevese is unbearable to me. Their love of equality
is but a desire to drag everybody down; their liberty is insolence, and
their morality is boredom.'

In January 1791, exasperated by Geneva, Germaine accepted an invitation to Lausanne from Madame Cazenove d'Arlens, a cousin of Benjamin Constant (whom she was not to meet until three years later). Rosalie de Constant, the favourite among Benjamin's innumerable cousins, who later detested Germaine, was enchanted by her on first acquaintance:

> She is an astonishing woman. The feelings to which she gives rise are different from those that any other woman can inspire. Such words as *sweetness, gracefulness, modesty, desire to please, deportment, manners,* cannot be used when speaking of her; but one is carried away, subjugated by the force of her genius. It follows a new path; it is a fire that lights you up, that sometimes blinds you, but that cannot leave you cold and indifferent. Her intelligence is too superior to allow others to make their worth felt, and nobody can look intelligent beside her. Wherever she goes, most people are changed into spectators.

And yet, at the same time: 'It is astonishing to find in this singular woman a kind of childlike good humour which saves her from appearing in the least pedantic.'

All those who knew Germaine intimately, stressed, when speaking of her, this outgoing, good-humoured, unstilted quality, in which she formed a striking contrast with her mother. Still, with all her unpretentiousness, the drawing rooms of Lausanne seemed to her an intolerably narrow stage. It was not enough to have spectators; one also needed room to act.

A few days after her visit to Lausanne, Germaine left her parents to their 'infernal peace' at Coppet and drove off to the heavenly noise of Paris.

Although in retrospect Madame de Staël's role in the French Revolution appears negligible, it may be said that 1791 was her year. Thus, at least, it appeared to some of her contemporaries and, no doubt, to her. It also was the crucial year, for it was the year when the French lost faith in their King, when the idea of a constitutional monarchy was tested in France and died stillborn.

The Constitution, a compromise which satisfied no one, was the work of Siéyès and La Fayette rather than of Madame de Staël, who objected to many of its features. Siéyès was a steady fixture in her salon: she admired him and quarrelled with him in equal doses. As for La Fayette, her opinion of him was low. The defects to which she was blind in her father she noticed acutely in the general. La Fayette, who in his letters to Washington marvelled modestly at the phenomenon of his own unshakable popularity, was described in Staël's reports to Stockholm as inadequate to his task, dominated by flatterers, incapable, and untrustworthy. Germaine remarked of him and of Bailly, the mayor of Paris, 'Those gentlemen are like the rainbow; they always appear after the storm is over.' However, La Fayette's politic l aims were close to Germaine's, and he was a friend of Narbonne's. His craving for popularity and glory interfered with her plan, no doubt; but he possessed the virtue of not being terribly clever and could be outmanœuvred with ease.

Her plan was, very simply, to arrest the course of the Revolution and to consolidate its gains. The Constitution, with all its defects, was the only guarantee of freedom. It could be amended later: for the present, it must be supported. Only a strong and intelligent leader could accomplish the transformation of France into a constitutional monarchy, and that leader was to be Narbonne. Anything to the right of such a programme would lead to the restoration of absolutism; everything to the left, to mob rule.

Her analysis was, of course, thoroughly reasonable. The several moderate political groups might disagree on a number of fundamental points—the royal veto power, for instance, or the status of the Church —but this was no time to quarrel, when the fate of the monarchy hung in the balance. So long as rational men were in control, rational solutions could be worked out; what had to be avoided at all costs was the rule of fanatics. It was a position to which Germaine adhered consistently throughout her life.

Working on the assumption that intelligent men cou d always find a basis of agreement, Germaine made her salon the forum of all shades of moderate opinion and brought together such disparate personalities as Brissot and Condorcet on the leftist extreme of the spectrum and Barnave, the brothers Lameth, and Malouet on the other end. Her own group—the triumvirate of Talleyrand, Narbonne, and Montmorency, reinforced by François de Jaucourt, Lally-Tollendal, and others—held less influence than did these men in the inner councils of the Assembly and the clubs; but if Germaine could win the support of the politicians for them, their independent position would work in their favour.

Germaine possessed a marked talent for political intrigues of the short-range variety—that is, the variety which, though successful for a moment, soon reveals itself as utterly futile. As Napoleon was to remark later, she not only united all opinions in her salon but also conferred with their representatives singly. The tortuous negotiations by which she eventually succeeded in having Narbonne appointed minister of war would do credit to any professional lobbyist in twentieth-century Paris or Washington. If she failed to reap the expected results, the fault was not so much in her overestimating Narbonne (he was vastly superior to La Fayette, for instance, and Napoleon later praised him as his ablest diplomat) as in her underestimating the forces at play to the right and to the left of her coalition.

Secret though her negotiations were, it was plain to everybody that Madame de Staël's salon was a centre of politicial intrigue. The extreme right and the extreme left, though irreconcilable on every other issue, united in attacking her with all the venom and sarcasm they could muster—and both factions had writers who were extremely gifted along those lines.

As early as 1790 a pamphlet entitled *King Necker* had quipped, on the subject of Germaine: 'She spares no effort, no effort whatever, to make men for her father, and her father refuses nothing to the men she has made for him.' In the *Acts of the Apostles*, published by the royalist Rivarol, she appears as the 'Bacchante of the Revolution', the only person in Europe 'capable of deceiving the public on her sex'. This unchivalrous allusion to her physical appearance Rivarol soon followed up with more specific charges. His *A Little Dictionary of the Great Men of the Revolution* (1790) was dedicated to Madame de Staël. 'We take the liberty,' the dedication ran, 'to place your name in front of our collection, for to publish a dictionary of the great men of the day is merely to submit to you the list of your adorers.'

A comedy, *The Intrigues of Madame de Staël*, was circulated in pamphlet form early in 1791, in which Germaine was shown as a nymphomaniac who stirred up riots to keep her lovers. A later poem, satirizing her attempts to unite all the parties, shows her as receiving the royalists in the morning, the Girondists for dinner, the Jacobins for supper, 'and at night, everybody'.

Germaine was wounded but not intimidated. The amount of abuse she was able to take is truly impressive; as long as she was riding the crest of the wave, she seemed impervious to it.

The tragedy which foredoomed the success of her policy occurred at a time when she was visiting her parents in Switzerland, from May to September 1791: the attempted escape of the royal family, and their arrest on June 22 at Varennes, was one of the few events of the Revolution in which she played no part. However, it was an event which had its origins in a policy that was dear to her heart and for which her friend Talleyrand was to a large degree responsible. Louis XVI was ready to accept almost everything, but he drew the line at his religion. The Civil Constitution of the Clergy, which created a schism in the Catholic Church from 1791 until 1801, divided the French clergy into those who refused to take the civil oath and to recognize the 'constitutional' bishops, and those who took the oath and incurred papal excommunication. At the head of the second group stood Talleyrand. Madame de Staël, who saw in the Civil Constitution the first step leading to her dream of a Protestant France, seemed unaware of the disastrous consequences that must follow from splitting a nation along a single political and religious line.

The reasons that decided Louis XVI to attempt flight were complex; there can be little doubt, however, that he was motivated chiefly by his religious conscience. The thought of hearing Mass said by an excommunicated priest, of confessing to a schismatic, was more than he could bear, and he yielded to those who had been pressing him for some time to flee and join the *émigré* princes. His arrest and return, his acceptance of the completed and amended Constitution, which was to become operative in September 1791, did not augur well for the Constitution's success. The nation could not trust a captive king.

After a summer in Switzerland, spent recovering from a bout of scarlet fever and suffering her usual agonies of boredom, Germaine arrived in Paris in time for the opening of the Legislative Assembly. Since, for reasons that will be shown presently, the Swedish embassy could no longer serve as a political meeting place, Germaine transferred her activities to the house belonging to her father and to the salon of Madame de Condorcet, wife of the philosopher and mathematician who was then playing a leading role in the new Assembly. The Marquise de Condorcet, whose social and political power were as great as her beauty, shared Germaine's admiration for Narbonne, and together the two women worked in his interest with efficiency and skill. The time was ripe, for war was in the air and a war policy was the one area of agreement between the party groups which Germaine sought to unite behind her chosen hero.

Brissot and the Girondists wanted war to consolidate and extend the Revolution. The Queen wanted war to be saved by her brother, Emperor Leopold, from the Revolution. La Fayette and the other 'Americans'—Rochambeau, Custine, Luckner, the Lameths—wanted war to acquire more glory, to restore military discipline, and to strengthen the Constitution against the extremists of either side. Madame de

Staël wanted war for the same reasons, and to offer Narbonne the opportunity to play the roles of the elder and the younger Pitt combined. The *émigrés*, in the meantime, were inciting the reluctant princes of Europe to a crusade against the Revolution. The outbreak of hostilities with Austria and Prussia was a foregone conclusion, and it was a wonder they were delayed for as long as they were.

Despite all the backing Germaine had secured for Narbonne, the royal couple stubbornly opposed his nomination. 'Rather perish,' said Marie Antoinette, 'than be saved by La Fayette and the Constitutionalists.' Narbonne's closeness to La Fayette and to Madame de Staël, the two *bêtes noires* of the Court, would have made his nomination impossible if Barnave—who since Varennes had gained increasing influence over the Queen—had not been drawn into his camp by Germaine and Madame de Condorcet. By some obscure manœuvres, the minister of war, Du Portail, who advocated a peace policy, was persuaded to resign, and Barnave convinced Marie Antoinette that Narbonne was the monarchy's last hope of salvation. On December 5, the Queen in a note urged her husband to nominate Narbonne immediately; on December 6 Narbonne was installed at the War Department. On December 7, he addressed the Legislative Assembly and received its enthusiastic acclaim—led, from the diplomatic box, by the Swedish ambassadress.

The Queen was under no illusions. To Fersen she wrote on the same day:

> At last Comte Louis de Narbonne is minister of war, since yesterday. What glory for Madame de Staël, what joy for her to have the whole army at her disposal . . .! He may turn out to be useful, if he wants to, since he is clever enough to rally the Constitutionalists and since he has the right tone for speaking to the army such as it is today.

What joy indeed! The Assembly voted an appropriation of twenty millions for the army. Within a month, Narbonne promised, 150,000 men would stand ready at the frontiers. He then departed to inspect the troops, accompanied by Mathieu de Montmorency, a liaison officer between the high command and Madame de Staël. The inspection tour was a triumph; the soldiers cheered the new hero and his flamboyant speeches, and a martial spirit of confidence settled over the country. The third lover, Talleyrand, was dispatched to London with the delicate mission of securing a promise of English neutrality in case of war. Nor was Monsieur de Staël allowed to go idle: to Gustavus III,

E*

by now the leading spirit of the anti-revolutionary crusade, the ambassador praised, in report on report, the messianic qualities of his wife's lover.

While her several satellites were thus employed on the military and diplomatic fronts, Germaine was meditating a bold stroke which, had it succeeded, would have snatched from the gathering anti-French coalition the military hero who was to command the allied forces in the coming war. The 'mad idea', as Marie Antoinette called it, was to offer the supreme French military command to the Duke of Brunswick, a nephew of the great Frederick and a hero of the Seven Years' War. Whether this notion originated with Narbonne or Germaine it is difficult to say; certain it is that, despite La Fayette's opposition, they secured the approval of the foreign minister, de Lessart, to send an emissary to Brunswick. The emissary was young François de Custine, son of the general, an admirer of Narbonne and a worshipper of Madame de Staël.

The idea, mad perhaps, was also ingenious. The Duke of Brunswick, though he later was to become in the eyes of the Jacobins the very embodiment of reactionary tyranny, was of a liberal disposition. His family ties with Prussia, England, and the House of Orange might have kept these powers out of the war; or, perhaps, his appointment would have prevented a war altogether. (Such was Louis XVI's hope when he consented to making the offer.) The Duke himself, though he finally declined the offer, negotiated seriously throughout January 1792.

Narbonne returned from his inspection tour flushed with optimism. The defences, he announced to the Assembly on January 25, were ready, the army's discipline and morale magnificent, supplies assured. When he finished his report, Brissot rose to move that, unless Austria disavowed the Declaration of Pillnitz[1] by March 1, France was to consider herself at war with her. From the diplomatic box, Germaine saw the Assembly rise in unanimous applause.

Actually, the declaration of war came only on April 20, when Louis XVI appeared before the Assembly and demanded, in a tone of voice about as expressive as if he were ordering a cup of coffee, that war be declared on 'the King of Hungary and of Bohemia'. The war Germaine had so desired was to last for twenty-two years, to cost the lives of several million soldiers, and to change the face of the world, without bringing about a single one of the results she had hoped from it. By

---

[1] The declaration, issued by Emperor Leopold II and by King Frederick William II of Prussia, calling on Europe to restore Louis XVI to his former authority.

April 20, however, things had changed quite radically for Germaine and her hero.

The King, with the stubborn instinct that sometimes served him as a substitute for intelligence, had never trusted Narbonne. In the cabinet Narbonne's position became increasingly insecure. The royalist minister of marine, Bertrand de Molleville, opposed him outright; the foreign minister, de Lessart, withdrew his support. Narbonne's principal strength came from the backing of the Girondists, for whom he actually had little sympathy. To end this precarious situation, Narbonne decided, upon Germaine's advice, to appeal directly to the Queen, to place his political programme before her, and to persuade her to support his nomination as prime minister. Received in private audience, he assured her of his loyalty; his alliance with the Gironde, he said, was temporary, and his military preparations were intended to strengthen the throne against the republicans as much as to defend France against potential foreign enemies. The Queen was not impressed. Since the Constitution did not provide for a prime minister, the King could not nominate him to that post, she replied, and dismissed him.

If not prime minister, Narbonne and Germaine decided, then at least foreign minister. Germaine, in her enthusiasm, wrote a four-page letter to de Lessart, advising him that in the interest of the King and of the state he should resign his post to the more capable Monsieur de Narbonne. De Lessart had the malice to read the letter aloud at a cabinet meeting: for this he was to pay with his life.

That manœuvre having also failed, Narbonne on February 24 submitted to Louis XVI a memorandum, written in part or in its entirety by Madame de Staël, inviting the monarch to break with his false friends, the 'Aristocrats', and to place his entire trust in the propertied bourgeoisie, whose sole aim it was to preserve its newly won advantages and to maintain law and order. The memorandum concluded with a phrase Germaine was to echo on a much later occasion: 'The thing that must be preserved in all situations whatever,' she admonished the King, 'is the reputation of one's character.' Years later she wrote to a friend: 'One must, so long as there is any life left, back up the character of one's life.'

Louis XVI, on this occasion, was faithful to the reputation of his character: he did nothing. Narbonne's hostile colleagues in the cabinet tried, in the meantime, to buy off a majority in the Legislative Assembly, a manœuvre which Narbonne lost no time in publicizing. On March 3, prompted by La Fayette, he formally announced that either he or

Bertrand de Molleville must resign. Bertrand did not resign. Narbonne and Germaine played their last trump: La Fayette, Rochambeau, and Luckner, who by a strained coincidence had happened to leave their respective commands in order to report to the minister of war, were induced to address three identically worded letters to Narbonne, in which they begged him to remain at his post and threatened to resign their commands if he were dismissed. According to Fersen, the text had been drafted by Germaine. At any rate, Germaine had them published (without Narbonne's knowledge, it seems) in the *Journal de Paris* of March 9, 1792. Louis XVI was forced to act at last. The King's note to Narbonne, delivered by a simple valet in the evening of March 9, was laconic: 'This is to inform you, sir, that I have just named Monsieur de Grave to head the Department of War. You will hand him your portfolio.'

For Germaine this was the exact repetition of July 11, 1789. Would there be another Fourteenth of July? If it had depended on Germaine, there would have been. The fall of Narbonne marked one of the few occasions, perhaps the only one, in her life on which she showed herself vindictive. Narbonne had barely received the King's note when, on March 9, the leaders of the Gironde and of the Fayettists assembled in her drawing room to hold a council of war. Brissot, Guadet, Narbonne, Fauchet, and Madame de Condorcet resolved upon the downfall of the cabinet. The attack was launched on the following morning in the Assembly by Brissot—the same Brissot who had invited her father to resign and die. The foreign minister, de Lessart, was the chosen target. Brissot charged him with nothing less than high treason: the minister had failed to communicate the Assembly's war resolution of January 25 to the Court of Vienna and, instead, had betrayed the national dignity in his negotiations with the Emperor. The accusation was endorsed by a nearly unanimous vote; de Lessart was arrested; the rest of the cabinet resigned without awaiting their turn.

In her vengeance Germaine had triumphed, but in her hope to see Narbonne restored she failed utterly. The King and Queen would sooner have appointed the Devil than Narbonne or La Fayette. The Devil was, in fact, appointed in the shape of a Girondist ministry, whose guiding spirit was not Madame de Staël but Madame Roland. Between the two ladies no love was lost. Narbonne had intended to use the Gironde as a stepping-stone to power; the roles had been reversed— the Girondists had used Narbonne, and they were to treat him as unkindly as he had planned to treat them.

In her *Considerations on the Principal Events of the French Revolution* Germaine devoted exactly two short paragraphs to Narbonne's rise and fall, and not a single word to her own activities. Since modesty was not her outstanding virtue, one may surmise that this was the one episode in her life in which she felt at fault.

While the Swedish ambassadress was thus making and unmaking the ministers of Louis XVI, the King of Sweden was working in an altogether opposite direction. It was Gustavus himself who planned the escape of the royal family after his arrival at Aachen on June 16, 1791. It was Big Axel Fersen who drove the royal carriage out of Paris, while Gustavus, impatient to meet the august refugees, was waiting for them at Spa. When he learned of their arrest at Varennes, Gustavus began to pose openly as Europe's God-appointed champion against Jacobin tyranny. On June 27, in a sternly worded note to Little Staël, which he had published in all the newspapers of Europe, he ordered his ambassador to extend all possible aid to the royal couple; forbade him to confer with 'the so-called minister of foreign affairs'; and declared that Louis XVI was to be regarded no longer as a free agent but as a prisoner acting under duress. Finally, Gustavus admonished Staël 'to avoid with the most scrupulous care any occasion that might compromise your person or your dignity. The deepest grief must reign in the interior of your household. . . . I expect from you courage, firmness, and prudence.'

Staël obeyed to the extent of closing his embassy to social functions— thus forcing Germaine to hold her conclaves in Necker's house or at Madame de Condorcet's—but he obstinately continued to confer with the revolutionary leaders to whom his master had issued a virtual declaration of war. His flagrant disregard of Gustavus's orders, his ridiculous praises for his wife's lover, were more than Gustavus could tolerate. A letter from Germaine, in which she tried to exonerate her husband by dissociating him from all her activities, left the King unmoved; early in January 1792 Staël received his formal recall. Gustavus instructed him to keep his order secret and advised him to use the pretext of a visit to his parents-in-law in order to explain his absence until the King saw fit to formalize the break of diplomatic relations. Staël ignored this advice as well as Necker's offer of a refuge at Coppet and delayed his departure from Paris until early February. What impelled him to return to Sweden is a mystery. A letter from Gustavus, forbidding him to set foot on Swedish soil, barely missed him at

Hamburg. He landed about March 10 or 12. On March 16, at a masked ball, Gustavus was shot to death.

The circumstances of this event are familiar to opera-goers: Verdi's *Un Ballo in Maschera*, which has one of the most improbable plots in operatic literature, represents them quite faithfully; even the sorceress is historic.

Of the three principal conspirators, it was Count Horn who pointed out the King to the assassin, Count Anckaeström, by placing his hand on Gustavus's shoulder, with the words, 'Bonjour, beau masque'. Anckarström fired immediately afterwards from a pistol wrapped in wool. The master mind of the plot, Count Ribbing, 'the handsome regicide', will be met again, in close connection with Madame de Staël.

The King lingered on for two weeks. On his death, Duke Charles of Sudermania, sole possessor of the Truth, assumed the regency for Gustavus's son. One of the first things he did was to void Gustavus's decision to break with France. Monsieur de Staël, ambassador again, was ordered back to Paris. Thus turns the wheel of fortune. Staël was, however, in no hurry to return to his post. By the time he came back to Paris, his wife had fled, the Jacobins were in power, Louis XVI had been guillotined, and Marie Antoinette, to whom he owed his good fortune, was on trial for her life.

On June 20, 1792, 'twenty thousand men of the lowest class of society, armed with pikes and lances, marched on the Tuileries without knowing why,' writes Madame de Staël, who, as usual, was there.

> These twenty thousand men penetrated into the King's palace. Their physiognomies were marked by that moral and physical coarseness which inspires unsurmountable disgust even in the most philanthropic-minded. If they had been animated by some genuine grievance, if they had come to protest against injustice, against the high price of bread, against the increase of taxes, against conscription—in a word, against everything that power and wealth cause the poor to suffer, against the rags that were their clothes, against their work-blackened hands, against the premature old age of their women, against the brutalization of their children—then everything in them would have raised pity. But their frightful oaths and shouts, their threatening gestures, their murderous weapons, offered a horrifying spectacle which could forever destroy the respect which the human race should inspire.

Madame de Staël had not inspected them so closely when they had carried her father on their shoulders. The mob, murderous though it

looked, was content with placing the red bonnet on the King's head.
The men who, half a year later, cast their votes for the King's death
were not ruffians; a number of them had seen the inside of Madame
de Staël's salon.

On July 14, when the fall of the Bastille was once more celebrated
on the Champ de Mars, Germaine again was there. 'The expression
on the Queen's face will never be blotted from my memory. Her eyes
were red from crying.' The King, for the second time, swore to abide
by the Constitution.

> My eyes followed in the distance his powdered hair amid all those dark-
> haired heads; his coat, embroidered as in times past, contrasted with the
> clothes of the populace that was pressing around him. When he ascended
> the steps to the altar, it was as if a holy victim were offering himself
> voluntarily to be sacrificed. . . . From that day, the people did not see
> him again except on the scaffold.

On August 10 Germaine received word that her compatriots of the
Swiss Guards were having themselves massacred in the courtyard of
the Tuileries. The royal family had sought asylum with the Legislative
Assembly. Germaine leaped into her carriage to get the news on the
spot; at the bridge the carriage was stopped by some men who, with a
silent but expressive gesture, signified to the coachman that on the
other side of the Seine people in coaches were likely to have their
throats cut. She could not pass but was informed, by and by, that all
her friends among the Swiss officers had escaped alive. That evening,
on foot, she made the round of the various 'obscure houses' in which
she had found temporary refuge for them, stepping across the bodies
of drunken patriots.

The royal family were imprisoned in the Temple. Germaine, who
in Talleyrand's words delighted in drowning people so she might enjoy
the pleasure of fishing them out again, had offered the King an elaborate
escape plan about a month before the events of August 10. 'Here is my
plan,' she told Malouet, who was to act as her go-between. 'It can be
carried out in three weeks, if we begin with the preliminaries in two
days. There is an estate for sale at Dieppe. I shall buy it, and every time
I go there I shall be accompanied by a reliable servant, whose build
is about the same as the King's, by a woman of the Queen's age and
general appearance, and by my son, who is about the age of the
Dauphin. You know how popular I am with the patriots. When they
have seen me make the trip with this retinue a couple of times, it will

be easy for me to take the whole royal family with me on the third trip, for I might as well travel with both my maids, and Madame Elizabeth might impersonate one of them. See if you can transmit this proposition. There is no time to waste. Bring me the King's answer tonight or tomorrow.'

La Fayette had promised his co-operation. Narbonne, who was to take charge of the execution of the plan, would drive the coach, as Axel Fersen had done a year earlier. It might have worked: far more unlikely escapes have been managed. But the Queen, who preferred to perish rather than be saved by La Fayette and the Constitutionalists, refused even to see Germaine's emissary. The King and Queen, she let Malouet know, were grateful to Madame de Staël for her kind intentions, but there was no compelling reason for them to leave Paris.

After August 10 there was nothing left for Madame de Staël but to save her Constitutionalist friends from the imminent catastrophe. There was little she could do for Stanislas de Clermont-Tonnerre, who on August 10 had been thrown out of a window and trampled to death, but at least she might try to prevent her other friends from suffering similar unpleasantness.

Narbonne, for whom an arrest warrant had been issued, was hiding at the Swedish embassy, and so was, for a few days at least, Mathieu de Montmorency. François de Jaucourt and Lally-Tollendal had been arrested, among thousands of 'aristocrats'.[1] Being exceedingly well informed, Germaine was aware that behind these arrests there lay a sinister purpose and that careful plans were being made for organizing a spontaneous massacre of all political prisoners by outraged patriots. The organizers of the September Massacres had a twofold aim: to remove their political rivals and to provide the nation with scapegoats for the French defeats at the hands of the Austro-Prussian Coalition— for it was only with the cannonade of Valmy, on September 20, that the tide turned in favour of the revolutionary army.

To save Narbonne from arrest was Germaine's chief concern. One day late in August a search patrol appeared at the Swedish embassy; detachments of soldiers were stationed at either end of the block.

---

[1] The term 'aristocrat' was a party label and did not necessarily connote noble birth. The counterpart of an aristocrat was not a commoner but a democrat. In the Reign of Terror chambermaids were guillotined as aristocrats while former marquises and counts sat with the democrats in the Convention. Madame de Staël's friends were noblemen and favoured a constitutional monarchy, but it was decidedly unjust to accuse them of being aristocrats.

Monsieur de Narbonne, the officer in charge explained, was said to be hiding on the premises. Germaine, who with the help of the embassy chaplain, Pastor Gambs, had just hidden her lover under the altar before which she had been married (by the same pastor), planted herself at the entrance of the embassy and began to lecture the patrol on the sanctity of international law, the inviolability of embassies, and the extraterritoriality of their occupants. Sweden, she asserted with bravura, was one of the mightiest nations of Europe, situated directly across the Rhine from France; its friendship for France was known, but if the patrol dared set foot in the house, Sweden would wreak terrible vengeance. The men seemed undecided. Germaine recalled later:

> With death in my heart I had the courage to joke with them about the unreasonableness of their suspicions. Nothing pleases men of this class better than jokes; for in their boundless hatred of the nobles they enjoy being treated by them on an equal footing. I thus led them back to the door and thanked God for the strength he had given me at such a moment.

She had, by that time, met a young Hanoverian physician, Erich Bollmann, who later with the help of an American acquired some fame by engineering the abortive escape of La Fayette from the fortress of Olmütz. Bollmann made his apprenticeship as Scarlet Pimpernel under Madame de Staël, whose appeal to his chivalry was irresistible. He offered to supply Narbonne with the passport of one of his friends, also a German, and to see him safely to England. He kept his word: on August 20 the two men reached the English coast.

With Narbonne rescued, Germaine turned her attention to the fate of Jaucourt and Lally-Tollendal, which was in the hands of the Commune of Paris. Among the leaders of the Commune she shrewdly singled out one Manuel, who dabbled in literature, as the point of least resistance. She requested an audience with him. Manuel asked her to call at his apartment on September 1, at seven in the morning—'a somewhat democratic hour,' she commented. 'I arrived before he had risen and waited for him in his study, where I saw his own portrait standing on his own desk. This gave me hopes that at least he might be vulnerable if attacked in his vanity.' She was right: to be petitioned by Madame de Staël flattered his vanity immensely. 'Save Monsieur de Lally and Monsieur de Jaucourt,' she cried to him when at last he had got out of bed. 'Store up this act of kindness and be solaced when you remember it at a time when you in turn will be proscribed!' Manuel was guillotined in the following year. Whether the thought of having saved Lally and Jaucourt gave him solace, it cannot be said.

The two prisoners were released the same day. There remained another friend in hiding, the abbé de Montesquiou. Germaine promised that on the following day, when she planned to leave for Switzerland, she would take him with her, disguised as a servant. The abbé was to wait for her on the highway.

On the morning of September 2 the well-prepared spontaneous mobs burst into the prisons of Paris and several other cities, and the massacre began. It was this day the ambassadress chose to leave her house in her berline, with six horses, with her postilions and servants in grand livery. It was her notion that, seeing her thus, no one would think that she was about to leave the country. The carriage had not moved four steps when 'a swarm of old women, issued from hell, threw themselves on my horses and screamed at me to stop, that I was taking the gold of the nation with me, that I was about to join the enemy.' A crowd collected; several toughs seized her postilions and ordered them to drive to the assembly hall of the revolutionary 'section' of her quarter. Arrived there, she succeeded in secretly dispatching a servant to Montesquiou. The abbé, thus informed, eventually made his way to safety.

At the section, her passport was examined and found inaccurate: one of the servants listed (the same she had sent to find Montesquiou) was missing. A gendarme was ordered to take her to the Hôtel de Ville.

Through the murderous crowd, step by step, the carriage-and-six, postilions and all, threaded its way under police escort. The trip took three hours, to the incessant accompaniment of threatening screams. The Place de Grève, facing the Hôtel de Ville, was a bedlam: 'I stepped out of the carriage, surrounded by an armed mob, and made my way through a hedge of pikes. As I mounted the stairway, which was also bristling with lances, a man pointed his pike at my heart. My policeman fended it off with his sabre. If I had stumbled at that moment, it would have been the end of me.'

The ambassadress entered the headquarters of the Commune. The hall was filled to bursting with men, women, children, all screaming patriotic slogans, while the committee, on a raised platform, were deliberating: Robespierre, Collot d'Herbois, Billaud-Varenne—'the latter had not shaved for a fortnight to be more secure from any suspicion of aristocracy'. When her turn came, Germaine was beginning to explain the rules of diplomatic immunity to the men on the platform, when, providentially, Manuel arrived. 'He was very much surprised to find me in this sad situation; he immediately vouched for me until the Commune had judged my case, made me leave that horrible place, and locked me into his office with my chambermaid.'

They had to wait for six hours, without food or drink. From the window Germaine could see 'the murderers returning from the prison, their arms naked and covered with blood, shouting horrible screams'. In the middle of all this, grotesquely, stood the carriage-and-six, protected from looters by a soldier of the National Guard. It was evening before Manuel rejoined the two women, and it was night when he escorted them back, still in the coach-and-six, to the rue du Bac.

Manuel informed Germaine that a new passport would be issued to her, valid only for herself and her maid. A gendarme was to escort them to the border. On the following morning an emissary of the Commune arrived to take her as far as the Paris toll-gate. He was Tallien, who two years later overthrew Robespierre. 'Several persons who were very much compromised in those days were in my room,' Madame de Staël reminisced. 'I begged Tallien not to mention them to the authorities; he promised it and kept his word. I stepped into the carriage with him, and we parted without being able to tell each other what was in our minds. The circumstances froze one's words on one's lips.'

While Germaine was rolling towards Coppet, on September 3, 1792, Marie Antoinette, in the Temple, looked up when she heard a roar and saw, swaying on the end of a pike, at a level with her window, the head of her bosom friend, the Princesse de Lamballe, who had just been hacked to pieces on the very spot where Madame de Staël had closely brushed the same fate.

8

THE HEARTBREAK AND THE TERROR [1]

B Y September 7, when the ambassadress stepped out of her carriage at Coppet to fly into her father's arms, 1,368 prisoners, including forty-three children, had been butchered in Paris alone. At Orléans Monsieur de Lessart, awaiting trial since the day he had fallen victim to Germaine's wrath, expiated his crime with his life. In Geneva, a few miles from Coppet, the local Jacobins were preparing a revolution of their own. Savoy across the lake was being occupied by the revolutionary army. Necker, no longer feeling safe at Coppet, made arrangements through Gibbon to move into a house belonging to Gibbon's friend Sévery, at Rolle near Lausanne, where the entire Necker family took up residence in early October.

Germaine's emotional state was suicidal, but the political events contributed to it only indirectly. All her thoughts revolved around one single aim—to join Narbonne in England. She would have followed him directly from Paris but for two reasons: her financial dependence on her father and the fact that she expected to bear a child—Narbonne's child—in November. She was determined to leave for England as soon as the child was born, and to divorce Monsieur de Staël if necessary. To such mad notions her parents, particularly her mother, were vehemently opposed; at the same time Monsieur de Staël announced the happy news that, by a stroke of luck, he had repaired his fortunes, that he would enjoy an income of 80,000 francs a year, and that he would soon join his wife at Coppet.

Madame Necker, to whom Staël had addressed this news, handed his letter to Germaine. Germaine, affecting a casual tone of voice, replied that she was pleased to see part of her debts paid, since she would be by

[1] For the hitherto unknown information contained in this chapter I am indebted to the Henry W. and Albert A. Berg Collection of the New York Public Library, which graciously permitted me to make use of Madame de Staël's unpublished letters to Narbonne and to quote fragments from them. I also am obliged to M. Georges Solovieff for the use I made of his excellent Columbia University Master's essay, 'Madame de Staël et Narbonne' (1957).

that much less of a burden to her father; whereupon Madame Necker retreated from the room in a huff and summoned her husband to talk reason to their child. Without giving her father time to attack, Germaine declared that she intended to leave for London immediately, pregnant though she was; that the dangers she would run in crossing France were nothing compared to the danger of giving birth to her child with her husband present, at a date that would seem most extraordinary to him. (They had last met almost ten months before the child was due.) He would call Auguste his son, an idea that revolted her, and her parents would want to reconcile them, which was equally revolting. She was resolved to take on one of two journeys before January 15: 'either to England or to the bottom of the lake'.[1]

Though shaken by her tears, Necker replied that Monsieur de Staël's continuing position as ambassador would have certain advantages for her that she would not despise. Germaine objected that she had no right to share her husband's fortune since she had ceased to share his bed; nor did she care to live in Paris if her friends were exiled from it. Her mind was made up; since her parents would give her no peace, she would leave the next morning at four for Paris and London. This threat, to which she kept returning, frightened Necker a great deal, Germaine reported to her lover. Realizing that she would persist unless he promised to take her side against Monsieur de Staël, Necker began to yield. But since he was not, as Germaine put it, in the habit of saying anything that might commit him, he also temporized: if her love could survive a three-month separation from her 'magician', she would not be expected to live with a husband she hated or to tear herself away from 'the object of a constant and tried affection'. He would, if she passed this test, provide for a separation—or for what he called, euphemistically, a different arrangement—and thus end these quarrels, which he was beginning to find unendurable. 'I took him up on these words,' says Germaine, 'so that he was more committed than he intended, and then I yielded.' The idea of a three-month test of a sentiment that had lasted for four years made her, she confessed, laugh a little. She did not show her amusement, however, and instead, 'listened submissively' to a long sermon he felt in duty bound to make, in deference to Madame Necker, about the impetuosity of her character. The conversation ended with Germaine declaring her firm intention to break with Monsieur de Staël.[2]

[1] Madame de Staël to Narbonne, October 2, 1792, unpublished (Berg Collection).
[2] The scene is described in the same letter.

Despite this pact with her father, the family quarrels continued with rising bitterness. Here she was 'in this hole of Rolle', she complained to her lover, 'with a mother who is unimaginable and a father whom I love but who hides from me'. However, it was not only her parents she threatened with dangerous journeys and suicide. When Narbonne left her without news, she warned him that if his silence continued she would go to England, though eight months pregnant; she would die of it, and this would serve him right. 'Despite her pregnancy and her recent shocks, her enforced rest gives her less pleasure than you might think,' Madame Necker wrote to Gibbon in a characteristic understatement. 'She talks, wildly enough, of visiting England this winter,' Gibbon relayed to Lord Sheffield. 'Her friend the Vicomte de Narbonne is somewhere about Dorking.'

'Somewhere about Dorking' was the mansion of Juniper Hall, at Mickleham, Surrey, which Germaine had rented, through the intermediary of the Duchesse de Broglie, to serve as refuge for Narbonne and her other friends. After a stay in London and in Wales, Narbonne had moved there; with him came a whole colony, including Mathieu, Jaucourt, Théodore de Lameth, Bollmann, and General d'Arblay. The newcomers were well received by their neighbours and established particularly cordial relations with the Locks of Norbury Park—friends of Joshua Reynolds, Thomas Lawrence, and the late Dr. Johnson—and with Dr. Burney and his two daughters, Susan Phillips and Fanny Burney. It was here that the flirtation between Fanny and d'Arblay began, and when they were married a year later Narbonne was the groom's best man. The Juniperians lived modestly enough—largely at the expense of Germaine—but they enjoyed their peace, and their high spirits did not betray the inner anxieties that were devouring them.

Indeed, while Germaine, at Rolle, directed all her thoughts to Juniper Hall, the Juniperians' thoughts were monopolized by the events in Paris. Two events, above all, threw them into consternation: the King had been put on trial for his life, and a law had been passed ordering all *émigrés* to return to France or to forfeit their property. Both events exerted a strong gravitational pull on the Juniperians. Before the year was out, Mathieu was back in France to avoid confiscation. Narbonne, accused of treason by the Jacobins in Paris and of Jacobinism by the *émigrés* in London, sought to appease his guilt feelings and to justify himself to the world by calling on Pitt to intervene on behalf of Louis XVI and by offering to testify in person at the King's trial. Germaine regarded these moves as a personal outrage to her. Furious, she ordered him to go neither to London nor to France, to abstain from politics, to talk to no one. 'Do wait for me at Juniper Hall; my soul is all there already. My pregnancy cannot last forever—at least I do not imagine that your child requires ten months of gestation—and as soon as I am well I shall leave.'[1]

Albert was born on November 20. Monsieur de Staël, much to everyone's relief, had not come. 'You see me now the mother of the Gracchi,' Germaine wrote to Gibbon, 'and I hope that my two sons will restore liberty in France.' There was this difference, however, between Germaine and the mother of the original Gracchi, that Cornelia bore children only to her husband and had no lover somewhere about Dorking. The new Cornelia, in a series of pressing letters to the historian of the *Decline and Fall*, obtained his promise to use his influence with the Bernese authorities in order to secure a residence permit for Narbonne in case she could not join him in England.

She was still recovering from childbed when news eached her of Narbonne's offer to the Convention to testify for Louis XVI. Such inconsiderateness passed all bounds. He had no right to tear her heart to pieces, she informed him. He was more anxious to be in the public eye than to be useful. 'I can no more. I hate you, I despise you, and I am dying with the tortures of the damned.' What right had he to risk his life, which she had saved, for the sake of a mere king? In truth, she found, people had exaggerated notions about the King's fate. The mere title still produced a magic effect; one would do better, she pointedly reminded Narbonne, to mourn the victims of the September Massacres.

There was no more time to waste: she must go to England if she wanted to keep Narbonne. As December drew to its end, the family arguments reached a climax. Necker predicted that she would be murdered by the brigands on her way through France; Madame Necker accused her of breaking her father's heart, of deserting her children, and of bringing upon herself the wrath of God. To all this Germaine opposed stubborn resistance: England or the lake. On December 23 she wrote to Narbonne:

> The moment has come to choose between you and the rest of the universe, and it is to you that my heart compels me. May the gift of my life embellish yours! May I never be diminished in your eyes because of the very sacrifices I bring to my passion for you! And if my reputation is ruined forever, may you continue to esteem the woman who has recognized no law but that of love![1]

[1] Unpublished letter in the Berg Collection of the New York Public Library.

About Christmas Germaine told her parents that she was going for a brief visit to Geneva. She did not return. Leaving Geneva on December 28, she continued to Paris; from there Mathieu escorted her to Boulogne. After a few days in London, she arrived at Juniper Hall.

Announcing Germaine's departure, Necker wrote to his friend Meister: 'I have made every effort imaginable to keep her from it, but in vain. . . . One must resign oneself to what one cannot prevent; but, in every respect, I am very unhappy these days.' Cured of all ambition, he returned to nursing his wife, to writing books on the French Revolution and on religious ethics, and to defending, in an ineffectual memorandum, the life of Louis XVI.

On January 21, about the time Germaine arrived at Juniper Hall, the head of Louis XVI fell into a basket.

Monsieur de Narbonne, says Fanny Burney, was 'almost annihilated' by the news of the King's execution. The arrival of his mistress had an almost identical effect. He no longer loved her; if he had to reproach himself for having been instrumental in the King's downfall, it was Germaine he could blame for guiding him into a political course with which, at bottom, he had never sympathized. Now she exacted love as payment for having saved his life when his honour demanded that he die with his King. He was expected to 'continue to esteem the woman who had recognized no law but that of love'—but if she had risked her reputation it was not at his bidding; in fact, he had exhausted every possible pretext to discourage her from coming. Still, he had neither the courage nor the will power to break off. Courteous, dignified, and grave, he continued to accept her money and to live under her roof.

As long as she was near her lover and her friends, Germaine was appeased and in good spirits. Despite Narbonne's brooding fits life at Juniper Hall was gay and active. The Burneys and the Locks were enchanted with the new arrival. 'She is one of the first women I have ever met with for abilities and extraordinary intellect,' wrote Fanny Burney, comparing her favourably with Mrs. Thrale; as for Narbonne, he bore 'the highest character for goodness, parts, sweetness of countenance, and ready wit.' Talleyrand came for frequent visits from London: 'His powers of entertainment are astonishing, both in formation and raillery.' Oblivious of their exile, oblivious of their poverty and uncertain future, those *émigrés* would jest, argue, play games, with such abandon and verve that their English friends were dazzled and awed. How could one enjoy oneself so much without a steady income?

The time was spent in conversation, in reading aloud from work in progress, in calls and return calls, in drives around the countryside. For all the inhabitants of Juniper Hall, the only conveyance was a two-seated cabriolet; Germaine sat in the covered part, while Narbonne or Talleyrand rode in the dickey, or outside seat, leaning back to converse —for the glass partition had been knocked out to facilitate communication.

Germaine's social day began the minute she wakened. Recalling a morning visit to her bedroom, Dr. Bollmann describes her as dressed 'in a short petticoat and a thin shirt and twisting a piece of paper between her fingers. (She cannot do without one: she rises with it and goes to bed with it.) In this condition she began to praise and defend Narbonne in a speech remarkable for its warmth and for the extraordinary flow of words.' At other times Bollmann recalls her 'playfully singing very languid Italian airs' for him while accompanying herself on the piano. What impressed him above all was her energy:

> This Staël woman is a genius—an extraordinary, eccentric woman in everything she does. She sleeps only a few hours and spends the rest of the time in uninterrupted and furious activity. . . . She spends one third of her day writing, even while her hair is being dressed or while she is having breakfast. She is too restless to revise what she has written.

The work Germaine was then engaged on was her first truly original book, *On the Influence of Passions on the Happiness of Individuals and of Nations.*[1] The well-known apology for suicide contained in the book probably had been written at Rolle, when Germaine's morale was at its lowest. At Juniper Hall she read her chapters to the assembled company as soon as she had finished them. 'She has suffered us to hear some of her works in MS.; which are truly wonderful for powers both of thinking and expression,' wrote Fanny Burney; but Talleyrand criticized her monotonous singsong in reading prose. 'Madame de Staël was very gay and Monsieur de Talleyrand very *comique*,' Susan Phillips asserts in relating the scene, perhaps unaware that the monotonous prose Germaine had been reading was a cry of despair over Narbonne's vanishing love.

Before many weeks had passed the idyllic relationship between the Juniperian colony and their neighbours became a little strained. Not everybody approved of them. Horace Walpole, who frowned on 'unmarried couples' (besides Germaine and Narbonne, there were Jaucourt and Madame de La Châtre), refused to receive them at Strawberry Hill,

---

[1] This work is discussed in Chapter 11 below.

where seventeen years earlier Germaine and her parents had been his guests. And Dr. Burney warned his daughter to be careful: Germaine's morals were not pure, and her politics had helped to bring about the horrors that were taking place in France.

Although in her forties, Fanny Burney was shocked at the revelation of such wickedness. 'This intimation concerning Monsieur de Narbonne was . . . wholly new to me, and I do firmly believe it a gross calumny,' she wrote to her father.

> She loves him even tenderly, but so openly, so simply, so unaffectedly, and with such utter freedom from all coquetry, that if they were two men, or two women, their affection could not, I think, be more obviously undesigning. She is very plain, he is very handsome; her intellectual endowments must be with him her sole attraction. . . . Her whole côterie live together as brethren. . . . Indeed, I think you could not spend a day with them and not see that their commerce is that of a pure but exalted and most elegant friendship.

Elegant friendship or not, Fanny was terrified of losing her pension from the Queen; she refused all further invitations to Juniper Hall. In vain Germaine tried to reassure her that far from being Jacobins, she and her friends had 'barely escaped the Jacobins' knives'. When Susan Phillips tried to explain her sister's conduct, Germaine was dumbfounded: 'Do you mean to say that in this country a woman is treated as a minor all life long? It seems to me that your sister behaves like a girl of fourteen.'

Fanny Burney's behaviour towards Germaine was symptomatic of a general hostility among right-thinking circles, fanned by the spiteful aristocratic *émigrés* in London. Germaine tried to defend herself: surely, she thought, no one in an enlightened country like England could seriously believe that the political opinions of a few young women could be counted among the causes of 'a revolution that centuries have prepared and twenty-nine million people have desired'.[1] She repeatedly went to London to explain her political views to the men in power. Lord Sheffield, who as a favour to his friend Gibbon received her and introduced her to the highest circles, gave a dispassionate account of her to the historian: there was a great deal of prejudice against her as an intriguer and a democrat capable of setting the throne on fire, and he found it difficult to make people admit her agreeable and brilliant, though a little ridiculous, qualities. The Lord Chancellor, he reported,

---

[1] Draft letter, no date, no address. The sentence contains in germ the principal thesis of Madame de Staël's last work, the *Considérations sur . . . la Révolution française.*

had been astonished when she disputed with him on principles of politics.

Fear and suspicion had reached hysterical proportions in England; there were secret parliamentary investigations of alleged subversives and Jacobins; the Alien Bill was in preparation; a state of war had existed between England and France since February 1. The whole existence of the Juniperian colony was threatened. At the same time both Necker and Monsieur de Staël, who had resumed his ambassa-dorial post in Paris on March 3, were putting pressure on Germaine to force her return to the Continent. By early May Germaine had to acknowledge that her own and her friends' position in England was untenable. She agreed to return to Switzerland, provided her friends— particularly Narbonne and Talleyrand—gave her their solemn promise to follow her there as soon as she had made arrangements for their stay.

She had given up her resolution to 'break off all ties' with her husband. It was only too clear that her lover would show no gratitude for such a sacrifice. Instead, Germaine planned to take advantage of Monsieur de Staël's diplomatic status, set up house with him if he came to Switzerland, and under the cover of official respectability invite Narbonne to live with them. She even consented to adopt a 'new system' in their relationship, which would leave Narbonne 'absolutely free'. Narbonne seemed to fall in with the plan, but the strain between the two was sensed even by outsiders. 'Their minds,' wrote Susan Phillips on May 14, 'in some points ought to be exchanged, for he is as delicate as a really feminine woman, and evidently suffers when he sees her setting *les bienséances* aside, as it often enough befalls her to do.'

On May 25 Germaine, sobbing, took leave of Mrs. Lock at Norbury Park. Narbonne escorted her to Dover. He promised to join her within four months. At Ostend a secretary of the Swedish embassy awaited her to escort her through the war zone into Germany. After sending Nar-bonne a draft for £50, Germaine was on her way, through Brussels, Frankfurt, and Basel, to Coppet. From Basel she wrote to Gibbon, on whose intercession with the Bernese government she pinned her hopes of having Narbonne's stay authorized. 'I am not exalting my mind with romantic notions,' she declared in anticipation of Gibbon's objections, 'and I believe in every argument that reason has produced against them since the beginning of the world.' But, she continued, the French Revolution, which had drawn her and Narbonne so closely together, also had cut away the very basis of these reasonable arguments. 'The so-called proprieties, along with every social duty and privilege, have been reduced to a despised heap of ruins'; in such circumstances why should she sacrifice her happiness to conventions of a bygone era? The argument could not have impressed the moderately sensible Mr. Gibbon, who loathed the Revolution in all its works; all the same, out of friendship, he did what he could.

At Berne, on June 10, Germaine was met by her husband. After signing, in the middle of the Reign of Terror, a military and commercial pact with France, he had failed to obtain his own government's ratification of the treaty, and since it would have been pointless to stay on in Paris in these circumstances, he had chosen to await further developments in Switzerland. The couple had not met for well over a year. After their first talk Germaine reported to Narbonne that the ambassador seemed to be as much in love with her as ever. She would have no difficulty in making him do what she wanted; but was this really what she wanted—the presence of an eternal third party instead of the 'sweet and delightful abandon' of Juniper Hall?

'The mother of the Gracchi is here, with her pretty children and with her husband, for whom I have a great deal of affection,' Madame Necker primly informed Gibbon, who knew all about it. The younger of the Gracchi, Albert, was seven months old; Germaine had left him with a wet nurse five weeks after his birth. The older, Auguste, was in his third year; he, too, had spent more time with his grandparents than with his mother. The new Cornelia treated her jewels with something less than the Roman Cornelia's jealous preoccupation. What did preoccupy her was the absence of letters from the lover somewhere about Dorking. All the agonies of the preceding autumn commenced once more as if they had never ceased. Germaine appealed to d'Arblay, beseeching him to make Narbonne join her, or at least write to her. Narbonne himself received frantic letter upon frantic letter; Germaine was sick, she had a fever, she suffered from fainting spells, and all this because of his cruelty. Beginning on June 30 a few letters from him drifted in, all vague, all full of evasions. He even sent his table linen, as token of his impending arrival, but he made no move to leave Juniper Hall. In late September, with the reluctant consent of the Bernese bailiff, the Staëls moved into a house they had rented near Nyon, a few miles from Coppet. The house soon filled up with friends, but neither Narbonne nor Talleyrand was among them.

The agonies Germaine related to her lover by no means took up all her time, and while she ordered Narbonne to abstain from politics she threw herself into dangerous political ventures. In the summer of 1793, the revolutionary tribunal was preparing the trial of Marie Antoinette. Germaine had barely returned to Coppet when she wrote, at white heat, her *Reflections on the Trial of the Queen, by a Woman*. The anonymity of the author deceived no one. From the first page ('Women of all countries, of all classes, listen and be moved as I am') to the last ('I turn once more to you, women: for if her tender motherhood were struck, you all would be the victims. . . . Your sway will be lost forever once ferocity reigns. . . . Defend the Queen with all the weapons nature has given you'), the pamphlet is directed frankly at the readers' emotions rather than at their sense of justice. Even if her emotions had not been genuine, Germaine's approach would have been the only effective one, for legality was no longer a consideration of any weight whatever. But her emotions were genuine: no matter what grudges she may have borne the Queen, Germaine could not help identifying herself with her, for the accusations put forward against Marie Antoinette would have been unthinkable but for the fact that the Queen was a woman and a foreigner—precisely like Germaine herself. A man might have been accused of treason, but not of meddling and intrigue; and no man, no matter how immoral his private life, would have been faced with the obscene charges that Fouquier-Tinville manufactured against the Queen. Germaine's plea was more than a generous, futile gesture: it was, like everything else she wrote, a manifesto for sensibility against brutality—which comes to saying a manifesto for freedom.

It might be said that, coming from the island of safety that was the Republic of Berne, Germaine's plea for the Queen was not the heroic action it was advertised to be. This would be an injustice: fearlessness is a trait even her severest critics must concede to her. What is more, for Germaine, to whom Paris was the centre of existence, who had most of her fortune tied up in France, and who had nothing to hope for from the royalists, the publication meant a grave risk without any expectation of personal gain. Germaine was merely making a last, desperate attempt at fishing out of the water a queen she had helped to drown. Both the drowning and the rescue operation were essentially altruistic, for the sake of glory.

The Queen's head fell into the basket on October 16, 1793. Germaine's rescue efforts were more successful when she employed herself for personages of less exalted station. Indeed, she organized, operated, and financed a veritable rescue agency, whose exploits rivalled the fictitious ones of the Scarlet Pimpernel in effectiveness if not in derring-do. The method was, essentially, simple and safe. A Swiss man or woman (depending on the sex of the person to be rescued), would set out for Paris with two sets of passports; one of them was genuine, entitling him or her to go to Paris and to return; the other a forged passport, without the visas. This person would get the genuine passport visaed at the border and again in Paris, as the procedure demanded, then hand it to the person to be rescued, along with his or her Swiss citizenship papers. Both rescuer and rescuee would return by separate routes; the rescuer would have to forge the necessary visas; in case there was any difficulty at the border, the officer of the Swiss border guard, who had an understanding with Germaine, claimed the rescuer as a Swiss citizen. No mishap ever occurred.

Some of Germaine's rescue agents were volunteers, but most of them worked for money. This 'traffic in human flesh', as she called it, cost her dearly; one of the rescues cost her 40,000 francs. It was not for the love of humanity that Germaine took these risks but for the sake of friendship: all those she rescued were either friends or persons close to her friends. Among them were Mathieu de Montmorency, Jaucourt, Jaucourt's nephew Achille du Chayla, Malouet, the Marquise de Simiane, the Princesse de Noailles, the Duchesse de Broglie.

The Bernese government had no objection to most of these noble refugees, but some of them, whose political past was tainted with revolutionary activities, it tolerated only tacitly. Mathieu and Jaucourt resided at Germaine's house at Nyon under Swedish names; Narbonne was expected to arrive under a Spanish name. 'Berne knows it, Berne tolerates it,' Germaine wrote to Meister, 'because I live absolutely alone in the countryside, and because it has been proved that we wish to live in the most obscure retirement.' But Berne drew the line at the 'bishop'; Talleyrand, Germaine was informed, would be expelled from Bernese territory if he set foot in it. Could Meister secure the consent of the government of Zurich for Germaine to reside there with her two Swedes and the bishop? The two Swedes would never set foot outside her garden; they were 'two friends of limited monarchy, of freedom within order': surely she would not be subjected to unpleasantness on their account?

Meister's reply was cautious. The Spaniard she expected did not turn up: to all Germaine's appeals Narbonne replied with silence or evasion. Her friendship for him would be like that of a man for a man; he would find it as agreeable as Monsieur d'Arblay's, she promised him early in 1794. But a few weeks later, suddenly suspecting Mrs. Phillips of detaining him at Juniper Hall, she changed her tune: she would come to England under a false name, she threatened; she would fall at his feet in front of Mrs. Phillips and remind him of his promise to join her; if he came with her, she would forgive him; if he refused, she would die.

If Narbonne broke his pledge, it was not out of callousness. 'It seems to me,' Talleyrand wrote to Germaine, 'that he rather lacks courage, he finds it so difficult to make a choice. . . . He stays here because that's where he is. . . . You must give him support when he is back with you. Our situation depresses him too much. You must get him away from himself to make him happy.' This was excellent advice, but it did not make Narbonne go to Switzerland. As for Talleyrand himself, expelled from England under the Aliens Bill, instead of availing himself of Germaine's proffered aid, he left precipitately for the United States. 'They won't catch me again at making revolutions for other people,' he had exclaimed in 1792, when he saw the coast of France receding in the distance; forced to leave his refuge, he preferred to be forgotten in America until the storm had blown over, rather than be drawn back into it by Germaine. Germaine was disconsolate. 'Since the Revolution began, this has been the heaviest blow,' she wrote to Meister on March 12.

By that time her house had lost most of its inhabitants. The French secret agent Venet, who wrote fairly detailed reports on Madame de Staël's 'original life near Nyon', noted on March 14: 'Of all the Swedish merchants she has surrounded herself with, only Mathieu de Montmorency is left.' Venet was mistaken: Mathieu, too, had gone by then, sent ahead by Germaine to reconnoitre the hospitality of Zurich.

Monsieur de Staël had left about the end of 1793, and slowly made his way to Stockholm to look for new employment. He stopped at Zurich to unload his soul to the mystic pastor Lavater, inventor of the science of physiognomy, father confessor to the *Sturm und Drang* movement, and friend of Goethe. Lavater, one of the first men to have made *naïveté* into a successful career, promised his help in restoring marital harmony between Eric Magnus and Germaine; his letters produced little effect on her. However, her correspondence with her husband (she did not see him again until May 1795) was fairly cordial; she even asked Talleyrand if Philadelphia would be a suitable post for Monsieur de Staël. No, replied Talleyrand, 'America is too unimportant a post for Monsieur de Staël.' Meanwhile, the ambassador acquitted himself creditably in a special mission at Copenhagen, waited for calmer times to return to France, continued to pay Mademoiselle

Clairon's stipulated pension, got himself back into debt, and yearned for spiritual perfection.

With Talleyrand gone to America, Narbonne glued to England, Mathieu and Jaucourt threatened with expulsion from Bernese territory, and the Terror in France at its climax, Germaine was utterly at loose ends. Should she return to England to throw herself at Narbonne's and Mrs. Phillips's feet? Or move to Zurich, where Mathieu, still in Swedish disguise, was looking for a suitable hiding place? Or go to America, where Talleyrand would console her? 'I am beginning to detest Europe,' she wrote to Meister—her first hint at her plan to settle in the United States, with which she was to toy on and off for the next seventeen years. Necker had begun negotiations which led to the purchase of $38,000 worth of land in New York, and Germaine herself came to own, in the course of years, a sizeable part of upper New York State. However, America, that last resort, was never to be resorted to.

For the time being Germaine still pinned her hopes on Zurich. She no longer could appeal to Gibbon for aid: having returned to England just about the time Germaine had left it, he died on January 17,1794— 'poor Gibbon, the only man who could make me like Switzerland'. But she expected much from Meister's intercession, and in early April she left for Zurich, although her mother was dying. All she achieved was to spend a few days with Mathieu. The account the burgomaster of Zurich gave of her visit to the French ambassador shows the futility of her exertions: 'She took a lively interest in Monsieur de Montmorency, and she gave herself infinite trouble to prove that we must let him reside here for at least six months, unless we choose to be barbarians.'

In her despair Germaine was even thinking of returning to Paris in the middle of the Terror. 'I hold all Switzerland in a magnificent horror,' she wrote to her husband. 'Sometimes I think that if one had in Paris a title that people are obliged to respect [read: if you were again ambassador to France], one might be of service to many people, and my present life makes me brave anything.' Better dead in Paris than alive in Switzerland. These projects were cut short, however, by the news that her mother's worsening condition demanded her immediate return. By May 1 Germaine was at Lausanne, where the Neckers had rented the château of Beaulieu. The political situation in Geneva and the presence in Lausanne of the celebrated Dr. Tissot had played about equal parts in their move. She arrived none too soon.

Madame Necker died on May 15. Necker for days had remained at

MATHIEU DE MONTMORENCY
From a contemporary engraving

TALLEYRAND
After a portrait by François Gérard

BENJAMIN CONSTANT
From a portrait by Mademoiselle L. Vallier at the Musée de Versailles

her side. 'I saw him,' recalled Germaine, 'remaining motionless for hours on end, standing upright, without changing position, for fear that the least movement might awaken her.' Every evening, on Madame Necker's wish, musicians were called to the château, 'so that the impression created by the sound might inspire her soul with those elevated thoughts which, alone, give death a character of melancholy and peace'. One evening, when no musicians were available, Necker asked his daughter to play the piano. She played a few pieces, then sang an aria whose words were evocative of the situation. Necker burst into tears. 'I was obliged to stop, and I saw him yielding, for several hours, to his deep emotion, at the feet of his dying wife.'

A few hours after her mother's death Germaine, on entering her father's room, saw him standing at his window, gazing at the distant Alps, in the glow of the rising sun. 'Her soul, perhaps, is soaring there,' he said, and fell silent. Germaine's comment, on recalling these words, is significant. 'Ah! Why could he not have spoken the same words over me!'

Germaine made no pretence of mourning. Her preoccupations were centred entirely on the question of where she could rent a house and how she could reunite her friends. The spy Venet, after reporting that Madame Necker had 'ordered her body to be preserved in alcohol like an embryo', remarked in his report to the French ambassador that 'Madame de Staël has shown no reverence for her mother's memory.'

The embalmers and the architects came to embalm and entomb Suzanne. Until mid-September, when the tomb at Coppet was ready, Madame Necker's corpse remained at Beaulieu, and Necker stayed with it—alone: three days after her mother's death Germaine was already installed in separate quarters.

The château of Mézery, near Lausanne, which Germaine had rented, had been Gibbon's residence in 1763, when Germaine's mother made her last desperate appeals to the cold embers of his love. Gibbon and Suzanne had died within four months of each other. The rooms where they had so often met, where their love had ended in cruel banter, in pretended levity and indifference, the rooms through which the whole eighteenth century had passed and left nothing but memories, ghosts, regrets, disenchantment—the same rooms now were to receive Suzanne Curchod's daughter and her extraordinary group of friends and lovers, with their arguments, their quarrels, their jealousies, their fears and recriminations, while beyond the lake, beyond the mountains, the blade of the guillotine came whistling down on the heads of parents, friends, and brothers.

To Mathieu, who had joined her, she had to impart the news that his brother was among the victims. His wife and his mother, imprisoned and waiting for their turn, were saved only by the downfall of Robespierre on July 27. It was during these summer weeks of 1794 that Mathieu underwent the crisis which made him turn against his liberal past and expiate his guilt at the foot of the altar. With every day bringing news of more arrests, more deaths, the little colony at Mézery sank into a dejection and despair such as only those who have experienced a similar cataclysm can imagine. When the Terror came to an abrupt end on 9 Thermidor, they were too stunned to rejoice.

In August 1794, a few days after the Thermidorian coup, Narbonne at last appeared at Mézery. Since about mid-April, with rather surprising suddenness, Germaine had ceased to persecute him; her letters had been friendly and calm. This sudden change had its cause not only in the chastening effect of the Great Terror but mainly in the fact that another man—this time a genuine Swede—was occupying Germaine's heart. He was Count Ribbing, who had planned the assassination of Gustavus III and who was wandering in romantic exile, under an assumed name, across Europe. Germaine had met the handsome blond regicide some time early in 1794, had met him again at Zurich, and had enticed him to Mézery, causing Monsieur de Staël to explode when he heard the news. Narbonne, too, although no longer in love with Germaine, was vexed to find himself succeeded so soon. One morning, after exchanging some unfriendly words, Narbonne and Ribbing left the château at dawn. Germaine, convinced they were about to cut each other's throats, spent the morning crying convulsively until both returned for breakfast, hale and in excellent spirits, carrying a huge catch of perch. When Mathieu's mother and Narbonne's former mistress, Madame de Montmorency-Laval, came to join the colony at Mézery after her release from prison, Narbonne, much to Mathieu's displeasure, renewed his former relationship with her, and life flowed on as harmoniously as it could in the rather unconventional circumstances.

The inhabitants of Mézery had barely begun to breathe more freely after Robespierre's fall when the Bernese government broke up their several idylls by signifying its intention to expel them. By September, Germaine was on the road again, accompanied by Narbonne, trying to find asylum for her guests elsewhere in Switzerland. Returning alone by a circuitous route, she tarried at Coppet with her father for two or three days, admired her mother's tomb from the outside, and, these duties done, climbed into her carriage to return to Lausanne.

About half an hour after her departure a man arrived at Coppet and asked to see Madame de Staël. Told that he had just missed her, he leaped back onto his saddle and, with characteristic impulsiveness, galloped off in the direction of Lausanne to catch up with her carriage. He had never laid eyes on her before, nor had he anything of importance to say to her, nor was there any reason why he could not have come back another day. When, on the spur of the moment, he made up his mind to gallop after Madame de Staël, he rushed into fifteen years of slavery —fifteen years spent largely in meditating his escape.

He caught up with her at Nyon and introduced himself: Benjamin Constant—of all the Constants, the only one Germaine had never met. His appearance was striking: tall and gangling, in his late twenties; a pale, freckled face surmounted by a shock of flamboyant red hair, braided at the nape and held up by a small comb; a nervous tic; red-rimmed myopic eyes; ironic mouth; a long, finely curved nose; long torso, poor posture, slightly pot-bellied, long-legged, wearing a long flapping riding-coat—a decidedly gauche, unhandsome, yet interesting and attractive figure of a man, certainly somebody altogether out of the ordinary. Germaine invited him to continue the journey in her carriage. By the time they reached Rolle, Germaine knew that her companion was the most fascinating talker she had ever met. They dined at the house of some of Germaine's friends; at table they had their first argument. Germaine complained against a newspaper which had attacked her father; she was going to have the paper suppressed. Benjamin burst into an impassioned speech in favour of the freedom of the press. Germaine was delighted: this young man had possibilities. They continued their trip to Lausanne, completely absorbed in each other's conversation. When they arrived, Germaine invited him to Mézery, to continue their talk.

Thus began what must have been the most eloquent love affair in history.

9

BENJAMIN

T HE Constants were a family whose numerous offspring dotted the shores of Lake Geneva from Geneva to Lausanne, with offshoots in many distant places. The Constants of Geneva and Lausanne alone, with the allied families of Crousaz, Chandieu, Nassau, Charrière, Gallatin, Langalerie, and Cazenove, constituted a nation to itself; and there were Constants in London, Constants in Paris, Constants in Brussels, Constants at The Hague, Constants even in China. They were noble; they were, for the most part, rich; they owned town houses and country estates; they held colonelcies and generalcies in the service of the United Provinces of the Netherlands; they were gifted, clannish, eccentric, literate, articulate, and long-lived. Benjamin's great-grandfather David and his three brothers accumulated, among the four of them, a total of 362 years; his grandfather, General Samuel Constant, lived eighty years; his father, Colonel Arnold-Juste Constant de Rebecque, eighty-six years. There was a fibre of toughness in the family. But Benjamin's mother died a few days after she had given birth, on October 25, 1767, to her first child.

His father was a captain in the Dutch service when Benjamin was born; a large part of the Dutch troops were Swiss, and service under the Stadhouder was a Constant family tradition. Juste was disliked by his fellow officers. Distant, cold, ironical, inclined to cynicism—thus he appeared to those who knew him; Gibbon, who was close to his brother Constant d'Hermenches, detested him more perhaps than any other man in Lausanne. Yet Juste was, in truth, merely timid and hypersensitive; there was nothing he feared more than to expose his feelings. In his autobiographical novel *Adolphe* Benjamin Constant wrote of his father:

> Unfortunately his attitude was noble and generous rather than tender. . . . No confidence ever existed between us. His mind had some intangible ironic quality which did not agree with my character. . . . I found in my

father, not a censor, but a cold and caustic observer, who would begin by smiling at me with pity, and who soon after would end our conversations with impatience. I do not recall having had, during the first eighteen years of my life, a single hour's talk with him. . . . I did not know that, even with his son, my father was timid, and that often, after having long waited for some show of affection from me, which his apparent coldness seemed to forbid, he left me with tears gathering in his eyes, and complained to others that I did not love him.

Juste Constant was, in addition, more than a little eccentric. In 1761, before he was married, he had taken a fancy to a nine-year-old girl, Jeanne Suzanne Magnin, whom he had met in the neighbourhood of Lausanne. One day in October that year, Juste drove up to her village, put the girl into his carriage and drove off with her to Holland. Both his family and the child's remonstrated in vain; Juste took complete charge of the girl, gave her an excellent education, made her his mistress when she was grown up, and eventually married her (or, at least, solemnly promised to marry her) in 1772. It was to Marianne, as she was known to her intimates, that Juste entrusted the education of five-year-old Benjamin. At twenty Benjamin still was unaware of his father's relationship with Marianne, and his subsequent discovery that Marianne had borne him a brother and a sister was one of the great shocks in his life.

To trace an itinerary of Benjamin's childhood would require many pages. Lausanne, Geneva, Brussels, and points between—Benjamin was passed around from hand to hand, from mistress to grandmother, from grandmother to aunt, from aunt to father, from tutor to tutor. His precocity was prodigious. At seven he was fluent in Greek and an accomplished pianist; at twelve he had written a tragedy in verse and five cantos of a heroic romance. The darling and pride of the family, he was encouraged and admired; no one doubted that he would become a great man of letters, like his uncle Samuel's friend Voltaire, or his uncle d'Hermenches's friend Gibbon.

Clearly such a child deserved the most careful education. Yet if Juste Constant had bent all his energies on scouring the universe for the most eccentric rascals in the teaching profession, he could not have succeeded better than he did. Benjamin's first tutor, a German named Stroelin, regularly beat him, then smothered him with caresses to extract his promise not to tell. He also taught him a game—to invent an alphabet, a vocabulary, and a grammar. The language thus invented turned out to be Greek, and Benjamin had progressed in it considerably when Herr Stroelin, caught in one of his sadistic fits, was chased from the household. Benjamin was five years old.

Benjamin was seven and staying at Brussels when his second tutor, a Frenchman named Lagrange, took charge. Monsieur de Lagrange was a fanatic atheist, tried to rape the daughter of Benjamin's music master, and finally took his pupil to live with him in a bordello. Colonel Constant got wind of this, hastened to Brussels, and chased out Monsieur de Lagrange.

Next Benjamin was put to board with the music master, who left him to his own devices. The boy spent eight to ten hours a day in a local lending library which specialized in anti-religious propaganda and pornography. He read everything he could find, 'from La Mettrie to Crébillon', ruining his eyesight for the rest of his life.

The next mentor was an ex-lawyer, Monsieur Gobert, who had left France to escape some scandal and who, in partnership with his mistress, had founded an educational establishment in Brussels. Under Monsieur Gobert, Benjamin spent more than a year copying a historic work his master had written; but since Monsieur Gobert was dissatisfied with his pupil's penmanship, Benjamin had to begin anew each day and never got beyond the Preface. When Colonel Constant was informed of Monsieur Gobert's background, he hastened to Brussels and brought his son back to Switzerland.

Next came a defrocked monk named Duplessis. He was good-natured and competent, but Colonel Constant took a dislike to him, openly showed his contempt, and eventually dismissed him. The good monk soon afterwards became mad over an unhappy love affair and put a bullet through his head. Benjamin was thirteen by then, and his father decided to send him to Oxford.[1]

With such an education, Benjamin acquired an early knowledge of the world. 'What do I care what the ancients thought,' he wrote to his grandmother when he was ten, 'since I am not going to live with them. . . . I sometimes see an English girl of my age whom I prefer to Cicero, Seneca, etc. She teaches me Ovid, whom she has never read or heard of but whom I discover in her eyes. I have written a little novel for her.' His age was, let it be repeated, ten years. At twelve, he regaled his grandmother with an account of his life at Brussels:

[1] M. Gustave Rudler, the authoritative historian of Benjamin's youth, made a search of the University's archives but was unable to find any record of Benjamin's matriculation. He surmises that Benjamin, because of his extreme youth, was only conditionally admitted. It also is possible that Benjamin went to Oxford merely in the hope of being admitted. See G. Rudler, *La Jeunesse de Benjamin Constant* (Paris, Armand Colin, 1908), pp. 113–15 and notes.

I rise at seven; I breakfast; I work and put Horace on the rack . . .; I take a lesson in accompaniment and composition; I read with Monsieur Duplessis; I take a dancing lesson and dine with a good appetite; I hop around, run, and amuse myself; I read Quintus Curtius; I write Latin verse; I take a harpsichord lesson; I go into the park; I sometimes go to visit a pretty English girl; . . . back at home I play cards, have supper, go to bed at nine, and sleep ten hours without interruption. Meanwhile I am composing an opera, both words and music. . . .

. . . Do you know, my dear grandmother, that I go into society twice a week? I have a fine frock coat, a sword, a hat under my arm, one hand on the chest, the other on the hip, and I stand as straight and look as much like a big fellow as I can. I watch, I listen—and so far I do not feel tempted by the pleasures of high society. They all look as if they did not like one another much. However, the gold I see rolling on the gaming tables causes me some emotion. I should like to win some to satisfy a thousand needs that people call whims.

Before he was out of his adolescence, Benjamin was a confirmed gambler.

For reasons unknown (perhaps because of his extreme youth), Benjamin had to leave Oxford after only two months of studies. With a young English tutor, Mr. May, he spent the following year and a half (1780–1) travelling in Holland and Switzerland. Whenever Benjamin had a tutor who was not a rascal and a pervert, Colonel Constant found him uncouth and ridiculous; thus it happened with Mr. May, with the result that Benjamin spent eighteen months making fun of his companion, who was eventually sent back to England. While in Gertruidenberg, where his father was stationed, Benjamin, not yet fourteen, fell in love with the commandant's daughter, wrote her endless letters which he never sent, and left without declaring his love. At fourteen he matriculated at the University of Erlangen, where he stayed for eighteen months and 'studied much'. Erlangen was the residence of the Margrave of Ansbach-Bayreuth, who shared his rule with his mistress, the ubiquitous Mademoiselle Clairon. The Margrave was, to say the least, peculiar. His neglected wife—who, in Mademoiselle Clairon's words, 'was born dying and lived dying from that moment to this day'—was pleased with the diversion offered by the fourteen-year-old prodigy who had been recommended to her court, and so was the Dowager Margravine, who vied with her daughter-in-law in spoiling Benjamin. Thus indulged, Benjamin felt in duty bound to keep a mistress. 'I chose,' he says, 'a wench of rather bad reputation. . . . The bizarre part of the thing was that I, on the one hand, did not care for the girl, and that she, on the other hand, did not give herself to me. I am probably the only man whom she resisted. But the pleasure of hearing it said that I was keeping a mistress was a consolation.' This was too much for the Dowager Margravine, who had a personal grudge against Benjamin's mistress's mother; Benjamin, banished from the Court, was ordered by his father to return to Brussels, and was sent on from there to the University of Edinburgh. He was not quite sixteen.

The two years Benjamin spent at Edinburgh were beyond doubt the happiest of his life. With a faculty that included Adam Smith, William Robertson, Dugald Stewart, Adam Ferguson, and Lord Kames, the University provided prodigious intellectual stimulation. An active member of the Speculative Society, Benjamin formed friendships with such men as Sir James Mackintosh and the brilliant John Wilde, whose promising career was to be cut short by dementia. The freedom, independence of thought, seriousness, and simplicity he found in this circle determined his goals as a thinker and politician. Unfortunately, his acquaintanceship was not limited to them. He also fell in with an Italian who operated a faro bank, lost large sums, and left heavy debts when his father recalled him early in 1785.

Colonel Constant's scheme was to complete his son's education at Paris by having him board with the critic Suard, who was about to take over the editorship of the *Journal de Paris*. Suard's rationalism, scepticism, and Anglomania harmonized with the disabused *Weltanschauung* of Benjamin in his eighteenth year. But Benjamin, though he frequented the Suards, did not live with them. His room not being ready on his arrival, he took lodgings at a hotel, fell in with a rich young Englishman, tried to keep up with his frenzied pace, and after four weeks was up to his chin in debts. Colonel Constant, to remedy this situation, found nothing better than to place him under the supervision of yet another tutor, a certain Baumier, with whom Benjamin made the rounds of the Paris bordellos, paying both his own and his mentor's expenses. When they fell out, Baumier had the cheek to write to Colonel Constant, complaining of his ward's dissolute ways. Colonel Constant hastened to Paris, got hold of his son, took him to Brussels, and left him there.

Benjamin was eighteen. He had never had a family life; he had no home, no country. He had been brought up and had learned to think in three languages. He had known every vice and corruption, had learned to respect no one, to distrust everyone. Only in Edinburgh had he known the sweetness of friendship and the love of studies—but these had no place in the society of Paris and Brussels. Hiding his sensibility behind a mask of irony and frivolous nonchalance, he impressed those who knew him as a monster of arrogance and egotism, sharp-tongued, amusing, and inclined to ridicule all those he knew behind their backs, not caring whether they learned of it or not. It was at this time, in Brussels, that the veteran whoremonger of eighteen had his first, perhaps his only, happy love affair. Madame Johannot, unhappily married to a Genevese husband,

> was a woman of about twenty-six or twenty-eight, with a very seductive face and a very distinguished mind. I felt attracted to her without quite admitting it to myself when, by a few words which at first surprised me even more than they delighted me, she gave me to understand that she loved me. At the moment I am writing this, twenty-five years have passed since I made this discovery, and I still experience a feeling of gratitude in recalling the pleasure it gave me. Madame Johannot . . . holds in my memories a place apart from all the other women I have known. My liaison with her lasted a very short time only and did not amount to much. But she did not make me pay for the happiness she gave me by any admixture of agitation and suffering.

To make love thus naturally, simply, without fret and fuss, with a woman who was grateful, maternal, undemanding—this remained the ideal experience Benjamin sought to recapture throughout his life. He forgot that there are things that must be allowed to happen by surprise.

Back in Lausanne in November 1785 and still pining for Madame Johannot, Benjamin sought to duplicate what cannot be duplicated. Mrs. Trevor, wife of the English ambassador to Turin, was spending the season in Lausanne, where she kept a lavish house. She was about thirty-five, 'and still had pretty eyes, superb teeth, and a charming smile'. She also was extremely coquettish and lived separately from her husband. Benjamin, bent on making her conquest, declared his love in a long letter. When he sent the letter, he was still in cold blood; by the time her reply came, he had worked himself 'into a kind of fever which bore a close enough resemblance to the passion I had at first meant to feign'. Mrs. Trevor offered him her friendship. Benjamin, in despair, called on her, rolled on the floor and beat his head against the wall as soon as the cruel word 'friendship' crossed the lady's lips.

> I kept at ten paces from her as she approached to calm me down or to console me, and I drew back repeating to her that, since she felt only

F*

friendship for me, there was nothing left for me but to die. For four hours she could not get anything else out of me, and I departed leaving her, I believe, very much annoyed at a lover who disputed over a synonym.

For four months Benjamin returned to the assault. Mrs. Trevor answered all his letters, received him alone, let him stay until three o'clock in the morning. 'But she gained nothing from it, and neither did I. I was excessively timid, and carried away by frenzy. I had not yet learned that one must not ask but take; I kept asking and never took.'

He was still disputing over synonyms when his father arrived in November to take him to Paris. Benjamin and Mrs. Trevor embraced, spent nights crying, promised to write each other; then Benjamin was pushed into a coach and driven away. He met Mrs. Trevor three months later, in Paris, and experienced no emotion whatsoever.

In Paris Benjamin stayed with the Suards, where he met all the scientific and literary celebrities. 'When I recall what I said there, and the calculated contempt I displayed towards everybody, I am still at a loss to understand how they could tolerate me.' At the same time he continued to gamble. He had met an elderly woman, Madame de Bourbonne—'a reckless gambler, but otherwise quite kind and rather original: she gambled while riding in her carriage, she gambled in bed, she gambled in her bath, mornings, nights, evenings'. Benjamin gambled with her, and lost. To borrow some money, he addressed himself to Madame Saurin, a lady in her sixties who presided over a literary salon and who had kindly feelings towards him. Embarrassed, instead of asking her point blank, he beat about the bush. Madame Saurin misunderstood his intentions. 'She covered her face with both hands, and her whole body began to tremble violently. I saw clearly that she had taken everything I had said to her for a declaration of love. My blunder, her emotion, and a huge bed, covered with damask, at two steps from us, threw me into an unutterable panic.' Brutally he explained his errand. Madame Saurin remained motionless, then took her hands from her face, rose, and without a word counted out the money. Benjamin did not recover his power of speech to thank her; he left in silence—with the money in his pocket.

These things were trifles. Of far greater consequence was the liaison he had begun with a woman who was his senior by twenty-seven years, one of the most extraordinary women of her time—Madame de Charrière, also known as Belle van Zuylen, the Zélide in Boswell's diaries.

Born in 1740 into an aristocratic Dutch family, Isabelle van Tuyll van Serooskerken was, with all her beauty, charm, and wit, doomed to a life of unhappiness and frustration. As a girl in her twenties, she had known Benjamin's uncle, Constant d'Hermenches, and made him the confidant of her abysmal introspections: her letters to him leave nothing unsaid. Morbidly sensitive, her soul was the battlefield of all-pervasive sensuality, and all-paralysing intellectuality. In rebellion against her family, against her surroundings, she consumed her youth in unhappy passions that left her permanently scarred. Her habit of spending entire nights reading or writing kept her nerves in a state of tension which, at the age of twenty-four, she began to relieve by taking opium. Her marriage projects, her infatuations, all came to nothing—either because the men were frightened by her, because her dowry was too small, or because her family disapproved of her choice. 'I would prefer being my lover's laundress and living in a garret to the arid freedom and the good manners of our great families.' She had passed her thirtieth year when she married Monsieur de Charrière, a Swiss gentleman who had been the tutor of her brothers. She married him almost as an act of despair, against her parents' wishes, and at a time when she no longer loved him. Unable to raise her husband to her own emotional level, she had, in her forties, fallen violently in love with a much younger man, more remarkable for his looks than for his wit, who abandoned her for a younger woman. To this last and most shattering experience she owed her literary fame, for it inspired her with the theme of her novel *Caliste*, one of the many neglected minor masterpieces of her century. It was at this time that Benjamin met her in Paris, and her influence over him soon was complete.

Controversy has long been raging whether or not Benjamin slept with Belle van Zuylen. Yes, says Sainte-Beuve; no, says Gustave Rudler; a middle position is hardly possible. To call the question academic would be a misuse of the adjective; but unimportant it is. There may have been some intimacy in the early stage of their acquaintance; but, if there was, it played little or no part in their friendship, which was of a far less innocent nature than mere adultery. 'Madame de Charrière', says Benjamin, 'had so original and lively a manner of looking at life, so deep a contempt for prejudice, so powerful an intellect, and so vigorous and disdainful a superiority over the common run of men, that in the disposition I was in, at the age of twenty, bizarre and arrogant like her, I discovered in her conversation a pleasure I had not known before.' And so they sat up entire nights, 'drinking tea and talking about every

possible topic with inexhaustible energy'. Since 'all of Madame de
Charrière's opinions rested on her contempt for all proprieties and
conventions', they made it a game to disparage everything. 'We became intoxicated with our jests and with our contempt of the human
species'.

The result was, in Benjamin, a studied pessimism combined with a
total abdication of responsibility. Whether he was here or there, alive
or dead, respected or despised, loved or hated, sensible or ridiculous,
made no difference:

> Perhaps I have the misfortune of feeling too acutely what so many
> writers have kept repeating, while they went on acting as if they did not
> believe in what they said: that all our quests, all our efforts, all the things
> we attempt, do, or reform, are mere games of a moment and cannot lead
> to anything but to an imminent annihilation.

Partly pose, partly nature, Benjamin's pessimism prefigured Byronism
and nihilism all wrapped in one. No matter what his antics with regard
to others, absolute frankness was the rule between Belle and Benjamin.
'No phrases' was their motto. 'There is absolutely no phrase in this
letter' became a recurrent phrase in his letters.

It was under Madame de Charrière's guidance that Benjamin perfected himself in detached self-observation. The observer Constant
could analyse the actor Constant with scientific objectivity, while the
actor Constant went on behaving as if unaware of the observer. If his
character has been judged severely, it was he himself who furnished his
critics their weapons: few men have laid their innermost workings as
bare as did Benjamin Constant in his novels and diaries.

While Benjamin spent most of his time philosophizing with Madame
de Charrière, he still found ample opportunity to make a fool of himself
elsewhere. Having learned of his son's accumulated debts, Colonel
Constant notified Benjamin by letter that, unless he succeeded in
marrying a rich heiress, he would have to leave Paris. The heiress in
question was the pretty sixteen-year-old daughter of a financier, Jenny
Pourrat. She had been promised to another suitor, but the engagement
was by no means final. Instead of proceeding in the usual manner,
which would have been easy since he was on excellent terms with the
girl's mother, Benjamin put it into his head that Mademoiselle Pourrat
must elope with him. In letter after letter he promised to save her from
marriage with a man she did not love, and proposed the most extravagant schemes of elopement. His methods of love-making baffled

Mademoiselle Pourrat, who was not in the least reluctant to marry Benjamin's rival. Benjamin topped his inexplicable behaviour by making the girl's mother his confidante. For hours he was closeted with Madame Pourrat, relating in detail his unsuccessful attempts to make her daughter elope with him. Now Madame Pourrat had a lover, a Monsieur de Sainte-Croix, who in his ignorance of the true state of affairs took umbrage at Benjamin's intimacy with his mistress. As he burst in on them one evening and gave vent to his feelings, Madame Pourrat took Benjamin by the hand and begged him to explain the truth of the matter. Rather than admit his ridiculous love affair to a stranger, Benjamin resorted to a desperate expedient. 'By chance,' he relates, 'I happened to have in my pocket a small bottle of opium which I had been carrying about for some time.' Madame de Charrière had given it to him. While Madame Pourrat besought him to answer her leading questions, the thought flashed through his mind that swallowing the opium would relieve him of the necessity of answering them. He had swallowed half the contents of the bottle before Sainte-Croix tore it from him. The household was in a turmoil. Benjamin was made to swallow antidotes, which he took with docility, for he was 'totally indifferent to the outcome'. Saved from a most uncertain death, he was being lectured on the impropriety of committing suicide when Mademoiselle Pourrat entered the room, unaware of what had happened and all dressed for the opera. Asked to join the party, Benjamin accepted and spent the evening at the opera in high spirits. Thus ended Benjamin's first marriage project. His father dispatched a lieutenant of his regiment to Paris, with orders to bring his son to 's Hertogenbosch.

The lieutenant had never seen Paris, and Benjamin offered to show him around before they left. He took him to dine at the Palais-Royal, where he ran into an acquaintance. Leaving the lieutenant behind, Benjamin approached the man, whom he knew but superficially, and poured out his heart to him. He had no desire to go to Holland, and sometimes he felt a strong urge to end his troubles by running away. Benjamin's reluctant confidant listened with only one ear. 'Where would you go?' he asked.—'To England, of course.'—'Well, why not, it's a fine country, and there's a lot of freedom.'—'Everything would be all right again by the time I came back,' said Benjamin.—'Of course,' said the man; 'in time everything turns out all right.' Benjamin returned to his table. After he had finished his meal, he ran into his acquaintance once more. 'Well, haven't you left yet?'

The next day, with 600 francs in his pocket (borrowed from Madame de Charrière), Benjamin gave his lieutenant the slip, took refuge in the apartment of a girl 'of medium virtue', asked her to hire a chaise for him, ordered champagne, and went to sleep. The next morning he was rolling towards Calais, with 540 francs left. Within an hour after his arrival at Calais he was on a boat to Dover. When he reached London he had 300 francs left. Of these he spent 40 on the purchase of two dogs and one monkey. Back in his lodgings, he found the monkey uncongenial. He tried to beat him to teach him manners; the monkey resisted; and Benjamin took him back to the pet shop where he exchanged him for a third dog. Two of the dogs soon disagreed with him, and he sold them. The third loved him passionately and followed him all the way from London to Edinburgh, thence back to London, and thence to Dover. The two weeks he spent at Edinburgh were, he relates, a continuous feast, thanks to his hospitable friends. Far from repaying his old debts, Benjamin left Edinburgh owing ten guineas more. By the time he reached London he was penniless. A letter from his father, which he found there, ordered him to return immediately. Benjamin applied for help to a friend named Kentish, who, after treating him in the most humiliating manner, ended up by giving him ten guineas to be rid of him. Benjamin had his revenge: arrived at Dover, he confided his dog to a postilion, with orders to take him to Kentish, along with a note to the effect that since Kentish had treated his friend like a dog, he hoped that he would treat the dog like a friend. This done, he took the boat to Calais.

At 's Hertogenbosch, Benjamin found his father playing whist. 'Ah! There you are,' said the Colonel. 'How did you get here?' Benjamin explained: partly on horseback, partly by coach. 'You must be tired,' said the Colonel, having finished the rubber. 'Go to sleep.' He noticed that Benjamin's coat was torn. 'I always feared this would come of this excursion,' he added. He never mentioned the matter again: Benjamin felt crushed.

A few days later Benjamin arrived at the Charrières' manor at Colombier, near Neuchâtel in Switzerland, cured of his love for Mademoiselle Pourrat and with a resplendent case of syphilis. He was only passing through on his way to Lausanne, but returned two months later to stay and nurse his wounds. Again he stayed up nights with Madame de Charrière, talking and drinking linden tea. But his health did not improve, and he had to move to Neuchâtel for more radical treatment. While Dr. Leschaux combated his spirochetes as best he could, Benjamin employed his enforced repose in reading the collected works of

Restif de La Bretonne, the 'Rousseau of the gutter', who among all pornographers up to this day was undoubtedly the most gifted. In his daily bulletins addressed to Belle, Benjamin gave an exact accounting of his symptoms and of his readings, requesting her at one point to send him the first fifty or sixty volumes of Restif's epic, which Monsieur de Charrière had in his library. At the same time he meditated his *History of Polytheism* which he had begun in 1785 and was to write and rewrite during the remainder of his life. In the meantime, also, his father had found a position for him: Benjamin had been appointed *Kammerjunker*, or chamberlain, at the court of the Duke of Brunswick. It was a position that no one could have taken very seriously, least of all Benjamin.

He arrived at Brunswick in February 1788, still feeble, his face decorated with patches of plaster, and accompanied by his bitch Flora, for whom he had once fought a duel with a Swiss lieutenant whose dogs had molested her. Benjamin's sole official function at the ducal court consisted in this: that, in the absence of the Grand Marshal of the Court, it was his duty to seat everyone according to rank and etiquette. For this he received a gold-embroidered habit, a sword, 1,330 francs a year, and the profound contempt of the Duke, who detested courtiers.

The Duke, the Duchess, and their offspring, half of whom were mentally deficient, soon came to dislike Benjamin intensely. The local nobility, on whose rusticity the French culture of the court made hardly a dent, changed their linen once a month, ate sausage and raw bacon, and massacred the French language. The bourgeoisie never mixed with the nobility. Only his indefatigable reading, his correspondence with Madame de Charrière, and his friendship with Jacob de Mauvillon, a German man of letters of Huguenot origin, preserved Benjamin from intellectual starvation; but there remained enough idle time to commit new follies. Benjamin fell head over heels in love with one of the Duchess's ladies-in-waiting, Wilhelmina von Cramm, who was nine years older than he, ugly, penniless, vile-tempered, and furiously intent on getting married. She knew how to play on Benjamin's craving for love and understanding. The Duke and Duchess, anxious to marry off an impecunious but noble spinster, encouraged the romance. They were married on May 8, 1789, at a time when Benjamin was engulfed in a family disaster.

In August 1788 Colonel Juste Constant had lost the first round of the monumental lawsuit, or rather of thirteen interconnected lawsuits, which had grown out of an act of insubordination of his regiment's officers. The complexity of the suits, countersuits, appeals, and counter-appeals is so enormous (the records of the affair take up a respectable number of volumes) that they defy analysis. Constant, suspended from his command and threatened with financial ruin, at first lost his head and disappeared altogether, thus adding the charge of desertion to all the previous charges. He eventually turned up at Lausanne, when his family had hopefully given him up for dead. The subsequent five years were spent by Benjamin in continuous and frantic efforts to extricate his father from the nightmarish legal net. The affair gradually took on international proportions, with the Duke of Brunswick intervening with the Prince of Orange, and with an exchange of increasingly unfriendly notes between the governments of the United Provinces and of Berne. At times Benjamin touched the bottom of despair; it was no doubt on such an occasion that he computed, in a letter to Madame de Charrière, the precise budget required to run a plantation in the Carolinas. 'O for £300 a year, my Minna, and a cottage!' he exclaimed to her in English. It was only in 1796, when Juste Constant had retired to a small estate in the French Jura, that the judgment was reversed and the ex-colonel reinstated, with the rank and pension of general.

While his father's troubles continued to occupy most of Benjamin's time, the dream of Minna and a cottage dissolved. 'I love my wife for 1,000 good qualities which she has, but the great discouragement into which I am plunged has estranged her from me; whenever I want to show her some trust or warmth, she is either cold or unconcerned, and to avoid explanations beyond my strength, I am silent and go away.' Things became worse. 'My wife no longer loves me; she loves another man,' Benjamin announced in 1793 to Madame de Charrière, who was not displeased to learn it. 'She neither desires nor is able to keep herself occupied: a crowd of cats, dogs, birds, friends, and a lover—these are her company.' He fell back into his Hamlet pose:

> Blasé about everything, bored with everything, bitter, self-centred; endowed with a kind of sensibility that merely tortures me; unstable to the point of passing for mad; subject to fits of melancholy that stop short all my projects and make me act, while they last, as if I had given up everything; persecuted moreover by external circumstances . . .: how do you expect me to succeed, to please, to live?

In *Adolphe*, years later, he put this more succinctly: 'I found that no objective was worth the trouble of making an effort.'

During such fits of *Weltschmerz* Benjamin was most vulnerable to the illusion of love. In January 1793 he met Charlotte von Hardenberg, the woman who, he wrote twelve years later, changed his entire life. She did, in fact, change his entire life twice—the first time in 1793-4, the second time in 1806.

When Benjamin met Charlotte in 1793, she was twenty-four and had been married for five years to a Baron von Marenholz, who was twenty years her senior. Without being pretty she possessed to a large degree that sensual sentimentality which irresistibly attracted Benjamin whenever he despaired of knowing happiness. Charlotte was unintellectual, understanding, and tender in a simpering way. Benjamin, 'for a few days', was passionately in love with her. Even her foolishness, he wrote to Madame de Charrière, was a *witty* foolishness. *Charlottechen's* love for Benjamin lasted for more than a few days, and it soon began to frighten him: 'One wanted to marry me by might and main. . . . If one could not marry me, one wanted to follow me, to live only for me. . . . Female heart, female mind, or [blank]—what caused all this fury?' Strangely enough, even at the height of their infatuation they did not, during that stage of their relationship, indulge their senses. Was it Charlotte who refused or Benjamin who did not ask? 'It gives them so little pain, and us so much pleasure,' Colonel Constant used to say to his son about love and women; but the intermittent love that Benjamin had for Charlotte in the course of the following twenty years was to give her a great deal of pain and himself very little pleasure.

Charlotte was ready to divorce Herr von Marenholz, but Benjamin, his first passion spent, showed no inclination to marry her. In the circumstances Brunswick was not a good place to be. Benjamin washed his hands of the matter ('What will her husband do with her? . . . Well, that's her business'), and in the summer of 1793 shook off the dust of Germany to return to Lausanne. He found every single member of his family exasperating, a feeling which was altogether reciprocal; by September he was once more with Madame de Charrière at Colombier. He installed himself quite thoroughly, ordering his library to be sent to him—between three and four thousand volumes. The clouds which had thrown many a shadow on his friendship with Belle seemed to have dissipated; Benjamin returned to his conversations, to his studies. The French Revolution, to which in the midst of his trouble he had paid scant attention (although his master the Duke was the generalissimo of the Coalition armies), now began to absorb him and to turn him towards politics.

He returned to Brunswick in April 1794, largely to make a separation settlement with his wife. He found the Court hostile, Minna embattled, and Charlotte still counting on his marrying her, especially after he initiated divorce proceedings against Minna in June. (The divorce became final only in November 1795.) In August Charlotte divorced Baron von Marenholz. Whether or not he married Charlotte, his position at Brunswick had become untenable. The Duke, weary of a *Kammerjunker* who for five years had been the scandal of the town, asked Benjamin to resign. For all these developments Benjamin's letters of that period have a single recurrent comment: 'Je m'en fous—to hell with it!' In this frame of mind he left Brunswick in July 1794. Charlotte was not to hear from him for nine years.

He was nearly twenty-seven years old and—with all his gifts, connections, and intelligence—a failure. His relatives either made him their laughing-stock or tortured him with good advice. From the moment he entered the age of reason, his life had been a succession of follies. A case of arrested precocity, the former child prodigy had nothing to show for his years but a collection of vices, disease, emptiness, and nihilism.

He took stock of himself. The result was rebellion, rebellion against his pessimism, against his negativism—consequently, rebellion against Madame de Charrière. 'Believe me, my dear aunt,' he wrote to Madame de Nassau in May 1794,

> you do me an injustice if you think I am insensitive. Remember my education, this vagabond, torn-up life, these vain ambitions with which I was nursed in my childhood, this ironic tone which is the style of my family, this affectation which consists in deriding all sentiment and in prizing only intellect and fame—and then ask yourself whether it is surprising that my young mind has modelled itself on these patterns. . . . I am tired of my own persiflage, tired of surrounding my heart with a joyless atmosphere of indifference which deprives me of the sweetest sensations. . . . To this fatal wisdom . . . I prefer the madness of enthusiasm.

As early as 1793 Madame de Charrière had written to Benjamin, 'If I knew a young and robust person who would love you as much as I love you, and who is no more stupid than I am, I would have the generosity of saying "Go to her!" ' Madame de Charrière did not believe there was such a person. There was, however, and it seems a miracle that Benjamin had escaped meeting her thus far. He could not, at any rate, have met her at a more critical moment: the young man who had just escaped from the slough of nihilism in order to affirm the supremacy of enthusiasm over wisdom was ripe for Germaine de Staël.

10

'THIS MISERABLE GYPSY LIFE'

We promise to consecrate our lives to each other; we declare that we regard ourselves as indissolubly bound to each other, that we will share forever and in every respect a common destiny, that we will never enter into any other bond, and that we shall strengthen the bonds now uniting us as soon as lies within our power.

I declare that I am entering into this engagement with a sincere heart, that I know nothing on earth as worthy of love as Madame de Staël, that I have been the happiest of men during the four months I have spent with her, and that I regard it as the greatest happiness in my life to be able to make her happy in her youth, to grow old peacefully by her side, and to reach my term together with the soul that understands me and without whose presence life on this earth would hold no more interest for me.

[Signed:] BENJAMIN CONSTANT

THIS document bears no date. It would be only reasonable to suppose that Germaine and Benjamin exchanged its curiously worded vows in the first flush of their new love; but such a supposition would betray ignorance of the nature of their relationship. The document is not a freely given profession of love, but a promissory note, dictated by Germaine, and signed under duress.[1] It probably was written in 1797, when Benjamin, wearied to death by the vagrant and strenuous life Germaine forced him to lead by her side, first rebelled against her domination and began to look for a wife and peace—the year when Monsieur Necker cried out in anguish and disgust over his daughter's incessant wanderings, 'What a miserable gypsy life!'

'A miserable gypsy life'—the expression aptly describes Germaine's entire career from 1792 until her death a quarter of a century later; but to no period in her life can it be applied more justly than to the years 1794-9. Having emerged from her shattering experience with Narbonne, she sought, as she put it in her treatise on the *Passions*, to 'begin

---

[1] See a similar document on p. 298.

life anew, but minus hope'. Not only her heart was ravaged: France was, too. For Germaine the years of the Reign of Terror had been a double traumatic experience. And the political chaos which intervened between the fall of Robespierre and the accession of Bonaparte, a chaos in which she had her brief moments of triumph and long months of remorse, was paralleled by the chaos of her new friendships and loves.

Benjamin, when he met her, was also ready to begin a new life. Until their first meeting he had seen her through the eyes of Madame de Charrière, with whom Germaine had been in contact since 1793. (Germaine had tried to enlist her aid in a complicated scheme to free La Fayette from his imprisonment at Olmütz.) Madame de Charrière had judged her harshly: 'Her wit lacks simplicity and sometimes sharpness, and her sensibility is mere wit,' she wrote to Benjamin. Germaine's morality, she suspected, was merely a 'higher morality' which could dispense with the more lowly decencies of common mortals. 'Perhaps she has taken Catherine II as her model. . . .' Benjamin himself, on reading Germaine's *Reflections on the Trial of the Queen*, had commented: 'All these antitheses and cadenced phrases, when one has before one's eyes the image of such long and horrible sufferings! I spit on it.' Undoubtedly these judgments were deserved. But the simplicity and honesty of seventeenth-century classicism, which Madame de Charrière upheld so heroically against the onslaughts of the romantic rhetoric of the late eighteenth, had rested on a positive faith. Without that faith it led to the most arid nihilism: everything was false, illusory, foolish, ridiculous, dishonest, except the certitude that all ends in the void. With this ruthless nihilism Benjamin had been indoctrinated, and against it he at last rebelled. Four weeks after meeting Germaine he had thrown to the winds all that Madame de Charrière had taught him; triumphantly, brutally, he announced his emancipation to his former mistress:

As for me, I have for some time had the joy of repulsing all sterile sensations, and I do not like to wallow in the past when I believe that there still is hope in the future. . . . She [Madame de Staël] is the second woman I have met who could have replaced the entire universe for me, who could have been for me a world in herself. You know who was the first. . . . In a word, she is a being apart, a superior being, such as appears but once in a century, such a being that those who can be close to her, who can know her and be her friends, must not demand any other happiness.

Madame de Charrière's reply was straightforward: 'Love her! Get enthusiastic! You are free to do so, just as I am free to write to you no longer.'

Despite his declaration that to be near Madame de Staël was happiness enough, Benjamin asked for more than her mere presence; nor was he satisfied with being merely one of her friends. But though she never tired of his intellect, Germaine felt repelled by his physique. Neither in appearance, nor in manners, nor in birth was he a match for the four handsome aristocrats who then were occupying her heart: Narbonne, whom she still loved, though without hope; Mathieu, whose charm was not diminished by his incipient halo; Count Ribbing, the fair regicide; and the sensitive, brilliant Chevalier François de Pange, whom she was to pursue, passionately and without success, until his premature death in 1796. Ribbing had left for Paris. Narbonne and Mathieu were settled at Neuville, on the Lake of Biel, with several other ex-Constitutionalist *émigrés*, among them de Pange. Germaine could not bear life without them for long: there were frequent trips and meetings, and Mathieu came to stay briefly at Mézery early in 1795. In all these comings and goings, and in the social whirl that surrounded Germaine at Mézery and at Lausanne, Benjamin was but one among many. In one respect only was Benjamin closer to her than the others: he had become her political collaborator. Preparing her return to France, Germaine planned to re-enter the political scene in a spectacular way by uniting the moderates of right and left behind the Republic and by mediating a peace between revolutionary France and the European Coalition. A complete identity of political thinking between her and Benjamin made him the ideal collaborator in the writing of the pamphlet which was to open the campaign—Germaine's *Reflections on Peace, Addressed to Mr. Pitt and to the French*. The pamphlet was printed secretly at a small plant operated by de Pange, whom the angelic Mathieu assisted as printer's devil. But it was to her printer, not to her collaborator, that Germaine felt attracted.

Benjamin was not the man to sigh discreetly. At an early stage in his relationship he made up his mind that he would become her lover. In this resolution he was encouraged by the Machiavellian Madame de Laval, Mathieu's mother, who despised no means to separate her lover Narbonne from Germaine. But Germaine held out steadfastly: friendship, yes; love, no. It was the drama of Mrs. Trevor all over again, and Benjamin played his role in the accustomed style.

It was midnight, and the guests at Mézery had retired to their rooms;

suddenly the house was filled by screams and moans, which, upon investigation, were found to emanate from Benjamin's quarters. An empty bottle of opium stood on his bedside table; he was dying, but he wanted to say a last farewell to the hostess. Madame Rilliet-Huber ran off in quest of Germaine while one of the guests irrupted into Mathieu's room, to inform him of the tragedy. Monsieur de Montmorency was in his dressing-gown, calmly reading the *Confessions* of Saint Augustine. 'Throw that man,' he cried, 'out of the window. All he does is disturb the peace of this house and bring dishonour on it by a suicide.'

With dignified calm he lighted a taper and proceeded to the scene of the disturbance. He found Benjamin writhing on his bed, moaning and screaming, surrounded by the entire household, masters and servants. 'You wretch! What have you done!' cried Germaine as she burst into the room. 'Call the doctor!'—'Ah! it is you,' sighed Benjamin. 'You are calling me back to life . . .'—'Live! Live, my dear Monsieur Constant, I beseech you,' Germaine insisted, and Benjamin lived. 'Since you command it, I shall try,' he murmured generously, seized her arm, and covered it with passionate kisses. The doctor, who came at this juncture, found him cured. 'My God, what a comedy!' said Mathieu, relighted his candle, and returned to Saint Augustine. The audience followed him discreetly, leaving Benjamin alone with his saving angel.

But when Germaine returned to her boudoir, where Madame Rilliet was waiting for her, she washed her arm with eau de cologne and remarked, 'I feel that this man would inspire me with an invincible physical antipathy.'

Still the effect was not entirely lost on her; nor, for that matter, was the lesson: the 'Coppet dose' of opium, as Sainte-Beuve calls it, became one of her chief weapons against the man who had taught her its use. Whether it was shortly after this incident, or only a year later, as the Comtesse de Pange would have it, that Germaine overcame her repugnance is a matter for Staëlian and Constantian scholars to quarrel about. It is certain, however, that even if Germaine surrendered to Benjamin's importunities at an early date, she did not openly admit her liaison until the summer of 1796. Until then her association with Benjamin was, as far as the world could see, a political partnership. This partnership became official when, on May 15, 1795, the first anniversary of her mother's death, Germaine bade farewell to her father and her Gracchi and, with Benjamin, went off in her carriage to conquer Paris.

Monsieur Necker was apprehensive. His daughter's republicanism was not at all to his taste, and the conquering gleam in her eye presaged nothing good. As was customary between them, he gave her his farewell thoughts in writing. 'I fear that you have . . . the secret intention of playing a public role. How is it possible to carry out such projects without innumerable inconveniences! Remember the persecution to which you exposed yourself once before this.' The guardian angel, in his perplexity, delegated his functions to Benjamin. 'Allow me,' he continued, 'to ask Monsieur Constant to refrain from pushing you and to give you, on every occasion, a lesson in prudence and patience.'

It is difficult to decide which was worse—the holy madness of the Great Terror or the moral bankruptcy of its aftermath. When Tallien, one of Germaine's old friends, engineered the overthrow of Robespierre on July 27, 1794—the 9 Thermidor in the Revolutionary Calendar—the rule of idealist fanatics came to an end and a new set of men rose to power. These men had howled with the wolves while the Reign of Terror lasted, but since their sole aim was to acquire money and to keep their skins, they were the kind of men with whom respectable people can do business. Their greed and corruptibility was unlimited, and their political convictions began and ended with an instinct of self-preservation against enemies on either the right or the left. 'The new revolution which has just occurred,' wrote Germaine a few weeks after the 9 Thermidor, 'has put the villains-for-the-love-of-profit in the place of the villains-for-the-love-of-crime.' One of the first acts of the new government was to repeal the maximum price laws. The result was runaway inflation. The *assignats* soon were worth less than the paper they were printed on; citizens with fixed incomes literally starved to death; those who owned land, or had something to sell, or had hard currency with which to buy, grew rich overnight. The government was bankrupt; the governors were millionaires; the soldiers fired into rioting workers at home while they died for liberty, equality, and fraternity on the Rhine and in the Alps.

The France Germaine and Benjamin discovered when they set out for Paris in May 1795 has been vividly described, not by them, but by Germaine's arch-conservative friend Meister, who visited it in the same year. What struck him above all was the drabness, misery, and apathy of the masses. Between Basel and Paris he met exactly two coaches on the road. Everywhere he noticed 'malaise, worry, fatigue, discontent, and at the same time a great deal of indifference towards the success or failure of the new order'. Entire districts of Paris were deserted. In the Faubourg Saint-Germain the great town houses of the aristocracy, confiscated by the government, were plastered with signs announcing 'National Property for Sale' in huge black and red letters; inside they were stripped of furniture, draperies, wainscoting, everything. Marble saints, removed from churches, were on sale in front of the Dôme des Invalides. Pavements were lined with objects for sale—clothes, furniture, linen, everything that might bring cash for the next meal. 'The capital of the world,' observed Meister, 'looks like an immense junk shop.' After nightfall the streets, once thronged with carriages and pedestrians bound for pleasure, were deserted: 'To meet a carriage is an adventure; it is rare even to meet with pedestrians, except foot patrols.'

The police records of the period show a sharp rise in suicides and mendicity. One's position in a queue before a bakery sometimes determined life or death. On May 3 'a woman, at the sight of her desperate husband and of her four children who had not eaten for two days, threw herself into the gutter beating her head against the curbstone and tearing out her hair'. On May 10 a young man, finding the bakery out of bread, went up to his fifth-floor room and threw himself out of the window. On May 20 an immense crowd gathered shouting for bread. They were charged with bayonets, a cordon of troops was placed around the workers' quarters, and 10,000 arrests were made. At the same time 644 public ballrooms were operating in Paris; restaurants, jewellers' shops, and bordellos had never done more business; young men sporting extraordinary clothes and strong canes spent fortunes of mysterious origin; female fashions followed the lead of Madame Tallien—as little as possible, worn as loosely as possible; cemeteries were used for dances and orgies in memory of guillotined relatives; and the people's representatives in the National Convention were preparing to draft a new constitution under which none could vote except substantial property owners.

For the new men in power the Revolution had reached the precise point where they wanted it immobilized. The 'gains of the Revolution' —a phrase which covered both the newly won liberties and the ill-gained profits—had to be consolidated, and for this purpose it was necessary to guillotine democrats, shoot royalists, and make peace with the foreign enemies. Peace negotiations with Prussia and Spain had begun at Basel early in 1795; of the great powers only England and Austria held out.

Madame de Staël and Benjamin arrived in Paris on May 25, 1795, five days after the workers' massacre of 1 Prairial. Germaine moved back into the Swedish embassy; Benjamin took lodgings near by. Their political programme had preceded them in the shape of Germaine's *Reflections on Peace*; they were determined to back the Thermidorian government.

Madame de Staël had not given up her belief that politics must rest on morality; yet she consciously supported the régime of the 'villains-for-the-love-of-profit'. Tallien, Barras, and the rest of the Thermidorian crew, as corrupt a gang as can be found in history, were Germaine's friends. That her political line coincided with her material interests (and even more so with Benjamin's) was, of course, no accident; yet the monstrous alliance between virtue and vice which she proposed was not a mere rationalization of her interests. The grounds on which she called all men of good will to the defence of the Republic were eminently sane and valid. They owe much of their sanity and lucidity to Benjamin. The *Reflections on Peace* is a masterly plea, drawing on every possible argument and addressed with equal persuasiveness to every shade of opinion save the extremes, in favour of the acceptance of the revolutionary *status quo*. In the first part of her pamphlet, ostensibly addressed to Pitt, the leader of the Coalition powers, Germaine shows that the French nation, no matter how split, was united in its determination to resist the foreign invader. The French victories had been national victories, not party victories; the tyrants of the Reign of Terror, 'with the help of democratic ideas, had commanded enthusiasm in the name of fear, and had reaped, at the same time, the advantages of free consent and of coercion'. No doubt France was on the brink of ruin; but her ruin would also engulf the victors: 'If France crumbles, Europe must crumble. . . . Even America would feel a shock against which neither water nor space can cushion it.' No doubt the Revolution had made so many victims, so many enemies, that without a stable government a civil war was inevitable; but 'the destiny of France must be decided by the French; as long as one persists in pitting foreigners against them, they will fight, they will win; their government will be kept going by the very impulse of the external obstacles put in its way, and no one can tell how far their victories will lead them.' The rulers of the anti-revolutionary Coalition should beware: there were malcontents in their countries who were the natural allies of the French; continued French victories would lead to world revolution.

The pamphlet then subjects the past policies of the Allies to severe criticism. The Allies had persistently encouraged the Jacobins by siding with the extreme reactionaries against the moderates. 'One day the attempt will be made, perhaps, to reveal the secret treaty between the

Jacobins and the Aristocrats for the total annihilation of the entire interval of reason that separates them.' The governments of Europe never made any decision from foresight: 'All their resolutions have followed events instead of forestalling them. Nobody was willing to yield what he could not help losing.' The champions of legality and humanity had forfeited the very basis of their moral standing by exceeding the Terrorists in lawless cruelty. 'When one sees the agents of Spain in Santo Domingo surpassing the September Massacres . . . one finds some difficulty in believing that the foreign governments have sincerely adopted the system which might have swayed public opinion in France in favour of the Allied powers.'

However, Germaine concludes, let bygones be bygones. All Europe was crying for peace (that Germaine had done her best to precipitate the war was another bygone she was willing to forget), and making peace with a government does not necessarily mean approval or sanction of the form of that government. All the Allies had to do was to recognize the unshakable fact that the French Republic existed. If, under a stable government, France was allowed to recuperate from her wounds, if prosperity were allowed to return, the danger of revolution from the lowest, the unpropertied, classes would disappear and society would be consolidated on the basis of private property, which is the precondition of all social order. With moderate and wise counsels prevailing, it could then be decided which of the only two workable systems was to be adopted—a limited monarchy or a republic modelled on the United States. Only peace could restore social order; nothing but further revolution could result from war.

In the second, and by far shorter, part of the pamphlet, Germaine sings the same words to the French nation, but to two entirely different tunes: one for the ears of the republicans, one for the ears of the royalists. The performance does not lack virtuosity, yet there was no intent to deceive. The Republic, such as it was, was not only a lesser evil than either the reaction that would attend a Bourbon restoration or a victory of the fanatics on the left; it also kept open the door to change, which either of the extremist factions would have bolted. The Republic was one thing, the men who ran it another; Germaine endorsed the institution rather than the men.

Germaine's political line was practical, and it succeeded. The time of her return was extremely favourable to her purposes. Her ostensible reason for remaining in Switzerland until May was that she supervised the printing, at Lausanne, of a collection of short pieces, including her

Essay on Fiction and *Zulma*. But a more compelling reason was that she could not safely return without diplomatic immunity. Her husband had returned to Paris in January and, without official instructions, had begun negotiations with the Republic. On April 22, in a solemn ceremony, he presented his credentials to the Convention and thus became the first representative of a foreign power to give recognition to the First French Republic. It was an occasion of historic significance, the crowning point of his career, and, needless to say, entirely in harmony with his wife's wishes.

On their way to Paris, Germaine and Benjamin halted at Yverdun, where they met Narbonne, Mathieu, and Jaucourt. The purpose of the rendezvous was not merely to take leave; before continuing on her way, Germaine convinced her constitutional-monarchist friends that their only course was to rally to the Republic; she would try her utmost to have their names removed from the list of *émigrés* and thus make their return possible. For the Republic that now was governed by vice needed men of virtue.

At no time since the first year of their marriage had Monsieur and Madame de Staël been seen in such outward harmony as during the spring and summer of 1795. The apparent reconciliation had, no doubt, a variety of causes; but a sufficient cause was the fact that Germaine's presence in Paris hung by the precarious thread of her husband's ambassadorship. Anything that might cause Staël to lose his post would mean, to her, another exile at the very least. Thus, when, for once in his life, he put his foot down and forbade her to have any further dealings with Count Ribbing, Germaine complied like a good wife. This beautiful harmony lasted as long as their political interests were more or less identical—to be precise, for three months. The couple were seen together everywhere, and every *décadi* (the substitute for Sunday in the Revolutionary Calendar) the salon in the rue du Bac assembled the leading politicians and publicists of the post-Thermidorian period—Barras, Tallien, Cambacérès, Siéyès, Boissy d'Anglas, and, among the writers, Rœderer, Suard, and Marie-Joseph Chénier, brother of the martyred poet André Chénier. Through Chénier, who never refused her anything, she made possible the return of most of her friends. She had not been in Paris for five weeks when she was once more deep in politics.

While Germaine made politics in her salon, Benjamin surveyed the economic scene and found it enchanting past belief. Of breadlines and suicides not a word. 'Never was it possible to live so cheaply in Paris,' he wrote to his aunt, Madame de Nassau. 'For my flat—four large rooms —I pay one silver écu a month.' To be sure, it helped to be a Swiss and to have silver écus. 'One louis,' he informed his cousin Rosalie, 'is worth 950 livres in *assignats*.' 'A small part of your fortune,' he burbled to Madame de Nassau, 'would be worth a Peru here.' Exhilarated, he sold property in Switzerland and with the hard cash thus realized purchased land—the confiscated estates of the Church and the *émigrés* which the government sold at ridiculous prices. 'I have just made a bargain such as it is difficult to imagine! I have bought an estate for 30,000 [Swiss] francs which guarantees an income of 8,000 francs. . . . What things a man could do here with 200,000 francs in cash!' The miracle was possible, he explained with loving detail, because his tenants had to pay their rent in produce. France was a paradise, and no measure was too severe to chastise the spoilsports who spoke of famine and injustice. 'Everything is quiet,' he informed Rosalie on June 14; 'today they are guillotining the ringleaders of the Prairial uprising, and the Constitution is about to be published.'

Fifteen years later, reporting to the same Rosalie on the harsh treatment of the unemployed in Germany, Benjamin wrote: 'It is war—not, as it used to be, a war of the have-nots against the haves, but of the haves against the have-nots—and since the Revolution has given them a taste of fear, they are putting a great deal of firmness into their measures.' As a disinterested observer, Benjamin tended to sympathize with the have-nots; but when his gambler's instincts were roused by the temptation of quick gains, firm measures against the have-nots seemed in order. Germaine was torn by no such conflict: in none of her writing is her complete indifference to the condition of the masses more evident than in her *Reflections on Internal Peace*, which she had printed in 1795 but withheld from publication on the advice of de Pange. This pamphlet is a hymn to the sanctity of property and to the political rights of the propertied. Let all classes enjoy equal civil rights, but let those who have the largest stake in the government run it. Constitutions should not be made by metaphysicians like 'Thomas Paine, who has just written a book in order to raise demagoguery into dogma'. In the science of politics 'inventiveness is childish, practice sublime'. There is poetic irony in the fact that not long afterwards Bonaparte, basing himself on these very principles, vented his wrath on the metaphysicians and demagogues, 'that blackguard Constant', and 'that hussy Staël'.

The new constitution which Benjamin mentioned to Rosalie was in harmony with Germaine's wishes. It provided for a five-man directorate, a cabinet, a bicameral legislature, and a suffrage limited to the rich. Its text had been thoroughly discussed both in the Convention and in her drawing room. There was, however, one feature in the constitution that worried the Conventionals who had drafted it: the necessity of holding new elections at a time when the predominantly anti-republican provinces were sure to elect a royalist majority. To remedy this situation and to maintain themselves in power, the Convention proposed an electoral law by which two thirds of the deputies of the new legislature would be chosen from among the members of the outgoing Convention. This law did not meet with the approval of Madame de Staël, who hoped to see the Thermidorians replaced by men of her own more conservative camp. It was in support of her views that Benjamin began his political career. On June 24, 25 and 26, in the *Nouvelles Politiques*, a paper directed by Suard, there appeared three unsigned articles severely attacking the proposed electoral law. To his surprise and embarrassment their author, Benjamin, saw himself acclaimed by the royalists. Benjamin decided that this would never do. The real danger, he convinced Germaine, was not the Jacobins, who had grown fat and manageable, but the royalists, who were lean and hungry for revenge. On July 25, in what was the first but by no means the last about-face in his political career, Benjamin published in the *Républicain Français* an article signed 'B.C.', in which he pledged himself 'to fight and die' with the very men he had attacked a month earlier.

The subtleties that lay beneath Germaine's political conduct escaped the more coarsely formed minds of several of the Conventionals. Her friendships with ex-noblemen such as Jaucourt, Pange, and Mathieu, whose sympathies for a constitutional monarchy were known, increased their suspicions. On August 18 the deputy and ex-butcher Legendre rose in the Convention and, attacking Madame de Staël in the most indelicate terms, accused her of heading an anti-republican conspiracy as well as of cuckolding the Swedish ambassador. The speech won loud applause. Shortly afterwards the Committee of Public Safety gave Monsieur de Staël the friendly advice that, in his wife's interest, it would be best if she left Paris until the political situation had calmed down. The ambassador took the hint with almost unseemly alacrity; Germaine left Paris, but she did not go far. As Mathieu's guest at his château of Ormesson, she carried on precisely as in the rue du Bac.

Meanwhile the tension between republicans and royalists was nearing its breaking point. Germaine had information that the royalists, counting on the support of the starving masses, were planning an uprising; the knowledge that several of her intimates were, at the very least, sympathetic to the conspiracy filled her with dread. In an attempt to calm the hot-heads, she summoned her friends to a dinner and a lecture. 'The workers and the whole Jacobin populace have fresh grievances against the Convention,' she admitted in a euphemistic allusion to the Prairial reprisals. 'But,' she added, shrewdly, 'they hate you more and have hated you for a longer time; they will rush to the aid of the Convention. . . . I foresee only bloodshed—the blood of my friends shed in vain.' The speech advised her friends to spare their own lives for a better day, for even under the new electoral law their chance would come eventually. Germaine's friends heeded her warning, but the bulk of the rightist opposition did not. On the morning of 13 Vendémiaire (October 4) Paris was in a state of insurrection.

Shortly before these events the Staëls' friend Barras had got rid of a mistress and passed her on to an unemployed young general who seemed ready to do anything that would advance him. Her name was Josephine de Beauharnais, and his Napoleon Bonaparte. When, on the morning of 13 Vendémiaire, Barras found the Convention paralysed by fear and indecision, he knew exactly what sort of man was needed: a man who without the least scruple could order a battery to fire into a crowd. Bonaparte did not bother with firing blanks; thus he explained much later on Saint Helena, the rabble merely are made to feel that they will not be hurt, and you end up by killing more than necessary when you have to shoot in earnest. With his famous 'whiff of grapeshot', the general saved the Republic within a matter of hours. It was a more effective method than after-dinner speeches.

The Man of the Hour had solved the problem in accordance with Germaine's wishes, but the rank and file of the victorious Conventionals, bewildered by her frequent shifts and by her suspect friendships, were convinced that she stood at the centre of the ill-fated conspiracy. Two of her friends, Benjamin and de Pange, were arrested while they inspected the street fighting. With the help of Chénier, Germaine's habitual intercessor, they were released after a few hours. Benjamin sputtered with indignation. To arrest him, to suspect him of disloyalty—'me, when I have put three-quarters of my fortune into the acquisition of national property!' De Pange took the events of the 13 Vendémiaire more philosophically; they merely confirmed what he had noted in his diary a few days earlier: 'As long as a Revolution lasts, nothing solid can come into existence except tyranny.'

While it was possible for the Republican leaders to have Germaine's friends released from gaol, they could not afford to ignore the renewed and increasingly violent attacks directed at Germaine herself by the rank and file in the Convention. Germaine was ordered by the Committee of Public Safety to leave France within ten days. Monsieur de Staël lodged a formal protest against the order, but he obtained its suspension (not its revocation) only after promising that he would persuade his wife to leave Paris temporarily of her own accord. He pleaded his case with remarkably little conviction, and the Committee was left under the perhaps justified impression that by removing Germaine from the scene it was doing him a favour. With her friend, Madame de Beaumont, Germaine departed in mid-October for the watering place of Forges, near Dieppe in Normandy. She did not in the least abandon politics; indeed, wherever she went, her residence took on all the aspects of a headquarters, with a constant coming and going of friends, emissaries, and messengers. In December the suspended sentence of exile was reaffirmed by the government. Summoning Benjamin to her side, Germaine retraced her steps to Coppet. They arrived on New Year's Day of 1796.

It was not only in politics that Germaine had suffered a setback. She also had, once more, pursued happiness, and once more she had been defeated. Whatever her relationship with Benjamin at the time, it was not to him she looked for happiness but to the gentle Chevalier de Pange.

She had known François de Pange since 1786, when, a cavalry officer of twenty-two, he frequented the houses of the Suards and the Staëls; but at that period the studious, lanky young man had made no impression on her. Born in Lorraine, the second son of a marquis, de Pange felt drawn towards a quiet life of scholarly study rather than to a military career, to which he seemed destined by his birth, or to the pursuit of literature, in which André Chénier, his classmate and lifelong friend, sought to encourage him. He soon gave up poetry, and in 1789 he resigned his commission. By the time the Revolution broke out, he had studied astronomy, shorthand, Sanskrit, and the Zend-Avesta, among other things, and he somehow had also managed to learn the printing trade. The Revolution tore him from these absorbing occupations. His school years at the Collège de Navarre had taught him to hate a system

in which 'rebellion is the only crime, obedience the only duty'. He
enthusiastically hailed the advent of what he called 'the government of
the people by the people'. When the Revolution turned to violence, he
criticized the violence but remained faithful to the Revolution, refused
to admit that there existed 'any necessary connection between abstract
ideas and murder', and vowed not to share the passions of those whose
system he applauded. The distinction proved impracticable, and early
in 1794 he fled abroad. Yet even then, with his brothers serving in
Condé's army and with half of his relatives and friends gaoled or
guillotined, de Pange refused to take up arms against the Revolution.
Instead, he went to Switzerland, joined Madame de Staël's little colony
of liberal Constitutionalists, and served their cause as a printer.

In de Pange Germaine found a kindred intellect. Her political pamphlets show his influence (though not to the same degree as Benjamin's),
and his manuscript *Essay on the Causes and the Effects of the Progress
and Decadence of Literature* clearly inspired her later *On Literature
Considered in Its Relation to Social Institutions*. But their affinity was not
merely political and literary. De Pange possessed a set of contrasting
qualities that invariably exerted on her an ill-fated attraction. With a
solid, hard-headed intelligence he combined emotional enthusiasm for
ideas; with manly courage, a virginal reserve and a delicate physique.
(He was suffering from advanced tuberculosis.) Germaine was still
stunned by the blow of Narbonne's desertion; her liaison with Ribbing
was a passing affair; her attachment to Benjamin had not yet taken root.
In de Pange she saw the man who might give her happiness after all,
and set out to conquer him with every weapon at her disposal.

De Pange did not reciprocate her passion. 'Happy and cautious
youth,' André Chénier had once apostrophized him in a poem, 'gentle,
amiable, and tranquil even in his loves.' The plural 'loves' was poetic
licence; from his adolescence, de Pange had loved only one woman, his
young married cousin, Madame de Sérilly. During the Great Terror he
had received news that she had been executed with her entire family;
happily, this news turned out to be inaccurate. Madame de Sérilly had
escaped the guillotine by declaring herself pregnant. Not only was she
alive but also a widow and free to marry him. De Pange had no intention of letting his friendship for Germaine stand in the way of his
marriage. Yet by jealously defending his independence against Germaine's intrusions he merely increased her hunger for something more
than the chaste friendship he offered her.

De Pange preceded Germaine to Paris in January 1795. From her

MADAME DE STAËL
After a portrait by François Gérard

MADAME DE STAËL AS CORINNE
After a painting by Elizabeth Vigée-Lebrun

arrival on May 25 to her semi-exile at Ormesson in August, she saw him almost daily. His sinking health increased his attractions, but Germaine was unwilling to let sickness stand between her and him. Recommending the curative powers of goat's milk, she hoped to set him up sufficiently to be able to respond to her vigorous advances. 'I am not surprised at Madame de Staël's continued importunities,' wrote Anne-Marie de Sérilly to her friend Madame de Beaumont, 'but I admit that I should be very much surprised if they proved successful. They seem clumsy to me. One does not carry off a heart by assault. Such openly advertised intentions must, it seems to me, inspire a wish to resist rather than . . . to surrender.'

How he resisted, and how this resistance exacerbated her passion, may be gathered from a letter Germaine addressed to him from Ormesson, at midnight of September 11, 1795:

> I am so upset by your letter that I don't know how to express or how to contain a feeling which is capable of producing on you an effect so contrary to the desires of my soul. What expressions you are using! 'Breaking off a friendship—avoiding a commitment—not knowing when you will be able to come—believing me happy where I am.' Ah, Monsieur de Pange, has love taught you nothing except its injustice, its forgetfulness, its inconstancy? . . . You have no right to torture me. Remember what you have said to me about friendship. What life there is left me depends on that friendship; for the past four months I owe everything to it and, what is worse, I need everything still. I have no intention of intruding on your independence. . . . But if to need you means to disturb you, then you have a right to be afraid of me. . . . You know as well as I do what is missing from my happiness here, but you cannot know as well as I know that you are perfection itself in the eyes of those who know you, that you are, to me, something even more desirable than perfection, and that I should find in your friendship all the happiness there is for me in this world, if only you removed that sword that hangs over my head.
>
> I beg you on my knees to come here or to meet me in Paris or at Passy for just one hour. . . . I refuse to give up what I have won; this friendship is to me a *necessity*—I do not care if it is not one for you. Give me what you can spare, and it will fill my life. . . .

Germaine begging on her knees could no more be resisted than an order of the Emperor of Turkey. De Pange relented and met her, but the thing that was missing from her happiness he did not give. A month after her exile, in January 1796, he married Madame de Sérilly. At Coppet the news caused an explosion, but Germaine quickly

G

decided to make the best of a bad bargain. His marriage, she wrote to him in a letter that followed hard on the heels of the first, explosive one, was not the result of passion; 'consequently, it is not an enslavement, and in some ways you have gained more freedom than you have lost'. She had come to think of him as being impervious to love— hence, she explained, her first shock at the news:

> When I realized that you were one of ours, it seemed to me that I had missed my chance, that you could have loved me about as much as another. Why should I feel this, when it was friendship that drew me to you? . . . It is vitally important to me to know whether I shall see you as much as I used to, and whether your attitude toward me is unchanged.

De Pange's reply was an exercise in semantics:

> Your imagination has created a world that is quite different from the one within which I contain mine, and yet we give the same names to the objects with which we have filled those worlds. How can we speak of them and understand each other? . . . In the entire realm of concepts, no two ideas could be more dissimilar than the ones we have formed about happiness. . . . You see it in a grand passion in the midst of tumultuous events, of anxieties and pleasures and sacrifices. . . . I ask nothing for my happiness except peace.

Germaine, answering him, rejected his antithesis. She too desired nothing more than the passage from passion to gentler affections:

> I have seen all my past life smashed into pieces, and now at the age of twenty-seven I must either start anew in the career of passion or make a beginning with what ought to be its sequel. . . . Whatever choice I make is painful: to regret all my past feelings and to work at my destiny makes me feel the lassitude of labour and the torment of passion.

No doubt her despair was sincere, even though she was at the time starting a new career of passion with Benjamin—and three years older than twenty-seven.

At the end of 1795, when Germaine, ordered out of France, returned to Switzerland with Benjamin in tow, she bore the Republic no grudge. It was all a misunderstanding that she would soon clear up with the help of her friends. As for Benjamin, his loyalty to the Republic was above suspicion: an annual income equivalent to about £4,000 depended on its continued preservation. 'My daughter has arrived after a long journey,' Necker wrote to Meister. 'Monsieur Constant has escorted her. They both come with a fabulous cargo of republican notions and expectations, and they are a little too ready to forgive the means used by the regime for the sake of its aims.'

'The universe is in France; outside it, there is nothing,' Germaine wrote to de Pange after twelve weeks at Coppet. The nothingness of the outer spaces comprised her father and Benjamin. She hoped to be back in Paris by April; as it turned out, she was to spend the entire year in the 'magnificent horror' of Switzerland. Even Geneva was out of bounds, for a strip of French territory separated it from Berne; moreover, the Genevese aristocracy had emigrated *en masse* when the Jacobins had seized power.

Her father was 'kind, very kind', but he bored her. Her conversations with him were a series of false starts. Benjamin's 'inexhaustible kindness' for her was enchanting, she conceded, but his presence did not affect her sense of solitude. 'You see that I am absolutely alone,' she wrote to a friend a few months later, 'with my father and with the White Devil [Benjamin]. It is a terrible ordeal for all one's feelings to have to look at each other face to face. One needs company to be bright, company to be in love, company for everything. . . . As soon as one is two, one needs to be many more.'

Two is solitude; a crowd is company. Hence the many trips to Lausanne, which was not Paris but at least was not a solitude. 'A man from Zurich who has just returned from Lausanne says that at a grand ball given for Madame de Staël she appeared in flesh-coloured pantaloons that clung very tightly to her skin, and covered only with gauze, like the ballerinas at the Opéra,' reported General de Montesquiou. 'I believe our traveller has lied,' he added, probably correctly, but there is no doubt that Germaine relieved her boredom by making a spectacle of herself.

The pleasures of Lausanne were not her only distraction. During the winter and early spring of 1796 everybody at Coppet was busy writing—Germaine on *The Passions*, Benjamin on *The Strength of the Present Government in France and on the Necessity of Supporting It*, Necker on religious morality. The publication of Germaine's treatise was to prove, among other things, that she was not concerned with politics and that she had been maligned. 'Condemned to be famous without being known, I feel a need to let the world judge me by my writings,' she declared in the Preface, dated July 1. Benjamin's tract, on which she collaborated to a large extent, was to prove their loyalty to the Republic; also, it was to give a measure of his ability as a propagandist whom the government could employ with profit. As for Necker's pieties, they seemed out of keeping both with the times and with what was going on under his roof, but Necker wrote for the ages rather than for the day. Upon Benjamin he looked with inexplicable fondness; upon 'Minette', as he called Germaine, with pained resignation; and his daily tête-à-têtes with his pickled wife made him look at things from the sublime vantage point of eternity. Shaking his head at the young people's republican enthusiasm, he conceded that times had changed, and lent Benjamin 35,000 francs to furnish an abbey he had bought, at Hérivaux near Paris, for a song.

Benjamin left for Paris early in April, and Germaine expected to follow him shortly. Instead, on April 22 the French minister of police, complaisantly named Cochon, signed a warrant for her arrest if she set foot on French soil; Rewbell, one of the Directors, added detailed instructions on how she was to be spirited away from the border; and, to make triply sure she would not slip through the fingers of the police, the French minister-resident at Geneva, Desportes, planted a spy in her household. A former Presbyterian minister, named Monachon, the agent was engaged by her as a valet; since it was he who carried her mail to and from the post office, reading it on the way, the French secret service was well informed. Its vigilance seemed well justified, for apart from her continued friendship with royalists of various shades, Germaine had mysterious dealings with the English ambassador to Berne, who even came to Morges, near Lausanne, for the express purpose of an interview. Perhaps the subject of their conversation was quite innocent, but appearances were against her, and so were four of the five Directors—the lone exception being Barras.

Germaine was not aware that French spies were watching her as a dangerous counter-revolutionist, or that the Bernese government kept her under strict surveillance as a Jacobin subversive. If an official in the French police had not slipped up, she might never even have suspected the existence of an arrest warrant until she was caught. On May 17 she learned that her name appeared on a printed list of suspects and criminals that had been sent to the border police. Thus Cochon's cloak-and-dagger scheme of spiriting her into a French gaol if she as much as touched the border collapsed miserably. Germaine, indignant, stormed off to Geneva, escorted by her uncle, to demand an explanation from Desportes. 'My honour demands that I return to France immediately,' she declared to the crestfallen minister. 'Do not believe, sir, that the Directory will not see me there with pleasure: they know that I am in part the author of the work of Monsieur Benjamin Constant, that this work has been written entirely in my house and under my eyes, and that consequently they cannot suspect my devotion to their cause.'

Desportes advised calm and patience. No doubt it was all a mistake and would be straightened out. But calm and patience were not Germaine's outstanding qualities. 'It is imperative,' she wrote to her husband,

> that by a prompt trip to Paris I destroy the effect this news will produce in France. I assume, therefore, that you will not only authorize this trip but even exact it for the sake of your honour. If my presence should compromise your position, half of my fortune is at your disposal at all times to compensate you for the sacrifice you bring to our honour. . . . But the instant you hesitate, I must request you to dispense me from doing you the injustice of bearing a name you are unwilling to protect.

Faced with this ultimatum, Monsieur de Staël had no alternative. The French government responded to his request for an explanation by rescinding the warrant; the appearance of Madame de Staël's name on the list was due, they said, to a typographical error. But the order of exile was not lifted; Germaine would not be gaoled if she crossed the border, but she would be sent back. To obtain its repeal Germaine began to resort to rather roundabout and mutually contradictory manœuvres. On the one hand, she sought to prove in endless memoranda that she was a French citizen by birth and consequently could not be exiled; on the other hand, she begged Meister to intercede with the government of Zurich to request the French government to pass a law by which foreigners owning property in France could not be forbidden to reside there. Neither approach proved successful.

At about the time when she learned of the arrest warrant against her, Germaine also received news that de Pange was close to death. The thought of his dying before she could see him again increased her despair. Resignation was not in her nature: 'Try not to be changed by your illness or your marriage; either would hurt me a great deal,' she instructed him from Coppet in May. 'What I need is to embrace you, to press you to my heart, to make you play the last piece of music I heard you perform. In a word, give me back the past, which is my only future! . . .' And in June, one month before his death: 'You are the only man who has made me understand that it was possible to love without expecting as much in return.'

The object of her love, while waiting to die, was working on the outline of a remarkable project: a 'history of man', as opposed to a 'history of events'. Such fragments of his notes as have been published make one regret the early death of a subtle thinker. The history of events, he noted, showed only what man had attempted for or against men.

> What is not shown is the spectacle of a far more interesting struggle—that of man against nature. Nature created man an animal and savage; he made himself a thinker and a social being. He is condemned to keep up this struggle continuously, and to desire unceasingly to perfect himself. It does not matter whether he succeeds or not, whether or not his mind is pursuing a chimera: to perfect himself is the principal business of man. His whole history is that of his victories and setbacks in this enterprise.

In his final days, sitting in the sun at a table on his lawn, de Pange still reflected on the lessons of the tempest through which he had passed. His last thoughts on the Revolution were disabused: 'I have long believed in the power of reason . . . but every day my faith diminishes; every day my discouragement increases.' Reason, he admitted, had not succeeded in guiding the Revolution, nor would it succeed in stopping it. Yet, though disabused, he would not admit defeat. Man's principal business was still the same. Since the rational *élite* had failed, 'it is the mass of the people that must be enlightened'. This final conclusion of a dying idealist Germaine was to hand on to the nineteenth century.

The news of de Pange's death arrived at Coppet at about the same time as Benjamin, who was bubbling over with projects, and as Monsieur de Staël, who was weighed down by care. As early as June Eric Magnus had hinted, in his letters to Germaine, that he was deep in trouble and might soon have to join her at Coppet. How serious his troubles were Germaine did not yet know.

Sometimes the most tremendous causes can have the most insignificant effects. A marriage had been arranged between young Gustavus IV of Sweden and a granddaughter of Catherine II. The project (which eventually failed when the eccentric king walked out on his bride) necessitated a reorientation of Swedish foreign policy. Relations with France cooled off, Staël was relieved once again of his post, and a simple chargé d'affaires was appointed in his stead. Once again Staël rebelled; he refused to vacate his post, and persuaded the Directors to ignore the chargé. The Swedish regent retaliated by cutting off the funds of his obstreperous ambassador. Staël held out for a few weeks, but although he could defy his government, he was in no position to defy his creditors, who were laying siege to his residence. Early in September he arrived at Coppet at last, on his way to take the waters at Aix in Savoy. 'He is ruined by debts, and very unfriendly to me,' Germaine wrote to her friend, Adrien de Mun. 'We were rather ill at ease together. It is better to be united at a distance.' And to another friend, Pictet-Diodati: 'He has not made the least effort on my behalf; all he has to offer is to ruin me by making me pay his debts. I am not tempted.'

It was only after his return from Aix in October that he acquainted his wife with the finality of his recall. 'This new development,' she wrote to Pictet, 'makes my voyage to France almost a necessity. I must protect my fortune from the innumerable creditors who will show up.' Feeling that his presence gave no one pleasure, Staël went on to Basel to wait for further instructions from Stockholm.

Germaine's announcement that her return to Paris was almost a necessity was made just about the time she dispatched Benjamin to Paris with a consignment of copies of her book *On the Influence of Passions*. She expected great things from it, and her friends were enlisted to make sure it received the proper attention. Mathieu, according to General Montesquiou, made the rounds of Paris, 'from journalist to journalist, beseeching them to say that Madame de Staël's book is the finest work to have been published in our century.' With Suard, Chénier, and Rœderer among her friends, this was not difficult to accomplish. The work was highly praised—as in many ways it deserved to be—and by December the government relented; if she remained at a distance of eight leagues (about twenty miles) from Paris, she could return to France unmolested, although the order of exile would not be formally repealed. Benjamin having arrived at Coppet with news of this victory, the couple without wasting any time slipped out from under the paternal roof. On Christmas day they blew into Paris—'like a zephyr', said Montesquiou. They merely were passing through. In January they were installed at Benjamin's abbey of Hérivaux, which had been fitted out luxuriously with the help of Monsieur Necker's loan.

Germaine had accepted de Pange's death with far greater equanimity than his marriage. She rarely resigned herself to letting go of the living, but, excepting her father, she never lingered over the dead. 'The greatest happiness,' she wrote in one of her last letters to de Pange, 'is to transform one's feelings into action': such a transformation required a living object. There was no lack of admirers. Even in her exile, she never ceased to be surrounded by a set of bright young men; but though she might flirt and jest with them with shocking familiarity, it was Benjamin through whom she expected to transform her feelings into actions. How carelessly she flouted conventions may be gathered from the letters of Rosalie de Constant, who reported the doings of the *trop célèbre*, as she called her, at Lausanne:

> *Lausanne, May 24, 1796.*—The all-too-celebrated arrived at the party with her whole barnyard—her T[racy], who looks like a famished little fox meditating a snatch, and her M[un], who resembles a pretty kitten purring and fawning, each at one of her ears, not to mention the rest of them. She talks of nothing but Benj[amin]; she seems very much pre-occupied with him.
>
> *Lausanne, August 23, 1796.*—I called on them [Germaine and Benjamin] the day before yesterday. I found her between the fox, the cat, and him; she was leaning against one and holding the head of the other, while the third was tickling her neck and calling her his good little kitten. This tableau disgusted me a little, as did their jokes about the ambassador.
>
> *Lausanne, October, 1796.*—She speaks of him [Benjamin] without the least reticence—'the man whom I love most in the world, the man whom I desire with all the life that is left me'—without realizing the scandal she creates.

What Rosalie did not know when she wrote these lines was that Germaine had just discovered she was with child. For once Germaine might have claimed with some degree of plausibility that the child was begotten by her husband, who had spent a few days with her in September. However, although she officially maintained Monsieur de Staël's paternity of her daughter Albertine, she apparently did not discourage Benjamin's belief that he was the real father.[1] In October 1796, her first month of pregnancy, Germaine once again began to talk of divorce, and there was widespread gossip of her marrying Benjamin. Benjamin's family were shocked by these rumours, except Rosalie,

---

[1] In her book, *Monsieur de Staël*, the Comtesse de Pange (Albertine's great-granddaughter) argues that Albertine was indeed Monsieur de Staël's child. Her chief arguments are: (1) that the letters Germaine wrote to her husband after his September visit contain allusions to a renewal of intimacy between them; (2) that Benjamin seems to have been sterile; (3) that the alleged resemblance of Albertine to Benjamin—notably her red hair—could also be established between Albertine and Monsieur de Staël. I find none of these arguments conclusive. The allusions in Germaine's letters are very ambiguous and vague; Benjamin would not be the only man to have begotten only one known child; Monsieur de Staël was more blond than red, and the resemblance between Albertine and Benjamin is striking to any unprejudiced eye.

who felt that Germaine owed it to Benjamin's reputation to marry him
—as if Germaine had been a Lovelace and Benjamin a Clarissa:

> It seems to me that since she has dragged B[enjamin] on the stage, since
> she has made him the spectacle of all Europe, she owes him some com-
> pensation by allowing him to share the pleasures of her existence and
> her large fortune. . . . But I do not think that that lady will have the
> courage to take such a step; it is easier for her to continue her present
> way of life.

Germaine's cousin, Madame Necker de Saussure, and Mathieu de
Montmorency were equally concerned about the rumours of divorce
and marriage. Neither was over-fond of Benjamin, and both had
solemnly promised each other in the spring of 1795 to 'protect Germaine
from those first impulses, whether in love or in politics, which can no
longer result in anything but danger without bringing happiness'. But
in December 1796, after talking earnestly with Germaine about her
projects, Mathieu could report, with evident relief, that he had found
Germaine quite unenthusiastic on the subject of another marriage.
Rosalie was correct in predicting that the lady would find it easier 'to
continue her present way of life'.

It was easier indeed, even if it meant spending the winter in a
monastery, face to face with Benjamin, while waiting to give birth to
her child. Monsieur Necker was no happier with the situation than were
the Constants. He refused his daughter's demand to send her son
Auguste to her and remarked, in a letter to his niece: 'I believe that
Hérivaux is very bad for your cousin. I think that the place is a little too
secluded. I believe that the local population does not like this succession
of two Protestants to the ecclesiastics. Finally, I detest this unconven-
tionality—but that would be the same anywhere.'

The solitude at Hérivaux was almost complete. Only pious Mathieu
came to visit Abbot Benjamin and his new Héloïse. Not that the couple
had secluded themselves to be undisturbed in the joys of love; their
discretion was, rather, a matter of diplomatic prudence. The political
winds had shifted once again. The royalists were on the counter-
offensive, and the elections of March 31 gave them a majority. Germaine, exiled in 1795 because of her association with royalists, was
threatened with another expulsion in 1797 because of her association
with republicans. France, she wrote to Meister, was 'a democratic
republic where one risks being stoned if one is not for the aristocrats.
. . . The Republic exiles me; the counter-revolution hangs me.'

G*

Germaine's spite reflected that of Benjamin. He had just failed to get himself elected by his commune because of the chicanery of the French government, which insisted that he was not French. His claim to French citizenship was based on an article in the Constitution of 1791, allowing descendants of French Huguenots to recover their nationality. The difficulty was (1) that Benjamin had not availed himself of this opportunity while that constitution was in force; (2) that his ancestors, although religious refugees, originated from Artois, which was not French territory when they emigrated in the sixteenth century. Benjamin's setback, however, was a trivial matter compared to the royalist electoral victory. Germaine was waiting only for the end of her pregnancy to intervene in this state of affairs.

With the tacit consent of the authorities, Germaine returned to Paris to give birth to her child. She took up residence at the Swedish embassy, where Monsieur de Staël had returned late in 1796, despite the ambiguity, to say the least, of his diplomatic status. Albertine was born on June 8. Monsieur de Staël, Germaine confided to Mathieu, behaved 'very well' on the occasion—'without any show of emotion, but with sympathy and solicitude'. General de Montesquiou, who called on her, reported, 'Madame de Staël has at last given birth to her daughter, and at no time did she have fewer than fifteen persons in her room.' Three days after her delivery, he found her in bed, 'talking and holding forth as usual', while Mathieu rocked the cradle.

Less than a month after getting this tiresome business out of the way, Germaine swung into action to rescue the Republic. The most immediate necessity was to persuade the Directory that action was imperative. Facing a royalist majority in both chambers, under the efficient leadership of the Club de Clichy, the Directors were well aware of the danger, but they were paralysed by a fundamental difference of opinion among themselves. The difference of opinion was itself concerned with a dilemma which has, since then, paralysed many a democratic régime and delivered it, unresisting, into the hands of its enemies. It might be formulated thus: When, by legal, constitutional means, a legislature passes into the hands of a majority which seeks to overthrow the constitution and to introduce a form of government radically different from that which allowed it to be elected, has the executive branch of the government the right, or even the duty, to take unconstitutional measures against this majority, for the sake of preserving the basis of the constitution? Perhaps the most fateful example of this dilemma in recent history was seen in Germany in

January 1933, when the German government, answering the question with a No, handed its powers to its assassins.[1]

Of the five Directors, Carnot and Barthélemy answered the question with a No; Barras, La Revellière, and Rewbell, with a Yes. Their positions rested less on theoretical grounds than on personal preferences and interests. To counteract the royalist Club de Clichy, the loyalist Constitutional Circle, or Club de Salm, was founded in June. Benjamin was the chief organizer, and Madame de Staël, rising from childbed, stepped from the role of a political exile into that of hostess to its leaders.

Her position was logical. 'I am not, I think, particularly liked by the republicans or by the Directory,' she wrote to the publicist Rœderer. 'But do you not realize that by undoing them you are undoing yourselves?' The republicans, she agreed, were ignorant and unjust—but they could be influenced; the royalists could not. 'The only danger comes from the side of the aristocrats.' This also was the import of Benjamin's latest book, written with Germaine's collaboration at Hérivaux and published in May—*On Political Reactions*. If this work was not what Germaine called it—'the greatest work ever to appear in our language'—it was, at any rate, a masterly statement of the liberal position and still merits to be read as such.

Logical as it was in political terms, Germaine's choice was contrary to her personal loyalties: the Club de Clichy contained many of her former friends, the Club de Salm many of her recent enemies. Montesquiou accused Benjamin of having 'dragged her into the worst possible company. . . . This Benjamin is an evil man.' But Benjamin's role in Germaine's conversion has been exaggerated; it was the similarity of their outlooks which led to their association, rather than the other way round. Most of the opposition press was not concerned with the question of which of the two was influencing the other but roundly heaped insult on both as a unit. Montesquiou after a few weeks caught the tune of the newspapers: 'Madame de Staël says she is going to Switzerland next month. May she never leave it again, nor her Benjamin either! Switzerland is the only country where this couple is not a public calamity.'

Germaine had no intention of going to Switzerland when Montesquiou wrote this in August 1797. She was doing very well in Paris. Benjamin had become the main mouthpiece of the Club de Salm; and

[1] This question should not be confused, as it often has been, with the question of how a democratic government should deal with an anti-democratic *minority*.

she had just succeeded in placing an ex-lover in the ministry of foreign affairs.

'The bishop,' as Germaine persisted in calling Talleyrand, had been allowed to return to France, thanks to her intercession, in 1795. As unhappy as a man can be in Philadelphia, he nevertheless proceeded prudently, thanked his benefactress in cautious terms, and took his time. In the summer of 1796 he arrived in France at last, but it was only in the spring of 1797 that Germaine saw him again. He was in desperate need of suitable employment, and Germaine spared no effort to aid him. Besieging Barras, she persuaded him that in order to strengthen the government a new cabinet must be appointed, consisting of loyal supporters of the Club de Salm. She was so successful that, one July morning, the council of ministers found itself dismissed and replaced; Talleyrand received the portfolio of foreign affairs and held the dominant position. Among the ousted ministers was Cochon, thus duly punished for the effrontery of signing a warrant of arrest against Madame de Staël. Benjamin, in a letter to his uncle, claimed some credit for this upheaval. He was ill rewarded for his pains. The first secretary-ship in the foreign ministry was the least he expected, but Talleyrand was admirably self-controlled when it came to checking his sense of gratitude. Benjamin obtained nothing.

A change of cabinet was not enough. To assure a republican victory, the backing of the army was needed. Barras and Rewbell sent an appeal to the man whose shadow was reaching all the way from Venetia to France—General Bonaparte, whose victories had made him the hero of Europe. The hero was only too willing to take up the defence of the Republic. 'A band of men covered with ignominy and saturated with crime are agitating and plotting in Paris at a time when we have triumphed at the gates of Vienna,' reads his Proclamation to the Army of Italy of July 14, 1797. 'The armies must pacify France.'

Germaine herself had entered into a one-sided correspondence with Bonaparte. The letters have not been preserved. According to Napoleon, Germaine compared him to both 'Scipio and Tancred, uniting the simple virtues of the former with the brilliant deeds of the latter.' 'This woman is mad,' the hero allegedly commented. 'I don't want to answer such letters.' No doubt these quotations are apocryphal, but Germaine's letter to Meister of July 24, 1797, is not; in it she called Bonaparte 'the best republican in France, the most freedom-loving of Frenchmen'.

The most freedom-loving of Frenchmen approved of the plans of the Club de Salm and entered into an interesting correspondence with Citizen Talleyrand on constitutional reforms. Late in August Barras concentrated 30,000 troops near Paris, and Bonaparte dispatched General Augereau from Italy to take their command. On September 4 —the 18 Fructidor—at three o'clock in the morning, Augereau's troops surrounded the Tuileries, where the deputies had been summoned in emergency session by the respective chairmen of the two chambers. Rarely was a *coup d'état* handled with such efficiency. On the 19 Fructidor it was all over: Carnot and Barthélemy expelled from the Directory, 198 deputies deprived of their seats, the anti-clerical laws of the Reign of Terror restored, the press placed under police censorship, the opposition papers suppressed, 165 citizens deported to French Guiana—among them Barthélemy (Carnot had escaped), some forty deputies, and a platoon of journalists.

In later years Germaine disclaimed all responsibility for these events, which had not endeared her to those who survived their ordeal in Guiana or to the relatives of those who died there. Her role in the steps leading up to the 18 Fructidor, she claimed, was limited to the appointment of Talleyrand, and as soon as the reprisals began she did everything within her power to rescue its victims. That she successfully interceded for several of her friends—at considerable risk to herself—is perfectly true; it was upon this occasion that Talleyrand made the remark that Madame de Staël liked to throw people into the water for the pleasure of fishing them out afterwards. She did more: she rescued friends even before the *coup d'état* took place. Thus she had sent Mathieu to Switzerland as early as June. In October documents were discovered in a captured ship proving that she had systematically helped her royalist friends to escape in the course of the summer. That she was unaware of the impending *coup d'état* is most implausible, and that she furthered the policies leading to the *coup d'état* is incontrovertible. Talleyrand, with characteristic terseness, summed up her role with the words, 'Madame de Staël has made the 18 Fructidor but not the 19.'

'But who entrusted you with the mission you are carrying out among us? Who has asked you to meddle in matters of no concern to you? . . . Miserable hermaphrodite that you are, your sole ambition in uniting the two sexes in your person is to dishonour them both at once!' The apostrophe, which reflected the usual tone of the press towards Madame de Staël, came from the pen of a royalist editorial writer shortly after she had Talleyrand appointed. Perhaps the writer had time to ponder the answer to his question in the jungles of Guiana; others in the republican camp continued to ask it in France. Indeed, no sooner had she triumphed in the *coup d'état* of 18 Fructidor than she found herself at odds with the victors. As others shifted with each change of régime to side with the party in power, so Germaine, with lifelong consistency, shifted to be in permanent opposition. By October she was attacked with equal vehemence by the royalist press abroad for having instigated the *coup*, and by the French press for having helped the royalists to escape it. However, since Barras himself had been her accomplice in engineering these escapes, the government was obliged to smooth things over. Her position was precarious, but outwardly she seemed in control. Once again her salon was the meeting place of cabinet ministers, politicians, writers, and diplomats.

It was on December 6, 1797, that she met, for the first time, Napoleon face to face. He had just returned from Italy, having made a victorious peace which changed the map of Europe, and Talleyrand had arranged for a grand reception at the foreign ministry. 'He paid little attention to her,' Talleyrand recalled. She paid a great deal of attention to him, and his brief, modest speech impressed her as sublime. Four days later Germaine saw Bonaparte again, at his solemn reception by the Directors in the courtyard of the Luxembourg Palace. An altar to the Fatherland, covered with captured flags, had been erected, and the Directors, dressed in ancient Roman costume, stood ready to receive the hero, who appeared in simple uniform. Talleyrand made the welcoming speech, praising Bonaparte's 'insatiable love of Fatherland and humanity', his contempt of pomp, his love of Ossian. 'Ah! far from fearing what some would call his ambition, I feel that the time will come perhaps when we must tear him away from his studious retreat.' Indeed, Bonaparte, freshly elected to the Institute of France, was posing as a man of peace, desiring nothing but a life devoted to study: 'I shall bury myself in a retreat, and labour to deserve one day the honour of being a member of the Institute.' A few days after first seeing him Germaine set out to make the conqueror's conquest.

There can be no question that, at least until 1800, Germaine wooed Bonaparte and praised him hyperbolically. However, she was never sparing of hyperboles, and if she pursued him, it was not to sit at his feet in adoration. Doubtless, she felt that the greatest living man and the greatest living woman owed it as a duty to humanity to conjoin in spirit and, if at all possible, also in the flesh: however, it had to be an equal partnership. Napoleon sensed this immediately. The notion struck him as repulsive, ludicrous, and frightening, and he responded at first coldly, then coarsely, and finally with the ferocity that comes with panic. As for Germaine, she never completely trusted him, hyperboles notwithstanding, but she hoped, fantastically enough, to be able to guide him. When he repulsed her as a woman, that hope vanished, and when his conduct justified her suspicions, the cult changed into abomination.

In 1797 Bonaparte seemed the very essence of the hero; love of glory, passion, genius—he embodied all the qualities Germaine sought in men. He had had literary ambitions—had, in fact, been a protégé of the same abbé Raynal who had encouraged her own earliest literary efforts—and his youthful writings, filled with the rhetoric of the time, reveal sentiments (though not talents) similar to hers. When Necker was appointed minister in 1788, Lieutenant Bonaparte had not only hailed him but even written him several letters pleading for the independence of Corsica; in 1797 he still had a high opinion of the Sage of Coppet, whom he soon was to call a senile madman. His earnest republicanism, his moderate political views, his well-acted indifference to honours save those earned in the arts and sciences—all this could not help but seduce Germaine. She had her doubts, however. In September 1797, when Augereau came to Paris, she asked him if it was true that Bonaparte thought of making himself King of Lombardy. 'Surely not,' said Augereau, 'he is much too well-brought-up a young man for such a thing.' Was she convinced? An unpublished manuscript of a tragedy in verse, *Jan de Witt*, which she wrote that year, contains a portrait of William of Nassau whose resemblance to Napoleon is so striking (and so devastating) that it cannot be accidental:

> I fear his character, even his wisdom. This unshakable calm in so young a heart, far from reassuring me, fills me with terror. Already now his feelings are dictated by his sole interest: nothing can be seen in him that is not controlled by his will. Each step has its purpose, each word its enigma; his features, barely touched by twenty years, already seem jaded by a lifetime of memories; old age is placed on them side by side with childhood. From his earliest years he has coveted power; before his mind was formed, artifice took hold of it and strangled the nascent voice of nature.

Cold calculation against the warm impulse of nature—the whole antithesis between Napoleon and Germaine is prefigured in these few lines.

Her ludicrous pursuit of the hero has been told mainly by the hero himself and by his admirers; nevertheless, the episodes they relate seem authentic enough. At a dinner party given by Talleyrand in December

1797, Germaine, placed next to the general, asked him, 'Who is the greatest woman, alive or dead?' Smiling, Bonaparte replied, 'The one that has made the most children.' Germaine was flustered. Another time (if one is to believe Napoleon), Germaine asked to be admitted at his house in the rue Chantereine. The butler explained that the Citizen General was naked in his bathtub. 'No matter,' cried Germaine. 'Genius has no sex!' Napoleon, who in certain matters had curiously Victorian notions, did not relish this kind of wit. He eluded her whenever he could, and even declined her invitation to a grand ball in his honour.

Her pursuit had not only heroic motives. In fact, it could be argued that in her advances Germaine herself was not free of calculation. General Bonaparte was among the foremost advocates of a scheme proposed to the Directorate by Frédéric César de La Harpe, a fellow countryman of Benjamin, who plotted the liberation of Vaud from Bernese tyranny with the aid of French arms. La Harpe, freshly arrived from St. Petersburg, where he had been the tutor of the future Tsar Alexander I, was animated by motives that ought to have appealed to Madame de Staël and to Benjamin much more than to General Bonaparte: his was an ardent, reckless libertarianism of so infectious a quality that it took Alexander twenty years to shake it off. Alas! Those who see money as the mainspring of human motivation will here find a case to illustrate their thesis. General Bonaparte, who disliked revolutions and who, a few years later, was to restore the Swiss conservatives to power, advocated the armed 'liberation' of Switzerland because he intended to defray the expenses of his Egyptian venture with the gold of Berne—as indeed he did. Germaine, on the other hand (and Benjamin with her), much as she loved freedom, was acutely aware of the fact that her father, the Baron of Coppet, depended financially on the maintenance of the *status quo*. She had, in France, defended every stage of the Revolution except the Reign of Terror. But when there was talk of the Vaudois imitating the French example, her reaction was unequivocal: 'Let them have anything they want,' she said, 'except the suppression of the feudal dues.' With the family income threatened, she even succeeded, by autosuggestion, in mustering a temporary love for Switzerland. She made a direct appeal to Bonaparte:

> I tried to temper his republican ardour as much as I could, by pointing out to him that the Vaudois were perfectly free as far as civil rights were concerned, and that, when civil liberty existed *de facto*, there was no necessity, in order to secure it *de jure*, to expose the country to the

greatest of misfortunes—foreign invasion. . . . I insisted once more on the happiness and on the beauty of Helvetia, on the peace she had enjoyed for several centuries. 'Yes, no doubt,' interrupted Bonaparte, 'but men need *political rights; yes*,' he repeated, as if he had learned the words by heart, '*yes, political rights.*'

Bonaparte pleading for political rights against Madame de Staël is one of the more piquant situations in history.

Her efforts failed. The invasion had been irrevocably resolved upon, and there was nothing left for her but to hasten back to Coppet, to be at the side of her father when the invaders came. All she had accomplished was to delay the blow, but this merely gave her additional reason for fearing its severity. 'It is this Staël woman who by her intrigues has prevented the report [on the invasion project] from being presented earlier,' wrote La Harpe to a friend. 'She is leaving. I wish they'd start out by setting fire to her castle of Coppet, for that woman is an infernal slut.'

When she left in 1798, the press was scarcely more polite: 'The baroness among baronesses,' jeered the *Ami des Lois*, 'the pearl of her sex, the divinity of the oligarchs, the favourite of the God of Constancy, the protectress of the émigrés, in a word, the universal woman has at last left France. . . . Hapless Frenchmen, you will not see her again.'

'Madame de Staël arrives for the brawl,' wrote Suard to Meister on January 24. 'She is not afraid of them [the French], her father writes me. . . . What does she think now of the glorious 18 Fructidor?'

The brawl began on January 27; it was over fairly quickly. Switzerland was reorganized under French occupation as the Helvetic Republic, Geneva annexed to France, the gold of Berne carried off to Paris to outfit the Army of the Orient. 'It was then,' Germaine wrote much later, 'that for the first time I prayed for a French defeat.' If this is true, she changed her mind quickly. In her book *On the Present Circumstances Capable of Ending the French Revolution*, written in 1799 but unpublished until 1906, she referred to Bonaparte as 'that intrepid warrior, the most profound thinker, the most extraordinary genius in history'. She had been told that the hero had read her book *On the Influence of Passions*, she wrote to her father in May 1799; and Necker replied: 'So there you are, glorified on the shores of the Nile. Alexander of Macedon gathered the philosophers and sophists from all the corners of the world to make them talk; the Corsican Alexander, to save time, communicates only with the spirit of Madame de Staël. He knows his business.' Judging from his tone, one must conclude that even Monsieur Necker had been infected by the style of the press.

Germaine's reconciliation with the French may be explained, in part, by the fact that the invading troops had treated the lord of Coppet not only gently but even respectfully. Monsieur Necker continued to collect his rents, and no one set fire to the castle. However, if Germaine was reconciled to the French government, the French government was not reconciled to her. Throughout 1798 and 1799, her repeated forays into France were regularly frustrated. In the summer of 1798 she ventured to Saint-Ouen (the château, confiscated in 1792, had been returned to Necker); by November she was back at Coppet, prudently taking a hint from the police. On January 1, 1799, she took an apartment in Geneva; six weeks later she was back at Coppet. In April she joined Benjamin in France. He had once more run for election—this time as candidate for Geneva, whose citizenship he claimed since its annexation to France, in sublime disregard of the fact that he neither had been born nor ever had resided there—and again he was disqualified. In July the old order of exile, never revoked, was once more revived; Germaine, formally expelled, returned to Coppet.

The French government was decidedly unfriendly; it was moreover tottering, undermined by corruption, civil war in the Vendée, and defeats at the hands of the new Coalition in Germany, Switzerland, and Italy. Germaine's growing admiration for Bonaparte (who, having conquered Egypt and failed to conquer Syria, did not know what to do next) happened to harmonize with the sentiments of a minority group within the French government. Led by Siéyès, one of the new Directors, this group had as its principal objective its own overthrow.

Whether by prearrangement or—as official historiography has it—by lucky coincidence, Bonaparte returned from Egypt at the precise point when Siéyès and his allies needed him most. All the way from Marseilles to Paris he was beset by hangers-on: he was the man of destiny, the 'invincible son of the god of war'. He must establish a strong government, end factionalism, turn the tide of the war, and restore French power and prosperity on the foundations of order, authority, and peace. Bonaparte saw quite clearly that these men, all solid middle-of-the-roaders, regarded him as a mere instrument, politically naïve and inexperienced, that could be manipulated as long as it proved useful and discarded afterwards. Thinking his own thoughts, he graciously allowed them to stage the *coup d'état* of 18–19 Brumaire, which made him the master of France.

Germaine's latest manuscript (*On the Present Circumstances*) was entirely in line with the official programme of the Brumairians: to end the Revolution, to stabilize the government, to extend a general amnesty for all past political offences. Moreover, even if she had no direct part in the preparation for the *coup d'état*, she was most certainly well informed of its coming. It was, perhaps, not an accident that she precipitately left Coppet late in 1799 and arrived at the outskirts of Paris in the evening of the 18 Brumaire (November 9). Benjamin had come to meet her. Together they awaited the outcome of the *coup d'état*, which very nearly miscarried because of Napoleon's fumbling on 19 Brumaire. To Germaine a Jacobin victory would have meant another exile, perhaps arrest. But her friend Lucien Bonaparte, Napoleon's brother, saved the day; the recalcitrant deputies were dislodged with bayonets, and Bonaparte, Siéyès, and Ducos were made Consuls. Germaine's enthusiasm was boundless. 'Your nerves are overwrought,' her father admonished her by letter. 'Unfortunately, everything rests on the life of one man; but he is young, and Fortune will preserve him for us. . . . I congratulate you on the happiness you find in his glory.'

Germaine's 'miserable gypsy life' of the years 1795–9 was to the taste of neither her father nor Benjamin. As early as May 1797, one month before Germaine bore him a daughter, Benjamin wrote to his aunt, Madame de Nassau: 'I must give some happiness to somebody. . . . I ask you to find me a wife. I need one to be happy.' His pathetic struggle to break loose from his mistress was to be the main content of his life for thirteen years—thirteen more years of gypsydom. He could not give happiness to Germaine, for she was not capable of happiness. In her quest for that elusive goal she had got no further in 1800 than she had been at the outset; in her quest for glory she had attained mere notoriety. Only in 'camouflaging life', as she put it, had she been successful, thanks to her perpetual motion. The astonishing thing was that she had found time to mature, and that despite the frenzied agitation of the years to follow she would find the means of expressing her mature genius in works of lasting value. All told, she had gained despite all her defeats and with majestic aplomb she had weathered all the storms—indestructible, unsinkable, impervious to intimidation, persecution, abuse, mockery, betrayal, and even repudiation.

The same could not be said of her husband, whose final disintegration remains to be related.

At the news of Monsieur de Staël's return to Paris late in 1796 his creditors moved in for the kill. Germaine at the time estimated his debts at 150,000 Swiss pounds, a figure which turned out to be optimistic. To satisfy the most pressing demands, he took to borrowing at 3 per cent per month and to haunting every gambling den in Paris. Only one obligation he fulfilled with punctilious regularity: the payment of Mademoiselle Clairon's annual pension of 5,000 francs and fifty quintals of wheat. He also had bought her a house about 1793, in which an apartment was reserved for his use. In 1797 she presented him with a bill for 46,000 francs for roof repairs and the concierge's wages; Monsieur de Staël disbursed.

In July 1797 a ray of hope appeared. Talleyrand, made minister by Madame de Staël, hinted to the Swedish government that her husband's reinstatement would be received favourably by the French foreign office. In Sweden the pendulum had again swung towards France; after lengthy negotiations Gustavus IV decided to appoint a minister plenipotentiary, and Monsieur de Staël, no longer in a position to haggle over titles, was given the post in April 1798. It was a short-lived triumph; a few months later the unpredictable monarch changed his course again. Diplomatic relations were virtually broken off, and on October 10 the hapless Staël was notified of his final dismissal. The letter in which he imparted this news to his wife was pathetic. 'I must add,' he commented, 'that this misfortune is not the greatest I have experienced.' In reply Monsieur Necker sent his son-in-law 18,000 francs to pay for his return to Sweden.

Staël had no intention of giving up Paris, not even as a favour to Monsieur Necker. Leaving the glories of the rue du Bac, he rented a small apartment on the Place de la Concorde and, as far as his wife and father-in-law were concerned, disappeared from view. In November 1800 Necker received a letter from a Monsieur du Buc, who identified himself as a friend of Staël's. Not only was Monsieur de Staël destitute; he also was sick, alone, uncared for. 'Monsieur de Staël lacks the barest essentials. I have, from my own modest means, given him 1,000 francs, with which for the past month he has paid for his food and medicine.' Thus Monsieur du Buc.

The guardian angel was sceptical: 'Monsieur de Staël never writes to me. . . . I had no idea of his predicament, and several details made it seem inexplicable, if indeed it is such as you believe it to be.' He had sent him 20,000 francs over the past thirty months, Necker continued. 'My house was open to him as a refuge; he was free to return to his wife; his furniture, I understand, has an appearance of luxury. . . .

I have requested one of my friends to look into the matter and to provide for his wants.' To console his son-in-law, the guardian angel sent him, without awaiting the result of his inquiry, a copy of his *Course of Religious Morality*, fresh from the printing press. Staël thanked him in a tearful letter, praised the book, and continued with several paragraphs of clinical description.

Germaine was in Paris when, on March 19, 1800, the First Consul addressed the following letter to his brother Joseph Bonaparte, with whom Germaine was on the most cordial terms:

> Monsieur de Staël is in the most abject misery, and his wife gives dinners and balls. If you continue to see her, would it not be proper to suggest to that woman that she ought to pay her husband an allowance of 2,000 francs per month? Or have we reached an age in which one may, without incurring the blame of decent people, trample underfoot not only all morality but even duties more sacred than those that unite children and parents? . . . Let Madame de Staël's conduct be judged as if she were a man; but would a man who is heir to Monsieur Necker's fortune, who for a long time has enjoyed the privileges attached to a distinguished name, and who leaves his wife destitute while he lives in abundance— would such a man be the kind one wishes to associate with?

For different reasons than Bonaparte's, Necker also was pressing for a settlement. A separate maintenance decree seemed to him essential to prevent his son-in-law's debt from swallowing up a substantial part of his fortune. The settlement was negotiated through a lawyer. Without meeting face to face, husband and wife put down their conditions on a sheet of paper, which passed back and forth between them. Germaine stood pat on her original terms, which her husband was forced to accept: 10,000 francs in a lump payment and an annual allowance of 3,600—less than one sixth of the amount suggested by the First Consul.[1]

One would like to report that Monsieur de Staël lived out his remaining years on this modest but secure pension, in his apartment on the Concorde, surrounded by his luxurious furniture. Unfortunately, one cannot. He had to stop his payments to Mademoiselle Clairon. The septuagenarian, to whom he had brought back the 'sweet and innocent illusions of her youth', sued him in court. The bailiffs came to the apartment on the Concorde and carted away the luxurious furniture. Then he suffered a stroke.

[1] In addition, the Swedish government agreed to pay him a pension of 10,000 a year; but there is no indication that it actually was paid.

In the spring of 1801 Germaine went to investigate rumours that her husband was not as well as he might be; she found a feeble-minded, hideous-faced, slobbering paralytic. She decided to take charge of him. Pity and fear of scandal overcame revulsion.

He lingered on. In the spring of 1802, when she was about to leave for her annual visit to Coppet, she made up her mind to take the invalid with her and leave him there. Monsieur Necker, himself no youth, was not enchanted with the idea. Why did she not take her husband into her own house in Paris? he inquired. Since the French government was again threatening her with exile, it was unwise, he suggested, to bring him to Coppet; in Paris Monsieur de Staël's hulk could still serve a useful purpose: 'You could always say, at any rate, "I must live here in order to take care of Monsieur de Staël." '

Perhaps Germaine felt that in her house Monsieur de Staël would not look decorative. She disregarded the advice of the author of *Religious Morality*, loaded her husband into her carriage, and drove off to Switzerland. The trip was uncomfortable for the patient. They arrived at Poligny, in the Jura mountains near the border, where his symptoms took an alarming turn. Germaine decided to stay overnight at the local inn. The next morning he was worse and his physiognomy most unaesthetic. There was no question of resuming the journey. Germaine stayed at his bedside. On the night of May 8 she left him sleeping. On the morning of the ninth a servant found him dead. Germaine made her entry into Coppet followed by a hearse.

She was moderately affected. In reply to a letter of condolence she wrote:

> It is true that I felt much more pain than I would have felt in any different circumstances. I had found real happiness in making up through my care for the sentiments I had been unable to give him. I had spent six weeks doing nothing but putting his affairs in order, and I was going to present him, as a result, with his pension from Sweden and with ours, i.e., 10,000 pounds a year, without any deductions. I shall continue to make every effort and sacrifice to see his debts paid, but I shall find no more pleasure in this duty. Also I am very much affected by this death, and I shall never find any consolation for my inability to make him happy for a little while when he had abandoned himself to me. Besides this feeling, there was the horror of being alone with him, alone with his sad remains. I never had seen death from so close, and for twenty-four hours I experienced the most painful and, at the same time, the most fantastic impressions.

It is easy to imagine what were those painful and fantastic impressions: a vision of her father on his deathbed.

About the sad remains of Monsieur de Staël less fuss was made than about Madame Necker's. He was buried in the cemetery of Coppet and promptly forgotten. When, some time in the last century, the cemetery was condemned, Madame de Staël's heirs made no effort to salvage his bones. Monsieur de Staël disappeared altogether; he has no grave.

In 1877, for the price of 50,000 dollars, Sweden sold back to France the island Monsieur de Staël had obtained from Marie Antoinette so that he might marry Mademoiselle Necker's millions.

Part Three

TWO TYRANTS

*There are only two powers in the world—the sword
and the spirit. . . . In the long run, the sword is
always beaten by the spirit.*

NAPOLEON TO FONTANES

*Intellect does not attain its full force unless it
attacks power.*

MADAME DE STAËL, *De la littérature*

*I have never known a woman who was more continuously
exacting without realizing it. . . . Everybody's entire
existence, every hour, every minute, for years on end,
must be at her disposition, or else there is an explosion
like all thunderstorms and earthquakes put together.*

BENJAMIN CONSTANT, *Journaux intimes*

11

IDEOLOGY

IF Madame de Staël had died in 1799, she would be remembered, if remembered at all, as a curious period piece. Her efforts to force the revolutionary deluge into rational and utilitarian channels by means of her pamphlets, her lovers, her drawing-room conspiracies, were consequential enough to bring her to grief, futile enough to be ludicrous. Her writings before 1800, despite flashes of brilliance, would not even have earned her a footnote in the history of French literature. To be remembered as a passionate heroine, she lacked in her love affairs an essential tragic dignity, simplicity, and honesty.

But Madame de Staël lived until 1817, and few women left so deep an impression on their time. As a political figure, as a writer, as a woman, she was to embody a principle. In her lifetime she held a position comparable to Voltaire's fifty years earlier. *Ecrasez l'infâme!* was the battle cry with which the Patriarch of Ferney had exhorted his faithful; the Matriarch of Coppet might, with equal justice, have adopted the motto, *Résistez l'infâme!* in defiance of Napoleon's threat, *Je l'écraserai*—'I shall crush her.' Later in the century, when liberalism became the established doctrine of the Western world, soon to degenerate into complacency, the significance of Madame de Staël became blurred; in our own times it is possible to see her again in the intense light of her relevancy.

Nothing happened in her personal life in the year 1800 that would explain so sudden a transformation. In truth she was not transformed at all: nothing could change her except, in her last two or three years, physical disintegration. Like a spinning top, she derived her stability from her own inner movement, but every change of direction came from an impulse outside her. To stand still was death; what strength she had she owed to the activity which exhausted others. But before 1800 her activity had taken place amid constant flux: the top had been spinning on an ever-shifting plane. With each new impulse she had changed direction, opposed what she had helped to create, seemingly animated by the sole desire to undo whatever had been done. Her inner consistency could not become apparent unless the outer setting was stabilized; what she had learned in ten years of turmoil could not take on a consistent shape unless an unyielding outer force imposed consistency on her.

As far as lay in his power, Napoleon Bonaparte did her this favour. It was he who happened to Germaine in 1800. He could not impose consistency on her heart, and her loves continued as turbulent as ever; but he did arrest the Revolution, and he stopped all outlets to ambition save one—to serve him, or his order, on his own terms. Perhaps Germaine was willing enough to serve him, but only on her terms. His uncompromising hostility met her intransigent resistance, and in the fourteen-year-old duel between the Emperor of Matter and the Empress of Mind (as Sainte-Beuve called them), the Emperor ended up without any matter, while the Empress had broadened and sharpened her mind.

Her struggle with Napoleon made her the Conscience of Europe; her equally relentless fight to dominate the men she loved made her its spectacle. Two wars of such magnitude conducted simultaneously should have left her little time for anything else; yet this was the period in which she wrote her epoch-making works—*On Literature, Corinne,* and *Germany*—besides others scarcely less important or voluminous. These works were her heaviest weapons in both her wars; through them she helped to found a new ideology; because of them she is remembered. The episodes of her wars must form the subject matter of her biography. The preceding chapters have dealt with the personal experiences that shaped and influenced her thought. The following chapters must, perforce, continue the narrative of events. It remains for this chapter to define the essence of Staëlian thought and to place it in the framework of the forces that shaped it and of the forces it helped to shape.

Germaine de Staël is invariably presented as the pioneer of Romanticism. Romanticism, in turn, is commonly regarded as a reaction against the Enlightenment. There is no question that Madame de Staël helped to spread German Romanticism, even if the importance of her role has been exaggerated; but her first visit to Germany took place only in 1803, and in all its essential features her thought was fully developed in 1800, when she published her book *On Literature Considered in Its Relationship to Social Institutions.* She never departed from any of the fundamental principles she had laid down in that work. These principles, far from clashing with the philosophy of the Enlightenment, represented its ultimate conclusions and passed them down to later ages as the heritage of liberal idealism. If Romanticism was in conflict with that heritage, then Madame de Staël did not understand Romanticism.

To look on Madame de Staël as a novelist and literary critic is to misunderstand her; she was, above all, a political thinker, a moralist, and a philosopher of history. Every work she wrote wrestles with the same ideas, and these ideas had little to do with literature, unless literature is understood in her own broad definition—'everything concerned with the exercise of thought in writing, excepting the physical sciences' (*De la littérature*, Preliminary Discourse).

She was a pure product of intellectualism and rationalism. Whatever could not be rationally apprehended and expressed—music, for instance —was mere entertainment or, at best, a stimulation to reverie. In the eighteenth century, she declared, literature had 'ceased to be a mere art; it had become a means to an end, a weapon in the service of the spirit of man'. For a government to patronize literature 'is to consider literary genius as separate from the social and from the political scene; is to treat it like the talent of music or of painting, or of any work which is not thought itself, that is to say, all of man'. 'The truly beautiful is that which makes man better.' When Henry Crabb Robinson, a young Englishman, declared that she would never understand Goethe, she replied, 'Sir, I understand everything that deserves to be understood; what I don't understand is nothing.' Most baffling, perhaps, is her pronouncement on Mozart's *Don Giovanni*: 'Of all composers, Mozart probably has shown the greatest ingenuity in marrying music and words. . . . This witty alliance of musician and poet also gives a kind of pleasure—but a pleasure that originates in the mind, and this kind of pleasure does not belong to the marvellous sphere of the arts' (*De l'Allemagne*).

Madame de Staël approached literature not as 'a mere art' but as a means to a moral or social end: to civilize mankind—to free it from ignorance, superstition, brutality, and injustice; to develop its innate sense of virtue by the cultivation of reason and sensibility, of enthusiasm and the generous passions. This was, of course, the ideal of the Enlightenment, the intellectual and emotional climate in which Germaine had grown up.

Germaine's cult of sensibility, of the passions, and of enthusiasm

did not conflict in the least with the commonplaces of the Enlightenment. To ascribe this cult to the exclusive influence of Rousseau is a
persistent error. It was Locke, not Rousseau, who first vindicated the
just demands of the passions. It was Shaftesbury who argued, before
Rousseau, that man had a natural sense of right and wrong and an
innate sympathy for his fellows; who extolled the benevolent passions;
and who wrote a *Letter Concerning Enthusiasm* that anticipated everything Madame de Staël said on the subject. It was Diderot, Shaftesbury's translator and commentator, who pleaded, even more eloquently
than Rousseau, the case for the natural passions of man. Diderot was
one of the familiars of Madame Necker's drawing room; his collaborator, Raynal, whose immensely popular *Philosophical History of the Two
Indies* is a treasure house of anecdotes illustrating the noble passions
among exotic savages, had earnestly conversed with Germaine almost
from her infancy. Bernardin de Saint-Pierre had read his *Paul et Virginie*
for the first time in Madame Necker's salon, though it is true that the
audience fell asleep.

Rousseau, then, was not in conflict with the 'rationalists' over the
necessity and beneficence of the passions. It was Rousseau, however,
whom Madame de Staël singled out to acknowledge her intellectual
debt, thus promoting the misconception about her spiritual affiliation.
There was, in a sense, good reason for this.

Rousseau, usually described as anti-rational and as inconsistent, was,
paradoxically, the only one among the *philosophes* who achieved a
synthesis of reason and feeling. This achievement was possible because
his temperament enabled him—indeed, forced him—to rebel against
his age and to place himself outside society. Diderot, no matter how
boldly he criticized his age and its institutions, needed society as much
as food and air. It was not anything that Rousseau wrote which caused
the break between the two men; what Diderot could neither forgive
nor understand was that a man should cut himself loose from all social
bonds. Rousseau frightened him: 'I thought I saw a damned soul,' he
noted after their last interview. And a damned soul he was, for the
clearer he made his position, the more he was bound to be misunderstood. There is no need to discuss the psychological reasons of the
malaise Rousseau experienced in his contact with modern civilization.
It is enough to say that he found it insincere, artificial, loveless, constricting, destructive of life.

> Where is he, this natural man who lives a truly human life? Who,
> caring nothing for the opinions of others, acts only in accord with his

impulses and reason, without regard for the praise or blame of society?
In vain do we seek him among us. Everywhere only a varnish of words;
all men seek their happiness in appearance. No one cares for reality,
everyone stakes his essence on illusion. Slaves and dupes of their self-
love, men live not in order to live but to make others believe that they
have lived![1]

In order to live in accord with his impulses and reason Jean-Jacques
broke with society, as Thoreau was to do after him. It should be noted
that he wrote impulses *and* reason. There must be no conflict between
natural impulse and reason, between conscience and law, between
individual freedom and social community: to reconcile these elements
Rousseau wrote the *Discourse on Inequality*, *The New Héloïse*, *The
Social Contract*, and *Emile*. The result was a complete revaluation of
all values. Laws, society, institutions, morality, such as they were, were
neither lawful, nor social, nor orderly, nor moral, nor reasonable; in
fact their purpose was the perpetuation of the very opposite, for they
served only to cover up the pursuit of self-interest and power under the
cloak of law and morality.

Like all followers of Rousseau, Germaine took from him only what
suited her. His break with the conventions of society suited her; his
withdrawal from society itself did not. She could no more have lived
unsociably than Diderot could. Rousseau's belief in the innate virtue
of man, in the concord of natural feeling and reason, suited her too,
but the radical utopias of the *Social Contract* and *Emile* did not: mankind must strive towards virtue by cultivating reason and sensibility,
not by remaking society from the bottom. Rousseau's rebellion against
the frivolity of his time suited her, but his onslaught on the arts and on
science did not. In every respect but one she accepted Rousseau when
he was in obvious accord with the Enlightenment and rejected him
when he seemed to deviate from it. The one exception is that Germaine,
like most of her contemporaries, was profoundly affected by that new
note of indefinable yearning, of cherished melancholy, which Rousseau
introduced into the literature of Europe. It was the image of a watered-
down Rousseau that she shared with her age, not of the true Rousseau,
Diderot's damned soul, in whose gigantic shadow the world still stands.
For this sentimentalized image, Rousseau would have had nothing but
a sneer—and his sneers were ferocious.

* * *

[1] *Rousseau juge de Jean-Jacques*, Third Dialogue. 'It looks as if people, in the present state
of society, had almost no use for the simple gift of life,' Germaine echoes Rousseau in
Corinne.

Sensibility, passion, enthusiasm, exaltation, happiness, sadness—
these words recur constantly in Madame de Staël's writings, along with
love, friendship, kindness, nobility, generosity, virtue; along, also, with
reason, light, progress, freedom. All vague words, taken singly, but
together they define her spiritual climate and contain all that was sacred
to her. When, upon her marriage, she met the world with its mask off,
she discovered that the world held all these notions in contempt. The
shock lasted a lifetime. Contemptuous laughter at the expense of a
generous, idealistic impulse or thought was, to her, the sin against the
Holy Ghost. The 'tyranny of ridicule', she explained in *De la littérature*,
characterized the final years of the *ancien régime* in France and was the
product of an aristocratic court society in which men were judged
according to what they *appeared* to be rather than what they *were*.
Every departure from accepted behaviour was its target; 'it laughs at
all those who see the earnestness of life and who still believe in true
feelings and in serious thought. . . . It soils the hope of youth. Only
shameless vice is above its reach.' Before the Revolution this 'discouraging mentality' was, at least, kept in check by a polished taste and
the refinement of manners; the Revolution did away with the taste and
the manners, leaving only the jeer of those who held money and power
to be the one reality, and all the rest a dangerous and contemptible
illusion.

It is a singular tribute to Germaine's courage and toughness that,
although this jeer wounded her in the depths of her soul, far from
shunning it, she bravely provoked it every day of her life. Of enthusiasm, the sacred spark, she made her religion, and the scoffers became,
in turn, the objects of her scorn. In one of her earliest works of fiction,
the short novel *Adélaïde et Théodore* (first published in 1795), she
caricatured the frivolity of the *ancien régime* in the figure of Baron
d'Orville, 'an amiable man, easy to live with, but so lacking in seriousness that it would have been impossible to obtain his attention for a
quarter of an hour even if the object was to save half his fortune. This
disposition made him most amusing. In his youth, his insouciance was
regarded as folly; in his old age, it was called philosophy: the effects
were the same, only the name had changed.' This representative of a
society which had been destroyed because of its inability to devote
fifteen minutes' thought to its own survival, reappears unchanged,
twelve years later, in the Comte d'Erfeuil, one of the characters in
Corinne. Penniless and exiled by the Revolution, d'Erfeuil has lost
nothing of his levity. Good-natured, doing good and evil indifferently,

'capable of sharing pleasures and dangers but not griefs', d'Erfeuil is no better than those tepid souls in the antechamber of Dante's *Inferno*, on whose gruesome punishment Virgil comments, *Non ragionam di lor, ma guarda e passa.*

It was to the emotional climate of Rousseau's ideas, rather than to the ideas themselves, that Germaine responded—the *New Héloïse* rather than the *Social Contract*. And even in this respect she selected only what was congenial to her. Sensibility and enthusiasm, yes; undefined yearnings for the unlimited, yes; melancholy, yes; love freed of the artificial shackles of society, yes, and again, yes. But all this was only Rousseau in the abstract. The real Rousseau was a brusque and loutish fellow who in order to escape human company would leave his house at sunrise with his dog, sneak around a corner, and wander into the fields, where he would lie down, daydreaming or merely absorbing physical sensation—the smell of the grass and brush, the warmth of the sun, the colours, the sounds as they changed according to the hours of the day; it is difficult to visualize Madame de Staël doing this, and yet it was this which was the root of Rousseau's rebellion. As Ernst Cassirer has pointed out, Rousseau began his philosophy when he threw away his watch.

This Rousseau Madame de Staël did not understand. She made a great deal of the correspondence between landscape and the state of the soul in Rousseau's writings; yet to the landscape of the *New Héloïse* —the Lake of Geneva, the Alps—she preferred the gutter of the rue du Bac. In *Corinne* she succeeds admirably, it is true, in establishing a correspondence of moods between characters and surroundings, but only when the surrounding landscape is a city, Rome. This is no accident. Rousseau's landscapes have no history; Madame de Staël, when putting Corinne—herself—in a suitable setting, could not have chosen a better setting than Rome, which is not 'a mere collection of buildings, but the history of the world symbolized by various emblems and represented under various forms'. 'The most beautiful landscapes in the world,' Germaine remarks elsewhere in *Corinne*, 'if they evoke no memory, if they bear no trace of a remarkable event, are uninteresting compared to historic landscapes.' Immediacy of feeling and experience, the goal of Rousseau's quest, was made impossible for Germaine by the interposition of the intellect.

History was the very element of Madame de Staël, and she contributed mightily to making the nineteenth century the most historical-minded century to date. Apart from being in love, nothing intoxicated

H

her more than being in history; and even love she viewed, like everything else, as a social historian. In this respect her mentors were not
Rousseau but Voltaire and Montesquieu, especially Montesquieu.
From them she learned that institutions, laws, mores, all manifestations
of the human mind, were the products of man's environment, were
related to one another, and went through historical phases: these—
not wars, marriages, and successions—were the stuff of history.

The sensibility, the melancholy, the yearning that appealed to Germaine in the *New Héloïse* she also found in *Werther*, in Richardson,
in the melancholy English poets—Gray, Young, Thomson—and in
Macpherson's *Ossian*. In the classic literature of France, she found not
a trace of it, except in two of Voltaire's tragedies, *Zaïre* and *Tancrède*,
the first inspired by Shakespeare, and both by medieval themes.
Historic-minded, given to classification, and applying to sensibility and
literature the principles Montesquieu had applied to laws and governments, Germaine formulated, even before her first contact with the
German Romantic School, the theory that two contrasting principles
were at play: on the one side, clarity, sunlight, a happy, colourful,
sensuous imagination, the southern, pagan, classical Mediterranean
world; on the other, the misty, cloudy, melancholy, sensitive, Christian,
northern world. How she tried to reconcile the numerous contradictions arising out of this dichotomy will, to some extent, be shown later.
The important point here is that, by intellectualizing sensibility, Germaine established a relationship between history and feeling, between
social and political institutions and the human heart.

This relationship occurred to her fairly early and, as it were, spontaneously. It was in the air. Her father's tendency to subordinate all
things, including the national budget, to a system of liberal Christian
morality no doubt played its part in the process, as did his Anglomania.
Her own origin, Swiss and Protestant, and her thorough knowledge of
at least one foreign language and literature—those of England—saved
her from the self-centred provincialism of the French, one of the most
frequent targets of her wit. The novel notion that the French might
learn from other nations, rather than serve as their model and cynosure,
had been disseminated by Montesquieu and Voltaire; Madame de
Staël by no means discovered it. But this notion, fairly popular just
before the outbreak of the Revolution, had fallen into sudden oblivion.
As under Louis XIV, so under the Revolution and under Napoleon,
the French once more regarded themselves as models and lawgivers.
Madame de Staël did not go along with this; the more absolute became

the hegemony of France, the more she held other nations, especially England and Germany, up against France—to the point where her books were banned as 'un-French'. However, in this respect as in many others, her loyalties were divided. Her ideas were cosmopolitan—un-French. But her tastes were French—not only French but Parisian.

The point of departure of Germaine's thought was, as it had been for Rousseau, an emotional reaction. Her early writings—the *Letters on Rousseau*, the *Eulogy of Guibert*, the dramas *Sophie* and *Jane Grey*, the novelettes *Zulma, Mirza, Adélaïde and Théodore*, and *History of Pauline* —are the protests of enthusiasm against the weary frivolity of eighteenth century society, of sensibility against cynicism, which is the callousness of the refined. They also were, no less significantly, the protests of a superior woman against a society which, though singularly indulgent to all other feminine weaknesses, reserved its punishment for the crime of superiority. Like Delphine and Corinne, so her early heroines—Zulma, Mirza, Adélaïde, Pauline, Jane Grey—ended tragically because they possessed superior ideals, talents, passions, and sensibilities. Her object was not merely to exhibit or justify herself; rather, it was to criticize a society that stifled generous impulses and that discouraged half of mankind (the feminine half) from developing its gifts.

The initial phase of the Revolution seemed to offer the fulfilment of Germaine's aspirations. Reason and sensibility, carried on a wave of enthusiasm that drowned out all scoffers, would create a free society ruled by talent and virtue, rather than by privilege and self-love. The United States, it was thought, was such a society of the future, and its existence was proof enough that the ideal was not Utopian. Conditions in France were, of course, different from those of the American wilderness, and there was argument on how democratic, how republican a society would be suitable for France. Germaine, if she regarded America as the ideal, nonetheless clung to England as the model, to the Revolution of 1688 as the precedent.

The exhilaration of the opening stage soon soured. Obviously the generous and benevolent passions were not the only ones at play, and pure Virtue, as personified by Monsieur Necker, was not in control of the historic forces. Fanaticism, greed, ambition, vindictiveness, 'personal interests disguised as metaphysics', and plain cruelty were also passions to be reckoned with. Germaine had to readjust her ideas.

There is, among disappointed liberals, a tendency to turn against their past. Enthusiasm for justice and virtue had led to crime and vice; for equality, to the enrichment of a few profiteers; for liberty, to the

Reign of Terror; for fraternity, to a world war; for the Rights of Man, to mass executions; for life, to death. Whose fault? As Victor Hugo's Gavroche was to put it, *C'est la faute à Voltaire, c'est la faute à Rousseau!* Or, as Napoleon put it, the guilty men were the ideologists, the meta-physicians, the irresponsible intellectual subversives who had unleashed the masses without being able to deliver what they had promised; Monsieur Necker he placed at the head of his list. Or, as Edmund Burke said, the French nation had broken with the sacred traditions and institutions of its past, had torn to shreds the living organism that made it a nation, and sought to replace it with the tyranny of an artificial system. After a wave of enthusiasm, a general revulsion seized Europe against the French Revolution; among its former supporters, breast beating became epidemic; a few isolated voices—those of a Kant, a Herder, a Thomas Paine, a Mackintosh, a Fox, who refused to damn the Revolution and all its works—were denounced as belonging to senile metaphysicians, hot-heads, cranks, or traitors. Such was the climate of opinion Germaine met in England and Switzerland after her flight from Paris in 1792.

She might have done penance and joined in the conservatives' litanies to tradition and the God-given order according to which the well-born must govern and the rest stay in their places. This she most decidedly did not do. She did, indeed, call the Jacobins beasts and hangmen; did write in defence of the Queen; did exert herself in saving the victims of the Reign of Terror: but she did not deplore the Revolution or recant her beliefs. The Revolution had got into the wrong hands and taken the wrong direction—that was all. The fault was not exclusively the Revolutionists'; many of their crimes had been provoked, had even been imitated, by their adversaries. When Robespierre fell, her first concern had been to save the positive accomplishments of the Revolu-tion and to prevent reactionary reprisals: her *Reflections on the Peace* had no other aim.

To turn against the ideals of the Revolution would have meant to turn against her father and against enthusiasm for virtue. Either was unthinkable. Her father might have made mistakes, and so might she; so might anybody. But her innermost convictions could not have been in error. Just so might a woman make a mistake in giving her love to a man unworthy of it, but surely it was not a mistake for a woman to love a man. The two questions, of politics and love, unrelated though they may seem, were not unrelated in the mind of Madame de Staël. Both, to her, lay in the field of ethics, and ethics was, as with most French intellectuals, her predominant interest. Her book *On the Influence of Passions on the Happiness of Individuals and of Nations*, of which she completed only the first part (published in 1796), is an intensely personal and, to the modern reader, an exasperating work; exasperating because of the tiresome anguish she pours out in wave after wave of rhetoric. Yet it shows her, barely disguised behind its impersonal trappings, in a frantic, chaotic effort to overcome her moral crisis.

The Revolution had sought happiness for mankind and created an inferno; Germaine had looked for happiness in love and found agony. In both cases passion had dictated the quest, and passions had prevented its fulfilment. It is the passions, Germaine deduced from this premise, 'that is to say, the impulsive forces that sweep man with them whether he wills or not, which are the real obstacle to individual and political happiness'. As individuals those who lack passions are immune to all sufferings save those resulting from material circumstances: 'they never are agitated or dominated by any impulse stronger than they themselves'. Their vegetable bliss being in no need of a physician, Madame de Staël dismisses them. As members of a social community, passionless individuals present no problems either:

> It is obvious that the most despotic forms of social organization would be suitable for inert men who are satisfied with the station fate has placed them in, and that the most abstract form of democratic theory would be practical among sages guided only by their reason. The only problem is to what degree it is possible to excite or to contain the passions without endangering public happiness.

Before proceeding further, Germaine distinguishes two kinds of happiness: happiness such as it is desired and happiness such as it can be obtained. Such as it is desired, happiness is 'the reunion of opposites': hope without fear, liberty without instability, etc.—in other words, each good without its concomitant evil. Clearly this kind of happiness is impossible. The other kind, the kind that can be had, 'can be acquired only by studying the safest means of avoiding the great sorrows'. It was this study the book proposed to make, and Germaine might as well have written a treatise on how to keep eaten cakes intact, or on how to lift oneself by one's own boot straps. Her failure is lamentable. To begin with, she admits that the book will do no good to any passionate soul younger than herself (twenty-five, she said, being thirty); it is only for those who have followed their passions and who, feeling the ground give way, want to overcome them. In the second place, whereas it is true that all passions, noble and ignoble, bring suffering on those they move, it would have been useless to give advice to self-seekers, gamblers, drunkards, or criminals. As a result, the book is only for those who suffer from the generous passions—love of glory, or love, for short—and in the end Germaine admits that she has not succeeded in persuading even herself that a generous, passionate soul is capable of renouncing the generous passions, no matter what unhappiness may result from them. The ultimate aim is to depend solely on one's own inner resources. To reach it one must pass through an intermediate stage, in which the passions are sublimated as it were: love becomes friendship or conjugal tenderness; love of glory, the desire to immortalize oneself, is transmuted into religion. Yet at the same time Germaine admits that passions cannot be compromised with, and the course of her reasoning is caught in so many contradictions that her failure to follow her own precepts is scarcely astonishing. Happiness exacted too great a sacrifice. She had begun the book when Narbonne had ceased to love her and when her political influence had been destroyed; she finished it when she was in love with de Pange (or was it Benjamin?) and when her return to the political scene seemed assured. Hence the curious effect of her leaving a loophole open to the passions she had proposed to banish. Writing the book had helped her out of her crisis but had not solved it.

The political ideas in Madame de Staël's treatise on the *Passions* were far more original and fruitful than was her attempt to find a way to personal happiness.

There is a fundamental difference between the happiness of an individual and the happiness of a nation, she begins. The quest for individual happiness must aim at the complete mastery of the passions, whereas political liberty (which she equates with happiness on the national plane) must be founded on a calculus which takes into account the existence of a certain quasi-constant quantity of passions among the population. The stability of a form of government (she intended to show in the second part of the book) is a function of its ability to give as free a field to the natural passions of man as is compatible with its own conservation. The development of the calculus of probability and of statistics made it possible to determine and to predict human behaviour, human passion, in the aggregate. The larger the aggregate, the more accurate the calculation. In certain states, she points out, it is possible to predict the number of murders and divorces that will take place in a given year. This idea, first stated in the introduction to the treatise on the *Passions*, she developed further in *De la littérature*, where she declares in so many words that politics can and must be made into a science.[1]

From this premise, which she was among the first to state explicitly, Germaine drew a startling but logical deduction. Ideal happiness, the reunion of opposites, though a senseless quest for the individual, is the goal towards which the legislator must strive. The individual is powerless to act on the forces that shape his destiny; not so the government, 'for it holds, so to speak, the place of fate with regard to the nation; since it acts upon the mass, its results and its means are predictable'. Not that perfection can be attained, she hastens to add, but it must be the ideal goal of the social order.

This is hardly the doctrine of an anti-rationalist romantic. Like Rousseau, Madame de Staël had achieved a synthesis of passion and reason, but whereas Rousseau's synthesis was what social scientists would call a theoretical model, realizable only in a completely transformed society, hers was conceived as a historic process taking place in real life.

The introduction to the *Passions* was written in 1796; Germaine's grand conception of history, of which that book contains the germs, was fully formulated only in *De la littérature*, published in 1800. The thinkers to whom she was most indebted for her intellectual development in that period were not the precursors of the 'romantic reaction'; they were, in fact, the very torchbearers of the Enlightenment: d'Alembert, Turgot, Montesquieu, Condorcet, Condillac, Godwin, Bentham, Étienne Dumont.[2] They also were, one and all, men of a practical, scientific, down-to-earth turn of mind, far removed from Monsieur Necker's seraphic platitudes; three of them—Turgot, Condorcet, and Dumont—had been among Necker's sharpest critics.

When she was nineteen, while her father was writing *On the Importance of Religious Ideas*, Germaine was reading Condorcet's *Essay on the Application of Analysis to the Probable Outcome of Decisions Taken by a Plurality of Votes*. The work struck her imagination: 'He subjects all moral ideas to algebraic calculations. Henceforth triangles . . . shall be the poetic figures with which I shall embellish my discourses.' In the

---

[1] The best-known statement of this idea is in Buckle's 'General Introduction' to his *History of Civilization in England* (1856). As can be seen, it was not novel in Buckle's time.

[2] Madame de Staël's friendship with Dumont, Bentham's collaborator and propagandist, began during the French Revolution and lasted through her life.

course of the nine years that remained for the Marquis de Condorcet to live, he combated Germaine's father, struck up a temporary alliance with Germaine in the days of Narbonne's ministry, was led, by the 'partisan passion', the ideological fanaticism that Germaine could never forgive him, to become a fellow traveller of the Jacobin extremists, and paid for his passion by being imprisoned as an 'Aristocrat' by his allies. Yet he no more than Germaine was able to disavow the Revolution; dying in his cell, convicted by the forces of darkness and brutality, he saw as his last vision the ascent of humanity to light and humaneness.

The work which was crowned by this vision was the *Sketch of a Historic Table of the Progress of the Human Spirit*, in which Condorcet predicted that the tenth and final epoch in the progress of man, which would lead to his ultimate perfection, had begun with the French Revolution. The theory of history as a progressive development of the human faculties did not begin with Condorcet. It had originated, at the end of the seventeenth century, in the literary quarrel between the 'ancients' and the 'moderns'. Even earlier Bacon had proclaimed the New Science, and at the halfway mark of the eighteenth century d'Alembert in his 'Preliminary Discourse' to the *Encyclopédie* had sketched the progress of the sciences, which according to him had entered into their mature phase only with Bacon and the experimental method. Turgot had foreshadowed Condorcet's division of history into progressive epochs; in Germany Lessing and Herder were reaching similar conclusions; Saint-Simon continued where Condorcet had left off; and Comte, dividing history into the religious, the metaphysical, and the positivist ages, formulated the doctrine which, in its essential features, is still widely held. What has become doubtful is not the progress of human knowledge but the progress of morality, which was expected to go with it. Madame de Staël was as influential as anybody in popularizing the idea of progress; and her work seems more relevant to the doubts and misgivings of the present age than does the historicism of a Condorcet or the Utopianism of a Saint-Simon.

Condorcet, Saint-Simon, and after them Hegel and Marx, saw the historic process as determined by some universal dynamic law and as leading to a culminating stage where further perfection was impossible. Madame de Staël was both more and less optimistic. The process, in her view, has no predictable term. It is merely a trend. The study of history confirms the trend and makes it possible to predict how certain institutions must affect it. She might venture a few guesses about the future shape of political institutions or of literature, but she would not predict the precise organization of Utopia. Utopia was impossible because human passions were a constant factor, and Utopianism led to fanaticism, which of all the passions was the most pernicious to freedom and progress.

Even more directly than by Condorcet, she was influenced by de Pange. In his projected *History of Man*, it may be recalled, de Pange had made it his central idea that 'to perfect himself is the principal business of man'; that history is the record 'of his victories and setbacks in this enterprise'. History was the record of a sustained effort—not the outcome of an inescapable law.

If Germaine chose literature as the peg on which to hang all her ideas, she did so, in part, because literature seemed an innocuous subject on which a woman could write without being gaoled or exiled. But another, and equally strong, reason was that she regarded literature, in its widest sense, as the most significant record of the evolution of the human spirit, and that she was convinced of its growing importance and responsibility in an age which, she prophesied, would be dominated by philosophy and science.

'The study of history, it seems to me, leads to the conviction that all important events tend towards the same end—the civilization of mankind.' This conviction is the guiding thought of her book *On Literature*. But not all human faculties are capable of the same degree or rate of perfectibility. Since knowledge is cumulative, the progress of the human spirit is most evident in the sciences. Feeling, too, is capable of refinement: 'There is a certain kind of sensibility which increases in proportion with the world of ideas.' But the purely creative arts—the 'imaginative arts', as Madame de Staël calls them—are not capable of surpassing certain standards of beauty which the Greeks had already reached. However, while imagination and beauty cannot progress, the scope, the thought content, the psychological and emotional depth of artistic creations must increase as knowledge progresses and sensibility is refined. By the same token, morality is capable of advance. Virtue is an innate sense which society may, as Rousseau had taught, either foster or corrupt; the more it is enlightened by reason and sensibility, by science and feeling, the greater the progress of morality. Cato, with all his virtue, was inhuman to slaves, and regarded as natural actions that would have shocked the average Frenchman of the eighteenth century.

H*

Civilizations, says Madame de Staël, tend to pass through three stages. The stage of epic poetry and mythology leads into a more reflective, questioning stage, in which the creative arts reach their flower and ethics and philosophy begin to develop. This age, which in literature finds its fullest expression in tragedy, gives way to an age where artistic creativeness is replaced by philosophy and science. The Age of Pericles is succeeded by that of Aristotle, the Age of Michelangelo by that of Galileo, the Age of Shakespeare by that of Bacon and Newton, the Age of Louis XIV by the French Enlightenment. Since artistic creativeness cannot advance beyond a certain level, while thought and knowledge accumulate indefinitely, a general progression of the human spirit from the mythological to the scientific stage is logical.

Civilization must not only rise; it also must spread. 'Every time a new nation, America or Russia for instance, advances towards civilization, the human race perfects itself; every time an inferior class emerges from enslavement and degradation, the human race again perfects itself.' Greece shone brightest in a barbarian world; but its population was small, and half of it enslaved. Rome diffused the light among hundreds of millions. Roman philosophy and ethics were superior to those of the Greeks; Aristotle did not regard slaves as human beings, but Seneca did.

Christianity and the barbarian invasions, far from retarding the progress of civilization, helped its spread. Christianity introduced the idea of the equal dignity of all human beings; it sanctified marriage and ennobled love; its morality stressed sympathy rather than strength, service rather than independence. What is more, it was the only force capable of bringing about 'the fusion of the spirit of the North and the Spirit of the South'. It was ideally suited to counteract the moral decay of the southern peoples and the ferocity of the Germanic warriors. Offering a hope, a centre of enthusiasm for both national groups, it hastened the civilization of the barbarian invaders and prevented the destruction of all the values of ancient civilization. The meeting of the two distinct spirits produced a new literature which, although less perfect than that of the Greeks and Romans, was superior in its ideals and sensibility. The conception of love in the age of chivalry, the respect shown for women in the times of feudalism, were proof that 'delicacy of feeling' had progressed immensely. The descendants of the jaded, corrupt Romans and the descendants of the savage, brutal Germans had, through the civilizing action of Christianity, discovered new ideals that inspired them with enthusiasm and that tempered the crudeness of their times.

Nor were the barbarian invasions a calamity in the long run. Each time a culture is destroyed by invaders from outside or from the lower ranks, as in the fall of Rome or in the French Revolution, the destroyers absorb the civilization they have conquered. A less destructive method of spreading civilization would be more desirable and speedier; on the other hand, as civilization widens and deepens, the danger of destruction by invaders from outside or below grows less.

In this connection, Madame de Staël takes issue with the theory of organic growth and decay of empires and civilizations. Decay is not a necessity. The chain of progress 'may be broken by accidental events which obstruct future progress, but these events can never be the consequence of past progress'. On the contrary, the Roman Empire could have been saved if it had had a more advanced technology: 'One of the causes of the destruction of empires in antiquity was ignorance of several important scientific discoveries. These discoveries have placed nations as well as individuals on a footing of greater equality. The decadence of empires is no more in the natural order of things than is the decadence of literature and science.' If the Romans had known printing, they would not have lost their traditional virtues and their freedom; if they had had gunpowder, they would not have succumbed to warlike savages.

Madame de Staël was among the first to reject the idea that the Middle Ages were a period of darkness and stagnation. Even metaphysics and scholasticism, for which she had no use, prepared the ground for 'the greatest stride ever made by the human spirit', that is, the replacement of *a priori* philosophizing by the scientific method. If scientific thought had stopped in 476, the appearance of Galileo and Bacon twelve hundred years later would be difficult to explain. Actually there must have been slow and steady progress in the interval; the Dark Ages are dark only to us, because we know so little about them. Scholarship certainly has borne out Madame de Staël.

One of the most influential generalizations made by Madame de Staël—first in *De la littérature*, and at greater length in *De l'Allemagne* —was the division of the European peoples into two groups, whose literatures are 'completely distinct': the serene, brilliant, imaginative, balanced, form-conscious, light-hearted South, which in *De l'Allemagne* she identified with Classicism, and the cloudy, gloomy, meditative, form-breaking, boundlessly striving, melancholy North, which she

identified with Romanticism. Following Montesquieu's lead, she explained these national characteristics by climatic and geographic conditions. Like all such dual classifications, Madame de Staël's was a
useful if question-begging device, intended to express a complex set of
ideas, which became pernicious when repeated after her as literal fact.
Some of her followers tended to forget that Madame de Staël believed
these two spirits to be distinct but not irreconcilable. Far from it, she
regarded their fusion as essential to the progress of civilization.

The fact that Madame de Staël did so much to introduce German
literature and philosophy to the world has given rise to the impression
that she wholeheartedly favoured the Romantic spirit of the North and
rejected the Classicism of the South. Actually the North won out only
by a narrow margin, and never completely. Her reasons for believing
that the North held more promise for the age she lived in were partly
rational, partly emotional, and they are intimately linked with her
doctrine of progress.

It is curious how high a value Madame de Staël, whose lifelong quest
was for happiness, attached to melancholy. The ancients, she says, had
not yet attained the age of melancholy. The Romans were sadder, consequently wiser, than the Greeks. Christianity is the religion of suffering,
consequently superior to paganism. The spirit of the North is more
given to melancholy reverie than is the Southern temperament, consequently more receptive to Christianity. Melancholy, yearning, dream-
ing, brooding are more conducive to philosophizing than is a serene
acceptance of things as they are. Hence the spirit of the North favours
philosophy, freedom, reform, activity—in short, progress. The spirit of
the South, passionate in its quest for pleasure and beauty, is placid
in its acceptance of injustice, oppression, superstition, immorality, and
ignorance, unless it is fired by enthusiasm for virtue, as were Republican
Rome, Revolutionary France, and reawakening Italy.

A melancholy temperament, moreover, was more capable of sensibility than a happy one. The ruling classes of a republic or constitutional
monarchy tend more towards seriousness than does the pleasure-hunt-
ing *élite* in an absolute state. 'The life of famous men was more glorious
in antiquity; the life of obscure men is happier in modern society.'
As mankind becomes more civilized, the few are sadder, the masses
happier. 'Happy the land where the writers are sad, the merchants
satisfied, the rich melancholic, and the populace content.' The effects
of equality were not all happy ones, Madame de Staël felt. It gave
power to the mediocre and forced the talented to be either hypocritically

self-effacing or persecuted. Still, the price was not too high. Two generations later, Nietzsche, starting from the same premises, reached the opposite conclusion.

The literature and spirit of a nation, Madame de Staël held, are profoundly affected by its political institutions. In democratic Athens writers addressed the entire people; poets, statesmen, and heroes alike competed for applause and glory. This public character is imprinted on all Greek literature. Republican Rome was aristocratic; Roman writers wrote not for the nation but for a small *élite*. The rationalistic, practical, and calm dignity of senatorial deliberation marks most of their works. Under oppressive governments a strict separation between literature and social and political activity is the rule. Absolutism encourages the fine arts, poetry, music, architecture, and science, but discourages philosophy, ethics, history—anything that might lead to the application of thought to action. This explains the high achievements of Italy in the arts of the imagination and in the sciences, and the paucity of its contributions to social thought. The refined court aristocracy of France, while it perfected good taste, made a tyranny of conformity and thus stifled originality and enthusiasm. Under free governments—republics or constitutional monarchies—thought can be translated into action. The fine arts, music, the perfection of literary taste, are less developed under them. On the other hand, their literature has a more moral and philosophical tone: Shakespeare's plays, Richardson's or Fielding's novels, teach lessons that one would seek vainly in Racine. It was no accident that fiction first flourished in England; fiction and drama, being most akin to philosophy, were the literary forms of the future. But the first place in a free society must belong to the political, the moral, and the physical sciences. Through them society perfects itself; through them freedom is safeguarded.

The French Revolution had been blamed on the philosophy of the Enlightenment; consequently, its critics held, all new ideas, all enthusiasm for improving the lot of mankind, were dangerous: the wisdom of hallowed tradition was greater than the wisdom of system makers. Madame de Staël did not deny that the Enlightenment had inspired the Revolution. She was to deny, in her last work, the *Considerations*, that the régime which the Revolution had overthrown represented the French tradition. The French tradition was older than Louis XIV, and though held in check by centuries of oppression, it was a steady tradition: the struggle of the burgesses, of the Third Estate, for liberty. On this theory the liberal school of French historians—Thierry, Guizot,

Michelet, Lamartine—was founded. In her book *De la littérature* Madame de Staël contented herself with pointing out that an ideal could not be abolished every time a crime was committed in its name. Nor could enthusiasm for generous causes be suppressed without suppressing all good instincts. 'From the severity with which philosophy, liberty, and reason have been censured, one might conclude that prejudices, servility, and lies never did humanity any harm.'

It was difficult to accept the fact, Madame de Staël admitted, that humanity in the Age of Enlightenment and Sensibility should have revealed itself in all its bestiality and savagery, as it did in the Reign of Terror. She never found a satisfactory explanation for this phenomenon, which is the principal puzzle of the twentieth century. In the treatise on the *Passions* she blamed it on the ambition of the demagogues and on fanatical party spirit; in *De la littérature* she is more convincing in pointing out that the masses had not reached the level of rationality and sensibility of the *élite*. It was not the Enlightenment that had caused the atrocities; rather, it was the ignorance and brutishness in which the masses had been kept. The cure was not in less freedom, less enlightenment, but in more freedom and more enlightenment. Whatever its crimes, the Revolution had made this cure more possible than had the system of the *ancien régime*.

However, by coarsening the whole social fabric of France, the Revolution had created another danger—a vulgar, materialistic society of calculating and ambitious men who respected only money and power, a society combining the worst features of the jungle and of civilization. Unless Europe regained its faith in the ideals of the Enlightenment, nothing would be left except 'the most greedy calculations of selfishness and vanity'. It was the task of writers to restore taste and sensibility and 'to serve the development of all generous ideas'. But it was the sciences that opened up the greatest hopes. Even the most reactionary régimes and the most selfish men would encourage the physical sciences, since they would profit from them; the task of philosophy was, therefore, to apply the scientific method to the moral order. 'I shall go further: scientific progress makes moral progress a necessity; for if man's power is increased, the checks that restrain him from abusing it must be strengthened.'

Politics must become a science. 'Why should it not be possible some day to compile tables that would contain the answers to all questions of a political nature based on statistical knowledge, on positive facts gathered for every country?' If specific political questions could be decided by mathematical evidence on the basis of known data, the vast majority of men would submit to them, and one large area of conflict would be removed.

However, in submitting political questions to calculation, one must never reduce men to figures. A calculation which would sacrifice the lives of a few for the good of the many is inadmissible. Politics must be in accord with morality, and the aim of morality is the conservation of the happiness and rights of every individual. 'Morality must guide calculation, and calculation must guide politics.'

Calculation may be in error, but morality cannot err so long as it rests on the concord of instinct and reason. Here Madame de Staël completes a full circle and ends where she began—with Rousseau. She agrees with Condillac that a scientific ethics is possible, but such an ethics must not take the place of feeling. She agrees with Bentham and Dumont that morality is always in accord with the true interests of man, but she has two important objections to the utilitarian doctrine as applied to individual conduct. First, 'if a man had only his personal interest to guide his conduct, even if this guide were never to deceive him . . . the source of all generous actions would dry up in his heart'. Second, 'it is not true that self-interest is the most powerful motive of human conduct; pride, vanity, and fury easily make men sacrifice their interests'. The ultimate criterion must be the voice of virtue, which is inborn. Compassion is as natural to man as the instinct of self-preservation. Reason and feeling teach the same morality, but if reason is in conflict with virtue, then the reasoning is faulty.

Madame de Staël concluded her book on the *Passions* with a chapter on compassion; she concluded her *Considerations on the French Revolution* with a chapter on liberty; she concluded her other two great works of non-fiction—*De la littérature* and *De l'Allemagne*—with chapters on enthusiasm. Without enthusiasm virtue cannot live. Enthusiasm may, as it did in the French Revolution, lead to criminal excesses. Whenever this happens, the fault lies in the reasoning, not in the emotional impulse, that led to the action. Human nature being imperfect, even the most disastrous errors must be forgiven if they proceed from generous impulses, if 'the mark of greatness is still imprinted on the brow of the offender and his virtues shine through his passions'. This is the last word of Madame de Staël's philosophy. No crimes, no errors can stop the spirit of man in its ascent; reason and virtue are its guide, but the fire of enthusiasm is its very life.

.   .   .

De la littérature was an influential book. There is scarcely an idea of the eighteenth century which it does not transmit, scarcely an idea of the nineteenth century which it does not contain in germ. More, it accomplishes precisely what it set out to do: it is an inspirational tract for left-of-centre liberals whose faith is weakening under the onslaught of reaction. A liberal writer who would wish, in the mid-twentieth century, to draw up a brief for his beliefs could borrow all his arguments from Madame de Staël's arsenal.

However, like all of her works, the book is very uneven, shining with all the virtues and swarming with all the defects of a brilliant conversationalist and improviser. There are faults of logic. Thus, after rejecting *a priori* reasoning, she justifies virtue as supreme arbiter on *a priori* rather than on pragmatic grounds. But more striking are the ineptitude of many of her literary judgments and the facility with which she generalized on subjects of which she knew next to nothing. Her chapter on Italian literature, in which Dante receives one passing and disparaging mention, is an outrage which she quietly repaired in *Corinne*; for her chapter on Germany, based on superficial second-hand information, she atoned in *De l'Allemagne*. But she never corrected her absurdities on Arabic literature, and she was convinced until death that Ossian was the father of English literature, and that the Irish were Germans.[1] Her knowledge of history was shaky, and often she illustrated a valid assertion with the wrong examples. A conservative writer who would wish to draw up a brief against the liberal faith in progress could borrow all his arguments from Madame de Staël's mistakes. (He would, of course, be beside the point.)

Her German critics gently took her to task for her superficial scholarship, though conceding that for being French and a woman she was uncommonly profound and serious. But if it is true that these defects and her Frenchness prevented her from truly understanding much of German literature and philosophy, which she forced into the strait jacket of her North-South dichotomy, there were deeper reasons why she could never fully accept Romanticism. She championed Romanticism because it fitted into the theory she had formulated in *De la littérature*, and only to the extent to which it fitted the theory. She remained distrustful of German metaphysics, hesitatingly toyed with mysticism only to discard it in the end, recoiled from the glorification of Catholicism, and looked to the Middle Ages as an inspiration rather than a model. In no respect is the cleavage between Madame de Staël

---

[1] In *Delphine*, she calls Spinoza an Italian.

and the arch-romantics so striking as in their attitudes towards medieval Catholicism. She believed in indefinite progress; they believed in a return to the past. Her romanticism was never reactionary.

Her French critics—being, unlike the German critics, as superficial and ignorant as she was—attacked not the weakness but the strength of her book. With an unerring instinct for wrong timing, Germaine had chosen to publish *De la littérature* in April 1800. Bonaparte, still shaky in his power, had resolved to silence the critics, particularly those on the left—the ex-revolutionists, the 'Ideologues', by which term he designated not only the followers of Condillac and Condorcet but all intellectual troublemakers in general. Though written mostly before he had seized the power, Madame de Staël's book contains phrases which seem specifically aimed at him. This may have been accidental, but there is reason to believe that some of the sharpest barbs were added at the last minute, and the preface to the second edition, a few months later, leaves no doubt about the identity of the foe.

It is all the more surprising that Germaine expected her book to improve her position in France. So did Necker. 'I expect great things from this manifestation of the Sublime You' (*cette manifestation du Haut Toi*), he wrote to her in the bizarre jargon they had adopted with each other. Her situation was, indeed, in need of improvement, for it was not only in her writings that she had given offence to the First Consul. If Germaine believed that her book would strengthen her position, she must have counted on rallying a strong resistance rather than on appeasing the dictator. But it is not clear to what extent she still entertained illusions about Bonaparte. If one is to believe the testimony of her correspondence with her father in the years 1800–3, these illusions were slow in dying; Count Haussonville, who published the correspondence, arrives at that conclusion. It is not in Germaine's letters, however, but in Necker's that we find references to Germaine's continuing admiration for Bonaparte; and it seems plausible that Necker inserted them for the benefit of the secret police who might be reading her mail (as indeed they were).

Be this as it may, Napoleon's and Germaine's thinking were not altogether at odds, and it would be understandable if Germaine was slow in realizing the abyss that separated their temperaments.

Like Madame de Staël, Napoleon was a child of the Enlightenment intellectually and a romantic emotionally. 'Love of glory' was an expression equally dear to both; only Madame de Staël called Napoleon's love of glory ambition, while Napoleon called hers meddling. Like Germaine,

Napoleon hated mockery; her witticisms at his expense pained him as much as his at hers pained her. Like her, he believed in the cumulative progress of the sciences, in the spread of the liberal principles of the Revolution to all of Europe, in the need for increasing public and private morality; like her, he wanted to end partisan strife and unite all Frenchmen regardless of political past; like her, he adopted the slogan of equal opportunity for all; like her, he saw property as the foundation of the social order; like her, he believed in salvaging the best of the past without attempting a return to the past; like her, he believed that enthusiasm was the mainspring of all greatness; like her, he appreciated art only for its thought content; like her, he had a cult for the immense, the melancholy, the infinite. He even loved *Ossian* and *Werther*, like her. At least this can be gathered from his utterances. But he tolerated no greatness but *his* greatness, no enthusiasm but enthusiasm that was useful to him. 'He wanted,' says Madame de Staël, 'to put his gigantic self in the place of humankind.' He did not love men but despised them; he had no use for anyone whom he could not use. He believed that men prized equality higher than freedom and gaining advantage over others higher than equality. Germaine appealed to men's virtue, Napoleon to their greed and vanity. 'There is only one thing to do in this world,' she quotes him as saying, 'and that is to acquire money and more money, power and more power—all the rest is illusion.' He prided himself on always suspecting the worst in men, on basing all his decisions on cold calculation, on being capable of infinite deception. He hated intellectual women, regarded love as a pastime, had no friends, and in his lonely grandeur arrogated to himself the right to sacrifice the lives of millions for some vision of national splendour. In no man had so much grandeur been combined with so much cynicism. As Tocqueville remarked, he was as great as a man can be who lacks the least shred of virtue.

No sooner was *De la littérature* published than the press went to the attack. 'The masses must be led by a well-informed government,' wrote Fontanes, reviewing the book for the *Mercure de France*. 'But if the masses themselves marched forward, as our innovators would have them, we would relapse into anarchy and ignorance in the name of the progress of the human mind.' This was mild. An article in the *Journal des Débats*, inspired or dictated by the master himself, made clear his displeasure. 'He does not lose himself in futile theories,' declares the article, referring to Bonaparte. 'He knows that men have always been the same, that nothing can change their nature, and it is from the past that he will draw his lessons in order to regulate the present.' To his brother Lucien he remarked that he had studied the book 'for at least a quarter of an hour' (it is six hundred pages long) and could not understand it. 'The devil take me if I have been able to decipher, I won't say the words—there is no lack of them, and big words at that—but with all the concentration of my intelligence I failed to discover a meaning in any of these ideas that are reputedly so profound.'

He was not speaking the truth. He had understood her only too well, and he soon saw to it that she should understand him, too.

12

THE IDEOPHOBE DEFIED

MADAME DE STAËL had returned to Paris on 19 Brumaire of the Year VIII (1799) without the authorization of the government. It was thanks to Bonaparte, who overthrew the government on the day of her arrival by the simple expedient of having his troops charge the Council of Five Hundred with bayonets, that she was allowed to stay. While the deputies scrambled out of the windows, Germaine slipped into the Faubourg Saint-Germain.

Within seven weeks, Germaine's salon was back in its former glory, and Benjamin was in the government. One more week, and Germaine was ostracized. Two more years, and Bonaparte vowed that he would crush Germaine. Three more years, and she was in exile.

Madame de Staël and Bonaparte were fundamentally incompatible —this much has been shown. Why, then, did Napoleon allow Germaine's return, knowing that she would make trouble? Why did Germaine support the establishment of a régime she feared? Why was Bonaparte afraid of a woman whom, in substance, he could accuse of nothing but talking? And why did Germaine risk the realization of her worst nightmares rather than stop talking? The answers to these four questions are intimately linked with one another.

Bonaparte, for the first few months after his return from Egypt, was the creature of certain individuals and interest groups that had little in common save three objectives: to overthrow the tottering Directory before either the Jacobins or the royalists had a chance to overthrow it; to make a victorious peace; to establish a non-partisan régime that would protect those who had come out on top of the Revolution from fanatics of either Right or Left. The groups who agreed on these objectives included bankers, industrialists, acquirers of 'national property'; ex-Jacobins grown fat and ex-royalists grown lean; all those politicians who had made all they could out of politics and who only stood to lose by further politics; job-hunting ex-*émigrés*; and those whose close connection with Bonaparte afforded infinite possibilities of power and wealth for themselves—his generals and his family, for instance. Among each of these groups Germaine had powerful friends and protectors: Napoleon's brothers Joseph and Lucien; Barras, who generously committed political suicide to make the 18 Brumaire possible; Siéyès, chief organizer of the *coup d'état* and father of the new constitution; Talleyrand, whom Bonaparte made foreign minister; Fouché, ex-monk, ex-Jacobin, and police minister; Generals Junot, Murat, Bernadotte; the Swiss banker Haller, who had made a fortune as commissary of Napoleon's army in Italy and with whose firm the Necker fortune was intimately linked; and publicists such as Suard, Fontanes, Rœderer, and Benjamin himself.

Since Bonaparte depended on these men at the outset, it would have been difficult for him to refuse them the favours they asked for Madame de Staël. At the same time, he knew very well what they meant when they called him 'the man of the hour', or what Madame de Staël meant when she compared him to George Washington. He had not the least inclination to serve as their tool for an hour and then be put away in a Mount Vernon. But it was only after his victory at Marengo, in June 1800, that he was in a position to show who was master.

Germaine's contention in *Ten Years of Exile*, her memoirs, that she had long foreseen and dreaded a military dictatorship is only partly disingenuous. She foresaw it even while she applauded the *coup d'état* which brought it nearer. But, like all the supporters of 18 Brumaire, she regarded Bonaparte as a necessary choice and as a lesser evil. Bonaparte's dictatorial tendencies could be kept in check by those who placed him in power, and she had an influential voice among them. The Directory, on the other hand, had kept her in exile; a Jacobin or a royalist régime would have ended all her hopes.

Germaine could not at first understand how the constant nagging she directed at the government could be misunderstood as disloyalty. Her salon, as she saw it, was not a rallying point of the opposition but a sounding board of public opinion. It was not committed to any faction or clique but was hospitable to all convictions: why, then, should the First Consul fear her? Why should the 'favourite son of the God of War' be afraid of a weak woman who merely got intelligent people to exchange their ideas in a drawing room? Why indeed?

The reason is simple: his position was weak, weaker far than Madame de Staël's.

Napoleon once observed, without concealing his envy, that Emperor

Francis of Austria could afford to lose a war and several provinces without losing the loyalty of his people; Francis could lose the battle of Austerlitz and be cheered on his return to Vienna—not because the Viennese enjoyed defeats but because they were glad to see him back. If he, Napoleon, lost a single important battle, he could not dare to show his face in Paris. Those who owed him most—his brothers, his generals, the entire ruling class—would be the first to desert him.

He had refused to be a tool of others and had made them into his tools. He was independent enough to impose his will, but still he could not do without the tools. Men, he said, were guided by fear and self-interest; only by being continually successful could he hold them in fear and satisfy their greed. From the moment he took power until his abdication in 1814 he was driven by the absolute necessity of taking risk upon risk. 'Politics is fate,' he observed to Goethe.

If Germaine's salon in the rue de Grenelle had been the meeting place of an opposition party, he would not have feared her. It was, however, something much more elusive and dangerous. Germaine could not head an opposition, since she was disliked by as broad a spectrum of political groups as was Bonaparte himself. The most prominent of her regular guests were drawn not from among the enemies of his régime but from its *élite*—his ministers, officials, generals, and family. It was this which disquieted him. In Madame de Staël's house the schoolboys were encouraged to be disrespectful of their master; they unlearned the fear on which his power rested; they were corrupted by ideas that undermined his discipline. Just as Germaine thought that to Napoleon nothing was sacred, so Napoleon thought that to Germaine nothing was sacred; they disagreed on what was sacred, but they shared a common hatred of sacrilege. Germaine radiated disaffection. That his own brothers and most intimate associates should become accomplices to her persiflage on the new order and its slogans was intolerable: it amounted to a chronic state of latent mutiny. After every attempt to silence her he was besieged by his brothers, ministers, and generals pleading her cause: their interventions merely doubled his irritation and eventually gave Germaine an importance in his eyes that was altogether obsessive.

If Germaine had known this, she might have acted more discreetly. But she counted on her friends in the Napoleonic *élite*, and she miscalculated the character of this *élite*. When it came to the test, even her best friends found the surly charm of a man who could make or break generals, councillors of state, prefects, and kings, more irresistible than the charms of Germaine, who had nothing to offer but her friendship and wit. As a lady of the *ancien régime* aptly remarked, 'Kings are always more or less beautiful.'

Germaine had no desire to earn martyrdom—and to be exiled from Paris was, for her, martyrdom. The least taste of it threw her into a panic, yet step by step she walked right into it. Nor did Napoleon wish to persecute her: as he saw it, she forced his hand. During the early days of the Consulate, he asked Joseph to find out what he could do to gain her good will. 'My brother complains about you,' Joseph told her. 'Yesterday, he again said to me, "Why does Madame de Staël not rally to my government? What does she want? Is it the restitution of her father's deposit? I'll have it done. The right to stay in Paris? I'll grant it to her. What *does* she want?" '—'Good lord,' said Germaine, 'it's not a question of what I want but of what I think.' There could be no compromise. No matter how often she resolved to stay away from politics, to live in obscurity, to stop writing books (her letters are full of such resolutions), she simply could not help thinking, and she was congenitally unable to refrain from at least hinting at what she thought.

Napoleon put no faith in her promises, and he was not interested in her assurances of loyalty. Loyalty to him meant silence and obedience. A loyal opposition was possible in England, where the government was firmly established. In France things were different. Whoever was not for him was against him. 'Tell the newspaper editors,' he wrote to Fouché, 'that I shall hold them responsible not for their criticism but for their failure to praise.' Insincere praise was preferable to loyal criticism. Since all men were potential traitors, only his successes and their fears could keep them in line. Madame de Staël had nothing to gain from his successes, and her urge to say what she thought was stronger than her fear. To allow her to function as a symbol of public conscience, of public opinion, would be suicidal. Public opinion in Paris was too vital a matter to be left in the hands of private persons. He did not care, he repeatedly declared, what she might say against him in Vienna, London, or New York, but in Paris he feared her. In Paris her loyal opposition might inject courage into his disloyal supporters. In Paris she was digging tunnels through his feet of clay. Madame de Staël understood everything about Napoleon except how weak he was.

The new constitution, as drafted by Siéyès and emasculated by Bonaparte, offered certain bizarre features that no constitution before or since could boast of. One of these features was the establishment of a

Tribunate, whose members were to discuss the laws proposed by the
government without voting on them, and of a legislature that was to
vote on the laws without discussing them. Benjamin Constant, still
claiming French citizenship in the name of a mythical Genevese
citizenship, made up his mind that he would rather discuss without
voting than vote without discussing: he wanted to be a Tribune.

His candidacy had, of course, Germaine's full support. She asked
Joseph Bonaparte to promote it, and Joseph worked on his brother with
such persistence that he wore him down. At the same time she asked a
politician, Chabeau-Latour, to present Benjamin to the First Consul.

The interview, according to Chabeau, began with the General com-
plimenting Benjamin on his writings. Benjamin countered by compli-
menting the General on his genius. He then expressed a strong desire
to be a Tribune. 'Why not?' said Bonaparte. 'Yes, it could be done.
I'll see about it.'—'You realize,' said Benjamin, 'that I am your man. I
am not one of those ideologues who want to do everything with
theories; I am all for being *positive*, and if you nominate me, you can
depend on me.'

As Benjamin and Chabeau descended the stairs, Chabeau mentioned
that he was about to call on Siéyès, who lived across the street. Benjamin volunteered to accompany him. Two minutes later he was talking
to Siéyès: 'You know how I hate force. I will not be a friend of the
sword. What I want is principles, ideas, justice. You may be sure that
if I obtain your vote you can depend on me, because Bonaparte has no
greater enemy than me.'

On December 24, 1799, Benjamin received his nomination. On
January 1, 1800, the Tribunate held its first session. On January 3 the
Tribune Duverrier, close to the Staël circle, called Bonaparte a 'two-
weeks' idol'. On January 5 Benjamin was to make his maiden speech,
on a rule, proposed by the government, which would oblige the Tribunate to discuss each proposed law on a fixed day. The speech, a sharp
blast against the government, had been drafted under Germaine's eyes.
On the evening of January 4 there was a brilliant gathering at Germaine's
house. Since half of Bonaparte's cabinet and family were among the
guests, she received a first-hand account of the master's reaction to
Duverrier's speech. The First Consul, it was clear, would not tolerate
'opposition for opposition's sake'. 'Tonight,' Benjamin whispered to
Germaine, 'your drawing room is filled with people whom you like. If
I make my speech, it will be deserted tomorrow.'

'One must follow one's convictions,' Germaine replied.

Benjamin made his speech. Accusing the government of 'presenting its propositions to us on the wing, in the hope that we shall be unable to catch them,' he concluded that, without an independent Tribunate, 'there would be nothing left but servitude and silence—a silence that all Europe would hear'.

Germaine had planned a dinner in Benjamin's honour that evening. By five o'clock she had received ten notes in which her guests begged off. She took the first ones in her stride; the tenth left her in a condition comparable only to that of Niobe after the loss of her last child. The refusal that hurt most came from Talleyrand.

At the Tuileries the First Consul gave one of his exhibitions of 'calculated rage'. 'There are, in the Tribunate, twelve or fifteen metaphysicians fit to be drowned. They are a vermin I carry on my clothes, but I shall shake them off.' The blast was echoed from all sides, and its main target was not Benjamin but Germaine. 'It is not your fault that you are ugly,' said the pro-Jacobin *Journal des Hommes Libres*, 'but it is your fault that you are an intriguer. . . . You know the road to Switzerland. . . . Take your Benjamin with you. Let him try his talents in the Swiss senate.' The royalist *L'Ange Gabriel*, published abroad, also belaboured 'the Curchodine': 'She writes on metaphysics, which she does not understand; on morality, which she does not practise; on the virtues of her sex, which she lacks.' Continuing in this chivalrous tone, the journalist placed the following programme into her mouth: 'Benjamin will be Consul; I'll give the Treasury to Papa; my uncle will be Minister of Justice; and my husband will be given a distant embassy. As for me, I shall have the supervision of everything, and of course I shall rule the Institute.'

Germaine was stunned. 'This persecution is a veritable madness,' she complained to Rœderer. 'What woman has shown herself more consistently enthusiastic for Bonaparte?'

Fouché summoned her to the Police Ministry. The First Consul, he explained, held her responsible for Benjamin's speech. Germaine indignantly denied the charge. Monsieur Constant, she declared, was intelligent enough to think for himself. Besides, his speech merely defended liberty; it did not attack the First Consul with a single word. Was the First Consul opposed to liberty? Fouché did not contradict her. If she went to the country for a few days, he advised her, the storm would soon blow over. Germaine went to Saint-Ouen.

Fouché's relations with Madame de Staël throw an interesting light on that mysterious man, who switched sides with every change of government from Robespierre to Louis XVIII and whom posterity remembers as the ruthless organizer of the first modern police state. He loved intrigue and power but not cruelty and oppression. He possessed, in Madame de Staël's words, 'a transcendental intelligence in matters revolutionary'; he hated mistakes, and doing any evil beyond the strictly necessary was a mistake. 'It's worse than a crime; it's a blunder,' was his comment on Napoleon's execution of the Duc d'Enghien. 'Often,' says Madame de Staël, 'he referred to virtue as an old wives' tale. Nevertheless his remarkable sagacity made him choose the good because it was reasonable, and his intelligence at times led him to the same results that others would have reached under the inspiration of their conscience.' He liked to wield power mildly and to cast bread upon the waters: in a world as unstable as the one he lived in it paid off more handsomely in the long run to oblige people than to gaol them. With a compulsion to peer into everybody's secrets he combined an inclination to look the other way, which he indulged to the point of courage. As long as he remained police minister, Germaine and hundreds of others benefited from his dedicated lack of zeal. Germaine was right in looking to him for protection.

Fouché was mistaken, however, in thinking that a few weeks at Saint-Ouen would be enough to repair the damage. When she returned to Paris, Germaine discovered that she was ostracized. It was then that she began to pursue the fixed idea that a personal explanation with the First Consul would convince him of her innocence and end the persecution. She begged Talleyrand, 'in the name of our old friendship', to send her an invitation to a ball Bonaparte was to attend. 'In the name of our old friendship', Talleyrand begged her to stay away. At another ball, to which she had been asked only because the hostess knew that Bonaparte, though invited, would not come, Germaine experienced all the primitive brutality society is capable of when it decides to shun one of its members. She arrived in high spirits and was greeted by silent stares. When she approached a group, it broke up or faced the other way. A circle of emptiness seemed to travel with her shadow. She backed into a corner, where she could be seen sitting 'all alone, with her enormous slate-grey dress', as a lady recalled in her memoirs, until her friend Delphine de Sabran came to her rescue and sat by her side for the rest of the evening. Out of this traumatic experience the idea of *Delphine* was born; the scene is described twice in the novel,[1] and the name of its heroine is a monument of gratitude to a simple gesture of kindness.

[1] In Part I, Letter XXX, where a Mademoiselle de R. is the victim and Delphine the rescuer; and in Part IV, Letter XXIX, where Delphine herself is ostracized.

Before returning to Coppet for her annual visit Germaine played her last trump—the publication, in April 1800, of *De la littérature*. Its reception proved that she was still a power: she might be ignored in a ballroom but not in the newspapers. At about the same time Bonaparte left Paris to head his army across the Saint Bernard. On June 14, on the battlefield of Marengo, he gambled the future of his power, lost it, and, as the sun was setting, won it back.

Germaine, who almost followed on his heels, leaving Paris for Coppet on May 7, was holding her breath. 'I wanted Bonaparte to be beaten,' she confesses in *Ten Years*. At her request the Prefect of Léman (as the Geneva region was called during its annexation to France), sent her a courier to Coppet every hour, relaying the military news. France, for her own good, needed a defeat: this was her conviction. And indeed one may wonder what would have been the history of France and of Europe if, in the late afternoon of June 14, 1800, Napoleon had not, by an incredible fluke, won a battle that was already lost.

Marengo was a blow to Germaine's hopes, both political and personal, but she had not placed all her bets on an Austrian victory. When Bonaparte, on his way to Italy, had passed through Geneva, Monsieur Necker had called on him to intercede on behalf of his daughter. The interview lasted for two hours. 'The First Consul,' Germaine asserts in her *Considerations*, 'made a rather good impression on my father.' Necker made a less favourable impression on Napoleon: 'A dull, bloated pedant,' was his verdict. Even so, he promised to let Madame de Staël reside in Paris, provided she behaved herself. The news of Marengo, the memory of her ostracism, the advice of her father, and her yearning for Paris—everything strengthened Germaine's resolve to behave herself indeed.

'One must, in one's life, make a choice between boredom and suffering,' Germaine wrote to her friend Claude Hochet in the summer of 1800.[1] Her decision was emphatically in favour of suffering, which after all was a pleasure compared to boredom; nevertheless, every year from May to November was largely devoted to the boredom of Coppet and the happiness of being with her father. 'Except for my happiness, I do not like it much here,' she informed the same correspondent in 1801. To Necker, Germaine's visits were not a source of unalloyed pleasure. All those who were close to her, says Benjamin in his diary,

---

[1] An official in the Conseil d'Etat and a minor littérateur, Claude Hochet (1772–1857) was a confidant, friend, and go-between both for Madame de Staël and for Benjamin Constant. Germaine's and Benjamin's letters to him were first published by Jean Mistler as *Lettres à un ami* (Neuchâtel: A la Baconnière, 1949).

experienced in various degrees the same continuous tension demanded by their efforts to 'disengage their lives from hers'—and among them Benjamin specifically mentions Necker. It seemed to Germaine that if Necker made a determined enough effort, he could put an end to her persecution. With mounting insistence, she begged him to move to Paris. His presence, she believed, would be a shield to her, while he, venerable and immune, would crown his career by playing the role of elder statesman. Perhaps a place reasonably close to Paris—Saint-Ouen, for example—could replace Coppet during summers. But Necker had lost his illusions: he knew that he was, at best, a curious relic and that his advice would be ignored or ridiculed. Also, he could not bear the thought of ceasing his daily visits to his wife in her alcoholic container. All Germaine achieved with her tears and tantrums was to sadden the last years of her father's life.

Coppet meant a reunion not only with her father but also with her children. Auguste she discovered 'already a gentleman though barely ten years old', on her arrival in 1800. Suddenly conscious of her role as a mother, Germaine began to give lessons to the two boys. (Albertine was only three years old.) The instruction was erratic: she would interrupt her lessons at every instant, giving orders to servants, dictating letters, or receiving visitors, and then expect her pupils to take up again where she had left off. Auguste, a plodding lad, succeeded; Albert, scatterbrained, showed little taste for study. The interests of both boys were in science and mathematics, of which Germaine knew nothing; only in Albertine was she to find the sensibility and interests she expected in a child of hers.

Since Germaine could spend only part of the year with her children —and even then she made frequent and prolonged side trips to Geneva and Lausanne—she engaged a tutor for her sons, a young German pastor named Gerlach. With more time on her hands than she cared for, she decided to take German lessons from him. Germaine made little progress with her German, which she continued 'with resignation', as she wrote to Meister; and Gerlach made even less progress with Germaine; that he had fallen in love with her she noticed only two years later when Gerlach died on her hands of a combination of tuberculosis and a broken heart.[1]

[1] His death, three weeks after Monsieur de Staël's, shook Germaine more than her husband's. 'Every day I cry more bitterly over that poor young man,' she wrote to Hochet on June 28, 1802. 'Ah! If I had known him better, he would perhaps still be alive, and I would not suffer from bitter remorse!' One wonders what is concealed behind this exclamation.

The summer of 1800 passed quietly enough. 'In three months,' she wrote to Hochet on August 17, 'I shall see you again; but three months are counted drop by drop when spent in solitude, and when Benjamin leaves, this solitude will be complete. I shall not go back to Geneva but shall wait for Paris.' Benjamin had indeed left Paris to spend the summer with his family in Geneva, where Germaine joined him, and in Lausanne, whither she followed him. Their relationship had long ceased to be—if ever it had been—one of sensual passion, but this change did not imply the usual consequences of a cooling love. As far as Germaine was concerned, Benjamin woed her every duty and regard a lover owed his mistress, including 'the language of love', even though they no longer were lover and mistress. Such demands Benjamin regarded, not unreasonably, as unreasonable; in return, Germaine accused him of being harsh, insensitive, and selfish.

In her thirty-fifth year, Germaine looked back on a life spent in quest of love and saw nothing but brief glimpses of bliss, followed by disillusionment and betrayal. 'I live with a wound in my heart as others live with a physical ailment,' she wrote to the philosopher de Gérando that summer. 'Do you think that after these experiences a new beginning is possible? The three men I have loved most since I was nineteen or twenty are Narbonne, Talleyrand, and Mathieu. The first is only a graceful husk, the second has not even salvaged the husk, and the third has lost his grace, although he has retained his adorable qualities. New friends have become dear to me, but it is the past which stirs my soul and imagination.' Why had she missed her chance of happiness, whose remembered glimpses made her shudder? Why could not she, like other women, hold a man?

The men around Germaine saw her quite differently from the way she saw herself. No man loves a woman for long who makes ceaseless, uncompromising demands on all his faculties. After a short period of intoxication (four to six months, in almost all cases), her lovers began to tire. Thus they started on a thought process which, invariably, ran along these lines: Germaine had no sense of duty or responsibility. For services of questionable value she exacted love or friendship like a pound of flesh. What, in fact, did they owe to her? She had made Narbonne minister of war to glorify her own ambitions, led him along a road he lived to repent, and saved his life only to dispose of it as her exclusive property. She had saved Benjamin from obscurity only to make him an object of notoriety. She insisted on bringing trouble on herself and made it a test of friendship. She asked for a happiness that can be found only in tranquil domesticity, and refused to sacrifice fame and ambition. She did not realize that to demand love, friendship, or gratitude was to forfeit it, and that scenes, threats, and tears relieved a man from any further obligation. 'Pursued by her incessant reproaches, always in the public view because of Germaine's situation, and never holding the tiller of my own life,' Benjamin expostulated in his diary. Having established their moral right to abandon a woman, the lovers (except Benjamin) calmed their remaining scruples by telling themselves that Germaine was not really a woman at all but man enough to take a little rough handling.

To Germaine the problem appeared in a different form, which may be summed up something like this: 1. Germaine is an extraordinary woman. 2. Society hates everything that is extraordinary, but while extraordinary men can impose themselves on society, society is absolutely intolerant of extraordinary women. 3. Men are less capable of love than women, because men always remain under the influence of society. 4. If a man loves an extraordinary woman, he enters into conflict with society. 5. In this conflict, instead of sacrificing the demands of society to his love, he will ask his beloved to sacrifice her extraordinary qualities to the demands of society. 6. The extraordinary woman, though ready to defy society, is unwilling and unable to sacrifice these qualities; after all, if the man loves her, he should love her for her qualities, not for being like any other woman. 7. With the poison of society working in him the man loses faith in the woman, misconstrues her motives, listens to insinuations, yields to public opinion, and kills their love. 8. Extraordinary women are fated to be unhappy. 9. Germaine is the most extraordinary woman of her time. 10. No one ever suffered what Germaine suffers. Q.E.D.

This reasoning Germaine was to illustrate in three volumes, entitled *Delphine*, which she supplemented five years later with three more volumes, entitled *Corinne*. The theme of *Delphine* was to be the punishment inflicted by society on nonconformity in a woman; Germaine would be its heroine, Narbonne its imperfect hero, and Talleyrand its villain. She began the novel in the summer of 1800. 'I am continuing my novel,' she wrote to Hochet in October. 'It will be finished in a year, I believe, and there will not be a single word of politics in it, although it is laid in the later years of the Revolution. What will they say of such abstinence?' As usual, Germaine was deluding herself: *Delphine* might be called the ancestor of the political novel. She did, however, steer clear of current politics. Announcing her impending departure for Paris in the same letter, 'I intend to keep quiet this winter,' she promised, 'because the arrival of a cousin whom I love [Madame Necker de Saussure] will force me to spend all my time at the theatre and at concerts. I shall make myself frivolous, although I am making a late start at thirty.'

In the first days of December Germaine interrupted her novel and her German lessons, bade farewell to her father and children, and from the window of her berline waved her handkerchief at Coppet. In January Benjamin could report to his cousin Rosalie, 'The fair lady, recently arrived from Geneva, is caught in a whirlwind of balls, feasts, and parties. She drags me along at times, but more often I manage to swim to safety.'

Germaine kept her promise: the winter of 1800–1 was spent in a continuous round of visits, receptions, opera, theatre, balls, suppers, and week-end parties at Joseph Bonaparte's estate at Morfontaine. At her soirées 'the lambs grazed with the wolves', as she put it in a letter to Joseph: ex-Jacobins rubbed elbows with royalists and returned *émigrés*, the ambassadors of Austria, Spain, Prussia, Russia, and Sweden with the brothers and sisters of Bonaparte. At Morfontaine the time was spent in feasts and games. Count Cobenzl, the globular, cross-eyed Austrian ambassador, organized theatricals and charades with extraordinary enthusiasm, and Germaine, on quieter evenings, read aloud from the work of an unknown author—Chateaubriand's *Atala*. While the Master sat meditating at Saint-Cloud, the children played at Morfontaine, forgetful of his shadow.

Germaine met Bonaparte only once that winter, at the house of General Berthier. It was the last time they came face to face. Since Napoleon's presence had the miraculous power of rendering her tongue-tied, Germaine had prepared in advance her answers to the questions she anticipated. She had sought this opportunity for a year, and she did not intend to waste it. Bonaparte, passing through the throng with Lucien at his side, stopped in front of Madame de Staël and scrutinized her imposing *décolletage* as if he were inspecting the battle scars of a grenadier. 'No doubt,' he said brusquely, 'you have nursed your children yourself?' Germaine had not anticipated that question; she was petrified. 'You see,' said the First Consul to his brother, 'she doesn't even want to say yes or no.'

Bonaparte's temper had become increasingly short over the winter. On Christmas Eve, while driving to the Opéra for the première of

Haydn's *Creation*, he was very nearly blown up by a time bomb concealed in a water wagon. He took this in ill humour but made the best of it—that is, he placed the blame on the Jacobins and had 130 of them deported without legal procedure. Then Fouché inconsiderately submitted proof to him that the plot was the work of royalists. The First Consul's annoyance changed into anger. The Jacobins, he pointed out to Fouché, were criminals by definition, and this was a good opportunity to get rid of them, whereas the royalists were to be conciliated. This new conception of justice moved Benjamin Constant to speak out, in February, against arbitrary procedure. This time Bonaparte lost all patience, turned editorialist, denounced the 'sarcasms and insane notions of a dozen or so befogged metaphysicians', in the *Journal de Paris* and the *Mercure de France*, and threatened them with extinction. In April, still brooding, he suppressed several newspapers, exiled a few more Jacobins, and sent warnings to Madame de Staël that, for her own good, she should stop inciting her Benjamin. Thus, despite her efforts, and through no fault of hers, Germaine was no more in favour when she left for Coppet in May of 1801 than she had been the year before.

She resumed *Delphine*. She also resumed her onslaughts on her father. Though adamant in his refusal to move to Paris, Necker let her persuade him to write his 'swan song', as Germaine called his *Last Views on Politics and Finance*. Inspired by her, this work was intended not only to establish its author's immortal genius but also to accomplish the magic trick of regaining the First Consul's favour while pointing out a road by which France could avoid his dictatorship. That a person of Germaine's intelligence expected *Delphine* and Necker's *Last Views* to bring anything but disaster on the authors' heads seems incredible.

Just before her return to Paris in November, Germaine wrote to Joseph that the Consul Lebrun had praised her highly to Bonaparte, and that Bonaparte had replied, 'Why, yes, to be sure, I believe you, since I haven't heard any talk about her of late.' No sooner was she back in Paris than trouble started. Benjamin resumed his harassing tactics against the government. 'I do not think it is possible to carry on if the constituent authorities are made up of enemies,' Bonaparte informed his colleagues Cambacérès and Lebrun on January 24: he had just expelled Benjamin and nineteen others from the Tribunate. A month later, with peace about to be signed with England, the First Consul wrote to Fouché: 'Being now free to devote more time to police matters, I wish to be informed of everything with the greatest detail, and work with you at least one hour, and often two hours, if necessary, every day.'

When Bonaparte said 'with the greatest detail', he meant precisely that. Everything that was said in the salons of the Faubourg Saint-Germain reached his ears. Fouché was by no means his sole informant: Madame de Genlis, Germaine's literary rival, who had been the mistress of the Duke of Orléans and the governess of his children, acted as the First Consul's special agent in the Faubourg.[1] He knew whom Madame de Staël saw, what she did, and what she said—or at least what she was quoted as having said. When told that, alluding to his sarcasms on the 'ideologues', she had called him an 'ideophobe', he was stung to the quick. Seated in his bathtub, he took his brothers Lucien and Joseph to task for defending such a woman. Joseph denied she had ever called him an ideophobe. 'I can smell Madame de Staël from a mile away,' countered the First Consul. 'A fine thing! It's war she wants. Ideophobe! Charming! Why not hydrophobe? One can't govern a country with people like that.' As he ranted on, his indignation grew until, to illustrate what he would do to people like that, he hit the bath water with his fist, splashing Joseph from head to foot. 'Serve notice to that woman,' he concluded, while a valet dried off the future king of Spain, 'serve notice to her illustrious highness that I am neither a Louis XVI, nor a Barras. Advise her not to block my path, no matter what it is, no matter where I choose to go. Or else, I shall break her, I shall crush her. Let her keep quiet, it's the wisest course she can take.'

The message was relayed to her. It frightened without intimidating her. 'There is,' she said, 'a kind of physical pleasure in resisting an iniquitous power.'

Witticisms were not her only crimes in his eyes. He was unable to accuse her of any overt action, yet he was convinced that in some manner she was at the centre of every trouble, and his inability to prove guilt merely increased his irritation, like that of the wolf in the fable. 'They say she talks neither about politics nor about me: but somehow it so happens that after having been with her one always likes me less,' he said, stating an undeniable fact. 'The arrival of this woman, like that of a

---

[1] Madame de Genlis was living down a scandalous past by writing novels promoting religion and describing sin in an unfavourable light. Napoleon said of her, 'Madame de Genlis speaks of virtue as if she had just made a discovery.' She had known Germaine from girlhood and found her an ill-bred and 'a most embarrassing person'. Two of her novels, *Mélanie, or the Female Philosopher* (1803), and the posthumously published *The Château of Coppet in* 1807, are direct attacks on Madame de Staël.

bird of ill omen, has always been the signal for some trouble,' he wrote
a few months later.

The trouble Bonaparte referred to in 1802 was of a very specific sort.
His Concordat with Pope Pius VII was about to go into effect, the
Catholic clergy to be restored, and Bonaparte himself to be nominated
Consul for life. Republicans and royalists alike saw themselves betrayed
by the man on whom they had pinned their hopes. Germaine, who called
her house a 'hospital for defeated parties' united the leaders of both the
extreme factions in her drawing room in what amounted to a conspiracy
of the extremes against the middle. 'At the time of the Concordat,'
Napoleon reminisced at Saint Helena, 'she suddenly united the aristocrats and the republicans against me. "You have not a moment to
waste," she cried to them. "Tomorrow the tyrant will have 40,000
priests at his command." ' Graver still, she was aware of, if not an
active participant in, the so-called 'Generals' Plot' of twelve of Napoleon's comrades in arms to overthrow the Consulate. That she was
closely associated with Bernadotte, its leader, she admits in her
memoirs. The conspiracy came to a head, and was squashed, only after
Germaine had left for Coppet with her dying husband. A few arrests
were made, but the leaders escaped with a stern warning, which Germaine chose to ignore.

On May 8, 1802, the day Monsieur de Staël died at a roadside inn,
Napoleon's term was extended for ten years; on August 2 a plebiscite
made him Consul for life; two days later he was given the right to
choose a successor. At this timely juncture two works emanating from
Germaine's closest circle reached the public: in July Camille Jordan's
The True Meaning of the Plebiscite for the Consulate for Life, and one
month later Necker's *Last Views on Politics and Finance*. Jordan's
pamphlet filled Germaine with such enthusiasm that she learned
passages of it by heart. 'I never read anything that was closer to my
innermost feelings,' she wrote to the author. 'I have a ring, made of
my hair, which used to belong to poor Monsieur de Staël; I wanted to
send it to you, but you seem to be so fond of the blonde hair of Madame
de Krüdener that I felt embarrassed about my dark locks.' The pamphlet had barely been confiscated when Necker sent a copy of his swan
song to his friend, the Consul Lebrun, who was to present it to the
First Consul with the author's compliments.

Bonaparte read the book, he said, 'from cover to cover'. The Bard
of Coppet, he discovered, not only called him 'the necessary man', an
expression Bonaparte correctly interpreted as 'necessary evil', but also

criticized the new constitution, warned against the concentration of power in the hands of the military, proved that Bonaparte could never succeed in establishing a monarchy under a new dynasty, and ended up by presenting three alternative constitutions of which Bonaparte would be the 'guardian'. 'His rage,' a friend reported to Madame de Staël, 'pretended to be extreme. Above all, it was brutal and coarse.' As usual the main blow fell on Germaine, whom Bonaparte accused of inciting and misinforming her father—'as if it were possible,' remarked Germaine, 'to guide the pen of a man who thinks so nobly.' Napoleon had sworn, her friends informed her, that she would never be allowed to set foot anywhere in France except Geneva. Germaine could not believe it. 'I shall defy his fury,' she wrote to Jordan. 'He fears me,' she told Lacretelle. 'This is what makes my joy and pride, and terrifies me at the same time. I must make this confession: I am exposing myself to persecution, and yet I am ill-prepared even for the tedium of my exile. . . . I have a woman's fears, but they cannot make me into a hypocrite or a slave.' 'What matters in a character,' she wrote to Hochet, 'is not whether one holds this or that opinion: what matters is how proudly one upholds it.' In this state of *hubris* she published *Delphine* in December, concluding her preface with an undisguised insult to Bonaparte. She was not concerned, she declared, with the official reception of her book, which was predictable; she had chosen her public, and that public was 'the silent but enlightened France'.

With the public *Delphine* was an instantaneous success, in silent France as well as in England and Germany. Bonaparte had a digest made of the novel; having read it, he turned anonymous literary critic and damned it in the *Journal des Débats* for its 'completely wrong, anti-social, dangerous principles and its total lack of a moral aim'—reproaches which Germaine countered in the second edition by prefacing it with a long note on the moral aim of *Delphine*. Bonaparte's article was restrained compared to that of Joseph Fiévée, in the *Mercure*:

> Take a close look at these women, and you will see that their desires are always violent . . . and that it is even more difficult to be their friend than their lover. Listen to them carefully, and you will learn that everybody has wronged them; you will hear them exhale their profound melancholy in deep sighs at every moment. . . . Behold them: they are big, stout, fat, hefty. Their faces, glowing from an excess of good health, show none of the traces that the sorrows of the heart inevitably leave behind. Indeed, the only sorrow they ever experience is the humiliation of their vanity. In a word, they are simply exalted egotists.

These words hurt: they might persuade even Germaine's friends, who found it difficult to reconcile her professed suffering with her evident resilience. There was truth of a sort in Fiévée's caricature, yet at bottom his indictment amounted to but a single count: that Germaine was a woman unlike other women. The combination of a feminine sensibility with unfeminine behaviour was inadmissible. Thus Fiévée, with the skill of a paid assassin, struck at the very heart of the book and its author.

'I believe,' says Germaine in her *Reflections on the Moral Aim of Delphine*, 'that it was useful and compatible with the strictest morality to show how, with a superior soul, one can commit more errors than a mediocre person could, unless the power of passion is matched by that of reason; and how, with a generous and sensible heart, one is apt to become guilty of many sins if one does not submit to the most rigid morality. . . . But I also wanted to show to what extent the blame must rest on the rigour that society shows towards Delphine.' What is needed above all else, she points out, is understanding and compassion; and two pages later her dialectic leads to the desired result: 'Kindness and generosity . . . form the true morality of human actions.'

There is an inescapable contradiction in a superior soul pleading for compassion with the mediocre herd; yet it is the essence of tragedy —the hero on the stage eliciting the pity of the groundlings and the chorus. The thing becomes annoying only when the hero is someone you know personally, and he is performing his tragedy in your living room. There is enough of Germaine in her heroines to produce this disagreeable impression of histrionics. 'Stop being superior,' we are tempted to say, 'and we shall pity you; or be superior and do not ask for pity.' But Germaine, being a woman, shifted the problem to another plane. A woman, she says in substance, needs even more sympathy when she is superior than when she is not; for the fact of being a woman renders her defenceless against society, and the fact of being superior earns her the hatred of society. 'The entire social order . . . is arrayed against a woman who wants to rise to a man's reputation,' she wrote in *De la littérature*; and when that book came under attack, 'Oh, if I could make myself into a man!' she exclaimed. 'How I would settle accounts with those *antiphilosophes* once and for all!' She was right. Had she been born a man, three quarters of her talents would not have been spent in combat to hold affection and to justify her right to be herself; the role she played and the work she left, though remarkable, are only a fraction of the potential she could have realized without the handicap of her sex.

In *Delphine* the heroine's superiority is not so marked as it was to be in *Corinne*. Delphine, to be sure, is a dazzling conversationalist, but she is not creative. Her superiority is not so much of the intellect as of the heart. In fact, all her faults are excesses of virtues: her impulses are too generous, her love too passionate (though chaste), her kindness too imprudent, her trust too naïve, her enthusiasms too exalted. All the mistakes she makes, and the ruin she brings on herself and on her lover, are the results of her generous impulses—or, rather, of the wrong interpretation society places on these impulses. She loves Léonce de Mondoville, who, unlike her, has one flaw; he is too easily influenced by public opinion, too ready to sacrifice happiness to an artificial code of honour. In point of sensibility he is impeccable; unfortunately, he also wishes to be impeccable in the eyes of the world and expects the same of Delphine. Instead of relying solely on his own reason and heart, as Rousseau taught, he looks on himself with the eyes of others. The parallel of his character with Narbonne's is inescapable. This 'other-directedness', to use a fashionable term, was in Germaine's eyes a characteristically male flaw. A woman wants happiness, and she concentrates happiness in love; a man prefers reputation to happiness, and his love is never unqualified. 'Delphine's love is more perfect than Léonce's. It cannot be otherwise, since she loves and she is a woman.' Thus women are not only punished for being superior: they also are superior because they are women. The unpleasant consequence of this state of affairs is that superior women are condemned to love men who, at least in their capacity for love, are their inferiors. Lesbian love, the only way out of this dilemma, was not to Germaine's taste, although, in an altogether platonic manner, she came close to it in her relationship with Madame Récamier.

It is not clear whether Madame de Staël considered the possibility of a society in which this incompatibility between the sexes could be resolved. Being averse to Utopian dreams, she probably did not. However, she advocated a society in which women would not be judged by a different code from men. She was not interested in equal political or legal rights; her feminism was concerned solely with the right of women to be themselves. The indictment of society for refusing that right is the chief theme of *Delphine*.

Germaine had promised that there would not be a word of politics in her novel. If politics is understood in its narrowest meaning, she kept her promise. But Bonaparte and his press quite correctly interpreted the word in a broad sense, for every criticism directed at the constitution and laws of society, rather than merely at its vices and abuses, is political. The action of *Delphine* takes place from 1790 to 1792—the critical period both of Germaine's adventure with Narbonne and of France's adventure with the Revolution. The principal characters of the novel not only are modelled on real persons but also embody the various attitudes of Frenchmen towards the Revolution. Delphine-Germaine is a disciple of Rousseau and welcomes the Revolution as an idealistic force. The aristocratic gossips, male and female, who ruin Delphine's reputation represent the old society and are unanimously hostile to the Revolution. Monsieur de Valorbe, Delphine's unsuccessful suitor, whose love, turned into brutal vindictiveness, precipitates the final tragedy (and whose character, one suspects, is modelled on that of Monsieur de Staël), embraces the Revolution from vulgar ambition. Monsieur de Serbellane (Count Melzi) personifies the liberal idealism of the pro-revolutionary nobility. Monsieur de Lebensei, Delphine's Protestant and Anglophile friend (an idealized Benjamin Constant), embodies the practical, independent-minded humanitarianism of the English reformists; he supports the aims of the Revolution and rescues its victims.

The hero himself, Léonce-Narbonne, is a divided personality. His upbringing and code place him on the side of the established institutions and values; his natural sensibility draws him to the side of Delphine. He wavers from his first appearance to the end. In love with Delphine, he credits rumours accusing her of scandalous conduct instead of listening to his inner conviction of her purity, and marries a woman he does not love, the beautiful, arid, bigoted Matilde de Vernon; when he discovers Delphine's innocence, his passion flares up with doubled violence and is kept in check only by Delphine's self-denying virtue (a trait not borrowed from real life); but when his faith in Delphine is again put to the test by her independent conduct, he reverts to his ready-made code. Delphine, in despair, retires to a Swiss convent, where an unscrupulous abbess, Léonce's aunt, tricks her into taking vows. Sure enough, Léonce at this point discovers both her loyalty and her hiding place. His wife (whom, upon Monsieur de Lebensei's repeated advice, he was ready to divorce as soon as divorce was introduced by the revolutionary government) has conveniently died; Léonce storms off to Delphine's convent and persuades her to renounce her monastic vows. 'Come to the altar,' he cries, 'come this very instant! When I shall possess you, I shall feel nothing but the ecstasy of happiness. Follow me, let this instant decide our lives! There are decisions that must be made in the heat of passion, without giving bitter reflections the time to revive!' But the instant Delphine gives in, he is transformed. He leaves her without an explanation, and the next thing she hears of him is that he is about to join the *émigré* army: the code has won again. Delphine in a frenzy dashes after him to Verdun, the *émigré* headquarters, only to learn that he has managed to be taken prisoner even before joining the army and is about to be executed as a traitor. Thus, by his inability to choose between the code of his peers and the code of his conscience, he destroys his own life as well as Delphine's and is shot for a crime he did not commit—for, characteristically, he still was undecided at the moment of his capture whether he would join the *émigré* army or not. Delphine tries to save his life; having failed, she takes poison, then accompanies Léonce to the execution ground and, the instant he falls before the firing squad, expires.[1]

Thus, although the Revolution merely forms a background for the action, its influence is decisive, and the political overtones can be heard clearly throughout the novel. In addition, the book is a ferocious attack on marriage unsanctified by love, a satire on Catholic bigotry, a brief for divorce, and a plea for the rights of women. Small wonder that the book enraged Bonaparte, who at the very moment of its publication was trying to impose a conventional morality which prefigured that of the Victorian age, forcing Talleyrand to marry his mistress, Madame Tallien to wear clothes, Josephine to keep respectable company, school children to learn the Catechism, and women to stay in their place. Equally bad, *Delphine* reasserted the philosophy of the Enlightenment and held up England as a model to France. Reading it must have seemed to Napoleon like watching a parade of his *bêtes noires*.

To realize how much *Delphine* is a political novel, it is useful to compare it with its antipode in literature, *Pride and Prejudice*, written about the same time and laid in the same period. Jane Austen's readers would never suspect that the world of the Bennets is troubled by revolution and war. News of these events surely must have penetrated into Hampshire, but Jane is not concerned with them. Jane's world is stable, Germaine's in flux; Jane satirizes manners, Germaine attacks

[1] Madame de Staël later replaced this ending with a different one, in which Delphine dies a natural death and Léonce dies fighting in the Vendée. This ending appeared in the edition of her complete works (1820). The reason for changing the ending is made plain in her *Reflections on Suicide* (1813), in which she recants her earlier defence of suicide, explicit in her book on the *Passions* and implicit in *Delphine*.

society; the Bennets' problems are of the commonplace or eternally human variety, while the problems of Germaine's characters are those of her age and place. Germaine found Jane's novels contemptible, and Jane probably found Germaine's novels ridiculous. Jane is still read, and Germaine is not.

Madame de Staël did not, like Jane Austen, write for her private amusement; nor did she expect her books to be read in ages to come. Her aim was to gain recognition, to explain herself to her contemporaries, and to influence the age in which she lived. It is easy to dismiss her novels as dated. Yet their emotional intensity, intellectual power, and originality of conception raise them high above other, no less dated novels. There are great bad novels, and there are worthless good novels; Germaine's belong to the former category. What is more, for better or for worse, they influenced the development of fiction.

In her *Essay on Fiction* (1795), a work much admired by Goethe, who translated it, Madame de Staël predicted that the novel of the future would deal no longer with a single passion—love—but with all the passions within the framework of the social scene. Neither of her own novels realized her prediction: it fell to Balzac to write the *Comédie Humaine*. But *Delphine* does show an entire society; it does show a variety of passions at play in it—love, greed, vanity, jealousy, politics; it subjects to radical criticism both the old society that has perished and the new society that has emerged; it reasserts faith in the ideals of the Enlightenment—reason, sensibility, and justice. Now the novel as an instrument of radical social criticism barely existed at the time. Richardson's novels, Rousseau's *Nouvelle Héloïse*, Goethe's *Werther*, Choderlos de Laclos's *Liaisons dangereuses*, each had represented steps in that direction, and it is significant that in *Delphine* Germaine adopted the epistolary form, in which all of these are written: it is a very convenient device for social criticism as well as individual characterization. But Germaine's *Delphine* attacked a wider variety of problems than did her predecessors, who wrote in calmer times. To the public *Delphine* had all the sentimental appeal of the *Nouvelle Héloïse*, the novelty of a shocker, and the timeliness of a political manifesto. In addition, its author was better acquainted with the high society she described than her predecessors had been, and the novel itself was a *roman à clef*—an undeniable attraction.

This is not to say that *Delphine* is devoid of distinction as a work of fiction. It contains many pages of acute psychological observation; it is studded with brilliant epigrams whose wit rests on subtle nuances rather than cheap paradox; and the characterizations, except those of the hero and heroine, are convincing. One characterization stands out above all others, that of Madame de Vernon.

Madame de Vernon, the mother of Léonce's wife, Matilde, is Delphine's most intimate friend. Under the mask of exquisite sensibility and charm, she conceals ruthless egotism and greed. It is Madame de Vernon who, by keeping silent about what she knows, confirms Léonce's distrust of Delphine in order to snatch him for her own daughter. Delphine's confidence in her is unlimited, and so is her generosity, which has saved Madame de Vernon from ruin and provided Matilde with a dowry. Madame de Vernon, it will be remembered, is Talleyrand. No one has described his, or her, charm more convincingly:

> Only the most intimate qualities of the soul can inspire that perfection of delicacy which, in everything she says, even the most trivial words, makes the discourse of Madame de Vernon so seductive. . . . She fell in with my [Delphine's] impressions in order to attenuate them; she never contradicted any of my feelings, but she knew how to modify them insensibly. Without knowing why, I was less sad when I was near her.

Of herself Madame de Vernon writes to an accomplice:

> Nobody knows better than I do how to put indolence to use: I make use of it to undo quite naturally the activity of others. . . . I have not bothered to will anything more than three or four times in my life; but whenever I make up my mind to take that trouble, nothing can deflect me from my aim, and I reach it, you may be sure.

Yet Madame de Vernon never forfeits the reader's sympathy, for she too is a victim of society. Near death, she writes to Delphine, telling the story of her life to explain her conduct. When still a girl,

> I soon noticed that the feelings I expressed were turned into jests, and that my intelligence was silenced, as if it were improper for a woman to have any. Thus I locked up in myself everything I felt. I early acquired the art of dissembling, and I stifled my natural sensibility; only one of my qualities escaped my endeavour to control them all: pride. When I was caught in a lie, I never gave any excuse or explanation; I kept silent. . . . I was, and I still am convinced that women, being the victims of all social institutions, are destined to misery if they make the least concession to their feelings and if, in any way whatever, they lose control of themselves.

It will be objected that Talleyrand was not a woman. True—but Talleyrand was, from childhood, a cripple. In eighteenth-century

1*

society this amounted to the same thing. Psychologically, making Talleyrand a woman was not only defensible but ingenious.

The scene in which Madame de Vernon admits her treachery to
Delphine is undoubtedly the best part of the book. When Delphine
reproaches her for having abused her confidence, Madame de Vernon
retorts that it was inexcusably naïve to expect her to act against her own
interests. When Delphine accuses her of having influenced Léonce,
Madame de Vernon replies that 'nobody can ever be influenced in a
sense contrary to his character'. When Delphine mentions the dowry
she provided for Madame de Vernon's daughter, Madame de Vernon
interrupts her: 'Delphine, nothing is more indelicate than to reproach
people for favours one has done them.' True, admits Delphine, but
friends do not repay friendship with ingratitude. 'Ingratitude,' says
Madame de Vernon, 'is a big word that is much abused. I help you
because I like you; when I stop liking you, I leave you. Whatever is
done in life is done either for gain or for pleasure: I don't know what
gratitude has to do with either.'—'Is it true, then,' asks Delphine, 'that
for six years our conversations, our correspondence, our intimacy,
everything was a lie as far as you were concerned?' Suppressing her
emotion, Madame de Vernon replies coolly: 'Everything is finished
between us two. With your character, you will never look at anything
sensibly. You are too exalted; it is impossible to make you understand
the facts of life.'

Undoubtedly, a conversation like this one had taken place between
Talleyrand and Madame de Staël. If he did accuse her of refusing to
understand the facts of life, he was mistaken. She understood them
perfectly well. What she refused was to accept them.

There is in *Delphine* a long portrait of Henri de Lebensei—that is,
of Benjamin Constant—in the form of a letter written by Madame de
Lebensei, his wife, who in this passage may be assumed to be speaking
for Madame de Staël. Monsieur de Lebensei, she says, has the most
remarkable mind to be met anywhere. He combines a solid education
and vast knowledge with a lively imagination and originality of views.

> A kind of savage and proud timidity often makes him taciturn in com-
> pany. His spirit being lively and his character rather serious, the more
> intimate our circle becomes, the more charm and resourcefulness does he
> display in his conversation, and when he is alone with me he is even
> more engaging than he has ever shown himself to others. For me he
> reserves treasures of thought and grace. . . . Do not believe that this

eagerness to entertain me is merely the result of his love for me. . . . What gives me absolute confidence in my happiness with him is my complete knowledge of his character as it is, independently of the feelings I inspire in him, and the fact that I am the only person in the world with whom he has developed both his virtues and his faults to their fullest extent.

With all her confidence Madame de Lebensei seems to be worried, or else she would not enumerate all her reasons for not fearing the loss of her happiness. His charm and sense of humour, she continues, require the 'familiarity of intimate feelings' to blossom out:

When intimacy has reached the point where one finds happiness in childlike games, in standing jokes, in innumerable small details whose meaning is known only to you two, then the heart is captive in a thousand ties, and a single word, a gesture, the most fleeting allusion to such sweet memories would suffice to recall it from the end of the world.

After giving several additional motives for her certitude, she makes this final point:

Beneath a cold and sometimes harsh exterior, he is more accessible than anyone else to pity. He conceals this secret, lest one take advantage of it. But I, I know it and rely on it. No doubt I would be very unhappy if only the fear of hurting me prevented him from leaving me; but while I rejoice in the love I inspire in him, I am glad in the thought that two virtues guarantee my possession of his heart—truthfulness and kindness.

One sometimes suspects that Madame de Staël's novels are collections of private messages, fully intelligible only to the addressees; their advantage over messages delivered by word of mouth or by letter is that the recipient sees himself being judged by the public at large and by posterity. Nothing is more intimidating than to receive communications from a person in the room next door by way of novels sold at the Leipzig Fair. Germaine had been reading in Benjamin's thoughts; it was not so much herself she wished to reassure as him she wished to cow.

By the end of 1802, when *Delphine* was published, Germaine's relationship with Benjamin had, for several years, been entirely platonic. Benjamin noted in his diary on January 6, 1803:

For a long time now, I have felt no love for Germaine. A great adaptability of character helps me to make up for this lack without being insincere. A great intellectual rapport draws us together. But can this

last? My heart, my imagination, and above all my senses crave love. I
need a being whom I can protect, who will follow me, whom I can hold
in my arms, whom I can make happy without effort.

He had craved love all his life. His mother had died when he was
a week old; his father had withheld his affection behind a mask of
irony; his successive tutors had initiated him into the most sordid,
loveless aspects of love. Abnormally timid, afflicted with that paralysis
of the will which is the disease of the modern intellectual, incapable of
asking for love in a normal manner, he gradually atrophied his ability
to love. An elusive image obsessed his mind, a composite of quiet
motherly understanding and of a soft, moist, languorous sensuality, undemanding, submissive, grateful, and yielding. A vision of 'beautiful
physical forms' was ever floating before his red-rimmed, myopic eyes,
and an obsessive sexual urge, more psychological than physical, drove
him in quest of love to the sanctuary of the timid, the brothel. Yet try
as she may, a prostitute is an unsatisfactory substitute for a mother.
The craving continued, without a concrete object, until it became unbearable. Then the ideal image crystallized around the nearest object
at hand. 'I have often thought,' he wrote in his diary,

> that love has nothing to do with the object one loves. It is a need of the
> heart that makes itself felt periodically, at longer intervals than physical
> needs but in the same manner; and just as the sexual urge makes one
> look for a woman one can enjoy physically, no matter what woman, so
> the need of the heart requires an object which attracts either by its
> sweetness, or by its beauty, or by any other quality which the heart uses
> as a pretext to justify its choice to the mind.

The transfer of an image to a real person is not an uncommon process
in the genesis of love. But in most people this transference is involun-
tary, unconscious. With Benjamin it was a deliberate plunge, a hopeless
gamble, a temporary suicide of his inhibiting rationality. All in vain:
it could not generate love. Passionate frenzy was followed by icy lucidity, which in turn was followed by a different kind of frenzy—the
frenzy of the man who has locked himself up and thrown away the key.
All this was bewildering to the victim of his craving for love. The wild
wooing was unusual enough, the sober reaction came as a shock. Still,
after recovering, she might have regarded herself as another victim of
male lust and faithlessness if Benjamin had actually left her at this point.
This he almost never did. He was equally incapable of loving and of
breaking off. For one thing, his passion was apt to flare up again

periodically, sometimes after years. A fleeting allusion, a word, a gesture, as Germaine had observed, were enough to make him repeat the whole process all over again. For another thing ('I know it and rely on it,' said Germaine through Madame de Lebensei), he was 'more accessible than anyone else to pity.' His pity, to be sure, was no more genuine pity than his love was genuine love. He could not bear to see the suffering he was causing. Instead of putting an end to the torture, he yielded, marked time, compromised, made promises, and committed himself even more deeply. This process normally took place simultaneously with two women; the resulting complications were staggering, but they were further complicated by another factor. His perpetual perplexity whether he should remain with Madame de Staël, marry someone else, or regain his independence and, with a mistress to satisfy his needs, lead a life of study—a perplexity that filled ten years of his life and several hundred folios of his diary—resulted to a large extent from his attempt to reconcile his sentimental with his financial needs. Not that he loved women for money; but in his eminently rational weighing of pros and cons in the post-passionate stage, material advantage had its rightful place.

His sense of guilt was the real source of his pity, and like his craving for love it dated back to childhood. His relatives had always regarded him as a monstrous egotist; the women who loved him reproached him with cruelty, deceit, and calculation; Germaine, for ten years, made scenes to him lasting until four o'clock in the morning, using 'the most atrocious' expressions, sometimes several times a week. 'There were moments,' says Sainte-Beuve, 'when he thought of himself as a monster in the eyes of the universe. "When I come back to Paris," he said in all seriousness, "I raise the carriage windows because I am afraid that people will point their fingers at me." ' Yet he knew that he was not such a monster, to be pointed out with abhorrence by his fellow men. If Germaine, instead of threatening to expose his shame to the world, had been more tolerant and understanding, she might have held him. There were fleeting moments of such tenderness, and after every one Benjamin, overcome with memories of her kindness, decided to stick it out. But Germaine, though unwilling to let go of him, could not accept him on his terms, as a big boy. The first woman capable of doing this, capable of asserting his kindness, his goodness even while he was driving her close to suicide, was also the woman who after five tenacious years pried him loose from Germaine. *Adolphe*, which he wrote late in 1806 under the impact of that woman's love, is not merely an account of his sentimental impotence, or of his enslavement to Germaine: it is, above all, an attempt to explain that his soul was not monstrous but sick.

His first attempt to break loose occurred in the autumn of 1800, when he fell violently in love with Mrs. Lindsay. The career of Anna Lindsay, *née* O'Dwyer, 'the last of the Ninons,' as Chateaubriand called her, is too picaresque to be related here. She had passed through many hands, had even known prostitution; since 1791 she had lived with Auguste de Lamoignon, scion of an illustrious family, with whom she emigrated to London and who, after their return to Paris in 1800, thanked her for her uncounted sacrifices and devotion by refusing to make her his legal wife. Chateaubriand, who frequented her in London, described her as a noble soul and intellect. Refined, elegant, clever, well educated, and unhappy, she was at thirty-seven still beautiful. Benjamin met her at the house of his intimate friend Madame Talma, the divorced wife of the celebrated actor, who knew her from London days. It is easy to conceive how Benjamin's ideal image crystallized around Anna Lindsay: like him, she had been disabused of life, and like him, she was yearning for stability and affection; her love promised sensuality and repose, the joys and the peace of the womb.

He courted her in his usual manner. 'I love you like a madman,' he wrote to her, adding clinical details on his trembling hands, perspiring forehead, pulse rate, and nervous symptoms. 'It is impossible, physically impossible, for me to bear this situation one more week.' Astonished, Anna surrendered; Benjamin offered marriage. At this point, in December 1800, Madame de Staël arrived in Paris. Paying no more attention to Benjamin's passion than if he had been a puppy dog straining on the leash, she ordered him to resume his place at her court. Her mere appearance was enough to convince him of the utter preposterousness of his dreams of freedom. Meekly he obeyed, slipping away whenever he could, and finding it increasingly difficult to explain his conduct to the bewildered Mrs. Lindsay. Sobriety had set in once more: he was not really in love with Anna; the idea of marrying a woman of her age, with her past, with two bastard children, and with less money than he thought, was utter folly. Still, he did not want to hurt Anna. The time was not ripe, he explained to her, for marriage; things would have to be managed diplomatically, and by stages. 'The position you two are in is by all odds the most complicated imbroglio that ever was,' Madame Talma wrote to Benjamin in February 1801. The imbroglio never had a clear-cut dénouement. Benjamin and Mrs.

Lindsay continued to see each other, to write to each other, and, sporadically, to make love to each other—even as late as 1805; but Germaine could return to Coppet with the conviction that she had rescued Benjamin from yet another disaster.

Germaine was certain that, with a little supervision, she could forever bar to Benjamin the exit from her Venusberg. The powers she held over him were formidable. She could appeal to his 'pity' by her truly astonishing ability to summon up tears, nervous crises, and even fever at will; she could accuse him of abandoning a persecuted woman at the moment of her greatest need and threaten to expose him as the monster he was; she could hold out hopes of marriage; she could remind him of the material advantages he enjoyed with her, of the money he owed her, of the brilliant society to which he had access through her and from which she could banish him; she held him through Albertine, whom he adored; above all, she held him through herself.

The relationship that bound them together was not love. Benjamin was enslaved to her even while carrying on the most paroxysmal affairs with others; and Germaine was to threaten him with suicide if he left her at the same time as she was threatening other men with suicide if they did not join her. There was between them an absolute rapport of sensibility and intellect which enabled them to stimulate each other's nervous and intellectual faculties to the highest pitch. 'No one has known Madame de Staël unless he has seen her with Benjamin Constant,' their friend Sismondi reminisced after Benjamin's death in 1830. 'He alone had the power, through an intelligence equal to hers, to bring all her intelligence into play, to enhance it by competition, to kindle an eloquence, a depth of feeling and thought that she never revealed in all their brilliance except in his presence; neither was he ever himself except at Coppet.' Carnal thraldom is nothing beside these cerebro-nervous ecstasies. What other woman, once she had sated his sensual needs, could satisfy him after he had known Germaine? What other man, among all those she still was to love, could replace Benjamin?

Why did they not marry each other? The question was debated repeatedly between them after Monsieur de Staël's death, and Benjamin more than once faced her with the ultimatum of either marrying him or setting him free. It was Germaine who refused. The reasons she gave—that she would lose rank, that her children's inheritance, her sons' careers, her daughter's marriage would be compromised by such a change of station—were undoubtedly valid and sincere; but the decisive reason, one suspects, was that Germaine still dreamed of happiness in a marriage of love. This happiness, she knew, Benjamin could not give her: even while she demanded that he speak 'the language of love' to her, she knew that the faculty of love had died in him, as an organ may die of a disease.

After reading *Adolphe* in 1816 Sismondi wrote to the Countess of Albany:

> When I knew him [Benjamin] he was exactly like Adolphe—just as loveless, just as tempestuous, just as bitter, and then again just as eager to flatter and to deceive, by some gesture of kindness, the woman he had been lacerating. . . . This apparent intimacy, this passionate tyranny, during which they lashed out at each other with every insult that fury and hatred can inspire—this was their story.

It is difficult to say when this inferno began, for none of Benjamin's diaries anterior to January 1803 has been found.[1] That it had become unendurable by that time is written with burning words on every page of the diary. 'Scenes upon scenes, tortures upon tortures,' says the entry for March 8—and a dozen others would do as well:

> For three days Germaine has been in a fury. . . . It is a terrible relationship—a man who no longer loves and a woman who does not want to stop being loved. . . . As always happens, the idea of losing me makes Germaine more anxious to keep me. . . . The least word of ambiguous reassurance calms her fears in this matter, and since I really still love her, her anguish when she fails to find in me the feeling she needs is extremely painful to me.

The winter of 1802-3, which Benjamin and Germaine spent in Geneva, was a critical time for both. Surveying his past and staring into the future, as men will at thirty-five, Benjamin could not find a single reason to be satisfied. Chained to Germaine, he was being dragged along in her wild and erratic course, which already had cost him his government position and which was keeping him from his studies and his literary occupations. He was tired of being 'swept away in her whirlwind', of being swallowed up in an unwanted celebrity, of sharing the blame and the scandal of her conduct, of being kept up late every night either by scenes, or by social gatherings, or by both. His eyes smarting and half blind from the glare of chandeliers, and with only a furtive excursion to the brothel now and then to slake his burning

---

[1] On January 26, 1803, he wrote in his diary: 'For eight years Germaine has forced me to live in a perpetual storm, or rather a complex of storms. . . . Since the time when, after capturing me, she subdued me by violent exhibitions of her sufferings, I have not spent a single day or night without raging against her and myself.'

fantasies, he dreamed once more of silent women waiting for his love in dark bedrooms at Christian hours. He had to get married, he decided, if only in order to get enough sleep. In this wholesome sentiment his family supported him vigorously. Benjamin spent the whole winter trying to fall in love with one of the candidates recommended by his family, Amélie Fabri, heiress to an old and rich Genevese family, but despite the most heroic efforts, he balked at her stupidity, which might have been charming in a young girl but not in a woman of thirty-three. Germaine, who got wind of the affair, told him that if he married Amélie, his imagination would 'reverse itself': now he was seeing only the disadvantages of a too intellectual, too celebrated woman; let him marry, and he would feel the disadvantages of 'an insignificant woman, who, for all her insignificance, would be no less demanding or complaining'. Benjamin had to do justice to this reasoning; he acknowledged all the advantages, social and intellectual, that Germaine gave him. And yet: 'I cannot go on living as we do. . . . I need women. Germaine is not sensual. . . . I thus positively need a wife. It is a political necessity'—and so on, *ad infinitum*. 'What a cruel thing indecision is!'

Benjamin called Germaine by two nicknames: Minette, which was the name her father used, and Biondetta, after the heroine in Cazotte's novel, *The Devil in Love*. 'To separate yourself from me, Alvare,' says, Biondetta in the novel, 'all you require is an act of the will.' 'When a man does not want to give happiness to a woman,' Germaine once said to Benjamin, 'he must have the courage to break with her.' 'What do you want me to do?' Benjamin has his heroine Ellénore say to Adolphe. 'Leave you? Do you not see that I lack the strength? It is up to you, since you do not love me, to find that strength.' Benjamin had neither the will, nor the courage, nor the strength.

Germaine, too, was passing through a crisis of despair, but unlike Benjamin, who bottled up his agonies in a secret diary, she vented them on those closest to her—her father and, above all, Benjamin. The more feelings she vented on him, the more he had to bottle up. The cause of her despair was the usual one: Paris once more was closed to her, and Geneva gave her the physical sensation of suffocating. The First Consul, infuriated by Necker's book, seized the opportunity of the publication of *Delphine* to strike at Germaine. 'I hope,' he said, 'that Madame de Staël's friends have advised her not to come to Paris; I would have to have her taken back to the border by the gendarmes.' In his vindictiveness he went so far as to request the Elector of Saxony to forbid the sale of *Delphine* at the Leipzig Fair, the centre of the

European book trade, and the Elector complied. With very few exceptions, the French press attacked her with a brutality such as has rarely been directed at a woman. Like Talleyrand, her enemies seemed to believe that Germaine had merely disguised herself as a woman and was capable of taking as sound a drubbing as a man. Her cries for help could be heard all the way from Geneva to Paris. It was all a case of mistaken identity: she really *was* a woman, and would her friends please tell their friends to stop beating her?

When her friends' answers continued to be discouraging, she prevailed on Necker to join his voice to hers. How many scenes must it have taken before the old man swallowed his self-respect and penned his abject letter to the Consul Lebrun? Knowing that the letter would be shown to Bonaparte, he asked the Consul to take pity on Germaine, wasting the best years of her life in 'the austere solitude of Coppet or some small town in its neighbourhood' (what a strange circumlocution for Geneva!), and apologized for her 'careless utterances', which were not to be taken seriously. If necessary, he himself would move to Paris to ensure her good conduct.

Lebrun's reply was a slap in the face: 'Although the First Consul is not afraid of society gossip, he does not care to be thought so weak and imprudent as to allow his administration to become the butt of sarcasms. You will see that, in the circumstances, every further attempt is useless. . . . My sincere condolences.' Obliged to postpone her departure from month to month, still waiting for the least word of encouragement to take a chance and to test the seriousness of Bonaparte's intentions, Germaine was in a state of indecision no less agonizing than Benjamin's. Sleepless from impotent worry, she began to take opium, on which she became increasingly dependent. 'Germaine is the best woman in the world,' noted Benjamin, 'but she has such a need for activity and such a capacity for suffering that I cannot live happy as long as I remain in her dependence.'

She had the gift of convincing those whom she was torturing with her unhappiness that any unhappiness beside hers was negligible. It was her unhappiness which made living with her intolerable and leaving her impossible. But there were short periods when Germaine seemed appeased, and an entirely different personality—was it her true personality?—revealed itself. The week Benjamin spent with her at Coppet before his departure for Paris on April 10 was such a period. 'How graceful she is! How affectionate! How devoted! How intelligent!' With these feelings Benjamin left.

'Madame de Staël is in good faith in a thousand conflicting directions in quick succession,' wrote Benjamin in 1815; 'but since at each particular moment she is genuinely sincere, the person she is addressing is completely spellbound by the ring of truth that vibrates in her words.' Throughout the autumn, winter, and spring of 1802–3 Benjamin and Necker were fully convinced that Germaine had reached the bottom of despair. Undoubtedly she had—when she talked or wrote to them. But she could not have been desperate when, in September 1802, she invited Camille Jordan to accompany her on a trip to Italy, all expenses paid, 'to forget everything with you, whom I love profoundly!' If he agreed, she added, she would 'suspend [her] anguish for six months'. When Camille politely declined, she was not hurt. 'Let us forget it,' she wrote. Of this neither Benjamin nor Necker knew anything; on the other hand, they could not help noticing a handsome young Irishman named O'Brien who, throughout the winter months, never seemed to leave her side. Germaine, a local memoirist asserts, 'sought to divert him from conjugal fidelity'—with what success he does not say. 'No doubt,' he adds, 'she thought that this was a privilege of kings and of the great of this world', thus giving a fine specimen of the spirit in which Germaine was judged by Geneva.

After Benjamin's departure she switched from the Erse to the Scots. (Geneva, during the interval of peace in 1802–3, was overrun by visitors from the British Isles.) Lord John Campbell, later Seventh Duke of Argyll, arrived in Geneva in April, seeking solace from an unhappy marriage which, in the words of his son, had caused him to suffer 'not only in spirits, but in health'. A physician, Dr. Robertson, accompanied him. They were introduced to Germaine at the Necker de Saussures' house on April 16. 'She appears to be near forty,' John Campbell noted ungallantly in his diary, adding three years to her true age. 'Her eyes are dark and expressive, her features coarse, and her person tolerably good. She invited us to supper Monday next.' Between the two young Scotsmen and Germaine an intimate friendship developed, which in the case of Robertson appears to have been far more than friendship.

When a renewal of war with England seemed imminent, Germaine invited her friends to Coppet, on Swiss territory. There the romance continued for several days, Necker watching it with the resignation of a lifelong Anglophile. Then, throughout June, the trio moved about from place to place, with Germaine guiding them to the sights and beauties of western Switzerland. Even for Germaine this unconventional mode of travelling was extraordinary, and it attracted the attention of the police. In the meantime, another Scotch admirer of Germaine, named MacCulloch, madly jealous of Robertson, had teamed up with Ferdinand Christin, a Swiss diplomat in Russian service, who long had loved Germaine with only partially requited passion. MacCulloch, to whom she had admitted 'a confusion of feelings', was resolved to settle the matter with Robertson 'in the only honourable way'. On June 25 Christin and MacCulloch caught up with Germaine, Campbell, and Robertson at an inn at Yverdun. Only Germaine's eloquence prevented a holocaust. By now, the police were thoroughly alarmed. Three British subjects, a Russian agent, and Madame de Staël in secret conference at a remote inn—there was enough to arouse anyone's suspicion. Campbell, alerted to the danger, resolved to leave for Germany. He and Robertson had not yet reached the border when one morning an officer of the French occupation forces came to arrest them. Campbell managed to escape disguised as a woman; Robertson was released for lack of evidence and followed his patient to Vienna. Christin was less fortunate. He was arrested in Geneva on July 25; released upon Germaine's intercession with the Prefect Barante; rearrested on August 20 upon the special command of Bonaparte (who severely reprimanded Barante), and held in solitary confinement in Paris for sixteen months. It took the intervention of Pope Pius VII to set him free.

During his imprisonment Germaine wrote to him regularly. Her letters, Christin wrote to her from the Temple, were 'the oil that keeps alight the dying lamp'. Obliged to flee his native land in 1805, he spent his remaining thirty-two years in Russia, living with the memory of Germaine. 'I love you more than I ever have loved anyone, more than I have told you, more than I shall ever tell you. . . . During my worst sufferings, your image never left me for an instant; it was always there like a consoling angel.' Thus, on his road to exile, he addressed the woman he might have blamed for all his misfortunes. Germaine did what she could to help him, but there is no indication that she ever felt remorse.

The episode, with its tragicomic complexities, was of virtually no significance in Germaine's life. It is precisely in its insignificance to Germaine that its significance lies. Blaming Christin's fate on Bonaparte's tyranny, she was free to concentrate once more on the uniqueness of her own sufferings.

In the late summer of 1803 Germaine received private assurances that, if she settled quietly at ten leagues' distance from Paris, the First

Consul would raise no objection. On September 16 she left Coppet, accompanied by Mathieu de Montmorency, Auguste, and Albertine. Albert remained at a boarding school in Geneva.

She left with anguished premonitions. Ahead of her lay uncertainty and danger; behind she left her father in his seventy-second year. To avoid a farewell scene she wrote to him on the eve of her departure:

> These separations rend my heart. Is my great anguish a warning Heaven sends me that we must not separate? . . . I implore you, in the name of this life of mine which you want to preserve for my children's sake, to take the most painstaking care of your health. . . . I know, this very instant, that if I were to lose you I should die in the convulsions of despair. . . . I am more shaken, more torn than ever before in my life. Forgive me if in my insane fits I have used absurd expressions toward you. God knows that I love you, that I adore you, and that I do not even feel any bitterness over your not going to France.

Following her instructions, Necker called on his daughter at breakfast, spoke about business matters, avoided any mention of her farewell letter, left the room without a word of parting, and went to his study to read the newspapers while her carriage rolled out of the courtyard. What to do with a person who, against her conscience and for no rational motive, left comfort and duty for trouble and adventure, and who on top of all this threatened suicide if he were so careless as to die? 'My dear Minette,' he wrote to her four days later, 'you are beyond all doubt the most lovable and the most intelligent person in all the known world. With all this, is there nothing we can do to make you happy?'

On September 26 Germaine reached her official destination, a small country house, rented from her lawyer, at Mafliers, north-east of Paris, not far from Benjamin's estate 'Les Herbages'. She found it small, depressing, chilly, and dark. To stay there through the winter was unthinkable—but then she was not thinking of it. On the day of her arrival she wrote a letter to Bonaparte:

> A few kind words you have said about me . . . convinced me that my exile has lasted long enough in your eyes and that you are willing to take into consideration certain family reasons which make my return to Paris an absolute necessity. However, I am stopping at an estate ten leagues from Paris, for I do not wish to return without knowing your intentions concerning me.

She knew his intentions well enough: she was not to cross the ten-league limit, under pain of expulsion. Germaine's technique of requesting an unconditional ell for every conditional inch was transparent to the point of impudence. She wrote to her father on September 27, from Mafliers:

> In two weeks I shall arrive [in Paris] on the pretext of my daughter being sick. I shall write to Lebrun only, for since the First Consul has said, 'I shall not answer her,' I think it would be improper to write to him again in case he turns me down—that is, if he sends me an order to leave. I shall not take a mere hint. I am like the Irishman who kept coming back until he was thrown out of a fourth-floor window.

So confident was she of not being defenestrated that she rented a house at 540 rue de Lille.

While Germaine was waiting for the First Consul to change his decision (or, according to her, to make a decision), Bonaparte was receiving exaggerated reports of Germaine's activities. Her country house, he heard, had become a general meeting place. Benjamin and Mathieu lived in the vicinity; Madame Récamier had moved to nearby Saint-Brice; Morfontaine was not far away. The road to Mafliers, Madame de Genlis reported, was thronged with carriages; Germaine herself had made furtive visits to Paris; and, at any rate, Mafliers was only six leagues from the capital.

Madame de Genlis's reports were untrue. Mafliers was close to ten leagues from Paris, and Germaine's daily letters to her father, which form a detailed diary, show that she did not go to Paris and that her callers were few. Much of her time was given to untangling, with her lawyer, the formidable maze of debts her husband had left across Europe. Her company was often limited to that of neighbouring gentlemen, whose docile parroting of the official propaganda line horrified her. But neither the monotony of French conversation nor the fact that two plays in which she was satirized were enjoying successful runs at the Vaudeville theatre could deter Germaine from sighing her soul towards Paris, as Troilus towards the Grecian tents. On October 4 she wrote to Joseph Bonaparte. To prolong her stay at Mafliers was out of the question, she explained, begging Joseph to press his brother for a clear-cut decision: Paris or exile. 'It is one of the great misfortunes, for those who are persecuted, that they are obliged to beg for the air they breathe.' To the First Consul it seemed that air was plentiful and free outside a ten-league radius from the Tuileries. Through the intermediary of his minister and Madame de Staël's friend, Regnault de Saint-Jean d'Angély, he informed her that Mafliers was inside the forbidden circle, and that if she was still there on October 7, he would have her escorted back to Coppet by four gendarmes.

Refusing to believe the dictator capable of so unheard-of an outrage to womanhood, Germaine dispatched Benjamin to see Fouché. The news, Fouché said, was only too true; four gendarmes were to call on her the following day. 'How about you?' asked Fouché. 'Haven't you received any orders?'—'No, why should I?'—'Why, why! A fine question! Does anybody in this country ever ask why?'

On Saturday, 15 Vendémiaire (October 7), Germaine left Mafliers with Albertine and a maid to hide in the house of Madame de La Tour, a few miles away. She barely knew the lady, to whom Regnault had recommended her. (Napoleon's complaint that his ministers did not serve him well was not groundless.) Two days later Germaine moved on to Saint-Brice, where Juliette Récamier gave her asylum and where she awaited the results of appeals she had addressed to Napoleon and to Joseph. Her letter to the First Consul proves dramatically that, no matter how high the stakes, she was incapable of asking a favour without seeming to exact her due. Beginning modestly enough, she worked herself, with rising pride and indignation, into the role of a moral blackmailer:

> I was living peacefully at Mafliers, relying on the assurances you kindly had conveyed to me that I could stay there, when I was told that I was to be arrested there with my two children. Citizen Consul, I cannot believe it. Your deed would earn me a cruel fame: it would give me a line in your history.
>
> You would pierce my venerable father's heart. Despite his age he would, I am sure, wish to come and ask what crime I have committed, what crime his family has committed, to deserve so barbarous a treatment. If you want me to leave France, let me have a passport to go to Germany and grant me one week in Paris, so that I may get money for my journey and take my daughter to see a doctor; she is six years old and the voyage has tired her.
>
> There is no country in the world where such a request would be refused. . . . I beseech you once more, give me the benefit of your leniency and allow me to live in my father's house at Saint-Ouen. . . . I shall leave in the spring, when the season will allow my children to travel safely.
>
> To conclude, Citizen Consul, stop to think for a moment before you inflict such suffering on a defenceless person. By a simple act of justice you will inspire more genuine gratitude in me than you will perhaps obtain from others by showering them with favours.

Joseph informed her, in a letter dated 15 Vendémiaire, that the First Consul had rebuffed his intercession and was about to have her formally exiled. Yet Germaine still had not received an official order on October 12; hoping once more that Napoleon would not carry out his threat, she returned to Mafliers. Hope alternated with fear and indecision. The sound of horses' hooves under her window made her pale; in every man on horseback she saw a gendarme. She had not even decided where to go if the order came. Some friends had advised her to go to Germany, where *Delphine* had met with immense acclaim, and thus restore her prestige. 'I do not know,' she complained to Necker, 'where to find money or a carriage. My head reels. My heart draws me to you, but everyone is of the opinion that after saying that I wanted to go to Germany I must stick to it.'

But to stay would be best. 'Let me die in France, so long as it is near Paris, at ten leagues, and I shall thank *him*, I shall pray to *him* as if he were God Himself!' Joseph, to whom she addressed this cry, forbore to remind her that if that was what she wanted, she could have had it but for her demanding more. It was too late: on October 13 Bonaparte signed an order enjoining Madame de Staël to remove herself, within twenty-four hours after it was served, to a distance of forty leagues (110 miles) from Paris.

On October 15, at four in the afternoon, Germaine was sitting in her drawing room at Mafliers with several friends, among them Madame Junot. Optimistic again, she was waiting for word from Joseph, who had promised to make one last effort. From her seat, through the tall windows, she kept an eye on the highway and the entrance to the garden, waiting for the messenger. She had just picked up a bunch of grapes from a bowl before her when her guests saw her freeze. At the gate a man on horseback, wearing a grey riding coat, was ringing the bell. Germaine turned white and, for a moment, speechless. 'They have come to arrest me,' she stammered at last, still holding the grapes in mid-air. Then she rose to meet the visitor in the garden. He introduced himself as Lieutenant Gaudriot, of the gendarmerie of Versailles, produced the order signed by Bonaparte, and explained, with the utmost courtesy, that he had been ordered to wear civilian clothes and to treat her with all the deference and discretion due to her station.

Still trying to convince herself of the reality of the scene, Germaine gazed at the garden, bathed in the slanting rays of the October sun and the perfume of the last flowers of the year. Her senses absorbed every impression as intensely as if she just had learned her death sentence. But she quickly pulled herself together. A woman with two children, she declared, could not be ordered to move at twenty-four hours' notice like a recruit. She needed three days in Paris to wind up her affairs. The lieutenant consented but insisted on going with her. A few minutes later Germaine, her children, and the gendarme were rolling towards Paris.

Gaudriot had been picked for the assignment as being, in Germaine's words, 'the most literary of gendarmes'. He complimented her on her writings. 'You can see for yourself, sir, what being an intelligent woman leads to,' replied Germaine. She asked him to stop at Saint-Brice, so she could take leave of Madame Récamier. Her appearance in such circumstances caused consternation. General Junot, who happened to be with Madame Récamier, promised to hasten to Saint-Cloud for a last attempt to soften the First Consul. Regaining courage, Germaine continued to her house in the rue de Lille, where she had hoped to spend the winter.

At Saint-Cloud that evening Junot appealed to his former comrade-in-arms. 'What makes you take such an interest in that woman?' Bonaparte cried and stamped his foot. 'The same interest I would take in any weak and suffering being,' Junot replied nobly. 'Besides, she would worship you, General, if you only let her.'—'Oh, yes, yes, I know her,' said Bonaparte. 'But *Passato il pericolo, gabbato il santo* [when the danger's gone, the saint's forgotten]. She has only herself to blame; let her bear the consequences.' After Junot, Regnault, Fontanes, Lucien, and Joseph went to the assault. A note from Joseph, written at midnight, informed Germaine that his brother's determination was unshakable.

Still Germaine played for time. Her house was full of callers, as if she had established herself permanently. She could not make up her mind where to go. Bonaparte had indicated that she could reside freely at Bordeaux or Lyons; Germaine was still trying to meet Bonaparte halfway—a place twenty leagues from Paris. 'I still do not know where to turn,' she wrote to Necker. 'All I know is that twice a day I receive the visit of my disguised gendarme, who reminds me of Bluebeard crying, "Are you coming down soon?" ' In the midst of her perplexity came a respite in the form of an invitation from Joseph to visit him at Morfontaine. 'Bizarre destiny,' commented Germaine, 'to be exiled by one brother and to go visiting the other.'

At Morfontaine she found half of Napoleon's court. 'The terror he inspires is inconceivable,' she reported to Necker. 'He keeps saying that he is at five days from Berlin, eight days from Vienna, and that is his only answer to any objections or representations that are made to him. . . . One has the impression of an impetuous wind blowing about one's ears when one is near that man.'

Her attempts at bargaining failed utterly. Germany it had to be. Her passport was delivered. She gave her father a forwarding address in Strasbourg. 'I would give everything in the world to see you again— but not in the place where you are.' Before the letter reached him, she had again changed her mind; she would go to Metz rather than Strasbourg. Benjamin, all his resolutions thrown to the winds at the news of Biondetta's distress, had hurried to her side. He would accompany her to Germany.

On October 24 her carriage left. The travellers stopped at the inn of Bondy, just beyond the tollgate. Perhaps the First Consul would have a last-minute change of mind. Germaine decided to wait for a word from Junot. Incapable of remaining still, she spent the waiting period driving around Paris. Her grief became hysterical as she watched, from the carriage window, the immense city stretched out before her. As Benjamin tried to calm her, her children watched in timid awe. At last, when on the next day there was still no news, Germaine wrote her last message from France to her father, and ordered the driver to make for Châlons.

'Farewell! I am getting into my carriage at a place three leagues from Paris, seeing it from here, leaving my friends that are there—by force —oh God!'

Her letter crossed a message from Necker: 'Lift your head high in adversity and permit no man on earth, be he ever so powerful, to hold you under his boot.'

13

WEIMAR, BERLIN, AND FATE

———

AVING travelled two hundred miles in two days, Germaine and her party—Benjamin, Auguste, Albertine, and two or three servants—reached the Hôtel de Pont-à-Mousson at Metz late on October 26. There was a reason for her haste, but that reason was by no means her anxiety to see Germany.

When, in 1796, her friend Meister invited her to Zurich to meet Wieland, who was visiting there, Germaine replied: 'To go to Zurich for the sake of a German author, be he ever so famous, is one thing you shall not see me do. I think I already know everything that is said in German, and even what will be said fifty years from now.' All she had read was *Werther*, and she did not know a word of German. In 1797 Goethe sent her a magnificently bound copy of *Wilhelm Meister*; Germaine admitted that all she could admire was the binding. The thought that German literature and philosophy had something new to say brushed her only in 1798, when a French *émigré*, Charles de Villers, began to publish a series of articles on German thought and letters in the *Spectateur du Nord*, in Hamburg. Germaine's inadequate chapter on Germany in *De la littérature* drew almost exclusively on Villers' articles. She took up German lessons with her children's tutor, Gerlach, and after her return to Paris late in 1800 frequented many *émigrés* recently returned from Germany, among them Camille Jordan, who was translating Klopstock, and Gérando, who, with Villers, introduced Kant to the French. Through them and through the Swedish chargé d'affaires, Baron Brinckmann, she met several eminent members of the German colony. The philosopher Jacobi put her in touch with Villers, and the learned Wilhelm von Humboldt continued her German lessons. By 1801, according to Humboldt, she knew German tolerably well; no doubt he meant that she could read German—for in 1804 she still was incapable of conversing in that language.

Germaine had corresponded with Villers for several years, and an

intellectual flirtation had sprung up between them. 'Villers is writing
me letters in which his love for Kant and his love for me are manifest,
but Kant has his preference.' Shortly after receiving her order of exile,
she learned that Villers, whom she had never met, was on his way to
Paris and would stop on his way at Metz. Impulsively she changed her
itinerary to spend a week in Metz, absorbing information on Germany
from her correspondent.

Villers, at twenty-eight, had become a fanatical Germanophile.
Though known chiefly as an exponent of Kant, he had moved far
beyond the Königsberg philosopher, whose admiration for the French
Revolution he did not share, into the arch-romantic camp of Schelling,
and looked with pained contempt on the incurable superficiality and
immorality of France. In these sentiments he was maintained by his
travelling companion, Frau Senator von Rodde, who with her children
occupied the entire first floor of the hotel, forcing Germaine and her
suite to occupy more cramped quarters on the second. He had loved
Frau von Rodde before her marriage, when he was a student at Göttingen, and Herr von Rodde did not object to his continuing to love her;
but Frau von Rodde, less tolerant, objected to the prolonged and
animated tête-à-têtes between her lover and Germaine.

In the six days Germaine had planned to stay at Metz, and which
she extended to twelve, an argumentative flirtation between her and
Villers sprang up. It was argumentative, for Germaine was never more
devoted to France than when she had just been expelled from it, and
Villers' disparagement of her Paradise infuriated her. 'Everything seems
frivolous and superficial to him compared to his good little bunny,' she
complained. On the other hand, the heat of their arguments, which
were not always monitored by Benjamin and the bunny, generated a
mutual attraction. Germaine even considered the possibility of weaning
Villers from his 'big German woman'; Benjamin, she wrote to her
father, was too 'incomplete in his feelings and character' to satisfy her
needs. Nevertheless, she repulsed Villers' advances. 'I am exclusive in
my feelings, though catholic in my good will,' she explained after one
of his more ardent attacks.

When she arrived at Metz, Germaine was still, as she put it, holding
on to her soul with both hands: should she stay in Metz, push on to
Germany, or return to Geneva? But Metz, she soon decided, would
be 'ridiculous', and the very thought of Geneva was too dreadful; in
Germany, Villers assured her, she would be given a triumphal reception. Yet when, on November 8, she left Metz for Frankfurt, her fore-

bodings were more intense than ever. A few days before her departure she had visited the cathedral and the synagogue of Metz: 'Those tombs in the cathedral,' she wrote to Mathieu, 'those piercing wails in the synagogue, everything acted upon my nerves and I was seized by an indescribable agony of terror. It seemed to me that death was threatening my father, my children, my friends.' Thus, in gloom and fear, began the voyage which was to end, after six months of triumphs and glitter, with a scream of despair.

On a bleak November day Germaine stood shivering by the dark grey waters of the Rhine, waiting for the ferry. 'My French servants,' she later recalled, 'were impatient at the German tempo and were astonished that nobody understood them when they spoke the only language they thought was admitted in a civilized country.' Fidgeting, Germaine observed an old peasant woman stolidly enthroned on her cart. 'You are very calm,' said Germaine. 'Yes,' answered the woman. 'Why make a fuss?' The reply left Germaine pensive.

On the other shore Germaine was greeted by 'the shrill and false notes of the postilion's horn, which seemed to announce a sad departure towards a sad sojourn.' There was snow on the ground; in the small windows along the road heads appeared, staring at the passing carriage. Despite Benjamin's efforts to amuse the company, the gloom deepened as they penetrated into Germany. 'My dear Papa,' Albertine wrote to her grandfather, 'I am bored in Germany; I would be much happier seeing you again. I like France much better. Without Benjamin, who plays with me, neither of us, Maman and I, would know what to do in the middle of all those Germans.'

At Frankfurt Albertine came down with a fever. The best doctor in town was summoned. He took one look at the child: scarlet fever, he declared, in French. Albertine began to cry. Switching to English, Germaine asked if the disease was dangerous; unperturbed, the doctor related how a girl had died of it in the house next door a few days earlier. Without Benjamin, Germaine wrote to her father, she would have lost her head. The 'scarlet fever' turned out to be a bad cold, which she blamed on the German mania for overheating. 'What a heap of German brutality this doctor is!' she added.

All Frankfurt seemed a heap of German brutality. Of a triumphal reception there was no sign. The notables of Frankfurt were prosaic merchants and bankers; they did not care to discuss Kant, and they were afraid of compromising themselves by displaying too much interest in a person who had just incurred Bonaparte's wrath. 'It is in the character of the Germans not to be incautious,' she noted. They locked away their thoughts and feelings 'like objects never to be used, not even on Sundays'. Their attempts at humour were even more oppressive than 'the tedium of their grave and monotonous formality' —'a dreary playfulness which places its paws on your shoulders with heavy familiarity'. 'All they do is eat, and all they talk about is food.' All in all, 'except for the educated minority, the Germans, if judged by French tastes and sensibility, barely belong to the human race'. German women were affected; they were insulted, Germaine noticed, when she consulted them on children's diseases instead of discussing literature. They also were sentimental. At that, they were superior to the men.

> There is nothing more clumsy, nothing more smoke-filled in the moral as in the physical sense, than German men. . . . I still am at a loss to understand how those women can turn their feelings toward anything but an ideal object, for there is no sadder reality than the German men, whom, for want of choice, they are obliged to marry.[1]

These utterances were not dictated by a preconceived hostility. The hostility and the prejudice were on the German side. Reporting on Germaine's stay at Frankfurt to her son, Goethe's mother wrote: 'She oppressed me like a millstone. I avoided her wherever I could, refused all invitations to gatherings she was to attend, and breathed more freely when she left. What does this woman want from me? I never wrote a dictionary in my life.'

Frankfurt boded so ill that Germaine refused to let Benjamin return to Paris, as had been originally planned. 'I am keeping him hidden in my hotel like a prisoner,' she wrote to Necker. Benjamin agreed to accompany her to her next destination—Weimar. Early in December they were on the road. The journey took them across the pine-clad, snow-covered mountains of Thuringia, through tiny, medieval towns huddled in the valleys, through Eisenach, Luther's birthplace, where they watched the young men singing Christmas carols under the frosted, yellow-glowing windows, their black cloaks sharply outlined against the snowy, deserted street. This was quite a different Germany from Philistine Frankfurt. Germaine was strangely moved by the indefinable poetic atmosphere—'that interior life, that poetry of the soul, which

---

[1] These quotations are taken from letters written in November and December 1803. Germaine's travel diary (a fragment from which the Comtesse de Pange has published in the *Nouvelle Revue Française* [October 1957]) confirms these impressions.

characterizes the German people'. At least, thus she recalled it in her book on Germany, but her letters show that Germaine was sensitive not only to the poetry of Germany. She wrote to Villers:

> May I, like a true Frenchwoman, after barely two days, describe my impressions of a country I do not know? I was at an inn, in a little town. In the small, smoke-filled room, where woollen clothing had been put to dry on an iron stove, I heard furious piano playing. This is the way everything appears to me: music in a smoke-filled room. Everywhere you find deep, poetic feeling, but no grace of outer forms. . . . There is a strange contradiction between the elevation of the Germans' thoughts and the vulgarity of their forms. One is almost tempted to believe that it is the vulgarity which is their true nature.

In her book on Germany all this was transmuted. Almost all Germans were musical, Germaine asserted. 'At times, entering a humble, smoke-blackened dwelling, I found not only the housewife but also her husband improvising on the spinet, just as Italians improvise poetry.' The contradiction was sacrificed for the sake of idealization.

Be this as it may, somewhere between Frankfurt and Gotha Germaine acquired a taste for German folk music in its most soulful and unsophisticated form: she bought a mouth organ and, during her two days' stay at Gotha, took lessons in playing that humble instrument. The image of Madame de Staël, stately in low-cut dress and turban-crowned, blowing upon a harmonica on her way to see Goethe and Schiller, is inexpressibly endearing. Small wonder that she surprised Weimar by her simplicity and naturalness.

'Intellect personified is being called to arms to receive me,' Germaine reported to her father on the day of her arrival at Weimar, December 13. 'I shall let you know my first impressions. At any rate, I am in a civilized place. I cannot help thinking so, since *Delphine* is known here to the entire reading public and I am told in wretched French: "*La Delphine est charmante*." '

She was, indeed, preceded by a tremendous reputation. Three different German translations of *Delphine* had sold out, and the press was issuing daily bulletins on her progress across Germany. The sleepy little capital of a pocket-sized duchy, happily complacent in its geographic and spiritual remoteness, Weimar looked forward to her arrival with nervous apprehension. The court and court society anticipated a bluestocking, a dangerous republican, an affected pedant who tried to seduce men by wit and erudition since she could not seduce them by beauty and feminine charm. Intellectual Weimar saw in her the representative of Parisian salon civilization who would force them to put away their spiritual working clothes and take their uncomfortable Sunday best out of mothballs. It was rumoured, moreover, that Bonaparte had exiled her for her intrigues. This earned Germaine little sympathy in the Germany of 1803. Germany despised French civilization, which Germaine represented, and fawned on French power, which Germaine defied.

It was not quite true that 'intellect personified had been called to arms' to receive her: intellect had either taken to its heels or gone to ground. Goethe, on a thin pretext, had left for Jena—not so much from fear of Germaine, whom he invited to join him there, as from fear of the social whirl her presence would stir up at Weimar. Schiller, who had barely one more year to live, was terrified at the prospect of having to interrupt the writing of *William Tell*; also his French was very poor. 'To expound our religion to her in French and to stand up to her volubility will be a hard task,' he wrote to Goethe, and it was only on the Duke's command that he undertook it. Herder was on his deathbed when Germaine arrived, and Goethe somewhat callously expressed his envy of such an easy escape. Karoline von Wolzogen, who was to introduce her into Weimar society, was away on a trip. Undismayed, Germaine undertook the conquest of the court.

She presented herself at the palace on December 14; she had barely appeared when all the court's apprehensions vanished. Duchess Louise, ordinarily of a chilly nature, voiced the surprised enthusiasm of the entire court when she described Germaine as 'unique in her kind', completely natural and unaffected, 'without the least trace of pedantry', and 'willing to speak with everybody about any subject he is interested in'. The surprise could not have been greater if the Queen of Sheba had suddenly evinced an interest in baby care. Germaine's politics, although a little too free for the Duke's taste, were far from Jacobin, and she was tactful enough to speak of Bonaparte with moderation. It was absolutely untrue that she spoke only to men; she was not a 'man-woman'; she was a good mother; and the rumours about her relationship with Monsieur Constant were malicious inventions.

The court's discovery that Germaine was one of theirs meant relief not only from apprehension but also from boredom. Duke Charles Augustus and his family had ambivalent feelings towards the intellectual giants with whom they had surrounded themselves. They felt a little uneasy, a little awed, at times a little annoyed, and not infrequently puzzled. If, in order to entertain Germaine, a Schiller or a Goethe had to be put to a little inconvenience, the Duke took an almost malicious pleasure in putting them to it. Schiller was summoned and appeared in full court uniform (Germaine mistook him for a general); Goethe, under pressure from both the Duke and Germaine, had to leave his Jena refuge; Professor Böttiger was commandeered to supply Germaine with a précis of German literature in French; balls, suppers, large parties, and intimate gatherings alternated with command performances at the theatre, put on specially for Germaine to acquaint her with German dramatic literature. When Schiller had finished *William Tell*, he had to read scenes from it. When Germaine wished to uphold the honours of French drama, all Weimar had to listen to her recite the fourth act of Racine's *Andromaque*, the dream of Athalie, and the principal scenes of *Phèdre*. Her greatest success was with the Duchess Dowager. Formed in the age of Voltaire, Anna Amalie delighted in Germaine's company, which seemed to bring back a gayer and more gracious past. Almost nightly she had Germaine and Benjamin to her private supper and to cards. Another warm admirer was the hereditary prince of Saxe-Gotha, who showered her with poems. The court's enthusiasm was duly taken up by all Weimar society: even Germaine's dresses, which the Parisians called ridiculous, enchanted the ladies of Weimar as being Parisian. As she put it, she was treated 'like a sister of the First Consul'.

To reap this kind of success had been Germaine's chief aim in coming to Germany. Through the newspapers and through her letters, it was sure to reach the First Consul's attention; and how could the First Consul persist in banishing from Paris a woman who was acclaimed abroad as the glory of French civilization? But this was not her only aim, especially in Weimar. 'I shall amuse you for some time to come with my reports on Germany,' she wrote a friend in Paris. 'Absolutely nothing is known about this country in France, and yet there is a gold-mine of ideas which a Frenchman might put to clever use.' By February she had begun to plan for a book on Germany. 'I regard this trip through Germany as a course in new ideas.' She made no secret of her notebook in which she recorded her conversations for future use.

But the conquest of intellectual Weimar was not so easy as that of the court. Germaine got along best with Wieland; something like a flirta-tion sprang up between her and the septuagenarian author of *Oberon*. But Wieland, a relic of the Voltairian age, was not representative of the Weimar of 1803. Between Germaine and the Weimar of Schiller and

K

Goethe there was a barrier which she could breach but never break down. Schiller complained:

> She wants to explain everything, apprehend everything, measure everything. Wherever her torch cannot penetrate, nothing exists as far as she is concerned. As a result, she has an unbelievable aversion for idealism, which in her opinion leads to mysticism and superstition. . . . For what you [Goethe] call poetry, she has no sense at all. Of such works she will appropriate only the generalizing, rhetorical, and passionate elements; however, she never esteems any false values and always recognizes true ones.

Thus, for Schiller, she represented 'French intellectual culture in its purity'—a vast over-simplification, just as her conception of Schiller as a pure Kantian idealist was an over-simplification.

What shocked both Schiller and Goethe was Germaine's belief that the ultimate problems formed a fit subject for social chatter. Wrote Goethe:

> To philosophize in a social setting means to indulge in lively conversation on insoluble problems. This was her true joy and passion. Quite naturally, she usually carried speech and repartee to matters of thought and feeling which by right should never be discussed except between the individual and his God. . . . Because of all this the evil genius in me was provoked, and whatever subject came up, I addressed myself to it in a spirit of contradiction, dealing with it dialectically and problematically. My obstinate contrariness often drove her to despair, but it was then that she was at her most amiable and that she displayed her mental and verbal agility most brilliantly.

Her first meeting with Goethe, on Christmas Eve, was a disappointment. Forgetting his age, she had expected to meet a Werther; instead, she faced 'a stocky man, with an undistinguished physiognomy, who likes to act like a man of the world but only half succeeds'. Also he slept with his housekeeper. In their subsequent three meetings they clashed. Germaine's notebook gave him an uneasy, exploited feeling. He resented her criticism of his plays; perhaps it had been reported to him that she had called his *Natural Daughter* 'a noble bore'. At any rate, after their meeting on January 2 he let it be known that he had a cold and could see nobody. Germaine, though she had planned to go to Berlin early in January, decided to outlast his cold.

Relations were resumed only three weeks later, and from then until the end of Germaine's stay they improved steadily. Their conversations took on the teasing tone which is possible only in a flirtatious friendship. 'At one time,' says a witness,

> Madame de Staël would make a pronouncement on art, and Goethe would be paralysed with shock; then Goethe would make a cutting remark on false sentimentality and the confounded moralizing intent that soiled the purity of art, and Madame de Staël would shake with indignation at such heresy. Attraction and repulsion alternated between them, and thus the conversational minuet continued along endless diverging lines until it ended with two deep bows.

Schiller was entirely correct in saying that Germaine had no sense whatever for poetry as he and Goethe understood it. Her translations from Goethe are conclusive proof: as if intentionally, they transform every concrete, intimate shading into a vast glittering generality. Whatever could be expressed only by indirection or symbol escaped her: everything had to be intellectually apprehended. Thus, even when she had mastered the German language, the essence of German poetry remained unknown territory. The same was true of German music. In her travel diary she admitted that the Germans had good instrumental music, but she found their interminable and complicated sonatas unbearably dull; only a nation as patient as the Germans could resign themselves to enduring them. In aesthetics Germaine was a Philistine: art was a social function. The ideas she found at Weimar were utterly strange to her; they were, indeed, revolutionary.

Where Germaine thought that the artist's function was to communicate with the public, Weimar held that art was autonomous, an aspect of Reality. In his sphere the artist's powers were limited only by his duty to his art. Whenever Germaine or Benjamin criticized some fault of taste in one of Goethe's plays, Goethe calmly replied, 'The public will get used to it.' When somebody mentioned the wave of suicides his *Werther* had precipitated, Goethe said, 'When I do something that suits me, the consequences are of no concern to me,' and went on to expound Schelling's ideas, that the secret of morality is to be at one with one's self.

Determined to get to the bottom of the new doctrine, Germaine began to take lessons from a young Englishman, Henry Crabb Robinson, a Schellingian disciple. (It was to him she remarked that 'whatever I don't understand is nothing'.) Robinson became a familiar at Countess von Werthern's haunted house, where Germaine was lodging. He taught Germaine philosophy in the morning, when 'she was sitting, most decorously, in her bed', and he often ate at her table, over which Benjamin presided paternally. An entry in Benjamin's diary, summing up Robinson's part in one of their conversations, provides the key to the new creed which neither Benjamin nor Germaine could understand: 'Art for art's sake, and without aim. Any aim denatures art. But art attains the aim it does not have.'

If Germaine refused to adopt the German metaphysical outlook, she nonetheless appreciated the immense fertility of Germany in utterly novel, revolutionary ideas. She was not so French as Schiller thought: she was tired of the stereotypes of French writers and thinkers; she sensed that the new German philosophy would dominate the century. Hence, when in France, she made it her responsibility to explain German philosophy in terms that Frenchmen could understand; when in Germany, she sought to moderate the undisciplined flights of metaphysics by opposing them with French clarity. As one of her Weimar admirers put it aptly, 'Since she understands what she is saying, she naturally wants to understand the person with whom she is talking just as completely, and for this purpose she makes use of a peculiar talent in being midwife to the birth of others' ideas.' If she had been content to watch the Germans thinking ineffable thoughts, she could not have made these thoughts intelligible either to herself or to her countrymen.

On March 1, after ten weeks of stimulating discourse on the ineffable, Germaine and her retinue left Weimar for Leipzig; from there she would go to Berlin, while Benjamin returned to Lausanne. Both had cause to be satisfied with their stay. 'It is not without sadness I am leaving Weimar,' Benjamin noted in his diary. 'I have studied there. I have lived in security. I have not suffered much. I ask no more of life.' The erudition of German scholars had impressed him immensely, and he threw himself into a titanic programme of studies preparatory to recasting his *History of Polytheism*. To resist the ferment, the creative outburst, of early Romantic Germany was impossible: everything had been assumed to be known; now, suddenly, it was discovered that everything remained to be discovered. It was as if a child had found all his familiar toys magically transformed into entirely new and strange ones, with infinite possibilities of blissful games no mortal before him had suspected. Benjamin and Germaine were too worldly-wise to be carried away by the Romantic intoxication, but it did stimulate their minds. A few drops of the magic potion, brought back to France as samples, would be enough to make all Frenchmen gape with astonishment.

Germaine had found what she had sought—acclaim and new ideas—but she was not happy. 'All this,' she wrote to Necker, 'gives me release from pain but no real pleasure. Pleasure would be love, or Paris, or power. I need one of these three things in order to exalt my heart, my mind, or my activity. All else gives me only metaphysical pleasure when available, or very real pain when missing. What do you think of this faithful portrait of my innermost me?'

With such preoccupations, the journey from Weimar to Leipzig, which to a Romantic would have been full of excitement and charm, was to Germaine merely a fatiguing displacement. The travellers halted as Naumburg, whose cathedral has some of the finest Gothic sculpture in Germany; they did not stop to inspect it. 'There are few remarkable buildings in Germany. For the most part, all one sees in northern countries is Gothic monuments,' she wrote in *De l'Allemagne*; as for sculpture, 'it has not been cultivated very successfully in Germany', the Germans lacking both marble and gracefulness. There was heavy snow, but the idea of being snowbound in Naumburg for even one day was intolerable. The party set out twice on March 2, once by carriage, once by sleigh; each time the snowstorm drove them back. On March 3, over atrocious roads, they doggedly drove on to Leipzig, which they reached at nine in the evening.

Two days were enough for Leipzig: a visit to the museum library, a tour of the booksellers, a few calls on university professors. The impending separation from Benjamin terrified Germaine; he was her last link with France, with Necker. A dread of solitude and of abandonment seized her. Benjamin, too, was overcome with affectionate emotion: he promised her never to marry another woman. Appeased, Germaine departed for Berlin on March 6. 'She has left,' reads Benjamin's diary entry for that day. 'There is no more kind, loving, intelligent, and devoted creature. And Albertine! . . . I am profoundly sad. Solitude is rather a disagreeable cold shower at first. But I am sure I shall get used to it.' On March 7 he offered himself a prostitute. On March 9 he began his journey to Lausanne by comfortable stages. He arrived on April 7. On April 11 he was back on the road to Germany; on April 22, having broken several carriages *en route*, he saw Germaine again at Weimar to bring her news: Necker was dead.

To come from Weimar to Berlin was like stepping from a cloister into a ballroom. Germaine had scarcely taken lodgings at the Hotel Stadt Paris when she was drawn into the dazzling and deafening finale of the social season, for which the birthday of Queen Louise of Prussia served as pretext. The newspapers made her visit a public event; the court of Weimar recommended her to the court of Berlin with unstinted enthusiasm; after a few days even the French ambassador, Laforest, received instructions to treat her with all the honours due to an important traveller.

Invited to the Queen's birthday ball on March 10, Germaine had a new dress made in twenty-four hours, spent three hours at her toilet, and, after being presented to the Queen Mother, took her place among the two thousand guests in the grand ballroom. The Queen, radiantly beautiful, made her entry amid a fanfare of trumpets and cymbals. 'I hope, Madame,' she said when Germaine was presented to her, 'you are aware that we have enough good taste to be flattered by your presence in Berlin. I have admired you for a long time, and I have been impatient to make your acquaintance.' Germaine quoted the exact words of the Queen to everyone she wrote to; the Berlin press quoted them too. What would Bonaparte say to that?

The King complimented her most graciously. Several of the royal princesses, whom she had met at Weimar, embraced and kissed her. At a costume ball given four days later in the Queen's honour, Germaine supped at Louise's table. 'Half Berlin paraded by me in order to contemplate me,' wrote Germaine; 'if celebrity is a pleasure, I have had my fill of it.' In the letter she wrote to Necker on the day of his fatal attack Germaine outlined the social programme of a typical week: Thursday, lunch with the French ambassador and dinner with Princess Henry of Prussia; Friday, dinner with the Princess of Orange; Saturday, lunch with the brother of the Duke of Brunswick and dinner with Princess Louise; Sunday, luncheon with Prince Belmonte, the Swiss historian Johann von Müller, the Swedish minister, and the Russian ambassador, and dinner at the Spanish embassy. 'This will give you an idea how time rushes by, painlessly, joylessly, without either thought or boredom. . . . But I would just as lief spend my life moving from place to place as spend all my time dressing, drinking, eating, playing cards, and watching Müller, Prince Louis, and the Duke of Öls getting drunk every night. Ah, poor France, poor beloved France!' 'Society in the large cities of Germany imitates Paris, and Paris in German loses a great deal in the translation,' she wrote to Joseph Bonaparte. The name of her hotel, Stadt Paris, was symbolic.

Germaine did not like Berlin. 'The two classes of society—the scholars and the courtiers—are completely divorced from each other,' she wrote to Madame Necker de Saussure. 'As a result, the scholars do not cultivate conversation, and mundane society is absolutely incapable of thought.' To Jacobi she expressed this even more forcefully, almost prophetically: 'The thinkers are soaring in the empyrean, and on earth you find only grenadiers.' The thinkers themselves, she noted elsewhere, accepted this social rigidity without questioning: in the ideal world they were carrying out a revolution bloodier than that of France, and nothing was safe from their attacks; on earth they bowed to rank, title, and authority.

Germaine's relations with the Prussian court cooled a little after the first honeymoon. It was bad enough that, at a children's ball, Albertine had slapped the Crown Prince and called him a snotty brat (exactly what one might expect from a republican education, the royal parents remarked), but Germaine's apologies were accepted and Albertine was released from room arrest upon the intercession of Frederick William III. A more serious matter was the news of the kidnapping and murder of the Duc d'Enghien on Bonaparte's orders. The incident placed Germaine in a difficult position. Her anti-Bonapartist sentiments were a matter of public knowledge, but so was her republicanism. The Prussian court, on the other hand, was torn between fear of Bonaparte and indignation, not so much at the crime itself, as at its having been perpetrated by an upstart on a person of royal blood. While Prussia clung to its neutrality, anti-French and reactionary sentiments were vented with impotent rage. Germaine was neither anti-French nor reactionary; moreover, she was tactless enough to blame Bonaparte's despotism on those Frenchmen and those European powers who accepted it supinely. This, however, she did only privately. Officially she avoided anything that might compromise her claim to French citizenship or prolong her exile. In the circumstances she naturally enough thought of shortening her stay in Berlin. First, however, she had to terminate a very delicate negotiation.

It seems paradoxical that German Romanticism, a movement which extolled medieval Catholicism and chivalry, the childlike and folklike poetry of the German soul, the dark and mysterious forces symbolized in the German forests, should have its headquarters in Berlin, the most prosaic, modern, secular, and Frenchified of all German cities, and that its founders should congregate in the salons of people named Levin, Herz, and Mendelssohn. But the paradox is merely apparent, for the German Romantics were sophisticated, city-dwelling intellectuals reacting against themselves.

In Weimar Germaine had found little sympathy with the new movement. Goethe was still flirting with it; the incense the young Romantics
burned to him did not displease his Olympian nostrils, and their ideas
could be poetically utilized; but to the rest of Weimar the Berlin school
was anathema. To Germaine, its Catholic, mystical, and authoritarian
tendencies were repulsive, but its idealistic enthusiasm attracted her.
To study the movement, Berlin was a better place than Weimar.

The time she chose to visit Berlin was unfortunate. Novalis was
dead; Tieck was absent; Brentano, Arnim, Hoffmann had not yet
arrived; Kleist was there but unknown; Schelling was teaching at
Würzburg, Schleiermacher at Halle, Hegel at Jena. Of the two chief
hostesses of early Romanticism, one—Henrietta Herz—had closed her
salon because of her husband's death, and the other—Rahel Levin—
had not yet reached her zenith. Germaine did meet Rahel at the house
of the Swedish minister, Baron Brinckmann, was very much taken by
her, and flattered herself that the sympathy was mutual. 'Poor woman,'
wrote Rahel after their first meeting, 'she has seen nothing, heard
nothing, understood nothing.'

At Brinckmann's house, Germaine also met Fichte, notoriously the
least comprehensible of all German philosophers. He had scarcely been
introduced when she invited him to explain his Absolute Ego (*Ich-Ich*),
'as briefly as possible, in a quarter of an hour for instance'. Fichte
swallowed, spoke for a few minutes, then was interrupted by Germaine.
'Oh, that will do, Monsieur Fisht,' she remarked with a charming
smile; 'I understand you completely. Your system may be illustrated
admirably by one of the tales of Baron Munchausen.' While Fichte
looked thunderstruck and the guests studied their shoes, she explained
how Baron Munchausen, having come upon a large river, had managed
to cross it by firmly taking hold with his right hand of his left sleeve
and swinging himself to the other shore. 'This, if I understand you
correctly, Monsieur Fisht, is exactly what you have done with your I.'

No doubt Fichte believed, like Rahel Levin, that the poor woman
was a fool and had understood nothing. The truth is that she had
understood more than most.

> For Fichte [she wrote to Jacobi] the very word *man* is an erroneous
> concept, and all words in general appear to him much too material for
> his ethereal metaphysics. I must admit that so far I am keeping to Kant,
> and that I find in him a felicitous synthesis of realism and idealism—a
> synthesis which unites in itself the freedom of the individual and the ties
> of the community.

In other words, Germaine stuck to the Enlightenment.

The one man in Berlin who was best equipped to introduce Germaine to the ideas of the 'new school' was its foremost spokesman and critic, August Wilhelm Schlegel. Schiller had winced at the very mention of his name; Wieland, when she wrote to him from Berlin that Schlegel was not half bad, begged her never to mention him again; but Goethe had given her a letter of introduction to Schlegel on the day she left Weimar. She had been in Berlin for two weeks when the fateful meeting took place. On March 23 she wrote to her father:

> I have met here a man who in literary matters is better informed and more ingenious than almost any other person I know: it is Schlegel. Benjamin will tell you that he enjoys a high reputation in Germany, but what Benjamin does not know is that he speaks French like a Frenchman and English like an Englishman, and that he has read everything in the world, although he is only thirty-six. I do whatever I can to persuade him to come with me. He would not be the tutor of my children [Germaine was desperately looking for one], he is too distinguished for that, but he could give lessons to Albert during the months Albert spends at Coppet, and I too would benefit a good deal from his presence for the book I am planning.

Born at Hanover in 1767, August Wilhelm Schlegel was, like so many German men of letters, the son of a pastor. He matriculated at Göttingen as a student of theology but soon changed to the study of ancient languages. To supplement his allowance, he took up tutoring, first at Göttingen, then—from 1790 to 1795—at Amsterdam. Although his position in Holland appears to have been far from brilliant, he succeeded during these years in acquiring some literary distinction as a critic and translator, and when he returned to Germany Schiller invited him to come to Jena and to collaborate on his periodical, *Die Horen*.

While at Göttingen, Schlegel had met Caroline Böhmer, the widowed daughter of a university professor. He was twenty-three, she twenty-seven. Schlegel fell in love and offered marriage, but Caroline had had enough of marriage. Instead, she went to Mainz with a friend. When the Prussians recaptured Mainz from the French, Caroline was gaoled because of her close association with the pro-Jacobin Georg Forster, her friend's husband. Worse, she was pregnant—by whom, no one knows. Her family got her out of gaol and housed her near Leipzig, where she gave clandestine birth to her child. August Wilhelm's younger brother, Friedrich, met her there and promptly fell in love. At about

K*

the same time August Wilhelm, back from Holland, met his old love
again, proposed again, and was accepted.

August Wilhelm came to Jena with his wife, his wife's daughter by
her first marriage, Augusta Böhmer, and his brother Friedrich, still
burning with love. Almost as soon as his association with Schiller began,
the two men were quarrelling. Schiller had a low regard for Schlegel's
character, detested his theories, and could not put up with his arrogance. The quarrels soon led to a complete break. By then, however,
the Schlegel household had become the gathering place of a younger
generation of writers—Schelling, Novalis, Tieck—the brotherhood of
the early Romantics and as brilliant a constellation of talents as ever
united into a literary clique. Having left *Die Horen*, the Schlegels
succeeded in realizing a long-standing dream: they founded a periodical
of their own, *Das Athenäum*, in 1798. The influence of this short-lived
magazine cannot be overestimated. Every literary theory since its time
may, at least partly, be traced to its seminal ideas.

Meanwhile Friedrich's love for Caroline had, if anything, become
more passionate. Since all three lived together in the same house, and
since outpourings of the heart were *de rigueur* among the Romantic
brotherhood, the emotional climate of the household was delicate and
intense. Finally, in his novel *Lucinde*, published in 1800, Friedrich
boldly proclaimed his passion to the world at large. The novel, one of
the first to glorify the cult of experience, created something of a scandal.
It was, after all, even though very deep, a little naughty. As far as
Friedrich was concerned, however, it helped him to transcend his
experience by means of romantic irony (which he invented), and freed
him to fall in love with Brendel Veit, the wife of a Jewish friend and
the daughter of no less a personage than Moses Mendelssohn. Brendel
left Veit, and went to live with Friedrich; in 1804 in Paris, she was
baptized, christened Dorothea, and married him. The minister performing the double ceremony was, by a curious coincidence, the same
Gambs, pastor of the Swedish embassy chapel, who had married Germaine and Baron de Staël in 1786 and who had hidden Germaine's
lover Narbonne under his altar in 1792. It was, indeed, a small world.

Friedrich having paired off with Brendel, Caroline was left, as it were,
empty-handed. Fortunately, at this point, Schelling stepped into the
breach. Indeed, it was August Wilhelm's fate to need reinforcement by
other men in his relationship with women. He loved women, but
apparently there was something lacking in his love that his friends felt
they could supply. Thus Schelling took Friedrich's place, and things

would have continued as before but for the sudden death of Caroline's daughter. August Wilhelm was deeply attached to the child; her portrait never left him through the rest of his life, and her death seemed to symbolize to him all unfulfilled promise—not only the child's but his own, and that of life, as well. Caroline was more easily consoled. 'I doubt,' wrote Novalis, 'that she will take it as she ought to: frivolity is an immortal child.' The death of the mortal child broke up the romantic fraternity, which had devoted something of a cult to Augusta. One month after she was buried the last issue of the *Athenäum* came out. Novalis died in 1801. In the same year August Wilhelm and Caroline separated, and August Wilhelm went to Berlin to lecture on literature. Their divorce became final in May 1803. One month later Caroline married Schelling. August Wilhelm's love life remained, so to speak, *en famille*: in Berlin he began his liaison with Sophie Bernhardi, the sister of his friend and protégé Tieck.

Schlegel's exodus from Jena caused little regret in the duchy of Saxe-Weimar. As vain and quarrelsome as he was learned and intelligent, he lacked the redeeming features of his confrères in the Romantic coterie: he wanted the poetic, creative genius and depth of Novalis or Schelling, the fantastic wit of Tieck or Brentano, the originality of his brother Friedrich. Every school needs its pedants, and A. W. Schlegel was the pedant of Romanticism. In one respect, however, his literary virtuosity stands unrivalled: by 1804, when Germaine met him, he had already translated sixteen of Shakespeare's plays; through him Shakespeare was naturalized in Germany and became, in a sense, part of the German literary heritage, just as the Authorized Version of the Bible became the literary heritage of the English-speaking world. This was one of the most remarkable accomplishments of the nineteenth century. Germans have been known to prefer Schlegel's Shakespeare to Shakespeare's. To those who prefer the English version, Schlegel's versification may sound a little too smooth, too elegant—Heine said it made him think of whipped cream—a little too precise and well tailored, like Schlegel's own impeccable wardrobe. There was something mincing, something too self-satisfied, something too flexible about the man.

As a guide and interpreter through the Romantic mazes, Schlegel could not be surpassed. His mind was logical, lucid, precise: Germaine could understand him. Still, her enchantment was not unmixed with criticism. 'I am increasingly enchanted by Schlegel,' she wrote to Necker, 'and I have decided to bring him to you. . . . It must be admitted, though, that his intelligence is purely bookish; as for the rest, I regard him as a stranger. . . . He is thirty-six; he is small and rather ugly, but he has very expressive eyes.'

To tear Schlegel away from Berlin, from a brilliant career, from Sophie Bernhardi, was a delicate matter. It seemed odd for a person of his prominence to take the position of private tutor, even if Germaine offered him social equality, a light teaching schedule, a yearly salary of 12,000 francs, and, after a certain number of years, a life annuity. Schlegel hesitated. He was famous, but he was poor. He had no fixed position. Madame de Staël would introduce him into the most exalted spheres of the European *élite*. This might be better than giving lectures in Berlin. To seize the opportunity of converting Germaine to Romanticism and German culture was almost a patriotic duty. What was more, her easy familiarity, her flirtatious philosophizing, and her magnetic charm combined in seducing him. If one is to believe his later recriminating letters, she encouraged him to fall in love with her and concealed her relationship with Benjamin. Nothing but extraordinary conceit could have given him such a notion, but that he fell in love there is no doubt.

Schlegel's hesitations were cut short dramatically. On April 18, at the house of Princess Radziwill, where she spent much of her time, Germaine received a message requesting her immediate return to Coppet; Monsieur Necker was gravely ill. 'He is dead!' cried Germaine. She drove home, packed her trunks, and dashed off a note to Schlegel: she would call for him the next morning, in her carriage. When she called at 9 a.m., Schlegel was ready for the trip. Thus, on the impulse of a moment, the rest of his life was decided. 'You were unhappy,' he wrote to her later, 'and everything was decided in an instant.'

Necker became delirious on April 8. The thought that he might die before Germaine's return terrified him. 'Give me only six more days,' he begged his doctor. He died the next day. Benjamin, barely arrived at Lausanne, sped to Coppet. 'He is dead!' he wrote in his diary. 'What will become of her? . . . Poor wretch! To die would be better than what she will suffer. And he himself, I regret him. He was so good, so pure, so noble. He loved me. Who will now guide the existence of his daughter?' He read Germaine's letters to her father, which had come too late. 'She is gay and calm—and in one week—! Poor Minette, how she will be punished for lacking the strength to do her strict duty! . . . Nothing counts in life but to do one's duty.'

Benjamin did his duty. On April 21, after a week on the road, he was waiting for Germaine at Weimar. The news of Necker's death had been kept from her until he could break it. But Benjamin could not bear to inflict suffering: he arranged with one of the ladies of the ducal court to perform that task.

Germaine arrived at Weimar the following day. Schlegel was present at the terrible scene, which he described in a letter:

> She fell to the ground with a piercing scream; they had to hold her arms tightly to prevent violent movements; she continued screaming as if she had lost her reason. It was almost impossible to give her any sedative, because she pushed everything away from her. . . . With a great deal of effort she was at last carried to bed. . . . We had arrived at half past four, and only at nine o'clock she calmed down a little. . . . Until then she never ceased reproaching herself bitterly for her journey and her absence. At night, she lapsed into exhaustion. Constant, tired by his journey, was persuaded to go to bed, and I kept vigil. She was incapable of closing her eyes for a few seconds without starting up convulsively. Only at dawn did she sleep for a quarter of an hour.

Germaine's room was filled with visitors bringing their trivial condolences. 'He was not my father,' cried Germaine to one of them. 'He was my brother, my child, my husband, my All!' The commonplaces nevertheless seemed to produce a good effect on her, Benjamin noted; but she had not yet apprehended the reality of her loss.

She stayed at Weimar nine days, to regain strength for the rest of the journey. The Duke and Goethe called on her on April 25. 'The Duke,' says Benjamin, 'was touched to tears by her grief; and he is one of those people who are said to be hard-hearted.' Benjamin, while still carried away by compassion, was beginning to recover his critical faculties:

> Minette is reproaching herself bitterly for the past, and I cannot deny that in part these reproaches are well-deserved. Perhaps I would be less severe if I did not see clearly that this terrible crisis will change nothing in her character. She does not make the least application of her remorse to the future. . . . Her remorse will be sterile. At least, I shall have done my duty.

On the following day, April 26, he made a shocking discovery: 'I believe that Minette feels attracted to Schlegel. Attracted! At this moment! She has sent me away to be alone with him this evening. She did so with some embarrassment, but she could not deny herself.' By April 28 Minette and Benjamin had started quarrelling again, and Benjamin was back at his indecisions: within a year, he noted on May 1, he either would marry Biondetta or leave her. On May 2, at an inn at Schmalkalden, he confirmed this resolution: 'My decision is irrevocable. It must be all the more irrevocable since Biondetta is deceiving me. At the moment of my writing, in the room next to this one, where she thinks I am in bed, she is talking with Schlegel, whom she pretended to dismiss for the night.'

On May 5 the party arrived at Würzburg. 'Seen the palace of Würzburg,' says Benjamin's diary. 'Vast, beautiful, in the worst possible taste.' So much for the glories of German Baroque. With Schlegel he went to see the other glory of Würzburg, Schelling. 'Never did a man produce a more disagreeable impression on me.' All the same, Benjamin and Schlegel stayed up talking until one in the morning with Schelling and Schlegel's former wife, now Frau Schelling—a bizarre encounter, to use Benjamin's favourite adjective.

The dreary journey continued the next morning. To distract Germaine, Benjamin and Schlegel engaged her in conversation and read aloud. Half of Benjamin's time was spent in playing with Albertine. On May 7 their efforts to distract Germaine were successful: everybody began to quarrel. 'For the second time I have noticed,' says Benjamin, 'that Schlegel's theories have become so personal a matter with him that when he is attacked he suffers physically. As he was talking of Cervantes, he became pale and his eyes filled with tears. . . . Dispute between Minette and him on the subject of jesting. She does not realize that to attack a man for his manner of jesting is to attack his vanity at its most ticklish point.' Thus in the carriage rolling from Blaufelden to Aalen, the Coppet atmosphere of the next few years was prefigured.

At Zurich the travellers were joined by the Necker de Saussures. At Berne Benjamin managed to find a brothel. On the road between Berne and Payerne Schlegel and Benjamin quarrelled about religion. Between Payerne and Morges Benjamin came to reflect that Schelling's system threw an interesting light on certain puzzling aspects of fetishism. On May 19 the travellers were approaching Coppet.

It was early morning. Germaine was silent along the whole way. At Nyon she became convulsive. The driver could not go fast enough. Every few seconds she looked out of the window, until, despite her protests, her companions lowered the shades. The carriage, without slowing down, sped through the little town, where a crowd had collected to watch her arrival, then thundered over the cobblestones of the courtyard and came to a stop. 'She did not descend, she fell out of the carriage,' writes Schlegel, 'and never in my life have I heard a more piercing scream than when she was carried, half unconscious, by her servants into the house.'

The crisis lasted for several hours. Then she asked for Necker's papers and manuscripts and began to read.

14

THE ISLE OF CALYPSO

I counted on him to make good my mistakes. Nothing seemed beyond remedy as long as he lived: only since his death have I known what real terror is; only then did I lose the confidence of youth, which relies on its own strength to attain all its desires. In his strength I found my strength; in his support, my confidence. Where is he now, my protecting genius? . . . Will he guide my steps? Will he spread his wings over my children, whom he blessed with his dying voice? And can I gather up enough of him in my heart to consult him still and listen to his voice? . . . . . . And yet I exist. . . . Pain gives forth only more pain; time does not stop mid-way; and life, barer from day to day, returns, such as it is, each morning.

GERMAINE had turned thirty-eight when her father's death cut her adrift. For twenty years the thought of losing him had obsessed her; every death was *his* death; yet she was utterly unprepared for the actual event.

It is tragic to have to face life for the first time after having lived so much.

'I counted on him. . . . Nothing seemed beyond remedy as long as he lived'—thus, in the long, pathetic lament that concludes her essay on *Monsieur Necker's Character and Private Life*, did she candidly admit that she had been irresponsible for thirty-eight years. There could be no danger so long as he was with her, no guilt so long as he forgave her, no loss of youth so long as she was his child. Now there was terror, and also guilt. She had had premonitions, and had not heeded them. While the helpless old man was struggling with death to give her time to return, she was dancing in Berlin. The spectacular violence of her first reaction on learning his death was an explosion of guilt feeling: to have failed one's father, brother, husband, child, and All at the most decisive moment, a moment anticipated for twenty years, is enough to crush the most robust of consciences. It did not, however, crush Germaine's: from his grave, the Guardian Angel forgave her.

Her first activity at Coppet was to read her father's last manuscripts and letters. 'My child,' Necker had written, just before his stroke, 'enjoy all the pleasure you can find in the society of Berlin and do not worry, for I have not felt in such good health for a long time.' 'He blessed my three children,' writes Germaine; 'he also blessed his daughter. Placing his hand on his heart, he repeated several times . . .: "She has loved me much." Oh yes, no doubt she has loved him much!' Her conscience was appeased—not completely, to be sure, but enough for her to resume functioning. Much had been forgiven her because she had loved much.

Reading and sorting her father's papers was her chief occupation throughout the summer of 1804. Even her mourning required activity: she arranged a collection from Necker's unpublished writings, prefaced it with her essay on her father's private life, and had the volume published in Geneva. The eulogy, despite its extravagant estimate of Monsieur Necker (she placed him beside Voltaire as a writer), is a moving document, moving especially in its final pages, where the pathetic outcry of the heart pierces through the fatuous Neckerian self-righteousness. Yet even in grief, pride was not forgotten:

> If anyone should take pleasure in the observation that 'we are a family who praise one another', let him say so gaily in the presence of death. Yes, we have loved one another; we have felt the need to say so; and, feeling that it was below our dignity to defend ourselves against the attacks of our enemies or to make use of our talents against them, we have faced them with a steadfast sentiment of elevation and pride, of which I alone remain the grieving but faithful trustee.

Alas, the Neckers had not merely loved and praised one another; in their collective pride they had raised themselves, in their own eyes, above human criticism. Necker's death confirmed rather than shook Germaine in that self-exaltation. Benjamin had been right: her character was unchanged; her remorse had no 'application to the future'. Several of her biographers have seen in Necker's death a turning point in her life, an awakening to a sense of duty and the beginning of a religious conversion. It was nothing of the sort. In one respect only was the event a turning point: Germaine accepted her father's fortune and estate as 'a sacred trust' and managed it with a prudence one might not have expected of her. Amid the most tempestuous passions of her soul there never ceased to be a pool of calmness in which she conducted her business transactions. She was by no means avaricious; all testify to her generosity. Her way of life was lavish, though not extravagant, but her personal needs were simple, and she never lost count of a penny. Her children probably inherited more than Necker had left her.[1]

Except for her American investments, which had to be sold at a loss by her heirs when it turned out that upper New York State would not be the goal of millions of pioneers, Germaine's investments appear to have been exceedingly cautious: mostly real estate in France and Switzerland and government bonds. Only the New World seems to have tempted her to speculation, and she had reason to trust her American advisers—Gouverneur Morris; the bank of LeRoy, Bayard, and McEvers in New York; James LeRay de Chaumont, one of the principal developers of upper New York State; and her agent, Judge Cooper, father of James Fenimore. That she did not hesitate to place even American real estate speculation on an exalted level may be seen from one of her letters to Judge Cooper. 'I am sure,' she wrote to him in English in 1804, 'that you will not consider this transaction as a mere affair of interest, but that you will take pleasure in increasing the fortune of a mother of three children and a daughter of M. Necker.' A similar sentiment is expressed in the words she wrote on the first page of an account book in 1804: 'I pray that by the grace of God I may piously transmit to my children the fortune left me by my adored father. I regard it as a trust. I do not want the fruit of such a man's labours to be destroyed.'

Along with financial responsibility, Germaine accepted responsibility for her children's education and careers. Her intentions were no doubt excellent, and she spared no effort, but they were offset by the manner in which she chose to manage her own life. There was a clash of duties —the duty she owed her children and the duty she felt she owed herself. The latter duty was the same as it had always been: 'to keep up the

---

[1] In the absence of a documented account of the Necker fortune, its amount may only be guessed at. In 1808 Madame de Staël declared that she had a yearly income of 120,000 francs and owed not a penny. Estimating 5 per cent as a conservative yield of the period, this would mean a fortune of about 2,400,000 francs—not a huge fortune, but a considerable one in that period. To this should be added the 2,000,000 francs owed her by the French government, which were repaid to her (without interest) in 1816; at least 80,000 francs owed her by Benjamin (never repaid); and vast holdings in St. Lawrence County in upper New York State, which at her death amounted to 35,000 acres but which yielded as good as no returns, having been acquired for speculation. She gave her daughter a dowry of 2,000,000 French francs in 1816 and left 408,000 Swiss francs in specie to her youngest child alone.

character of one's life,' as she put it once; to confront the world with a 'steadfast sentiment of elevation and pride'. In politics as in love, this pride was to lead to catastrophic results, for which each of her children paid dearly.

Thus, Necker's death was decisive in Germaine's life, not because it changed her characteristics but because it intensified them. Her restlessness no longer found temporary appeasement; her pursuit of love became a panic race; her horror of ennui was no longer checked by the obligation to spend several months a year in relative inactivity by her father's side. All her life she had evaded the thought of living without him. She had hoped to die before him, or assumed that she would not survive him but die of grief, kill herself, go mad. Yet she did none of these things. As she remarked with surprise, she existed. Time had not stopped mid-way. Like the trees in the park of Coppet, which she could see as she wrote those words on an October day, life became barer from day to day, and before her there stretched an opaque fog of immense boredom. All summer and autumn she had been able to combine her need for activity with the need to prolong Necker's life in the act of writing it. This done, only one more evasion remained: to camouflage not only life but death itself. 'She was bored by her own grief,' Benjamin once observed cruelly.

She felt 'more lacerated' every day, she complained to her friends; her health was ruined; she trembled like an old woman; life had become indifferent to her. At the same time, she inquired if it was true that Napoleon would grant a general amnesty on his coronation, and whether exiles would be comprised in it. She went further, asking her intermediaries to convince the government of her hostility to the Bourbons and her loyalty to the Bonapartes. 'I pronounce myself in favour of the present dynasty,' she grandly informed Hochet. While waiting for a pardon, which would allow her to return to Paris, she postponed her projected trip to Italy from month to month. Joseph had promised her to do what he could: 'If I do not succeed, nobody will.' All he obtained from his brother was the assurance that Madame de Staël could go to Italy with a French passport and under the full protection of the French government. In the first week of December, while Paris was celebrating Napoleon's coronation, Germaine resignedly took the road to Italy.

Even in the summer of 1804 life at Coppet was by no means subdued and withdrawn. Ten days after her arrival Benjamin already complained to his diary of the 'continual company and the perpetual distraction'. For the following six years, whenever the chatelaine was in residence, there never was, to put it mildly, a quiet moment.

The years 1804–10 were the 'great days' of Coppet. 'Her house at Coppet,' Napoleon declared on Saint Helena, 'became a veritable arsenal against me. One went there to win one's spurs.' This was true, but Coppet was more than a centre of political intrigue and opposition. It was a literary and dramatic workshop, a permanent seminar and debating club, a laboratory of ideas, and a Circean menagerie. Like a capricious and tyrannical fairy queen, Germaine held sway over the most ill-assorted crowd of admirers, lovers, friends, and slaves ever assembled in a castle. Under the majestic and eternal calm of the Alps they argued, quarrelled, loved, hated, wrote, acted plays, organized feasts and parties, rebelled, submitted, intrigued, and agitated themselves in an unceasing dance of grand and petty passions. Each guest-room concealed its own drama; but through the pattern of secret jealousies and frustrations, of confidences made to diaries and letters, of furtive exchanges and explanations, there broke at times the naked violence of tragedy in the grand style, with Germaine as its heroine and with an unusually large cast of principals.

The souvenirs and memoirs of Coppet left by its guests give the impression that life at the castle was a continuous, brilliant feast. Naturally, the guests assumed that during their absence things at Coppet continued the same as during their stay. The impression is mistaken. Roughly, out of the seventy-eight months from May 1804 to October 1810, Germaine spent only about forty-five months in Switzerland. Of these forty-five months, she spent at least half not at Coppet but in Geneva (which then, of course, was in France), and even while residing at Coppet she interrupted her stay by numerous trips to Geneva and Lausanne. She travelled in Italy from December 1804 to June 1805; spent the year from April 1806 to April 1807 in France; travelled in Germany and Austria from December 1807 to June 1808; made a foray to Lyons in June 1809; and transplanted her court to Chaumont and Blois from April to October 1810. What characterized these years, then, was not Coppet but the restless straying from it; and what characterized Coppet while she was there was her desperate effort to forget that she was there.

Life at the castle was played in grand style. The kitchen personnel alone, according to the testimony of the laundry woman, amounted to at least fifteen servants. During the summer season the table was laid for thirty guests every day. The leftovers were sufficient to feed the poor of the neighbourhood, many of whom came regularly. 'Madame de Staël often asked for their news,' recalled the laundry woman. 'She was well loved by them and liked to talk with them when she met them.'

Except for the meal hours nothing had a settled routine. The life of the guests was strangely informal and erratic. Nobody knew where to find anybody, says one of the guests, the Comtesse de Boigne, and there was no fixed place for anything. All the doors to all the rooms were continually open: one wandered about the house, and 'wherever a conversation developed, one set up camp and stayed for hours or for days, without being interrupted by any of the normal routines of life. Talking seemed to be everybody's chief business. . . . Madame de Staël worked a great deal, but only when she had nothing better to do; the most trifling social amusement always had priority.'

Madame de Boigne might have said 'talking and writing'. People wrote books at Coppet who had never written before. One read one's writings to one another or in company; one praised, one criticized, one argued.

Breakfast was between ten and eleven. Then the guests were left to their own devices, while Germaine devoted herself to her business correspondence, her accounts, the administration of her estate, and, if there was time, to reading or writing. To her guests it seemed that she was doing nothing, for she was able to busy herself with several matters at a time, and interruptions, which were continuous, did not set her back. She took notes while riding in her carriage, kept up running conversations while dictating letters, and worked at her books no matter where she happened to be or what was going on. Even to those closest to her it was a mystery how she could write so much when there seemed to be no time for writing. The secret was not in any special organization of time; rather, it was in absolute lack of organization. Most men expend the larger part of their time on trying to concentrate and on resting from the effort; between preparation and relaxation there is hardly time left for action. Madame de Staël, always concentrated, never at rest, was endowed with a brain that could, in an instant, adjust itself to whatever demanded her attention.

Dinner was served about five and was followed, sometimes by a walk in the park or an evening drive, more often by music, conversation, and games. At eleven supper was served, but conversation often continued until the morning hours, at least for Germaine and her intimate circle. Like all insomniacs, she resented fatigue in others as a manifestation of disaffection. Sleep came only with opium.[1]

Apart from conversation, Germaine's favourite pastime was to act. A small but quite professional stage was installed in the 'gallery' on the ground floor (since then transformed into a library), and great care was lavished on the wings, the backdrops, the costumes, and the properties. The actors were amateurs and of uneven quality, but the audience, who flocked to Coppet from as far as Geneva, Lausanne, and Berne, were conscious of the privilege of seeing a cast comprising Madame de Staël, Madame Récamier, Benjamin Constant, and August Wilhelm Schlegel. The theatre of Coppet had its heyday from 1807 to 1809. Apart from Voltaire and Racine, the theatre offered some novelties. Zacharias Werner's *Der vierundzwanzigste Februar*, a brooding tragedy of fate, had its first performance at Coppet, in German, in October 1809. A monstrously long comedy by Elzéar de Sabran, one of the regular guests, was performed in 1807. 'Madame Récamier played in it, and she was beautiful, as beautiful as can be,' wrote one of the spectators. 'Nevertheless . . . it was a relief to see the curtain fall, especially for those who had been standing from 3.30 until 10.30.' Indeed, Sabran's comedy had been preceded by a play written by Madame de Staël, *Geneviève de Brabant*, in which she appeared with her three children. For the same cast, plus an angel impersonated by Juliette Récamier, she had written the drama *Hagar in the Desert*. The angel helped a great deal in its success. In another Biblical drama written by her, *La Sunamite*, Benjamin held the role of Eleazer, Albertine of the young Shulamite, and Germaine of her mother. The heroines of the three plays, needless to say, were the projections of Madame de Staël, but the high point of self-dramatization was reached at the celebrated performance of *Andromaque*, on August 22, 1807, when Benjamin played Pyrrhus to Germaine's Hermione.[2]

The dramatic performances kept the guests occupied. In addition to conversing, quarrelling, making love, and writing, they could be seen wandering all over the estate, learning their lines by heart. Besides giving them something to do, the pastime had the advantage of forcing

[1] Taking opium or opium derivatives was a widespread habit in an age when sedatives, barbiturates, and pain-killers were unknown. Madame de Staël took opium as one takes sleeping pills. It is true that the habit undermined her health; at times of stress, when she increased her doses, it often stupefied her for days.

[2] This performance did not take place at Coppet but at a place Germaine temporarily occupied at Ouchy, near Lausanne. It was repeated at Coppet on September 19. See Chapter 16.

them to stay for protracted periods. One day Guizot, then still a youth, called on Germaine while passing through, and read aloud Chateaubriand's daring article in the *Mercure* of July 4, 1807, attacking Napoleon in barely disguised terms; Guizot declaimed the rolling periods with such magnificent emphasis that Germaine, placing her hand on his arm, interrupted him to exclaim, 'Do stay with us, Monsieur Guizot. I have a part for you in *Andromaque*!' Unfortunately, Guizot excused himself; others were less cautious.

Germaine's talents as an actress have been judged diversely. In her declamation she tended to overstress the caesura and to drop her voice at the end of each alexandrine—surely grievous defects—and in the passionate passages she forced her voice beyond its means. On the other hand, in those roles with which she could identify herself completely—the great Racinian tragic roles—she was unsurpassable. 'Her principal talent,' said one spectator, 'is to play everything with her soul, and often she sweeps you along with her, especially in the jealousy scene [of *Phèdre*].' After the performance of *Andromaque*, Rosalie de Constant wrote, 'Never was the role of Hermione played with more fury or truth.'

The cast of the larger drama at Coppet was very diverse and requires some classification. The barony united the qualities of a feudal manor, an aristocratic salon, a bohemian summer colony, a grand hotel, a family seat, and the Isle of Calypso; in each of these aspects it had its distinct cast. The permanent residents and dependants—servants, tenants, and local tradespeople—formed a sort of rustic chorus in the background. When Germaine arrived from a journey, she was welcomed by a band concert in the park; on Sundays she attended, according to local tradition, the ancient Gothic church of Coppet; afternoon snacks for the Coppetans and their children were a regular custom; the sick and poor of the neighbourhood depended on her charities. Germaine was very much the chatelaine, even if her writings and published correspondence ignore that aspect of her life. The château itself employed a huge staff—some of them no doubt only seasonally. They were ruled by Germaine's factotum, Joseph Uginet, familiarly known as Eugène. Uginet, who spent his last years as superintendent of the Tuileries palace, enjoyed Germaine's complete trust and was employed at times on the most delicate missions, which took him to Paris for months at a time. He was her business agent, diplomatic courier, liaison officer, and even, on at least one memorable occasion, when he tried to bring the reluctant Benjamin back to Coppet, truant officer. Eugène is mentioned in thousands of letters to and from Madame de Staël, but his personality remains elusive.

Visitors fell into three groups—local callers, who might come only for a few hours as dinner guests or as spectators at the theatrical performances; transient guests from all corners of Europe and even from America, who might stay from several days to several weeks; and the permanent family in the larger meaning of the word: Germaine, her children, their tutors, Benjamin, and a handful of loyal satellites. The local callers comprised members of the neighbouring gentry, usually invited only for the larger functions, and a number of friends and relatives from Geneva and Lausanne. Among the latter, two were particularly close to Germaine—Madame Rilliet-Huber, Germaine's girlhood friend, and Madame Necker de Saussure, Germaine's cousin and first biographer.

Albertine de Saussure, daughter of the great naturalist and Alpinist, Horace Benedict de Saussure, was born the same year as Germaine. In 1784 she married Jacques Necker, Germaine's first cousin, a man to whom she was in every respect superior. According to Sismondi:

> Married to a very mediocre husband, she wanted to make a distinguished man out of him, and succeeded. She began by writing all his books. He was nominated Auditor of our Republic [Geneva]: she wrote all his reports, did all his work. Then he was appointed professor of mineralogy: she wrote all his lectures and took great care to hide in his shadow—but while she gave him a reputation before he deserved it, she also inspired in him the ambition of deserving it. He ended up by knowing what he was teaching and became a rather good naturalist. . . . Madame de Staël said of her: 'My cousin has all the intelligence I am reputed to have and all the virtues I lack.' Madame Necker's intelligence was, however, of an entirely different cast from Madame de Staël's, much more serious, much more virile, but not nearly so brilliant.

Not only was Madame Necker de Saussure intelligent, erudite in the most varied fields, gifted with acute psychological observation, and capable of writing in a limpid, unmannered style that Germaine might have imitated with profit—she also was very beautiful, and of a beauty that age did not affect. 'I would gladly give you half the wit I am credited with for half of your beauty,' Germaine once said to her. She had other qualities that Germaine lacked: self-control, tact, and a virtue above reproach. Perhaps it was her deafness, which increased with the years, that gave her an air of aloofness; even so, for a passionate soul, Madame Necker de Saussure must have seemed a little too perfect, a little too poised, a little too precise, a little too well adjusted not to be a little irritating. Punctiliously faithful to the pact she had concluded with Mathieu, she bore with the most extravagant manifestations of Germaine's disorderly passions and never ceased trying to protect her from herself. There was in the relationship between the two women something of the generous indulgence that friends have for each other when in fact they do not like each other.

Their friendship had its ups and downs until 1804, when the successive deaths of Jacques and Louis Necker drew them closer together. M. Necker de Germany, Albertine Necker's father-in-law, died only four months after Germaine's father. He had ill chosen his time: after the great Necker's death his was an anticlimax.

Transient guests from more distant places may be classified into those who were invited or invited themselves (sometimes a difficult distinction to make) and those who were summoned by subpoena. Among the former were Prince August of Prussia, who lost his heart to Madame Récamier; Mr. Middleton, a young American art student, who did likewise; the German philanthropist Baron von Voght, 'the fattest of all sensible men', who did likewise; Frederika Brun, a Danish poetess writing in German, whose poems were so obscure that she provided them with footnotes; the Danish dramatist Oehlenschläger; a constant procession of eccentric Germans; Guizot; Chateaubriand; the Duchess of Courland; Prince Belmonte; two Russian admirers, Baron Balk and Prince Tuffiakin; Prince Sapieha; Madame Vigée-Lebrun, who painted Germaine's portrait as Corinne;[1] the philosopher Gérando; and, a category all to herself, Madame de Krüdener. The list could be prolonged indefinitely—a sizeable proportion of Europe's aristocracy and world of letters passed through Coppet, where cosmopolitanism was preached and practised on an unrivalled scale.

Those who came because they were subpoenaed were the friends and lovers. Of the original triumvirate—Talleyrand, Narbonne, Mathieu de Montmorency—only Mathieu remained faithful. Since Monsieur de Staël's death, he was the legal guardian of Germaine's children. Unlike Talleyrand and Narbonne, he never surrendered to Napoleon's blandishments. Apart from his membership on the boards of various public and private charities—the Hospital for the Blind, the celebrated Institute for the Deaf Mute, and the like—he stayed away from public life, and in the summer of 1804, just before joining Germaine at Coppet, at a family council, he made the entire Montmorency clan swear never to

[1] Reproduced facing p. 161.

serve at Napoleon's court. Armed with rosaries and resignation, he appeared without fail whenever summoned by Germaine. Indulgent to her errors, he hoped against hope that her very unhappiness would force her to face herself and to find peace in religion. In this his conduct differed sharply from his sternness to his charity wards: two women whose subsidies he had cut off because of their obdurate immorality were found one day hanging from a rafter in their garret. But Germaine he still half loved, and the virtuous Madame Necker de Saussure he more than half loved, and his wife was a shrew—a combination of circumstances which helps to explain both his indulgence and his faithful attendance.

Other friends and lovers were to appear at Coppet and complicate its amorous tangles; they, however, were almost interchangeable. Germaine's friendship with Madame Récamier, whose disturbing and seductive figure is intimately associated with Coppet, was, however, unique.

Julie Bernard was born at Lyons in 1777, the daughter of a lawyer. She was fifteen when, in the middle of the Reign of Terror, she married the banker Jacques-Rose Récamier, of Lyons, her senior by twenty-seven years. There was a mystery about her marriage. Monsieur Récamier, it was rumoured, had been the lover of Juliette's mother, and Juliette was his daughter; fearing for his life, he made sure that his fortune would pass to his daughter, in case he was guillotined, by marrying her. The rumour may be discounted, as may be that other rumour, spread by Mérimée, that Juliette was physically incapable of losing her virginity. Still it is undoubtedly true that, at least until 1818, she did not lose it.

She was afraid to death to give herself, and Monsieur Récamier, though not the most sensitive of men, 'respected her susceptibilities', as he put it once. Her virginal beauty and charm, combined with a sensuousness, an almost voluptuous gracefulness, exerted an irresistible attraction on men. But to fall in love with that angel was an infernal experience. Sentimental and frivolous in turns, playing with passion but terrified of surrendering to it, she tormented even those among her lovers whom she wanted to love; those with whom she merely flirted— a category embracing virtually every man she knew—and who were incautious enough to allow themselves vain hopes could say of her, as did Benjamin Constant: 'She has played with my happiness, my career, my life. May she be cursed!' Only one man, Chateaubriand, thought differently; but when he and Juliette met and loved, she was forty and he fifty.

Germaine first met the Récamiers in 1798, when Juliette's husband was interested in buying a house that Necker owned in Paris. Monsieur Récamier purchased the property, and it was here, in the house on the rue du Mont-Blanc, that Juliette enjoyed her first great triumphs. Its ostentatious luxury set off her simple Grecian robes, flowing white and unadorned from a narrow gold or blue ribbon that gathered them beneath her virginal breasts. Intimate friends might be shown into the sanctum, her bedroom: the bed, raised like an altar and adorned at either end with gilded bronze swans, was an awe-inspiring sight. The same privileged few—Madame de Staël was among them—might, if she felt inspired, see her perform the Dance of the Shawl, an invention of Madame de Krüdener which Juliette brought to its ultimate perfection. So impressed was Germaine by Juliette's dance that she described it twice—in *Corinne* and in *Delphine*:

> In every movement there was a suppleness, a gracefulness, a mingling of modesty and voluptuousness that suggested the powerful hold the Hindu dancing girls exert on the imagination. . . . An indefinable impassioned joy and a heightened sensitivity of the imagination suddenly electrified the witnesses of this magical dance and transported them into an ideal existence where one dreams of a happiness that is not of this world. . . . She seemed animated by the enthusiasm of life, of youth, of beauty, and one could not help being convinced that she needed no one to be happy.

> Sometimes, when the music became gentler, Delphine walked several steps, inclining her head and crossing her arms, as if some memories, some regrets, had suddenly intruded on the splendour of a feast; but soon resuming her light and airy dance, she draped herself in an Indian shawl, which, as it outlined her figure and floated with her long hair, transformed her whole person into an enchanting tableau.

Indeed, at that climactic moment, Juliette by loosening a pin concealed in her hair, let her dark waves float languidly in harmony with the diaphanous shawl, then stopped and, slightly out of breath, disappeared into her boudoir to receive the company's compliments while resting on the couch that David's painting made famous.

Identifying Juliette with the eternally virginal, youthful, and feminine, Germaine felt drawn to her with the impetuousness of a lover. The attraction was mutual, but Juliette was reserved. 'I hope,' Germaine wrote to her in the spring of 1802, 'that you have lost that singular timidity you used to feel when writing to me. Could you not see plainly that I love you?' Even after Juliette had lost her timidity, Germaine was left in the role of a suitor: 'Why, whether in love or in friendship, is one never necessary to you?' No one but Juliette was necessary to Juliette.

The tone of Germaine's letters to Juliette often is astonishing. 'I believe I can sense your charm like a lover. . . . I love you more than friendship can love. . . . I kneel before you to embrace you with all my soul,' are examples of her ardent language. Theirs was decidedly not an ordinary friendship; yet, despite all the burning words, there emanates from the correspondence a feeling of chastity and innocence. Germaine's demands on Juliette were imperious, like those of a lover; but except when Juliette encroached on her own domain, Germaine was not jealous. The love she gave to and demanded from Juliette was more sisterly and girlish than erotic. But it was the contrast that attracted her: if Germaine embodied the principle of motion, Juliette embodied that of calm. The attraction of opposites inevitably engenders a tension which, regardless of sex, is an erotic tension.

In their conversation, in their interests and ideas, there was a perfect rapport between them. Intellectually no less than physically and emotionally, Juliette's femininity contrasted with Germaine's maleness. Her intelligence was essentially receptive. Benjamin, in recalling their conversation, speaks of the speed with which Germaine emitted new ideas, and the speed with which Juliette seized and judged them: of 'that powerful and virile intelligence that uncovered all' and 'that delicate and sensitive intelligence that understood all'. Far from eclipsing each other, each enhanced the fascination of the other in the eyes of the onlooker—a fact of which they were quite conscious and which no doubt contributed to the growth of their friendship.

Politics helped to strengthen their alliance. After repulsing the ardent advances of Lucien Bonaparte and of Adrien de Montmorency (Mathieu's cousin), Juliette had the temerity to refuse the brusque offers of the First Consul himself. Madame de Staël's arrest and expulsion in 1803 convinced her that 'a man who could send a woman, and such a woman, into exile could never appear to me except as a despot'. The opposition sharpened after the arrest and trial of Moreau, who had ties of friendship with Juliette's family, and it grew into active hostility when Juliette refused Napoleon's offer, made through the intermediary of Fouché, of the position of lady-in-waiting. (What the offer really implied, Fouché made quite plain. 'The Emperor,' he said, 'has not yet met a woman worthy of him.')

Madame Récamier's refusal put her on Napoleon's blacklist. His opportunity for revenge came when Monsieur Récamier, as a result of the financial crisis of 1805–6 and of his own over-ambitious operations, was found to be in debt by about one million francs. For a bank as great as his this would have been a minor matter in normal times; but there was a rush on the banks, and he was obliged to ask the Bank of France for a loan to tide him over the crisis. His request was referred to Napoleon, then campaigning in Germany. 'I am not Madame Récamier's lover,' the Emperor said to Junot, who had put in a word for her. 'I don't come to the rescue of financiers who spend 600,000 francs a year. Understand that, Monsieur Junot!'

Monsieur Récamier went into bankruptcy; the house in the rue du Mont Blanc was put on sale; Juliette sold her silver and her jewellery. She uttered not even a murmur of complaint. Truth to tell, she still had a small private fortune, and her husband was entrusted by his creditors with his own liquidation. In 1809 he was back in business, though on a more modest scale. The Récamiers were by no means reduced to mendicity, nor even to dishonour. It was perhaps the only instance in history that saw a bankrupt banker hailed as a hero; for several days after the catastrophe, the whole Faubourg Saint-Germain filed through the Récamiers' house to leave their visiting cards. A more stylish protest against tyranny there never was.

The first news of the Récamier disaster reached Germaine at Coppet, on November 17, 1805. 'If it were possible to be loved more, to be the object of even more sympathy than you have been until now, this is what would have happened,' Germaine wrote in an effusive letter.[1] The bankruptcy procedure took a long time and was not complete until the end of 1806. On January 20, 1807, Juliette's mother died, to whom she had been devoted; her death made it possible for Juliette to accept Germaine's often-repeated invitation to spend the summer in Switzerland. On July 10, after a nearly fatal carriage accident while crossing the Jura, Juliette arrived at Coppet for the first of three turbulent visits.

If credit were given for faithful attendance at Coppet, the first prize would, beyond any doubt, go to Charles-Victor de Bonstetten. Born in

[1] The date-line of the letter reads merely '17 novembre'. Nearly all biographers of Madame de Staël and Madame Récamier date it as of 1806, when Germaine was in Rouen. But the letter contains the passage, 'enfin, du moins à Lyon ou jusqu'à mes *quarante lieues* j'irai pour vous voir', which makes sense if Germaine was at Coppet, but not if she was at Rouen; and B. Constant's diary entry for November 17, 1805, reads: 'Banqueroute de M. Récamier. Pauvre Juliette!' This seems conclusive.

1745 into a patrician Bernese family, he displayed from adolescence an ebullience and volatility that seemed decidedly out of place in staid and ponderous Berne. He studied in Geneva, in Holland, and finally at Cambridge, where he enjoyed the friendship of Thomas Gray. A stay in Paris in 1770 acquainted him with the pleasures of high society; a trip to Italy followed. He dabbled in writing—pastoral idylls, a treatise on the butter trade—entered the Grand Council of the Republic of Berne, served as bailiff of Their Excellencies at Nyon from 1787 to 1793. His acquaintance with Madame Necker dated from adolescence, when he used to accompany her and Pastor Moultou on their Saturday visits to the Sage of Ferney. At Paris he became a frequent guest of the Neckers at Saint-Ouen. One day, walking in the park, he was startled by a sharp blow across his back; whirling about, he found a small girl, half hidden behind a tree, a stick in her hand. 'Mama wants me to exercise my left arm, so I was trying it out.' Friendships have begun under even worse auspices.

The proximity of Nyon to Coppet made Bonstetten a familiar visitor after Necker's retirement in 1790; he became an even more assiduous guest of Madame de Staël's after her flight from Paris in 1792, and in 1794, being no longer bailiff, he moved in with her altogether, spending the winter in the company of Narbonne, Mathieu, and Benjamin at her court at Mézery. When the French invaded Switzerland in 1798, Bonstetten emigrated. He had begun a lifelong friendship with Frederika Brun, the Danish poetess, in 1791, and it was at her house in Copenhagen and at her country seat, Sophienholm, that he spent the years 1798–1800. Married to a rich philistine of a merchant, Frederika cultivated her frustrated sensibilities by taking opium and writing poetry. Overwrought, sentimental, platonic, and three-quarters deaf, she regarded herself as a poet of genius. Her house was a literary centre; Oehlenschläger, the future national poet of Denmark, made his début there. Under Frederika's influence Bonstetten began to write in German, which he had nearly forgotten. He returned to Switzerland in 1801, was nursed back from a near-fatal sickness under the care of Necker and Madame de Staël, and then proceeded, as Sainte-Beuve puts it, to rejuvenate. Madame Brun appeared in Geneva at about the same time. On her first visit to Coppet she arrived at dawn, was overcome by the splendours of nature, burst into a quotation from Ariosto, and was sent to bed by Germaine. She was a frequent guest from 1802 to 1810, bringing Oehlenschläger and the German poet Matthisson in her wake.

Bonstetten had been married once, but this is a condition in which it is difficult to visualize him. His wife's death caused him little sorrow, but when his younger son, whom he adored, became fatally ill in 1809, it seemed that Bonstetten would never be able to bear his loss. Late in 1810 the blow came; it scarcely touched him. He could cry as inconsolably as a child, and forget the cause of his tears as quickly. 'He never abandoned a friend; to be sure, he forgets them every moment of the day,' his best friend, Sismondi, said of him. It cannot be denied that with every death of a friend—and he survived them all—Bonstetten's nature became more happy, carefree, and ebullient. When he was in his seventies, he was known to leap out of his window into the garden in order to escape boring visitors; at eighty he expressed his pleasure at the unexpected visit of the writer Zschokke by seizing him around the middle and waltzing him around the room. His frivolity, being good-natured and tempered by sensibility, attracted rather than offended Madame de Staël. 'Believe me,' she said to him, 'wit and grace such as yours are without an example.'

'She alone understands me,' Bonstetten wrote to Frederika about Germaine. 'Never in my life have I seen a greater intelligence.' Indeed, Germaine had discovered Charles-Victor's literary gift. He was working, in 1803, on a book based on his earlier travels in Italy—a description of Latium, which he had visited with a copy of Virgil's *Aeneid* as his Baedeker. He was writing it in German. Germaine, after hearing him read some pages he had written, declared herself enchanted, advised him to write in French, and promised to find him a publisher. In 1804 the book was finished; it was published in the autumn, at Geneva, as *Voyage sur la scène des six derniers livres de l'Enéide*. Germaine reviewed it in a literary journal in Paris. 'His vanity,' noted Benjamin, 'has been so stimulated that he cannot stop talking about his writings. The joys of literary self-satisfaction partake of a species of physical pleasure. The whole physiognomy lights up and a visible voluptuous titillation pervades the body.' A woman who, by a few flattering words, could procure a man such voluptuous titillations was a redoubtable woman. Perhaps Frederika Brun showed some alarm. At any rate, Bonstetten thought it politic in 1804 to temper his praise of Germaine in his letters to Madame Brun: 'I have just returned from Coppet [to Geneva], and I feel completely stupefied . . . and exhausted by the intellectual debauches. More wit is expended at Coppet in a single day than in many a country during a whole year. I am so tired of it that I am lying down half-dead, and my room seems like a tomb.'

·   ·   ·

'I know very well which woman is always a woman, even when she has the eloquence of an orator, the depth of a philosopher, or the inspiration of a prophetess. And I also know how she is loved, how one must love her forever.' Thus wrote of Germaine, nineteen years after her death, Jean-Charles-Léonard Simonde de Sismondi. Among those whose names are intimately linked with Madame de Staël's, Talleyrand, Benjamin Constant, Prosper de Barante, A. W. Schlegel, and Sismondi possessed beyond doubt the most remarkable minds; and Sismondi probably owed her more than the rest put together.

He was born in 1773, seven years after Germaine, the son of Gédéon Simonde, a Genevese pastor descended from an honourable but not quite patrician family; the 'de Sismondi' he added to his name only in 1800. As a child, he was 'the Solon', so Rosalie de Constant relates, of an imaginary republic called Consigal, whose name combined those of its three founders—Victor de Constant, Simonde, and one of the Gallatin boys. They met under the statue of Rousseau and made imaginary constitutions. This idyll ceased when Simonde's father lost the larger part of his money in the government loan floated by his compatriot Necker. Simonde had to forgo a higher education and entered a Genevese bank at Lyons as a bookkeeper. The beginning of the Reign of Terror forced him to return to Geneva in 1792; he found that Geneva, too, was having its Reign of Terror. The whole world seemed to be playing under Rousseau's statue making imaginary constitutions.

The Simonde family fled to England in 1793, but returned a year later because the climate did not agree with the health of Madame Simonde. After selling his property, Gédéon and his family moved on to Italy, where they bought a farm near Pescia in Tuscany. Gédéon did not stay long. Leaving his wife, son, and daughter behind, he returned to Geneva and tried to recoup his losses by devices that might have led to riches in America but merely caused raised eyebrows in Geneva. He tried dairy farming, and was seen driving his milk wagon through the streets, tooting on a cowherd's horn to notify the housewives of his passage. Later he combined a wine retail business with a bookshop, but these more heady pursuits succeeded no better than the dairy farm; in 1800, Simonde senior returned to Pescia, where he lived unobtrusively till his death ten years later. About the time he left Geneva his son returned, transformed into Monsieur Simonde de Sismondi.

The earth rarely bore a man more honest than Sismondi. But he had genuinely convinced himself that he was descended from the powerful

THE CHÂTEAU OF COPPET

ALBERT DE STAËL
From a charcoal drawing attributed to Firmin Massot at Coppet

AUGUSTE DE STAËL
*From a portrait by Anne Louis Girodet
de Roucy-Trioson at Coppet*

ALBERTINE DE STAËL
From a portrait by François Gérard

Sismondi family of medieval Pisa; the addition of the 'de Sismondi' to his name appealed to the future historian of the Italian republics; and since his father's ungentlemanly pursuits had cost his family some of its status, the new name might help to restore it.

During his five years at Pescia, Sismondi had tried his hand at gentleman farming, studied and written about the agricultural economy of Tuscany, and been imprisoned twice—first by the revolutionists as an aristocrat, then by the Austrians as a revolutionist. The bigoted, stupefying atmosphere of Italian provincial life made this and his later briefer stays a torture. Although his sister married a local notable, the Protestant Sismondis remained strangers in their new home, and their isolation may be in large part responsible for Sismondi's anti-Catholic bias in his *History of the Italian Republics*. No one who was brought up as a Calvinist, even if like Sismondi he becomes an agnostic, can quite escape the influence of the Calvinist ethos; at heart Sismondi remained his whole life a Genevese, Protestant, and republican.

Although Geneva had become a French provincial town in 1798, he hoped to make a modest career in it. He became secretary to the Chamber of Commerce; in 1809, when the publication of the first volumes of his Italian history had earned him a *succès d'estime*, he was appointed professor of moral philosophy at the Academy of Geneva. (He gave only one course, in 1811–12, on the literature of southern Europe.) Until about 1805 he also operated a small printing plant, where Madame de Staël once printed a sheet with her own hands.

Sismondi had several counts against him: socially, despite his adoptive ancestry, he never was quite accepted as an equal in the high spheres he was to enter—not even by Germaine, who opened these spheres to him. Intellectually, despite his exceptional gifts, he suffered from the handicaps of being self-taught. In addition, he was poor, ugly (though not unattractive), and proverbially awkward and clumsy. Unfortunately, dancing was his passion, and there was no way to prevent him from it. Women made him their pet; perhaps, had he asked for love more aggressively, they might even have loved him.

He met Germaine in 1801 or 1802, and his first letter to her, dated January 1801, took her defence against the critics who had attacked her *De la littérature* for accepting the Ossianic poems as authentic. Sismondi supplied her with arguments to confound the critics (surely a case of the lame leading the blind) and furthermore, in support of her doctrine of progress, asserted the superiority of Necker over the Church Fathers as a moral guide. No doubt this sentiment predisposed her in

L

his favour, but it was as an economist and a lover that he attracted her attention. In 1802 he published his first important work, *On Commercial Wealth*, and fell in love with a penniless girl. His book, strongly influenced by the English economists (from whom he later dissented), contained a good deal of implicit criticism of Bonaparte's policies. It impressed Germaine, who promised to use her influence to help his career. Sismondi, a regular guest at Coppet from then on, confided his sentimental dilemma to Germaine: should he marry his Lucile, who besides being poor was consumptive and of inferior social status, despite his mother's opposition?

Germaine's advice to the lovelorn was not what one had a right to expect from the author of *Delphine*. To marry Lucile, she told him, would hinder his career, prevent him from achieving financial independence, and close society to him. Sismondi admitted that all this was true, but what of love? No matter how passionate one's love, Germaine replied, an intelligent being must always preserve 'an inner self-critical faculty'; she herself, whenever she had been in love, had felt that there were two beings inside her, one of which mocked the other. 'This conversation greatly upset me,' Sismondi noted in his diary.

Lucile's death in 1803 relieved Sismondi of his dilemma. 'It was from her ice-cold corpse that I obtained my first kiss,' he wrote to Germaine, adding that he was not particularly unhappy but merely hoped to die. Sismondi's loves were chaste, his physical needs easily controlled; he was forty-six when he finally married, two years after the death of Germaine, who once wrote to a freshly married friend, 'I do not like my friends to get married.'

His devotion to Germaine became passionate in the summer of 1804. What Coppet, what Germaine meant to him he summed up after her death:

> It is all over, then, with the place where I have lived so much, where I was so sure of feeling at home! All over with this vivifying society, this magic lantern of the world, which I first saw light up there and that has taught me so much. . . . There is no one to whom I owe more than to *her*.

It was at Coppet that the awkward, self-taught young provincial was introduced to a new world which at first dazzled and frightened him. His conversations with Germaine, Benjamin, and Schlegel shocked him into an awareness of how little he knew. 'The good Sismondi is completely upset,' noted Bonstetten. 'I had to cheer him up. He would like to go to Germany to see the great geniuses himself.' One of the geniuses, the historian Johann von Müller, came to Coppet that summer. It was he who inspired Sismondi's ambition to become a historian. Sismondi began to write his *Italian Republics* in 1804; he finished it in 1817. Without Germaine's encouragement and criticism, he might well have abandoned the enterprise soon after starting it, for his task was nearly insuperable, and no one has attempted it since.

To be sure, by guiding Sismondi into history Germaine led him away from the field for which he was most gifted—economics. She was passionately interested in history and shared Sismondi's enthusiasm for political freedom—his theme as a historian—whereas she had only primitive notions of economics, and her complete identification with the propertied classes would have made it difficult for her to endorse his views. In his *New Principles of Political Economy* (1819) Sismondi attacked the 'liberal orthodoxy' which Germaine accepted without question: 'The social order we are now entering,' he wrote thirty years before Marx and Engels, 'is a state of war between those who own and those who work.'[1] As an economic thinker Sismondi clearly belonged to the Industrial Age; a chasm separated him from Germaine's eighteenth-century views. It would be idle, however, to deplore her diverting him into more literary than scientific channels. His Italian and French histories, though not of the first rank, are very influential contributions, and his *Literature of Southern Europe*, though less brilliant than *De l'Allemagne*, is a more solid work and was perhaps even more important in the formation of French Romanticism. Coppet was Sismondi's school; since he was a man of outstanding talent rather than of genius, it is likely that without that 'magic lantern of the world' he never would have achieved anything worthy of note.

But Sismondi had to pay a price for his schooling: he fell in love with his teacher. 'Believe me,' he wrote to her on December 11, 1804, when she had left for Italy, 'believe me that I love you more than I ever told you, more than I shall ever say.' He joined her at Milan in January and accompanied her to Rome and Naples. After leaving her at Rome he wrote from Pescia:

> I can no longer visualize an existence away from you. . . . I do not want to let myself go any further—you would take it for a declaration of love, and this would make you feel obliged to laugh at me. Do not laugh, I beseech you, at my attachment: it is the most serious sentiment of my life.

[1] Marx owed more to Sismondi than he admitted, but the remedies Sismondi proposed were not Marxist. As late as 1897 Lenin attacked Sismondi in his *Characteristics of Economic Romanticism: Sismondi and Our Russian Sismondists.*

Sismondi was not, of course, of the physical type that inspired passion in Germaine. But even if he had been, a love affair would have been unthinkable: it is a statistical fact that Germaine never fell in love except with aristocrats. This partiality may be explained only in part by rank consciousness. It had a deeper cause: Germaine loved only men who had a certain elegant recklessness, or dash, or at the very least a manner that showed they took their place in society for granted—in other words, men of the world. Her efforts to polish those among her friends whose social education had been neglected—a Sismondi, a Schlegel—were at once touching and cruel. Be this as it may, Germaine soon succeeded in containing Sismondi's feelings within the bounds of a cordial friendship.

It took Sismondi a little while to bury his hopes. When he discovered that a French official in Italy had mistaken him for Benjamin, he was elated. 'Is it possible, is it true,' he wrote to Germaine, 'that there is something in the way you behave to me that might justify his mistake?' Undoubtedly, there must have been: Germaine's exalted friendships lent themselves to misinterpretation.

Germaine had one rival in Sismondi's heart—his mother, who dominated him even more than Germaine. Comparing them, he once wrote naïvely: 'Madame de Staël has more genius, more intellectual brilliance, but my mother yields to her in nothing where tact, sensibility, and imagination are concerned.' As the years went by, and Germaine's lack of tact became more and more pronounced, Sismondi knew moments of rebellion. As he confided to his diary in 1809:

> She often is too resentful and contemptuous. Power seems to warp everybody's mind in the same manner. The power of her fame . . . has made her acquire several of Bonaparte's faults. Like him, she is intolerant of all opposition, insulting in disputes, and very prone to wound people by cutting remarks—not to vent her anger but to enjoy her superiority.

His sharpest condemnation of Germaine he reserved for his letters to his mother. In flattering the maternal jealousy he could, at the same time, avow feelings he otherwise sought to suppress. 'Madame de Staël never puts herself in the place of others,' he wrote one day. 'With all her intelligence she cannot understand anything that is not she herself. But then, if one were to believe the rich, nobody is unhappy but they. It is a curious way they have of monopolizing everything.' Nothing could be truer: but it is interesting that Sismondi was the only man to attribute these defects to Germaine's social and economic status.

Germaine's increasing interest in the mystical ideas of Romanticism, which Schlegel encouraged, often caused her to clash with Sismondi. It was in such clashes that each brought out the best in the other. A visitor at Coppet in 1808, Karl Ritter, found Sismondi expounding his opinion that religion must be substantially morality. Otherwise, he said, t rested only on feeling and became fanciful and fanatical; religion needed a firm rational foundation. Germaine naturally defended the opposite view. 'Her inspiration,' relates Ritter, 'lasted nearly an hour. Never in the whole course of my life have I felt more nervous agitation. I had cramps even to my fingertips. There was in her something of the power which Alcibiades attributes, in the *Symposium*, to the word of Socrates.' To be drowned out by such eloquence day after day was frustrating enough; to see Germaine espousing the metaphysical fantasies of a German schoolmaster was intolerable. Sismondi was not jealous of Germaine's lovers ('I believe Sismondi loves me with his love for Minette,' Benjamin once observed), but he was jealous of those who interposed a spiritual barrier between her and himself, and most specifically of Schlegel, 'a presumptuous pedant', whom he held responsible for Germaine's alienation from common sense.

The friendship that tied the flighty Bonstetten and the earnest Sismondi was both touching and comical. Neither was uncritical of the other, but they became almost inseparable and took lodgings in the same house at Geneva. Whenever 'Bon' received a letter from Frederika Brun, he would stamp his foot, thereby notifying 'Mondi' in the room below to come up and have it read to him. 'As soon as Mondi or I have anything amusing or sad to communicate to each other, we are running up or down the stairs.' The friendship cooled down only when Bonstetten—who said he was beginning to feel old because the women kissed him first—gallantly asked Sismondi's mother in marriage in 1811. Madame Sismondi fled back to Pescia, while her son deplored the old man's levity.

It was their common detestation of Schlegel which established a spirit of camaraderie between Sismondi and Benjamin. In Sismondi this antipathy resulted partly from his instinctive realization that Schlegel's position with regard to Madame de Staël was very similar to his own.

Schlegel too loved Germaine. When, on April 19, 1804, he impulsively jumped into her carriage and threw in his lot with hers, he was under the illusion that her heart was free and accessible to him. Between Weimar and Coppet he discovered that 'older ties' bound her to another. Instead of Germaine's lover, he found himself the tutor of her children. This was, of course, what had been agreed upon, but in his amatory *hubris* Schlegel had not taken the agreement literally. It is true that he did not over-exert himself; Germaine gave many of the lessons and corrected the children's translations and compositions, so that his teaching load amounted to three and a half hours daily for five days a week. But in a foreign country and an alien social environment he found it difficult to be tutor in the afternoon and man of the world in the evening. His position was all the less enviable because he had been fool enough to hint to his German friends, and even to his brother Friedrich, that he had come to Coppet as a successful suitor rather than a humble tutor. The rumour soon spread through German literary circles that Schlegel was earning his living honestly, and his reputation was on the brink of ruin. 'You must do everything in your power to refute so harmful a rumour by deeds,' Friedrich wrote to him. 'Even if you want to draw up the study plan for the young people, you must in no manner busy yourself in person with an activity that would . . . lower your dignity.' It is not clear what Friedrich meant by 'deeds'. Was he exhorting his brother to seduce the Baroness of Coppet in order to maintain his dignity? Not exactly: appearance, in this particular case, would be as good as reality. August Wilhelm, it must be said to his credit, did not follow this advice. To Sophie Tieck, the friend he had left in Berlin, he admitted that he was at Coppet for a salary. He also informed her that he would be able to put aside several hundred thalers a year, since he had no expenses except his clothing and tips for the servants. 'I should like to give them large tips in order to insure my prestige in the house.' He had a comfortable room, between the library and the boys' quarters. The library was fitted out to serve him as a study. The food was excellent and wholesome. There were too many guests. The local wine was palatable; he did not mix it with water, but he had given up opium (was there anybody in 1804 who did not take opium?) and he was toying with the idea of giving up strong liquors. Thus the seraph of Romanticism to his distant beloved.

Germaine had brought August Wilhelm to Coppet as a kind of trophy, a showpiece of German erudition and philosophy. Schlegel, vain to begin with and made more aggressive by his frustrations and insecurity, surpassed her expectations. Methodically, professorially, with all the rancour of an oppressed minority, he held forth in the drawing room, contradicting everybody, running down France, extolling Germany, and revelling in paradoxes. The guests were not pleased;

Germaine, somewhat brusquely and in presence of the company, undertook to teach Schlegel the elements of polite intercourse. On June 6, 1804, Benjamin noted in his diary:

> Quarrel between Minette and Schlegel yesterday, about the spirit of conversation. How can one push the pedagogical mania to the point of educating a tutor! And what a bore for the others! They ensconce themselves, face to face, amid universal silence, Schlegel congratulating himself on his contempt for society and she congratulating herself on her conversational genius. The rest of the audience is reduced to the entertainment of this exchange of panegyrics, not of each other but each of himself at the expense of the other.

The scene was frequently repeated. In teaching Schlegel politeness Germaine was often quite rude. Annoyed by his pedantic assertiveness, she would contradict him flatly, even if she was completely ignorant of the matter in question. Then Schlegel would swallow his tears, retire to his room, and address long epistles to her, mixing lamentations with erudite disquisitions on the point in dispute: 'There is no need to spare my feelings; if there were, I would have left your house long ago. If you only knew how indifferent I am to those little public insults! I have the honour of drawing your attention to the fact that to call a language dead or living—' and so forth. Every time Germaine assuaged his wounded feelings, for at bottom she had a kindly disposition; but with equal regularity she made Schlegel her whipping boy when she felt irritated, and often Wilhelm caught the tail end of her scenes with Benjamin. 'I am all submission and compliance,' he complained in another midnight note, 'and yet you never cease rebuffing me in a manner that no human being could stand for long. What is your intention in acting thus?'

Apart from the children, who felt a tolerant affection for him, Schlegel was surrounded by enemies. 'Walk with Simonde and Schlegel,' noted Benjamin on May 25. 'They regard each other as madmen.' Summing up Schlegel's character on August 25, the diarist wrote:

> Constant preoccupation with himself, and excessive cowardice. This does not surprise me much, despite his pretensions to virility, horsemanship, and courage. He is a man who is swallowed up by self-love and who derives from self-love all his good and bad qualities—his enthusiasm, his irritability, his gentleness. When self-love abandons him, which happens whenever danger is imminent . . . all that is left is a typical man of letters whom a life of studies has weakened in body and soul.

As usual, Benjamin was right. Fussy, hypochondriac, ineffectual, arrogant, servile, brooding over real or imaginary wrongs, heavily humorous, tediously argumentative, Schlegel was not the ideal of the well-rounded man.

He tried to develop his physique. He took riding lessons; he went swimming; he marched the boys on epic walks around the lake and through the Alps. Perhaps all this improved his health, but it did not change him into an athlete. He also polished his manners—so much so that, when he returned to Germany after Germaine's death, he was regarded as a Parisian dandy. Heinrich Heine, who attended his lectures at the University of Bonn in 1819, described him thus:

> Herr August Wilhelm Schlegel wore kid gloves and was dressed according to the latest Parisian fashion. . . . He was elegance personified. And when he mentioned the Lord Chancellor of England, he added 'my friend'. Next to him stood his servant, in the livery of the baronial house of Schlegel [he had been ennobled], trimming the wax candles that were burning in silver candelabra, which had been placed on his lectern next to a glass of sugar water.

An impressive sight, no doubt; but in Paris Schlegel was still just a German professor. As a result, he regarded the French as a hopelessly frivolous race.

Besides his schoolteaching and his own literary work (he translated Shakespeare and Calderon at Coppet), Schlegel's chief activity was as literary adviser to Germaine. His impact on her has been exaggerated, but Germaine's friends were not mistaken in attributing to him a powerful influence on her thought. To convert her to the Romantic creed he called on reinforcements. His brother Friedrich came to Coppet on October 2, 1804. Benjamin says:

> He is a little roundish man, immoderately fat, with a pointed nose protruding from between two shiny cheeks, a mouth that smiles in rather honeyed fashion under that pointed nose, fine eyes, a subaltern bearing (especially when he is not speaking), and an icy expression when he is listening. His ideas are as absurd as his brother's. The part of Germany he likes best is Vienna, because there is no freedom of the press.

Having spent a year in Paris with his Dorothea ('*née* Mendelssohn and runaway Veit', as Heine liked to call her), Friedrich was deep in the study of Sanskrit. He had just discovered Hindu philosophy and was well on his way to Catholicism. Benjamin, who in his distaste for either brother lumped both under the collective designation of 'Schlegel', thought that he had discovered the motives of their strange theories:

Their entire doctrine is a purely personal affair. They declare themselves for Catholicism because the Protestant philosophers make fun of them. They do not like the governments that allow freedom of the press . . . because people have taken advantage of it in order to write against them. They bear a grudge against the princes who favour enlightenment because those princes have not called on their talents.

Germaine's judgment was equally to the point: 'In every respect they are two very remarkable men,' she wrote to Johann von Müllr. 'If they had been able to be remarkable without trying to be extra-ordinary, they would have been more remarkable still.' Benjamin and Germaine respected common sense; the Schlegels despised it. Wishing to be original and right at the same time, they were equally offended by agreement and contradiction, and they prefigured the authoritarianism of the rebel, the schoolmaster on a rampage.

Friedrich left on November 8. A few days later he wrote to Germaine, from Paris, a letter in which he called her 'my kind protectress' no fewer than six times. 'I believe this man to be dissembling, ambitious, self-seeking, and ungrateful,' wrote Benjamin with absolute accuracy.

Soon after Friedrich's departure Germaine, accompanied by Wilhelm, left for Italy. If Schlegel hoped that in Benjamin's absence his chances as a lover would improve, he was mistaken. At their return in 1805 Schlegel found that, instead of losing a rival, he had acquired two more. In the resulting turmoil he got short shrift. He had, he thought, borne as much as a man could bear, and he let Germaine know it in a pathetic letter. After recapitulating his past—the death of his stepdaughter, his love affair with Sophie Tieck—he came to his meeting with Germaine: 'For the first time in my life I thought that I was favoured by fortune.' Then he had discovered her relationship with Benjamin. Amid the whirlwind of Coppet he felt isolated. 'Often I spent my days sadly in a noisy solitude.' Worse, Germaine had taken sides against him in his disagreements with her friends. 'I can say truthfully that all those who surround you, friends or mere acquaintances, have constantly con-spired against me and tried to banish me from your house like an intruder.' For her he had left his fatherland and his friends, only to discover that another possessed her heart. No matter—his life was a failure; he was willing to sacrifice what remained of it to her. 'Whatever there is of value in my learning, my abilities, my talents, take it, it is yours, but be indulgent to what you call my shortcomings. . . . Tell me my defects, but "*Do not hurl them in my teeth.*" '

Germaine took fright. She might treat Schlegel like a dog, but the

L*

thought of the dog running away was intolerable. There is no record of what she said to him. To surmise an all-night scene is not unreasonable. The result of the conversation was this document:

> You wanted a written promise, adorable friend. You thought I would hesitate. Here it is:
> I declare that you have every right over me and that I have none over you. Dispose of my person and of my life; command, forbid—I shall obey you in everything. I desire no other happiness than what you see fit to give me. I want to own nothing; I want to owe everything to your generosity. I easily would consent to give up all thought of fame and to devote all my knowledge and talents to your personal use. I am proud of being your property.
> ... I do not know whether ... it is right to surrender so completely to another human being. But you have over me a supernatural power; it would be futile to resist it. ...
> Do not abuse your power. You might easily make me miserable, while I would be defenceless against you. Above all, I beseech you, do not ever banish from your presence your slave
>
> A. W. Schlegel

18 Oct. 1805.

Whatever may be said or thought of August Wilhelm Schlegel, he kept every word of his promise until Germaine's death and beyond.

Thus Germaine ruled over Coppet, like Venus over the damned souls in the Venusberg, like Calypso over shipwrecked travellers, like Circe over her menagerie. Much as the caged animals might growl and snap at each other, there was among them a species of solidarity. Benjamin summed it up in a terse entry of his diary, dated July 22, 1804:

> Minette went to Geneva for the day. Bonstetten, Blacons, Simonde, Schlegel, and I dined together like schoolboys when the master of studies is away. Strange woman! She exerts over everything around her a kind of inexplicable but very real power. If she could govern herself, she might have governed the world.

15

CORINNE AND ADOLPHE

Oswald Lord Nelvil, a Scottish peer, left Edinburgh in the winter of 1794–5 in order to travel in Italy. He had noble, handsome features, a good deal of wit, a great name, and an independent fortune; but his health was undermined by a deep sorrow, and his physicians, fearing consumption, had prescribed a southern climate. He followed their advice, although he cared little for the preservation of his life. He hoped to find, at least, some diversion in the variety of the scenes he was going to see. The most intimate of griefs, the loss of a father, was the cause of his illness. There were some cruel attending circumstances—remorse inspired by delicate scruples—that intensified his regrets, to which were added the figments of his imagination. A person who suffers is likely to convince himself that he is guilty, for violent sorrows bring disorder even into one's conscience.

THE opening paragraph of *Corinne*, here quoted, would require few substitutions to be applicable to Madame de Staël herself as she left for Italy in the first week of December in 1804. It is true that, unlike Lord Nelvil, she travelled with her three children and their amorous tutor and that she was thirteen years older than her hero. Also Lord Nelvil had no intention of turning the trip into a book. This, however, despite all her sorrow and indifference to life, was precisely what Germaine intended. As early as August 8 she had written to her friend Claude Hochet, 'I shall write a novel about my Italian journey.' Not a diary, not a travel book, but a novel—*un roman*. This seems odd, but then everything about *Corinne* is odd. Never was conscious self-dramatization carried to such extremes: Germaine lived a novel in order to write one; began to write it while still living it; and ended up by writing it in order to live it.

Since the publication, in 1807, of *Corinne, or Italy*, critics have remarked that there is a break in that novel. The break, however, is not caused by the reasons usually given—shift of scene, transformation of character—but by an intensification of tone. *Corinne* begins as a novel of ideas; neither its hero nor its heroine can be identified completely with anyone in Germaine's real life; then, rather suddenly, Oswald becomes one specific man (Prosper de Barante), Corinne one specific woman (Germaine), and the novel turns into an act of confession and revenge. So powerful was the explosion which brought about this change that it set off, by sympathetic detonation, the writing of another novel, also autobiographical, also lived while written—Benjamin Constant's *Adolphe*. Two more different works it is difficult to imagine, but they strangely complement each other.

With Schlegel and her children, Germaine crossed the Alps in deep snow, spent a week in Turin and three weeks in Milan, where Sismondi joined her, then continued by way of Parma, Modena, Bologna, and Ancona to Rome, where she arrived on February 3 or 4, 1805. She found the Italian winter north and east of the Apennines a dreary experience. The huge marble palaces, 'whose owners look like pygmies in the dwellings of giants', were glacial; at night, in the inns, she could hear the rain falling on the roofs like a deluge. 'It penetrates into the houses, and water pursues you with the energy of fire.' Only after crossing the Apennines did she find the Italy she had imagined.

The warmth of her reception made up for the damp climate. She wrote to Hochet from Bologna:

> My vanity ought to be satisfied by this journey. I surely did not suspect that I enjoyed even a quarter of the reputation I am enjoying in Italy—but this country is all the more eager to appreciate literary accomplishments because it cannot hope ever to attain any other kind. And even those accomplishments are drowned in rhetoric, as they must be in any country where words are permitted but things are not.

After one month, Germaine had formed a fairly set opinion of Italy:

> If one hour's work is enough to govern France, four minutes is all that is needed for Italy. There is no nation more easily frightened; even its poetic imagination predisposes it to fear, and they look upon power as on an image that fills them with terror. The sciences are cultivated here with admirable conscientiousness. Ridicule is unknown, because there is no society. Yesterday I went to visit a woman here [in Bologna] who is a professor of Greek.[1] In her unheated room she received all the university professors, who kept their overcoats on; her old teacher, a

---

[1] Clotilda Tambroni (1768–1817) taught Greek at the University of Bologna.

Spanish monk, showed us in with a little lantern. Well, all this does not cause so much as a smile in a people which laughs at grotesqueness but not at contrasts in rank, manners, or behaviour. These contrasts go unnoticed. There were a female physician, a female lawyer, and right with them some women who barely could read—but there is no such thing as a conventional education such as we know it. Either one knows twenty-eight languages here or else one cannot even spell one's own. . . . In Milan there is more of a social tone, but everywhere there is a mixture of wealth and poverty, of love for the fine arts and of bad taste, of education and ignorance, of greatness and pettiness—in a word, this is not a nation, because there is no coherence, no truth, no vigour in its life.

These first impressions later went into *Corinne* almost unchanged; in some ways they anticipated Stendhal. The absence of *amour-propre*, of the preoccupation with oneself as one appeared to others, attracted Germaine at the same time as the reason for its absence alienated her. In *Corinne* she says:

Unhappy love in Italy is not complicated by the sufferings of wounded vanity. Thus one is likely to meet men who are either passionate enough to stab their rival from jealousy or considerate enough to accept, gladly, a secondary role near the woman whose company pleases them. . . . There is in this country a bizarre mixture of *naïveté* and corruption, of dissimulation and frankness, of good nature and vindictiveness, of weakness and energy, which explains this general rule: that all the good qualities spring from the fact that nothing is ever done here to satisfy one's vanity, and all the bad qualities from the fact that a great deal is done to serve one's interests—love, ambition, or money.

This was a pleasing contrast with France, where—according to such diverse witnesses as Madame de Staël, Napoleon, and Stendhal—vanity and artificial values reigned supreme.

Germaine travelled through Italy, visiting churches, museums, galleries, palaces, without more than a passing glance at any of them. 'As you know,' Sismondi wrote to Bonstetten, 'Madame de Staël is bored if she has to pay any attention to *things*; they seem to keep her from pursuing her thoughts.' It was Schlegel who suddenly discovered an interest in matter rather than pure ideas. He could not get his fill of paintings, statues, and architecture. When he visited them by himself, says Sismondi, 'the domestic peace remained undisturbed. But when we go on expeditions in a group, it rarely happens that his enthusiasms do not lead to a quarrel. . . . One has become much harder on poor Schlegel. One allows him four paradoxes per day at the utmost, and when he starts on a fifth, the oncoming thunderstorm can be heard rumbling.'

Though Germaine might quarrel with Schlegel, her aesthetic guide, and presumably also, though more rarely, with Sismondi, her sociological guide, she made ample use of their ideas in *Corinne*.

Until her stay in Rome Germaine met scarcely anyone whose conversation interested her, although she was surrounded by a crowd at all hours. At Milan she tried to convince herself of the superior qualities of Vincenzo Monti, who by default passed for the greatest Italian poet of his time.[1] The only things her mother loved in Italy, observed seven-year-old Albertine, were 'the sea and Monti'. Germaine's letters to the poet sound passionate enough ('I have found myself in you; I have sensed my own nature in yours. . . . The sound of your voice still echoes in my heart'), but the expressions she used were her standard vocabulary of enthusiastic friendship. To those she really loved she never wrote letters as uniformly friendly as to Monti. She was less favourably impressed by the other Italian poets—there were thousands of them—who showered her with a dozen sonnets every day. But it was flattering and amusing to be the recipient of so much 'meaningless sound', and no doubt Germaine smiled benignly upon the versifier who introduced himself as 'an insect on Parnassus'. 'I must admit that I like it here because I am so marvellously well treated,' she confessed to Hochet from Rome. 'What would Geffroy and Fiévée [two hostile journalists] say if they saw the cardinals calling on me daily?'

The crowning glory of Germaine's stay in Rome was her public reception as an honorary member of the Accademia dell'Arcadia. After a spate of speeches Germaine read her French translation of a sonnet by Minzoni on the death of Christ, which was received with an ovation and followed by a cloudburst of sonnets in her honour. Prince Chigi concluded an elegy on a recently defunct cardinal with a pretty compliment to the Academy's new member; Count Alborghetti managed the feat of improvising a poem on her book *De la littérature*. Germaine reported every detail of the occasion in a letter to Benjamin. 'Much good may it do her,' Benjamin grumbled into his diary. 'There really is something of the mountebank in her behaviour.'

Literary triumphs, cardinals, sightseeing, midnight visits by torchlight to Canova's studio, being lionized by the Roman aristocracy and the foreign colony—all this was entertaining: but Germaine was more

[1] Alfieri was dead; Foscolo, Leopardi, and Manzoni had not yet produced their mature works.

than entertained. 'Would you believe it possible that I could love another city than Paris?' she asked Hochet when she was about to leave Rome.

> In fact, it is not so much the city I loved as a kind of musical, poetic, picturesque, aerial way of life that has opened up to me a new sphere of ideas and sensations—those monuments, those memories, this beautiful sky—the barren countryside surrounding Rome, which is not arid but which seems to mourn its former owners—all those works of art that reinvigorate the despondent soul—those harmonious songs one can hear in every street—this social freedom, which lacks the dignity of political freedom but has a charm of its own in every-day life—those Italians, all of them witty, all of them gay without malice, all amorous if you give them the least chance, all adorers of women (a little too much for their own dignity but not too much for rendering the women's life agreeable)—all this is so strange, so young, so sweet, that nowhere else is it possible to live in quiet and obscurity as happily as here. . . . What attracts me in this city is a mystery that does not reveal itself on first acquaintance, a sensation of the South that is completely unknown to those who have not been there, a certain sympathy between nature and man that cannot be imagined anywhere else—and a noble and calm image of death in the tombs and the traces of great men.

What caused this torrent of rhapsodic praise? Germaine had fallen in love.

Dom Pedro de Souza e Holstein, future Duke of Palmella and prime minister of Portugal, a young man who at twenty-four was bored with life, chanced to be present at Germaine's reception into the Arcadian Academy. He introduced himself; she asked him to accompany her home, along with Prince Chigi and Cardinal Consalvi, Pius VII's secretary of state. When Madame de Staël embarked on a romance, she usually did so in style.

Dom Pedro was exceptionally handsome; he combined nobility and sensibility; he was a poet, and not a bad one. Germaine, to borrow Gibbon's expression, saw and loved. Dom Pedro, who believed that at twenty-four he had known all that life has to give, could not resist the novel experience of being loved by a woman of genius who, at thirty-nine, was afraid that she might never know life again. Germaine swept him away to Naples—not alone, as Corinne does with Lord Nelvil, but with Schlegel, Sismondi, and Albertine.[1] That Schlegel

---

[1] The boys were left in the care of the Roman banker Torlonia. Several writers assert that Sismondi did not accompany Germaine to Naples, but his letters (especially one addressed to her and dated May 6, 1805) make it plain that he was of the party.

made no attempt to hide his feelings is clear from Germaine's correspondence; Sismondi, who tended to love Germaine's lovers, found
Souza 'a charming man'.

The sensuousness of the Neapolitan countryside overpowered Germaine. The heavy perfume of the flowers rising at nightfall, the
nightingales singing in the rose bushes, the softness of the air—she
remembered it all in *Corinne*. 'As you approach Naples, you experience
a sensation of absolute well-being'—a well-being not unmixed with
melancholy, 'but even in this melancholy there is no dissatisfaction, no
anxiety, no regret'. For once, and for three short weeks only, Germaine
let herself live. She explored the city, the slums, the ruins of Pompeii.
In a palanquin she made the ascent of Vesuvius in eruption, escorted
by Dom Pedro on horseback, and after nightfall she watched with him
the glowing stream of lava flowing, 'like a royal tiger, stealthily, with
measured steps'.

What had distressed her in Italy until then appeared to her excusable
at Naples. 'The people of Naples conceive of happiness as nothing but
pleasure.' The beggars were too lazy even to ask for alms; they simply
gestured to the passer-by. There was an absolute lack of dignity; in
fact, the Neapolitans were, 'in certain respects, not even a civilized
race'. With splendid equanimity, she ascribed their misery to the fine
climate and to the fertility of the soil, which made life too easy. Unlike
French misery, Neapolitan misery was artistic and picturesque. Thus,
leaning on the arm of Dom Pedro de Souza e Holstein, Germaine de
Staël passed through hell on earth and thought it Paradise.

Germaine was received in private audience by Queen Marie Caroline.
'What would the aristocrats in Paris say,' she wrote to Hochet, 'about
the Queen of Naples presenting me to her whole family and spending
several hours alone with me in her private apartment?' What the
aristocrats said after Hochet duly relayed this information is not known.
What the Emperor thought about it may be surmised easily enough.
Germaine had an infallible flair for boasting of her intimacy with
people whom Napoleon regarded as his worst enemies—first with
Queen Louise of Prussia, then with Cardinal Consalvi, and now with
the proud sister of Marie Antoinette, to whom he was writing menacing
letters and whom he was about to drive from her throne.

Back in Rome with Dom Pedro, Germaine spent her remaining weeks
in the enchantment of his company. It was April. Together they saw
the ceremonies of Holy Week and visited the monuments, the palaces,
the ruins, and the tombs. They met during the day and, to be alone,

again at night. 'If you come back tonight, at eleven o'clock, we might go together and see the Coliseum in the moonlight,' she wrote to him one day in May, and continued in verse: it was through him that the past spoke to her; it was his youthful promise that revived her faith in the virtues of antiquity; he was not one of those 'sterile hearts without freshness at dawn, without vigour at noon, that coldly calculate both life and happiness;

'Their wretched bliss I spurned and pushed away:
Love, pain, and thought have filled my every day.'

Pain and thought filled her even then. She had no illusion on the durability of Dom Pedro's attachment. 'If you are the person I think you are,' she wrote to him, 'you will go on loving me for some time. Not forever: destiny has not made us contemporaries.' There was in his character a reserve which attracted and disquieted her. 'I am all movement; you are all reflection. Everything I feel, I say; your feelings are all hidden by a veil.' This contrast in their characters passed into the characters of Oswald and Corinne, but she had used almost the same language with Narbonne and was still to use it with others.

After one last walk through the moonlit streets of Rome Germaine gave Dom Pedro a ring, then parted from her lover. She wrote to him from Florence on May 14:

My whole soul was bursting with regret, tenderness and admiration. We were of the same age in the face of the ruins of centuries. We were united by the same cult for beauty; and in Heaven my father forgave me a happiness mixed with so many tears and threatened by dark clouds. I wrote down a few of the things you said to me then. I shall never invent anything better, and I like to think of the secret understanding that will spring up between us when you read *Corinne*. You will recognize yourself in that book exactly as you are. . . . Rome and you are inseparable in my memory. Only through you have I understood its delights. . . . I loved you, and everything became alive for me. . . . Two months of my life are your work.

Thus the first part of *Corinne* had been lived, and Germaine had already discussed its outlines with Dom Pedro. But she had not yet begun to write it; she could not then have planned its unhappy ending. As originally conceived, *Corinne* must have been a sentimental *Cicerone*, a view of Italy as seen by two contrasting but sympathetic temperaments, hung on a simple and flexible plot. As it turned out, it became that and many other things besides.

Corinne is the worst great novel ever written—ineptly plotted, hysterical, and romantic in a ludicrous sense. Having acknowledged this, one remains faced with the product of an extraordinary mind and temperament, lucid and chaotic in turns, but always relentlessly intense, and if one attempts to analyse the intentions of the work one finds oneself in a maze of fascinating problems. The problems can merely be sketched or suggested, but even to do this a brief outline of the plot is necessary.

The idea of making her heroine an *improvvisatrice* probably came to Germaine on the day after her reception into the Arcadian Academy, when she witnessed Isabella Pellegrini, one of the most famous Italian improvisers, demonstrate her art. The *improvvisatrice*, usually a woman, would choose a theme, perhaps one suggested to her, and after collecting her thoughts while preluding on a harp—in *Corinne* it is a lyre—declaim melodiously in verse whatever inspiration dictated. Improvisers might be well-educated or illiterate; they were held in high esteem, and there was about them a mystic quality reminiscent of the Pythian priestesses, which often was ascribed to Germaine herself. A god was in them and spoke through them: they were, in the original meaning of the word, *enthusiasts*.

Corinne is such an improviser and poetess. Oswald sees her first in Rome as she receives the laurel crown at the Capitol with much pomp and fanfare. They meet; they are attracted to each other. But Oswald, the melancholy traveller from the North, is repelled by the sensuous Italian scene, and Corinne, to overcome his prejudice (and also to monopolize his company), shows him the sights of Rome and the Campagna, explains Italy, its past, its art, the character and beliefs of its people, and gradually brings him to share her enthusiasm for her country.

Oswald's Anglo-Saxon reserve melts under Corinne's eloquence, and they mutually confess their love. Yet each withholds a secret from the other. Corinne's existence is a mystery: she is beautiful, young, wealthy, the centre of a brilliant society, but except for her discreet maid no one knows her real name or her place of birth. Oswald's only clue is her perfect command of English. He himself is ridden by remorse for some secret guilt that threatens their future relationship. An explanation is inevitable, but Corinne, fastening on the happiness of the passing moment, deliberately delays it. She proposes a trip to Naples, alone with Oswald. At the foot of Vesuvius, at dusk, Oswald at last makes his confession. While travelling in France during the Revolution he had fallen madly in love with a French noblewoman, whom he intended to marry and for whose sake he disregarded his ailing father's pleas to him to return to Scotland. The woman turned out to be unworthy, but this discovery came too late: he had barely landed in England when he learned from a newspaper that his father was dead. His anguish at the thought that he could never make good his fault was only intensified when he found, among his father's papers, several moving pages on the disregard of children for their parents. Oswald asks Corinne to read them and, when she has done this, ' "Corinne," cried Lord Nelvil in agonized pain, "do you believe it was against me that he wrote those eloquent complaints?"—"No, no," answered Corinne, "you know that he loved you, that he did not doubt your love. And I know from you that he wrote these reflections long before you committed the wrong with which you reproach yourself." ' As if to confirm the reader's surmise, Madame de Staël in a note identifies the late Lord Nelvil's 'eloquent complaints' as quotations from Necker's *Course of Religious Morality*.

Corinne's hopes of calming Oswald's scruples are dimmed when, on the following day, she learns that his father had intended him to marry an English girl, Lucile Edgermond, who happens to be Corinne's half-sister. Plainly the time has come for a fuller explanation. Before giving one, however, Corinne takes Oswald to Cape Miseno, where she has arranged a rustic feast in his honour. At the end of the feast, overcome in the middle of a dance by a sombre foreboding, she walks alone to the extreme point of the cape, where Oswald and the guests find her and persuade her to take up her lyre. Gérard's well-known painting of 'Madame de Staël as Corinne on Cape Miseno' shows Germaine as she describes her heroine, seated on a rock, lyre in hand, under a pale moon, at dawn, with the Bay of Naples and Vesuvius in the background. She is surrounded by her friends, and, at a slight distance, by the peasants who have left the dance.

As Benjamin had noted, there was something of the mountebank in all this. Yet Corinne's improvisation, its harmonious prose stanzas rising to a crescendo of passion and despair, cannot be denied a certain tragic power.

> Fate [says Corinne] persecutes the exalted souls, the poets whose creative power springs from their capacity for suffering and love. . . . Why did the ancients speak of destiny with terror? What power has this destiny on vulgar and contented souls? They follow the seasons, and docile they travel on the common paths of life. But the priestess through whom the god spoke was shaken by a cruel power.

Soon after this Corinne hands Oswald a written account of her life. She is the daughter of Lord Edgermond by his first wife, an Italian. She was born in Italy. When she was ten, her mother died; after staying in Florence for five more years with an aunt, she was called back to England by her father, who had in the meantime married an Englishwoman and retired to an estate near a small Northumbrian town. English provincial life could not be painted in bleaker colours than by Corinne. The tea chatter of the local ladies makes Jane Austen's most insipid gossips sound like inspired conversationalists. 'Birth, marriage, and death made up the entire history of our society, and these three events bore an even closer resemblance to one another there than anywhere else in the world.' The second Lady Edgermond, Corinne's stepmother, combines the horrors of British rectitude with the most hateful characteristics of Germaine's own mother. When Corinne stayed in her room 'to cultivate her talents', Lady Edgermond was annoyed. ' "What is all this good for?" she said to me. "Will it make you any happier?" ' Among the narrow-minded and the mediocre, Corinne observes, 'duty means to sacrifice whatever talent one has, and intellect is a sin that must be atoned for by leading exactly the life of those who have none.'

Corinne's father planned to marry her, when she was twenty, to the son of his best friend. His best friend was Oswald's father. But the older Lord Nelvil was disquieted by Corinne's foreign and too lively ways; in a letter he informed Lord Edgermond that Oswald was too young to marry, and later he expressed the wish that Oswald should marry Corinne's half-sister Lucile when Lucile was old enough.

Corinne's life becomes intolerable when her father dies; she flees to Italy, assumes a new name, and allows Lady Edgermond to spread the rumour of her death. With her independent fortune she is able to cultivate her talents, to surround herself with friends of her choice, to live the life of a famous poetess. It is thus Oswald finds her, and with him she first knows love.

Oswald is shaken by this recital, as Corinne feared he would be. He vows never to marry any woman but her and gives her his ring as a pledge; but grave doubts, at first barely admitted to himself, arise in his mind whether he is free to marry her. The memory of his father, which is in reality the voice of the conventions of his society, warns him against marrying a woman so utterly incompatible with the Anglo-Saxon ideal of a wife; his heart and mind tell him that his prejudices are liars. He wavers, becomes evasive.

With all his exceptional virtues, there was a great deal of weakness and irresolution in Oswald's character. These defects are never noticed by him who has them, and with every changing circumstance they take on a new disguise in his eyes; at one moment, prudence makes it advisable to postpone a decision and to prolong an ambiguous situation; another time, it is sensibility or delicacy; almost never does one realize that it is one's own character which attributes the same kind of difficulty to all circumstances.

It is well to interrupt the story of Corinne and Oswald at this point, leaving the rest to be told in the proper context of Germaine's life. The Oswald just described is no longer the Oswald of the beginning. Not that there is a break in his character; but whereas his more positive qualities are prominent at the beginning, his weakness and irresolution dominate in the end. In a general sense, Oswald is all the men Germaine ever loved; in a specific sense, the Oswald who emerges in the middle of the book takes on the recognizable traits of Prosper de Barante, with whom Germaine fell in love on her return from Italy.

But *Corinne* is not merely a disguised confession. Even a complete identification of fictional with real characters is impossible except towards the end of the story. Corinne clearly is Germaine throughout, but an idealized Germaine. At the beginning, when she dances the shawl dance, Germaine and Juliette Récamier are conjoined in her person; at the end, she is Germaine undiluted, while some of Juliette has passed into Lucile Edgermond. But there is also a great deal of Germaine in Oswald himself; it is into him that she projects her feeling of guilt towards her father, into his mouth she places her negative reactions to Italy. Even in the Comte d'Erfeuil, her caricature of the conventional Frenchman, there are traits of Germaine; Sismondi's description of her, breezing through Italy and liking nothing, tallies comically with Germaine's description of d'Erfeuil. There are other manipulations of Germaine's actual experience that shed an interesting psychological light on the book: for instance, her triple rejection of her mother—first, by presenting her in a vicious caricature; second, by making her a stepmother; third, by making Corinne run away from her. The word Lady Edgermond never tires of repeating is *duty*, and the word Corinne never tires of repeating is *genius*: more sharply than in *Delphine*, the conflict between a woman's conventional place in society and her right to fulfil her destiny becomes a guiding theme of *Corinne*. When Corinne approaches the Capitol to be crowned, in a chariot drawn by four white horses, the crowd exclaims, 'Long live Corinne!

Long live genius! Long live beauty!'—and at that moment, says
Germaine, 'she produced the impression of a priestess of Apollo
approaching the temple of the sun and at the same time of a perfectly
simple woman in all the ordinary circumstances of life.' Elsewhere she
has Corinne declare, 'In seeking glory I always hoped to find love.'
To be priestess of Apollo and an ordinary woman whom men could
love like an ordinary woman—this seems scarcely possible, and Byron
was only half joking when he told Madame de Staël that her books were
immoral.

The personal problem dealt with in *Corinne* is merely an elaboration
of the problem treated in *Delphine*—but in a larger context. Madame
de Staël confronts not only the extraordinary woman with the ordinary
man; she confronts the North with the South, Romanticism with
Classicism, reason with passion. In this sense, *Corinne* is *De la littérature*
in fictional form. But it seems that at times Germaine got her polarities
mixed. Corinne herself she made a hybrid of North and South. This
was logical enough, since she regarded herself as such a hybrid. But by
combining the polarity of individual happiness *versus* social pressure
with the polarity of Classical South *versus* Romantic North, Germaine
obliged herself to side with the South against the North. There is a
tendency to extol the pagan serenity of the Latin South, which accepts
life and death, where even melancholy is untainted by 'dissatisfaction,
anxiety, and regret', and to oppose it to the introspective, metaphysical
North, where man, instead of living life, rejects its joy and beauty in the
name of morality, duty, and other abstractions. In Corinne instinct
balances the intellect (she is, be it remembered, a hybrid); in Oswald
thought kills instinct and abstractions paralyse action. The antithesis
might almost be reduced to one of male and female; and in this connection, too, it is useful to recall that in *Corinne* Germaine represents herself as a hybrid of North and South.

One faculty alone can bridge the gap. 'There are only two distinct
classes of people on this earth,' says Germaine: 'those who espouse
enthusiasm and those who despise it.' And enthusiasm she equated with
love. 'Love, supreme power of the heart,' declaims Corinne on Cape
Miseno, 'mysterious enthusiasm that encloses in itself all poetry, all
heroism, all religion!' This was forever Germaine's last word, but
never that of the Oswalds in her life.

Benjamin had left Geneva on November 26, 1804, about a week
before Germaine's departure for Italy. His destination was Paris, but

he intended to stop at Brévans, near Dôle, where his father lived in retirement with his second wife—the Marianne he had abducted half a century earlier—and his two children, whom Benjamin called, un-lovingly, the bastards. On the eve of his departure Germaine had asked him, impulsively, to meet her at Lyons (where she stopped to spend a few days with Camille Jordan) before he continued to Paris and she to Italy.

On his way to Brévans, Benjamin had time to reflect on a variety of problems. At seventy-eight Juste Constant was no more approachable to his son than he had been at sixty; on the contrary, the barrier of their timidity had been reinforced by conflicting material interests. At the time of his epic lawsuits of 1788 Juste had taken the precaution of transferring the bulk of his estate to his son in return for an annuity, but after his rehabilitation he claimed that the transfer had been ficti-tious and began to harass Benjamin with lawyers. Benjamin, who attri-buted his father's move to the cupidity of Marianne, agreed to increase the general's annuity but stoutly maintained the validity of the transfer. Since the general had a mania for litigation (he had an average of four to five lawsuits going at any one time), Benjamin had reason to believe that between the lawyers and the bastards his inheritance would vanish quickly if his father had control of it.

To be chronically threatened with suicide by one's mistress and with a lawsuit by one's father was especially disagreeable if one had appro-priated one's father's fortune and owed the mistress 80,000 francs. The sovereign remedy would be marriage with a rich woman, provided she also was loving, pretty, sensual, submissive, silent and undemanding, and provided neither Madame de Staël nor General Constant ruined his chances by some spectacular theatrical gesture. The next best thing would be to marry Madame de Staël and take a mistress who was loving, pretty, etc. Since his last week at Coppet had been spent in comparative peace, this alternative seemed to him workable and attractive. After four days at Brévans, spent entirely in talk about money, he joined Germaine at Pont d'Ain, and *en route* to Lyons he began to talk mar-riage. Germaine gently objected that she could not marry him until her children were grown up and provided for. Benjamin, while ap-preciating her motives, noted in his diary that a secret marriage would serve his purpose.

As always when she was about to leave France, Germaine during the five days she spent in Lyons was affectionate with Benjamin. 'She loves me more than ever,' he discovered. 'She clings to me as to her last attachment, her last tie on this earth.' On December 11 she left, almost fainting with grief. Benjamin was moved. 'It is a strange feeling I have for her. I am much happier away from her, yet to console her when she suffers I would sacrifice my life. Now for five or six months I shall be on my own.' That evening and the next day he slept with a prostitute.

He arrived in Paris on December 22. On Christmas Day, after a visit to a bordello, he reconsidered his situation. He had received from Germaine a 'touching and affectionate letter'. There was, he reflected, only one difficulty in their relationship—his need for women:

> I cannot do without them. I cannot start again the kind of life I have been leading, in this respect, at Weimar and Geneva. I need either a large city, where I can easily find beautiful physical forms, or a mistress. With her susceptibility, how can I manage this while she is in exile? As for marriage [with another woman], it would be madness. To break with the best of all beings, a being who has nothing left in the world that is homogeneous with her except me, would be cruel to her and ill-advised for me. The wisest and happiest course would be to allow her to come back and to live in Paris with her. If that is impossible, I shall have to see what else can be done. It would be impracticable to fall back on the abstinence of Coppet and the resources of Geneva.

Soliciting permission for Germaine's return and finding 'beautiful physical forms' were his principal pursuits under these Christmas resolutions. He also planned to spend much of the winter revising his *History of Polytheism* for which purpose he had installed his library at his estate, Les Herbages. As it turned out, of his six months of freedom from Madame de Staël Benjamin spent, in all, only a little over one month at Les Herbages and made no appreciable progress in his work. His efforts on behalf of Madame de Staël bore no fruit. He called on Regnault de Saint-Jean d'Angély, on Fouché, and on a dozen others of only slightly less exalted rank; they listened sympathetically, made vague promises, and did nothing.

Under the date of December 26, 1804, Benjamin's diary contains this fateful entry: 'Written to Madame du Tertre.' Madame du Tertre was Charlotte von Marenholz, *née* von Hardenberg, whom he had loved at Brunswick. After divorcing her husband to marry Benjamin, she had waited for five years; at last she gave up Benjamin and married a French *émigré*, General du Tertre, who took her back to Paris in 1802. During his trip to Germany Benjamin had received a letter from her; a desultory correspondence followed; now, at last, he would see her again. Her answer arrived on December 28, at the same time as a letter from

Mrs. Lindsay. 'I knew she still loves me,' was his comment on Anna's letter. 'I must answer her. I shall be as affectionate as possible, since this no longer commits me to anything.' And on Madame du Tertre's reply: 'At last I shall see her again, the woman who has changed my entire life and whom I have loved so passionately for a few days. I feel rather curious at the thought of this interview after twelve years of separation.'

He found her still pretty at thirty-five, and she made no attempt to conceal that she still loved him. Her husband, jealous, frivolous, mediocre, made her unhappy. Benjamin sensed danger. 'She might keep me busy through the winter, but she would make me waste my time. Good-bye, poor manuscript, if I yield to this temptation!' Yet despite his resolution to flee to Les Herbages, he returned to Charlotte the next day, and the day after that, and the next. At the same time he resumed his visits to Mrs. Lindsay. 'I daresay,' he admitted to himself, 'that no man ever was more polite to the women he had abandoned.' His politeness exceeded, perhaps, the proper bounds. Thus his journal entry for March 8 reads: 'Spent two hours at Mrs. Lindsay's. I have regained complete possession of her. $\pm$. Tuesday, I shall go to the country to rest from my women and my idleness.'[1] This episode remained without a sequel, which cannot be said of his daily calls on Madame du Tertre, even though Benjamin made no attempt to possess her. On December 31, three days after their reunion, Charlotte offered Benjamin her entire liquid fortune, 100,000 francs. 'I shall not take advantage of this, but it is a touching offer,' he commented. 'Women are good, honest creatures.' Two days later: 'This woman loves me passionately, and I could make her do whatever I want, but where would this lead? To more trouble. I want none of it.'

Charlotte began to show signs of impatience at Benjamin's reserve; her husband was infuriated by his assiduities: the situation was quite typically Benjaminian. Caught in a new dilemma, Benjamin gradually abandoned the ambitious plans he had formed for his six months of independence and sank back into his old abulia, or moral paralysis. He would begin his day by lying in bed for hours in a state of near-catatonic depression. Once risen, a spurious activity took hold of him, and he began a round of social calls which, combined with visits to the brothel, Mrs. Lindsay, and Charlotte, would fill his day. By the end of winter the empty automatism of his life had eroded his will power; then two events struck at him which unhinged him completely.

On March 15, while he was at Les Herbages, a messenger brought

[1] $\pm$ is Benjamin's symbol for sexual intercourse.

him news that his boon companion, the Marquis de Blacons, had just blown out his brains. The police had found him with 3 francs and 65 centimes in his pocket, a sum he had just borrowed from his janitor. Benjamin had eaten, drunk, gambled, and whored with Blacons; he even had lent him a few francs—but apparently not enough, so that for several days he regarded himself as responsible for his friend's death. He was shattered; even the bordello brought no comfort: 'Never, never shall I forget him. $\pm$. Useless attempt. I am just as sad as before.' By and by he convinced himself that nothing could have saved poor Blacons, but in the meantime an even worse piece of news had reached him: his old friend Julie Talma was dying.

On March 19, when Benjamin was already deep in his depression, Charlotte informed him that Monsieur du Tertre was in a mood approaching homicidal mania. If Benjamin kept up his visits, the general might go berserk. She begged him to stay away, cried, promised to write, and, when Benjamin agreed to all this unprotestingly, cried even more. Charlotte's manœuvre was an ill-disguised invitation to elopement, but if she expected the initiative to come from him, she was mistaken. 'Once and for all,' he wrote in his diary, 'I want no more of these warmed-up conquests.'

He spent the last days of March and most of April staying away from Charlotte and watching the slow dissolution of Madame Talma. The former actress had been deserted by her husband; she had lost her three sons within three years; she had nothing to hope for from life, and, being completely areligious, nothing from death either. Yet in her final weeks her noble stoicism gave way. She refused to face death and with incredible energy began to scheme a thousand small plans on the assumption that she would live on for years. Around her inheritance there grew up an intrigue of Balzacian proportions in which her friend, Mrs. Lindsay, and Mrs. Lindsay's lover, Auguste de Lamoignon, played unpalatable parts. Madame Talma herself, thinking perhaps that she could trick death, began to sell her estate for life annuities. Benjamin watched this strange spectacle with a mixture of detachment and fascination, contempt and pity. When, towards the end of April, Charlotte called at his apartment to let him know that for a reasonable share of her fortune General du Tertre would consent to divorce her, Benjamin was scarcely surprised. There was nothing men would not do for money. Charlotte suggested that, after her divorce, she could marry him. 'I don't think this is feasible,' mused Benjamin. 'If it were, at least I would get some rest.'

For temporary rest he escaped to Les Herbages. There he accidentally came across some old letters from his former wife. Two nights later, he

> dreamed all night of love—sentimental love, young love, love such as I experienced it at twenty. Three times in my life similar dreams were the harbingers of a violent passion. Once, especially, for Madame de Marenholz, now poor Madame du Tertre. But I still have no clear idea with whom I could fall in love. It is true that love is a feeling one places, whenever one feels the need of placing it, on the first object that happens along.

Back in Paris on May 2, he received a note from Charlotte, asking to see him because she had important news. He worked a little on his history of religion in the morning, went to his bordello in the afternoon, then dined with Madame Talma. 'Her death is close,' he noted. The next day came a letter from Germaine, 'violent, exaggerated, tempestuous', because Benjamin had not responded with sufficient alacrity to her order to await her return from Italy at Lausanne. In an instant, all his old fury against his slavery revived. 'If I had received this letter yesterday, I would have written more tenderly to Madame du Tertre.'

On May 4, Benjamin settled down by Julie Talma's sick bed to watch her end. 'I am studying death itself.' Naïvely he sought the answer to Hamlet's ultimate question. 'Is there a part in us that survives? . . . All the arguments of my habitual ideas are against; but the spectacle of death makes me glimpse possibilities in favour that until now I never suspected.'

He tore himself from the side of death to face Charlotte, who announced that her husband agreed to let her obtain a German divorce decree and that she placed her fate in Benjamin's hands. 'I was dominated by my astonishment,' says Benjamin, 'but I believe I told her enough to encourage her.'

Next day, May 5, Julie Talma died under Benjamin's eyes. Lucid to the end, she rose up violently in her bed, with a final gesture of protest and flight, when death pushed her back onto her pillows. A 'bizarre, greedy, and sombre curiosity' led Benjamin back to her lifeless, naked body: 'Eyes half-closed, mouth ajar, head fallen back, hair in disorder, hands contracted, nothing gentle left in her expression, nothing that resembles her!' Benjamin's obsessive thought returned with all its force: that all must end there, that nothing mattered in life because of death.

Madame Talma was buried on May 7. 'In silence the earth opens up,' Benjamin wrote years later, 'in silence it closes again, and as its surface resumes its uniform aspect it leaves our questions unanswered and our regrets uncomforted.' After the funeral Charlotte called at his flat. She could not have selected a more favourable time for her purpose, which was to inform him of her impending departure for Germany to obtain her divorce. Benjamin agreed to everything she said. 'I surrender myself to fate,' he wrote in his diary. The same afternoon a letter from Germaine ordered him to leave Paris on June 1 and to meet her at Lausanne. 'It is all the same to me at this point,' he commented. While Charlotte was in Germany, he would join Madame de Staël, calm her down, and await further developments. With this resolution, or rather abdication of his will, he ended his diary. Only an abbreviated journal covers the period from May 8, 1805, to April 12, 1808. It is partly written in number code. The code tells more of Benjamin than anything else could in so little space:

  1 = Physical [i.e., sexual] pleasure.
  2 = Desire to break my eternal chain [with Madame de Staël].
  3 = Reconciliation with this bond, because of memories or a momentary charm.
  4 = Work.
  5 = Disputes with my father.
  6 = Tenderness for my father.
  7 = Travel projects.
  8 = Marriage projects.
  9 = Tired of Mrs. Lindsay.
  10 = Sweet memories and revival of love for Mrs. Lindsay.
  11 = Irresolution in my projects with regard to Mme du Tertre.
  12 = Love for Mme du Tertre.
  13 = Indecision about everything.
  14 = Plan to settle at Dôle [with his father] to break with Biondetta.
  15 = Plan to settle in Lausanne for the same purpose.
  16 = Projects for a voyage overseas [i.e., America]
  17 = Desire to make up with certain enemies [i.e., Napoleon].

Numbers 9 and 10 gave Benjamin some slight trouble during his remaining weeks in Paris. On July 3, after receiving a letter from Germaine which prompted him to write fourteen 2's in a row, he left for Coppet.

On May 26, 1805, Napoleon was crowned King of Italy at Milan. Though tempted to approach the tyrant while he was in a clement mood, Germaine stayed away from Milan until the coronation festivities were over. When she arrived in early June, she was well received by Empress Josephine, but her hope to obtain redress was disappointed. By way of Florence, Venice, Milan, and Turin, Germaine and her suite returned to Coppet late in June. On July 8 Benjamin, Claude Hochet, and Prosper de Barante arrived together from Paris to lighten her solitude; Chateaubriand came in August. Another Coppet season had begun.

As Germaine told Chateaubriand, who owed much of his reputation to his sonorous admiration of Nature, what she really longed to see was the gutter of the rue du Bac. She had wheedled Hochet into coming to Switzerland for very practical reasons. As Secretary of the Department of the Interior of the Conseil d'Etat, that amiable six-footer was in an ideal position for promoting her two principal objectives: repeal of her order of exile and—the *basso ostinato* of her life—restitution of Necker's two millions. A new approach was devised. Her eldest son, Auguste, would be sent to Paris to enter a boarding school and to prepare his entrance examinations for the Ecole Polytechnique. This plan would both open a career for Auguste and supply his mother with an additional argument in favour of residing in Paris. Five weeks after Hochet's arrival he left again, accompanied by Auguste and well provided with tactical instructions.

Germaine's letters to Auguste show her as exacting towards her elder son as she was indulgent to the younger. If the fifteen-year-old boy had been her lover, she could not have treated him more roughly. His letters were too short, she complained; they lacked sensibility and refinement; they ended with detestable references to bells ringing for class or to the mail being about to leave; they were uninformative on such subjects as friends, curriculum, and scholastic progress, and they were not frequent enough. 'I order you to write to me two letters every week, Thursdays and Sundays, of four pages each, and I mean of the size of this sheet. I am sorry if I am obliged to prescribe to you the measure of your sentiment, but it is the lesser evil to impose it on you as a duty until you are aware enough of what I want to do it as a pleasure.' Writing letters, she informed him another time, 'is an exercise of the mind and of the heart'—a pretty formulation, and no doubt Auguste's indolence deserved some criticism; but the mind staggers when one reads what other things she expected of the boy. She ordered him to speak of her 'interests' to various high-placed persons and to take letters from her to Prince Joseph and to the Emperor himself; and when he evaded those

frightening missions, she sent him crushing rebukes. 'The kind of shyness that prevents you from being of any service to me distresses me a
little. . . . It would have been very good for you to overcome your
natural timidity, either out of love for me or even as a duty, for it will
be a great obstacle to you.' Sound advice again; but ordering a timid
adolescent to face Napoleon seems too heroic a remedy for shyness.

All these manœuvres were futile. Napoleon had issued specific instructions to Fouché on August 29, 1805: 'Madame de Staël pretends
I gave her permission to go back to Paris. . . . Order her back to Coppet.
You realize I am not such an idiot that I would rather have her in Paris
than at twenty leagues away from it.' As for the two millions, without
ever rejecting Germaine's claims, the Emperor protracted negotiations
indefinitely: in the policy of the stick and the carrot he was an accomplished practitioner.

'I have had the visits of the Elector of Bavaria . . . of Prince Esterhazy,
of all Europe—but what good does all this do me?' Germaine wrote to
Hochet on September 4. From her lamentations one might think she
was confined on an aristocratic Devil's Island. Her work, her estate, her
guests, her correspondence, her children, her daily quarrels—all this
could not fill the void inside her. And so it was that she fell in love; the
second part of *Corinne* remained to be lived and written.

Her affair with Dom Pedro had been little more than a passionate
flirtation. If she tried to retain his affections, she went about it by strange
means. Thus, writing to him from Florence to invite him to Coppet,
she made this extraordinary declaration: 'I shall be the knight who will
set [your mind and feelings] free. I shall teach you to know yourself, to
show yourself as you really are. Then, having become even worthier of
love than you are now, you shall leave, and I shall dream that perhaps
one day you will marry my daughter.' She was not jesting, she added.
His natural gifts being combined with indolence, he needed the society
of a superior woman who would stimulate his intelligence and sensibility—'for what better things has this earth than to think and to feel?'

Dom Pedro was in no hurry to join a mistress who wanted to be his
knight, muse, and mother-in-law all in one. He remained silent. Yet
when Germaine learned, late in October, that Dom Pedro was to marry
a Mademoiselle du Perron, her reaction was surprisingly mild: 'I did
not think you would settle down so young. Your choice seems excellent.' As it turned out, Souza did not marry the lady, but this Germaine
could not know; if she acted so calmly, it was for two reasons: she had
never counted on Oswald I, and she had discovered Oswald II.

Prosper de Barante, the future historian of the dukes of Burgundy, was in his twenty-fourth year when he fell in love with Germaine, who was in her fortieth. His father, Claude-Ignace de Barante, Prefect of the department of Léman, had been among Germaine's admirers for many years. He had paid court to Germaine assiduously, perhaps not altogether without amorous intentions. His good relations with Madame de Staël ended up by making him suspect to his superiors. Prosper, attached to the Ministry of the Interior, had first come to Germaine's attention in 1804. He was young, elegant, intelligent, reserved, of delicate health—all qualities she liked in young men. When he journeyed to Geneva in the company of Hochet and Benjamin in July 1805, he was on extended leave for reasons of health. By early September Germaine confided to Hochet that every day she found Prosper more worthy of her attention. In the same month Prosper addressed to Germaine a note which leaves little doubt on the progress of their relationship:

> Adieu, I kiss you and I love you: I am happy. Sometimes, when I hold you in my arms, I feel regret at not being able to be yours completely. But when I listen only to my heart, I tell myself that nothing can be added to my feelings and that I need nothing more to declare myself yours forever.

'Not being able to be yours completely' is a puzzling phrase, following as it does on 'when I hold you in my arms'. Whether it was marriage or herself that Germaine was refusing him, no one can say with certainty, but there is no question that Prosper wanted to marry her. This, too, was strange; for, as he wrote to her three years later, the woman of his dreams had always been, 'a mixture of ignorance, weakness, and inexperience'—a virginal image to which Germaine bore no resemblance. Admitting to thirty-five years, stout, formidable, and prognathous, she had nothing to redeem her appearance except her eyes and her smile. But those expressed intelligence, kindness, and idealistic fire, not ignorance, weakness, and inexperience. Now Prosper, like many men endowed with talent and sensibility, was balanced between two opposite poles of attraction: on the one hand, the clinging vine (it takes little effort to hold up a vine); on the other, some incarnation of Lady Macbeth. Germaine might be selfish, tyrannical, preying; but if she fastened upon a man, she would awaken and stimulate every ounce of his latent capacity and make him conscious of his every gift—an experience more intoxicating than mere sensual delight. 'I shall teach you to know yourself.'

In the long run, men are more comfortable when operating somewhat below maximum capacity, but in the autumn of 1805, Barante the son was still intoxicated with the self revealed to him and spell-bound by the revealer. Barante the father was not only sober but also terrified. The disparity of age and wealth, he pointed out to Prosper, was bound to lead to domestic unhappiness if they married. The Emperor, on whom Prosper's fortunes depended, would be antagonized. Prosper himself would be crushed under the weight of Germaine's personality and fame. These excellent arguments sank in, but their effect was not immediate. Prosper defied his father, and Germaine, in a tearful scene, implored the Prefect not to 'deprive her of all hope of happiness'. Claude-Ignace, who was not a barbarian, allowed the romance to continue, putting his trust in the effect of time. To Germaine the present sufficed. 'I do not know,' Prosper wrote to her at the time, 'what will happen after this month of friendship we shall spend together. I shall try not to let thoughts of the future spoil the enjoyment of the present.' One is reminded of this dialogue between Oswald and Corinne: 'I swear,' says Oswald, 'that I shall not leave you before three months are out. And even then, perhaps—' 'Three months!' exclaims Corinne. 'Then I still have all that time to live. I had not hoped for so much. . . . Three months is a future.'

Unfortunately, while Germaine was enjoying her month of happiness with the new Oswald, the old Oswald intruded on the scene: Dom Pedro, in a delayed reaction to her proddings, appeared suddenly in Geneva, where she had moved for the winter. This awkward complication has no parallel in the novel. Germaine was not in the least embarrassed by it. The two months he spent in Geneva with Germaine, Dom Pedro asserts in his diary, were among the most agreeable in his life. Prosper was puzzled. He could put up with Benjamin; he resented Schlegel, who 'rolled his eyes' at him 'with ridiculous hatred'; he probably did not even know of Sismondi's low-powered passion—but Dom Pedro was something else. Before the season was over, Prosper's diary began to bear an astonishing resemblance to Benjamin's.

Thus surrounded by an ex-lover whom she refused to let go, by the two models of Oswald, by Schlegel, who had signed a pledge of lifelong slavery, and by the discreetly sighing Sismondi, Germaine spent the winter of 1805–6. To amuse the dreary solitude of her exile, she plunged herself into what Benjamin called the 'fury of spectacles'—that is, she rented an apartment on the Place du Molard, remodelled it into a stage, and offered a full-fledged theatrical season. The stage was low ('The

MADAME RÉCAMIER
From a portrait by François Gérard at the Musée de la Ville de Paris

THE CHÂTEAU OF COPPET, GRAND SALON

THE CHÂTEAU OF COPPET, MADAME DE STAËL'S BEDROOM

only role we could offer you,' Prosper wrote to the giant Hochet, 'is that of a Caryatid'), but the scenery was professional and the performances well rehearsed. The season opened with Voltaire's *Mérope* on December 30. On January 27 *Mahomet*, also by Voltaire, was on the bill. On March 31 the season ended with Germaine's preferred vehicle, *Phèdre*, with Prosper, appositely enough, as Hippolytus. Four days later Prosper left for Paris to take his new post as auditor in the Conseil d'Etat. 'Prosper gone, Schlegel overjoyed,' reads Benjamin's diary entry for April 4, 1806.

With a ruler draw on a map a straight line from Geneva to Paris; with a compass draw a circle with Paris at the centre and a radius of forty leagues: the circle will intersect the line at a point very near the city of Auxerre. This is where Germaine went two weeks after Prosper's departure, with Schlegel, Albert, and Albertine in tow. The two objectives of her strategy were Prosper and Paris; the strategy itself was a circular system of successive approximations, with long halts at each newly conquered position to consolidate her gain and soften up the next objective. Her first step—obtaining permission to re-enter France proper—had been facilitated by Barante *père*, who avowed to Fouché that for the past year she had been 'very reserved and circumspect'. On April 28 she arrived at Auxerre. There and at the nearby château of Vincelles, which she had rented from a friend, she was to spend the next four months.

It took Auxerre, situated in a treeless, chalky plain, to make Germaine babble of greenery and nature. Finding no resources in the town, where French provincial life crept on imperceptibly in a desolation of the spirit, she sat in her room cramming herself with opium, issuing the customary summonses and appeals to friends, and starting up each time she heard the sound of a coachman's whip, hoping it meant a letter or a visitor. Souza, Mathieu de Montmorency and his cousin Adrien, Juliette Récamier, Camille Jordan, Hochet, Elzéar de Sabran—all came for visits of various duration: never had Auxerre seen so fashionable a concourse.

The most urgent summonses went out to Benjamin and to Prosper. Benjamin, still convalescing from broncho-pneumonia, left Geneva on June 1 and stopped on his way at Brévans. His stay was cut short by a bombardment of letters from Germaine. 'The universe is shaking and chaos on the move,' Benjamin wrote in his diary. 'All the volcanoes put together are less flamboyant than she.' Along with her letters,

M

Germaine sent her factotum Uginet, who collared Benjamin and delivered him at Auxerre on June 7. 'What utter disorganization!' was the diarist's comment on the reunion.

On June 15 Prosper arrived on one of his flying visits. 'She is furious,' noted Benjamin, 'because he is leaving tomorrow. I feel like setting up an altar to unreasonableness.'

Like Benjamin, Prosper came reluctantly. Not only did Germaine threaten to die from despair or an overdose of opium if he did not, but she also employed Mathieu and Juliette as intercessors. Cornered, he remonstrated:

> I have told you already: take care! I shall do everything to appease your suffering; I shall deliver into your hands the man whom you love— deliver him to you at the cost of his happiness. He will come to stay with you, unhappy and wretched; and to avoid your reproaches, to make your life easier, he will conceal as best he can his misery under a laughing mask.

If Prosper imagined that she would refuse him under such conditions, he was mistaken.

At his wits' end, Prosper resorted to the bizarre scheme of writing to his father and begging him to use his authority with Germaine; he was to persuade her to cease making demands on his son's love and to be content with his exalted friendship. Prosper even sent the Prefect a draft of the letter he was to write. At this, Claude-Ignace blew up:

> I am returning the draft of the letter you order me to write immediately to Auxerre. Extravagance and insanity cannot be pushed further. There is not a word, not a single word in your letter that does not reveal to me the horrible situation that woman has put you in. . . . Keep on . . . wasting your time and health on continuous journeys undertaken at the expense of your sleep and my money, for a woman who, as you told me and others, has not the least notion of what duty means! . . . Everything is possible in the horrible madness into which this woman has led you. . . . What sort of relationship is there between you? You give me your word of honour that you will never be her lover or husband. What do words matter to me if the feelings you are made to feel are more imperious even than love? Oh, how I pity you for not being able to break such a bond!

These accusations were undeniably true. Yet if one places side by side this letter, Prosper's diary, and the character of Oswald in *Corinne*, Germaine's (or Corinne's) behaviour becomes understandable; and, as Corinne says, 'To understand all makes one very indulgent.'

Talleyrand, Mathieu, Narbonne, de Pange, Benjamin, Souza, and now Barante—all had tired of Germaine because her demand for love exceeded their capacity. She had not, to be sure, loved them with all the exclusive faithfulness male vanity expects; yet if the love of any one of them had measured up to hers, perhaps this would have been different; and, at any rate, each share of her divided love exceeded in intensity the entire love that they could muster. But love as she understood it was incompatible with duty. Undoubtedly, common sense, responsibility, the public good are all on the side of the Oswalds; the egotism of romantic passion, so wise men tell us, is pernicious. However, one might question, with Germaine, whether the Oswalds are cold lovers out of devotion to the public good, or whether they are cold lovers because they are cold. Is there really a danger of enthusiasm becoming epidemic, Benjamin asked in an article in defence of *Corinne*; 'Is there a great deal of self-immolating going on on account of love? . . . Seeing so many writers hasten to the rescue of selfishness, one would think that it is in danger of extinction.' In truth, Corinne's *égoïsme à deux* and Oswald's sense of duty are but two aspects of selfishness. Barante eventually will marry Mademoiselle d'Houdetot, gentle and innocent, and become an ambassador; Oswald marries Lucile and, sooner or later, will be a Member of Parliament: the orderly progress of the world is assured. But, as the dying Corinne says of Oswald:

> He has soiled the object of my cult. He has deceived me, knowingly or unwittingly—it does not matter. He is not what I thought he was. What has he done for me? For one year he has enjoyed the feeling he inspired in me; and when the time came to take my defence, when he should have proved his feelings in action, did he act? Can he boast of a sacrifice, a generous gesture? He is happy now; he possesses every advantage the world prizes; as for me, I am dying. He should leave me in peace.

It is unlikely that Germaine would have changed a word in this tirade if she had read this entry in Prosper's diary:

> Assuredly, no one is more capable of love than she. But, all the same, there is a proper limit to love that must not be passed lest one become unhappy or guilty. She, on the contrary, believes that there is nothing better than to push love to its ultimate limit, and she has a real esteem for people whom love drives to frenzy and to crime.

In this argument there can be no last word.

In her novel Madame de Staël has Corinne follow Oswald to England, where he had been recalled to his regiment, just as she herself had

followed Barante to France. Unlike Germaine, however, Corinne gives
Oswald no sign of her presence. She observes him secretly—at Covent
Garden, at a military review in Hyde Park, at the house of Lady
Edgermond in Northumberland. Unseen, unsuspected, she observes
him falling in love with her half-sister Lucile, that mixture of 'ignorance, weakness and inexperience'. While Corinne is 'wandering alone
from inn to inn, without even seeing the man for whom she has
sacrificed everything, and lacking the strength to keep away from him',
Oswald, being without news from Corinne, begins to doubt her constancy. Yet faithful to his promise, he still resists his love for Lucile: he
cannot marry her as long as Corinne has his pledge, symbolized by the
ring he has given her. This Corinne does not know, but she can plainly
see Oswald's feelings for Lucile. A chance conversation with Oswald's
solicitor, who is unaware of her identity, reveals to her that she alone
stands in the way of Oswald's marriage. Hiding in the darkness of the
Edgermonds' park, while the mansion is illuminated for a ball in
Lucile's and Oswald's honour, Corinne is moved to self-sacrifice at the
aspect of Lucile's love. She hands a letter, containing the ring, to a blind
old man and asks him to deliver it to Lord Nelvil through a servant.
She watches the servant close the door;

> and when she no longer saw him, and she had reached the highway, and
> no longer heard the music, and even the lights of the castle had disap-
> peared from sight, a cold sweat broke out on her forehead, a deathly
> shudder seized her: she wanted to walk away, but her strength failed,
> and she fell unconscious on the highway.

After the wildly romantic and sentimental scene in the park, this
stark conclusion, a woman collapsing in cold sweat on a dark highway,
has the ring of truth. A similar incident seems to have occurred at
Auxerre. In the novel Corinne is picked up on the road by the Comte
d'Erfeuil, who chances by on his way to visit Lord Nelvil. D'Erfeuil
nurses her through eight days of 'fever and delirium', and sees her off
safely to Italy—all this as a matter of course and without the least
display of emotion. 'Thus,' remarks Germaine, 'it was the frivolous
man who cared for her, and the man of sensibility who pierced her
heart.' *Corinne* was barely off the press when Hochet complained to
Madame de Staël that he would be identified with the Comte d'Erfeuil
because of this particular episode in the novel. In her reply Germaine
denied the identification but admitted the factual basis of the episode.

Had Germaine really fainted on the highway, perhaps after taking leave from Prosper, and been found by Hochet? It surely would have been in character. It seems likely, at any rate, that Hochet had found her in a profound crisis of despair and cared for her material needs in an offhand, unsentimental manner—perhaps even saying 'I told you so', as d'Erfeuil says to Corinne. A crisis assuredly occurred late in July or early in August 1806, and it was succeeded by a temporary calm. Indeed, on August 26 Sismondi in a letter to Germaine expressed his gratification that her projects concerning Prosper had undergone a change. 'You would have ended up by losing Benjamin,' he added bluntly.

A common criticism of *Corinne* is that the entire plot rests on Corinne's implausible silence. If she had let Oswald know that she had followed him to England, Oswald would never have married Lucile and Corinne need not have died in despair. This criticism is very superficial. True, Corinne's silence is implausible if Corinne is equated with Germaine; but it is not implausible in itself. For Corinne it is enough to see Oswald's attraction to Lucile; she has seen enough to know that Oswald will never be happy with Corinne. Why should she disclose her presence to him? Undoubtedly he would come back to her, but he would condemn her unladylike action, and he would regret Lucile for the rest of his life. He is not what she thought he was. How much more noble to remove herself from the scene, to let Oswald marry Lucile, and to die in the knowledge that he would regret Corinne for the rest of his life!

These motives, though implicit, are not stated in the novel. When Corinne is on the brink of disclosing her presence to Oswald, what prevents her is, of all things, womanly modesty. This motive of Corinne's silence accords neither with Corinne's character nor with Germaine's conduct. There was no womanly modesty in Germaine's appeals to Prosper or to anyone else she loved; there was only the despotic truculence of the spoiled child. In her tantrum she *commanded* love, she *commanded* pity—the two feelings least responsive to commands.

The identity of Corinne and Germaine should not blind one to the discrepancies, not of character, but of conduct. Corinne has only one Oswald; Germaine had two. Corinne goes to England incognita; no one could help noticing Germaine's presence at Auxerre. Corinne magnanimously sacrifices her happiness to Lucile's; Germaine advised Juliette Récamier to keep her hands off Prosper. For Prosper, weary of the flamboyant Germaine, had begun to long for the demure Juliette.

It was Germaine herself who unwittingly introduced this new complication. She had asked Juliette to speak to Prosper in Paris, and to make him see his duty. Prosper noted in his diary on August 3:

> At eleven o'clock I called on Madame Récamier, who has written me again to ask me to her house so she could talk to me about Louise [i.e., Germaine].[1] She preached a good deal on the conduct I ought to follow; she asked me to visit Louise again in a few days, which I certainly shall not do. This disagreeable conversation is to be resumed day after tomorrow.

The interviews became more frequent and less disagreeable. Juliette did not speak only of Madame de Staël.

Germaine's suspicions were aroused. She wrote to Juliette:

> You say you will write to me more often, now that you see more of Prosper. I fear, I confess, that you let yourself be loved by him. This would cause me mortal suffering. . . . Do not do it, Juliette. . . . I have placed my faith in you; I am prodigiously inferior to your attractions: generosity forbids you to allow yourself the least coquettishness with him. Not that I have much trust in his love for me: . . . but if in addition to this misfortune I must think that I owe it to you, this would be a terrible blow to me. . . . Answer this letter at once, in which I have put my whole soul at your mercy.

The letter was written from Rouen, late in September 1806. A good many things had happened since her arrival at Auxerre that had little to do with Prosper and that found no place in *Corinne*. To see Prosper had not been Germaine's only objective in coming to Auxerre, nor was Prosper's coolness the only cause of her frenzied frustration. With her headquarters established on the periphery of the prescribed forty leagues, she had set in motion all her forces to obtain permission to reside in Paris, or at least close to Paris, and to recover her two millions. The road from Paris to Auxerre was never empty of emissaries going to and fro. At times the officials answered with cautious optimism; at other times they dashed all hopes. It was on Benjamin, if he was not away in Paris, that she then vented her fury. 'Bad news from Paris,' he noted on June 25. 'Veritable delirium. It is a torture to see her in this situation. Horrible day.' On July 30: 'Horrible, frightening, demented scene. Atrocious expressions. Either she is mad, or I am. How will all this end?' A short period of calm followed, perhaps thanks to Souza,

---

[1] Prosper called Madame de Staël by the second of her three given names (Anne Louise Germaine) either because he liked it better, or, more probably, because no one else did.

who arrived the following day. Germaine had made up her mind to take the waters at Spa; perhaps she might return to Paris from there; or, if the current rumours of a general peace were true, she might continue to England. All was ready for the journey when, on August 8, Schlegel came down with a tertian fever.

On August 10 Germaine and 'all her troops', as she called them, moved on to Auxerre. But Schlegel's condition became so alarming that they could not continue the journey. At the wretched inn the travellers took turns watching Schlegel's agues and made scenes to each other in the intervals. When not delirious, Schlegel enlivened the atmosphere with exhibitions of cowardice, self-pity, and 'incredible ill-humour'. 'For the love of God,' Sismondi admonished Germaine from Geneva, 'come back to Coppet, where the air is more wholesome for your patient and yourself, and stop this eternal camping under tents!'

But Germaine was a determined nomad. As soon as Schlegel improved a little, she dragged him on to Dijon and thence (having dropped the idea of Spa), to Rouen, where Fouché gave her permission to stay the winter. On her way, with Schlegel suffering a relapse, she halted at Etampes, where for three days she exchanged farewells with Dom Pedro, who was on his way back to Portugal. 'I cried last night when I heard the horses taking you away,' she wrote to him in the small hours of September 17; 'how happy you would make me if you returned. This is all I can think of, all I can think of.' This done, and with Benjamin again by her side, she bade Schlegel rise from his sick bed, and drove on to Rouen, where the party arrived the next day.

Soon afterwards, Dom Pedro de Souza e Holstein married Eugenia Telles de Gama. She was sixteen years old.

'I am especially glad to find you speaking in the past tense of sentiments which I thought were only too present,' Sismondi wrote to Germaine in October, alluding to her love for Prosper. Her letters seemed calmer, her spirits much improved. But Sismondi rejoiced too soon: the sentiments of which she spoke in the past tense were not past at all but merely found a temporary outlet in her novel, and a new crisis was building up with Benjamin.

After Charlotte's departure for Germany in May 1805 Benjamin had gone through his usual cycles of abandoned resolutions. In August a letter from Charlotte informed him that her husband's consent to divorce was not legally valid. 'I have wasted my time,' was Benjamin's only comment. Having abandoned 12 (love for Charlotte), he wavered between 2 (break with Germaine), 3 (reconciliation with Germaine,) and 8 (marriage with Antoinette de Loys, a Lausanne heiress whom his family sought to impose on him). His diary entry for September 29, 1805, is typical: 'Morning wasted. Horrible scene. 2 seems inevitable. Another scene. 3 impossible. 7 [voyage abroad] difficult. 12 abandoned. I must seriously think of 8.'

He had spent the rest of the winter in alternating fits of broncho-pneumonia and theatrical rehearsals, punctuated on December 30 by the news of Belle van Tuyll's death. ('I am profoundly depressed by the death of Madame de Charrière. 1.') The summer was employed in running errands for Germaine in Paris and listening to her rant at Auxerre. And yet, on August 26, he could write in his diary: 'After all her scenes and my resolutions, I feel that I am reverting to 3, I do not know why.' The persistence of his attachment to Germaine had indeed no rational explanation, for he was fully aware of her relationship with Prosper. He and Prosper even exchanged confidences. 'He suffers,' Benjamin wrote of Prosper on July 13; 'he is weary. Who wouldn't be? But he will manage to extricate himself from this, whereas I—'

On October 18, relieved from his post at Rouen by the arrival of Mathieu, Benjamin left for Paris. The following day he called on Charlotte, who had just returned and whose looks he found much improved, then dined with Prosper. What happened then is told in *Cécile*:[1]

> I went to dine with one of my friends. The excitement into which the sight of Cécile [i.e., Charlotte] . . . had plunged me continued and increased during the meal. The talk drifted to the subject of women and was of the kind that is normal among men. A kind of fatuous regret took hold of me. I reproached myself for having been loved by Cécile for thirteen years, without ever exacting conclusive proof of her love, and I returned to her determined to try all in order to obtain all, leaving the rest of my fate to chance.

His diary confirms the novel:

> *October* 19: Dinner with Prosper. Tonight I want to go as far as possible with Charlotte. Thirteen years of resistance is more than enough. Tomorrow I shall write down the result. . . .
>
> *October* 20: Charlotte has yielded. Thus 1. When it was over, I did what I could to calm her. I hope I succeeded.

---

[1] This barely disguised autobiographical novel, which Benjamin never finished, was first published in 1951.

In *Cécile* Benjamin elucidates:

> I felt almost as if I had robbed a blind man who has asked me to guide
> him, or killed a child that has trusted itself to me. As for Cécile, when
> she recovered from her surprise, she fell into a deep depression. She
> remained silent and motionless, and tears rolled down her cheeks. When,
> by talking to her, I forced her to answer, I realized that all her ideas had
> changed. She thought she had no more claims on me. . . . For a long
> time I was unable to make her give the least thought to the future.

Thus, after deciding from vanity to possess her, he committed his
future to her from pity, and persuaded himself that he loved. In the
evening he possessed her again. 'This time, there is no doubt left [of
her love]. God, how this thing attaches a woman to a man!' 1 again on
October 22, on October 23, and on his fortieth birthday, October 25.

> What an angel I have disdained! Love in all its violence has seized me
> again. . . . Delirium of love. What the devil is the meaning of this? For
> ten years I have felt nothing like it. . . . Everything is upside down. I
> want Charlotte, I want her at any price.

Still, Benjamin was not so carried away as to lose all gift of self-
analysis:

> Stupid animal that I am! I let myself be loved by women whom I do
> not love. Then suddenly love rises in my heart like a whirlwind, and an
> affair I wanted merely to pull me out of my boredom results in a total
> upheaval of my life. Should this be the destiny of an intelligent man?

'Unbelievable blend of pleasure and pain. Most delicious night in
my life,' noted Benjamin on October 28, adding that 12 was no longer
a question but a sacred duty. The morning after making this entry he
returned to Rouen, leaving Charlotte 'bathed in tears and in convulsions
of grief'. He found Germaine's household in deep gloom and felt a
little embarrassed.

On the day of Benjamin's arrival, Germaine wrote a letter to Claude-
Ignace de Barante. To remove his son from Germaine's influence, the
Prefect had induced the government to employ him on missions
abroad. Prosper had been to Spain in late August. He was about to
be sent to Germany. To add insult to injury Barante the father had
reproached Germaine for her obstinate attempts to return to Paris.
Hence the gloom. She wrote to the Prefect:

> I do not know what will become of me. France, for me, is he! Why blame
> me, if I am not to see him again? You, whom he loves so much, whom I

M*

love too, although you have hurt me so much, do give me your support if you can, and have pity on me if I cannot bear up under my misery.

Benjamin's excitement did not escape Germaine. Acting like a schoolboy, he was caught like one. On November 7, as he was writing to Charlotte, Germaine entered his room. She had long been in the habit, Benjamin says in *Cécile*, of reading his letters, and he had never tried to prevent her. This time he hastily hid what he had written.

> She asked me, in a rather imperious tone of voice, to show her my letter. I refused and, to cut the struggle short, burned it before her eyes. Her irritation increased, and in the course of the ensuing quarrel it occurred to me that if I told her all, I would be relieved both of the need to dissemble, which I found disagreeable, and of my yoke. This decision, which I made in the belief that it proved my strength, was perhaps merely the product of my submissiveness, which had become second nature. . . . She thus was apprised of my relationship with Cécile and of the promises I had made her. A storm broke loose which lasted without interruption through the entire day and the entire night.

Benjamin's diary confirms the veracity of *Cécile*: 'Burned my letter. Terrible day. Admission. 2 decided. Everything is finished. My head feels smashed. I want to leave. If I stayed, all I would get is scenes, and I would be regarded as a monster.' But already on the following day, his resolution was broken: 'Had a calmer talk. I must proceed with caution.' This was precisely what he did for three more years.

Benjamin was not alone in finding it difficult to break with Germaine. The following diary entries, made on the same days by Prosper in Paris and by Benjamin in Rouen, are suggestive:

BENJAMIN'S DIARY

November 17: Gentle, dear Charlotte, I shall make you happy. I cannot express the delight I anticipate in living with her. Its own worth will be enhanced by all the storms and privations of my past life.

November 19: Letter from Charlotte. I can guess at his [du Tertre's] conditions. They will be onerous as far as money is concerned. . . . I desire 2 so intensely that I shall raise no difficulties so long as they are not intolerable.

PROSPER'S DIARY

November 17: I have changed a great deal. Thought about my situation. Desire to marry, but only to love and be loved. Fear of seeking that pleasure elsewhere. I incline to seek this kind of relationship with Juliette.

November 19: Every morning I think with displeasure about this tyrannical *liaison*. Difficulty of breaking it up. Desire to be in a position to marry. I want to marry to be happy.

On November 29 Germaine moved yet another stage closer to Paris, into the château of Acosta, at Meulan near Versailles, which she had rented from a friend. Napoleon was campaigning in Poland, and Fouché, whose permission she anticipated, made no move to eject her. Having scored this tactical victory, she regained some of her calm. She had resumed working on *Corinne*. To write its conclusion was a catharsis and a revenge.

With Corinne back in Italy, broken-hearted and waiting for death, it remained for Germaine to prepare a suitably savage punishment for Oswald. He marries Lucile, who bears him a daughter, then he goes off to the wars in the West Indies. Returning after a lapse of years, he finds Lucile a model mother and wife but a poor substitute for Corinne. To make things worse, his solicitor, Mr. Dickson—the most blundering solicitor in all fiction—tells him calmly how Corinne has sacrificed her happiness to his. This information spoils not only the tennis game in which Oswald happens to be engaged but also the rest of his life. After Lady Edgermond, having savoured all the joys of dying, is laid in her grave, Oswald falls gravely ill. In his delirium he raves of the sun, the south, warmth, the coldness of the north, Italy, Corinne.

When Oswald recovers, Lucile proposes a trip to Italy for his health. She and her child will accompany him, she adds. Lucile is jealous of Corinne, but never mentions her. Oswald hopes to see Corinne, but never mentions her. A wall of unavowed thoughts grows up between them; they both are profoundly unhappy. If there is any part in *Corinne* in which Madame de Staël wrote with the persuasiveness of a skilled novelist, it is her chilling description of the dreary void of marriage without intimacy or communication. Let Prosper, let Benjamin shudder at the picture of themselves hitched to a sweet mediocrity, after having known the passion of a priestess of the sun!

Crossing the Alps and the rain-drenched plains in winter, Oswald and Lucile reach Florence in early spring. Here Corinne is living; here the sun grows warmer. But although Corinne consents to see Oswald's daughter and dispenses womanly advice to Oswald's wife ('You must be both you and I in one . . .'), she refuses to see Oswald himself until she senses the approach of death. It is not in her character to die on a forgiving note: 'Love and glory had always been confounded in her mind. . . . She wanted the ingrate who had abandoned her to feel once more that the woman he had killed was the woman who could feel and think more deeply than any other in her time.' Accordingly she invites all her friends, Oswald and Lucile among them, to hear her swan song.

She is too weak to improvise; a young girl reads Corinne's last poem to the assembly. Lord Nelvil swoons and is carried out. A few days later Corinne dies, with Oswald lying at her feet.

> Lord Nelvil [Germaine concludes] went on to live a most regular and pure domestic life. But did he forgive himself for his past conduct? Did the world, which approved of his conduct, console him? Was he content with mediocrity after what he had lost? I do not know. In this respect, I will neither blame nor exonerate him.

These pages are not the work of a novelist: they are the fantasies of glory and revenge of a spoiled child. 'When I am dead, you will be sorry,' Germaine might have said to Prosper—and not only to Prosper, for in her final rage it is against all the men she had known that she turned in the luckless Oswald. Prosper, to whom she sent a set of the three volumes after their publication late in April, reacted with understandable indignation:

> I have received *Corinne*. . . . I did not judge it: I remembered. All in all, I want no part of Oswald. He is loved more than anyone ever was loved, and it seems he should have been more deserving of that love. I think he is cold-hearted and unimaginative. . . . What should I say of the end, where he is shown wretched in his guilt, a guilt he has incurred without struggle, without uneasiness, without coercion? . . .
>
> You reproach me cruelly, and you have imprisoned me in that Oswald, in whom I am powerless to defend myself. Ah! if one day he should describe what he felt, it would become apparent how much he suffered. . . . His entire youth is ruined for having met Corinne. He too had his inner struggles, his moments of agitation, and there are times when he still has them. But he is not so unjust as to blame anyone; his remorse is enough for him. . . . What is more, he will not write a book on his feelings and sufferings. . . .
>
> I told you some time ago how upset my life was as a result of my having known you and of my having resisted my forebodings: you may make use of this too as material for a book. You can see that if *Corinne* is intended as an act of revenge it produces the desired effect and that I regard it as such. . . .
>
> Ah! do not speak to me of applause and of success, you who have lived on it, who have sought it in every way, who are not afraid of making books out of the most intimate experiences of the heart, of things that are so personal that a kind of modesty should forbid their use as an instrument to obtain success.

Most love affairs would have ended after such a letter; that of Germaine and Prosper did not.

On October 30, 1806, at Rouen, Benjamin wrote in his diary: 'I have started the novel that will be our story.' 'Our story' was to be the story of Benjamin and Charlotte; but soon an episode in Benjamin's life—his affair with Anna Lindsay—began to arrest his attention, and an entirely different novel emerged. As he progressed, the heroine, Ellénore, took on more and more resemblance to Germaine. As for Adolphe, its hero—or, rather, anti-hero—who cannot break away from a love he no longer feels, in fact has never felt, he is the pitiless portrait of the author.

Benjamin worked furiously on *Adolphe*, while Germaine was finishing *Corinne* at white heat. The thought of this couple, unable to live together, unable to part, each consumed by love and hatred of the other, each pouring his despair into a manuscript, inspires awe and pity. The themes of *Corinne* and *Adolphe* are identical: in each novel the heroine dies the victim of the hero's inability to make a courageous choice. But *Corinne* is a three-volume rhapsody of self-delusion, self-pity, and posturing; *Adolphe* is a long short story, concentrated, ruthlessly self-analytical, and uncompromisingly true. As one critic put it, there is not a wrinkle in it after 150 years.

Critics still argue of Ellénore's identity, but it is difficult to see why the question should generate so much passion between the Lindsayite and the Staëlite camps. In writing *Adolphe* Benjamin was concerned not with a particular woman but with himself in his relationship with women. Every woman who loved Benjamin was Ellénore: the heroine is a composite. It is clear, however, that Ellénore's character as it develops is Germaine's. Even more striking is the identity of Ellénore and Corinne in the concluding pages. After describing Ellénore's death (in terms lifted bodily from Benjamin's diary record of Madame Talma's agony), Adolphe quotes from one of her letters to him. The letter ends with these words:

> She will die, this importunate Ellénore whom you cannot bear to have near you, on whom you look as an obstacle. . . . She will die: you will be left to walk alone among the crowd you are so eager to mingle with! You will learn to know them, those men to whom you now are grateful for their indifference. And perhaps one day, wounded by their arid hearts, you will regret this heart of which you could dispose, that lived on your love, that would have defied a thousand perils in your defence, and that you no longer deign to reward with so much as a look.

Most of the letters Germaine wrote to Benjamin have been lost. It takes little courage to wager that, if ever they were found, among them there would be one from which Ellénore's letter was copied word for word.

Benjamin finished his novel in a few weeks. He withheld it from publication until 1816, but he had the folly to read it to Madame de Staël at Acosta. Her reaction was fulminating. 'Unexpected [*sic*] scene because of the novel,' says Benjamin's diary entry for December 28, 1806. 'These scenes now cause me physical pain. I coughed blood.' On the twenty-ninth the scene was renewed for two hours; on the thirtieth another scene until four in the morning; on New Year's eve two hours of convulsions, ending with a reconciliation. Thus another year opened.

On December 2, 1805, Napoleon won the victory of Austerlitz; on October 14, 1806, he crushed Prussia with a single blow at Jena; in the winter of 1806–7 news of dreadful battles came from Poland and East Prussia.

Germaine would not have been herself if she had allowed her sentimental preoccupations to interfere with her political passions. Napoleon's defeat might have meant the end of her exile, if her friends took the power, or the end of her hopes, if the Bourbons returned. And the winter of 1807 was a perilous one for the Emperor. That Germaine and her circle ardently desired a French defeat is beyond all doubt. That a spirit of resistance and disloyalty crystallized around her, was kept alive and encouraged by her, is equally evident. That she was at the very least aware of a plot to form a provisional government under General Malet if Napoleon was defeated is most probable. Yet Germaine believed naïvely that, because she abstained from overt acts, her role was not known to the government. She even believed, all previous experiences to the contrary, that her new book would restore her to favour. 'Dante hoped that his poem would end his exile,' she has Corinne say.

She did not know that her mail was intercepted, that the seals were removed, then resealed by expert hands, the contents of the letters copied and forwarded to the Emperor: on Saint Helena he still reminisced with awe about her fulminating missives to Benjamin. He followed her movements almost as attentively as she followed his. 'Do not let that bitch of a Madame de Staël approach Paris,' he wrote to Fouché from Pultusk on the last day of 1806. 'I know she is not far from it.' The order was ignored, and another warning came from Osterode on

March 15, at the very time when Germaine solicited Fouché's permission to buy an estate at Cernay a few miles beyond the city limits. On March 30 Benjamin visited Fouché on her behalf, and was flatly refused. If Madame de Staël were willing, Fouché suggested, to insert a few laudatory remarks on the Emperor in *Corinne*, then being printed, all obstacles might be removed; she might even recover her two millions. Germaine's response to this offer was true to her form: she was ready, she informed Fouché, to remove anything in her book that might give offence, but she would not insert a word of flattery.

Refusing to praise Napoleon in print was the only thing on which her mind was firmly made up. In every other respect, with *Corinne* finished, she was adrift, forming dozens of contradictory projects.[1]

Knowing that her days near Paris were numbered, Germaine in early April ventured into the city itself. After dark, unable to resist the temptation, she strolled through the streets with her friends, unaware that every step was being watched. The thrill was spoiled by the agonizing thought of the impending departure, for she was only waiting for the publication of *Corinne* to return to Coppet. On April 23 she dined with Mathieu and Benjamin at the suburb of Charenton, famous for its insane asylum. 'The name brought ill-luck,' Benjamin recorded. 'Never have I seen her so demented. Impossible! Impossible! After fits of veritable insanity, she finally settled on a plan. God knows if she will follow it. I doubt it very much, but if she has not left by Sunday, I leave on Monday.'

Her presence in Paris, completely unauthorized, nearly cost Fouché his post. On April 19, from Finkenstein in East Prussia, Napoleon addressed another diatribe to his police minister:

> Among the thousand and one things concerning Madame de Staël that came into my hands, here is a letter from which you can see what a fine Frenchwoman we have there. . . . It is my intention that she must never leave Geneva. . . . It truly is difficult to restrain one's indignation at the spectacle of all the [political] metamorphoses this whore, and an ugly one at that, is undergoing. I shall not tell you what projects this ridiculous

---

[1] Thus on February 26, in a 'bizarre conversation', she told Benjamin that if it were not for him she would marry Elzéar de Sabran. It seems unlikely that she seriously entertained the thought of marrying a man whose love she found repulsive although she welcomed his friendship—a 'man who . . . would gladly become my shadow if such a thing would not disgust me with myself', as she said of him six months earlier in a letter to Souza. Gossip about her impending marriage with Sabran circulated throughout Europe; perhaps Benjamin helped spread it. If Germaine considered the marriage at all, it was as a desperate expedient to end her exile.

côterie has already formed in case by a happy accident I should be killed, since a police minister may be assumed to be informed of all this.

Similar letters followed, showing increasing irritation with Fouché. Thus, on May 7: 'I see from your bulletin of April 27 that Madame de Staël left for Geneva on the 21st. I am displeased to see you so ill-informed. Madame de Staël was in Paris on April 24, 25, 26, 27, and 28, and probably is still there.' Actually, Germaine had left Paris on April 25; Benjamin escorted her to Mongeron, where they parted on the 27th.

Before leaving, Germaine had written to the Emperor. His reaction can be seen in a letter dated May 11, again to Fouché:

> This madwoman of a Madame de Staël writes me a six-page letter, in double Dutch. . . . She tells me she has bought an estate in the valley of Montmorency and draws the conclusion that this will entitle her to reside in Paris. I repeat to you that to leave such a hope to that woman is to torture her gratuitously. *If I showed you the detailed evidence of everything she has done at her country place during the two months she resided there, you would be astonished. Indeed, although 500 leagues away from France, I know better what happens there than does my police minister.*

In her own words Germaine returned to Coppet like a wounded pigeon; it was a pigeon who had left a time bomb behind. The sensation created by *Corinne* was explosive. The official press reacted as was to be expected, denouncing the book as anti-French, which it certainly is; but the general public was deaf to its political overtones, engrossed as it was in its sentimental and romantic aspects. Thus Germaine's political message was lost on those for whom she intended it, and seized upon by those who she had hoped would not notice it. In East Prussia Marshal Berthier, Napoleon's chief of staff, went into ecstasies over it; Napoleon skimmed through it and called it junk. Nine years later, on Saint Helena, he tried to read it again, then declared he could not finish it. 'I can see her,' said the Emperor, 'I can hear her, I can sense her, I want to run away, I throw down the book. . . . However, I shall persist; I want to see how it ends, for I still think that it is an interesting work.'

As a literary critic of the nutshell school, the Emperor was not at all bad.

16

FARCE, TRAGEDY, AND HISTRIONICS

ON April 25, 1807, the day Benjamin hustled her away from Paris, Germaine in her despair turned to an old friend: 'When shall we see each other again? My son will, I believe, go to America next year, and perhaps we all shall go. If this Old World of ours is to be nothing but a single man, what is the use of staying here?' The President of the United States, to whom the rhetorical question was addressed, answered cautiously. On July 16 Jefferson wrote:

> The grandson of Monsieur Necker cannot fail of a hearty welcome in a country which so much respected him. To myself, who loved the virtues and honoured the great talents of the grandfather, the attentions I received in his natal house and particular esteem for yourself are additional titles to whatever service I can render him. . . . He will find a sincere welcome at Monticello, where I shall then be in the bosom of my family.

Jefferson chose to ignore the hint that Germaine too might go to the United States. Perhaps he found the notion of Corinne in America too grotesque to be taken seriously, but more likely the evasion was diplomatic: the administration that was about to pass the Embargo Act was little disposed to invite trouble with Napoleon. Germaine, however, was quite in earnest. As she explained in a letter to Gouverneur Morris, written the same day as the one to Jefferson, she intended to increase her already vast holdings in America; Auguste would take charge of them and be naturalized an American citizen.

Morris took her at her word:

> You and your son will board ship at Nantes, for New York, in mid-April. As soon as you arrive, you will come here [to Morrisania] to drink milk and rest. Early in July you will start out to visit your lands. . . . By mid-September you will come back to rest from your efforts, pick peaches, go for walks, write poetry, novels, anything you like. When my retreat has

lost its charms, you will settle in town, where with the help of a good cook you will eat very well. The amusements of New Yorkers are, as elsewhere, to digest, to say witty things, to speak ill of their neighbours, and the rest. When all is said and done, Madame, life is pretty much the same everywhere.

Whether Morris intended it or not (most probably he did), this image of happiness threw a cold shower on Germaine's dreams of America. Morrisania was another Coppet, New York another Geneva—but how much farther from Paris!—and St. Lawrence County the wilderness. It was better to love America from a distance. Nevertheless, for the next four years, every time her other projects foundered, Madame de Staël returned to the idea of America. Her intention of sending her sons there was no doubt sincere; on the other hand, her often-announced and ever-postponed departures were useful in intimidating her friends and reassuring her enemies. When, in October 1810, her last hopes collapsed and her passport for America was in her hands, it was not to New York she went but back to Coppet.

The reception of *Corinne* throughout Europe (except Italy, where no one read books) soothed Germaine's wounds after her return to Coppet in May 1807. Goethe, who sent her word that he was 'enthusiastic', set the tone. There was no question that she had become the author of the day. Within a few weeks, Coppet had filled up with guests. Some had been summoned, some came from habit, some drifted in, some drifted through, some were snapped up on their passage. Madame Récamier arrived with Elzéar de Sabran on July 10. Prince August of Prussia, released by the Peace of Tilsit from captivity in France—a captivity spent, for the most part, in salons and boudoirs, on parole— came to Ouchy, near Lausanne, where Germaine had temporarily shifted her court, on August 11; he had planned to stay for two weeks and remained for two and a half months. 'The summer,' as Chateaubriand put it (although he was not there), 'was spent in feasts': feasts, dinners, stage rehearsals and performances, excursions on the lake, music, conversation, and romances. It seemed a not unpleasant way of spending one's exile, surrounded by the most magnificent scenery of Europe, while Europe bled and starved. A passing guest might bring with him the chill air of grimmer realities; thus Prosper de Barante, back from a tour of duty in Poland and Germany, spent a few days at Coppet in the autumn, telling of the atrocities he had witnessed in the occupied territories. Here, at the 'Grand Assizes of the Conscience of Europe', the conqueror was being judged no longer as a mere tyrant but as a criminal. While all Europe cringed before him, Coppet remained one of the few places where uncompromising resistance was kept alive, and it probably was the only place where resistance was grounded not in national or dynastic pride but in moral principles. This resistance could be no more than a state of mind; action was impossible; but the state of mind of the guests of Coppet determined public opinion in Europe.

Nature, little regarded by Germaine, received tribute from her familiars. Schlegel, partly to escape the commotion at the castle, partly because the presence of princes and duchesses relegated him to an inferior role, took off for a walking tour of Switzerland in the company of Albert, now fifteen, whose excess energies thus found an educational outlet. 'He has a strong wish to become a chamois hunter,' Schlegel wrote to Germaine when she complained of Albert's spelling; 'who knows if that is not his real calling?'

The greatest tribute paid to nature that summer was, however, Madame de Staël's and Madame Récamier's ascent of Mont Blanc. On July 23 Juliette had received news that Prince Pignatelli, with whom she had been cultivating one of her almost passionate romances, had died of tuberculosis. 'Juliette is sad. In a week her mind will be on other things and in a month she will be consoled,' prophesied Benjamin. To help console her Germaine and Elzéar drove her to Chamonix, where they hired a guide to take them to the Mer de Glace. The sun proved stronger than the ladies' diaphanous scarves and veils. They had not even reached the glacier when their low décolletage was burned to a crisp and their beribboned straw hats were limp with perspiration. They absolutely refused to take one more step uphill. The guide expostulated, giving a lyrical description of the grandiose spectacle that would be their reward. 'My dear,' Madame de Staël interrupted him, 'you could beg me to go in every language of Europe, and still I would not go.' Redskinned and exhausted, the ladies retreated to Ouchy, where within the period specified by Benjamin Juliette was to be consoled.

Such was the life at Coppet and Ouchy in 1807 as it appeared to any passing guest who was not acquainted with what lay under the surface. Reality, uneasily contained under its glitter, was grim.

Benjamin stayed in Paris for two months after Germaine's departure. His honeymoon with Charlotte continued more hectic than happy. On the one hand, there was 'that Fury who pursues me, foaming at the mouth, dagger in hand'—Germaine threatening him in letter after letter and spreading rumours of his monstrous conduct; on the other hand Charlotte, offering to break off, weeping, fainting, and throwing fits that invariably ended up with a reconciliation in bed. In addition his oculist, diagnosing incipient blindness, subjected him to a barbarous treatment. After one such session, his face still covered with blood, Benjamin received a particularly 'horrible letter' from Coppet. He decided that he had reached the limit: he would not return to Germaine. A week later Uginet arrived, bringing word that if Benjamin did not return immediately, Germaine would come and get him in person. Benjamin almost yielded. He went as far as Melun. 'If I go one mile farther, I risk losing Charlotte,' he suddenly realized; and, turning on Uginet, he vented his rage against Germaine in a scene more humiliating for him than for the servant. As soon as Uginet left the room, Benjamin broke down. 'A thousand memories tore my soul. Her good qualities, Albertine, so many ties! I cried like a child.'

Benjamin returned to Paris, where a tender and weeping Charlotte was awaiting him, along with another threatening letter from Germaine. Still undecided on their next step, Benjamin and Charlotte left Paris together on June 27. By the time they reached Châlons they had settled on a plan: Charlotte would go on to Germany and obtain her divorce, which had now been arranged; Benjamin would go on to Dôle and stay with his father until her return. This, of course, was an exact repetition of 1805.

At Dôle the bombardment by mail reached a new degree of intensity: Germaine was dying; she was taking opium; she would kill herself; Benjamin would stand before the world as her murderer. All this while the feasts of Coppet were proceeding gaily. Auxiliary batteries joined in; Schlegel advised him to resign himself to the inevitable; Auguste wrote a 'dignified letter' to the same effect. Praying God to preserve Charlotte for him, Benjamin modified his plans. He would leave all his manuscripts with his father, take with him only his notes and filing cards, appear at Coppet with an overnight bag, and leave at the first scene Germaine made. He was still perfecting these plans when Schlegel burst into Dôle. A 'violent conversation' took place. If Benjamin did not come to Coppet immediately, Schlegel declared, Madame de Staël would come to Dôle, swallow poison, and die at his feet. Benjamin flew into a rage: when he was in Paris, he exclaimed, his illness was of no account to Madame de Staël; that he also had some obligations to an eighty-two-year-old father meant nothing to her; her tyranny knew neither reason nor pity; she had forfeited whatever claims she had on him.

At such blasphemy Schlegel paled and grew fanatic. What was a father, what were comfort, repose, freedom, fame, reputation, when balanced against the love of a 'divine friend', a 'supernatural being'? To spare her two hours of suffering, the sacrifice of filial duty was not too much. As he pounded away at Benjamin, Schlegel worked himself into a frenzy: if Germaine had ordered him to strangle the man who refused to love her, the unique, divine being to whom he had sacrificed everything without any hope of a return, he would have strangled him with pleasure. The interview ended with Benjamin promising to leave the day after the morrow. Only the manacles were missing when the tutor grimly took his seat in the carriage beside the criminal. After travelling all night and day, they reached Coppet at nine in the evening of July 17. Germaine was waiting in the courtyard. Benjamin was hardly outside the carriage, stammering a few words, when she seized him by the arm, dragged him into the park, and began to scream every invective she had stored up while waiting. Overcome with fatigue, Benjamin kept absolute silence, which she interpreted as contrition. Before falling into bed that night, he concluded his diary entry thus:

> I am very calm; the very scene she made calmed me. There is nothing to it except her determination to dominate through terror. All I have to do is to calculate my best advantage. She does not want any consideration. Let us calculate, then.

Their conversations continued in a calmer mood during the next few days. Still, even that calm was only relative. Every day Germaine announced her intention to commit suicide.

> She will not let me out of her sight, and at my first attempt at going away, she threatens to kill herself. Her children, her servants, her friends, the whole world, have been drawn into the confidence of that threat, and they all regard me as a monster for not appeasing her sufferings.

In retaliation Benjamin threatened to die of unhappiness if deprived of his freedom; she would rather see him die, replied Germaine, than allow him to go.

> I am threatened with passing for a brute if I leave her, and for an egoist if I marry her; at the same time she reproaches me with bitter tears and cruel insinuations for my sadness and my discouragement, which are the results of my secret sentiments.

The day after Germaine left for her Alpine expedition Benjamin moved to Lausanne to stay with his relatives. Faithful to her word,

Germaine transported her court to Ouchy, a stone's throw from Lausanne, where she could keep him under close surveillance. While his
aunt de Nassau and his cousin Rosalie taunted him for his slavery to
Madame de Staël, Madame de Staël kept him up in stormy conversations until five o'clock in the morning, extracted 'tacit promises', and
announced to the world at large that she and Benjamin were inseparably
reunited. Benjamin did not contradict her. 'How can one tell the truth
to a person whose only answer consists in swallowing opium?'

It was at this time that he began to seek solace at the mystical gatherings of one of his innumerable cousins, the Chevalier de Langalerie.

Langalerie was the leader, in French Switzerland, of that Quietist
mysticism, derived from St. Francis of Sales, Jakob Boehme, Fénelon,
Madame Guyon, and Saint-Martin, which had so profound an influence
on the mystic revival among both Protestants and Catholics during the
first decades of the century. The Duc de Broglie, who was to become
Madame de Staël's son-in-law, described that remarkable man in his
reminiscences:

> He was a little man, exceptionally fat, round, and short, a little vain,
> something of a gourmand, not unlike the stock character, in the salacious
> novels of the last century, of a father confessor in a nunnery. . . . His
> saccharine, insinuating, nasal tone of voice was exasperating: but as soon
> as he entered on a purely spiritual topic, it was impossible not to admire
> the depth and delicacy of his ideas, the finesse and acumen of his ob-
> servations, the infinite resourcefulness and the marvellous agility of a
> dialectic which sometimes penetrated into a maze of arduous subtleties,
> without getting lost, and at other times rose to heights of eloquence.

Langalerie, seeing his cousin's deplorable spiritual condition, and
aware of his deep anti-religious convictions, attempted to show him the
way out of the Slough of Despond without so much as mentioning the
word *God*. 'You cannot deny,' he said, 'that there is a power stronger
than you outside yourself.' Benjamin was in no position to deny it.
'Well now, I'll tell you,' the Chevalier continued, 'that the only key
to happiness on this earth is to be in harmony with that power, whatever it is, and that in order to achieve this harmony only two things
are needed: prayer and abdication of the will.' But how could he pray
without believing? Benjamin wondered. All he had to do was try and
see what would happen, explained Langalerie. The change would take
place not outside but inside him. 'Is it not the same to you whether
what you will happens or whether what happens, you will? The important thing for you is that your will and events be in accord.'

To a man caught in a situation such as Benjamin's, this doctrine has much to commend it. He began to pray, ending all his prayers with the words, 'I fully renounce every faculty, all knowledge, all reason, all judgment', and felt immensely relieved. Four years later in *Cécile* he recalled:

> I slept, as it were, a moral sleep under the wings of an Infinite Being that watched over me. . . . I renounced, both in deed and in intention, every attempt to guide my destiny. I left my engagements with Cécile [i.e., Charlotte] up to God.

A strange mystic! An inspection of his diaries leaves one with the painful conviction that his resignation was fatalism of the crudest kind, and insincere at that; it was not even complete, for the diary pages are strewn with appeals to the Deity of the 'Please God, make such and such a thing happen' variety. 'O God,' he exclaims at one point, 'preserve me from the consequences of my miscalculations!'—surely one of the most extraordinary prayers ever uttered. The only result of his 'quarter conversion', as the Duc de Broglie calls it, was his moral sleep. Hoping to induce the same soporific effects in Germaine, he tried to make a convert of her, too.

> Often tired of herself and of the agitation that consumed her, she was tempted to imitate me and find some peace, but . . . her reason rebelled against her renunciation of self, and the only benefit we derived from our theological disputations was that time went by and that, occupied with general ideas, we suspended our quarrels and no longer devoured each other.

All this took place in between the rehearsals of *Andromaque*. Leaving the title role to Madame Récamier, Germaine had chosen the more congenial one of Hermione, which gave her the opportunity to berate Benjamin, in the role of Pyrrhus, for trying to run off with a Trojan woman. Benjamin, after the first rehearsal, took note of the parallel between Hermione and Madame de Staël—'an old lawyer, serpents coiled in her hair, suing in alexandrines for breach of contract'. The performance, on August 22, attracted a large audience, many from as far as Geneva. 'It seems incredible to me,' wrote Rosalie, 'that people should expose their situation thus openly.' What Benjamin had not dared tell Germaine in private, he flung at her publicly in Act IV:

> 'Yes, I shall wed a Trojan woman; yes, 'tis true
> That I shall pledge to her the faith I promised you.'

Hermione's tirade, when Pyrrhus accuses her of not having loved him, was spectacular: 'Not loved you, cruel man! What then have I done?' Germaine cried out. 'Even now, at this instant, when your cruel lips so calmly pronounce my sentence of death, even now, ingrate, perhaps I love you still.' To her plea to postpone his decision for at least one day, Pyrrhus remained silent. 'Ah, I can see, you are counting the minutes you are wasting on me,' Germaine spat at Benjamin, who blinked at her in terror.

> Your heart, impatient to join your Trojan woman, only reluctantly sub-
> mits to what another has to say. Your heart speaks to her, your eyes are
> seeking her: I shall keep you no longer—escape from this place; go and
> swear to her the faith you swore to me. . . . The gods are just; they will
> not forget that the same oaths have bound you to me. Go and take to the
> altar the heart that has deserted me—go, run; but beware, Hermione
> will await you even there.

On August 25, after extracting Benjamin's promise to join her in five days, Germaine returned to Coppet. When the five days were up, he wrote a letter informing her that all was finished and that he would never return; then he tore up the letter, and returned.

He was going to have it out. Either she must marry him or set him free. Since she was telling everybody that he had pledged himself to her at Leipzig in 1804, she could not refuse an offer of marriage. Directly he arrived at Coppet, he went to her room, faced her squarely, and ordered her to marry him without further delay. 'Her fury,' relates Benjamin, 'was as great as her surprise. She rang the bell. Her children came in. "Behold," she said to them, pointing at me, "behold the man who wants to ruin your mother by forcing her to marry him." '

The children stared at the monster. Benjamin, putting his hand on Auguste's shoulder, came back with the retort magnificent: 'Regard me as the vilest of men,' he said, 'if I ever marry your mother.' At this point, Germaine 'rose from her seat, threw herself on the floor with horrible screams, tried to strangle herself with her handkerchief—in a word, made one of those atrocious scenes that she can produce at will and which poor Benjamin cannot resist.'[1] Here was an opportunity to test experimentally whether it is possible to strangle oneself with a cambric handkerchief; instead of seizing it, Benjamin raised Germaine and calmed her with tender words. He then retired to his room, wrote a letter saying farewell forever, and after a sleepless night slipped out of the house at seven in the morning. He rode straight to Lausanne, where

---

[1] Rosalie to Charles de Constant, September 8, 1807.

he found asylum with a relative, Madame de Charrière de Bavois. Madame de Nassau and Rosalie joined him, to keep up his courage. Benjamin, in a state of terror, sat in the parlour staring at the clock, already waiting for the inevitable, when suddenly he heard Germaine's voice from downstairs. Rosalie leaped up to meet the enemy, locking the door behind her. She found Madame de Staël sprawled on the stairs, her bosom bared, the black coils of her hair sweeping the steps. 'Where is he? I must find him!' she cried. While Rosalie and Madame de Nassau were trying to take her into one of the bedrooms, assuring her that Benjamin was not in the house, Benjamin began to knock furiously at the door of the drawing room, shouting to Rosalie to unlock it. Rosalie had no choice but to obey; Germaine burst in, threw herself first into Benjamin's arms, then at his feet, and, writhing on the floor, screamed the most hair-raising accusations at everyone present. When the paroxysm was spent, she implored Benjamin to grant her two more months; after that, if he wished, he could have his freedom. Like an automaton, he followed her into the waiting carriage. At 7 p.m. on September 1, twelve hours after his flight, he was back at Coppet.

The universe of Coppet revolved around two suns—Germaine, flaming, explosive, commanding; and Juliette, cool, distant, and beckoning. Juliette, the more celestial body of the two, was still discreetly mourning Prince Pignatelli when, three weeks after Benjamin's prophecy, Prince August of Prussia appeared at Ouchy. A nephew of Frederick the Great, Prince August at twenty-eight was a dashing young officer who had earned for himself the nickname of Prince Don Juan. Meeting Juliette transformed him, for the remainder of his life, into a Werther. Juliette allowed him to adore her, and Germaine encouraged the romance with all her might. In Prince August, she hoped, Juliette would find at last the happiness in love she had sought and evaded all her life. Also she hoped to eliminate a rival: for Prosper, whom she had by no means given up, was expected in September. By the time Prosper arrived, on September 26, Juliette and the Prince were engaged. Taking advantage of the last days of summer, they had spent their time riding alone across the fields and vineyards of the countryside, or rowing together on the lake. One day the Prince, performing a feat of oarsmanship unique in the annals of royalty, rowed her to Clarens and the rock of the Meillerie, scene of the *Nouvelle Héloïse*. Something worthy of Julie and Saint-Preux was called for: they swore each other eternal love.

It was after a performance of *Phèdre*, in which she held the role of Aricie, that Juliette, still flushed with her triumph, admitted the Prince into her room and promised to become his wife. Since Monsieur Récamier, even then struggling, in Paris, to extricate himself from his bankruptcy, could not be ignored altogether, Juliette wrote to him and asked for a divorce. She hoped for a reply before the Prince's return to Berlin. 'We were convinced,' she confessed thirty-five years later, 'that we were going to be married, and our relationship was very intimate; even so, there was one thing he failed to obtain.' No answer having reached them on October 28, the day set for the Prince's departure, the lovers, in true Coppet style, exchanged written promises.

> I swear by my honour and by love to preserve in all its purity the senti-
> ment that attaches me to Juliette Récamier, to take all steps that duty
> allows to unite with her in the bonds of marriage, and to possess no
> woman as long as there is hope that I may join my destiny with hers.
>   AUGUST, PRINCE OF PRUSSIA

> I swear by the salvation of my soul to preserve in all its purity the senti-
> ment that attaches me to Prince August of Prussia; to do everything that
> honour permits to dissolve my marriage, to have no love nor flirtation
> with any other man, to see him again as soon as possible, and, whatever
> the future may bring, to entrust my destiny entirely to his honour and
> his love.
>
>   J.R.

They exchanged rings; August also gave her a gold bracelet and a gold chain with a ruby heart as pendant. The day after he left the postman brought Monsieur Récamier's reply. The banker was not enchanted, nor did he think that Juliette had well chosen her time in asking for a divorce when he was in misfortune. He would consent if she insisted, appealing at the same time to every sentiment of her noble heart, and expressed regret at having respected her virginal susceptibilities. The answer, which she well might have anticipated, plunged her into consternation. She must break with her husband, Germaine told her peremptorily; at the same time Germaine was reluctant to let Juliette leave for Paris. Glad to be able to postpone a decision, Juliette stayed on for a month at Coppet, where the American Mr. Middleton made life as pleasant for her as she would let him.

Germaine had for some time entertained the thought of spending the winter in Vienna and South Germany, which she had never seen; but there was talk of war between France and Austria, and the departure was postponed from week to week. On November 1 Benjamin's two months were up. Germaine begged him to stay until she left. Benjamin consented easily enough: his moral coma was deeper than ever. Charlotte, following his instructions, was on her way to meet him at Besançon, yet the thought that she would not find him there did not disturb his equanimity: 'Let time do its work,' he wrote in his diary. 'What is written in the book of destiny shall be accomplished.' His resignation was not the result of Quietism only. To occupy himself while waiting for Germaine's departure he had begun to write a tragedy, *Walstein*, an adaptation in five acts of Schiller's *Wallenstein* trilogy. The work progressed rapidly, and absorbed him increasingly. He had no desire to leave Coppet before it was finished. Once he had ceased to struggle, Germaine, 'the easiest person to live with in all small matters provided she has her way in the big ones', became an agreeable companion and an invaluable literary adviser. Unperturbed by Charlotte's heart-rending letters, Juliette's elegant despair, Monsieur de Sabran's nervous breakdowns, Schlegel's jaundiced eyes, and the lack of 'ı', he ground out his alexandrines with dogged determination. Germaine's habit of 'continually feeling the pulse of her own sensibility' occasionally irritated him, and there were small quarrels when he displayed insufficient interest in her 'self-analysis', but on the whole the period was spent calmly; the explosion of August 31–September 1 had cleared the air. At the end of November Germaine at last left for Vienna with Schlegel, Albert, Albertine, and Uginet. Benjamin went with them as far as Lausanne. On December 4, after a touching farewell, Germaine went on her way to Munich, Benjamin on his to Besançon, where Charlotte had been waiting for him for four weeks, at an inn, gathering fury with every passing day.

As he rolled across the snow-covered Jura, Benjamin stared ahead, motionless in a corner of his carriage. Before him, he saw 'all the spectres of the past rising up and growing larger'. Germaine, he reflected, had been 'the tyrant, but also the goal of my life. . . . I was about to cast from me all the good I might have done during more than one third of my existence.' As the carriage descended a sharp grade beside a 200-foot precipice, the harness broke; the driver was obliged to whip his horses into a gallop to avoid crashing into them.

> I believed [says Benjamin] that we were about to perish, and I experienced a great joy. . . . But our driver, who did not share my wishes, noticed a rather steep hollow to the right of the road, where he succeeded

in making the carriage overturn. The carriage was damaged, but the horses stopped.

He continued on foot to Ornans, whence he wrote a note to Charlotte, then resumed the journey in the carriage, which had been repaired. At one mile from Besançon, Charlotte and her maid stood waiting by the road, in a quagmire. Instead of being touched, Benjamin was infuriated. He jumped out of the carriage, took Charlotte by the hand. 'You are out of your mind,' he snapped at her by way of greeting. 'You might at least have come by carriage.' Charlotte stared at him incredulously. 'Continue in the carriage. I shall join you later,' she said at last. Benjamin got back into the carriage and drove off, leaving Charlotte to trudge back on foot.

He reached the inn one hour ahead of Charlotte. 'I employed this hour in writing the most passionate love letter Madame de Staël ever received from me,' he says.

Germaine, in leaving her son Auguste behind, had assigned him a special mission which, to a lad of seventeen, must have been frightening. On December 30, just about the time his mother reached Vienna, Auguste was waiting at Chambéry in Savoy, to be shown into the presence of Napoleon. The Emperor, who was only passing through, had granted the audience from which Germaine expected a double miracle—two million francs and a residence permit in Paris. Auguste was shown into a room where he found the tyrant finishing his breakfast, surrounded by his staff. In stating his request, the boy fell into the Neckerian error of bringing up the past, among other things Monsieur Necker's last book. At its mention the Emperor launched into an extraordinary tirade. 'Your grandfather was an ideologist, a madman, a senile maniac,' he barked at Auguste, who paled at the blasphemy and retorted that Necker had not been the only economist to write on constitutions. The Emperor, however, was in fine fettle, Auguste's obstinacy in arguing back inspiring him to brilliant flights of invective. Economists were not fit to be tax collectors in the remotest village of his empire; Necker was 'a stubborn old man who on his deathbed kept twaddling about the government of nations'. '. . . It was he who overthrew the monarchy and led Louis XVI to the scaffold. . . . Yes, I am telling you, even Robespierre, Marat, Danton have done less harm to France than Monsieur Necker. It's he who made the Revolution.' After ranting on in this manner for several minutes he suddenly stopped, turned to his staff, and smiled. 'In the last analysis, gentlemen, it isn't really up to me to speak ill of the Revolution, since I ended up by snatching the throne,' he remarked, then looked sternly at Auguste. 'The reign of the troublemakers is finished. What I want is subordination. Respect authority, because it comes from God. . . . Everybody must keep straight in politics.' At these words he rose, while Auguste, seeing his opportunity vanish, frantically appealed to the Emperor to end his mother's exile.

Napoleon stepped up to Auguste, pulled him hard by the lobe of his ear—a mark of imperial favour—and said, in a more kindly tone:

'You are very young. If you had my age and experience, you would judge things better. Far from offending me, your frankness pleases me. I like a son who pleads his mother's cause. Your mother has sent you on a difficult errand, and you have acquitted yourself intelligently.' All the same, he continued, nothing would induce him to call her back from exile. If she were in prison, that would be a different matter. Auguste objected that exile was as painful as prison. 'Romantic notions all this,' replied the Emperor. 'You must have picked that up from your mother. She's much to be pitied indeed! Except for Paris, all Europe is her prison.' But all her friends were in Paris, Auguste persisted. Napoleon, however, was convinced that she could make friends elsewhere. Why Paris? Why was she so eager to place herself under his tyranny? Why not London? Anywhere— 'But Paris, don't you see, Monsieur de Staël, Paris is the place where I live. I don't want anybody there who doesn't like me. . . . Your mother would promise miracles, but she won't be able to keep from talking politics.'

Auguste reassured him on that account. Her friends and literature were all his mother cared for.

'That's what it is! Literature, is it? I won't be taken in by this. You can make politics by talking literature, morality, arts, anything. Women should stick to knitting.'

'But, Your Majesty,' objected Auguste, 'if certain sacred duties should require her presence in Paris for a few days, couldn't she—'

'What do you mean, sacred duties?' interrupted the Emperor. 'What are you talking about?'

Auguste mumbled something about a 'sacred debt', an expression which seemed to amuse the Emperor. Every creditor thinks debts are sacred, he pointed out. It was for the laws to decide. Determined to get some concession, Auguste shifted his ground. Both he and his brother, he asserted, wanted to settle in France, but how could they decently do so if their mother was not allowed to live there? Napoleon was not impressed:

'I am not at all anxious to have you there,' he said. 'Go to England. There they love the Genevese, the quibblers and drawing-room politicians. Go to England, for I am warning you that in France I'll be against you rather than for you.' And without another word he left the room, entered his carriage, and drove off. After a long silence he remarked to Duroc, 'Wasn't I a little rough on that young man? I'm afraid so. Well, so much the better, all things considered. She won't send anybody else to try again. Those people disparage everything I do. They don't understand me.'

On her way to Vienna, Germaine stopped for six days at Munich, where she was received with hostility by a zealously pro-Napoleonic society. 'Her clothes,' a local diarist recorded, 'were ridiculous to the highest degree and rendered her natural ugliness even more hideous.' The world of letters received her more amicably. With Schlegel she called on Schelling, who found her 'outwardly as French as can be but inwardly much better'. Caroline Schelling, after reporting to a friend on the prosperous appearance of her former husband, Schlegel, continued with a description of Madame de Staël:

> She is a phenomenon of vitality, egotism, and intellectual activity. Her appearance is transfigured by her soul, and indeed stands in great need of it. She has moments—or, more exactly, clothes—in which she looks like a camp follower, and yet it is possible to imagine her in the part of Phaedra, in the most tragic sense possible.

But where Caroline could see beauty of soul shining through Germaine's coarse and heavy features, the frivolous crowd of Munich and Vienna society saw only ugliness; where Caroline discerned the tragedy of a woman in her forties still clutching at the hope of happiness in love, they laughed at the ridiculous spectacle of a woman who did not know her age. Her grand décolletage, baring fleshy arms and ruddy expanses of neck and bosom; her turbans and bird-of-paradise feathers; her loud voice; her incessant fidgeting and twiddling of bits of paper or twigs; her utter lack of self-consciousness—all this made her, throughout the five months she stayed in Vienna, an object of curiosity and, behind her back, of cruel fun.

Times had changed. The good-natured tolerance of eccentricity that characterized the eighteenth century—at least in high society—

had given way to a priggish snobbery and self-consciousness, an arrogant frivolity devoid of humane feeling though steeped in superficial sentimentality. Nowhere was this spirit so manifest as in Vienna, a city which traditionally combines sentimentality with derision. The Vienna which laughed at Madame de Staël also was laughing at Beethoven. At the time of Germaine's visit the population of the city proper —which was still quite small—formed one large family, headed by the imperial couple. There were more dukes, princes, and magnates per acre than anywhere else in the world, and although the social division between nobility and bourgeoisie was maintained with extraordinary strictness, there was a deceptive familiarity and intermingling of the classes. The familiarity was deceptive, for although the nobility condescendingly mingled with the populace at play—in the Prater, in the Redoutensaal, in the theatres, in the taverns—the bourgeoisie was absolutely excluded from the aristocratic society. The result was mediocrity on the cultural and snobbery on the social level. As Madame de Staël remarked in her book on Germany, the high society of Vienna made a rigid system out of frivolity and dissipation. The houses where conversation was least insipid, manners most natural, and talent most recognized were those of the Russian ambassador and of the Polish nobility—that is, the houses where French rather than German was spoken.

For the five months she spent in this most cosmopolitan and most provincial of capitals Madame de Staël was the principal object of gossip. For years afterwards the Viennese referred to 1808 as 'the year Madame de Staël was in town'. Nothing she did was right by Viennese standards. At the court of the new young Empress she committed the breach of etiquette of not confining herself to answering the Empress's questions, and was shunned thereafter. In the salons she talked to the men much too much, and she was too intellectual. She lacked all sense of propriety. Even the old Prince de Ligne, field marshal of Russia and of Austria, who attracted her because of his eighteenth-century wit and manners, judged her with a point of malice. While Germaine was preparing a selection from his papers, thanks to which he secured a minor niche in the literary pantheon, he composed a portrait of her which, amid some windy rhetoric, contains this barbed passage:

> She has more imagination than intelligence, and more intelligence than learning. . . . She makes pronouncements, decides everything, accumulates error upon error, and ends up by not knowing what she is saying when she talks about the arts, of which she is ignorant, and of religious

feeling, which she sees in everything. Her Christianity makes one wish to be a pagan, her mysticism makes one prefer matter-of-factness, and her love for the extraordinary makes one appreciate everything that is common and vulgar.

Despite her ridiculousness, or perhaps because of it, Germaine was much in demand. Her life was a round of the great houses—the Schwarzenbergs, the Liechtensteins, the Lignes, the Fürstenbergs, the Lobkowitzes, the Esterhazys, the Palffys, the Batthianys, the Potockis, the Zamoyskis, the Lubomirskis, in a word, the owners of half of Central Europe. Of the cultural life of Vienna she saw little, except for a few visits to the opera and the theatre. She heard Haydn's *Creation* and *Seasons*, Mozart's *Requiem* and *Don Giovanni*, Gluck's *Iphigenie*; but although she conceded that those composers were excellent, she wondered if what they had written did not exceed the proper bounds of music. She made no effort to see Haydn, and she made no mention of Beethoven, although she saw his patron Prince Lobkowitz several times a week. The play that most arrested her attention was a performance at the Kasperltheater, the Viennese version of Punch and Judy, to which she took her children. On the other hand, she spared no effort to acquaint the Viennese with her own dramatic talents: for a whole season Vienna went through an epidemic of private theatricals. Thus, on February 14 at the Zamoyskis' and again on March 8 at the Fürstenbergs', she performed *Hagar in the Desert*, with Albert as the Angel and Albertine as Ishmael; the audience was amazed at this family exhibition, at the vehemence of Germaine's declamation, at the expressivity of her bare toes. The play, remarked a wit, should be called 'The Justification of Abraham'. Her other family play, *Genevieve of Brabant*, she read at Countess Potocki's on March 14, 'with violent screams', and performed at the Liechtensteins' on March 30. After hearing its endless pious invocations, one spectator remarked, 'Well, now that we have said our prayers we can go to bed.' Her performances in Marivaux's *Legacy* and in Molière's *Femmes Savantes* were more successful; in comedy roles she acted without exaggeration and shouting.

Germaine's lack of self-consciousness, which prevented her from noticing that she was ridiculed even by those whom she regarded as her friends, also made her impervious to satirical attacks in the press and to the hostility and distrust with which she was seen both by the court and by the populace. The imperial family could not forget her role in a revolution which had led the Emperor's aunt to the scaffold; the populace simply hated her as a foreigner. Anti-French feeling was on the rise in Austria (a year later it was to lead to the ill-advised war of 1809), and in the patriotic hysteria Germaine was suspected of acting as a secret agent of Napoleon. There was indeed something puzzling in her conduct: a victim of Napoleon's persecution and an outspoken critic of his despotism, she nevertheless was well received by the French ambassador and a frequent guest at his house. The Austrian police, never inclined to consider a simple explanation where a tortured one would do, shadowed her closely throughout her stay.

The official in charge of Germaine's surveillance soon was able to notify his superiors that almost every night, after returning to her flat from her round of calls, she received the visit of a young man who stayed until the early morning hours. The caller, her junior by fourteen years, belonged to the high aristocracy and was an officer in the Austrian army; at times he could be observed, through the window, writing late at night under her dictation. Whatever sinister interpretations might be placed on these facts, the police also reached the more natural conclusion that 'their relations were not limited to intellectual conversation'. For the following three months the police minister could follow Germaine's love affair in circumstantially detailed but occasionally arch accounts, couched in the best bureaucratic style of Austrian officialdom.

The young man's name was Graf Moritz O'Donnell von Tyrconnel. His family had settled in Austria in the preceding century, and Maurice, born in Vienna in 1780, was a captain in the Engineers. Germaine had met him during the five days she spent in Venice in May 1805; Count O'Donnell, who appears to have been a hypochondriac, was on sick leave at the time. In a series of playfully flirtatious letters, she invited him to visit her at Coppet or Geneva, but O'Donnell turned a deaf ear, and their correspondence almost ceased between October 1805 and March 1807, when she began to think of visiting Vienna. Nothing in her letters of the time indicates passionate feelings, but clearly she counted on his presence in Vienna to keep her heart occupied.

Undoubtedly it was she who made the first advances, but when he responded she held out long enough to give him a sense of victory. 'Is it not the beginning of the story which is the most beautiful time for a woman? And you want to deprive me of my reign so soon?' she asked him, adding, 'Yours will come only too soon.' The notes that followed took on an increasing resemblance to all the letters she had ever written to all her lovers: threatening, pleading, and recriminating in turns. There is strong reason to suspect that O'Donnell was afraid of exposing himself to public ridicule. In company he affected to pay no attention to Germaine when she was talking; he openly flirted with the Prince de Ligne's granddaughter Christine (universally known as Titine); and he found all manner of excuses for not making his nightly visits. In this his hypochondria came to his aid: his eyes ached; he had the chills; his teeth ached. No captain of engineers was ever stricken with so many infirmities. Germaine sent him eyedrops, orangeade, broth, mouthwash, and a profusion of medical advice. No sooner did he venture to feel improved than new storms broke out. 'I am tormented at the idea that there was in your eyes an expression that was not entirely friendly,' she wrote to him after they had spent an evening in society. By March 29 the affair had taken on all the classical features of her past loves: 'I beg you on my knees for a hearing. . . . I shall not go to bed without seeing you. We shall have an explanation—but for pity's sake come and speak to me: you do not know how you hurt me, no, you do not know.' Her stay was drawing to a close when she sadly noted that

> it seems to me that every day we draw farther apart. . . . Alas! This is not the way we should spend our last days together if we want to make sure of meeting again. . . . The tenderness and respect I felt for you deserved an effort on your part to harmonize with my nature rather than to struggle against it. All the enthusiasm I have would have been for you. By trying to clip my wings, you prevent me from feeling and exalting your own distinction. There are people whose characters cannot be judged from their behaviour in society: I am of a solitary nature despite my liking for company. If you knew how much you hurt me you would be sorry.

Like all the others, O'Donnell had tried to 'clip her wings', reproached her for her celebrity, and questioned her love when she refused to conform to his conventional standards. To be loved by a woman of genius had seemed flattering at first, embarrassing and humiliating later. But as Germaine saw it, to ask her to reduce her stature was to reduce his own; the man who could accept her as she was would fill her whole life. Would Corinne never tire of repeating the same experience, the same disappointment?

Reading her letters to Benjamin and to Juliette Récamier during the same period, one wonders how sincere was her attachment to O'Donnell—in fact, if she was sincere in anything. Thus on May 15, when she was writing impassioned notes to O'Donnell, she wrote to Benjamin: 'I return with the same attachment for you. . . . My heart, my life, everything I have is yours if you wish and as you wish. Think about this. . . . Love me one hundredth as much as I love you.' In her letters to Madame Récamier, she took care to anticipate all rumours about the fine time she was enjoying in Vienna—rumours which might have unfavourable effects both with Benjamin and with those of her friends who were still trying to end the agonies of her exile. Her social life was 'a vague noise around my head that enters neither my mind nor my soul—a kind of opium I take while watching or listening and that tires me almost as much as the other kind'. 'I have dizzied myself as much as I could this winter, like an eighteen-year-old girl. Nobody came within a hundred miles of my soul.' Again, shortly before leaving, she begs Juliette to influence Benjamin in her favour. 'All the triumphs and honours in the world are worth less than Coppet with him there. I try to distract myself because he mistreats me; but there is a wound in my heart, and I can say without exaggeration that I would die if he left me. . . . I did not enjoy myself this winter.'

The manœuvre is only too transparent. Should one infer that Germaine did not love O'Donnell, that all her declarations and the agonies to come were mere histrionics? There can be no doubt that Germaine's love for O'Donnell was no more than an infatuation; that she was fully aware of his mediocrity. But, as she wrote to Juliette, 'Only one thing hurts me—but cruelly—and that is my fear of not being loved.' In such a state of mind one clutches at straws, knowing that they are straws. But once the straw had failed her, things changed; to be discarded by an insignificant little officer—that caused very real pain.

Watching the progress of Germaine's affair with Count O'Donnell, Schlegel might well have gone mad with jealous rage, if Germaine had not, by a master stroke, kept his vanity occupied elsewhere. In 1806, in France, he had written a brochure entitled *Comparaison de la Phèdre de Racine avec celle d'Euripide*. Published late in 1807 in Paris, the work had made precisely the effect he had hoped. 'My enthusiasm for this subject,' he had confided to his sister-in-law Dorothea, 'springs principally from the fact that it will infuriate the readers.' His contention that Racine's *Phèdre*, though an estimable play, was in every point inferior to Euripides', did indeed amount to overt *lèse majesté* in France. Nor did the book please uniformly in Germany, for it evidently was also intended to kick the dead body of Schiller, who had translated Racine's *Phèdre*. Schlegel's brochure created some flurries in Viennese literary circles, which he frequented while Germaine made the rounds of the princely houses, and he hit on the notion of giving a series of lectures on dramatic literature. Germaine helped him obtain a licence from the government, a hall, and two hundred subscribers at 25 florins apiece.

The lectures began on March 31. Contrary to assertions made by people who have not read them, they made no appeal to German nationalism in a political sense. They were exactly what they were announced to be —a course in comparative dramatic literature. That Schlegel sought to encourage a German national stage scarcely makes him a chauvinist. What surprised his fashionable public was his often contemptuous and always condescending treatment of the French stage. Seldom if ever was so much pedantry expended in an attempt to prove pedantry in others. But Schlegel's lectures on the Elizabethan and the Spanish drama remain milestones in dramatic criticism. To the eighteen princesses in his audience, so much learning about so many things they had never heard of and did not really care for must have been a piquant diversion. That there were precisely eighteen princesses we know from Schlegel himself, who counted them. 'I had an audience of more than 250,' he reported to a friend in Geneva, 'almost the entire high nobility, many courtiers, ministers of state, generals, eighteen princesses, and many beautiful and witty women.' The memory of this triumph never faded, and the eighteen princesses recur in his correspondence for several years. Travelling with Madame de Staël had some compensations.

Schlegel's lectures were still in progress when Sismondi arrived in Vienna in mid-April, invited there from Tuscany by Germaine. The first volumes of his *Italian Republics* had been published and greeted with a silence that would have been universal if Madame de Staël had not coaxed a few friends into reviewing them. Germaine paraded him in the great houses of Vienna along with Schlegel. While Schlegel charmed his princesses with 'eloquent flights of poetic ideas', Sismondi could buttonhole cabinet ministers to explain his views on paper money and the Austrian currency inflation; in the meantime, Germaine, in another corner of the room, would hold forth about mysticism and the Great Chain of Being—for, much to Sismondi's dismay, she had begun to use Schlegel's language—and then proceed abruptly to anecdotes on Napoleon's despotic love-making. 'He has Mademoiselle Mézerai come. He makes her enter while he is writing. "Sit down! Undress! Lie down!" ' Having finished her performance, Germaine would return to her rooms and, alone at her desk, write to O'Donnell in a mood of total discouragement. Her stay in Vienna was drawing to a close; there was no prospect of an end to her exile; more struggles, more loneliness awaited her at Coppet; she had lost all hope of happiness; she felt disgusted with herself; she was a 'soul condemned to eternal solitude'.

Germaine had planned to leave early in May, after placing Albert in the Vienna military academy;[1] yet despite her dissatisfaction with O'Donnell, the thought of parting and of resuming her wanderings terrified her. She postponed her departure until May 22. On May 21, according to the police report,

> Madame de Staël and Count O'Donnell drove to Laxenburg and came back only at 11 o'clock at night. . . . When she came home, she called all her servants and gave them strict orders not to mention that excursion. . . . Probably she attracted attention there by her behaviour with her friend.

Probably she did: Germaine and Maurice carved their names on the trees of the park.

Germaine journeyed to Dresden by way of Prague, barely stopping long enough along her route to write O'Donnell letters worthy of a sixteen-year-old. No sooner had she left Vienna than she made detailed plans for his visit to Coppet in the autumn. From Budweis she wrote:

> Oh God, for four months no door will open to let my Maurice in. . . . My friend, my friend, why did we separate, we must not leave each other, you will take me with you—everything is easy—to Poland, to the end of the world—but not to see you, that is inconceivable!

If this tone seemed calculated to alienate whatever there was left of O'Donnell's affection, Germaine's meeting at the baths of Teplitz with Friedrich Gentz cost her whatever sympathy she still might have expected from Napoleon. A disciple of Burke, that remarkable publicist was a known English agent and the most fanatical opponent of Napoleon; he soon afterwards became the Grey Eminence behind Metternich, the intellectual guide of the Holly Alliance, the chief theoretician of reaction, in a word, the 'secretary of Europe'. Germaine, who had been recommended to Gentz by the Prince de Ligne, spent seven hours with him in conversation; he accompanied her as far as Pirna in Saxony, where he met her again on June 4, she coming specially from Dresden and he from Teplitz. Of the nature of their talks nothing is known. Undoubtedly they did not see eye to eye on all things: in 1813 Gentz wrote to her, 'To dispute with you does me more good than to agree with anyone in the world.' They did agree in their opinion of Napoleon,

---

[1] This may have been an act of spite over Napoleon's refusal to admit her sons to the Polytechnique. When informed of her intentions by Fouché, Napoleon replied, 'I see no objection, since this woman is a foreigner. But henceforth the young man must always be regarded as a foreigner in France' (to Fouché, Milan, December 23, 1807).

but this was scarcely a matter in which Gentz needed encouragement. Nevertheless, it was upon receiving information of these two interviews that Napoleon began to persecute her in earnest. 'She is beginning to enter into a coterie that is inimical to the public peace,' he wrote to Fouché on June 28. On the same day he instructed his foreign minister to withdraw all diplomatic protection from her, forbade his envoys to see her, and placed her under permanent police surveillance. At the time, however, Germaine was equally unconscious of Napoleon's reaction to her friendship and of O'Donnell's reaction to her letters.

From Dresden Germaine wrote three times to O'Donnell. Mixed with her passionate declarations was the kind of chitchat that enlivens so many of her letters. 'Ah! how it hurts to be in love!' she exclaims, and then goes on to relate how a Prince Puttiakin, a Russian, 'has built himself a house here that is painted all over. He goes around in tin boots to avoid being bitten by mad dogs and works from dawn to night on a book which, he says, will save the human race.' Gentz's friend Adam Müller, the 'peasant prophet', hardly less mad than Prince Puttiakin, visited her daily at her hotel, and she showed him the finished parts of her manuscript on Germany.

At Weimar, her next stop, thirty letters awaited her, including eleven from Benjamin but none from O'Donnell. Goethe was absent, taking the waters, and Germaine stopped for only a week. At Gotha she still had no letter from O'Donnell; nor did she find one on her arrival in Frankfurt on June 25. The tone of her letters changed from reproachfulness to fury to pathos. 'My life is finished if you are not what I thought,' she wrote from Gotha. At Frankfurt, her depression had so affected her physical appearance that Bettina Brentano believed her near death.

Despite her not-so-secret agony, Germaine's progress through Germany was a triumphal tour. At Dresden a romantic customs official told her that now he had seen Madame de Staël he could die content. All along the route admirers showered her with manuscripts and books. 'The axle of my carriage is bending under the weight of all the literary gifts I have received in the past month,' she wrote to O'Donnell; 'in Austria my carriage would not run any such danger.' Whatever satisfaction Germaine derived from all this vanished when, upon reaching Basel on June 30, she still found no letter from her lover. The letter that awaited her at Coppet brought her no comfort: with the chances of war increasing daily, O'Donnell wrote, the odds were against his coming to Switzerland. Germaine replied immediately, in a letter dated July 7, that she would send him a draft on 125 louis (2,500 francs), which she begged him on her knees to accept. In case of war he might use the money for his health and comfort. If there was no war:

> You will come to join me and we shall discuss the future, or else you will go to Italy and I shall join you there. . . . If I were not afraid of displeasing you, I would have sent you four times as much. Do not forget that in my present circumstances I have a yearly income of 120,000 francs and do not owe a penny.

Her friends and lovers had never refused her generosity before. This time, apart from offering to defray O'Donnell's travelling expenses, she held out this thinly disguised enticement to marriage. While she waited for his reply, which came on August 5, her spirits rose. Her letters to him became more relaxed and chatty. She reported her first impression of *Faust*, which Goethe had just published; what she admired most was Goethe's 'grasp of the principle of evil, of irony, of ferocious persiflage' in the character of Mephistopheles, whom she regarded as the embodiment of anti-enthusiasm, a Napoleon of nihilism. She showed concern for Albert, whose supervision she had entrusted to O'Donnell: 'Do not show my son that you do not like his tutor [i.e., Schlegel]. . . . Is it true that Albert had a front tooth broken in a fist fight? Is he disfigured? This worries me a great deal.' She also gave an account of Benjamin, who had obediently joined her on her return. 'I had an explanation with him, and I believe that our summer will be calm, though necessarily sad.' Benjamin, she had found to her surprise, seemed changed: he was meek, docile, almost affectionate. Of the causes of this extraordinary change she had no idea until nearly a year later.

O'Donnell's reply was brutal. To understand its brutality one must keep in mind Madame de Staël's place in Viennese public opinion. Among the scandalous tales circulated about her after her departure from Vienna there was one to the effect that Maurice had offered to marry her and that she had turned him down; Germaine herself, Maurice was told, had spread the story. To be in love with a woman old enough to be his mother was ridiculous; to be suspected of trying to marry her for her money was worse. His honour, he felt, was compromised—that is to say, his vanity was wounded—and when the shower of Germaine's letters came pouring in, he openly complained of the persecution to which this woman was subjecting him. Germaine's money offer changed his annoyance into exasperation. Without any further regard for her feelings, he served notice on her that his honour obliged him to break off, and in a second letter, dated July 30, he went so far as to fling accusations of 'artfulness, dissimulation, and abuse of confidence' into her face. Indeed, his father had just been nominated minister of finance; to have one's career threatened by the amorous persecutions of an ageing woman was intolerable.

Germaine's reply to the first letter, though it indignantly denied his accusations, was conciliatory. His second letter, with its more specific charges, reached her while she was touring central Switzerland with Elzéar de Sabran, Mathieu, and Sismondi. The first instalment of her reply, written at Berne, takes up seven printed pages. Nothing but insanity could explain his conduct, she began; and, with an eloquence that has the proud ring of truth, she went on to straighten out the record. At Interlaken she added several more pages, this time pleading with him to preserve, at least, their friendship. O'Donnell replied that he was acting according to 'the code of honour', a subterfuge with which Germaine took issue: 'Your father's nomination has opened new possibilities of a career for you, either political or military, and perhaps also of an advantageous marriage. Instantly, you rid yourself of your ties with me.' The usual Corinne tirade follows, pointing out how much he had sacrificed for how small a gain: 'Now you are already blaming my intellect, my celebrity, etc. The talents I have are the talents that prove my soul. . . . Try to find among the new hangers-on of your good fortune an attachment such as mine. Adieu.'

Thus ended the last of Germaine's agonizing infatuations. She wrote twice more to O'Donnell before April 1809, when the war broke out and interrupted the correspondence. O'Donnell served with distinction; he was present at the useless Austrian victory of Aspern. The correspondence was resumed after the armistice in July, but no trace of bitterness remained, and when O'Donnell married Titine de Ligne in 1811, Germaine sent him her most cordial congratulations. O'Donnell rose to lieutenant general. He died at Dresden in 1843.

'There is no reality on this earth except religion and the power of love; all the rest is even more fugitive than life itself.' Germaine wrote these words to O'Donnell on September 22, 1808, and they betray a strange new spirit which had got hold of Coppet. If the summer of 1807 had been spent in feasts, the autumn of 1808 was spent in mysticism. 'You will see,' Bonstetten wrote to Frederika Brun, 'all those people will end up by becoming Catholics, Boehmists, Martinists, mystics—and all this thanks to Schlegel and the whole lot of Germans. . . . When

Madame de Staël is alone in her carriage, she reads mystical works!' Sismondi, too, was accusing Schlegel—but Schlegel was by no means the only influence that made Germaine explore the possibilities of mysticism; in fact, he was ill suited for such a task. The Chevalier de Langalerie produced a greater impression on her soul, and in the autumn of 1808 two eccentrics made their appearance at Coppet, who transformed the castle into what outside observers and half of the inmates regarded as a madhouse.

The first of these was Madame de Krüdener—the Baltic noble-woman who, seven years later, in one of the most implausible episodes of modern history, was to talk Tsar Alexander I into founding the Holy Alliance. Madame de Staël had first met her at Geneva in 1801. Julie de Krüdener was thirty-seven years old then; her husband, a Russian diplomat, had just died. After a wild and footloose life of amorous activity, she had lost her good looks—also, according to rumour, her celebrated blonde hair—and her Pietist upbringing began to reassert itself. However, before a conversion there must be a confession: in 1803 Julie published her autobiographical novel *Valérie*. The book was clearly intended to rival Germaine's *Delphine*, and this it did very successfully, for Delphine was tame and demure compared to Valérie. After reading Madame de Krüdener's novel, Madame de Staël wrote to Hochet, 'This book is such a caricature of the genre that one feels ashamed to make any further use of it.' But Julie was pleased with her success: women were standing in bookstores reading *Valérie* and weeping silently, she wrote from Paris to her friend Jean Paul Richter. Her new fame delayed her conversion. Paris, where she was then living with her two daughters, offered her a last dizzying round of feasts and pleasures. In 1804 she returned to Riga for a visit. One day as she was sitting by a window, she saw an acquaintance, who was passing in the street, raise his hat to her and drop dead. The grotesque episode was Julie's road to Damascus: she joined the Moravian Brethren. In 1806, after two years of prayer and good works, her old wanderlust seized her, and she set out on a prilgrimage through Germany. At Königsberg she attended the sermons of Pastor Mayr, who regarded himself as, at the same time, a Lutheran, Catholic, Jew, and Free Mason, and who ended up in an insane asylum; at Baden she came under the influence of the Councillor Jung-Stilling, an occultist and mystic who by a simple calculation could predict the certain date of the end of the world —1819; at Sainte-Marie-aux-Mines in Alsace she sat at the feet of the revivalist Pastor Friedrich Fontaines and of his sister Marie Kummer,

N*

who could give as detailed a description of the coming Kingdom of God as if she had lived there all her life. Thence she went on to Geneva, and late in September 1808 she showed up at Coppet. Being penniless by then, she did not refuse an invitation to stay.

She found Germaine in a deplorable spiritual condition, not unlike her own before her conversion. Julie, on the other hand, was happy as a lark. To attain such happiness, she told Germaine, she must allow God to come to her: 'Stay quiet; refuse nothing; flowers grow only because they tranquilly allow the sun's rays to reach them. You must do the same.' Germaine, who had been deeply impressed by a visit to a Moravian community near Weimar, and whose distaste for mysticism had been weakened by Necker's death and Schlegel's theories, was eager enough to exchange mortal turmoil for heavenly serenity, but a sustained effort at quietness was beyond her capacity. On leaving Coppet, Julie remarked, 'We must leave Madame de Staël to God; she will not be able to escape Him.'

Scarcely had Julie de Krüdener left when, on October 14, another evangelist arrived. His appearance was, perhaps, repulsive—cadaverous, ascetic, and wild, with features devastated by debauch and eyes burning with spirituality—but his theories of divine and worldly love were more suited to impress Germaine than were Julie's. Madame de Krüdener's ideas were nothing new to her; but a man who called God 'the Great Hermaphrodite', spoke of Saint Rousseau, called Germaine Saint Aspasia, pulled fistfuls of crumpled mystico-erotic sonnets out of every pocket, along with enormous, dirty, blue-checked handkerchiefs, and oozed religiosity and lechery from every pore—such a man was at least something novel.

Born in Königsberg in 1768, the poet and dramatist Zacharias Werner grew up in the same Evangelical and Pietist atmosphere (which is almost a part of the eastern Baltic landscape) as Julie de Krüdener. Unlike Madame de Krüdener, he had true poetic talent, occasionally even flashes of genius. His entire life, from adolescence to his conversion to Catholicism in 1810, was consumed in the struggle between religious, mystical drives and compulsive sexuality. He seemed to unite in his person every Romantic striving to an extreme degree, and the resulting hodge-podge of exalted paradoxes closely resembled madness. His road to conversion led through the most fantastic attempts to reconcile sexuality with mysticism, fanciful Masonic myths with Christianity; yet it ended in submission to the discipline of the Church in which his obsessive sense of guilt was laid to rest.

His lechery was pathological and impressive. He wrestled with servant girls at every inn or private home he visited in his wanderings from Warsaw to Paris, from Königsberg to Rome; his senses, aroused by their earthy charms, responded also to such sublime spectacles as the Falls of the Rhine, which struck his imagination as a symbol of orgasm; his address book might have served as the basis for a Baedeker to Europe's whorehouses. His three marriages (the first with a prostitute abducted from a Königsberg bordello) all ended in divorce. After his last divorce in 1805, he admitted in a letter to a friend that he could hardly blame his wife for leaving him: 'I am not evil, but I am a weakling, . . . a coward, moody, stingy, and dirty; you know me.' Werner's estimate of himself squared with that of his best friend, who, however, added the adjectives 'greedy', 'vain', and 'embarrassing'.

Werner's mother, the Pietistic widow of a university professor, had been ailing for years before her death on February 24, 1803. In the last stages of her illness she was under the delusion that she was the Virgin Mary and her son, Christ.[1] Werner, on leave from his civil service post in Warsaw, nursed her through those heartbreaking months, and it is scarcely surprising that his mother's death filled him with an intense consciousness of guilt and sin. Through Pastor Mayr he came into close contact with a mystical Masonic sect, among whom he seems to have won several disciples for the wild doctrine in which he sought to reconcile art, religion, and love. Mankind had to be saved through 'disenlighten-ment'; art and religion should fuse in a higher unity; art, itself a strange language of symbols, was to symbolize the divine element in man; religious faith sprang from the soul's dark urge for something higher, a yearning which only art could appease by establishing harmony in the soul and by giving form to the infinite; love was the mediator between God and man; 'death, which unlocks our prison, must be ecstatically embraced; putrefaction, which restores us to the infinite by uniting us with it, must be fervently desired.'

Such was the gospel Werner set out to preach. Since Werner believed that animal lust, being a form of love, brought mortal creatures closer to the Godhead, and that there was no connection whatever between religion and morality, his doctrine of 'Christlike and copulatory love' (as Herder's widow put it) found more scoffers than disciples. 'That queer bird,' reminisced another contemporary, 'made no secret of his

---

[1] E. T. A. Hoffmann, who spent his childhood in the apartment below the Werners', asserts in *Die Serapionsbrüder* that Frau Werner entertained her son in this sentiment from boyhood on. This is poetic licence.

doctrine that man's soul in its ascent must pass during its earthly life through the purgatory of female bodies.'

On moving to Berlin in 1805, Werner embarked on a literary career which, he hoped, would make him Schiller's successor as Germany's national dramatic poet. His first plays, *The Sons of the Valley* and *The Cross on the Baltic*, were turned down by the Berlin theatre because, said Iffland, its omnipotent director, the public would not stand the mysticism. Iffland proposed that he write a drama on a real German, non-mystical subject—Martin Luther. Though already then strongly attracted to Catholicism, Werner obliged Iffland without demur: *Luther, or the Consecration of Strength* was finished early in 1806 and had its première with Iffland in the title role. Despite the rather cloying mysticism Werner had smuggled into the play, *Luther* was fairly successful, and Iffland toured Germany with it. Werner was on his way to fame, but since fame brought little money, he began to wander through Germany in search of a stable position. He wrote two more plays (*Attila* and *Wanda*) and hundreds of sonnets, flattered the great, asked for money and protection with all the obsequious arrogance of unrecognized genius. His grotesquely deep bows, his emaciated figure and flashing eyes, his celebrated handkerchiefs, his hysterical readings, and his curious gospel of love impressed some and amused others. At Weimar Goethe treated him graciously, and the Duke favoured him as a kind of court jester, but his stay was cut short after a scandalous incident. Frau Schopenhauer had invited a circle of ladies to tea, to be uplifted by the discourses of the apostle of love. Werner was late. A maid, sent to fetch him, soon returned screaming rape. More wanderings followed, and August 1808 found him at Interlaken to witness the celebration of the five-hundredth anniversary of Swiss liberty. It was here he first met Madame de Staël, who at the time had reached the depth of despair over Count O'Donnell. Werner impressed her—no one could say that he was boring—and she invited him to her château.

Early in October, by leisurely stages, he made his way to Coppet. At Payerne he clumsily missed the conquest of a servant girl ('magnificent build, full bosom, rosy complexion, splendid lips, eyes swimming in lubricity'). At Yverdun he kissed Pestalozzi's hands while Pestalozzi kissed his. At Clarens he made a pilgrimage to the rock of the Meillerie, prayed to God and to 'Saint Rousseau', and scratched his name on the stone. At Saint-Maurice he contemplated the cattle in the Rhône valley,

> Where in their joyful urge to be like God
> The Alpine bulls are mating with the cows,

and on October 14 he bowed his way into Coppet. He stayed only a little over two weeks, but those two weeks remained vivid in the memories of all those present.

Among the guests of Coppet, Werner found Schlegel, Oehlenschläger, Benjamin, Sismondi, Bonstetten, Henriette Mendelssohn, Count Kochubey, who had been foreign minister under Tsar Paul I, the sculptor Friedrich Tieck (Ludwig's brother), who had made the bas-relief on the Necker mausoleum, Elzéar de Sabran, and a young Greek named Skinast. Conversation at the dinner table and in the drawing room struck uninitiated visitors as incomprehensible, chaotic, loud, and German. Everybody read and declaimed—Werner from his poems, Oehlenschläger from his tragedy *Axel and Walburg*, which he was then writing, Schlegel his translations of Calderon's *Constant Prince* and of Shakespeare's *Richard III*. They argued over Catholicism and mysticism. Werner discussed his next tragedy with Germaine, who showed him Madame de Krüdener's letters and asked for his advice, of which he gave freely and eloquently. Schlegel explained to him his theory 'that animals were the dreams, men the thoughts of Nature', that 'the earth and stars had life of their own as well as free will', that 'man since his existence has moved ever farther from the God of Light', and that Werner should read Saint-Martin, the 'Unknown Philosopher'. In a talk with Baron Voght Werner asked him suddenly, 'Do you know what a man loves in his mistress?' Voght hesitated. 'God,' said Werner. 'Ah!' replied Voght with an air of conviction, 'no doubt about it.' To Sismondi Werner explained that God was 'the greatest hermaphrodite of the universe', that 'religion was love of God —but if one could not rise so high, it was enough to love a man or a woman, for everything that love makes us do when we are with a mistress is done for the glory of God'. 'He is very talented and kind,' Sismondi wrote of Werner: 'it is a pity that he is completely mad.'

Oehlenschläger, jealous of the favour Werner found with Germaine, almost came to blows with him, packed his trunks to depart, and was kept back only by his hostess's pleas. On evenings when there were neither quarrels nor metaphysical discussions, Werner would waltz with Our Lady of Coppet, as he called her, or play chess with her. On November 2 he attended the performance of *The Young Shulamite*, which moved him profoundly. His description of Madame de Staël is characteristically enthusiastic:

> She is of middle height; her body, while not slim as a nymph's, is voluptuously beautiful, especially her breasts and neck. She is decidedly

brunette, and her face is not precisely beautiful, but all criticism is forgotten at the sight of her magnificent eyes through which there shines—nay, flashes with fiery flame—a great, divine soul. And whenever, as often happens, she lets her heart speak, and one realizes how the greatness of that noble heart surpasses even her vast and powerful intellect, then one must adore her.

Taking his leave on November 3, Werner knelt down before Germaine, and both broke into tears. He then went to Benjamin's room. He earnestly begged Benjamin to spread 'the religion' in France. Benjamin promised to do what he could. Then Werner, tears in his eyes, said, 'Do not leave that poor woman!' Benjamin, now also in tears, promised solemnly not to desert Germaine. Thus Werner left Coppet —'where, praise God, I have left many disciples behind'.

The Benjamin who, with tears of sincerity, promised the apostle Werner never to leave Germaine, had in fact been married to another woman for five months, during four of which he had lived peacefully under Germaine's roof. His wife was residing at a few miles' distance, and they had met furtively from time to time. This state of affairs requires some explanation.

When, on a December evening in 1807, Charlotte du Tertre caught up with Benjamin at her inn in Besançon, he had just mailed to Germaine the most passionate love letter she ever received from him. Charlotte, exhausted by an hour's walk through the mud, briefly gave news of her divorce: it was certain, but not yet final. Benjamin dwelt for some time on the probable delays; interrogated about Madame de Staël, he replied evasively. They spent the rest of the evening in silence. The next day, after praying God to take care of Charlotte, he asked her for permission to spend six more months with Germaine so that he might obtain her free consent to leave her. Charlotte sat silent with lowered head, nodding and staring. She seemed to have fallen into a stupor which made Benjamin fear that she had lost her mind.

Following up his plans, Benjamin took her to Dôle. On the road Charlotte fell into a deep faint. Benjamin tried to revive her, but she seemed cataleptic. For the rest of the way he held her in his arms; the colour had drained from her face, and her limbs were rigid. Next day she was writhing with stomach cramps. The physician, spending the night by her bedside with Benjamin, pointed out the approaching symptoms of death. She became delirious. 'That voice! That voice!' she cried as Benjamin spoke to her. 'That voice which has hurt me so! This man has killed me. Who is accusing him? They must not accuse him. He is kind, is he not, but not to me.' It was then that Benjamin prayed, 'O God, save me from the consequences of my miscalculations.'

Bled, stuffed with opium, and fed with milk, Charlotte slept for three days. On the fourth she revived; Benjamin promised to devote his life to her; they went to bed together. Soon afterwards, they left— for Paris. Charlotte had an indisputable advantage over Germaine: she was capable of falling into mortal illness at will and of recovering only when circumstances were favourable. Germaine never could stick to attacks of fever for more than two days, and even then she never put her whole mind to the business; she had too many other things to think about. Charlotte, who spent all her days doing nothing, could devote her whole time and energy to indefinite periods of catalepsy.

Another advantage was that she was with Benjamin, and Germaine was five hundred miles away. Her divorce being made final, she accompanied Benjamin to his father's estate at Brévans late in May 1808. On June 5 the Pastor Ebray married them in a secret ceremony— which, incidentally, was legally invalid, since the French Civil Code recognizes only the civil ceremony. But a civil ceremony could not have been kept secret, and Benjamin had persuaded his bride that the time was not ripe for breaking the news to Germaine; he would have to dissemble for some time longer, avoid spectacular scenes, and reach a satisfactory settlement of his 80,000-franc debt. The couple separated a few miles from Coppet. Benjamin went on to join Germaine; Charlotte, to Neuchâtel and thence to Lausanne and Geneva.

Having waited all these months for Benjamin to make the break he had promised, Charlotte was beginning to show some impatience and scepticism. She pointed out to him 'the unbelievable position' he had put her in with regard to her family. 'I wonder if you will ever recover the independence without which we cannot be happy.' That independence, she feared, was a kind of Lost Paradise which he would go on mourning for the rest of his life. She returned to Brévans in mid-December. Benjamin joined her there in January, leaving Germaine to another winter of boredom in Geneva, and together they went on to Paris. The situation was untenable indeed. By May, when Benjamin was expected back in Coppet, they agreed to go before Madame de Staël and tell her the truth. They stopped at the fashionable inn of Sécheron, just outside Geneva, where Charlotte wrote a note, under Benjamin's dictation, asking Germaine for an urgent interview. She signed it

'Hardenberg', with all her titles, and sent it off by a messenger on horseback. This done, Benjamin went into hiding at Ferney.

At ten in the evening, on May 9, Charlotte was bathing her feet in a bucket when Madame de Staël burst into her room without knocking. 'I have come,' she said, 'because you are a Hardenberg.' Charlotte gently apprised Germaine of the fact that she was a Hardenberg no longer but a Constant.

When Germaine left, at four o'clock in the morning, Charlotte sat down to write a report to Benjamin. From it the ordeal she had just passed through may be reconstructed with a fair degree of accuracy.

Germaine received the news with the violence that might be expected; but, says Charlotte, 'she had not the least symptom of convulsions in my presence. I virtually forced her, through my conduct, to be gentle towards me.' What Germaine really desired, despite all her expressions of grief, was a long delay in making the marriage public. And on this point—one feels incredulous writing it—Charlotte gave in, meekly, humbly, completely. 'I shall not refuse anything you two require,' she wrote to Benjamin. All she asked of him was that he see her before going to Coppet. That he had to go was a certainty: Charlotte having pretended not to know where Benjamin was hiding, Germaine had announced that she would send her people to search for him on every road.

Once Charlotte had yielded to her main wish, Germaine changed tactics: from tragic she became confidential. For several hours Benjamin's conduct and character were dissected.

> My conversation with her [wrote Charlotte] has left an impression on me which it will be difficult to erase. . . . I think that it would have been better, for your happiness and for my peace of mind, if we had not married. . . . Good God! After the thousand oaths you swore that all your happiness rested on me, did you have to make another woman believe that away from her there was no happiness for you?

Benjamin went back to Coppet. In Geneva, in Lausanne, rumours were circulating. Was Benjamin married? Was he not married? Benjamin's family no longer knew what to think: Benjamin insisted that he was married, but that for reasons of prudence and self-interest his marriage must be denied; Germaine pointed out that his marriage was legally invalid; and Charlotte compounded the confusion by announcing—in order, explained Benjamin, 'to put her situation in less bizarre a light'—that she had not yet married Benjamin but was going to marry him.

After two weeks at Coppet Benjamin left for Brévans, where Charlotte was awaiting him. No sooner had he arrived than the familiar orders arrived from Coppet: Germaine was going to spend a few weeks in Lyons, to see Talma act; Benjamin must join her, or else. Benjamin joined her. Hard on his heels, but without his knowledge, came Charlotte. When, on June 8, she unexpectedly entered his hotel room, Benjamin was indignant. What business had she to persecute him? She had better go straight back to Brévans or to Lausanne—anywhere she liked. Charlotte went to her own room. Soon after she sent a servant with a message for Benjamin. She was dying. She had drunk a glass of laudanum. Would he make sure she was not buried alive? Could she see him once more? 'But be quick. Quick!'

Benjamin reached Charlotte in time: the 'Coppet dose' was not lethal. As soon as Charlotte recovered, it was agreed that she must be got rid of somehow. Upon his promise that he would be back on the twenty-fifth, and that the Treaty of Sécheron was still in force, Germaine allowed Benjamin to escort Charlotte to Paris, where he left her in the hands of a physician. Benjamin kept his word: he returned to Lyons and then continued with Germaine to Coppet, where he stayed until October 19. It all sounded like a novel by Mrs. Radcliffe, declared his aunt de Nassau when apprised of this latest exploit.

Charlotte was not the only one to resort to the 'Coppet dose' that year. Juliette Récamier, after her return to Paris in December 1807, began to reconsider her romantic involvement with Prince August in a more sober mood. Monsieur Récamier remained firm in opposing annulment or divorce; in fact, after fifteen years of marriage, he even suggested that he was minded to consummate it. At the same time, August, sensing in Juliette's letters that her ardour had cooled, insisted on the execution of her written promise; and Madame de Staël, to whom he appealed, backed him up in her letters to Juliette. Yet if there was one thing Juliette was incapable of, making a choice between men was it. Suicide was a better way out, and attempted suicide better still— better, at any rate, than that fate worse than death, a consummated marriage. One day towards the end of winter Juliette wrote her farewell note to her husband: 'Determined as I am to end my life, I want to tell you that until my last heartbeat I shall remember your kindness, and never cease to regret that I was not for you all that I should have been'; and so forth. Before her she had a box full of opium pills. Did she swallow them? Did she merely contemplate them? Did her husband see the letter? One thing was certain: Juliette felt that she had gone as far as she could go. She had done her duty, she had looked at the pills, she was in a position to inform the Prince that she relieved him of his vows. The Prince's cries of treachery; his pleas to reconsider her decision; their rendezvous at Aachen, where he went and where she stood him up, sending her portrait instead; the Prince's unwavering and hopeless attachment to her until his death in 1843; his burial with the ring Juliette had given him at Coppet thirty-six years earlier—all this would make a splendid subject for a sentimental historical novel.

During the first stages of the Prince's romantic despair, Germaine stood firmly by his side—to the point of indiscretion, according to Juliette; Juliette stayed away from Coppet in the summer of 1808, fearing no doubt a plot of Germaine's to reunite them. Her fears would have been justified, for the already complicated imbroglio was even more labyrinthine than appears on the surface.

The situation in the autumn and winter of 1808–9 may be recapitulated as follows: (1) Germaine refused to give up Benjamin, who, unknown to her, had married Charlotte; (2) Charlotte refused to give up Benjamin, who was living with Germaine; (3) Prince August refused to give up Juliette, who was living with her husband; (4) while clinging to Benjamin, Germaine was dying of despair over O'Donnell's treachery and trying to regain the affections of Prosper de Barante; (5) Barante was explaining his love to Juliette Récamier; (6) Juliette, without depriving Prosper of hope, did nothing to fulfil it; (7) Germaine, in her letters to Juliette, suggested that Juliette was alienating Prosper's affections; (8) all correspondence between Juliette and Germaine ceased in November 1808.

While Juliette and Germaine sulked, Prosper in his letters to Germaine reproached her for questioning his fidelity (he still regarded himself as bound by his promises to Germaine); at the same time he reproached Juliette for her reserve. Among Germaine, Juliette, Charlotte, Benjamin, Prosper, and the Prince of Prussia there existed a system of conflicting and overlapping secret treaties, not one of which corresponded to any real sentiment or situation, but every one of which was invoked with all the self-righteousness of a nation wronged. Why should he not enjoy the company of Juliette, Prosper asked Germaine, since Germaine had for so long deprived him of happiness? 'In case this means anything to you, be assured that I have not pronounced the word "love" to anyone but you.' This may have been true, but if Prosper did not pronounce the word before Juliette, he hinted at the thing clearly enough, and at any rate his explanations infuriated rather than appeased Germaine. She asked Prosper to return her letters. He refused to seize this opportunity to regain his freedom. Instead, he persuaded Juliette to write to Germaine and exonerate both him and herself. Early in February 1809, Germaine received from Juliette a letter offering to show her Prosper's letters. 'Your letter, my dear Juliette, makes me want to throw myself at your feet,' Germaine replied. 'I do not want to see Prosper's letters—all I want is to be loved by you again.' Prosper, too, was forgiven, not only for loving Juliette but even for not mentioning, in his *Survey of French Literature in the Eighteenth Century*, the name of Jacques Necker. (Not without justification, Germaine regarded this omission as a gesture of submission to the Emperor, and indeed Prosper was made Prefect of Vendée soon after the publication of that very remarkable book.)

Thus reconciled, Juliette did not refuse Germaine's request to see her at Lyons in June 1809, and late in July she arrived at Coppet, escorted by her most recent admirer, the fat Baron von Voght. She was given her old room, next to Germaine's; Voght occupied the room formerly tenanted by Prince August. Life at Coppet resumed much as in the summer of 1807, and Germaine once again seemed victorious, having subdued the rebels, recaptured the deserters, intimidated the disloyal, and imposed her laws. Just so Napoleon had returned to Paris after crushing Austria at Wagram, seizing the Papal States, and expelling Wellington from Spain.

The feasts, the plays, the discussions began all over again. Zacharias Werner reappeared on September 6; Germaine had paid his travelling expenses. Out of his pocket he pulled, besides his famous handkerchief and gigantic snuffbox, the manuscript of his latest drama, a tragedy of fate, with only three actors—a kind of *Oedipus* in reverse, in which the father murders his son—entitled *The Twenty Fourth of February*.[1] Germaine was struck by its sombre power—indeed, the play is regarded as Werner's best—and decided to stage it. Werner and Schlegel took the male roles, a Fräulein von Jenner of Berne the third part. Coppet, it seemed, had become a German colony. A German play was being rehearsed and at the dinner table more German than French was spoken. Yet, as Werner observed, Madame de Staël's German entourage were not, 'as was stupidly supposed in Germany, engaged in forming her mind; on the contrary, they receive from her a social

---

[1] The day of his mother's death. It would be idle to dwell on the significance of his choice of date.

education'. This education was dealt out with a stern hand, witness Schlegel's continuing complaints in his midnight notes: 'Dear friend, I am not susceptible, but it hurts me to think that far from being of any use to you, I am made to understand at every moment that you regard me as disagreeable, bothersome, boring, and ill-bred. It is too late to undertake my education; I advise you to give it up.' Not only did she not give it up, but she even reproached the immortal translator of Shakespeare and Calderon for his failure to educate Albert (back in Coppet at that time), who at the age of fifteen had the handwriting of a six-year-old.

Nor did Benjamin's presence add harmony. When Germaine announced, from Lyons, that she would bring him back, Schlegel wrote: 'That he is a cause of discord between you and your friends is the least of his disadvantages. But every day you spend with him from now on is a waste of your talents and will merely delay the time when you can be happy again, or, at least, regain your tranquillity, forget, and put your noble faculties to work.' Nobody could have agreed with him more than Benjamin himself, but Benjamin no longer was exchanging confidences with anyone; he had embarked on a new system, which may be characterized as total deception of everybody.

Benjamin's family, unable to understand why he was back in Coppet, lent credence to the rumour that he was forcing Germaine to tolerate him at her house, where he stayed only for the sake of material comfort. This accusation he denied violently. On the contrary, he affirmed in a letter to Rosalie, Germaine's unhappiness at the idea of losing him was only too manifest. His friends accused him of having 'precipitated her into an abyss of suffering' from which she could never be rescued if he left her. 'Everybody here, every visitor, every letter, speaks to me in the same terms. She herself sends notes from her room to mine, any one of which would be enough to disprove what she is alleged to have said about me.' In other words, it was Germaine herself, according to Benjamin's relatives, who circulated the rumour that Benjamin was in Coppet on tolerance only. In the desperate phase the struggle had reached it would be useless to look for rationality, truth, or even decency. While Benjamin went as far as to promise Germaine to accompany her to America in the following year, he was secretly dispatching, in a steady stream of small and furtive parcels, all the books, papers, manuscripts, and notes he had accumulated at Coppet in the course of fifteen years. Then, on October 19, he was gone.

'He left a week ago,' Germaine wrote to Juliette, who had returned to France in September, 'and never in my life have I experienced such convulsive pain. . . . I know I cannot live without seeing him and talking to him.' On the same day, October 26, she wrote an astonishing letter to the Marquis de Châteaugiron, who was about to see their common friend, Prosper de Barante: 'You will see him, sir, and he will tell you everything that passed between us. . . . I beg you to plead my cause. Independence, glory, affection—all this I offer him. If he follows his own way he will tear my heart without finding, it seems to me, any happiness or dignity.' The letter continues chaotically, without punctuation, with a confusion of thoughts and feelings that defies translation. In her frenzy she also wrote to Mathieu, begging him to talk Prosper into marrying her. Mathieu, embarrassed and uneasy, carried out his mission. The result is summed up in one sentence of Prosper's letter to Germaine, in which he reports on Mathieu's visit: 'He will pray God to inspire us with a salutary resolution.' Mathieu's prayers were not heard.

On November 1 Zacharias Werner left Coppet after spending two months 'in the adoration of this image of grace, which truly works miracles for the salvation of pilgrims who, like myself, are persecuted both by fate and their own follies'. From the 'Shrine of Saint Aspasia', the pilgrim was making his way to Rome, stopping on his way at churches and bordellos, and ending up in priestly robes. Before parting from Our Lady of Coppet, he left her a sonnet entitled 'Love and Friendship', in which he admitted, with resignation, the superiority of the latter over the former. While weeping over Prosper and Benjamin, Germaine had been obliged to repulse Zacharias's advances.

After another month at Coppet Germaine transplanted her sorrows to the Hôtel des Balances in Geneva. Prosper, called to Geneva by his sister's death, saw her briefly in January, and his presence gave her 'miraculous relief'. 'Dear Juliette', she begged Madame Récamier after his departure, 'make him love me and not you. . . . At least, I hope that I shall suffer less from Benjamin, now that I shall suffer from Prosper.' Her hopes revived—but Juliette must keep this secret from Benjamin, whom Germaine suspected, not without reason, of having sinister plans.

Before leaving Coppet Benjamin had promised to keep his marriage secret for another six months, until Germaine's departure for America. But no sooner was he in Paris than he informed Germaine that he no longer could keep the secret. This information was largely responsible for Germaine's frantic pursuit of Prosper: the world must not think that she had been discarded, and only marriage with Prosper could save her from such a disgrace. Benjamin, for his part, was concerned with his own reputation. Only by placing all the blame for his conduct on Germaine could he expect to survive the crisis with his honour intact. In Paris he began a regular campaign against her, winning Hochet to his side and swaying even Juliette. 'Benjamin's conduct is atrocious, you may believe me,' Germaine wrote to her. 'Mine towards him is, I daresay, extraordinarily generous. I take his defence here, where everybody knows what he has done, and he attacks me in Paris while beseeching me not to let anyone know the truth.' Germaine was stating an objective fact. Benjamin's letters of the period, begging each of his friends to conceal some aspect of his conduct, border on the fantastic. At the same time he was gathering material for blackmail. Rosalie had hinted that she had information detrimental to Germaine—possibly about her relations with Barante. In a letter dated November 14, 1809, Benjamin begged her to disclose it. He had he knew not what baneful sympathy for Germaine: 'If I could d scover any evidence of duplicity, bad faith, or ill will, the spell would be broken.' In simpler terms, what he wanted was some weapon he could wield against Germaine when it came to accounting for the 80,000 francs he owed her. To state his case fairly, it must be said that Germaine had been blackmailing him morally for fifteen years and that even now she held his written promise to return to Coppet by February 1. He returned.

The purpose of his visit, he assured his aunt de Nassau, was 'to force Madame de Staël to accept' what he owed her. This could hardly have been true, since he had no money to pay her; the truth was that Germaine had asked him to pay his debt: 'It is incredible,' Charlotte wrote to him indignantly, 'that after showing such an attachment for you, after telling everybody within hearing that you are the father of her daughter, Madame de Staël should send you her bills and ask for the repayment of debts although she has all the money she needs.' After six weeks of haggling Benjamin and Germaine reached a settlement. In the instrument he signed on March 21 Benjamin acknowledged owing 80,000 francs to Madame de Staël and promised to inscribe her in his will to this amount, without interest, in case he should die childless; a mortgage Germaine held in a property of his was included in this sum. There was a price he had to pay for this unorthodox way of paying debts; its nature may be surmised from a passage in a letter to Hochet, dated March 31, from Coppet: 'Now that our struggle is ended, I am ready to admit that it was the faults of my character, as well as the force of circumstances, which prevented our relationship from being a harmonious one; it would hurt me much more if she were ill-judged on my account than if I were on hers.' One can almost hear Germaine's voice dictating: what Hochet knew, all Paris was bound to hear.

By Christmas 1809 Germaine had formally announced her plans to leave Europe in the summer of 1810. The project caused her friends profound misgivings. Schlegel, though determined to accompany her, dreaded the voyage, and Sismondi, who would be left behind, predicted that American materialism would not agree with her. The comment he read in an American newspaper on her impending arrival confirmed his fears: 'She is a very wealthy woman,' it read, 'who lives very nobly in her castle. She also has written several books which, being widely read in Europe, earn her a great deal of money.' But Germaine clung to the idealized eighteenth-century vision of the New World: 'I have no doubt,' she wrote, 'that America shall inherit the civilization of Europe.'

Early in 1810 she received her passport, which allowed her and Auguste to enter France for the purpose of boarding ship to the United States, without touching Paris. Before leaving the Continent, she was going to stop at Blois, meet her friends once more, and supervise the printing of her latest book.

She had, indeed, nearly finished a new book—a book which in the complete edition of her works takes up three volumes. The larger part of it she had written only after September 1809: Germaine might waste everyone else's time, but never her own.

With the nearly finished manuscript of *De l'Allemagne* in her luggage, Germaine left for France in April 1810.

17

THE SWORD BEATS THE SPIRIT

THE manuscript of the first volume of *De l'Allemagne* was already in Paris in the hands of the publisher Nicolle when Germaine left Coppet. Nicolle, whose business was not flourishing, was eager to publish the work as soon as possible; while Madame de Staël was still completing the last volume, the first was already in composition at Tours.

Late in April Germaine arrived at the castle of Chaumont on the Loire near Blois, taken from her American agent and friend, James LeRay, who did not expect to return from New York before autumn. Chaumont was conveniently close to her printer in Tours; manuscript and proofs were to shuttle back and forth all summer long. Schlegel, in a letter to his sister, described the historic castle:

> I am writing to you, my dear sister, from the banks of the Loire . . . in an ancient and handsome castle, guarded by indestructible round towers, once owned and inhabited by kings, rebuilt for the most part by Cardinal d'Amboise, the adviser of Louis XII, and in which a magician, on the request of Catherine de' Medici, conjured up the infernal spirits to prophesy the fate of her progeny. . . . This feudal castle stands on a high rock. The village lies at our feet; two hundred steps lead up to us. . . . Like the Elysian Fields, we are surrounded by flowery groves in which the nightingales are singing without cease. From our platform we command a wide view, not of the Swiss Alps, to be sure, but of a fertile cultivated plain. To one side, shaded by ancient trees, stands the rustic parish church, whose bell stirs pious emotions at the hours of the Mass, the Angelus, and the Hail Mary. On the river, small barks with sails are gliding by; they seem to entice our thoughts to the sea and to more dangerous navigation. All this would be beautiful and magnificent if it were not in France—to be precise, in the heart of France, supposing this country to have a heart. However, what can I do? I am following an alien star, and who knows how much time will pass before I can once more follow my own destiny, for better or for worse?

In this romantic castle, incongruously the property of an American speculator in landed property, Germaine assembled, for what might be the last time, all her friends, lovers, and vassals. In her immediate suite were her three children, Schlegel, a Neapolitan music master and guitarist, named Pertosa, and a new member of the household, Miss Fanny Randall. The last, who was to play an extraordinary part in Germaine's last years, was distantly related to Sismondi by marriage. Germaine had taken the English spinster into her family on a vague basis—as companion to Albertine, as confidante, as friend—partly out of pity, partly to please Sismondi. An unhappy love affair had disillusioned Miss Randall with all men; her father, from whom she expected to inherit £80,000, committed suicide and left only debts. She became attached to Germaine and Albertine with the fanatical devotion of English spinsters whom life has treated roughly. Taciturn, disagreeable to the point of rudeness in order to mark her independence, bitter and violent, she was to centre her whole existence in Madame de Staël, threatening suicide if she felt neglected, and ready to murder, poison, or lie for her idol if asked. She soon was to be called upon for services that required the greatest discretion.

The self-pitying German, the guitar-strumming Italian, and the sinister Englishwoman formed an odd enough assortment, yet no more odd than the other guests in Germaine's fairy-tale castle: Juliette Récamier, her American adorer Middleton, her German adorer Voght, her Russian adorer Baron Balk; Elzéar de Sabran; Mathieu and Adrien de Montmorency; Adelbert von Chamisso, expatriate Frenchman, botanist and poet, creator of *Peter Schlemihl, the Man without a Shadow.* Prosper de Barante spent several days at Chaumont late in April (I see him here like an illusion that colours my life,' wrote Germaine to Juliette); Barante *père* followed soon after, stopping on his way to his estate; and on June 10 Benjamin arrived, to stay for five weeks.

While Germaine was working on her book and her proofs, the other inhabitants of Chaumont yielded to the temptations of idleness, and Germaine herself reserved her evenings for conversation, music, and a strange game called *petite poste*, itself one of the forms assumed by the game of love. The stay at Chaumont was the last feast on Cythera before the embarkation for the United States.

Juliette Récamier was flirting, separately and collectively, with Schlegel, Middleton, Voght, Balk, Adrien de Montmorency, and Auguste de Staël, who suddenly fell violently in love with her; Albert had succumbed to a lady in Blois; Mathieu and Elzéar, though resigned, still were sighing for Germaine; Chamisso, finding that Germaine combined 'German seriousness, meridional fire, and French manners', fell in love with her and was not altogether discouraged; Germaine, while confiding her disappointments to Chamisso, still strove to regain her hold on Benjamin and wrote melancholy letters to Barante; and Schlegel was jealous of everybody. All these half-avowed sentiments found their outlet in the game of *petite poste*. The group would gather around a large table and, instead of conversing, write notes to one another. A number of these accordion-shaped papers have been preserved. Here is one:

> MME RÉCAMIER (*to Schlegel*): Do you believe that I am the woman of torments or the woman of desires?
> SCHLEGEL: You are a heavenly woman, slightly disguised to increase her charm.
> MME RÉCAMIER: Do you love me?
> SCHLEGEL: If I dared——
> MME RÉCAMIER: Dare!
> SCHLEGEL: I dare. What now?
> MME RÉCAMIER: I should tell you, sir, that I do not want to compromise myself *in writing*. But if you want to join me this evening for a talk, I shall tell you what I think.
> SCHLEGEL: I shall come to be rebuffed. It is true that I am used to it.
> MME RÉCAMIER: That goes without saying.
> SCHLEGEL: You are right, Madam, but you must be very clever if you should succeed in discouraging me. I am blasé when it comes to despair, for I have long since given up hope.
> MME RÉCAMIER: What to do with a man who can neither hope nor despair?
> SCHLEGEL: Alas, pity me, my time is past: I have no illusions on that head.
> MME RÉCAMIER: To run away from one illusion you are falling into another. Your time is not past. Your soul has what it needs to love and be loved. . . .

Folded inside the sheet there was a smaller one, in Juliette's hand. On one side is written, 'To M. Schlegel'; on the other, in English, 'I love you.' Another sample:

> AUGUSTE DE STAËL: Dear Juliette, I love you.
> MME RÉCAMIER (*returns the paper without an answer*).
> AUGUSTE: I implore you, dear Juliette, be kind to your friend. I am afraid of your terrible letter.

MME RÉCAMIER: What have you written? What is in the letter you got? I want to know everything. I am jealous, I am exacting, I am despotic, and I love you enough to make up for all these faults.

The *petite poste* was a dangerous game. In the park of Chaumont, recalls Chamisso, there were two walks which the inmates had christened *l'allée des explications* and *l'allée des réconciliations*. There, says Chamisso, the dregs of the *petite poste* were sifted by couple after couple. And the partners changed as in an elaborate dance. But for once there were no grand passions, no grand scenes. Germaine was too absorbed in her work—and she was absorbed in her work because she was almost resigned. Only Auguste forgot that love at Chaumont was a game.

The unreal quality of life at Chaumont was heightened by some incongruous and picturesque touches: Madame Récamier dancing and shaking a tambourine to the accompaniment of Pertosa's guitar; Chamisso, addicted to an enormous German pipe, obliged by the relentless Miss Randall to indulge his vice in the remotest chambers of the castle; or the baptism, at the parish church, on May 29, of 'a Negro born in Africa, belonging to the Baroness de Staël-Holstein, aged about twenty-two', with Mathieu de Montmorency and Juliette Récamier as his godparents. The parish register records the event, and Schlegel wrote a touching ode on it—but who the Negro was, how Germaine happened to have him in her possession, and what became of him, has never been discovered.

Amid these doings fell two successive bombs. The first, on June 3, was a laconic newspaper item announcing the dismissal of Fouché and his replacement by General Savary, Duke of Rovigo. The second was a letter from the lord of the castle, received by Germaine on August 8, announcing that he had landed in France with his entire family, servants, and baggage, and was about to return to his castle. 'Here I am,' wrote Germaine to the elder Barante, 'on the road again with my whole caboodle.'

By mid-August Germaine had found a new home for herself and her caboodle—the country residence of Fossé, near Blois, belonging to a royalist nobleman, the Comte de Salaberry. There was nothing feudal about the residence—it was just a big house. No sooner had they arrived, Germaine recalls in her memoirs, than Pertosa began to play his guitar and Albertine her harp to accompany Juliette singing a romance. 'The peasants gathered at the windows, astonished to see thsi colony of troubadours that had come to enliven their master's solitude'.

Not only the peasants were astonished. Whenever Germaine ventured into the streets of Blois on foot, the entire population followed to stare at her. Savary, the new police minister, disliked this publicity. Madame de Staël, he wrote to Corbigny, the Prefect of Loir-et-Cher, was surrounded by a court. The Prefect, himself in the process of becoming a member of the court, informed Germaine of Savary's displeasure. 'You may be sure at least,' said Germaine, 'that if I have a court I do not owe it to power.'

On September 23 Germaine corrected the last proofs of her book. Most of her friends had left; Germaine herself, afraid of a winter crossing, had as good as postponed her journey to America until spring and hoped to obtain the government's permission to spend the winter at Vendôme. In the back of her mind the old illusions were still alive: *De l'Allemagne* would so impress Napoleon that he would lift her exile; Prosper would come back to her; Benjamin would leave Charlotte. It was then that, with brutal suddenness, a blow of the master's fist shattered these hopes and destroyed the work of six years.

Of all the writings of Madame de Staël, three books can still be read with great profit. They are *On Literature Considered in Its Relationship to Social Institutions*; *On Germany*; and *Considerations on the Principal Events of the French Revolution*. Each of these books contains important elements also found in the other two; yet in some ways *On Germany* seems an apostasy from the liberal, rationalist position of *On Literature*, to which Madame de Staël returned in the *Considerations*. A careful reading will correct this impression, but the feeling will remain that in her book on Germany Germaine was neither completely sure of what she was doing nor completely honest.

On Germany stands midway between Voltaire's *Letters Concerning the English Nation*, published eighty-one years earlier, and Tocqueville's *On Democracy in America*, published twenty-two years later.[1] Like Voltaire's *Letters*, it is a protest against the suppression of intellectual freedom in France and a successful attempt to revitalize French thought by the injection of fresh ideas from abroad; like Tocqueville's book, it seeks to interpret a whole culture and to point out to a complacent public the dynamic direction taken by a new nation—for Germany was, in many ways, a new nation. But Tocqueville shunned wishful thinking, whereas Germaine's book is replete with ulterior motives, scarcely

[1] For reasons that will become apparent later in this chapter, the year 1813 is here taken to be the publication date of *De l'Allemagne*.

concealed propaganda, and wilful blindness. The theme of the monarchist Tocqueville's book is related to the themes developed by the republican Germaine in *De la littérature* and in the *Considérations*: 'that the gradual and progressive development of equality is both the past and the future of human history' (the words are Tocqueville's); but the theme of *De l'Allemagne* is essentially polemical and for the day, and in this it harks back to a much earlier book bearing the same title, Tacitus's *De Germania*. What imperial Rome was to Madame de Staël's favourite historian, Napoleonic France was to her. '*Solitudinem faciunt, pacem appellant*—They make a desert and call it peace', Tacitus has a British chieftain say of the Roman conquerors.[1] Just so Germaine regarded the graveyard silence of the Napoleonic order. As at Rome, so in 'silent France' despotism was breeding a nation of urbane parrots, ambitious operators, and submissive automata. Germaine could not say this in so many words, but she could, like Tacitus, hold up the Germans as a foil to vice. Whether Tacitus's hardy warriors or Germaine's night-capped dreamers, the Germans were the noble savages of Europe.

It was against this false image of Germany that Heinrich Heine protested twenty years later in his own *De l'Allemagne*. Heine clearly recognized three things to which Germaine was blind: that to Europe east of the Rhine and south of the Alps and Pyrenees Napoleon brought not despotism but liberalism, equality, and membership in the modern world; that German Romanticism was a refusal to accept the modern world; and that German idealist philosophy meant, in 'effect, the destruction of Christian morality. The day would come, Heine prophesied, when pitiless, unrestrained Kantians, armed Fichtean strong men, and savage *Naturphilosophen* or Schellingians would rise up against civilization and destroy it in an orgy of fighting for fighting's sake. Heine's prophecy, to be sure, placed too heavy a responsibility on German philosophers; but the daimonic forces of discontent with civilization were present in the non-philosophic population of Germany even in Germaine's time.

Other accusations have been levelled against Madame de Staël's *De l'Allemagne*. German critics found her treatment of philosophy superficial, her treatment of literature uncomprehending. Though justified, these strictures may be dismissed: Germaine was addressing herself to a French audience, and her aim was to present a huge mass of new and strange information in terms the French educated public could understand. The charge that she punished with silence those

---

[1] Not in *De Germania*, to be sure, but in his *Life of Agricola*.

who had not received her well is altogether unfounded. Nor is it true that she was unfamiliar with the literature she wrote about or that Schlegel supplied the knowledge she lacked and guided her pen: Germaine documented herself very carefully, despite her mediocre capacity for systematic reading, and she did not always take account of Schlegel's opinions.[1] Undoubtedly Schlegel guided her readings and gave critical advice, but this was all the part he had in *De l'Allemagne*.

One accusation, however, has not been raised, and it is more serious than the others: if one compares Germaine's letters—particularly those written during her two stays in Germany—with the book itself, one gains the distressing conviction that in many chapters she wrote things she did not believe. Her strictures of Germany are all there, to be sure, but diluted and softened, whereas the enthusiastic praise one finds in the book is largely absent from the letters. At times, no doubt, she was carried away by the enthusiasm one works up in writing; but at other times her determination to set up an idealized image of Germany in order to criticize Napoleonic France is only too apparent. Even more distressing are those manipulations of the truth whose end was the exact opposite of resistance to Napoleon. It was no accident that Germaine worked against time to publish *De l'Allemagne* in the year of Napoleon's marriage with Archduchess Marie Louise, nor was it an accident that her flattering chapters on Austria and Vienna belied her real impressions. Naïvely assuming that Marie Louise read books or was interested in Germany, Germaine clearly expected to gain the new Empress's favour.[2]

With all these reservations, *De l'Allemagne* remains an extraordinarily intelligent and admirable book; and while its general outlook is dated and was strangely irrelevant even to the Germany then in the making, it is full of incidental observations which have acquired significance in retrospect.

In Part One of *De l'Allemagne* Madame de Staël examines the geography, the mores, the institutions of Germany; this section concludes with a chapter on the festival of Interlaken, praising the antique virtues and liberties of the Swiss (with whom, however, she does not identify herself). In Part Two she addresses herself to literature and the arts; in Part Three to philosophy and ethics; in Part Four to 'religion and enthusiasm'.

---

[1] The Comtesse Jean de Pange has proved this conclusively in her *Auguste-Guillaume Schlegel et Madame de Staël*, a work to which I am greatly indebted.

[2] Napoleon, on Saint Helena, asserted that Germaine solicited a position as lady-in-waiting. Was it with this end in view that she had a copy of her *Reflections* on the trial of Marie Antoinette conveyed to the Queen's grand-niece?

To say that the first part of *De l'Allemagne* is a thinly disguised satire on France is scarcely an exaggeration. It could be shown that nearly every assertion made on Germany serves as a springboard for a critical disquisition on French society. The strictures, however, are the same she had always made; it is in the remaining three sections that Germaine departs from her previous beliefs. She joins in the Schlegelian strictures of Racine; espouses the theory that the French language is less suited for poetry than the German; attacks the English empirical and the French sensationalist philosophers, utilitarian morality, and the application of the empirical method to social and moral problems; and defends *Naturphilosophie*, mysticism, and even Catholicism, at least German Catholicism. The influence of Schlegel is very definitely felt here; six years of daily conversations and discussions could not have been wasted on the most talented brain picker of the age. At the time of the composition of the book, this influence was at its peak: her disappointments, her attempt to come closer to the Pietism of Madame de Krüdener and the Chevalier de Langalerie, even the strange Catholicism of Zacharias Werner—everything pushed her in the direction of a vague, self-indulgent emotional religion which she identified with German idealism, mysticism, and Romanticism.

Still, Germaine never espoused Catholicism; her chapter on mysticism shows that she did not even quite grasp the term, and her last deed in life was to reaffirm, in her *Considérations*, her faith in Enlightenment, freedom, and progress. Was *De l'Allemagne* a mere temporary aberration, half abdication of her rationality, half polemics against Napoleonic France? It was nothing of the sort. Rather, it was an experiment: Germaine, tempted to bathe in the Romantic Ocean, dipped her toes into it, proclaimed its delight, and returned to dry land as soon as she decently could. Her religion, remarked Mathieu, was 'merely another kind of poetry'.

Even in *De l'Allemagne*, there were certain aspects of Germany she decidedly rejected. She deplored the lack of good taste, of good conversation, of critical standards—all results, she thought, of the absence of true social cohesion. She pointed out the danger to liberty inherent in exclusive preoccupation with abstractions: 'The spirit of the Germans seems to have no communication with their character: the one cannot tolerate any limits; the other submits to every yoke.' She was astonished by the contrast between the 'warlike aspect of all Germany, where one sees soldiers everywhere, and the domesticated way of life'. The combination of eiderdown quilts, stocking caps, hermetically sealed windows, and the alleged bellicose nature of the Germans is striking indeed; Germaine diagnosed correctly that, unless exalted by a passing fever, the Germans were peaceful to a fault. Their respect for rank, their indifference to politics, their submissiveness to foreign occupation, the disunity of their many petty states, and the absence of liberty in all practical matters led her to deplore the absence of a German national spirit. Because of this, she was generally regarded by German nationalists in the nineteenth century as a prophetic precursor. There can be no doubt that the national spirit of Germany's 'War of Liberation' was the spirit Germaine hoped to see; but this spirit was composed of two very distinct elements—liberal patriotism and fanatic nationalism. When her mentor Schlegel joined the forces of the latter element, Germaine was horrified.

She criticized the belief, axiomatic with German nationalists, that the national regeneration of Germany began with Frederick the Great. To her the Prussian solution, a state 'founded on military strength and civil justice', was a hybrid of two irreconcilables. 'Frederick wanted his soldiers to be military machines, blindly obedient, and his subjects to be enlightened citizens capable of patriotism. . . . He wanted the military class to be dominant . . . and yet he would have liked the civilian class to remain independent side by side with force.' Such a thing was not possible. What Madame de Staël wanted Germany to be was a modern nation, like England or America. What she failed to recognize was that German Romantic nationalism was a direct refusal to be part of the times. 'The subject I am working on,' Schlegel once wrote to her, 'transports me completely into times of old, while I loathe the times we live in.'

If Germaine shared the Romantic enthusiasm for the Middle Ages, her reasons were completely different from those of the Romantics. She preferred Christianity and chivalry, as a source of literary inspiration, to Greek mythology and ancient history because they were more *modern*. What the heroes of Homer were to the Greeks, the heroes of the Crusades were to us: so, at least, she thought. While Schlegel escaped into the past, Germaine merely felt inspired by it and originated the liberal belief that the thread running through all medieval history was the struggle for freedom. There was a fundamental misunderstanding between Madame de Staël and the Romanticism of Schlegel, and a careful perusal of *De l'Allemagne* will show that in nearly every chapter she qualified her espousal of the 'new philosophy' with a 'but'. The 'whirlwind in petticoats', as Heine called her, was in fact characterized, as an intellect, by one predominant quality—moderation.

Germaine's flirtation with *Naturphilosophie* and mysticism becomes quite understandable if one reads her chapter 'On the Influence of Enthusiasm', which concludes the book. It is the key to her thought. What the Germans possessed, and the French had lost, was the faculty of enthusiasm. By enthusiasm, she understood the vivifying force of generous emotions—never fanaticism. The incredible creativeness of Germany in the age of Goethe would have been impossible without enthusiasm, as would have been its noblest synthesis—Schiller's 'Ode to Joy' in Beethoven's Ninth Symphony. It was here that the humane ideals of the Enlightenment, faith in the future, and Romantic enthusiasm—what else was that joy that Schiller sang?—found their unique expression; and this was the Romanticism that Germaine, despite her deafness to poetry and music, understood and defended.

De l'Allemagne, because of its absurd emphasis on national characteristics, was often cited in support of racial doctrines. Yet apart from warning specifically against a 'moral system based on national interest', Madame de Staël also emphasized the need for international cross-fertilization. This, in fact, was the repeatedly stated aim of the book. Germany had learned from France, now France could learn from Germany. 'I do not suppose,' she wrote in her introduction, 'that we have reached the point where we want to erect a Great Wall of China around intellectual France.'

Early in 1810 Napoleon established an office of censorship for books and placed it under Joseph Marie Portalis, who held the title Directeur de la Librairie. The procedure was the following: the first proofs were submitted by the publisher to the censor; the censor then either approved the book, or condemned it, or demanded certain changes. If a work consisted of several volumes, proofs might be submitted volume by volume, but until the last volume was approved, the censor's approval of the earlier volumes was merely conditional. The system had decidedly unpalatable features, but it was applied with moderation, and it gave authors and publishers a chance to revise their publications before they went to press and thus to prevent seizure after publication —all authors and publishers, that is, except Madame de Staël and Gabriel-Henri Nicolle.

On May 7 Nicolle submitted proofs of Volume I to the Directeut de la Librairie. Portalis was a friend of Madame de Staël. The volume was approved, subject to a number of minor deletions which Germaine accepted. On June 3 Fouché was dismissed and replaced by Savary; but

O

since the censorship of books, unlike that of the periodical press, was not under the police ministry, the change, though ominous, did not seem to affect Germaine's publication plans. On August 8 Nicolle sent Volume II to the censor, who approved it without change. It was the third volume Germaine was worried about, not without reason. Nicolle pressed her to send the remaining copy and to correct the galleys with the utmost speed, before the censor changed his mind. *Petite poste* and dances to tambourines and guitars notwithstanding, Germaine dashed off the last chapters on mysticism and enthusiasm like an inspired improvisation. But even before she corrected the last proofs, on September 23, trouble had started.

Nicolle, in his eagerness to win influential friends in the press, had given a set of proofs of Volume I to Laborie, one of the owners of the *Journal de l'Empire*. Laborie had read long passages aloud all over the Faubourg Saint-Germain, and the rumour that a new, extraordinary, and rather daring work of Madame de Staël was printing soon came to the Emperor's attention. Taking alarm, Germaine began to alert her friends to bring their influence to bear on the censors. Uginet, shuttling back and forth between Paris and Blois, carrying proofs, acted as her envoy and liaison officer, but the chief mission was entrusted to Madame Récamier. On September 25 Juliette left for Paris, carrying with her one set of proofs of Volume III, one complete set of bound proofs of all three volumes, and a letter from Germaine to Napoleon. The proofs of Volume III she was to convey to the poet and academician Esménard, one of the censors, who was also a department head in the police ministry; the versatile Esménard was well placed to smooth out all difficulties, and he was moreover sensitive to Juliette's attractions. The complete set and the letter she was to take to Queen Hortense of Holland, daughter of the ex-Empress Josephine and deserted wife of the ex-King Louis Bonaparte: Hortense was to take them to her step-father and brother-in-law, Napoleon. In her letter Germaine begged the Emperor to read her book and to grant her an audience for only half an hour.

By then the imprudent Nicolle had already printed 5,000 copies[1] of each of the two volumes, at the expense of 30,000 francs, not counting the 13,000 francs he had paid Germaine for the manuscript.

While Juliette was rolling towards Paris, Germaine left Fossé in the company of Mathieu, who had joined her in mid-September, to visit

---

[1] According to the Comtesse de Pange; Madame de Staël, in *Dix Années d'exil*, says 10,000.

an estate he owned in the vicinity. Returning in the evening of September 26, the party lost their way. They were still on the road at midnight when a young horseman who chanced by invited them to spend the night at his parents' château of Conan. On entering the castle, Germaine to her astonishment found herself transplanted into 'the luxury of Asia', mixed with the 'elegance of France': the owners, after spending many years in East India, had brought back a vast collection of Indian art. Fascinated, Germaine, despite the late hour, began to examine the strange objects. She did not notice a servant speaking to Mathieu, and Mathieu following him out of the room.

At the main entrance Mathieu found Auguste waiting for him. Wasting no words, Auguste explained that in the afternoon the Prefect Corbigny had presented himself at Fossé with an order from Savary, enjoining Germaine to leave within forty-eight hours for one of the Atlantic ports, there to await passage to the United States; furthermore, Germaine was ordered to surrender her manuscript and all proofs of *De l'Allemagne*. Auguste had left Fossé immediately to intercept his mother on the road. He too had lost his way in the monotonous plain of Vendôme; he had stopped at Conan to ask for directions, and upon mentioning his name had learned that he had stumbled on his mother. Begging Mathieu not to alert his mother before the morning, he handed him a note for her and sped back to Fossé at a gallop.

On the morning of September 27 Mathieu handed Germaine her son's note. It merely informed her of 'new complications' and advised her to return without delay. Only with difficulty was Germaine persuaded to tear herself from the Hindu art. After they had gone some distance Mathieu broke the news. Germaine made no scene. She only wept, then said: 'I shall have to conquer myself once more, despite everything.' And indeed, no one could have displayed more coolness than did Germaine for the next twenty-four hours.

Germaine's carriage was approaching Fossé when Fanny Randall intercepted it on the road. She gave further particulars on Corbigny's visit; no doubt she also informed her that Auguste had placed the manuscript in a safe place—and none too soon, for the house was surrounded by police.

Monsieur de Corbigny, obviously distressed, presented himself once again, repeated the orders, and asked for the manuscript. Germaine proceeded to lie with admirable aplomb: the manuscript was in Paris; she would write immediately to have it sent back; she would hand it over, along with her notes and the proofs, as soon as she had got everything together. As for the order to leave, immediate compliance was out of the question, and she would ask for a week's delay.

Monsieur de Corbigny was a gentleman. He did not order a search; he did not order Germaine to be taken away by force; and he did not believe a word she said. In his report he merely relayed her assertions. On September 29 Germaine handed him a set of proofs, which she said was the only one, and on October 3 she gave him a wretched copy of the manuscript. Still a gentleman, Corbigny accepted them as the genuine articles. He was dismissed soon afterwards, went into a depression, and died.

When Corbigny served her with Savary's injunction on September 27, neither he nor she had any idea of what had precipitated this sudden blow. Having staved him off, she held a council of war with her sons, Mathieu, Schlegel, and Miss Randall. They came to the conclusion that nothing was lost; the publication of the book was merely delayed, probably on the Emperor's intervention. Napoleon had not replied to Germaine's first letter; she would write him another, as well as a letter to Savary; Auguste would leave for Paris with Albert in order to conduct the campaign on the spot. Early on September 28 Germaine wrote the two letters and the two brothers went off to war.

In her letter to Savary Germaine declared herself ready to make any changes in her book that were within reason, informed him that she was appealing to the Emperor, and asked for permission to delay her departure. Her letter to Napoleon, conceived in the same self-righteous tone as her earlier communications, pointed out that she could have had the book published in Germany and that submitting it to French censorship proved the loyalty of her intentions. She begged the Emperor to judge for himself whether it contained a single word offensive to him and repeated her request for an audience.

Exactly what had happened is not quite clear. On September 24 Savary sent the order which Germaine received from Corbigny three days later; at the same time he sent orders to Tours, where on the following day the police entered the printing plant of Monsieur Mame to place all the plates and sheets of *De l'Allemagne* under seal. Mame immediately sent a protest to Portalis. Portalis, to whom all this was news, protested to the Minister of the Interior, pointing out that under the regulations the police had no right to seize the books until the board of censors had completed its report. As it happened, the censors' report on Volume III was made only on September 29, four days after Savary had issued his orders, and it authorized publication if certain passages (about eleven pages in all) were removed. Portalis's complaint was passed on to Savary, who sent him Esménard with an explanation: there was a 'special circumstance' which had forced the minister of police to take exceptional measures. The exceptional circumstance was a direct order from the Emperor himself. It may be surmised that Napoleon, informed that the censors were about to approve Madame de Staël's book, had decided to delay its publication so that a more rigorous examination could be made. A couple of days after Savary issued his orders, Queen Hortense gave Napoleon the bound proofs and Germaine's letter. The Emperor read the proofs, or at least a considerable part of them. On September 28 from Fontainebleau, where he was then residing, he wrote to Savary: 'I have returned Madame de Staël's book to you. Is she entitled to call herself a baroness? . . Have the passage concerning the Duke of Brunswick suppressed, as well as three quarters of the passages in which she exalts England. That unfortunate exaltation has done us enough harm already.'

Everything in these lines indicates that Napoleon was not then contemplating the complete suppression of the book. But Germaine would not leave well enough alone. At the very moment when Napoleon wrote these lines to Savary, Auguste and Albert were speeding to Paris to ask for justice.

They reached Paris at night. At seven in the morning on September 29 Auguste went to see Juliette Récamier; they spent the entire day rounding up the pro-Staëlian forces. Esménard, who acted as Savary's mouthpiece, reassured them: Madame de Staël would be granted the delay she asked for, and her book would be published once the desired changes were made. 'I told him,' Auguste reported to his mother, 'that you will accept all deletions so long as they do not disfigure your work, but that you would rather burn it than consent to adding a single line.'

This accomplished, Auguste went on to Fontainebleau. Early in the morning of September 30 he called on Regnault de Saint-Jean d'Angély, whom he asked to transmit Germaine's letters to the Emperor and to Savary. Regnault, after examining the letter to the Emperor, refused to deliver it; Germaine would have to rewrite it in humbler style; he would speak to Savary, however, to sound him out. Auguste then saw the Queen of Holland, who promised her support. This done, he dispatched Albert to Blois, with a long letter, on October 1.

On October 2 Albert, after riding all night, reached Fossé. Germaine rewrote her letter, leaving out the recriminations to which Regnault had objected; but her nature was stronger than her intentions. 'I have made all the changes indicated by Monsieur Portalis in the first two volumes, and I intended to accept his recommendations for the third one as well. What more could I do to conform with the procedure outlined in Your Majesty's own decree?' The argument was irrefutable, but irrefutable logic is misplaced in arguments with emperors. To this letter Germaine added one to Queen Hortense; then she sent Albert back to Paris, where he arrived on October 3, having covered two hundred miles in less than two days.

Auguste lost no time in returning to Fontainebleau with his new letters. He might have saved himself the trip: Germaine's friends had served her too well already. As so many times before, their constant solicitations had overtaxed the Emperor's endurance. After listening to Hortense's pleas, he asked to see the copy of the book again. In his hasty way he read a few pages here and there, became more and more irritated, and finally threw down the whole set—according to one account, into the fireplace. He then gave his final orders to Savary.

Paris, October 3, 1810

Madam:

I have received the letter with which you have honoured me. Your son must have informed you that I see no objection to your delaying your departure by a week or so. I trust this will be enough for you to make all your arrangements, because this is all I can grant.

You must not suppose that the order I sent you was motivated by your failure to mention the Emperor in your last book. You would be very much mistaken: there could not have been in it a worthy place for him. Your exile is the natural consequence of the course you have followed for several years. It seemed to me that the air of this country did not agree with you—and we have not yet reached the point where we have to model ourselves on the nations you admire.

Your last work is un-French. I am the one who stopped the printing. I regret the losses your publisher will take, but I cannot allow its publication.

You are aware, Madam, that we allowed you to leave Coppet only because you expressed the desire to go to America. If my predecessor [Fouché] allowed you to reside in the département of Loir-et-Cher, this was no reason for you to regard that act of tolerance as a revocation of the measures taken with regard to you. You now force me to see to their strict execution, and you have only yourself to blame.

I am instructing Monsieur Corbigny to carry out the order I have given him as soon as the delay I have granted you expires.

I regret, Madam, that you have obliged me to begin my correspondence with you by an act of severity; I should have preferred to offer you only the assurances of my high esteem.

I have the honour, Madam, of being your most humble and obedient servant,

[signed] THE DUKE OF ROVIGO

P.S. I have good reasons, Madam, to indicate the following ports of embarkation to you: Lorient, La Rochelle, Bordeaux, and Rochefort are the only ports where you are authorized to board ship. I request you to let me know which one you choose.

When Madame de Staël had *De l'Allemagne* published by Murray in London in 1813, she flaunted this letter in the preface.

What Savary did not say, and what Germaine learned only two weeks later, is what happened to the books. On October 11, a detachment of gendarmes surrounded Mame's printing plant, broke up the type from which the book had been printed, seized all the copies, counted them, and carted them away. The entire edition was then crushed into pulp and sold for 500 francs.

Germaine had spent the week from September 28 to October 5 in an agony of uncertainty. She did not even know if she should go to New York or Coppet. On October 5, writing to Juliette, she announced that she was leaving for Saumur, to say an 'agonizing farewell' to Prosper; from there she would go on either to America or to Switzerland. It is likely that she had no serious intention of going to America but merely kept up the fiction in order to motivate her westward progress, whose goal was not New York but Prosper. Indeed on the following day, writing to Juliette from Blois, she had given up America: 'I was unable to go to Saumur. The Prefect [Corbigny] told me brutally, "If you meet Prosper, he will be sacked immediately." There is such a cloud of pain surrounding me that I no longer know what I am writing.'

Instead of Prosper, she asked Benjamin to meet her at Briare on her way back to Geneva. Benjamin came, and with him Charlotte, who was no longer taking any chances. 'My two days at Briare were very strange,' Germaine reported to Juliette. 'I had proof that Benjamin still loves me, that he is unhappy with his lady, and she with him. . . . In matters of the heart, nothing is true except the improbable.'

Germaine was indulging in another delusion. Undoubtedly Benjamin was tired of his wife, but the explanation of what Germaine mistook for a return of love had nothing to do with love. His father was about to sue him for a settlement of accounts; his aunt de Nassau, on whose inheritance he counted, was incensed by his marriage with a double divorcée; in the impending showdown, it was essential to have Germaine on his side. Germaine did not fall in with his complicated schemes. Two days after her departure, in a panic attempt to restore his finances, he gambled away 20,000 francs in a single night—and this was a mere beginning.[1]

Germaine, comparing herself to a lame pigeon, returned to her coop, limping but unbowed. She heard the news of the destruction of her book almost without emotion and scarcely uttered a complaint. She repaid her advance to Nicolle. She seemed to have lost all interest in literature, politics, and even love. After a few weeks at Coppet she took an apartment in Geneva, the only place in France she was allowed to visit, and on November 13 her childhood friend Catherine Rilliet could report to Henri Meister, 'All I can say is that she is as lively and brilliant as ever—which proves the advantage of organizing one's heart in a system of multiple hiding places.'

The Genevese were surprised to see Germaine so gay in her misfortune who had been so unhappy before; but far more spectacular surprises were in store for them.

---

[1] In a note found by Sainte-Beuve among Benjamin's papers, he accused Germaine of having stopped at Brévans on her way to Geneva in order to talk General Constant into suing him. There is no evidence to back up this accusation.

Part Four

THE VANITY OF HUMAN WISHES

With these celestial Wisdom calms the mind,
And makes the happiness she does not find.
SAMUEL JOHNSON, *The Vanity of Human Wishes*

o*

18

CALIBAN

ON her way from Blois to Coppet Germaine had passed through Dijon, which was filled with Spanish prisoners of war in rags; through Auxonne, where the English prisoners were kept under guard; through Besançon, where she saw more Spanish prisoners; and crossed the Jura into Switzerland within sight of the dread fortress of Joux, where Toussaint L'Ouverture 'had died of cold'. All Europe seemed a prison camp. 'Nothing,' Germaine wrote in her memoirs,

> nothing can convey to the few free nations that remain on this earth the complete absence of security which was the normal condition of all human creatures under Napoleon's Empire. Other despotic governments have customs, laws, and a religion which the ruler never violates, no matter how absolute his power. But since in France, and in French-held Europe, everything was new, past traditions gave no protection, and one could fear the worst or hope for the best, depending on whether or not one served the interests of the man who dared make himself, and himself alone, the purpose of the entire human race.

Compared to what the world has known since, Napoleon's régime seems mild and humane; but to one who remained faithful to the hopes of the eighteenth century, the world of 1810 was a nightmare of brute force. War was permanent: it had gone on for eighteen years. From Spain to Poland, from Amsterdam to Corfu, French soldiers were garrisoned, levying tribute and imposing the will of one man. With the Continental System and the blockade war had become total, with no end in sight, engulfing all human energy: the arts had to glorify the régime; philosophy and education must function as tools of conformity; science was enlisted to create synthetic substitutes. Resistance was punished by demotion, exile, imprisonment, and, in the conquered countries, the firing squad. The year 1810 marked the beginning of a new phase in systematic oppression. Napoleon created state prisons where inmates were held without trial, decreed drastic new censorship laws, and deprived the Church of its last vestige of independence. The Pope himself was arrested and hustled off to Savona. If his plans had succeeded, said Napoleon in 1816, he 'would have become the master of the religious as well as of the political world'.

What could any individual do against such a man? Nothing could defeat him except his own folly. If one draws up the balance sheet of Germaine's resistance to Napoleon between 1800 and 1810, the credit side seems unimpressive: a great deal of subversive talk, oblique attacks in four or five books, and a few ineffectual drawing-room conspiracies. On the debit side, there are repeated attempts to come to terms with the tyrant, even offers to wield her pen in his support, provided he let her stay in Paris and returned Necker's two millions. Only a small fraction of her energies was spent in the political struggle, while super-human efforts were expended on imposing her own tyranny on Benjamin, O'Donnell, and Prosper.

Yet the little she did was more than most did. There are times when even drawing-room conversations can become acts of heroism and keep alive the spark of resistance. Germaine did not limit herself to subversive conversation: her books, read in the context of her time, were barely disguised manifestoes. However, until about 1808, Napoleon regarded her as harmless, provided she was kept away from the centre of his power. So long as he was master at home, Europe was at his mercy. But then he was forced to change his mind: in Germany secret patriotic societies were forming; Austria was preparing for war even during Germaine's stay at Vienna; Spain was altogether intractable; England showed no signs of weakening under the Continental System. Although Napoleon never grasped the significance and power of rising nationalism, he was aware of the presence of explosive forces in the conquered nations, and these forces Germaine was fanning by everything she said and wrote, by her very example. Reading *De l'Allemagne* in 1814, when Germany had risen in arms, Goethe remarked, 'The French police, intelligent enough to understand that such a work must bolster German self-confidence, wisely had it destroyed. . . . At the present moment, the book produces an astonishing effect. If it had been published earlier, one might have imputed the great events that just took place to its influence.'

Napoleon's downfall can hardly be imputed to the actions or ideas of individuals. Yet in keeping up the spirit of resistance among the social and intellectual *élite* of Europe, Madame de Staël did the most anyone can do against a tyrant while his star is high. Her example did not present all the dignity and consistency one might wish, but it was precisely from her rebellious pride and passions that she drew the power to resist at all: with all her contradictions, she was of one piece. To call the entire universe to witness the monstrous behaviour of Benjamin was extravagant and reckless. It diminished her stature as a fighter against tyranny. But without such extravagant recklessness she would not have fought tyranny and called upon the entire universe to witness the monstrousness of Napoleon Bonaparte.

Fouché's dismissal was the first step in the Emperor's new tough course. The man who replaced the defrocked monk was as brutal and loyal as his predecessor had been subtle and treacherous. 'If I ordered Savary to do away with his wife and children,' said Napoleon, 'I am sure he would not hesitate.' Concerning his appointment as police minister, Savary recalled in his memoirs, with evident satisfaction, that 'the news of an outbreak of the plague could not have caused greater terror'. When, on October 17, 1810, the Emperor notified him, 'I do not want to hear any more about that miserable woman or her book', Savary took the injunction quite literally. Every possible measure had to be taken to prevent the book from being published outside France, and its author had to be systematically isolated.

When the first edition of *De l'Allemagne* was destroyed, at least one set of proofs and several copies were found to be missing; the Prefect Corbigny paid dearly for allowing them to escape. No sooner was Germaine back in Coppet than Barante *père*, the Prefect of Geneva, was ordered to recover the missing proofs. Germaine wrote to him that the proofs were no longer in Switzerland,[1] that she was neither willing nor able to return them, but that she promised not to have a new edition published on the Continent. Barante relayed her reply to Paris; on December 2 he was notified of his dismissal and ordered to withdraw to his estate in Auvergne. Meanwhile Nicolle, Germaine's publisher, who had hoped to restore his credit by the success of *De l'Allemagne*, had filed his bankruptcy, showing a deficit of 900,000 francs. In view of the size of the sum, Germaine can hardly be held responsible for this disaster, which caused a panic in the French book trade, but Nicolle's fate served as a salutary warning to any European publisher minded to publish Germaine's book.

The dismissal of two prefects, one of whom died of chagrin, was calculated not only to encourage the others but also to serve notice to all

[1] Actually, Schlegel had stored them away in Berne.

concerned that they had to choose between the Emperor and Madame de Staël. Almost everybody opted for the Emperor. Baron Balk, who had promised to spend the winter with Germaine, wrote long letters pleading poor health; all but a few houses in Geneva closed their doors to her; her misfortune, as she put it, was shunned like a contagious disease. Of her intimates only Schlegel, Sismondi, Bonstetten, and Miss Randall were left—an odd and unsatisfactory crew.

The new Prefect, Baron Capelle, was handpicked for his task by Savary. Young and handsome like an operetta tenor—his colleagues nicknamed him Floridor—he had been dismissed as Prefect of Leghorn because he had found too much favour with Napoleon's sister Elisa, Grand Duchess of Tuscany; Savary made him understand that if he displayed sufficient zeal in his new post, he might recover the Emperor's good will. Capelle's instructions allowed him wide powers, but before applying them he gave Germaine one last opportunity to do penance. The Empress Marie Louise had just given birth to Napoleon's heir, the King of Rome: if Germaine would signify her submissiveness by celebrating the event in a poem or eulogy, Capelle told her, the persecutions would cease. Germaine refused, but Capelle persisted. What should he report to the minister, he asked—that she refused to make wishes for the King of Rome? 'Tell him, if you want to, that I wish him a good wet nurse,' said Germaine. The sublime retort cost her dearly.

In May 1811, after ordering Germaine back from an unauthorized excursion to Aix-les-Bains, Capelle served notice that she was not allowed to set foot anywhere on French territory except Geneva; that she was advised not to travel farther than two leagues from Coppet in any direction; and that, in order to preserve her from Schlegel's unhealthy influence, he ordered Schlegel to leave Coppet. Germaine, indignant, drove to Geneva and called on Capelle. Coppet, she pointed out to him, was in Switzerland. What jurisdiction had he in a foreign country? Capelle replied by asking whether she would prefer the orders to be transmitted to the Swiss authorities by the French ambassador; she might delay them by ten days in that manner.

Schlegel left, first for Berne, then for Vienna, where his brother Friedrich was then living, freshly converted to Catholicism. His object was to remove the manuscript (or perhaps the copy) of *De l'Allemagne* still farther away from Savary's reach, and to explore the possibility of finding a refuge in Austria: for Germaine had decided to take to flight. After a few days in Vienna Schlegel returned to Berne; this was to be his new home, except for intermittent stays at Coppet.

Despite her new restrictions, Germaine still hoped to reunite her faithful. In August Mathieu de Montmorency announced his impending visit. Defying Capelle's orders, she met him at Orbe, far beyond the prescribed limit, and thence set off with him for a mysterious journey to a Trappist convent near Fribourg, where Schlegel joined them. (Mathieu was, in all probability, acting as secret courier for the French clergy, possibly even for the captive Pope.) To compound imprudences Germaine made her way back to Coppet, with Mathieu, by way of the Valais, then annexed to France. A severe reprimand awaited her on her return, followed, a few days later, by a letter to Mathieu from Savary: Mathieu was exiled from Paris and a radius of forty leagues.[1]

Germaine 'cried in anguish'; she was all the more horrified because at that very moment Juliette Récamier, yielding to her indefatigable entreaties, was on her way to Coppet. Esménard had warned Juliette against the consequences of the trip. Germaine and Mathieu sent Auguste to meet her at the border, with letters advising her to meet them secretly and away from Coppet. Juliette, however, persisted; on August 30 the two women fell weeping into each other's arms. They had not been together for twenty-four hours when Juliette's nephew, a French official then stationed at Geneva, horrified at his aunt's boldness, abducted her. Capelle reported to Paris: 'Coppet is in mourning. So much the better: it will be a good lesson.' A week after Juliette's departure worse news hit Coppet: Juliette had been ordered to choose a place at least forty leagues distant from Paris and to stay there until the Emperor saw fit to revoke her arrest. Juliette chose Châlons-sur-Marne; in 1812 she was allowed to go to her native Lyons.

The pattern of persecution was clear now: Germaine was to be quarantined. Police spies were stationed in the village of Coppet. By bribing some of the servants, Capelle secured exact reports on all the happenings in the château itself, which he conveyed to Paris, where Napoleon read them with great amusement—for Capelle was a witty enough writer. The police of Geneva began a series of inane investigations: was there a link between Germaine and the Free Masons? What were those lectures on medieval Romance literature that Monsieur de

[1] Deeply implicated in a plot to free the captive Spanish princes, Mathieu would have been exiled in any case; but Savary seized on his visit to Germaine as a pretext in order to frighten, as it were, two birds with one stone. Mathieu spent his exile clandestinely spreading Pius VII's bull of excommunication against Napoleon through the provinces, without the least interference from the police.

Sismondi was giving at the Academy of Geneva? Were they subversive? The investigations proved unrewarding, but it became clear to Capelle that Germaine was meditating flight to England—by way of either Russia or America. Her correspondence, although written in a naïve code and addressed to Madame Uginet rather than herself, was read by her gaolers. Germaine's definition of exile as 'a tomb in which you can get letters' was no longer an exaggeration, and before her eyes there loomed, ever more menacing, the image of a fortress, a prison cell, and death. From September 1811 to May 1812 her letters, and particularly those to Juliette, were one long, lugubrious lament. And yet it was precisely then, in her forty-fifth year, that what she had desired all her life had come to her.

In 1788, the year Germaine became the mistress of Narbonne, there was born in Geneva Albert-Jean-Michel Rocca, known to all as John Rocca, who in 1811 became the lover of Germaine. John's mother died a few days after his birth. His father, the Councillor Jean-François Rocca, issued from a Genevese patrician family of Piedmontese origin, was a stern and taciturn Calvinist. 'We were afraid of talking to each other,' John wrote of his boyhood, 'and we lived side by side in a continuous silence which neither of us dared break.' This was not unlike Benjamin's relationship with *his* father; but in every other respect, John Rocca was as different from Benjamin as one could be. Physical nature was what John revelled in. A passionate sportsman, hunter, mountain climber, swimmer, the growing youth developed into a splendid animal, but an animal endowed with a poetic sensibility, a romantic yearning for danger, exertion, and adventure. Napoleon's victories stirred in him dreams of military glory for which his relatives showed no sympathy whatsoever. When he was seventeen, he no longer could resist: he ran away from home and enlisted.

After receiving his training, John joined the 2nd Regiment of Hussars in Germany. He probably took part in the battle of Jena. There was, the saying went, a marshal's baton in every French soldier's pack; John did not become a marshal, but he was promoted to first sergeant and, in 1807, to second lieutenant. In 1808, after a year's occupation duty in Germany, his regiment was transferred first to Spain, then to Holland, where the English had made a landing; early in 1810 it once more marched to Spain.

Spain cooled his enthusiasm for war. The atrocities committed by the French, the relentless guerrilla warfare of the Spaniards, the constant presence of danger, the unconcealed hatred of the civilian population, the whole nightmare that Goya was to record as an eternal indictment of war, all this made Lieutenant Rocca wonder if perhaps his notions of honour and glory had not been mistaken. On May 1, 1810, a column he was leading was ambushed by guerrilla fighters; Rocca received several bullet wounds. One bullet penetrated into his body, another fractured his left thigh. His beloved Andalusian horse, Sultan, also was shot, but both managed to escape. Sultan's wound healed completely, but Rocca had to walk with a crutch for the rest of his life.

After a long convalescence he was put on indefinite sick leave and, still with Sultan, returned to his family, whom he had not seen in five years. The prodigal was received more charitably than he expected; by 1810 even the Genevese patriciate had swung to the point of view that service in Napoleon's army was not a disgrace.

He was about to complete his twenty-third year. What little education he had received he had forgotten, and his manners were not the best. He was, however, very handsome. A portrait shows him dressed in the dashing uniform of a hussar lieutenant, with splendid moustache and side-whiskers, standing beside Sultan, and looking as fiery, proud, and vacuous as his horse.

It was in the early winter of 1810–11, at the house of his aunt, Madame Argant-Picot, that he first met Germaine, of whom he had no doubt heard a great deal. Majestically draped in a huge shawl and crowned by bird-of-paradise feathers, Germaine graciously addressed to him, as he recalled, 'a few words of pity'; asked him if he cared to attend the concerts at her home; and paid no further attention to him. Rocca spent the rest of the evening gazing at her, transfixed. It was passion on first sight.

No amount of psychology can explain why John Rocca, who could have chosen from any number of pretty heiresses, fell in love with a woman twice his age, ravaged by passion, opium, and grief, and even, at that time, forbidding of aspect and manner. She did nothing to encourage him—this much is certain.

Was it the mother in Germaine that attracted the boy who had never known one? Was it a yearning to be the Oswald of Corinne? After a motherless childhood and five years among the hussars, with no one to love except his horse, the prospect may well have turned his head. Perhaps there entered into his feelings a dash of the Quixotic: Madame de Staël was unhappy and persecuted, and he would be her knight and protector. Since he was not the most articulate of men, it is impossible to tell just what he felt; whatever it was, it took complete possession of him.

Here now was Phaedra in reverse—Hippolytus, the youthful sportsman, pursuing the middle-aged queen. He attended the concerts at Germaine's house; he attended the theatricals in which she appeared; wherever she was, he was. Though he was too timid to declare his love to her, Germaine could not help knowing of it, for he declared it to everyone else. 'I shall love her so much,' he boasted, 'that she will end up by marrying me.' His conversation was fatuous, his intellectual resources limited—but love does not depend on these to manifest itself. There was one thing John Rocca could do superbly: ride his horse. This he did daily, under Germaine's windows on the Grand' Rue, and on the steep steps leading up to it from the rue de la Corraterie. It was winter; the steps were covered with thin ice; if the poor young man continued to demonstrate his love in this acrobatic manner, he was bound to break his neck. What woman, at forty-five, after losing one lover after another, with a life of exile in prospect and the hope of happiness still burning in her veins—what woman would have allowed the young man to break his neck unrequited?

But Germaine was a long time in making up her mind—far longer than usual, and in the meantime John Rocca became a public figure of fun. Germaine, it was pointed out to him, was old enough to be his mother. Imperturbable, John replied that he was glad to have this additional reason for loving her.

While John Rocca performed his strange antics, Germaine passed through a chaotic mixture of feelings and expectations. The suppression of her book had not affected her as severely as might have been expected. There was, after all, more glory in its destruction than there might have been in its publication. When she arrived in Geneva, she still had reasons to believe in Prosper's attachment, and she counted on Benjamin's imminent escape from domestic bliss. Only gradually was the horror of her real situation brought home to her. The dismissal of Barante *père* filled her with remorse. She called on him, in tears, moving him to such a point that he consoled her for the misfortune she had brought on him. Then came Baron Balk's defection and a growing sense of isolation. Still, she persisted in the pose of gaiety and calm she had affected from her arrival, perhaps because she begrudged the Genevese the pleasure of seeing her defeated. To bear her boredom and unhappiness she resorted to two remedies which, had they been applied sincerely, would have been mutually exclusive: one was frivolous diversion, the other religious consolation. She read the *Imitation of Christ*, Fénelon, and Madame Guyon much as one might try the effectiveness of a new patent medicine: she thought she was beginning to feel the beneficial effects of religion, she reported to Juliette Récamier. Yet a more turbulent Quietist there never was. In between prayers and devout readings she enlivened Geneva society with as gay a wit as ever she had displayed, wrote and staged several little comedies, or rather skits—*Captain Kernadec*, *The Mannekin*, *La Signora Fantastici*. The Genevese could not make head or tail of her sudden switches of mood. She appeared to have accepted her defeat and to be the happier for it.

Toward the end of January Germaine reported to Juliette on Rocca in the following terms:

> The new sentimental interest which allegedly is occupying my time is a young man of twenty-three, beautiful as the day, who walks on crutches because of five bullets he received, or rather deliberately sought, in the wars. I thought his life was in danger and I nursed him. He fell in love with me passionately. But his mind is uncultured, and there is no future in this relationship. . . . You know that the love one inspires is a temporary consolation and distraction, but none of my projects is in the least affected by this affair, which is a mere jig in my life. . . . I needed a diversion to bear what I carry in the bottom of my heart.

If Germaine wrote these lines in sincerity—which may be doubted— Rocca's prospects were none too hopeful. But the same letter contains passages which go a long way towards explaining why the young man's assiduities soon were crowned with success. Barante *père*, Germaine reported, was employing every possible ruse to break up his son's correspondence with her; and Benjamin, who had gone to Lausanne with his wife in order to settle matters with his father, was 'playing at husband in a rather affected way'. 'He has changed a great deal since Briare,' Germaine added. In truth he had not changed at all, but his entire fortune depended on his wife's being accepted by his family.

In her next letter to Juliette Germaine reported the news that God was supporting her with His hand. 'I no longer suffer from those crises of despair that annihilated my whole being.' Inasmuch as the mystic doctrine she had absorbed from Langalerie and Madame de Krüdener prescribed serene surrender to the inevitable and took a lenient view of carnal sin, it is not inconceivable that Germaine's sudden serenity coincided with the fulfilment of Rocca's desires. As the winter drew to a close, no one in Geneva could entertain any further doubts about their relationship. Certainly Germaine made no secret of it. The

Marquise d'Axat records a dinner party at the house of Madame Argant-Picot to which both Germaine and Rocca had been invited. Rocca was late. Someone mentioned seeing him at his favourite pastime —making Sultan go down a dangerous ramp at a canter. Hearing this, Germaine fainted, came to, and ordered a general search for Rocca. At last he appeared, kissed her hand, and apologized for his lateness. After another scene of tearful reproaches Germaine forgave him. Relieved, the company sat down at table, when the hostess asked him to carve the joint. Rocca seized the carving knife. 'Madame de Staël,' relates the Marquise, 'gave forth a piercing scream, cried to us to disarm him, that he would kill himself, and fainted all over again. It was a regular comedy, and I felt ashamed for her.'

Perhaps the Marquise embellished her anecdote. However, such hysterical scenes were by no means rare with Germaine, and they cannot be regarded as mere comedies: even in her childhood her imagination bordered on the hallucinatory and the regular habit of opium had intensified it. It is entirely probable that Germaine actually *saw* Rocca brandishing his knife with suicidal intent: Benjamin, who knew her better than any man, was not entirely wrong in thinking her mad. At any rate, scenes such as this were hardly calculated to keep the relationship secret. And when, at another gathering, Germaine seized the arm of the Comtesse de Boigne and whispered to her, in apology for an exceptional inanity just uttered by her lover, 'Ah! Words are not his language!' her touching remark was interpreted otherwise than meant, and not altogether incorrectly.

At the first signs of spring Germaine returned to Coppet, bringing Rocca with her. Her friends present and absent were in a state of consternation. From the Vendée Prosper complained of the coldness of her letters, adding accusingly: 'Incidentally, I know that, among other amusements, you are dabbling in sentimental experiments in Geneva.' Chamisso, who was visiting, packed up in disgust and departed like Peter Schlemihl in his seven-league boots, leaving behind him a reproachful poem that begins with the words, 'Farewell, Corinne, farewell! I leave forever,' and ends with: 'My eyes have seen!' Schlegel, too, could see only too plainly, and none was more consternated than he. For the sake of a 'frivolous infatuation', Germaine was ready to renounce his friendship, he wrote to her in one of his room-to-room epistles. While she treated him like a criminal if he made any plans for an independent life, she was thinking of forming a tie that would banish him after he had devoted seven years of his life to an illusion.

'Every night, locked up in my room, I feel like a prisoner outside whose cell door people are going to and fro, jeering loudly at my plight.' In revenge he nicknamed the none-too-articulate but ever serviceable Rocca Caliban—a name which stuck for the rest of his life. Perhaps Rocca was not familiar enough with Shakespeare to repay Schlegel with the nickname Malvolio: it would have been even more apposite.

Rocca got on splendidly with Germaine's children, however; they accepted him as a combination of brother, companion, and informal stepfather.

To be loved as she was, with complete, passionate, and Caliban-like devotion was what Germaine had always proclaimed to be the goal of life on earth. Yet when this happiness came to her at the moment she least expected it, she showed little eagerness to accept it unconditionally. Caliban might console her in exile, but what figure would he cut in Vienna, London, or Paris? Apart from the discrepancy of age, there was the obvious discrepancy of intellect. Germaine could not hide from herself the fact that Rocca was dull in any language that required words. With touching optimism, she tried to widen his intellectual horizon, set him to work on a book about his experiences in Spain, helped him to express his thoughts—in a word, undertook his education. The pupil made marvellous progress, but clearly he never could replace Benjamin, nor even Schlegel. There can be no doubt that Germaine loved Rocca deeply and sincerely; if he had tried to leave her, she probably would even have loved him passionately. Yet something was missing. She had found the love she sought in life, but not the happiness she sought in love.

Rocca, however, had vowed that he would love her so well that she would marry him in the end, and he was a very tenacious young man. 'I want you completely,' he wrote to Germaine. 'I want you to bear my name, and I want a child from you who will really be a *Little Us*.' It took a hussar to make love like this. Germaine could not quite resist such an impetuous charge. On May 1, 1811, in the presence of a Protestant pastor and with Fanny Randall as the only witness, Germaine and John Rocca affirmed their intention to marry 'as soon as circumstances permitted'. Before God they regarded themselves as man and wife; from the world the bizarre engagement was held completely secret. Not even her children had the least inkling of it.

Rocca was earnestly determined to assert his new rights—so earnestly that he challenged Benjamin to a duel twice in one month. On April 18, after a supper in Geneva with Germaine and her old lover, he followed

Benjamin into the street and invited him either to cease seeing Germaine or to fight it out the next morning. Benjamin, perplexed, saw no choice but to accept, but it seems that Germaine succeeded in appeasing Rocca's thirst for blood before the duel could take place. Rocca again came face to face with his rival on May 10 at Lausanne, where Germaine had gone to say a last farewell before Benjamin and his wife left for Germany. He could not resist the opportunity of repeating his challenge, but this time Benjamin flatly refused.

One more bond had to be broken to satisfy the exacting Rocca: Germaine wrote to Prosper that he was relieved of his vows. Prosper in his reply, headed 'Oswald to Corinne' rose to the occasion:

> Returning from two months' absence, Corinne, the first word I receive from you is to tell me that we must break all the ties that unite us. You give me back my freedom—or rather, you take back yours.... Why have I ever known you, Corinne? Why have I lived with you that exalted, intoxicating life? . . . After having tasted of the food and drink of the gods, what burning regrets hark back to the lost pleasures!

All the same Oswald was quick in taking advantage of his newly won freedom. In August Germaine received notice of Prosper's engagement to the young Mademoiselle d'Houdetot, who might have served as a model for Lucile Edgermond; on November 20 he was married. 'I understand that he looked solemn [at the ceremony],' Germaine wrote to Juliette. 'Was he thinking of me then? Alas! I no longer have a right to wear the bridal veil.'

Germaine's surprising preoccupation with bridal veils is reflected in the prose sketch she wrote in 1811 for her unfinished tragedy, *Sapho*. Its theme: the impossibility of a pure love between an experienced woman of genius and a virginal youth. 'Could I keep his love forever,' says Sappho of Phaon, 'I who have known the fires of the marriage bed? He needs the love of a heart that has beaten for no one but him.' Whom was Germaine thinking of—Oswald-Prosper or Rocca-Caliban?

Sappho, says the legend, after renouncing Phaon, threw herself into the sea from a high rock. Germaine wrote an essay entitled *Reflections on Suicide*. A retraction of her statements on suicide in her treatise on the passions, the *Reflections* marshal every conceivable argument against self-destruction. The thought of death and suicide was her almost continual preoccupation through the winter of 1811-12; but since, as Sismondi noted, the terror of hellfire had been added to

Germaine's lifelong terror of death, she succeeded admirably in dissuading herself.

In her lamentations to her friends Germaine enumerated every reason for her depression except the principal one, which was unmentionable. She had brought suffering on all who loved her; she was little better than a prisoner; the sad remnants of her court gave little comfort.

> Schlegel has defects that sometimes hide his virtues from me. . . .
> Auguste has no intimate rapport with anyone but you [Juliette]; although
> I love him much, I do not understand him well. Albert is a harum-
> scarum. Albertine is too young. . . . I spend whole hours familiarizing
> myself with the idea of death. . . . As for my friends and my children, I
> can see that they all would be better off if I were dead.

The thoughts of death in her mind came from the stirring of life in her womb: Germaine was with child. It was late in August or early in September that she discovered the presence of the 'Little Us', the wretched, ill-fated child she was to bear her lover. Soon her looks horrified her friends when she returned to Geneva to spend the winter. Her features were haggard, her skin sallow; she had lost her liveliness; and she seemed deformed by dropsy. Dropsy was the official diagnosis; except for Germaine, Rocca, Miss Randall, and Doctor Jurine, no one knew the truth—at least not at first.[1]

It was at this awkward point that the government granted her the passport to the United States that she had been requesting for several months. A voyage during her pregnancy, and at a time when war between England and America was imminent, was unthinkable. Germaine asked for permission to go to Italy; the government refused. There was no choice but to wait until the child was born, conceal its existence, and then flee.

Towards the end of winter the rumour spread that Germaine's obesity had non-clinical causes. Capelle, who as usual was reliably informed, delightedly conveyed the news to his superiors. In the streets and shops of Geneva Germaine was publicly jeered at and cursed. It was she who had brought misfortune on the city by causing Barante's dismissal; now the Jezebel was seducing young men. Red-faced, but carrying her head high like a true Necker, Germaine pretended not to hear.

On April 7, at Coppet, Germaine gave birth to a boy, while Schlegel,

---

[1] There is evidence that, besides being pregnant, Germaine was genuinely ill. A letter of Sismondi, dated May 5, 1812, indicates that her doctor had prescribed digitalis for her. She never recovered her health after her pregnancy.

Albert, and Albertine went about their business, in the same house, without the faintest suspicion of what was going on.[1] Rarely was more self-control exercised by a person seemingly less capable of it.

The infant remained with his mother for five or six days, and still no one in the house knew of his existence, except Fanny Randall, who had acted as midwife. Then Doctor Jurine and Miss Randall, she carrying a bundle, drove to the village of Longirod, near Nyon, where the Pastor Gleyre was awaiting them. The child was entered into the register of baptisms as 'Louis Alphonse, son of Henriette, *née* Preston, and of Theodore Giles, of Boston.' Discreet arrangements with the pastor and his wife were then completed; the child remained in their care, and Miss Randall returned to Coppet without the bundle. Germaine was not to see 'Little Us' again until 1814. He was then a frail child, shy, silent, and retarded.

One day after the birth of 'Little Us', Father Zacharias Werner wrote to Germaine: 'I hear you have just had an attack of dropsy! What a terrible misfortune! Perhaps you are going to die! . . . Alas, I embrace your knees and I cry out to you, my sister, my benefactress, I implore you, become a Catholic, without delay, this very instant!' The letter must have reached Germaine about the time the child of Theodore Giles of Boston was christened at Longirod.

Meanwhile Capelle in his reports quoted the epigrams circulating in Geneva:

> Astonishing woman! How fertile her genius!
> Whatever she makes is destined to fame.
> Even her dropsy, O woman ingenious!
> Will live to perpetuate her name.

Two weeks after her child was born Germaine reappeared in Genevese society. She looked so ill that those who saw her dismissed the scandalous rumours they had heard. Capelle knew better, but he kept quiet, probably meditating blackmail. He knew that she had liquidated a large part of her fortune and was carrying it around with her in cash. He knew that she had transferred her assets in London to New York. He had no doubt that she would try to escape, and he watched her closely.

On May 23 at two in the afternoon Germaine, after ordering the dinner, climbed into her open carriage with Albertine, dressed for a short drive, with no other visible baggage than their fans. They did

---

[1] Auguste was in Châlons, with Madame Récamier.

not return for dinner until July 1814. The afternoon drive was an unusually extensive one: it took them to Vienna, Kiev, Moscow, Saint Petersburg, Stockholm, London, and Paris before they saw Coppet again.

Monsieur Capelle, with all his spies and precautions, discovered only on June 2, ten days after her departure, that Germaine was missing. By that time she had crossed into Austria.

19

DEFEAT IN VICTORY

O N May 9, two weeks before Germaine's flight from Coppet,
Napoleon left Paris for Dresden. There, in the royal palace, he
held court: his father-in-law, the Emperor of Austria, and six
kings—Prussia, Saxony, Bavaria, Württemberg, Westphalia, and Naples
—were in attendance like so many lackeys. Meanwhile, at Vilna, his
special envoy delivered the French ultimatum to Tsar Alexander. The
envoy was the Comte de Narbonne; he had gone a long way since the
days of Juniper Hall.

'Time and space are for me,' the Tsar said to Narbonne, pointing
at the map of Russia. He would withdraw to the remotest corner of his
empire and defend the most distant posts rather than consent to a
dishonourable peace. 'I am not attacking, but I shall not put down my
arms as long as a foreign soldier remains on Russian soil.'

Narbonne brought Alexander's answer to Dresden. 'It remains to
be seen,' Napoleon said to him, 'whether Alexander's resolution will
hold out against the test of events. Deluded by English advice, he wants
war. I shall make war.' The marching orders were issued on May 29;
500,000 men converged upon Poland; on June 22 they began to cross
the Niemen. 'The peace we shall make,' says Napoleon's proclamation
to the Grande Armée, 'will contain its own guarantee and put an end
to that fatal influence which Russia has exerted for fifty years on the
affairs of Europe.'

With Europe at Napoleon's feet, Russia about to be invaded, and the
United States at war with England, Madame de Staël seemed to have
ill chosen the moment of her flight. England was her goal—but how to
get there? She did not know. She even lacked a passport. Yet if the
time was singularly unpropitious, it is also true that Germaine's pregnancy had made it impossible for her to leave earlier, and the thought of
staying on in Coppet was to her unbearable. Apart from her fear of
actual imprisonment, there was the even greater fear of boredom. 'This

monotony, which can be counted by years, while old age is approaching, is a veritable torture,' she wrote to Hochet eighteen days before her flight. 'I feel as if I were on guard duty over my tomb.'[1]

Her flight was not well prepared; no doubt it was the absence of preparation which made it possible. She had taken the precaution of transferring the ownership of Coppet to her son Auguste, who was to return there after escorting her to Papiermühle, a village near Berne, where she was met by Schlegel: nothing else had been prearranged.

At Papiermühle Germaine's resolution almost broke down. Should she undertake the 'big trip' or simply go to the baths of Schinznach, near Zurich? Should she ask Rocca to join her? What to do with Albert? What to do about passports? Schlegel was prepared to accompany her to the end of the world, but when she asked for his help in obtaining an Austrian passport for Rocca, he bridled. If he had advised the flight in the first place, it was partly in order to separate her from Caliban. His assistance was indispensable, however, for he had conducted Germaine's negotiations with the Austrian minister in Berne, to whom she was just about to send Auguste with a letter from Schlegel asking for the passports. 'To get this letter from Schlegel,' she wrote to Rocca on May 25, 'I told him the entire truth of my sentiments for you, because I did not want him to torment me about an affection that will last for life.' The entire truth no doubt included the secret engagement and the birth of 'Little Us'. Schlegel must have been dumbfounded—but once again he surrendered to a superior will, and he wrote the letter. When Auguste returned from Berne with the passport —issued under a false name—Germaine, almost on the spur of the moment, made her final dispositions: she would go on to Vienna with Schlegel and Albertine; Rocca would join her in Austria; Albert and Uginet would follow with the baggage. Once Germaine was separated from her lover, she felt unable to deny herself his presence, though fully aware that she was committing a crime—in the technical sense, by inducing him to desert to the enemy, and in the moral sense, by forcing him to accept hardships that ruined his already weak health.

By way of Zurich and Saint Gall Germaine with Schlegel and Albertine entered the Tyrol, which Napoleon had made a part of Italy, and thence went on to Salzburg, which Napoleon had made a part of Bavaria. Halting briefly at an inn at Salzburg, Germaine was informed

---

[1] According to a letter written by Capelle on June 4, Germaine fled to escape the scandal of having borne a child to Rocca; but at the same time, Capelle correctly accuses Schlegel of having advised the flight—and Schlegel knew nothing of the child. The fact is that Germaine had planned her escape even before 'Little Us' was conceived.

that a French courier was looking for her. Germaine, terrified, expected to be arrested, when the courier reappeared and turned out to be Rocca. The travellers reached Vienna on June 6, but even here they were within reach of Napoleon's long arm. Following Auguste's injunction, Germaine avoided showing herself in Rocca's company. While she and the rest of her party took lodgings at the hotel *Zum römischen Kaiser*, Rocca was hidden away in separate quarters, from which he emerged only after nightfall to visit Germaine. She herself went out little: apart from old friends such as the Prince de Ligne, Gentz, and Wilhelm von Humboldt, few of her acquaintances cared to compromise themselves by receiving her. She called on Titine O'Donnell, whose husband, Count Maurice, had, it seems, already joined his regiment in Poland.

Germaine stayed sixteen days in Vienna and forty days on Austrian territory; the police reports on her activities during that period cover 114 large sheets. This time, no attempt was made to hide from her that she was under surveillance: a plain-clothes man was stationed at the entrance to the hotel; others followed her on foot or, if she took a carriage, in cabs, wherever she went. When, after a few days, the agents became aware of John Rocca's identity, the chief of the Vienna police called on Madame de Staël. This was a serious matter, he pointed out. What should the Austrian government do if France demanded Rocca's extradition as a deserter? Why, refuse, of course, said Germaine. 'But Madame, do you want us to declare war on France on account of Monsieur Rocca?'—'Why not?' said Germaine. 'He is my friend and will be my husband.'

While she tried to brazen it out, she was waiting with mounting anxiety for the return of the Russian diplomatic courier from Vilna, who was to bring a reply to her request for a Russian passport. In the meantime, other routes had to be considered in the event of the passport being refused or the border closed. Through Schlegel and Gentz she applied for an Austrian exit visa allowing her to leave the country either by way of Poland into Russia or by way of Hungary into Turkey. From Turkey she would make her way to England either through Russia and Sweden or by way of Greece, Sicily, Cadiz, and Lisbon. 'All the Turkish couriers are in my room,' she wrote to Rocca. Small wonder that Herr Seywalt, the agent in charge of her surveillance, became as confused about her intentions as she herself was. Madame de Staël, he wrote in his report, was planning to go to Stockholm *via* 'Riga, Malta, Asia, Greece, etc.'

Austrian bureaucracy proved too much for Madame de Staël. Regulations, she was told, forbade the issuance of exit visas by alternative routes. Without awaiting the return of the Russian courier, she left Vienna with her children and Rocca on June 22—the day of Napoleon's proclamation to his army—and went on to Brünn, the capital of Moravia. Schlegel and Uginet stayed behind to straighten out the passport matter. In Brünn she was politely informed by the Austrian governor that she was to proceed through Galicia into Russia without delay. Germaine pointed out that she must wait for her Russian passport; did he mean her to spend the rest of her life at Brody, on the border, unable to come or go? 'What you say is quite true,' said the governor, 'but these are my orders.' Things had reached this impasse, familiar to millions since her time, when on June 29 Uginet reported from Vienna, in a style worthy of *Corinne*, that the Russian passports had arrived. 'I am feverish with joy and anxiety,' his note concluded. While Uginet returned to Coppet, Schlegel hastened after Germaine with the precious papers, and the flight continued.

Crossing Galicia, Germaine had to report at every district police station to have her passport visaed. When she stayed overnight in the château of her friend Prince Lubomirski, a police agent insisted that, according to his orders, he had to spend the night in her bedroom. Only when Albert threatened to throw him out of the window did he agree, with a deep bow and a 'Ja, Herr Baron', to spend his vigil in the hall. There was, Germaine noted, 'a kind of brutality that can be met with only in subaltern German officials: only they can pass, without transition, from arrogance towards weakness to obsequiousness towards power'. Poland was, perhaps, a better place to study Germany than Weimar had been.

It was on July 14 that Germaine crossed into Russia, with a special permit given her by the governor of Lvov.[1] 'Thus, as far as I was concerned, the cycle of French history which began on July 14, 1789, was closed. When the barrier . . . was raised to let me pass, I swore never to set foot in any country which was in any way subject to Emperor Napoleon.' She greeted Russia as a land of freedom.

Madame de Staël spent altogether eight weeks in Russia. The advance of Napoleon's armies forced her to make a detour by way of Kiev, Orel, Tula, Moscow, and Novgorod to reach Saint Petersburg.

[1] Russia and Austria were, of course, in a state of war by then, but there was no fighting on their border.

She left Saint Petersburg for Finland and Sweden on September 8, the morrow of the battle of Borodino; one week later Moscow fell and went up in flames. She saw Russia at a moment in history when the nation's character revealed itself in its fullest strength. Neither she nor anyone in her suite understood a word of Russian, except a German physician who had offered to escort them to Moscow as interpreter; yet the ten chapters she devotes to Russia and Finland in her *Ten Years of Exile*—one third of the book—are among the most perceptive of her writings. No Russian Rahel Levin could have said of her, with a sneer, that she had 'seen nothing, heard nothing, understood nothing': Germaine saw and absorbed everything, with an intensity, a freshness, a directness, that one misses in her descriptions of Germany and Italy. Equally astonishing is the wealth of historic lore, for the most part fairly accurate, which informs her descriptions of places and monuments. Nothing gives one a more impressive demonstration of her ceaseless curiosity and activity; the mind staggers at the thousands of questions that must have showered from her mouth during these eight weeks, and at the imperturbable note-taking on the ever-ready portable green-leather escritoire.

For once Germaine's eyes were wide open. She saw the great wheat-growing plains of the Ukraine, 'which look as if they were cultivated by invisible hands, so sparse are the dwellings and inhabitants'; Kiev, which from afar looked to her like a camp, its wooden houses resembling Tartar tents, and, 'rising from the midst of these huts, the palaces, and above all the churches, whose green and gilded cupolas make a singular impact on the eye', especially at sunset, when 'one has the impression of a festive illumination rather than of a solid edifice'; the plains south of Moscow, with their birch forests and the sparse villages, 'made up of wooden houses all built on the same model'; Moscow before the great fire, with its wooden palaces, which she was one of the last to see, 'painted green, yellow, pink, and sculptured like dessert decorations'; the Kremlin, where she ascended the 300-foot bell tower of Ivan the Great, to see spread out beneath her the 1,500 churches of the city; Saint Petersburg, whose 'buildings still were of a dazzling white, and, at night, in the moonlight, seemed like great shrouded phantoms staring motionlessly upon the Neva'.

The human scene appears equally vividly in Germaine's pages on Russia. There are the coachmen, driving her with lightning speed 'while singing songs whose words, I was told, are compliments and encouragements addressed to their horses'; the Cossacks on the roads, 'joining the army each by himself, without order or uniform, carrying long lances and wearing a greyish kind of garment with whose vast hood they cover their heads'; the couriers darting along the highways 'at incredible speed', bouncing two feet in the air from the wooden seats of their little carts; the blue blouses and tight red belts worn by most Russian men, and the vivid colours of the women's costumes, which 'also have something Asiatic about them'. She was one of the first Europeans to report enthusiastically on Russian folk music and dances. She was struck by the natural grace of Russian women, by the metallic sonority of the Russian language, by the richness of the ruby- and diamond-studded icons. 'Magnificence is the characteristic of everything one sees in Russia.'

Like all travellers in Russia, she was overwhelmed by the hospitality she received everywhere and from all classes; like all travellers, she fearlessly generalized on the Russian national character. The Russians, it seemed to her, showed more affinity with the nations of the South and the Orient than with those of the North. 'Their nature is Oriental,' she says—but at the same time she stresses their energy and patriotism, which set them apart from the indolent Orient:

> It is characteristic of this nation to fear neither fatigue nor physical pain; they are at the same time patient and active, gay and melancholy. They unite the most striking contrasts, and this entitles us to expect great things from them: for only superior beings possess mutually opposed qualities. . . . Most noteworthy is the high degree of public-spiritedness in Russia. The reputation of invincibility which that nation has earned by its frequent successes, the natural pride of the nobles, the loyalty characteristic of the people, its powerful religious spirit, and its hatred of foreigners . . . which is in the blood of the Russians and which, when the occasion arises, reasserts itself—all these causes combine in making this a most energetic nation. . . . Diderot's famous quip, that 'the Russians became rotten before they matured', has been much praised: I cannot think of anything more false. Their very vices, with few exceptions, are the result not of corruption but of violence. A Russian's desire . . . is capable of blowing up a city; fury and ruse possess them in turn when they want to accomplish whatever they have resolved upon, be it good or evil.

It was this explosive, passionate, elemental vitality that impressed Germaine more than anything else in Russia:

> In every way, there is something gigantic about this people: ordinary dimensions have no application whatever to it. I do not mean by this

that true greatness and stability are never met with; but their boldness, their imaginativeness knows no bounds. With them everything is colossal rather than well-proportioned, audacious rather than well-considered, and if they do not attain their goals, it is because they exceed them.

Germaine was not blind to the faults of Russia. The monotony of the landscape, the primitive conditions of the roads, affected her much as they did the soldiers of Napoleon's army: it seemed to her 'that this country was the image of infinite space, and that eternity was needed to cross it'. There was fabulous luxury, but not 'what the English call *comfort*'. Because of the absence of a prosperous middle class, the aristocracy was, under a thin Western veneer, as raw and uncultured as the masses. The same lack of moderation characterized the nobles and the people. This made for 'a greater mutual sympathy' between the social extremes than could be found in other countries, but it also retarded civilization.

On the subjects of serfdom, autocratic despotism, and extremes of wealth and poverty, Germaine wrote with diplomatic caution. The general aspect of the peasantry struck her as prosperous, which is surprising. As for serfdom and despotism, she expressed faith—to all appearances, sincere faith—in Tsar Alexander's professed liberal and reformist intentions. Germaine wrote on Russia much in the same spirit as Western war correspondents in the Soviet Union during the Second World War; like them, also, she changed her tune once the Russian armies crossed the borders and swept across Europe. Yet what she saw was no less true for being incomplete: what she saw was the awesome strength of Russia in crisis, the strength of 1612, of 1812, of 1942: 'In the great crisis in which Russia found herself when I crossed her, one could not but admire the vigour and resignation which that nation manifested in its resistance and its sacrifices, and in the face of such virtues one scarcely dared to notice what one might have blamed at other times.'

There was even more than this to Germaine's enthusiasm for Russia: the Russian character, as she understood it, corresponded most intimately with her own. Like hers, it united the passions of opposite extremes, the vitality of the South, the melancholy of the North, the mysticism of the East. She too never attained her goal because she always exceeded it. What bore a closer resemblance to the impetuous violence of Russian desire, which was 'capable of blowing up a city', than that of Germaine's? Of whom could it be said with more truth that 'fury and ruse' possessed her in turn when she wanted to accomplish

SISMONDI
Medal by David d'Angers

ZACHARIAS WERNER
After a drawing by E. Schnorr von K. (Carolsfeld?)

Columbia University Press

MADAME DE KRÜDENER
From a pastel in the Rauch'sche Palais, Heilbronn

JOHN ROCCA AND HIS HORSE SULTAN
From a portrait by P. L. Bouvier at Musée Ariana, Geneva

LOUIS ALPHONSE ROCCA
Portrait by Arland in the collection of M. Léopold Boissier

what she had resolved upon? Who was more tyrannical and self-sacrificing? The very boredom that filled her soul recalls these plains that were 'the image of infinite space', and her intellect sent her ideas racing across it with the same lightning speed as the couriers that bounced along the highways of Russia. Here, as with Germaine, everything was extreme, exaggerated, savage, impulsive—and *never calculated*. And here she felt 'at the gate of another continent, close to that Eastern world whence so many religious faiths have issued forth and which still encloses in its bosom unbelievable treasures of perseverance and intellectual depth'. Germaine would have fitted better in a novel of Dostoevski's than she did into her own *Delphine* and *Corinne*.

These were affinities of temperament; intellectually and culturally, Germaine remained the child of the West, and in the last resort her intellect always won out over her temperament. When, at Saint Petersburg, the public hissed a troupe of French actors, 'The barbarians!' she cried out, 'Not to want to see Racine's *Phèdre*!' And the image of 'the Cossacks camping in the rue Racine' began to haunt her soon afterwards. It was the Russian victory, which she had hailed, that made her return to where she had started—the liberal Enlightenment.

But for the insistence of her travel companions, Germaine might not have crossed Russia at all. She was still in the Ukraine when news of the rapid advance of the French and their allies reached her. Terrified of falling into their hands, she thought of going to Odessa and Constantinople, and even advanced literary reasons for making this detour. In the winter of 1811–12 she had begun composing a prose epic on Richard the Lionhearted. The setting, she wrote, was to be 'the enthusiasm for the Crusades. Four heroes: Frederick Barbarossa, Philip Augustus, Richard, and Saladin—and, as dénouement, the prospect of English freedom in the Magna Carta.' The unfinished poem, on which she worked on and off until her death, was intended to celebrate 'that great epoch in English history when enthusiasm for the Crusades gave way to enthusiasm for liberty'. Germaine thought of pushing from Constantinople to Syria in order to familiarize herself with 'the customs and nature of the Orient', but Schlegel and Rocca convinced her that the hazards of such a journey were even greater than the risk of falling into French hands. It was thus that she came to gather firsthand knowledge of the enthusiasm for another crusade —that of Russia against Napoleon—and was led, by circumstances as much as by her will, to play an active role in current events instead of celebrating those of the past.

P

Russia received her like the commanding general of an allied power. At Kiev she was the guest of the governor, General Miloradovich; at Moscow of Governor Rostopchin, at whose country estate she dined six weeks before the great fire, which he is alleged to have instigated. Muscovite society, scattered in their summer homes, flocked back into the city to get a glimpse of her. 'Men and women came from all directions,' reports a lady memorialist published by Pushkin. 'They were disappointed: they saw a hefty woman of fifty whose clothes were inappropriate for her age. Her manner was not liked; her speeches seemed too long and her sleeves too short.' All the same, a dinner was given in her honour to which all Moscow was invited.

> She sat at the place of honour [continues the memorialist], elbows on the table, rolling and unrolling a little tube of paper. She seemed in ill humour. Several times she wanted to speak and could not say what she had to say. Our wits kept on eating and drinking as usual and seemed happier with their fish stew than with Madame de Staël's conversation. They rarely broke their silence, being convinced in their hearts of the nullity of their thoughts and intimidated by the presence of that illustrious European.
>
> The guests divided their attention between their sturgeon and Madame de Staël, waiting for her to make some witty sally. At last a double entendre escaped from her lips, and a rather risqué one at that. They all pounced on it, burst into laughter, and a murmur of admiration was heard. The guests left the table completely reconciled with Madame de Staël: she had made a pun! And they rushed out to spread it all over town.

Germaine's remarks on the superficiality of conversation and learning among the Russian aristocracy tend to confirm this narrative. At Saint Petersburg, however, where the Union Jack was flying on the Neva, she re-entered the Western world and the heady, bracing air of politics. With the Genevese banker Galiffe acting as her interpreter, guide, and general secretary, she made the rounds of the palaces, the embassies, the court. While Napoleon approached Moscow, the life of Saint Petersburg and its suburbs remained an uninterrupted succession of feasts and parties. Germaine attended them day after day, visited all the sights of the capital, admired the mammoth in the museum, read aloud from *De l'Allemagne* at Count Orlov's, discussed the future of Europe with Baron vom Stein at the Naryshkins' and with the English ambassador at the Foreign Ministry. Already at Saint Petersburg Germaine was horrified by the vindictive anti-French tone of the Allies, and she began to separate the cause of France from that of

Napoleon. When a toast was proposed at the Naryshkins' to the victory of England and Russia, she declared, with visible emotion, that much as she desired Napoleon's defeat, she could never wish for that of France. How the one could be brought about without the other it is difficult to see; for the following twenty months Germaine was to writhe in the dilemma.

In August 1812 to defeat Napoleon seemed the most immediate problem, and Germaine offered to play her share in the struggle. Exactly what passed in her two interviews with Tsar Alexander no one knows. The emotionally unstable Emperor was in an expansive mood, conversing with her, she says, 'like an English statesman, who relied on his own strength rather than on the barriers he might set up'. He was about to meet the Swedish Crown Prince at Åbo (now Turku) in Finland; on the outcome of that interview a great deal depended. The Crown Prince was, of course, Germaine's old friend and fellow conspirator Bernadotte, and she herself was planning to call on him at Stockholm, where she intended to spend the winter. Alexander realized what influence Madame de Staël could wield over Bernadotte, and he courted her accordingly. His immediate objective was to secure Sweden's assurance of neutrality and its renunciation of Finland; in exchange, he was willing to support Sweden's designs on Norway. Both men, however, had far vaster ambitions, and there is little doubt that they discussed these too at Åbo. The scheme was nothing less than the formation of a European coalition against Napoleon under Russian leadership and the establishment of a liberal monarchy in France with Bernadotte as king.

Germaine threw herself into the scheme with her customary enthusiasm. Savary asserts that she was 'the connecting link of the Åbo interview'. How much truth there is in this assertion it is difficult to determine; perhaps the answer lies buried in the Soviet archives. But there is absolutely no doubt that, after the Åbo interview, no single person did more to push Sweden into the Fourth Coalition as a full partner than did Madame de Staël; that by promoting Sweden's entry into the war she played a decisive role in Napoleon's defeat; and that she organized a veritable conspiracy to push Bernadotte's candidacy for the French throne.

The party which boarded a fishing boat at Åbo in mid-September of 1812 seemed strangely inadequate to the task of guiding the destinies of the greatest war Europe had seen till then: a dowdy, extravagantly dressed woman in her mid-forties; two young men, one of them lame, the other patently harebrained; a pretty red-haired girl of fifteen; and a middle-aged professor in breeches and silk stockings. Among the other passengers were the well-known German actress Henriette Hendel, her fourth husband, the historian Professor Schütz of Jena, and Madame Hendel's two daughters and newborn babe. The fishing boat had not sailed far when a violent storm began. Twenty-six years later Schlegel still remembered the occasion vividly. 'The sea,' he writes, 'swept over our fragile craft at every moment. In the midst of the general panic, Albertine kept up a brave and serene front and had no other thought than that of dissipating her mother's terror.' Forced to change his course, the captain took the craft to one of the Aaland Islands. No sooner did Germaine feel solid ground under her feet than her courage returned: waiting for the tempest to blow itself out, she and Madame Hendel organized, on the deserted beach, an impromptu theatrical performance, complete with 'living tableaux', recitations, dances, and pantomimes.

On September 24 Madame de Staël disembarked, at last, at Stockholm. The news of her arrival, the French chargé d'affaires reported to Paris, 'produced the effect of a bombshell'. She wasted no time in going about her business with Bernadotte, who received her 'like an old friend'. By September 28 the Crown Prince (who in fact reigned for his adoptive father, Charles XIII) had commissioned young Albert in the hussars of the royal guard and promised a position as aide-de-camp for Auguste. Soon afterwards he nominated Schlegel his private secretary. For it was Schlegel of all people—Schlegel the unworldly, impractical, hypochondriac professor, Schlegel the wet hen—who suddenly threw himself into politics and war with a furious energy which, though it may at first surprise, was entirely in keeping with his character. After years of humiliation and frustration he came into his own, with every opportunity to satisfy his smouldering hatred of France and his dreams of recreating the greatness of medieval Germany.

'Bernadotte,' writes Schlegel, 'began by fully confiding his political views to me.' He also asked him to draw up a memorandum on 'the state of Germany and on the means of organizing a national uprising'. Schlegel's memorandum is a fantastic document: he proposed the creation of a central German government, under the chancellorship of vom Stein and the military leadership of a 'great captain'—to wit Bernadotte; the princes were to give up their sovereignty so that a new, united Germany could be created; with this programme, the German people could be roused to take up arms against Napoleon. Bernadotte was impressed with the memorandum, parts of which he later utilized in his proclamations.

However, Bernadotte was as cautious as ambitious. The danger of losing Sweden while running after glory in Germany and France did not escape him. The French, Prussian, and Austrian diplomatic dispatches from Stockholm give an idea of the important role played by Madame de Staël in his final decision. 'She calls on the Prince Royal at all hours,' reports de Cabre, the French chargé d'affaires, on December 11; 'he tells her everything and she sometimes advises him.' Through Galiffe, she was in constant touch with the Russian government; the most important negotiations between Sweden and Russia were conducted, not through the embassies, but through Madame de Staël and Galiffe.

To Bernadotte she repeated almost daily her conviction—which, secretly, was also his—that he was the 'union of genius and virtue', the 'true hero of the century', that 'he alone could stem Napoleon's tide'; to Galiffe she repeated Bernadotte's complaints that unless Russia contributed the troops Alexander had promised him, he could not abandon his neutrality; to the British envoy, Thornton, she spoke of Sweden's need for financial subsidies. In her four-room apartment on the Arsenalgatan, facing the opera house, she received the entire diplomatic corps (except Monsieur de Cabre) at what Stockholmers soon came to call 'Madame de Staël's conversational dances'. On December 11 Cabre reported that she had succeeded in having the envoy of the Spanish Junta accredited minister, and on the same date she wrote to Galiffe: 'In the spring we shall wake up and make a terrible noise.'[1]

Napoleon by then was racing back to Paris by sleigh and carriage, leaving behind him the wreckage of an army of 500,000, to raise a new army before Europe could realize the extent of his defeat. In the first week of 1813 Bernadotte had a long conversation with the Prussian

---

[1] She even tried to make peace between the United States and England. In a letter to Jefferson, dated at Stockholm, November 10, 1812, she begged him to use his influence to end the War of 1812. America, she pointed out, was merely fighting Napoleon's war, and 'once Napoleon has destroyed English freedom, he will attack yours'. In his reply of May 28, 1813, Jefferson 'flayed both England and Napoleon as ruthless tyrants and declared that the United States was obliged to go to war with England because that country had respected neither the persons nor the property of American citizens' (R. L. Hawkins, *Madame de Staël and the United States*, Cambridge, Mass., 1930, pp. 51-2).

minister, von Tarrach, at Germaine's house; Sweden wanted Prussia
to join the Coalition, Tarrach reported to his government on January 8.
Six days later Schlegel wrote to his friend Count Sickingen to use his
influence with Emperor Francis to make him abandon his alliance with
France; the letter is full of the most extravagant praise of Bernadotte,
through whose 'noble simplicity, quiet dignity, and persuasive charm
. . . there shines the fire which fills his soul with passion for glory. . . .
Such a man is made to govern public opinion.' Swedish public opinion,
however, was not eager for adventures; in order to sway it into the anti-
French camp, Schlegel published a brochure, in French, on *The
Continental System in Its Relationship to Sweden*. The anonymous
brochure was generally ascribed to Madame de Staël, who had at the
very least a part in its composition and whose style and eloquence it
recalls. On March 3 Sweden and England concluded a treaty by which
Bernadotte, in exchange for a million rix-dollars and a free hand in
Norway, promised to land in Pomerania with 30,000 men; on March 17
King Frederick William reluctantly called Prussia to arms against
Napoleon; on May 18 Bernadotte landed at Stralsund, with Schlegel
as private secretary and Albert de Staël as aide-de-camp.

Surely the Fourth Coalition would have been formed without Madame
de Staël's intervention; on the other hand, the timing of Sweden's
accession to it—which she predicted five months ahead—was decisive
in Napoleon's defeat. On May 2 he had defeated the Prussians at
Lützen; on May 20 and 21 he defeated them again at Bautzen and
Wurschen; on May 30 Davout recaptured Hamburg from the German
insurgents: the fruits of these victories were destroyed by the presence
of Bernadotte's army in North Germany. Napoleon agreed to the
armistice of June 4 and to the holding of the abortive Congress of
Prague, which gave the Allies time to recuperate from their losses and
to pry Austria away from France; when hostilities were resumed in
July, Napoleon's situation had become hopeless. 'A Frenchman held
the destiny of the world in his hands,' Napoleon at Saint Helena said
of Bernadotte. 'He was one of the principal direct causes of our misfortunes.' If Germaine had lived to read these lines, she might have
felt complimented.

Germaine's complete success in the first phase of her campaign lent
some truth to the witticism which soon went round Europe: that there
were three great powers—England, Russia, and Madame de Staël.
With Bernadotte in Germany and Schlegel at his side, she was ready

to enter upon the second phase—to make Bernadotte King, or at least Regent, of France. One might expect that she enjoyed her triumph, that her feelings and thoughts were submerged in the tremendous excitement of the events she helped to fashion. The truth is that she was increasingly bored, increasingly unhappy, increasingly torn by a political and sentimental dilemma. To begin with, Stockholm had little to hold her interest; its aristocratic society still seemed to live in the eighteenth century, gaily and frivolously enough, an inadequate imitation of Parisian society in a vanished age. Apart from politics, Germaine found no occupation for her mind, and the brief sunless days and endless winter nights depressed her spirits and, she complained, her health.

Society, much as that of Vienna, looked at her with half-awed, half-mocking curiosity. The Swedish Baroness Sophie von Knorring, in an autobiographical novel entitled *The Illusions*, recalled Germaine's sojourn in Stockholm which she witnessed as a young girl. What struck her most was the family's complete lack of self-consciousness and their arrogant superiority to conventions. We are shown Germaine, enthroned in the director's box at the theatre, at one of the intervals during a performance of *Andromaque* by a French company, 'declaiming with her hands, feet, and lungs, to the great amusement of the entire parterre, who stared at her wide-eyed and open-mouthed, though continuing to eat apples'. Even more memorable an occasion was the ball of the Society of the Amaranth, where Germaine made her first public entry into Stockholm society.

> The door was thrown open, and she entered. . . . Alas! an illusion crumbled. There was nothing of a Corinne or Delphine in her. She was a corpulent person, very thickset, without any gracefulness in her movements. She always kept her head thrown back and never seemed to stop looking at the ceiling with her lively and mobile eyes; because of this attitude, her mouth was always half-open, even when she was not talking, which happened rarely. Of her clothes, one noticed only her heavy, voluminous, multi-coloured turban . . . which almost seemed to hang down over her neck.

As for Albertine, 'she was beautiful despite her carrot hair and her freckles. . . . She was draped rather than dressed, and every time her draperies slipped from her shoulders, Monsieur Rocca was at hand to replace them or, when her hair became undone, to repair it.'

When the traditional blows were struck on the door, the throng made its procession into the ballroom. Albertine, 'the most lively, natural,

and free person' Sophie von Knorring had ever seen, entertained her
dancing partners by comparing them unfavourably with the young men
of Saint Petersburg, so that after each dance Germaine (perhaps still
recalling Albertine's slapping the face of the Prussian Crown Prince)
apologized for her: 'She is a child, a flower of the fields, completely
natural!' Even more remarkable was Albert, who 'entered into the dance
like a hurricane', fully equipped in his new uniform, 'with his shako
under his arm and encumbered by his sword, cartridge pouch, sabre-
tache, and spurs'. As Sophie von Knorring aptly remarks, only the
horse was missing. 'I wish,' she adds, 'I could describe the mixture of
curiosity, astonishment, admiration, delight, mockery, and laughter
with which this family of strangers filled some of us, so that we forgot
everything else.'

The full account of the episode contains several inaccuracies, notably
the assertion that Auguste de Staël was also present. In fact, Auguste
was not at Stockholm but divided his time between Coppet and Lyons,
where he consoled Juliette Récamier, a circumstance which contributed
not a little to Germaine's unhappiness. The immediate purpose of her
long stay at Stockholm was not politics but to provide careers for her
sons. Bernadotte had given a commission to Albert and promised one
for Auguste—but Auguste, passionately in love with Madame Récamier, turned a deaf ear when his mother and Schlegel, in increasingly
imperious letters, summoned him to follow the path of duty and glory.
On January 26, Germaine appealed directly to Juliette: 'Give him, dear
friend, the strength to do what he must do.' Corinne in the role of
Oswald's father was something new.

Perhaps Germaine's appeals helped Juliette in making up her mind
to leave Lyons for Italy, which she did in February. As Schlegel put
it in a letter to Auguste, Juliette owed it to her lover to regard him 'as
an officer on duty, who cannot go on leave in the middle of a war or
refuse to join his regiment when it is ordered to march'. Having received his marching orders, Auguste by a vast detour made his way to
Sweden, which he reached in early May. He met Bernadotte at
Halsingborg, where he was about to embark for Stralsund, produced
an excellent impression on the Prince, and was encouraged to take
examinations for the diplomatic service at Stockholm. His career
seemed assured, which was enough for his mother, who saw no further
reason for remaining in Stockholm. In the last days of May, accompanied by Rocca, Auguste, and Albertine, she took ship at Gotenburg
for England. Stockholm without Bernadotte and Schlegel had seemed

to her oppressively boring: London held promises of new triumphs and activity, and in London she hoped to meet—there is no end to surprises —Benjamin Constant.

Benjamin had left Lausanne with Charlotte on May 15, 1811. On their way to Cassel, where Charlotte's relatives held high offices at the court of King Jérôme, they stopped at every gambling casino of Germany: Baden-Baden, Wiesbaden, Schwalbach. From June 25, when they arrived at Baden, to August 11, when they left Schwalbach— forty-six days in all—Benjamin spent thirty nights gambling. His diary marks small winnings on three occasions, 'mad' losses on sixteen occasions. Charlotte, far from attempting to restrain him, gambled with equal abandon, though slightly better luck. Besides this, bed, and her financial interests, which they had come to look after, they had nothing in common.

To escape his abysmal boredom and disenchantment, he plunged himself into work: the *History of Polytheism*, his perennial escape, once more went through a process of transformation. On November 2 he moved to Göttingen, in order to be closer to the university library. Here the stimulation of a scholarly society made life seem less empty, and his work progressed; but it would be difficult to call his life, and particularly his marriage, a happy one by any standards. Here are some extracts from his diary:

January 19, 1812: Finished Book Thirteen. Quarrel with my wife about [living in] Göttingen. Horrible life. . . . *February* 12: Worked. Quarrel with Charlotte. I would not wager that we shall finish our life together. . . . *February* 15: Worked. Excellent letter from Mme de Staël. Alas! Who knows! Acrimonious dispute with Charlotte about politics. . . . *February* 17: Worked. Ball. Quarrel with my wife. This cannot last. . . . *February* 18: Worked. Another quarrel. Boring. . . . *March* 17: Worked. My book is too confused. It bores me. Unexpected quarrel with Charlotte. I cannot make a step without her. My misfortune is my inability to love; and this makes even the easiest things difficult. . . . *March* 23: . . . Shall I forever sacrifice my life to feelings I do not have? . . . *March* 26: . . . Good letter from Mme de Staël. Who knows? . . . *April* 8: Charlotte's character is changing a good deal. From generous she has become avaricious; from gentle, exacting. Confounded marriage! Shall I get out of it? . . . *April* 17: . . . More serious and important quarrel than ever with Charlotte. I believe that at the bottom we are through with each other. . . . *June* 4: Worked poorly. Mme de Staël has left. My God! My God! . . . *June* 24: Worked. Her [Germaine's] voyage is in all the papers. Charlotte is the most boring creature the

P*

earth has ever borne. . . . *September* 14: Direct news from the traveller.
God be praised! . . . *October* 16: . . . The traveller has reached her temporary destination [Stockholm]. Bless God a thousand times. . . .
October 19: Worked. Slept too little, because Charlotte did not want to
go to bed. Among other things, I got married in order to sleep a lot with
my wife and in order to go to bed early. I almost never sleep with her,
and we stay up until four in the morning. . . . *November* 2: How I regret
Mme de Staël! . . . *December* 9: . . . I regret Mme de Staël more than
ever.

Germaine, too, felt regrets. She had not forgotten Benjamin, and
through war-torn Europe she managed to give him direct news. As
early as September 29 he received word, in veiled language, of her
scheme for 'the Bearnese'—Bernadotte. Benjamin rose to the bait. To
jump onto Bernadotte's bandwagon and to begin a new political career
—'I must give this serious thought,' he decided; 'I have nothing to
lose.' On November 14 Uginet arrived in Göttingen, no doubt with a
special message from Germaine. 'A great many thoughts,' noted Benjamin, 'are trotting through my head.' But it was difficult to rouse oneself
from lethargy in sleepy Göttingen, where even the news of the Moscow
fire was received 'without a single professor lifting his eyes from his
book'. Instead of following Germaine's appeal to meet her in London,
Benjamin lapsed into what he himself called 'a real impotence of soul
and moral paralysis', and to avoid making a decision he plunged himself
deeper into his work.

If Germaine tried to enlist Benjamin in the cause of the Bearnese,
it was not so much because she needed his help as because she needed
him. Rocca loved her, and she loved him, but besides being an inadequate substitute for Benjamin intellectually, he was difficult to live
with. He was proud, and he exasperated Germaine by lamenting the
necessity of living at her expense; he was, moreover, jealous and exclusive in his demands, qualities Germaine could not countenance in
either friends or lovers. Saint Petersburg and Stockholm put their
affection to a severe test. On the eve of her departure to England, with
Rocca almost at her elbow, Germaine meditating past and future, wrote
this to Benjamin:

> For two months I have had no news from you; for two years I have not
> seen you. Do you remember your promise that we would never separate?
> . . . I do not mind telling you this: you allowed a fine career to go to
> waste, not to mention all the rest. And I, what shall I become in my
> intellectual isolation? To whom can I speak? . . . I always have some

letters of yours with me. I never open my writing case without taking them in my hands: I gaze at the address. I shudder when I think what those letters have made me suffer, and yet I would like to receive still more. My father, you, and Mathieu remain in a compartment of my heart that is closed forever. . . . There I live and die. . . . Is it possible that you should have shattered all this? Is it possible that a despair such as mine did not keep you back? No: you are guilty, and yet your admirable mind still gives me illusions! Farewell. Ah, may you understand what I suffer!

On receiving this letter on July 7 Benjamin wrote in his diary: 'I am very much disturbed.' The following day: 'Done nothing. One of the worst days of regret and disgust I have had in a long time.'

Germaine's reception in London was triumphal. The Prince Regent, the Queen, the Duchess of York, the Duke of Gloucester received her. To meet a cabinet minister, wrote Miss Berry, one had to go to Madame de Staël's. At Lord Lansdowne's men and women climbed on chairs and tables to see her. After all, she was the only Continental power to have resisted Napoleon as steadfastly as England. Soon after her arrival, she signed a contract with John Murray, the publisher, who bought her manuscript *De l'Allemagne* for 1,500 guineas—not an inconsiderable sum for the time. Its publication in October made her the literary as well as the social and political lioness of the season; it sold out in three days. As usual, her triumph did little for her happiness. This time, however, about six weeks after her arrival in London, a very real blow struck her: her son Albert had been killed.

Albert had preceded Bernadotte to Stralsund late in April, with orders to wait for the Prince. Instead of waiting, he went to Hamburg, occupied since March 18 by three Cossack regiments under General Tettenborn, who was trying to hold it against the French under Oudinot. Schlegel, reporting his exploits to his worried mother, compared him to Hotspur. In truth, an examination of Albert's conduct during the last weeks of his life allows only one conclusion: either from insanity or from an excess of vitality he was bent on destroying himself by any available means within the shortest possible time. The Cossack life turned his head and Hamburg under Russian occupation was a wild place. Serving as aide-de-camp to Tettenborn, Albert gambled, drank and wenched with a frenetic abandon which made Admiral Hope, who watched him at the gaming table, predict 'a premature and unfortunate end'. In the intervals between excesses, he fought like a man possessed,

Cossack-style. Bernadotte, who brooked no nonsense where discipline was concerned, ordered him to return. Albert took cognizance of the order only after he had spent his last penny and after Hamburg was recaptured by the French. He was immediately placed under arrest, but Bernadotte, who reprimanded him in person, was content to punish him with a week's exile to the island of Rügen. Although Germaine had informed Schlegel that she refused to intercede on her son's behalf with Bernadotte, there can be no doubt that Albert would have got off less lightly if Madame de Staël had not been his mother. The lesson, however, was wasted on him. In July, as a mark of his favour, Bernadotte granted Albert a few days' leave at Doberan, a resort by the Baltic Sea whose principal attractions were a beach, a dance band, and a casino. Albert promised Bernadotte not to gamble, but he gambled. A Russian officer picked a quarrel with him; they agreed to settle the matter sword in hand. The duel, which took place in a clearing atop a wooded hillock —'a lovely grove,' Schlegel described it—did not last long: with one blow the Russian virtually cut off Albert's head. He was buried at Doberan before he had completed his twenty-first year. Germaine received the news one evening when she returned to her apartment from Covent Garden. The intensity of her grief cannot be measured by her expressions: she had lavished too many sobs on unworthy causes. Nor was there any noticeable change in her conduct: when the London season began in the autumn, Germaine was in the thick of it. A certain darkening of her mood may be detected in her letters, a growing weariness, confusion, and indecision; but although her son's death undoubtedly stunned and shocked her, she showed no such signs of convulsive despair as at her father's death; the death of Narbonne, Albert's father, in the same year, seems to have affected her almost as much as Albert's.

Nor did the tragedy bring her closer to her remaining children. 'There is no intellectual resource whatever in my children,' she complained to Schlegel. 'They are lifeless: strange result of my own fire! That poor Albert was alive in the wrong way, but at least he was alive!' The following letter to Benjamin betrays more self-pity than grief:

> Poor Albert! . . . Did you cry for him? I do not want to die before seeing you again, without talking with you as in the past. . . . But after that, I would like to die, for you have destroyed me in my innermost soul and you are destroying me still. . . . Farewell! Farewell! I am what I always have been, and even now you can tell yourself that I never shed tears except over the fate of my unfortunate child and over your letters.

Mathieu's comment on hearing the news was to the point, however one chooses to interpret it: 'Unfortunate mother—all the more unfortunate because her grief is not pure!'

 'I have been received like a princess,' Germaine wrote to Schlegel from London on July 2, 'but there always is such a crowd, such a quantity of women, such a monotony in society, that I feel more dizzied than amused.' On November 30 she could report that her book had been 'madly successful—but nothing can remove the weight that oppresses my heart: since our separation and Albert's death I feel isolated. In a word, life hurts me, and I know of no remedy except seeing you again. I always felt that it was you my father intended to close my eyes.'

This growing sense of isolation amid the dazzling society of Regency London was justified by very real sentimental and political causes. Rocca she had sent into exile at Bath immediately after her arrival, partly because of his ill health and partly in deference to English moral sensibilities. Benjamin, more from inertia than from conviction, evaded her repeated requests to join her. Schlegel, intoxicated with his military life, wrote increasingly seldom, and his politics soon put a barrier between them; Auguste, suddenly ambitious, tormented his mother in scene after scene to let him join Bernadotte's headquarters; when she finally yielded, she had to endure the humiliation of seeing his request turned down by Bernadotte. Of Albert's death she was reminded most unpleasantly by his many IOU's, which Schlegel kept forwarding to her for months. 'I shall pay the Hamburg debt,' she wrote to Schlegel, 'but I shall pay no more from now on. My dear friend, we must think of the future of ourselves and of those of our children who have been sensible and obedient.' This dry, practical tone became increasingly dominant in her letters and intimate conversations. She felt lonesome and burned out: to provide for her children, to marry off Albertine, were preoccupations that soon absorbed her more than love, literature, or politics.

Only those closest to her could sense that the fire was nearly burned out. The face she showed to the world might look haggard and tired; from her lips and eyes the fireworks shot forth as always. As she appeared in the eyes of London society, she was the familiar Germaine.

> She interrupted Whitbread [Byron reminisced in 1821]; she declaimed to Lord L[iverpool]; she misunderstood Sheridan's jokes for assent; she harangued, she lectured, she preached English politics to the first of

our English Whig politicians, the day after her arrival in England; and
... preached politics no less to our Tory politicians the day after. The
Sovereign himself, if I am not in error, was not exempt from this flow of
eloquence.

Byron himself, who met her innumerable times during the winter of
1813–14, delighted at first in baiting her, though his original hostility
soon changed into respect and even a teasing affectionateness. *Delphine*
and *Corinne*, he told her, were 'very dangerous productions to be put
into the hands of young women'; by representing all virtuous characters
in *Corinne* as dull and commonplace, she had struck 'an insidious blow
at virtue'. As Byron told Lady Blessington,

> She was so excited and impatient to attempt a refutation that it was only
> by my own volubility I could keep her silent. She interrupted me every
> moment by gesticulating, exclaiming—'*Quelle idée!*' '*Mon Dieu!*'
> '*Ecoutez donc!*' '*Vous m'impatientez!*' . . . I was ready to laugh outright
> at the idea that *I*, who was at that period considered the most *mauvais
> sujet* of the day, should give Madame de Staël a lecture on morals; and
> I knew that this added to her rage.

She clashed with Godwin, who defended Cromwell against her. 'It
is curious to see how naturally Jacobins become the advocates of
tyrants,' she remarked after Godwin left. What Englishmen resented
in her most was her admiration for England: Henry Crabb Robinson,
whom she had known from Weimar days, called her 'a bigoted admirer
of our government, which she considers to be perfect'. More fruitful
was her encounter with William Wilberforce, through whose influence
she spent much of her energies, in the years left her, in the fight for
the abolition of the slave trade. Wilberforce, after his first conversation
with her, at the house of the Duke of Gloucester, was profoundly
impressed: 'The whole scene was intoxicating, even to me. The fever
arising from it is not yet gone.' Her most intimate acquaintance in
intellectual London was Sir James Mackintosh, whom Benjamin had
befriended in his university days at Edinburgh, and who had recently
returned from India to serve in Parliament. The closeness of her friendship for Sir James, an almost daily caller at her apartment on Hanover
Square, was to have its repercussions in her relations with Rocca.

From October until Christmas 1813 Germaine spent a large share
of her time in a round of calls at the great country homes. One day,
invited to Lord Liverpool's estate at Coombe Wood, she missed her
way; only after she had visited what seemed half a dozen wrong

Coombes did she reach the right one, on foot and after nightfall. 'Coombe here, Coombe there, we have been through every Coombe in England,' she muttered as she sat down at table.

Although she was the most invited person of London, her manners surprised Londoners no less than they had surprised the Viennese and the Stockholmers. 'I shall never forget,' says Byron,

> seeing her one day at table with a large party, when the busk (I believe you ladies call it) of her corset forced its way through the top of the corset, and would not descend though pushed by all the force of both hands of the wearer, who became crimson from the operation. After fruitless efforts she turned in despair to the valet de chambre behind her chair, and requested him to draw it out, which could only be done by his passing his hand from behind over her shoulder, and across her chest, when, with a desperate effort, he unsheathed the busk. Had you seen the faces of some of the English ladies of the party, you would have been like me, almost convulsed; while Madame remained perfectly unconscious that she had committed any solecism on *la décence anglaise*.

In the middle of all this, an ordinary person would have found little time to be bored; but Madame de Staël was not an ordinary person, especially when it came to boredom. 'I turn this country over in every direction to see it as something other than a panorama, and so far I have been unsuccessful. . . . What I feel above all is boredom,' she wrote to Rocca. With somewhat more justification, Rocca in his exile experienced the same sentiment. In one of the first of her notes, Germaine traced a programme for him: 'I have received news from my bird and I am satisfied with what has happened. I am as melancholy as an owl over his absence. On July 26 he *must* be here, and his leg *must* be healed, and he *must* have learned English. *But above all he is not allowed to think of Benjamin!*' He must not think of Benjamin, but woe to him if he thought of some other things! 'I trembled when you spoke to me of those young ladies [at Bath]. Do not leave the old bird for them! Where would you find so much tenderness and gratitude as in my poor storm-beaten heart, which has found its only haven in your fidelity? . . . Dear companion of my life, do not abandon the old bird.'

By January 1814 Caliban had settled in London near the old bird; but to keep up appearances, 'Monsieur l'Amant' (as Byron called him) was never allowed to present himself at her apartment otherwise than with hat and cane in hand. At times he rebelled, letting days go by without calling. 'You treat me too cavalierly,' Germaine complained. 'This hurts and chills the heart. Goodbye. I tell you everything, and

you tell me nothing. I love you more than you love me. Bad Caliban!'
And again: 'Do not offend me any more! . . . You have a gift for irritating a person in cold blood for two hours on end, and in the end this
drives one mad.' He even refused to improve his mind. 'I have a right
to speak to you frankly. Yesterday, I suggested that you read a book
which had at least the merit of furnishing us with a topic of conversation. You refuse, with the most illogical reasons I ever heard in my life.
You do not derive any profit from my knowledge.' His politics compromised her: 'Lady Stafford said to the Duchess of Devonshire that
she had been told that you were so violently in favour of Napoleon that
I was afraid of speaking in your presence. Please do be more careful.
You will ruin me if you keep this up.'

Worst, he was jealous. In his simple-minded way he found it difficult
to conceive why Germaine, if she loved him as much as she said she
did, had to surround herself with people from morning to night; nor
why, if she was so surrounded, and had him by her side, she should
send desperate appeals to Schlegel and to Benjamin to join her. To
Mackintosh he behaved quite rudely. When, at a tea in Germaine's
apartment, he refused to greet his rival, Germaine was seriously
annoyed.

> When a man loves a woman [she lectured Caliban], he tries to make her
> happy. . . . I have given you proofs of my attachment that no other man
> has received. I prefer you to everybody, and I am ready to do anything
> for you [read: to marry you] once my daughter is married. But this
> attachment is due only to my feelings, for you have no regard for me.
> You do not know what you are trampling upon. You are too young and
> too presumptuous to know anyone's worth. . . . No matter how well off
> I may be in other ways, *I am dying from the need to be loved*, and because
> I have shown you this need you abuse my weakness.

Germaine's doctrine was, at bottom, very simple. She loved Rocca
more than anyone else, but not to the exclusion of everyone else. To
live she needed others. If Rocca loved her, he would not object to her
need for others. 'Only one thing in me matters to you: that I should
love no one else. But that I should be miserable because you have left
me sad and drained of feeling, that does not bother you. Jealousy comes
from self-love; the fear of being less loved by another is a more delicate
feeling, and that you lack.' In Germaine's metaphysics of love it is
difficult to see in what circumstances a man would be justified in being
jealous. Not even if she wrote to his rival, as she did to Benjamin on
January 8: 'If you had the character of the friend who is faithfully

devoted to me, I would have experienced greater happiness than I deserved. . . . To see you again would mean a rebirth of my spirit and of my ability to hope, which have died in me like all the rest.' She went as far as to promise Benjamin that 'M. de Rocca will conduct himself towards you the same way as towards M. de Montmorency. . . . He has changed completely, and you will recognize neither his manners nor his conversation. Do not think of him as an obstacle.'

In Caliban's innocent philosophy, to be counted as an obstacle by his mistress's friends was one of a man's prerogatives.

Exactly what it was Germaine wanted, no one could say, least of all she herself. At the same time as she asked Schlegel and Benjamin to join her she made projects about going to Germany, travelling in Scotland, in Greece, in Ireland; she seemed completely at a loose end. The course of the war threw her into an even greater confusion of contradictory wishes.

Until Napoleon's catastrophic defeat at Leipzig in October 1813, Germaine had steadfastly blinked an obvious but unpleasant fact: to defeat Napoleon France had to be defeated. When the Allies crossed the Rhine on December 21, it also became obvious that to defeat France, the war must be carried into France. Only then she realized, with sudden horror, that she was in the process of being lionized by the enemies of her country.

Her chief political preoccupation until then had been to defeat Napoleon and to prevent a Bourbon restoration by putting Bernadotte on the throne. To this end the cause of France had to be detached, in the minds of the French as well as of the Allies, from Napoleon's. It was she who wrote to General Moreau in America and, in the name of Alexander I and of Bernadotte, asked the hero of Hohenlinden to take a command against the Emperor whose glory he once had rivalled. Moreau came. He scarcely had taken the field when he was fatally wounded, on August 27; he died four days later. Germaine, though she expressed her 'heart-rending pity' for Moreau's widow in London, seems to have felt no pangs of conscience. The enterprise, however, had started off on the wrong foot. In London she found no supporters for Bernadotte: she abstained carefully from openly promoting his cause. Holland House was virtually Bonapartist; Lord Liverpool was committed to the Bourbons. The enterprise depended entirely on Bernadotte's adroitness and on Alexander's reliability—two feeble reeds.

But she was reckoned a power. In November Count Edouard Dillon called on her on behalf of Monsieur de Blacas, Louis XVIII's prime minister in exile. He invited her to 'lend her pen' to the cause of Louis's restoration. 'Whatever you desire,' he said, 'will be the reward of your condescension.' Germaine replied that she had no influence; Dillon protested that surely the woman whom the English papers called 'the first woman of Europe' could do almost anything. 'I do not mix in politics,' replied Madame de Staël. In conveying this information to Schlegel, she added a significant hint: Dillon had told her that if Bernadotte were willing to restore the Bourbons, he would be 'more King of France than the King himself'. Schlegel began to wonder whether Germaine was for the Bourbons or for Bernadotte.

Two or three weeks after her interview with Dillon the Russians, Austrians, and Prussians crossed the Rhine; even a Bourbon restoration now seemed to Germaine preferable to the ruin of France, especially since the Bourbons had made peace overtures to her. 'The Duc de Berry [Louis XVIII's nephew] came to see me, and I am on fairly good terms with the Bourbons,' she wrote to Benjamin on January 23. 'If they come back, we must submit rather than risk more troubles.'

Ironically it was precisely at this point, when Germaine began to waver in her ambitions for the Bearnese, that her two instruments, Schlegel and Benjamin, joined forces to work on the hero.

Schlegel had scarcely arrived in Stralsund when Bernadotte decorated him with the Order of Gustavus Vasa; henceforth, he instructed Germaine, her letters were to be addressed to the *Chevalier* Schlegel. The news of the armistice of June 4 threw him into a panic; the news of the resumption of hostilities on July 26 filled him with elation. From then on his letters spoke of nothing but horses, battles, marches, victories, and the exhilaration of soldiering. 'I am furious not to have secured a good horse in time,' he exclaims at one point. 'How annoying to be in the rear with the baggage train when the cannon thunders and the villages are burning!' But in the rear he was, from Stralsund to Oranienburg, from Oranienburg to Zerbst (where he proudly showed up at his godmother's, 'uniformed and decorated'), from Zerbst to Leipzig, where Bernadotte's army gave the Allies a decisive superiority in the gigantic three-day battle, and from Leipzig to Göttingen.

At Leipzig he published a fire-eating article in the *Leipzig Gazette*, which he sent to Germaine. His increasingly jingoistic tone had perturbed her for some time. The article was more than she could stomach. 'Prosperity has turned your head, my dear Schlegel,' she replied, and, after praising the eloquence of the article, continued:

All of you have now reached the critical point; what you have done so far was easier than what remains to be done. You want to make Holland an independent monarchy, invade Switzerland, attack France: no doubt as long as the *man* [Napoleon] lives, nothing is accomplished; but it is difficult to knock over twenty-four million people in order to strike at one.

When, on November 2, Bernadotte arrived at Göttingen, Benjamin was absent: his wife had induced him to make a short trip to Brunswick, and he cursed himself for a fool. But he caught up with the hero at Hanover and, between November 6 and 14, had eight interviews with him, notably a dinner tête-à-tête on the thirteenth. The immediate result of the interviews was Benjamin's drafting, on Bernadotte's request, a 'Memorandum on Communications to Be Established with the Interior of France'—a concise outline of a campaign of psychological warfare to isolate Napoleon from the French and to prepare France for a constitutional monarchy under Bernadotte. While still at Hanover, Bernadotte drafted a proclamation to the French, following Benjamin's outline closely, and a week later he notified the King of Prussia of his pretentions to the throne of France.

A series of interviews between Benjamin and Schlegel followed. For once the two saw eye to eye: they had a hatred in common—Napoleon; an aim in common—to make a career on Bernadotte's coat-tails. Encouraged by Schlegel, Benjamin began to work furiously on his celebrated book, *On the Spirit of Conquest and on Usurpation*, outlined already in his memorandum to Bernadotte: the book was to precede the publication of Bernadotte's proclamation to the French. *On the Spirit of Conquest* is unique in the literature of propaganda in that it survived the occasion for which it was written. It is perhaps Benjamin's most brilliant (and also his most prophetic) work; quite appropriately it was reprinted several times in the Second World War. Benjamin took the first chapters to the printer on December 13. On January 21, still at work on the last chapters, he noted: 'Time is pressing, if I want to be there for the kill.' On January 30 he released the proofs for the press: 'I have dropped the bombshell. God's will be done.'

In the first days of February Bernadotte, who in the meantime had campaigned against Denmark and snatched Norway in the Treaty of Kiel, was back in Hanover. The Order of the Polar Star was the only concrete reward Benjamin received for his labour. Still doubtful how far he should commit himself, hesitant also because he saw Bernadotte hesitate, Benjamin retired to Göttingen. But at the end of February, when Napoleon was near the end of his astonishing but futile defensive campaign, Benjamin could no longer stay put. He had to be in at the kill. On February 28 he was on his way to Liège, where Bernadotte stood poised but irresolute.

Bernadotte received him graciously but evaded him. 'I must hop on to another branch,' wrote Benjamin on March 11, the day after Auguste de Staël arrived from London. Prepared for any eventuality, he wrote new memoranda, some in favour of Bernadotte, others in favour of Napoleon's young son. He sent them to Germaine.

In London Germaine was in a moral agony. The Cossacks in the rue Racine! 'Is this a time for speaking ill of France, when the flames of Moscow are threatening Paris? Think well of what you are about to do!' she admonished Benjamin as early as January 23.

> One must not speak ill of France when the Russians are at Langres! May God banish me from France rather than let me return with the aid of foreigners! As for the *man*, what free soul could wish him to be over-thrown by the Cossacks? . . . What a combination of circumstances, that we must tremble at the defeat of such a man! . . . Has not France two arms, one to punish the enemy, the other to overthrow tyranny?

To a member of the British cabinet she said, in the same vein, 'I want Bonaparte to be victorious and to be killed in battle.' The rhetoric was splendid, the solution ingenious—but who had helped to bring the foreigners into France?

When she received one of Benjamin's memoranda, she replied, on March 22:

> I have read your memorandum. God forbid that I should show it. . . . I shall not turn against France in her misfortune. . . . Those burning villages lie on the road along which the women once fell on their knees to see my father ride by. . . . You are not French, Benjamin.

On March 25 Bernadotte made what Benjamin believed to be a 'final decision': he left for France incognito. If he had gone straight to Paris, he might have entered with the Allies on March 31, but he hesitated, stopped at Nancy, realized that his opportunity was lost, and returned. 'Paris taken,' reads Benjamin's diary entry for April 4. 'He comes back without having been there. What a fall! Talleyrand comes out on top. Divine justice! God's will be done.'

Indeed, it was Talleyrand, Germaine's first lover, who single-handed persuaded Tsar Alexander and the French Senate to proclaim Napoleon's deposition and the restoration of Louis XVIII. 'Liberty is not lost,' Benjamin consoled himself. 'Let us try to find a comfortable spot under a peaceful system.' He wrote to Talleyrand and, with Auguste, left for Paris. On April 9 at Brussels he learned of Napoleon's abdication. 'I always predicted it, but I am amazed.' On the fifteenth he was in Paris. He found Talleyrand favourably disposed towards him. 'Let us help the good cause and let us help ourselves,' Benjamin exhorted himself.

From London Germaine wrote to Auguste, 'The blow is cruel. All London is drunk with joy.' She was congratulated on being able to return, at last, to Paris, 'What are you congratulating me on? On my being in despair?' she answered. But she, too, was willing to make her peace. Liberty was not lost. 'The Emperor Alex,' wrote Auguste, 'who is the big wheel here, is, I believe, very well disposed towards you, and a letter from you to him, in the sense of your convictions, that is to say in favour of a free constitution under the Bourbons . . . might produce a good effect.'

With all her eloquent declarations, Germaine did precisely what Benjamin had done: on May 12 she was back in Paris. 'She has changed,' noted Benjamin. 'She is thin and pale. I did not allow myself any emotion. What good would it do?' And five days later, 'She has changed completely. She is absent-minded, almost arid, thinking only of herself, listening little to what others say, caring for nothing, not even for her daughter, except from a sense of duty—and for me, not at all.'

On this note concluded a struggle of nineteen years for Benjamin's love and of eleven years for the lost paradise of Paris.

20

NOT THE PORT BUT THE GRAVE

BENJAMIN was right in finding Madame de Staël completely
changed, but the change was apparent only to those who knew
her well.

To all outward appearances Germaine resumed her way of life
exactly as she had left it twelve years earlier, in the spring of 1802, when
her long exile from Paris began. In her flat at Clichy the victorious
sovereigns and commanders, with the 'Agamemnon of kings', Tsar
Alexander, at their head, attended her teas, her dinners, her balls, her
assemblies; Wellington, Schwarzenberg, Bernadotte, Canning, Gentz,
Talleyrand, Fouché, La Fayette met in her drawing room. The official
Germaine had not changed; nor was she to change to her dying
hour.

The political Germaine, too, remained faithful to the 'character of
her life'. Ostensibly she was at peace with the Bourbons: before leaving
England she had, at Hartwell, made obeisance to Louis XVIII.
Nevertheless, she predicated her allegiance to the restored dynasty on
the condition that it would rule under a liberal constitution. Her great
ally was no longer Bernadotte ('I would rather be wise than brilliant,'
he wrote to her) but Tsar Alexander, whose vehemently liberal pro-
nouncements astonished his fellow monarchs. Germaine did not allow
his enthusiasm to slacken; but when Louis XVIII, under the double
pressure of Alexander and of French public opinion, 'granted' the
constitutional Charter of 1814, Germaine was far from satisfied. Its
provisions, patterned on the English system, she welcomed warmly
enough. Yet by 'granting' the Charter, the King rolled history back to
1789: it seemed to the liberals that the French Revolution had established the nation as sovereign, and that a truly constitutional monarchy
would have to be founded on a contract between the King and the
sovereign people. No sooner had the Charter been promulgated than
Germaine began to attack it as a denial of the French Revolution and,

consequently, as opposed to the thousand-year struggle of the French people for freedom. To vindicate the Revolution as the fulfilment, not the destruction, of the French tradition, she began to write what was to become the Bible of French liberals under the Restoration—her *Considerations on the Principal Events of the French Revolution.*

There were other, more specific political questions that occupied Germaine after her return to Paris. She addressed an open 'Appeal to the Sovereigns Assembled in Paris' for an international convention outlawing the slave trade; spoke eloquently against Prussia's vindictive scheme of dismembering France; and secretly intrigued (largely as a favour to Madame Récamier) for the maintenance of Joachim Murat on the throne of Naples. The labyrinthine negotiations on behalf of Murat became known to Louis XVIII, who towards the end of the year sent her an emissary with the message: 'We attach so little importance to anything you do, say, or write that the government wants to know nothing about it; nor does it wish to give you any fear on this account, or even allow anyone to hinder you in any way in your projects and mysteries.'

Thus, despite the Cossacks camping in the rue Racine, despite the 'sabres and moustaches' of the foreign victors filling the opera house, despite the distressing spectacle of her beloved Paris under the occupation of barbarians, Germaine indulged her principal passion freely. 'I detest talking about politics,' Wellington told her one day. 'But talking politics is my whole life!' exclaimed Germaine. The Iron Duke had to submit, especially since he had fallen in love with Madame Récamier, and Germaine was playing Cupid.[1] In this respect, too, no discernible change had taken place in Germaine. Her passion for politics was the same as it had been in 1789, and it could be said of her, as Talleyrand said of the Bourbons, that she had learned nothing and forgotten nothing.

But her friends noticed a profound change. Her physical transformation was only too obvious: her thinness, her complexion, her weariness betrayed a complete breakdown of her health. If her energy did not flag, this was from sheer will power. Yet even more shocking was the change of her attitude towards her friends. Where once she had been too

---

[1] 'I waited for you last night, fair cruel one,' Germaine wrote to Juliette about that time, 'and Lord Wellington came for you. You will detach me from him if you do not keep your rendezvous with him.' 'Lord Wellington came to see me today to complain loudly about you and to tell me that he will call on me on Thursday to meet you.' From these and similar reproaches it would seem that Wellington was not a very successful suitor.

demanding, she now seemed almost indifferent. She could take them or leave them alone. She criticized them sharply; with Mathieu de Montmorency she almost broke because of his obnoxious Ultra-royalist views. If Benjamin and Prosper had feared that she would resume her pursuit of them as lovers, their fears had been needless. Germaine's friendship for them had become so 'dry', so distinct from love, that they felt a little vexed to see their wishes so well fulfilled. It was to Rocca, they noticed with astonishment, that Germaine was completely devoted—to Rocca, who was wasting away, destroyed by his tuberculosis. Love as she had always understood it, the love from which she expected happiness and serenity, the great elusive goal of her life, she had given up. This was the amazing change that had taken place in Madame de Staël: Corinne had died somewhere between Stockholm and Clichy. Instead of passion, happiness, serene old age, there was only a pathetic, ill-matched couple, a woman of forty-eight, a man of twenty-six, both slowly dying, each nursing the other in the fear of being the survivor.

Almost as intense as her preoccupation with Rocca's health was worry over money and over finding a husband for Albertine. The two million francs which the government owed her, and which she had spent half her life in claiming, now assumed an importance in her mind that sometimes overrode every other consideration. The political upheavals of the past two years had caused her heavy financial losses just at the time when she needed money most: for without a large dowry Albertine could not find a suitable husband. Not only was Germaine concerned over the future of her children, but also she could not marry Rocca until Albertine was married. She had, of course, pressed her claim against the government of Louis XVIII almost as soon as she was back in Paris. The government, though it promised its sympathetic attention, was in no hurry to examine the matter. In the meantime, a suitable candidate for Albertine's hand had presented himself—the young Duc Victor de Broglie, peer of the realm. His father, a liberal follower of the Revolution, had been guillotined in the Reign of Terror; his mother was an old friend of Madame de Staël, who saved her life in 1794. Victor himself was a man of intelligence, nobility, a dash of priggishness, entirely in harmony with Germaine's political views, and ambitious to play a part in his country's affairs. As Germaine wrote to Lady Davy, he was 'the only real *Englishman* in France'; he possessed every conceivable qualification to become the husband of Monsieur Necker's granddaughter save one: he was not rich. By Staëlian standards the courtship between the young people was tepid. Victor, it was rumoured, instead of making love to Albertine, entertained her about the Charter; and Albertine, despite her startlingly unconventional manners, was not a passionate soul. A constant witness to her mother's passions, Benjamin observed, she had grown up to be exaggeratedly sensible. 'Albertine is too reasonable,' Germaine complained; 'I shall force her yet to make a marriage of love.' Yet love or no love, without the dowry there could be no marriage. Albertine, haughty, ill-mannered, red-haired, freckled, and a little too intelligent, was not of the sort that easily find husbands; nor were there too many eligible young men who cared to have Madame de Staël as a mother-in-law.

In her despair Germaine turned to Benjamin. Could he repay the money he owed her, so that her daughter might marry? Benjamin was outraged. Had he not settled his debt by his promise to recognize it in his will? 'Madame de Staël,' he wrote in his diary on July 1, 'has suggested that I guarantee the payment of what I do not owe her. That's a bit thick.' All the same, he promised—or at least she later claimed that he had promised—to repay half the sum owed.

When, to the astonishment of her friends, Germaine left Paris in mid-July to spend the rest of the summer at Coppet, she was exhausted, her lover was deadly ill, her political hopes had been disappointed, and her financial worries were poisoning her existence. What kept her going was no longer hope but a mixture of restlessness and a sense of duty. So much remained to be accomplished, and idleness and solitude were so boring: 'I must keep on rowing,' she wrote to her cousin later that year, 'not until I reach port but until I reach my grave.' Port would have been happiness. There was no port in sight, but the oars had to be manned till they slipped from her lifeless hands.

The villagers of Coppet greeted her with fireworks, flowers, and songs. Geneva received her like a victorious hero and Rocca like the hero's mistress. Schlegel, who had joined her in London late in April, unpacked his military baggage in his book-lined 'Blue Room'; Bonstetten, Sismondi, and Miss Randall returned to their accustomed chambers. To be sure, there was no Benjamin, no Mathieu, no Juliette, no Prosper, no Elzéar; but all England appeared to have invaded the Continent and converged on Geneva, whence its cream flowed over into Coppet. 'I find it difficult to persist in the beautiful love of solitude that brought me here,' Germaine wrote to Madame Récamier—and, truth to tell, she did not persist for long, nor did she try to rest. The constant stream of visitors was not enough to fill her time, since her insomnia had become virtually permanent; she continued her work on *Richard the Lionhearted*, on *Ten Years of Exile*, on the *Considerations*. It was during that summer also that she helped to save the life of the man who had exiled her. One of her visitors having revealed to her a plot to assassinate Napoleon on Elba, Germaine sped off impulsively to the nearby château of Prangins, which her old friend Joseph Bonaparte had bought, and breathlessly offered to fly to Elba to warn the fallen Emperor. Eventually, a less glamorous messenger was dispatched —a Swiss named Boinaud—but Napoleon was informed of her gesture and had his appreciation conveyed to her. Whatever her faults, vindictiveness was not in Germaine's nature, nor was she able to let personal interest interfere with her impulses: her friendship for Joseph, her letters to Murat ('I worship you . . . because you are a true friend of liberty') were hardly calculated to please the Bourbons, on whom her fortune depended.

And yet money was the thought uppermost in her mind. With neither the French government nor Benjamin making the least move to pay their debts, it became a veritable obsession. Her friends could not even suspect the deeper motives of this greed: her fear of dying before she had confirmed her bonds with Rocca and legalized the existence of 'Little Us'. Her youngest child, now two years old, still lived its secret existence as Alphonse Giles, in the care of Pastor Gleyre at Longirod. There is not the least indication that Germaine felt affection for him, but she felt guilt and responsibility; and to Rocca, though he scarcely had ever seen his son, 'Little Us' was the only remaining bond with life. To be able to be near his child was the only wish of his final years. One or two furtive visits to Longirod was all he and Germaine permitted themselves. They found 'Little Us' a strangely quiet child, with a head a little too large for his size, methodical, grave, and timid. He could scarcely speak or understand; the great lady in her strange clothes, the coughing and limping gentleman only frightened him. 'Little Us', either congenitally, or because Madame Gleyre had let him fall on his head, or because he was brought up neglected and in isolation, was a backward child. It is not certain whether Germaine was aware of this. She scarcely knew him.

By September 30 Germaine was back in Clichy, with Rocca, Albertine, and Schlegel, whose dreams of independence had collapsed with Bernadotte's dreams of ruling France. She found the French treasury as evasive as ever; she found the Ultra-royalists in the ascendant; she found Benjamin in a state bordering on lunacy.

Benjamin's chase after success had yielded disappointing results. A new edition of *The Spirit of Conquest*, articles and pamphlets on constitutional government, on the liberty of the press, on ministerial responsibility—a series of brilliant productions that place him in the first rank of political thinkers—nothing brought him tangible rewards. He tried to attach himself to Tsar Alexander, hoping to be offered a position in Russia, since France spurned him. When no offer was made, he redoubled his attentions to Talleyrand and Fouché. These two defrocked ecclesiastics, after serving the Revolution, the Directory, the Consulate, and the Empire, now were the guiding spirits of the government of Louis XVIII. How had they succeeded, and why not Benjamin? 'I feel,' wrote Benjamin, 'that everybody despises me.' Even Madame de Staël loved him no longer, and his wife had stayed behind in Germany, letting herself be courted by the Duke of Cambridge. 'Six weeks from now I must be somebody,' he resolved on July 17.

Exactly six weeks after this diary entry, in the evening of August 31, Benjamin called on Juliette Récamier, who had asked him for a private interview on behalf of Murat's affairs. Summarizing his life in a few jottings of several years later, he related the interview in these words: 'Madame Récamier takes it into her head to make me fall in love with her. I was forty-seven. . . . Her way of acting that evening: "Dare it!" she says to me. I leave her house madly in love. My life completely upset.' For the twelve or thirteen years he had known Juliette, he had observed and judged her coldly and critically, without the least fluttering of love. The belated thunderbolt that struck him on August 31, 1814, was to deprive him of his wits for fourteen months—until November 2, 1815, when he recovered from his infatuation as abruptly as he had succumbed to it.

During the first two weeks of his affliction, Benjamin was still anaesthetized by the elation and hope of new love: 'I feel an unaccustomed heat in my veins,' the ageing sensualist noted with pleasure. But Juliette's immediate motive in arousing this heat was merely to enlist his pen in the service of Murat; when Benjamin responded with an ardour she had not expected, she combined the useful with the agreeable and, with all the virtuosity of a frigid coquette, kept him suspended for fourteen months between hope and despair. Rendezvous promised and not kept, or kept only in the presence of rivals; alternations of sympathy and frivolity, compassion and coldness; hopes held out, then withdrawn, then held out again; playing rival against rival—to these and all the other well-worn tricks Benjamin responded like a marionette even while he saw through them. When Germaine arrived in Paris at the end of September, he had lost all hold on himself. He sought oblivion in gambling, staying up all night at times; he spent entire days and nights in crying fits; he sought to cure himself of love through disgust: 'Another delirious night,' he noted on September 19, a typical entry among many. 'I cry without stopping. . . . I went to a prostitute. I shall sleep with another tonight, and again tomorrow, until the touch of any woman's hand disgusts me.' On October 17, when Juliette received him together with his chief rival, the painter Forbin, a bizarre scene took place: 'I talked with her in his presence, and we exchanged confidences, and both of us described our love to her. Suddenly, I was convulsed with laughter.' On the morrow, unable to contain himself longer, he called on Albertine to unburden his heart. Albertine listened sagely and reported every word to her mother. A week later, in the presence of Auguste (cured by then of his passion for Juliette), Benjamin made his confession to Madame de Staël herself.

Germaine seemed understanding and sympathetic. She also gave a dispassionate analysis of her angelic friend's character: Juliette, she told Benjamin, was incapable of physical love. All she wanted from a man was a substitute; she was stirred pleasurably only by the manifestations of male desire—'an emotion,' noted Benjamin, 'which my timidity often prevents me from giving her'. The more he showed his slavery to her, the more she would repulse him; he must follow a different approach, court another woman, any woman. 'A veritable female roué,' Benjamin commented on Germaine after listening to her advice (which, of course, proved futile). Roué or not, with all her exaltation of love, Germaine had a fairly realistic grasp of its functioning—more realistic than Benjamin's.

Benjamin's folly infuriated her more than she showed in the interview of October 26. Not only was he wasting his talents, which she had so carefully nurtured, for the sake of another woman, but also he was gambling away his fortune instead of paying her the promised 40,000 francs. To break up the love affair, she spoke ill of Benjamin to Juliette after speaking ill of Juliette to Benjamin. She complained of his unscrupulousness in money matters, of his bizarre conduct with Albertine, to whose dowry he refused to contribute but whose innocence he corrupted by his intimate confidences. 'Big fuss raised by Madame de Staël at Juliette's, who was furious against me,' Benjamin noted on

November 14. 'She [Germaine] is a serpent, and her vanity is ferocious. At bottom she hates me, and I pay her back in kind. I must protect my fortune from the claws of this harpy.'

If Germaine found Benjamin's claim that he had no money to spare inconsistent with the sums he lost at gambling, Benjamin found Germaine's financial worries equally inconsistent with her way of life, which continued on its usual lavish scale. Sismondi, then visiting in Paris, reports finding an assembly of about sixty persons at her house on January 14, with Wellington, La Fayette, and Richelieu among the guests; another large assembly on January 19; on February 4 a grand ball that lasted until four in the morning. Rocca, reduced to a skeleton, could not attend these functions; what strength remained to him gave out at midday, when he had to return to bed. But Germaine still clung to the illusion of possible recovery, and towards the end of February she even could hope that their situation would soon be regularized. The government had at last agreed to refund her money.

The prospect of soon receiving the longed-for two millions even restored some cordiality with Benjamin. A brief mirage of the port appeared before her eyes, blotting out the image of the grave. Then, on March 6, a bombshell shattered this vision: news of Napoleon's landing had reached Paris. 'Her consternation is complete,' noted Benjamin, who dined with Germaine on the seventh. 'I fear that her payment may be affected by this.' On March 10 the telegraph reported Napoleon's unopposed advance. 'The debacle is horrible,' wrote Benjamin, and indeed the demoralization of Louis XVIII and his entourage was past belief. Germaine, on the morning of the tenth, was speeding to Coppet, with Rocca, Schlegel, and Albertine, leaving Auguste behind to look after her interests. She felt, so she wrote later in her *Considerations*, as if the earth had opened up to swallow her.

While Germaine was fleeing to Coppet, Benjamin was debating with himself what course to take. The Bonapartist camp was making overtures to him—as, indeed, it also was to Germaine—to lend it the support of his pen. But Juliette was intransigently opposed to the 'Usurper'. He had to impress Juliette. On the day of Germaine's departure he wrote a fervently pro-Bourbon article for the *Journal des Débats*, offering to risk his life 'to repulse the tyrant'. On the nineteenth, the day of the King's ignominious flight to Ghent, a second article by Benjamin appeared, in which he surpassed himself in invective against the Corsican and the traitors who had deserted the King for him. Never, he swore, would he be seen passing into the camp of the wretched traitors, etc., etc. On March 20, amid general jubilation, the Emperor entered the Tuileries.

Benjamin took refuge at the American legation, where the minister, William Harris Crawford, gave him a passport. He had got no closer to America than Angers when he changed his mind and dashed back to Paris. He arrived on March 27, went to see Fouché on the twenty-eighth, and Joseph on the twenty-ninth. Joseph made tempting propositions. On the thirty-first Benjamin handed him an article supporting Napoleon; on April 4 it was published—anonymously—in the *Journal de Paris*. Ten days later: 'Interview with the Emperor. Long conversation. He is an amazing man. Tomorrow, I am to bring him a draft of a constitution.' Several more interviews followed. 'I wanted to rule the world,' the Emperor told the astonished Constant; 'who wouldn't have in my place?' But these dreams were finished; he wanted peace, a stable, liberal constitution. On April 19, after another long conversation, Napoleon announced to Benjamin his nomination to the Conseil d'Etat; he was to sit on the committee in charge of drafting the 'Acte Additionnel', in other words the new constitution; for all practical purposes, he was to write the constitution. Benjamin accepted.

That evening, at Madame Récamier's, he read aloud his novel—*Adolphe*. Victor de Broglie was present. 'We were a dozen or fifteen of us, listening,' he relates. 'The reading had lasted almost three hours. The author was tired. As he approached the end, his emotion increased, and his fatigue increased his emotion. At the end, he could not contain himself: he broke into sobs. The entire audience, itself very moved, was caught by contagion. The room was filled with sobs and groans. Then, suddenly . . . the convulsive sobs turned into peals of hysterical, irrepressible laughter.' Benjamin's own terse diary entry confirms the fantastic scene: 'Read my novel. Hysterics.'

This was the man who wrote the constitution for Napoleon's Hundred-Day Empire—*la benjamine*, as it became popularly known. On April 24 the constitution was in force. Calling on Benjamin, Sismondi was greeted by the sight of a new, gold-embroidered uniform, the uniform of a Conseiller d'Etat, draped over a chair. All was fine except for three things: the precarious situation of the Empire; Juliette Récamier; and Madame de Staël.

On April 20, the day after his nomination to the Conseil d'Etat and the strange reading of *Adolphe*, Benjamin received a letter from

Germaine. She blamed him for selling himself and invited him to pay his debt. 'She would like me to do nothing for my fortune and to give her the little I have,' he summed it up. 'A pretty arrangement. Neither one nor the other.' His reply to Germaine was a flat refusal. Germaine's reply was an outburst of incredulous indignation; she threatened to sue him. 'The war is on between us,' Benjamin noted. 'This suits me. I shall wage it with pleasure.' He advised Germaine to moderate her tone: he had all her love letters, and if she sued him he would make them public. 'I am waiting for her and I will crush her,' he wrote in his diary.

> This last stroke is worthy of you [replied Germaine], really worthy of you. To threaten a woman with intimate letters that could compromise her and her family, so as not to pay her the money he owes her, this is a device Monsieur de Sade has overlooked. . . . When proof is shown to all Europe that you owe me 80,000 francs (34,000 to my father for Hérivaux, 18,000 for your mortgage on Vallombreuse, etc., etc.), I shall declare that a woman cannot expose herself to the blackmail of a man who threatens to publish her letters, and this novel device of making money will be made known. . . . You tell me that for six thousand years women have complained of men who did not love them: but for six thousand years also men have loved money. . . . If you think that I owed it to you to pay you for the pleasure of your company, at least you cannot say that my father owed you 34,000 francs for it.

And then, the final blast: 'Money alone determines your entire life, political as well as private.'

A few days after Benjamin received this letter, the Emperor left for Belgium, to face the English and Prussian armies. On June 18 Benjamin dined at Madame Récamier's; there was talk of a victory—that of Ligny—at the very moment when Napoleon's army fled in a rout from Waterloo. On the nineteenth he went to the comedy and spent the evening with Juliette. On the twentieth he read *Adolphe* to Queen Hortense, then, on returning home, noted: 'A débâcle, it seems, on the 18th. God's will be done.'

The Emperor, back at the Élysée Palace, asked to see him on the twenty-first and again on the twenty-fourth. 'He speaks of his situation with astonishing calm and complete detachment,' remarked the gambler Benjamin on the gambler Bonaparte. While Napoleon fled to La Rochelle and his doom on Saint Helena, Benjamin sped to Haguenau, as a member of the commission sent by the provisional government to negotiate an armistice. He was back in Paris on July 4, succeeded in having himself struck from the list of exiles which the restored Bourbon government had drawn up, began to work on a memorandum to justify his conduct during the Hundred Days, and on July 31, after calling on Decazes, Fouché's successor in the police ministry, resolved in his diary: 'Let us seek election as deputy.'

Germaine's behaviour during the Hundred Days, though less spectacular than Benjamin's, was almost equally mystifying. To understand it one must keep in mind that, unlike Benjamin, she had no desire to play a role in the events; yet she could not entirely avoid taking a position. In her *Considerations* she represented herself as having unwaveringly opposed any attempt at coming to terms with Napoleon. This was not altogether true, but the complexity of her dilemma may excuse her simplification of the truth.

Her dilemma was political, emotional, and financial. 'If Napoleon wins,' she said after learning of his landing, 'liberty is done for; if he loses, national independence is done for.' But Napoleon, realizing that he needed the solid support of liberal opinion, posed as a new man, conciliated his enemies, and announced the advent of peace and liberty. Benjamin was his prize catch, but he also held out bait to Germaine. On March 24 Fouché—who had switched sides again—wrote to her of the interest the Emperor was taking 'in the delicate situation of Mademoiselle de Staël' and hinted strongly at the possibility that Germaine could recover her two millions. Joseph Bonaparte, too, assured her of his brother's gratitude for her generous conduct during his Elban exile. Benjamin's constitution won her grudging approval in several of her letters to friends, although there was no love lost at the time between her and its author and although she never believed that Napoleon would abide by it. In her scepticism she parted company with Sismondi, who, from Paris, was writing enraptured reports on *la benjamine*; with La Fayette, another trusting Benjaminite; with her prospective son-in-law, who likewise rallied to the Usurper; and with her son, who was graciously received by the Emperor and supported Benjamin. Germaine herself wrote to Joseph, probably not quite sincerely, 'the additional articles [i.e., Benjamin's constitution] are everything France needs, exactly what France needs. Your brother's return is prodigious and passes one's imagination. . . . I recommend my son to you.' Madame de Staël's family indignantly denied the authenticity of this letter; but no one can question the authenticity of the letter of April 17 to Madame Récamier: 'If he [Napoleon] accepts the liquidation [of the debt], he may be sure that my gratitude will prevent me from writing or doing anything detrimental to him.' Napoleon, who was short of cash, preferred, however, to continue dangling the money as bait.

Rumours of Germaine's negotiations reached Vienna, where the Congress, shaken into action by Napoleon's landing, was drawing up its final dispositions for Europe. Particularly disquieting was the inexplicable presence of Lucien Bonaparte at Versoix, a stone's throw from Coppet. 'What is he doing here?' the French minister in Switzerland wrote to Talleyrand at Vienna. 'He often meets Madame de Staël, who is almost as brokenhearted over the failure of the marriage as over the delay in her reimbursement. She is a real slut.' Talleyrand, alarmed, wrote to her on April 6 to sound out her disposition. It was easy for Germaine to deny any rumours accusing her of trying to sell her pen to Napoleon. If there was anything for sale, it was not her pen but her silence. Talleyrand need not have feared that Germaine might openly influence European public opinion in Napoleon's favour; caution, if no other reason, would have restrained her. That she attempted to influence events by indirect means cannot be doubted, however.

Whether or not she tried to dissuade England from resuming war on Napoleon will remain a debatable point as long as the mystery of the 'Crawford Letter' is not cleared up. Crawford, the American minister in Paris, was to return to America late in April by way of England. La Fayette, on Joseph Bonaparte's suggestion, asked him to take a package of letters to London in the diplomatic pouch. Crawford agreed. Accompanied by La Fayette, he called on Joseph, who briefed him on what he should say in England in order to encourage the pro-Bonapartist wing of the Whigs, and thus help to assure English neutrality. Among the letters Crawford took to London was one purportedly addressed to him by Madame de Staël but intended to be shown to Castlereagh or even the Regent. The letter argues that France, it left at peace, would develop under a liberal government, and that if war broke out, the whole French nation would rally behind Napoleon. It goes on with an estimate of the French military potential, and of the morale of the army and the civilian population—all highly favourable to Napoleon—and concludes with a plea for peace. As published in the *Letters and Dispatches* of Lord Castlereagh (Volume II, page 336), the letter swarms with errors in grammar that Germaine never would have made; on the other hand, these errors, and other discrepancies, may be due to faulty transcription by a Foreign Office clerk. Some recent authorities tend to accept the letter as genuine.[1] Even if authentic, it scarcely seems damaging to Madame de Staël. Another war and defeat, Germaine foresaw, would be disastrous for France and would result—as indeed it did—in a severe peace and in foreign occupation. Germaine owed no debt to the Bourbons, and a plea for peace did not necessarily signify a change of attitude towards Napoleon. All in all, if the least friendly interpretation is put on her actions during the Hundred Days, Germaine emerged with cleaner hands than most. Even the fulsome letter she addressed to Emperor Alexander ten days before Waterloo, exhorting him to be his own reincarnation—'In the name of you, always be yourself: this is my only prayer'—even this letter was, in the last resort, another plea for clemency towards France.

Whatever the truth about the 'Crawford Letter' and Germaine's stand on Napoleon, another letter, first published in 1931, shows that she was by no means eager for a second restoration of Louis XVIII. Addressed to Madame de Staël, it is dated from Twickenham, July 3, 1815, and its author is the Duke of Orléans, who as Louis Philippe became King of the French in 1830. Having inherited from his father, Philippe Egalité, a tradition of rivalry with the reigning branch of the Bourbon dynasty, he had also learned, during the long years of his exile in England and the United States, to admire the bourgeois liberalism which he was to promote in the first years of the July Monarchy. Already by 1814, when he returned to Paris with the Bourbons, Louis Philippe attracted the favourable attention of the liberal group who sixteen years later put him into power. He remained in Paris, unmolested, for several weeks after Napoleon's return. When it became obvious to Germaine that Napoleon's defeat was inevitable, she tried to cast Louis Philippe in the role she had given Bernadotte two years earlier. She sent Broglie and Auguste to him, and on June 12 she wrote to him personally: he was 'the hand God has chosen to carry out His designs'. The prince's reply, from which these facts are deduced, was polite, grateful, and firmly negative concerning her 'flattering dreams'. 'I am sorry to say,' he added in English (which he wrote better than French) 'that this is quite out of the question.' Like Bernadotte, Louis Philippe would rather be wise than brilliant. All the same, when he rose

---

[1] Notably Paul Gautier, *Madame de Staël et Napoléon*, pp. 386 ff. Madame Lenormant's argument against its authenticity, in *Coppet et Weimar*, pp. 295-9, still seems more convincing. Germaine was in no position to guarantee, as the 'Crawford Letter' does, that Napoleon would abide 'by every comma' of the Treaty of Paris of 1814 between the Allies and Louis XVIII.

to the throne thirteen years after Germaine's death, the men who raised him to it were her friends and political heirs.

While Louis Philippe bided his time at Twickenham, his distant cousin Louis XVIII returned to Paris for a second time. Germaine did not care to revisit Paris under Prussian occupation. Nor was Rocca in a condition to survive another winter in the capital. While Auguste, in Paris, continued to press her claim, she set out for Italy late in September, with Rocca, Schlegel, and Albertine. They were joined, at Pisa, by Auguste, Sismondi, and Victor de Broglie in January 1816. After twenty-seven years Monsieur Necker's two millions had at last been restored to his heir. Victor and Albertine were married on February 15 in a civil ceremony by the French consul at Leghorn, and again, on February 20, in a double religious ceremony, at Pisa, with papal dispensation. *Nunc dimittis*, Germaine might have said. But it was not in her nature to wait for death in idleness.

On September 11, 1815, on the Plain of Vertus, 150,000 Russian troops stood assembled to hear the Mass. The spectacle was watched by the Emperor of Russia, the Emperor of Austria, and the King of Prussia. At Alexander's side, in a blue serge dress and a straw hat, stood Julie de Krüdener, who had inspired the Tsar to hold that awesome ceremony. Ten days later the Holy Alliance was signed. Although Madame de Krüdener can scarcely be said to have been the creator of that strange treaty, she had acted as a catalytic agent and given the alliance its name; she returned to Paris as the prophetess of a new era; sovereigns, dukes, and men and women of fashion crowded her small apartment to hear her announce the fulfilment of the prophecies and describe the exact topography of Paradise. Even Madame de Staël, writing to Madame Récamier from Milan, acknowledged Julie de Krüdener as 'the forerunner of a great religious epoch which is dawning for the human race'.

On the morning of September 5, six days before her appearance on the Plain of Vertus, the prophetess received a strange communication: it was a letter by Benjamin Constant describing the misery of his thraldom to Madame Récamier. During the night of September 4 he had resolved to die. He spent the fifth without food. He was determined to present Juliette with an ultimatum: love me or kill me. If she loved him, he vowed to give 12,000 francs to the poor.

In the days following, Benjamin called on Madame de Krüdener repeatedly. Madame de Krüdener promised to establish a spiritual bond between Benjamin's and Juliette's souls, a task she proposed to accomplish by praying to God and talking to Madame Récamier. Benjamin prayed with rare fervour, sometimes alone, sometimes kneeling beside Madame de Krüdener. On at least one occasion, all three—Madame de Krüdener, Benjamin, and Juliette—prayed together. He felt appeased at times, and Juliette felt sporadic longings for religion and spiritual kinship; but then his 'paroxysms' seized him anew, and Juliette reverted to frivolity. On October 20, having received word from Madame de Krüdener that their prayers had been heard, he wrote her 'a letter of thanksgiving' and sent her some money for the poor. 'Pray God I have not thanked her too soon,' he added in his diary. The next day, at four o'clock, he had his rendezvous with Juliette, who asked him to return at seven, since she was entertaining Prince August of Prussia. He returned at seven, and was put off until nine; he returned at nine, only to hear Juliette tell him that he was compromising her and should stop forcing her to receive him. 'Madame de Krüdener was not a good prophet,' he noted sadly. 'All is finished, then.'

But it seems that not all was finished. If God did not help, perhaps the Devil would. The Duc de Broglie, an upright and truthful man, recounts in his memoirs how, on a black and stormy night, he rode from a country residence to Paris with Auguste de Staël and Benjamin in his carriage. To the accompaniment of the thunder rumbling and the sparks flying from the carriage wheels, Benjamin confided to them in detail his attempts to conjure the Devil and to sell his soul in exchange for Juliette's body.

> No doubt [says Broglie], he meant to pull our legs a little, but at bottom he was laughing at himself, and laughing on the wrong side of the mouth. He was pale, and a sardonic smile flickered across his face. He started out in the bitterly mocking tone of voice characteristic of him; little by little he became serious, and as he explained to us the antics he had performed, the futile experiments he had devised, his recital became so expressive and poignant that, when he had finished, neither he nor we felt inclined to laugh. . . . We reached Paris without another word being spoken.

Of this Benjamin's diaries say nothing, except perhaps for a mention of a 'foolish confidence' made to Auguste.

Fortunately for Benjamin, the newspaper articles he published in September and October got him into hot water with the government. A temporary voluntary exile seemed advisable, perhaps even imperative. God, and possibly also the Devil, having failed to bring Juliette into his arms, Benjamin on October 31 left Paris for the Netherlands. 'Well, I have left . . . I am all amazed.' On November 2: 'I emerge from my delirium.' This was the end of his love for Juliette. On December 1 his wife joined him at Brussels. A few weeks later they embarked for England. In London he revised *Adolphe*, which he read in nearly every drawing room. In May *Adolphe* was published. All Europe immediately identified its heroine with Madame de Staël.

To be in misfortune was a sure title to Germaine's forgiveness. Before Waterloo she had compared Benjamin unfavourably with the Marquis de Sade; after Waterloo she wrote to him conciliatingly, comparing him to Mirabeau, whose greatness was unimpaired by his susceptibility to bribes. 'He is wrong,' she wrote to Juliette, 'if he thinks I could wish him ill at a moment like this.' Even the publication of *Adolphe* left her at least outwardly unruffled. Ellénore, she explained to the sceptics, was plainly modelled on Mrs. Lindsay, not on herself. Her readiness to forgive was all the greater because she no longer needed the money he owed her. Shortly after *Adolphe* was published, Germaine returned from Italy to Coppet, with her son-in-law added to her party. Her two older children were provided for; it remained for her to provide for 'Little Us', now that all obstacles had been removed. Even Rocca's health seemed better; what was more, she wrote to Juliette, he had perfected his mind by reading eight hours a day during his illness. Germaine herself had not been idle: the *Considerations* were nearly finished, and with them her duty to posterity would soon be done too. Peace of a kind was coming to her, but not the peace she had wished. 'At my age,' she wrote to Juliette just before leaving Italy, 'life declines so much that no strong emotion is left except sadness.'

The summer of 1816 at Coppet was like a grand farewell party: the guests enjoyed themselves; the hostess surpassed herself, and when the guests had gone, was left with nothing but the trunks to pack. To entertain—or, at any rate, to titillate—her guests good luck had supplied her with the presence of the most talked-about man in Europe, Lord Byron. In early June, two weeks before Germaine's return, he had arrived in Geneva with Dr. Polidori and took the Villa Diodati, diagonally across the Lake from Coppet. Unlike Genevese society, Germaine welcomed the outcast. 'Byron, whom no one here receives except me, is nevertheless the man who occupies everyone most,' she wrote to the Countess of Albany. His first appearance at Coppet caused a bizarre incident: as he walked into the drawing room where his name had just been announced by a servant, he saw, to his surprise, one of the female guests being carried out in a dead faint. Entering, he 'found the room full of strangers, who had come to stare at me as at some outlandish beast in a raree show'.

The outlandish beast became a familiar guest. 'Since he boasted of his skill as a swimmer and sailor,' says Victor de Broglie in his memoirs, 'he incessantly crossed the lake in every direction and came to Coppet rather frequently. . . . Madame de Staël took a great deal of trouble to bring out the best in him, without succeeding. All in all, once curiosity was satisfied, his company was not attractive, and nobody was pleased to see him come.' Nobody except Germaine, and perhaps Rocca, for whom Byron had a good deal of respect and friendship. If Byron in later years recalled Germaine above all as 'a very kind' woman, it was out of gratitude to the one person in high society who did not regard him as a monster and who treated him with almost motherly solicitude. At the time he did not always repay her in kind. The temptation to tease her was invincible. Thus, when Germaine imprudently lent him a copy of *Adolphe*—a work he came to admire immensely—he mentioned to her, with what he called his '*aimable franchise*', that she was supposed to be the heroine. It 'rendered her furious,' he relates. 'She proved to me how impossible it was that it should be so, which I already knew, and complained of the malice of the world for supposing it possible.' He also told Germaine that there was more morality in *Adolphe* than in anything she had ever written (a not untenable contention), and that 'it ought always to be given to every young woman who had read *Corinne*, as an antidote. Poor de Staël! She came down upon me like an avalanche, whenever I told her one of my amiable truths, sweeping everything before her, with that eloquence that always overwhelmed, but never convinced.'

Byron's mockery was in truth a pose. In actual fact, when Germaine offered to mediate between him and his wife, in an attempt to bring about a reconciliation, he clutched at her proposal with desperate eagerness. There was no mockery in these lines he addressed to Germaine: 'The separation may have been my fault, but it was her own choice. I tried all means to prevent and would do as much and more to end it—a word would do so, but it does not rest with me to pronounce it. You asked me if I thought that Lady B. was attached to me? To this I can only answer that I love her.'

Germaine chose her go-betweens with singular maladroitness; her efforts were rebuffed by Annabella. Byron had left for Italy before the letters containing Annabella's answer arrived; 'but it is probable,' says his latest biographer, Leslie Marchand, 'that Madame de Staël sent them on to him, completing the corrosion of his feelings in regard to his wife'. It is difficult to see how Germaine could have helped forwarding the letters; nor is it likely that there was a person in the world who could have succeeded in the hopeless enterprise she had undertaken.

As in the summer of 1807, so in 1816 these delicate and secret negotiations were carried on against a background of feasts and talk. Among the guests Byron met at Coppet were Lord Lansdowne, Henry Brougham, Pellegrino Rossi, Etienne Dumont, Sismondi, several score of dukes and princes, English and continental, and every liberal in Geneva. The drawing room was a chaos; every language could be heard (though English predominated); the dinner table was too small to accommodate all the guests; the food and service were haphazard; the furniture was unsafe: but it would have been difficult to find a more brilliant assemblage or better conversation. This was the Indian Summer of Coppet, whose afterglow lives on in the nostalgic memoirs of the happy few privileged to witness it. 'She has made Coppet as agreeable as society and talent can make any place on earth,' said Byron. But when he left for Milan on October 5, few guests were left in Coppet. The autumn mists hung over the pale grey lake, and Germaine was packing her trunks.

Five days after Byron's departure Germaine, who had failed to mend his marriage, entered into a curious marital arrangement of her own. In a room of Coppet five persons were gathered: Germaine, John Rocca, Fanny Randall, John's brother Charles, and the Pastor Georges Guillaume Gerlach. After formally declaring their engagement of May 1, 1811, the birth of Louis Alphonse, and the reasons which had prevented them from legalizing their bond until then, Germaine and Rocca were pronounced man and wife by the pastor. The marriage certificate, signed by all five persons present, contains the deposition of the wedded couple; a specific recognition of their child; and the following paragraph:

> 5. [The two parties further state] that they wish to consecrate their union by a religious ceremony and that they are determined to live together as husband and wife and never to part; but that for the very plausible reasons by them enumerated, they are obliged to request that their marriage remain secret for a certain period of time.

'We have judged,' adds the pastor, 'that the moral reasons stated to us are sufficiently strong to omit the usual publicity.'[1]

[1] The document was first published by Pierre Kohler in 1916. Nearly all earlier accounts of Madame de Staël state erroneously that the secret marriage dated from 1811 or 1812, and the error is still being perpetuated.

The 'moral reasons' were implicit rather than explicit in the couple's statement. The existence of 'Little Us', if known to the world, would have created a scandal, as would the discrepancy between the age of the bride and that of the groom. The deeper reason for Germaine's secrecy was, however, her ineradicable revulsion against the loss of status and independence her marriage entailed. She had kept her promise to Rocca, and after her death their child would be recognized (he was, indeed, to become known as 'Madame de Staël's *opus posthumus*'); this much and no more she was prepared to do for the sake of duty—but the 'character of one's life' could not be compromised. Louis Alphonse remained with Pastor Gleyre, and Germaine continued to call herself the Baroness de Staël-Holstein, instead of Madame Rocca —or 'de Rocca', since she had bestowed, on dubious grounds, the *particule nobiliaire* on her secret husband.

Two days after her marriage, she made her last will, beginning with the following preamble:

> I commend my soul to God, Who has lavished His gifts on me in this world and Who has given me a father to whom I owe what I am and what I have, a father who would have saved me from all my errors if I had never turned away from his principles. I have but one counsel to give my children, and this is to have ever present in their minds the conduct, the virtues, and the talents of my father, and to imitate him, each according to his calling and his strength. I have known no one in this world who equalled my father, and every day my respect and love for him become engraved more deeply on my heart. Life teaches much, but to all thinking persons it brings ever closer the will of God—not because their faculties decline, but on the contrary, because they increase.
>
> I am secretly married to Monsieur Albert Jean de Rocca, as is proven by the marriage certificate joined to this testament. Our difference in age and political and private circumstances caused me to keep this marriage secret. But since a son was born from it, Louis Alphonse de Rocca, he must enter into his legitimate rights as my son by virtue of this document.

After this preamble, Germaine proceeded to the distribution of her fortune: to her husband, 82,000 Swiss francs, two estates in Normandy, and the equivalent of 24,000 francs in English funds; to Alphonse, 408,000 Swiss francs in specie; the remainder of the fortune (after deduction of various bequests, including one year's wages to all servants) to be divided between Albertine and Auguste at the ratio of 4 to 6. A codicil, dictated on June 21, 1817, assigned additional cash gifts to Rocca and to Fanny, three years' wages to two of her servants, and all her 'literary papers' to Schlegel. These two documents are the only ones she ever signed by her new name—'Necker de Rocca, my real name.'

Four days after signing her will, Germaine once more was on her way to Paris. This time she brought no hopes with her, only misgivings. The Ultra-royalists, though kept out of his government by Louis XVIII, were in all other respects masters of the field. 'I would speak my mind frankly and say things that are not fashionable these days,' she had written to Juliette late in 1815 to explain her absence from Paris. She had planned another winter in Italy, but her daughter's pregnancy upset her projects; she wanted to be near her when her grandchild was born. 'I am determined to keep silent,' she informed Juliette in the summer of 1816; 'but I can see from the very style of Mathieu what a horrible partisan spirit is reigning in France.' Mathieu, she noted sadly, was 'in the third epoch of his enthusiasms—first liberty, then religion, now ambition'. He soon was to serve Louis XVIII as foreign minister. Their friendship was to be severely strained, for into her trunks Germaine had packed the manuscript of her *Considerations*. As so many times before, her resolution to keep silent could not be taken very seriously, and although she said that she feared to face society, at bottom her heart longed for Paris. Rocca had 'fallen back into his sufferings'—but, she wrote to Juliette, 'I look forward with joy to seeing you again, and Mathieu, despite everything, and Prosper . . . and the streets!'

She arrived late in October, 'dead with fatigue' and 'worn out by opium', and moved into a flat in the rue Royale. Despite her fatigue, despite Rocca's alarming condition, Germaine's activity knew no respite. Her manuscript had to be revised for publication; into it she had put the creed of her lifetime; when she was in her grave and could row no longer, it would teach her successors how to pull on the oars for liberty. Her successors also gathered in her salon: Jordan, Barante, Guizot, Broglie—the men who became known as the 'Doctrinaires' and who eventually overthrew the Bourbon dynasty. At no time had she been as influential as during the decade that followed her death. All her life she had sought to influence the politics of the day; this time she worked for the future.

While she revised her manuscripts, indoctrinated the Doctrinaires, and nursed Rocca, Germaine continued to give her teas, dinners and

Q*

balls. She had time enough, since she could not sleep. 'Every night I suffer from my mother's illness [insomnia], and this lack of sleep makes life too long: there is not enough in it to hold one's interest for twenty-four hours,' she wrote to her cousin. Her heart, moreover, was weakening; her stomach had caused her agonies as early as during her stay in London; and her entire system was undermined by drugs. 'Madame de Staël,' wrote Catherine Rilliet-Huber to Meister, 'has reached the fulfilment of her dreams: her house is the most brilliant of all Paris and is as influential as she wishes to make it; she has no rivals. Her wealth is great. Her daughter is charming. Rocca is passably well. But her health is very poor. . . . She writes to me often, and she would like to come back to Coppet.'

Madame Rilliet's letter is dated February 14, 1817. One week later, on February 21, Germaine went to a reception given by Decazes, Louis XVIII's chief minister. She was walking up the stairs, when suddenly those near her saw her sway and fall. Broglie caught her in his arms; she seemed lifeless. She was carried into her carriage and brought home. Rocca, too ill to attend the reception, heard the commotion as she was carried in to her bed. When he saw her, her eyes were open, but she could neither speak nor move. A cerebral stroke had cut her down as she painfully ascended the steps amid the footmen's shouts and the glitter of the candles. She had not yet completed her fifty-first year.

'How much past there is in a life, however brief it be,' Germaine had written to Juliette one year earlier. In her life there had been more past, both good and bad, than in most: but what little life there was left her atoned, in its horror, for whatever bad there may have been.

She did not cling to life, but life clung to her. Her mind had remained lucid, and her speech returned; but while her craving for activity still possessed her, her body stayed paralysed. For ninety days she lay flat on her back, with continuous nervous cramps in her extremities and with three open bedsores. 'It truly is a punishment of heaven,' she wrote to Miss Berry, 'when the world's most active person finds herself so to speak petrified. . . . But I am not petrified in either mind or heart.' The treatments prescribed by the physicians, who for some incomprehensible reason diagnosed her illness as a liver ailment, defy description. Some of the remedies were merely disgusting (purée of crushed woodlice is a fair example); others, such as the vesicants that tore her flesh, were sadistic. When Jurine, her usual physician in Geneva, reached her bedside at last, her case was hopeless.

On March 1 Albertine gave birth to a daughter. Germaine, unable to come to her side, sent her a portrait of Necker, with this message: 'Look at him when you are in pain.'

When Albertine was again able to go out, the dinners and receptions were resumed on Madame de Staël's insistence, with Albertine doing the honours of the house. After the meals the guests came to Germaine's bedside; immobile, she presided over the conversation. Neither pain nor weakness, nothing short of absolute death could still the urge to think, to speak, to communicate, to inspire. Among her visitors in these last days was Chateaubriand. 'I have always been the same, lively and sad, I have loved God, my father, and liberty'—these were the last words he recalled her saying to him. Another visitor was George Ticknor, of Boston, who left a moving record of his visit. She apologized to him for not being as brilliant as she used to be, then prophesied of America: 'You are the vanguard of the human race. You are the world's future.' When alone, she read. A copy of Fénelon that belonged to her is marked with her underlinings—for underlining was all that her paralysed fingers allowed.

When spring came, her son-in-law moved her to another house, which had a garden, on the rue Neuve-des-Mathurins. Rocca, barely able to stand up himself, accompanied her as she was driven along the paths in a wheel-chair. The thought of outliving him terrified her; the thought of dying while asleep, without seeing him again, terrified her no less. As a result, she refused to sleep, refused even to take opium, despite her pains. At last Rocca devised a stratagem to entice her into sleep. 'He begged her to sleep for at least five minutes, and swore that at the end of the five minutes he would wake her. This he did. Then she slept for ten minutes. Rocca, watch in hand, waked her. Then twenty minutes. Thus, little by little, she became used to sleeping again.' Thus Bonstetten relates, to whom Rocca told the details of Germaine's last days.

On July 13 gangrene had begun to appear on her body. In the afternoon of that day Germaine was in the garden with Rocca; he broke some roses from their stems and placed them on her wheel-chair. After returning into the house, she received Mathieu. The Duke of Orléans also called on her. They talked politics. She expected the Duke of Wellington's visit the next day. In the evening she said to Rocca, 'This winter we shall go to Naples.' She still hoped that the sun would heal his chest. They bade each other good night. Fanny Randall stayed with Germaine, who begged her for a draught of opium. Fanny refused, but Germaine repeated her request for several hours. At last, about midnight, Fanny gave in. She made it a rather strong draught—stronger than the Coppet dose. 'Now are you going to sleep?' asked the spinster. 'Heavily, like a big peasant woman,' said Germaine. Both women fell asleep, Fanny in a chair by the bedside, holding Germaine's hand. A little after five Fanny woke up. Germaine's hand was ice-cold.

It was July 14, twenty-eight years after the people of Paris had carried her father's bust through the streets to witness the storming of the Bastille.

A few days before her death Schlegel received this note: 'I am very alarmed by what I hear. Is there no way to see Madame de Staël? . . . Others see her. . . . I cannot describe to you what I feel. . . . Is it that she does not want to see me? Believe me, the past is a horrible spectre when one fears for those one has made suffer.' The note came from Benjamin.

He was not admitted, for fear his visit might upset her too much. But on the evening of July 14 he was allowed into the house. With the Duc de Broglie he went into the room where Germaine's corpse lay. The two men watched by her side through the night, speaking of the past and of those great questions to which, of the three persons in the room, only the dead one knew the answer.

Schlegel and Auguste escorted the hearse to Coppet, where Rocca and the rest of the family had preceded them. On July 28, in the presence of the Duc de Broglie, a crew of workmen pierced the walled-up door to the Necker mausoleum. The Duke entered, alone. In the black marble basin, still half-full of alcohol, lay Necker and his wife, under a large red cloak. Necker's face was perfectly preserved; Madame Necker's head had sagged and was hidden by the cloak. Broglie stationed a man at the entrance to keep the curious out. Then Germaine's coffin was carried from the house by four municipal councillors of Coppet; only they, Auguste, and Broglie entered the monument. The coffin was placed at Necker's feet. Then the entrance was walled up again; it has not been opened since.

EPILOGUE

IN the summer of 1804, shortly after Necker's death, Madame de Staël allowed Benjamin Constant to examine the papers and correspondence her parents had collected in their lifetime. Here were the love letters of Gibbon to Madame Necker; here were letters and notes from Voltaire, d'Alembert, Diderot, Buffon; here were Madame Necker's diaries and Monsieur Necker's manuscripts; here, tied into small bundles, were the passions and the poses, the ambitions and aspirations, the wit and the folly of men and women who already then, so little time after their death, were legendary figures of a past forever lost. Benjamin, for whom the thought of death was a fist blow in the face of reason and meaning, remarked in his diary, after sampling the old papers: 'What strikes one most in these letters is the uniform stream of life, the interest each one brings to it in turn, and the profound silence that succeeds all this busy monotony.'

Busy monotony, profound silence: if four words can sum up the life and death of Madame de Staël, these are they. But the profound silence was not, in her case, the oblivion that follows the usual brief shock of bereavement. It is difficult to conceive of the effect her death produced on those whose lives she had transformed and dominated. The profound silence they felt reminded them, until they in turn died, of the intensely burning vitality that had been hers—a vitality that had fed on their own, lesser fires and that she had radiated back to them as if she were its sole source. They had come to rely, for their emotions, on her initiative, and when she was gone, they felt that their death, too, had begun. Ten, twenty years after her death, her intimates still mourned the period in their lives when she had been their centre; and to those who wanted to know what Madame de Staël had been like, they could only answer, half in pride, half in regret, that no one who had not known her, had not heard her, had not felt her power, could possibly form the least idea of what she was like.

Sismondi, upon hearing of Benjamin's death in 1830, wrote to a friend, 'When I saw him after Madame de Staël's death, his spirit was so extinguished that I found it difficult to believe he was the same man.' True, it was only after this extinction of his spirit that Benjamin was able to fulfil himself—as Deputy, as spokesman of liberalism, as a popular idol of the Revolution of 1830—and to attain the goal from which, during her lifetime, he had accused Germaine of keeping him: 'to accomplish something for liberty and for my glory'. But this self-fulfilment was in truth the fulfilment of Germaine's political legacy; scarcely a word he spoke or wrote was not dictated by her spirit. When his triumph was accomplished, his disillusionment was complete: his glory consisted in being besieged day and night by job hunters. With the victory of Germaine's libertarian idealism in the July Revolution, the reign of crass materialism had begun. Benjamin died a few months later, broken in body and spirit, and received the honours of a national funeral—a fitting reward for a man who believed that the answer to all human effort was death.

Of Germaine's family only Albertine and Alphonse survived Benjamin. Rocca had died six months after her, at Hyères, where he had gone with 'Little Us', his only interest in life. Subsisting on opium and 'health chocolate', he spent his last weeks watching his frail son through a glass partition. Alphonse, it seemed to him, was developing in body and mind, thanks to his care and to the open air. But although 'Little Us' did better than might have been expected under the care his half-brother Auguste lavished on him, he remained a pathetic, half-finished creature. Methodical to the point of mania, afraid of imaginary threats and dangers, the boy grew into a prudent, timid young man, married a granddaughter of Narbonne, and died in 1838, at the age of twenty-six, childless and unregretted. Auguste, after trifling away his few remaining years as a dilettante, had died in 1827. He too had married; his only son barely survived him. It seemed as if Germaine had drained her children of vitality. Only Albertine showed some of her mother's lustre and played a brilliant part in the political and literary society of Paris in the 1820s and '30s, and her descendants—statesmen, historians, scientists—made up in gifts and distinction what Germaine's sons had lacked. But in her cool virtue, her slightly bigoted piety, and her ostentatious dutifulness, the Duchesse de Broglie, with all her worship of Madame de Staël, bore a closer resemblance to Madame Necker than to her mother. The fire was lacking.

What was the nature of the brilliance Germaine had radiated, and after whose extinction the world seemed tarnished to those who had known her? Why was it that even her political ideals turned into dross as soon as realized? Calculation and selfishness, the qualities she had seen embodied in Napoleon, became the distinctive features of the bourgeois régime of Louis Philippe, which her writings had helped to bring into existence, while those who felt a need for enthusiasm and exaltation turned to the worship of Napoleon. What was it the liberals of 1830 lacked and that she had inspired in the liberals of 1817?

It was, undoubtedly, the faculty of enthusiasm. Byron, shortly after his first meeting with Germaine, wrote to a friend, 'She thinks like a man, but alas! she feels like a woman.' The 'alas!' is gratuitous. It was her feeling like a woman, her passionate feminine exaltation and emotion which communicated its power to her male rationality. There is scarcely any disparaging judgment passed on her by her contemporaries that has not a large element of truth in it: she was supremely egotistic, domineering, histrionic; she was superficial and self-contradictory in her thought; she tended to confuse politics with personal feelings; she exalted, at the same time, nationalism and cosmopolitanism, rationalism and mysticism, aristocracy and equality, utilitarianism and enthusiasm, sobriety and intoxication. The defects of her character, however, were by no means unique to her, though the power of her personality magnified them; and the inconsistencies of her thought have been misunderstood. What made her unique was that she sought essentially moderate goals by the most passionate means. Rarely was love more exalted than by her: yet the goal was not the agonizing passion she knew but the quiet happiness that eluded her. In politics and literature she never pursued extremes but always saw herself as mediator, as a channel of communication: 'The circulation of ideas is, of all kinds of commerce, the one whose benefits are most certain'—thus she declared in one of her last writings, her noble essay on 'The Spirit of Translation'. The circulator of ideas would defeat his own purpose if the ideas he circulated were consistent. Germaine was well aware that she often praised ideas springing from radically opposed principles. But she never ceased to believe that rational men, no matter how opposed in principle, can always agree peacefully on a vast area of ideas and measures, provided they remain free from fanaticism, which sees only the irreconcilable principles, and provided they are inspired by enthusiasm, which alone can vivify the spirit. Freedom, to her, was above all the right of the human spirit to progress; enthusiasm fed it, and fanaticism killed it. In a world where conciliation becomes increasingly difficult because of a fanaticism which is blind to the rational area of agreement and mesmerized by the opposition of principles, in a world where enthusiasm is usurped by fanaticism and where it has been lost by reason, Madame de Staël's passionate defence of moderation has only gained in relevance.

BIBLIOGRAPHIC NOTES

THE purpose of this essay is threefold: to indicate the principal sources used in this book; to acknowledge my heaviest debts; and to serve as a guide to the most important literature on Madame de Staël. I made no attempt to list all the literature known to me, since such a listing would, at any rate, be incomplete, nor even of all the works and articles I consulted, since many of them I found to have been superseded. If I listed only those works I actually cited, my lists would fail to include many works that I found very useful; if I listed all the works I actually consulted, my lists would include many works for which I found no use. I tried to strike a compromise, listing those works and collections of documents which I regard as the principal sources of this work, whether I quoted from them or not.

1. Biographies and General Studies

The first biographer of Madame de Staël was her cousin, Madame Necker de Saussure, whose *Notice sur le caractère et les écrits de Madame de Staël* appeared in 1820 in Volume I of the first and only edition of Madame de Staël's collected works. It is a masterpiece of tactfulness; yet despite its reticences it is by no means uncritical. Madame Necker de Saussure had several advantages over later biographers: she knew Madame de Staël; she possessed uncommon sensibility and psychological insight; and she was extremely intelligent. Recently published documents have brought to light aspects of Madame de Staël's personality with which Madame Necker de Saussure dealt only by indirection; knowledge of them enables one not only to know Germaine more intimately but also to appreciate more fully the penetrating intelligence of her first biographer. Madame Necker de Saussure's *Notice* exemplifies the superiority of well-bred restraint over the vulgar sensationalism of more recent schools of biography: a public character's dirty linen is not, after all, more significant than his public character.

Among later full-fledged biographies, three are particularly worthy of notice—none of them, strangely enough, by a French author. Abel Stevens, *Madame de Staël: A Study of Her Life and Times* (London, 1881), and Lady Charlotte Blennerhassett, *Frau von Staël, ihre Freunde und ihre Bedeutung in Politik und Literatur* (3 vols.; Berlin, 1887),[1] are indispensable to every student of Madame de Staël, even if their ponderous life-and-times approach makes them dull reading. They must be used cautiously, however, for they contain numerous errors of fact, and they have in many respects been superseded by more recently published specialized studies and documents. David G. Larg's two important biographical studies, *Madame de Staël: la vie dans l'œuvre* (1776–1800) (Paris, Champion, 1924)[2] and *Madame de Staël: la seconde vie* (1800–1807) (Paris, Champion, 1928), are stimulating (though often irritating), but they make no attempt at presenting a continuous biographical narrative.

Among authors of specialized studies, three Staëlian scholars stand out. Each has produced a body of work which, in its ensemble, constitutes a complete or near-complete account of Madame de Staël's life. Paul Gautier, besides a number of important articles (published, for the most part, in the *Revue des Deux Mondes* between 1899 and 1906), wrote the authoritative *Madame de Staël et Napoléon* (Paris, 1903) and the useful if less important *Mathieu de Montmorency et Madame de Staël* (Paris, 1908). Pierre Kohler, in his *Madame de Staël et la Suisse* (Lausanne and Paris, 1916), produced what amounts, despite its emphasis on the Swiss background, to a full-scale biography; it is a work of the most impressive scholarship and contains a vast amount of material unknown to earlier writers (and alas! apparently to many later writers too). Finally, the Comtesse Jean de Pange, a direct descendant of Madame de Staël, published a number of works to which I am deeply indebted: *Auguste-Guillaume Schlegel et Madame de Staël d'après des documents inédits* (Paris, Albert, 1938),[3] *Le Dernier Amour de Mme de Staël d'après des documents inédits* (Geneva, La Palatine, 1944), *Madame de Staël et François de Pange: lettres et documents inédits* (Paris, Plon, 1925), *Madame de Staël et la découverte de l'Allemagne* (Paris,

---

[1] English translation (abridged): *Madame de Staël, Her Friends, and Her Influence in Politics and Literature* (3 vols.; London, 1889).

[2] English translation: *Madame de Staël: Her Life as Revealed in Her Work*, 1776–1800 (London, Routledge, 1926; New York, Knopf, 1926).

[3] German translation: *August Wilhelm Schlegel und Frau von Staël* (Hamburg, Goverts, 1940). This translation has the original German text of documents that appear only in French translation in the French version of the book.

Malfère, 1929), and *Monsieur de Staël* (Paris, Editions des Portiques, 1931). All these contain a wealth of new documents from the family archives of Broglie and Coppet.

Among general literary studies of Madame de Staël, undoubtedly Sainte-Beuve's are the most famous; they also contain valuable biographic material and documents. Sainte-Beuve wrote no single large work on Madame de Staël, but he kept returning to her and to her circle again and again. His most important articles are conveniently grouped, in a new edition by Hachette, in a volume of the collection 'Les Grands Ecrivains français par Sainte-Beuve'; the volume is entitled *Madame de Staël* (Paris, n.d.). Sainte-Beuve's articles on Benjamin Constant are scarcely less important (see Section 3, below), and his *Chateaubriand et son groupe littéraire sous l'Empire* also deals at length with Madame de Staël. Other outstanding literary studies include Albert Sorel, *Madame de Staël* (Paris, 1890), and Chapter IV of Joseph Texte, *Jean-Jacques Rousseau et les origines du cosmopolitisme littéraire* (Paris, 1908). There is a superabundance of more specialized criticism—monographs, doctoral dissertations, articles in learned journals, and the like: much of it I have read; much of it I have not read; and none of it properly belongs in a selective bibliography.

2. *Memoirs and Documents*
As much as circumstances permitted, I have based this book on first-hand documents, such as letters and diaries, and on the testimony of contemporaries, mostly memoirs. Madame de Staël herself left important autobiographical writings, notably her *Considérations sur les principaux événements de la Révolution française* and *Dix années d'exil*, both posthumously published; others among her works contain autobiographical data, especially *De l'Allemagne*.

The contemporary memoirs consulted are listed below; their usefulness varies widely, and so does their reliability. Since many of them are available in several editions, and all of them are fairly readily available in the larger libraries, publication dates are given only where they may serve a useful purpose.

Duchesse d'Abrantès, *Mémoires*; George Douglas, eighth duke of Argyll, *Autobiography and Memoirs*; Prosper de Barante, *Souvenirs*; Comtesse de Boigne, *Récits d'une tante*; Charles Victor de Bonstetten, *Souvenirs*; Louis Antoine Fauvelet de Bourrienne, *Mémoires sur Napoléon*; Victor, duc de Broglie, *Souvenirs*; Lord Broughton (John

Cam Hobhouse), *Recollections of a Long Life*; Lord Byron, 'Some Recollections of My Acquaintance with Mme de Staël', *Murray's Magazine*, January 1887; Mme de Chastenay, *Mémoires*; Chateaubriand, *Mémoires d'Outretombe*; Benjamin Constant, *Le Cahier rouge*, *Mémoires sur les Cent-Jours*, and *Fragments des 'Mémoires de Mme Récamier'*; Constant, valet of Napoleon I, *Mémoires sur la vie privée de Napoléon*; Jean-Jacques Coulmann, *Réminiscences*; Marquise de Dax d'Axat, 'Souvenirs sur Madame de Staël', *Revue de Paris*, July 1933; Joseph Fouché, duc d'Otrante, *Mémoires*; J.-B. Galiffe, *D'un siècle à l'autre*; Mme de Genlis, *Mémoires*; Edward Gibbon, *The Autobiographies of Edward Gibbon* (2nd ed.; London, 1897); François Guizot, *Mémoires*; Théodore Iung, *Lucien Bonaparte et ses Mémoires*; Emmanuel, comte de Las Cases, *Mémorial de Sainte-Hélène*; Sir James Mackintosh, *Memoirs*; Pierre Victor Malouet, *Mémoires*; Claude François, baron de Méneval, *Mémoires pour servir à l'histoire de Napoléon Ier*; Metternich, *Mémoires*; Jacques de Norvins, *Mémorial*; Baronne d'Oberkirch, *Mémoires*; Adam Oehlenschläger, *Lebenserinnerungen*; Karoline Pichler, *Denkwürdigkeiten aus meinem Leben*; Mme de Rémusat, *Mémoires*; Catherine Rilliet-Huber, 'Notes sur l'enfance de Madame de Staël', *Occident et Cahiers Staëliens*, II (1934), 41–7, 140–6; Henry Crabb Robinson, *Diary, Reminiscences and Correspondence*; René Savary, duc de Rovigo, *Mémoires*; Talleyrand, *Mémoires*; Antoine Claire, comte Thibaudeau, *Mémoires*, 1799–1815; George Ticknor, *Life, Letters, and Journals*; Karl Varnhagen von Ense, *Denkwürdigkeiten*.

Several works of fiction in which Madame de Staël appears are so close to ascertainable facts that they must be included under the heading of memoirs. I do not consider Madame de Staël's own novels as belonging in this category, for she transformed her experiences into genuine fiction, but I do include, to some extent, Benjamin Constant's *Adolphe* and, most certainly, his *Cécile* (first published in 1951) as well as Madame de Genlis's *Le Château de Coppet en 1807* (Paris, 1831), and an episode from a Swedish novel by Baroness Sophie von Knorring, translated into French as 'Les Illusions' in *Occident et Cahiers Staëliens*, I (1932), 248–63.

As for documents bearing on Madame de Staël and her circle, a vast quantity of them remain unpublished in various family archives—notably at Coppet and Broglie—in private autograph collections, and in public libraries and archives: they are scattered over the world from America to Russia and from Sweden to Portugal. Most of them are letters by, to, and about Madame de Staël; others are police reports and the like. I do not know whether I regret or welcome the fact that I have been unable to examine any but a few of them: it is doubtful whether they would modify in any important way the image of Madame de Staël which the published documents make it possible to evoke; on the other hand, it is certain that several lifetimes would not suffice to track them down and absorb them. I must confess, however, that the few unpublished letters of which I was able to make use—Madame de Staël's letters to Narbonne in the Berg Collection of the New York Public Library—contain some surprising revelations, and that it would be rash to assume that further revelations are unlikely.

Nevertheless, the existence of this unknown material should not obscure the fact that a large body of new documents has been published in the last six decades which here is used for the first time in a full-scale biography. Some of them were published in the more recent works listed above under Section 1, particularly those of Pierre Kohler and of Madame de Pange; many are scattered in periodicals, notably the following:

Nouvelle Revue Française, October 1958: 'Textes d'un "Journal sur l'Allemagne" '; *Revue Bleue*, June 1905: letters of Mme de Staël to Nils von Rosenstein; *Revue d'Histoire Diplomatique*, 1890; letters of Talleyrand to Mme de Staël, from America; *Revue de Genève*, July–December, 1929: letters of Mme de Staël to John Rocca; *Revue de Littérature Comparée*, 1922: correspondence of Mme de Staël with Thomas Jefferson; *Revue de Paris*, 1897; correspondence of Mme de Staël with Tsar Alexander I; ibid., December 1923; letters of Mme de Staël to Adrien de Mun; *Revue des Deux Mondes*, June–July 1932 and March–April 1939: letters of Mme de Staël to M. de Staël; ibid., May–June 1934: letters of Charlotte von Hardenberg to Benjamin Constant. To these should be added the numerous documents published in *Occident et Cahiers Staëliens*, 1931 and years following, nearly all of which are of great interest. The publication, by Victor de Pange, of Madame de Staël's correspondence with the Duke of Wellington (*Revue des Deux Mondes*, January 1958) was, unfortunately, brought to my attention too late to be of benefit to me.

I also am heavily indebted to the following relatively recent works containing primary material on Madame de Staël:

Prosper de Barante *et al.*, *Lettres de Claude-Ignace de Barante . . .; de Mme de Staël . . .; de Prosper de Barante . . .* (Clermont-Ferrand, 1929; privately published for the Dowager Baroness de Barante); Benjamin Constant, *Correspondance de Benjamin Constant et d'Anna*

Lindsay, ed. by the Baronne Constant de Rebecque (Paris, Plon, 1933); Benjamin Constant, *Journaux intimes*, ed. by Alfred Roulin and Charles Roth (Paris, Gallimard, 1952; this edition supersedes all earlier ones); Benjamin Constant, *Lettres à Bernadotte*, ed. by Bengt Hasselrot (Geneva, Droz, 1952); Benjamin Constant, and Rosalie de Constant, *Correspondance*, 1786–1830, ed. by A. and S. Roulin (Paris, Gallimard, 1955); Edward Gibbon, *Le Journal de Gibbon à Lausanne*, ed. by Georges Bonnard (Lausanne, F. Rouge & Cie., 1945); Edward Gibbon, *The Letters of Edward Gibbon*, ed. by J. E. Norton (3 vols.; London, Cassell, 1956, and New York, Macmillan, 1956); Bengt Hasselrot, *Nouveaux Documents sur Benjamin Constant et Madame de Staël* (Copenhagen, Munksgaard, 1952); Othenin, comte d'Haussonville, *Madame de Staël et l'Allemagne* (Paris, Calmann-Lévy, 1928); Othenin, comte d'Haussonville, *Madame de Staël et Monsieur Necker* (Paris, Calmann-Lévy, 1925); Josef Körner, *Krisenjahre der Frühromantik: Briefe aus dem Schlegelkreis* (2 vols.; Brünn, Rohrer, 1936–7); Jean Mistler, *Madame de Staël et Maurice O'Donnell*, 1805–1817, *d'après des lettres inédites* (Paris, Calmann-Lévy, 1926); Gouverneur Morris, *Diary of the French Revolution*, ed. by B. C. Davenport (2 vols.; Boston, Houghton Mifflin, 1939); Elisabeth de Nolde, *Madame de Staël and Benjamin Constant: Unpublished Letters* (New York and London, Putnam, 1907); August Wilhelm Schlegel, *Briefe von und an August Wilhelm Schlegel*, ed. by Josef Körner (2 vols.; Vienna, Amalthea Verlag, 1930); C. L. Simonde de Sismondi, *Epistolario*, ed. by Carlo Pellegrini (4 vols.; Florence, La Nuova Italia, 1933–54); Mme de Staël and Benjamin Constant, *Lettres à un ami*, ed. by Jean Mistler (Neuchâtel, A la Baconnière, 1949); Mme de Staël, *Lettres à Madame Récamier*, ed. by E. Beau de Loménie (Paris, Domat, 1952); Mme de Staël, *Lettres inédites à Henri Meister*, ed. by Paul Usteri and Eugène Ritter (Paris, Hachette, 1904); Mme de Staël, *Lettres inédites à Juste Constant de Rebecque*, ed. by Gustave Rudler (Paris, Droz, 1937); Mme de Staël, *Lettres de Mme de Staël à Benjamin Constant*, ed. by P. L. Léon (Paris, Kra, 1928); Julie Talma, *Lettres de Julie Talma à Benjamin Constant*, ed. by the Baronne Constant de Rebecque (Paris, Plon, 1933); Zacharias Werner, *Briefe*, ed. by Oswald Floeck (2 vols.; Munich, Georg Müller, 1914); Zacharias Werner, *Tagebücher*, ed. by Oswald Floeck (Leipzig, Hiersemann, 1939).

Older works containing primary material—which, however, has been used in earlier biographies—include the following: Mme d'Arblay, *Diary and Letters* (6 vols.; London, 1842–6); Mary Berry, *Extracts of*

the Journals and Correspondence of Miss Berry (3 vols.; London, 1865);
Lady Blessington, *Journal of Correspondence and Conversations between
Lord Byron and the Countess of Blessington* (Cincinnati, 1851); Charles
Victor de Bonstetten, *Briefe an Friederike Brun* (2 vols.; Frankfurt,
1829); Benjamin Constant, *Lettres à Mme Récamier*, ed. by Louise
Colet (Paris, 1864); Benjamin Constant, *Lettres à Mme Récamier*, ed. by
Mme Lenormant (Paris, 1881); Benjamin Constant, *Lettres à sa famille*,
ed by J.-H. Menos (Paris, 1888); Baron A. Du Casse, *Mémoires et
correspondance politique et militaire du roi Joseph* (2nd ed., 10 vols.;
Paris, 1854–5); Baron A. Du Casse, *Supplément à la Correspondance de
Napoléon Ier* (Paris, 1887); Joseph de Gérando, *Lettres inédites et
souvenirs biographiques de Mme Récamier et de Mme de Staël* (Paris and
Metz, 1868); Johann Wolfgang von Goethe, *Briefwechsel mit den
Gebrüdern von Humboldt*, ed. by F. T. Bratanek (Leipzig, 1876);
Johann Wolfgang von Goethe, *Goethe-Jahrbuch 1884* and *Goethe-
Jahrbuch 1887* (Frankfurt, 1884, 1887); Fédor Golovkine, *Lettres
diverses recueillies en Suisse* (Geneva and Paris, 1821); Gustavus III,
King of Sweden, *Collection des écrits politiques, littéraires et dramatiques
de Gustave III, roi de Suède ; suivie de sa correspondance*, Vol. V (Stock-
holm, 1805); M. Isler, ed., *Briefe an Charles de Villers* (Hamburg, 1879);
Mme Charles Lenormant, *Coppet et Weimar : Madame de Staël et la
Grande-Duchesse Louise* (Paris, 1862); Mme Charles Lenormant, *Mme
Récamier, les amis de sa jeunesse et sa correspondance intime* (Paris, 1874);
Mme Charles Lenormant, *Souvenirs et correspondance, tirés des papiers
de Madame Récamier* (2 vols.; Paris, 1859); L. A. Léouzon Le Duc,
Correspondance diplomatique du baron de Staël-Holstein (Paris, 1881);
Thomas Medwin, *Journal of the Conversations with Lord Byron* (2 vols.;
Paris, 1824); Giovanni Monti, ed., *Lettere inedite del Foscolo, del
Giordano e della Signora di Staël a Vincenzo Monti* (Leghorn, 1876);
Thomas Moore, *Letters and Journals of Lord Byron* (2 vols.; London,
1830); Napoleon I, *Correspondance de Napoléon Ier* (32 vols.; Paris,
1858–70); Napoleon I, *Lettres inédites*, ed. by L. de Brotonne (Paris,
1898); Napoleon I, *Lettres inédites*, ed. by L. Lecestre (Paris, 1897);
Comte L. Remacle, *Relations secrètes des agents de Louis XVIII à Paris*
(Paris, 1899); R. G. E. Saint-René-Taillandier, *Lettres inédites de
Sismondi, de Bonstetten, de Mme de Staël et de Mme de Souza à Mme la
comtesse d'Albany* (Paris, 1863); C. L. Simonde de Sismondi, *Fragments
de son journal et correspondance* (Geneva, 1857); Jared Sparks, *The Life
of Gouverneur Morris, with Selections from His Correspondence* (3 vols.;
Boston, 1832).

3. *Other Works on Madame de Staël and on Members of Her Circle*
In addition to the works listed above, I am indebted, in various degrees,
to the following books, devoted either wholly or in part to some
specific aspect of Madame de Staël's life or to the men and women
closest to her:

Lucie Achard, *Rosalie de Constant* (2 vols.; Geneva, 1902); E. A.
Begin, *Charles de Villers, Madame de Rodde et Madame de Staël* (Metz,
1838); Dorette Berthoud, *La Seconde Madame Benjamin Constant*
(Lausanne, Payot, 1943); Jacques de Broglie, *Madame de Staël et sa
cour au château de Chaumont* (Paris, Plon, 1936); E. Caro, *La Fin du
dix-huitème siècle* (Paris, 1881); Edouard Chapuisat, *Madame de Staël
et la police* (Geneva, 1918); Edouard Chapuisat, *Necker* (Paris, Librairie
du Recueil Sirey, 1938); Emile Dard, *Un Confident de l'Empereur: le
comte de Narbonne* (Paris, Plon, 1943); Charles Dejob, *Madame de Staël
et l'Italie* (Paris, 1890); L. Dumont-Wilden, *La Vie de Benjamin
Constant* (Paris, Gallimard, 1931); Heinrich Düntzer, *Zwei Bekehrte:
Zacharias Werner und Sophie von Schardt* (Leipzig, 1873); A. Geffroy,
Gustave III et la Cour de France (2nd ed.; 2 vols.; Paris, 1867); Jean
Gibelin, *L'Esthétique de Schelling et l'Allemagne de Mme de Staël*
(Paris, Champion, 1934); Philippe Godet, *Madame de Charrière et ses
amis* (Geneva, 1906); Alfred Götze, *Ein fremder Gast: Frau von Staël
in Deutschland* (Jena, Frommannsche Buchhandlung, 1928); Othenin,
comte d'Haussonville, *Femmes d'autrefois, femmes d'aujourd'hui* (Paris,
1912); Othenin, comte d'Haussonville, *Le Salon de Madame Necker*
(2 vols.; Paris, 1882; Eng. tr., *The Salon of Madame Necker*, 2 vols.,
London, 1882); R. L. Hawkins, *Madame de Staël and the United States*
(Cambridge, Harvard University Press, 1930); Marie L. Herking,
Charles-Victor de Bonstetten (Lausanne, Concorde, 1921); Edouard
Herriot, *Madame Récamier et ses amis* (2 vols.; Paris, 1904); Constance
Hill, *Juniper Hall* (London, 1904); Ricarda Huch, *Blüthezeit der
Romantik* (2nd ed.; Leipzig, 1901); Pierre Jolly, *Necker* (Paris, Presses
Universitaires de France, 1951); E. J. Knapton, *The Lady of the Holy
Alliance: The Life of Julie de Krüdener* (New York, Columbia Univer-
sity Press, 1939); Pierre Kohler, *Madame de Staël au château de Coppet*
(Paris, Attinger, 1930); Heinrich Küster, *Die politische Rolle der Frau
von Staël in der französischen Revolution* (Greifswald, Hans Alder,
1931); Pierre de Lacretelle, *Madame de Staël et les hommes* (Paris,
Grasset, 1939); E. Lavaquery, *Necker, fourrier de la Révolution* (Paris,
Plon, 1933); Maurice Levaillant, *Une Amitié amoureuse: Madame de
Staël et Madame Récamier* (Paris, Hachette, 1956; Eng. tr., *The Passionate*

Exiles, New York, Farrar, Straus and Cudahy, 1958); Karl Morell, *Karl Viktor von Bonstetten* (Winterthur, 1861); B. Munteano, *Les Idées politiques de Mme de Staël et la Constitution de l'an III* (Paris, Les Belles Lettres, 1931); Sir Harold Nicolson, *Benjamin Constant* (London, Constable, 1949); Carlo Pellegrini, *Madame de Staël: il gruppo cosmopolita di Coppet, l'influenza delle sue idee critiche* (Florence, F. Le Monnier, 1938); Gustave Rudler, *Bibliographie critique des œuvres de Benjamin Constant* (Paris, 1908); Gustave Rudler, *La Jeunesse de Benjamin Constant* (Paris, 1908); Sainte-Beuve, articles on Benjamin Constant in *Causeries du lundi*, Vol. XI, *Nouveaux lundis*, Vols. I and IX, *Portraits contemporains*, Vol. V, and *Portraits littéraires*, Vol. III; Jean-R. de Salis, *Sismondi: la vie et l'œuvre d'un cosmopolite philosophe* (Paris, Champion, 1932); F. D. Scott, *Bernadotte and the Fall of Napoleon* (Harvard University Press, 1935); Georges Solovieff, 'Madame de Staël et Narbonne, ou "Quatre mois de bonheur échappés au naufrage de la vie" (unpublished Master's essay, Columbia University, 1957); Auguste de Staël, *Oeuvres diverses*, Vol. I (Paris, 1829); Maria Amalia Vaz de Carvalho, *Vida do duque de Palmella, d. Pedro de Souza e Holstein* (3 vols.; Lisbon, 1898–1903); A. F. Villemain, 'Monsieur de Narbonne', in *Souvenirs Contemporains*, Part I (new ed., Paris, 1855); Eugène Welvert, *Autour d'une dame d'honneur: Françoise de Chalus, duchesse de Narbonne-Lara, 1734–1821* (Paris, 1910; Eng. tr., *The Vicissitudes of a Lady-in-Waiting*, London and New York, 1912); H. Welschinger, *La Censure sous le Premier Empire* (Paris, 1882); Johannes Wickman, *Mme de Staël och Sverige* (Lund, 1911); Louis Wittmer, *Charles de Villers* (Geneva, Georg, 1908).

The preceding list does not include, for obvious reasons, works on such eminent acquaintances of Madame de Staël as Napoleon, Goethe, Talleyrand, or Lord Byron; nor does it include the large periodical literature, much of which undoubtedly has escaped my attention. Among those articles I found exceptionally useful are the following two: Dina Lanfredini, 'Le Secret de Corinne: Oswald et Prosper de Barante', *Occident et Cahiers Staëliens*, II, No. 3 (1935), 214–28, and Gabrielle Réval, 'Le Secret de Corinne: Oswald et le duc de Palmella', ibid., II, No. 3 (1935), 205–13, No. 4 (1936), 296–306.

4. *Works by Madame de Staël*

It is in Madame de Staël's own works as well as in her letters that she must be sought, and to them I have turned more often and more fruitfully than to her commentators. Paul-Emile Schazman, in his

Bibliographie des œuvres de Mme de Staël (Paris and Neuchâtel, Attinger, 1938), has produced a useful though not impeccable list of Madame de Staël's published works. The principal editions I have used are *Oeuvres complètes de Mme la baronne de Staël*, ed. by Auguste de Staël (17 vols.; Paris, 1820–1); *Oeuvres inédites de Mme la baronne de Staël* (3 vols.; 1820–1); *Dix années d'exil*, new ed. by Paul Gautier (Paris, 1904); and *Des Circonstances actuelles qui peuvent terminer la révolution et des principes qui doivent fonder la république en France* (written in 1799; first published Paris, 1906). A much-needed critical edition of *De l'Allemagne* is in preparation by the Comtesse de Pange. A complete edition of Madame de Staël's known correspondence is in preparation by Mrs. René Jasinski.

INDEX

Adélaïde, Madame, 91
Alborghetti, Count, 302
Alembert, Jean Le Rond d', 24, 68, 200, 461
Alexander I, Emperor of Russia, 176, 438, 443; and Mme de Krüdener, 361, 451; and Narbonne, 410; and Mme de Staël, 416, 419, 421, 438, 451; and Bernadotte, 419, 421
Anckarström, J. J., Count, 110
Anna Amalie, Dowager Duchess of Weimar, 256
Arblay, General d', 118, 124, 126
Arblay, Mme d', see Burney, Frances
Arfwedsson, Ulrica, 94
Artois, Comte d' (Charles X), 78-9
Augereau, P. F. C., 173, 175
August, Prince of Prussia, 281, 338, 345-6, 370, 452; romance with Mme Récamier, 345-6, 369-70
Austen, Jane, 232, 308

Bacon, Sir Francis, 200
Bailly, Sylvain, 102
Balk, Baron de, 281, 377 f., 398, 402
Barante, Claude-Ignace de, 244, 319 f., 322, 329, 377, 379, 397, 403, 407
Barante, Prosper de, 288, 319, 380, 391, 396, 397, 404, 406, 441; as Oswald in Corinne, 300, 309, 322-4, 331-2; infatuation with Mme de Staël, 319-21; at Auxerre, 322; and Mme Récamier, 325, 330, 370-1; and B. Constant, 330, 333; sent abroad, 338; on his role in Corinne, 332; at Coppet (1807), 338, 345; Mme de Staël's attempts to marry him, 377 f.; at Chaumont, 377-8; reaction to Germaine's liaison with Rocca, 404, 406; marries Mlle d'Houdetot, 323, 406; and Doctrinaires, 457
Barnave, A. P. J. M., 102, 105

Barras, P. F. N., Comte de, 153, 155, 158, 164, 171 ff., 174, 213, 225
Barthélemy, François, 171, 173
Beauharnais, Josephine de, see Josephine
Belmonte, Prince, 262, 281
Bentham, Jeremy, 199, 207
Bernadotte, Marshal (Charles XIV of Sweden), 213, 424 ff., 450; and 'General's Plot', 226; Mme de Staël's schemes for, 419, 421-3, 433 f.; her influence on him, 421; joins Coalition, 422; loses his nerve, 436, 438
Bernhardi, Sophie (née Tieck), 267-8, 294, 297
Berry, Mary, 427, 458
Berry, Duc de, 434
Berthier, Marshal, 223, 336
Bertrand de Molleville, A. F., 107-8
Besenval, Pierre Victor de, 83-4
Billaud-Varenne, Jean Nicolas, 114
Blacas, Pierre, Duc de, 434
Blacons, Henri François de, 298, 314
Boehme, Jakob, 342
Böhmer, Augusta, 266, 267
Böhmer, Caroline, see Schelling, Caroline
Boigne, Comtesse de, 277, 404
Boissy d'Anglas, F. A., 155
Bollmann, Erich, 113, 118, 121
Bonaparte, Joseph, 213, 215, 216, 223, 246, 262, 317, 442, 448; friendship with Mme de Staël, 181, 213, 224, 225, intercessions for her, 246, 247, 275
Bonaparte, Lucien, 179, 211, 213, 225, 249, 284, 449
Bonaparte, Napoleon, see Napoleon
Bonstetten, Charles-Victor de, 301, 360, 365, 398, 441, 459; biographic sketch, 285-7; and Sismondi, 290, 293
Boswell, James, 29, 138
Boufflers, Comtesse de, 56 f., 59

Brentano, Bettina, 358
Breteuil, Baron de, 71
Brinckmann, C. G. von, 252, 264
Brissot, J. P., 87, 102, 104, 106, 108
Broglie, Albertine, Duchesse de, *see* Staël, Albertine de
Broglie, Sophie, Duchesse de, 118, 126, 440
Broglie, Victor, Duc de, 3, 342–3, 440–1, 446, 450, 451, 454, 458, 460, 462
Brougham, Henry, 455
Brun, Friderika, 281, 286–7, 293, 360
Brunswick, Duke of, 106, 144–5, 146, 389
Buckle, Henry Thomas, 199 n.
Buffon, Georges Louis Leclerc de, 24, 36, 42, 50, 461
Burke, Edmund, 196, 357
Burney, Charles, 118, 120, 122
Burney, Frances, 118 ff.
Byron, George Gordon, Lord, 310; on Mme de Staël in London, 430, 463; in Coppet (1816), 454; on *Adolphe* and *Corinne*, 454; Mme de Staël's attempt to reconcile Lady Byron with him, 454

Calonne, C. A. de, 71, 74
Cambacérès, J. J. de, 155, 224
Campbell, John (7th Duke of Argyll), 89, 243
Canova, Antonio, 302
Capelle, G. A. B., 398 ff., 408–9, 411 n.
Carnot, Lazare, 171, 173
Castlereagh, Viscount, 396 f., 449
Catherine II, 59
Cazotte, Jacques, 241
Chamisso, Adalbert von, 377–9, 404
Charles, Duke of Sudermania (Charles XIII of Sweden), 94–5, 110, 166, 420
Charles Augustus, Duke of Weimar, 256 f., 269, 364
Charles XIII, King of Sweden, *see* Charles, Duke of Sudermania
Charles XIV, King of Sweden, *see* Bernadotte
Charrière, Mme de (Isabelle van Tuyll; 'Belle van Zuylen'), on Mme Necker, 49; on Mme de Staël, 52, 148; and Benjamin Constant, 138–40, 142, 143, 144, 145, 146, 148, 149; death, 328
Charrière de Bavois, Angélique de, 345
Chateaubriand, François René de, 223, 281, 282, 238; at Coppet, 100, 281, 317; on Mrs. Lindsay, 238; at Mme de Staël's deathbed, 459

Chayla, Achille du, 126
Chénier, André, 155, 159, 160
Chénier, Marie Joseph, 155, 159, 167
Chigi, Prince, 302, 303
Christin, Ferdinand, 244
Clairon, Mlle, 35, 94, 128, 135, 181
Clermont-Tonnerre, Stanislas de, 91, 112
Cobenzl, Ludwig von, 223
Cochon, police minister, 164, 172
Collot d'Herbois, J. M., 114
Comte, Auguste, 200
Condillac, Etienne de, 199, 207, 209
Condorcet, A. N. de, 71, 102, 199–201, 209
Condorcet, Marquise de, 104 f., 108 f.
Consalvi, Cardinal, 303, 304
Constant, Arnold-Juste de, 132–3, 134–44 *passim*, 136–7, 236, 311, 316, 392
Constant, Benjamin, 93, 101, 155, 156, 198, 212–13, 221, 222, 223, 224, 245 f., 268, 270, 276 ff., 280, 287, 290, 292, 293, 295, 296, 297, 310 ff., 321, 322, 323, 325, 326 ff., 341 ff., 365, 366 ff., 380, 400, 404, 406, 431 ff., 440, 441, 442–5; first meeting with Mme de Staël, 131; *Adolphe*, 132, 144, 240, 241, 300, 333, 447, 453, 454; family, 132; childhood and adolescence, 133–7; and Mrs. Trevor, 137; and Mme de Charrière, 138–40, 142–3; bogus suicide attempt, 141; escapade to England, 142; at Brunswick, 143; first marriage, 143; meets Charlotte von Hardenberg, 144–5; divorce, 145; first reactions to Mme de Staël, 148–9; on Mme de Staël, 148, 179, 240, 241, 295, 298; early relations with Mme de Staël, 148–50; swallows opium, 150; activities in Paris (1795), 152, 156, 157; arrested on 13 Vendémiaire, 158; in Switzerland, with Mme de Staël (1795–96), 162–3, 166; political writings, 163, 171; at Hérivaux with Mme de Staël, 169, 171; and Albertine de Staël, 168, 170, 239, 261, 270, 340, 379, 444; unsuccessful candidatures, 170, 178; organizes Club de Salm, 171; and 18 Brumaire, 179; tires of Mme de Staël, 180–1, 220, 221, 240; becomes Tribune, 216; fateful maiden speech, 217; threatened by Napoleon, 224; expelled from Tribunate, 224; as M. de Lebensei, in *Delphine*, 230, 234–5; and Mrs. Lindsay, 238–9, 313–14, 316, 333; his psychology of love, 236; love-hatred relationship with

Germaine, 237–8, 239; and Fouché, 247, 335; accompanies Germaine to Germany, 250–5; in Weimar, 256 ff.; leaves Germaine at Leipzig, 260; brings news of Necker's death, 261, 268; escorts Germaine to Coppet (May 1804), 270; and Schlegel, 269–70, 296 ff.; and Mme Récamier, 284, 443–5; financial disputes with father, 311, 316; with Germaine, at Lyons (1804), 311; in Paris (1804–5), 312–16; renewal of affair with Charlotte, 313–16; diary code, 316; summoned to Auxerre, 321; scenes with Germaine, 326; seduces Charlotte, 328–9; *Cécile*, 328–9, 343; at Rouen and Acosta: scenes with Germaine, 334, 335, 339; writes *Adolphe*, 333; sees Germaine off to Coppet (1807), 336; summoned back to Coppet (1807), 340; his reception, 341; takes up mysticism, 342–3; as Pyrrhus, in *Andromaque*, 343; escape to Lausanne and recapture, 344–5; writes *Walstein*, 347; meets Charlotte in Besançon, 348, 369; Germaine's letters to, from Vienna, 354; joins her at Coppet (1808), 365; secret marriage with Charlotte, 367; marriage revealed to Germaine, 368; agrees to stay with Germaine, 369; ruses and flight, 372 ff.; and debt to Germaine, 374; at Chaumont, 377; meets Germaine at Briare, 391; challenged by Rocca, 406; leaves for Germany (1811), 406; regrets for Mme de Staël, 425–6; her regrets for him, 426, 428, 432–3; joins Bernadotte's cause, 435–6; *On the Spirit of Conquest*, 435; opportunism, 436–7; reunion with Germaine (1814), 437; mad infatuation with Mme Récamier, 443–4, 451–3; quarrels with Germaine over money, 447; and Hundred Days, 446–8; Constitution, 446, 448; hysterical reading of *Adolphe*, 446; publishes *Adolphe* in London, 453; at Germaine's deathbed, 460; on opening Necker's papers, 461; death, 462

Constant, Charles de, 68 f.
Constant, Charlotte de (*née* von Hardenberg, divorced by Baron von Marenholz and by General du Tertre), 330, 333, 339, 340, 343, 370, 374, 388, 391, 443, 453; beginning of affair with B. Constant, 144–5; renewal of love affair (1804–5), 312–14; succumbs to Benjamin, 328–9; meets Benjamin at Besançon, 348, 369;

secret marriage, 367; meeting with Germaine, 368; suicide attempt, 369; Benjamin bored with her, 425–6
Constant, Rosalie de, 156, 223, 288, 345, 372, 374; on Mme de Staël, 101, 168, 169, 279, 344, 345
Constant, Samuel, 132
Constant, Wilhelmine de, *see* Cramm, Wilhelmina von
Constant d'Hermenches, 132, 139
Cooper, William, 274
Corbigny, Prefect, 380, 387–8, 390 f., 397
Correvon, M., 20 f.
Cramm, Wilhelmina von (Mme de Constant), 143, 145, 315
Crawford, W. H., 446, 449, 450
Creutz, Count, 26, 56–8
Curchod, Suzanne, *see* Necker, Suzanne
Custine, A. P. de, General, 104
Custine, François de, 106

Dante, 208, 334
Decazes, Elie, Duc, 448, 458
Delacroix, Eugène, 90 n.
Desportes, French resident in Geneva, 164–5
Diderot, Denis, 24 f., 40 f., 68, 190 ff., 415, 461
Dillon, Edouard de, 433
Ducos, Roger, 179
Dumont, Etienne, 199, 199 n., 207, 455
Du Tertre, Charlotte, *see* Constant, Charlotte de
Du Tertre, Alexandre, 312, 314, 330
Duverrier, Tribune, 216

Enghien, Duc d', 218, 263
Enville, Duchesse d', 20, 65
Esménard, J. A., 386, 389, 399
Eugène, *see* Uginet

Fabri, Amélie, 241
Fénelon, 342, 403, 459
Fersen, Count Axel, 56, 59, 73, 95, 105, 109, 112
Fichte, Johann Gottlieb, 264
Fielding, Henry, 205
Fiévée, Joseph, 227, 228, 302
Flahaut, Comtesse de, 90 f.
Fontaines, Friedrich, 361
Fontanes, Louis de, 210, 213, 249
Forster, Georg, 265
Fouché, Joseph, 213, 215, 217–18, 224, 225,

247, 284, 312, 318, 321, 327, 331, 390;
Mme de Staël on, 218; Napoleon's furious
letters to, about Mme de Staël, 335-6,
358; dismissal (1810), 379, 385, 397; in
1814, 438, 443; during Hundred Days,
448
Fouquier-Tinville, A. Q., 125
Francis I, Emperor of Austria, 214, 422,
451
Frederick William II, King of Prussia,
106 n.
Frederick William III, King of Prussia,
262 f., 422, 451
Frederick the Great, 384

Galiani, Ferdinando, abbé, 24 ff., 40
Galiffe, J. A., 418, 421
Galileo, 202
Gambs, Pastor, 113, 266
Gaudriot, Lieutenant, 248-9
Genlis, Stephanie Félicité de, 51, 225,
225 n., 246
Gentz, Friedrich, 357-8, 412, 438
Geoffrin, Marie Thérèse, 25
Gérando, J. H. de, 221, 251, 281
Gérard, François, 307
Gerlach, tutor of Mme de Staël's children,
220, 220 n., 251
Gibbon, Edward, 26, 38, 100, 116, 118 f.,
129, 132, 133, 461; and Suzanne Curchod,
12-19; Mme de Staël on, 22, 128; on
Mme de Staël, 51
Godwin, William, 199, 430
Goethe, J. W. von, 127, 214, 265, 269, 338,
359, 364, 385; *Werther*, 63, 194, 210, 232,
251; Mme de Staël on, 189, 250, 258;
translates her *Essay on Fiction*, 232;
Wilhelm Meister, 250; avoids Mme de
Staël, 256; on Mme de Staël, 258;
meetings with Mme de Staël, 258-9; Mme
de Staël on *Faust*, 359; on *De l'Allemagne*,
396
Goethe, Katharina Elisabeth, 254
Graves, M. de, 108
Gray, Thomas, 194, 286
Grimm, Melchior, 25, 26, 41
Guadet, M. E., 108
Guibert, Hippolyte de, 51, 72 f., 72-3
Guizot, François, 205, 279, 281, 457
Gustavus III, King of Sweden, 47, 57-8;
and Baron de Staël, 56-9, 92, 93-5, 105,
109-10; Mme de Staël's letters to, 69, 72,
75, 92-3; occult practices at his court, 94-

95; anti-revolutionary policy of, 109;
recalls Staël, 109; murder of, 110, 130
Gustavus IV, King of Sweden, 166, 180
Guyon, Mme, 342, 403

Haller, Emmanuel de, 213
Hardenberg, Charlotte von, *see* Constant,
Charlotte de
Haydn, Josef, 224, 352
Hegel, G. W. F., 200, 264
Heine, Heinrich, 267, 296, 381, 384
Helvétius, Claude Arien, 25
Herder, J. G., 196, 200, 256
Herz, Henrietta, 263
Hochet, Claude, 72 n., 219, 219 n., 227, 275,
299, 300, 302, 303, 304, 317-19, 321, 324,
325, 374, 375, 411; at Coppet, 317; at
Auxerre, 321 ff.
Hoffmann, E. T. A., 264, 363 n.
Holbach, Paul Henri d', 25 f
Horn, Count, 110
Hortense, Queen of Holland, 386, 389 f.,
447
Huber, Catherine, *see* Rilliet-Huber
Humboldt, Wilhelm von, 251, 412

Iffland, August Wilhelm, 364

Jacobi, F. H., 251, 263
Jaucourt, François de, 102, 112 ff., 118, 121,
126, 128, 155, 157
Jefferson, Thomas, 74, 75, 357, 421 n.
Johannot, Mme, 137
Jordan, Camille, 226, 243, 251, 311, 321,
457
Josephine, Empress, 158, 231, 317
Junot, Andoche, 213, 249 f., 285
Junot, Laure, Duchesse d'Abrantès, 248
Jurine, Dr., 407 f., 458

Kant, Immanuel, 196, 252, 264
Knorring, Sophie von, 423
Kochubey, Count, 365
Krüdener, Julie de, 226, 281, 283, 383, 403;
and Mme de Staël, 361, 362, 365; and
Holy Alliance, 451; and B. Constant,
451-2
Kummer, Marie, 361

La Châtre, Mme de, 121
Laclos, Pierre Choderlos de, 232
Lacretelle, Charles de, 70, 227

La Fayette, Marquis de, 112, 438, 445, 449; and events of October 5, 1789, 84, 85, 86, 86 n., 87; tricks Necker into resigning, 87–8; and Narbonne, 101 f., 105 f., 107, 108; at Olmütz, 113, 148; supports B. Constant's Constitution, 448

La Harpe, Frédéric César de, 176–7

Lally-Tollendal, Trophime-Gérard de, 102, 112 ff.

Lamartine, Alphonse de, 206

Lamballe, Princesse de, 44, 72, 115

Lameth brothers, 102, 104; Théodore de, at Juniper Hall, 118

Lamoignon, Auguste de, 238, 314

Langalerie, Charles Gentils de, 342, 361, 383, 403

Lansdowne, Henry, Marquis of, 427, 455

La Revellière-Lépeaux, L. M., 176

Launay, Marquis de, 82

Laval, Vicomtesse de, mother of Mathieu de Montmorency-Laval, 97 f., 130, 149

Laval, Pauline de, 98

Lavater, Johann Kaspar, 127

Lebrun, Charles François, 224, 226, 242, 246

Legendre, Louis, 157

Lenin, V. I., 291 n.

Leopold II, Emperor, 104, 106 n.

Le Ray de Chaumont, James, 274, 376, 379

Lespinasse, Julie de, 72

Lessart, Antoine de, 107, 108, 116

Lessing, G. E., 200

Levin, Rahel, 263, 264, 414

Ligne, Christine de, 354, 360, 412

Ligne, Prince de, 351, 352, 354, 357, 412

Lindsay, Anna, 238–9, 313, 314, 316, 333, 453

Liverpool, Lord, 430, 433

Lock, Mr. and Mrs., 118, 123

Locke, John, 190

Loménie de Brienne, E. C., archbishop of Toulouse, 42, 74 f.

Louis XIV, King of France, 194, 202, 205

Louis XV, King of France, 91

Louis XVI, King of France, 91, 104, 106–11, 225; and Necker, 28, 42 f., 72–4, 80, 81, 84; and Turgot, 41; signs Mme de Staël's marriage contract, 59; and Mme de Staël, 65, 93; opens States-General, 77; and events of October 5, 1789, 84–6; attempted flight, 104, 111; and Duke of Brunswick, 106; declares war on Austria, 106–7; dismisses Narbonne, 108; imprisoned, 111; rescue of, proposed by Mme de Staël, 111–12; trial, 118; execution, 120

Louis XVIII, King of France, 217, 434, 436, 438 ff., 445, 448, 450, 451, 458

Louise, Queen of Prussia, 262, 304

Louise, Duchess of Weimar, 256

Louis Philippe, King of the French (Duke of Orléans), 85, 451, 459, 463

Loys, Antoinette de, 328

Lubomirski, Prince, 413

Luckner, Nicolas, 104, 108

MacCulloch, admirer of Mme de Staël, 224

Mackintosh, Sir James, 136, 196, 430, 432

Magnin, Jeanne Suzanne, 133, 311 f.

Malet, Claude François de, 334

Malouet, Pierre Victor, 78, 111, 126

Mame, printer, 388, 391

Manuel, Pierre Louis, 113–14, 115

Marchais, Mme de, 39

Marenholz, Charlotte von, see Constant, Charlotte de

Marie Antoinette, Queen of France, 47, 72, 77, 83, 105, 108; 112; and Turgot, 41; and Necker, 42, 80; protects Baron de Staël, 57 ff.; signs Mme de Staël's marriage contract, 59; and Mme de Staël, 65, 72, 73, 93, 105, 125, 196; and events of October 5, 1789, 85; and Narbonne, 105, 107; turns down Mme de Staël's rescue offer, 112; trial, 125; executed, 125

Marie Caroline, Queen of Naples, 304

Marie Louise, Empress of France, 382, 382 n., 398

Marmontel, Jean François, 24, 36

Marx, Karl, 200, 291 n.

Matthisson, F. von, 286

Maurepas, J. F. de, 42

Mauvillon, Jacob de, 143

Mayr, Pastor, 361, 363

Meister, Henri 41, 51, 126, 127, 128, 165, 169, 172, 177, 220, 251, 392, 458; takes over *Correspondance Littéraire*, 41; describes post-Thermidorian France, 152

Mendelssohn, Brendel, see Schlegel, Dorothea

Mendelssohn, Henriette, 365

Metternich, Clemens von, 357

Michelet, Jules, 206

Middleton, John Izard, 281, 346, 377
Miloradovich, Mikhail A., 418
Minzoni, Onofrio, 302
Mirabeau, H. G. de, 71, 76, 77, 78, 79, 79 n., 80, 81, 453
Molleville, Bertrand de, 107, 108
Monachon, spy, 164
Montesquieu, 194, 199, 204
Montesquiou, A. P. de, 163, 167, 170 f.
Montesquiou, F. X. M. A., abbé de, 114
Monti, Vincenzo, 302
Montmorency, Adrien de, 284, 321, 377
Montmorency (Montmorency - Laval),
Mathieu de, 97, 102, 130, 149, 150, 155, 157, 169, 170, 221, 245, 253, 284, 286, 321, 328, 335, 360, 377, 387, 427, 429, 433; early career and character, 97-8; love for Pauline de Laval, 98; beginning of liaison with Mme de Staël, 98; hidden by Mme de Staël, 112; at Juniper Hall, 118 f.; escorts Mme de Staël to Boulogne, 120; rescued from Terror by Mme de Staël, 126; at Zurich, 129; religious crisis, 130; and Constant's 'suicide', 150; host to Mme de Staël, 157; tries to counsel her, 169; and 18 Fructidor, 173; at Coppet, 281; at Auxerre, 328; at Chaumont, 377 ff.; and suppression of *De l'Allemagne*, 387; exiled, 399; Ultra-royalism of, 440, 457; last visit to Mme de Staël, 459
Montmorency-Laval, Vicomtesse de, *see* Laval, Vicomtesse de
Montmorin, Armand, de, 78
Montmorin, Mme de, 76
Moreau, Jean Victor, 284, 433
Morellet, André, abbé, 24 ff., 41
Morny, Duc de, 90 n.
Morris, Gouverneur, 43, 52, 91, 92, 274, 337-8
Moultou, Paul, 16, 20 f., 286
Mozart, W. A., 189, 352
Müller, Adam, 358
Müller, Johann von, 262, 291, 297
Mun, Adrien de, 167, 168
Murat, Joachim, 213, 439, 442, 443

Napoleon I, Emperor of the French, 187, 188, 194, 195, 257, 262, 304, 316, 317, 318, 334, 335, 338, 353, 385, 412, 413-14, 417, 418, 463; on Necker family, xiii, 36-7; on Necker, 43 f., 181, 219, 348; on Mme de Staël, 156, 172, 181, 276,

349-50, 382 n.; on 13 Vendémiaire, 158; and 18 Fructidor, 173; Mme de Staël, on, 172, 174, 209-10, 359, 395; meetings with Mme de Staël, 174, 176, 177, 223; reception by Directory, 174; and 18 Brumaire, 178, 212-14; forces Mme de Staël into consistent position, 188; and Ideologues, 209, 225; reaction to *De la littérature*, 209, 210-11; affinities and differences with Mme de Staël, 209; reasons for enmity with her, 212-15; begins to persecute her, 217-19; turns on B. Constant, 224; threatens Mme de Staël, 224, 241; and Concordat of 1801, 225-6; on Necker's *Last Views*, 226-7, 241; on *Delphine*, 241-2; imprisons Christin, 244; ignores Necker's plea, 242; events leading to Mme de Staël's exile, 244-50; murder of Duc d'Enghien, 263; and Mme Récamier, 284-5; refuses residence permit to Mme de Staël (1805) 318; precarious position in 1806-7, 334-5; diatribes concerning Mme de Staël (1807), 335-6; on *Corinne*, 336; browbeats Auguste de Staël, 349-50; reaction to Mme de Staël's interviews with Gentz, 358; liberalizing influence of, 381; and suppression of *De l'Allemagne*, 386-7; nature of his regime and of Mme de Staël's resistance, 396; intensifies persecution, 397; invades Russia, 410; in Russia, 418 f.; Mme de Staël's role in forming 4th Coalition against him, 419-422; Mme de Staël's ambivalent attitude towards, after defeat of Leipzig, 433, 435, 436-7; Mme de Staël warns him of plot, 442; Hundred Days, 446-51; and B. Constant, 447, 448; and Mme de Staël, 448-51
Narbonne (Narbonne-Lara), Louis de, 46 n., 90-2, 97, 102, 103, 155, 198, 200, 221, 266, 281, 286, 305, 323, 400, 462; youth of, 91; beginning of liaison with Mme de Staël, 90-1, 92, 97; and Comtesse de Laval, 97, 149; minister of war, 103, 104-5; policy of (1791-2), 106-8; dismissal, 108; rescue of, by Mme de Staël, 112-13; Mme de Staël eager to join him in England, 116-19; and Mme de Staël, at Juniper Hall, 120-3; promises to join her in Switzerland, 123; procrastinates, 124, 126, 127; at Mézery, 130-1; effect of his conduct on Mme de Staël,

149; as Léonce, in *Delphine*, 222, 229–31; envoy to Tsar Alexander, 410; death, 428

Narbonne-Lara, Comtesse de, 91

Nassau, Anne Pauline Andrienne de, 146, 156, 179, 342, 345, 369, 374, 392

Necker, Charles Frédéric (Karl Friedrich), 4

Necker, Jacques, 1, 2, 10, 22, 32, 99, 100, 147, 163–4, 194, 199, 209, 241, 249–50, 261, 267, 288, 461; relationship with his daughter, 3, 22, 36–7, 38–9, 44–7, 62–3, 147; early career, 6–9; character, 8, 39–40; marriage, 9, 21; rise to prominence, 24, 40–1; appointed Director General of Finance, 27–8, 40, relationship with his wife, 37–9, 46, 50; first administration (1777–81), 40–3; early writings, 41, 43; *Compte rendu au roi*, 41, 42, 71, 74; as economist, 43–4, *On the Importance of Religious Ideas*, 49; as Comte de Sainville, in *Sophie*, 63–4; *The Administration of Finance*, 71; first exile (1787), 71–3; recall to ministry, 68, 74; second administration (1788–9), 74–9; dismissal and flight, 80–4; deposits 2,000,000 francs with Treasury, 81; recall and triumphal return (July 1789), 81–2, loss of popularity, 83–4; and events of October 5, 1789, 84–5; final fall from power (1790), 87–8; settles in Coppet, 99; offers asylum to Staël, 109; flees Coppet, 116; arguments with daughter, over Narbonne, 117–18; requests her return from England, 123; dealings in New York real estate, 128; and death of wife, 129 f.; distressed over daughter's conduct, 169; and Napoleon, 175, 178–9, 181, 217, 219, 224, 242, 348; conduct towards son-in-law, 181; *Course of Religious Morality*, 182, 307; stresses in relations with Mme de Staël, 220; *Last Views on Politics and Finance*, 224, 226–7; last parting with daughter, 245; death, 261, 268–9; posthumous papers, 271, 273; effect of his death on Mme de Staël, 272–5; tomb opened (1817), 460

Necker, Louis (Necker de Germany), 4–5, 7, 27, 164, 281

Necker, Suzanne (*née* Curchod), 9, 32, 116–17, 124, 286, 462; on Necker's character, 8; girlhood, 10–12; love affair with Gibbon, 12–19, 128; moves to Paris, 20; marriage, 21; birth of Germaine, 22–3; religious ideas, 23, 24; salon of, 24–7, 33–4; education of Ger-

maine, 24–5, 28–9, 30, 31, 33, 35, 47; caricatured in *Corinne*, 29–30, 309; relationship with Germaine, 29–31, 44–5, 46; relationship with husband, 37–9; tries to marry Germaine to Pitt, 46–7; last years and death, 49–52, 128–9; strange burial, 50–1, 129; negotiates daughter's marriage, 57–60; as Comtesse de Sainville, in *Sophie*, 63; and events of July 14, 1789, 81–2; scenes with daughter, 118; tomb opened (1817), 460

Necker de Saussure, Albertine, 72, 169, 223, 262, 270, 280–1

Nicolle, publisher, 376, 385, 386, 392, 397

Nietzsche, Friedrich, 205

Noailles, Princesse de, 126

Novalis, 264, 266, 267

O'Brien, admirer of Mme de Staël, 243

O'Donnell von Tyrconnel, Graf Moritz (Count Maurice O'Donnell), 364, 370, 396, 412; love affair with Mme de Staël, 353–9; breaks with her, 360, 370

Oehlenschläger, Adam, 281, 286, 365

Orléans, Louis Philippe, Duc d', *see* Louis Philippe

Orléans, L. P. J., Duc d' (Philippe Egalité), 85, 225, 450

Ossian, 175, 194, 208, 210, 289

Paine, Thomas, 156, 196

Pange, François de, 149, 157–9, 165, 198, 323; on 13 Vendémiaire, 158–9; early career, 159–60; Mme de Staël's unhappy love for, 159–63; illness, last writings, and death, 165–6; influence on Mme de Staël's thought, 201

Pange, Comtesse Jean de, 150, 168 n., 254 n., 382 n., 386 n.

Pellegrini, Isabella, 306

Pertosa, musician, 377, 379

Pestalozzi, J. H., 364

Phillips, Susan, 118, 121, 122, 123, 126–7, 128

Pignatelli, Prince, 339, 345

Pitt, William, 46–8, 57, 63, 73, 118, 153

Pius VII, 226, 244, 396, 399, 399 n.

Polignac, la Princesse de, 72

Portalis, Joseph, 385 f.

Pourrat, Jenny, 140 f.

Pourrat, Madeleine, 141

Racine, Jean, 30, 34, 205, 383, 417; Mme de Staël in tragic roles of, 257, 278–9, 321

R

Randall, Fanny, 377, 379, 387, 388, 398, 405, 407 ff., 441, 455, 457, 459–60

Raynal, Guillaume, abbé, 24, 26, 33, 36, 41, 175, 190

Récamier, Jacques-Rose, 282–3, 285, 285 n., 346, 369

Récamier, Juliette, 98, 246, 249, 278, 281, 325–6, 330, 339, 389, 399, 403, 408 n., 443, 446–7, 448, 451, 457; relationship with Mme de Staël, 229, 283–4; biographic sketch (to 1807), 282–5; elements of, in *Delphine* and *Corinne*, 283, 309; at Auxerre, 321; and Prosper de Barante, 325–6, 373–4, 377; excursion to Mont Blanc, 339; in *Andromaque*, 343; in *Phèdre*, 346; romance with Prince August, 345–6, 370–1, at Coppet (1809), 371; at Chaumont, 377–8; and Auguste de Staël, 378–9, 408 n., 424; at Blois, 379; tries to save *De l'Allemagne*, 386, 389; exiled, 399; and Murat, 439, 443; and Wellington, 439 n.; B. Constant's passion for, 443–5, 451

Regnault de Saint-Jean d'Angély, M. L. E., 246, 249, 312, 389

Reuterholm, G. A., Baron, 94, 95

Rewbell, Jean François, 164, 171, 172

Ribbing, Adolf Ludvig, Count, 110, 130, 149, 155, 160

Richardson, Samuel, 30, 194, 205

Richter, Jean Paul, 169, 232, 361

Rilliet-Huber, Catherine, 32–4, 150, 280, 392, 458

Ritter, Karl, 293

Rivarol, Antoine de, 103

Robertson, Dr., 243–4

Robespierre, Maximilien de, 76, 114, 130, 148, 151, 196, 217

Robinson, Henry Crabb, 189, 259–60, 430

Rocca, Charles, 455

Rocca, John, 441, 445; early years, 400–1; falls in love with Mme de Staël, 402; becomes her lover, 404–6; gets her with child, 407; joins Germaine in flight, 411 ff.; in Russia, 417, 418; at Stockholm, 423; to England, 424; difficulties with Germaine, 426; at Bath, 429, 431–2; in London, 432; quarrels with Germaine, 432–3; illness of, 440, 445, 453, 457, 458; at Coppet (1814), 442–3, (1816), 462; secret marriage with Germaine (1816), 455; and Germaine's last illness, 459; death, 462

Rocca, Louis Alphonse, 408, 442, 455–6, 462

Rochambeau, J. B. D. de, 104, 108

Rodde, Dorothea von, 252

Rœderer, Pierre Louis, 155, 167, 171, 213, 217

Roland, Mme, 108

Rosenstein, Nils von, 93

Rossi, Pellegrino, 455

Rostopchin, Feodor V., 418

Rousseau, Jean-Jacques, 288, 362, 364; intervention in Gibbon-Curchod quarrel, 16–17; *Emile*, 23, 28–9, 191; influence on Mme de Staël, 30, 49, 51, 96, 190–5 197, 202, 203, 207, 230; *Second Discourse*, 43, 191; *Nouvelle Héloïse*, 63, 191, 193, 194, 232; *Social Contract*, 191, 193

Sabran, Delphine de, 218, 218 n.

Sabran, Elzéar de, 278, 321, 335 n., 339, 347, 360, 365, 377–8

Sainte-Beuve, C. A. de, 98, 139, 150, 188, 237, 286, 392 n.

Saint-Martin, Louis Claude, 342, 365

Saint-Pierre, Bernardin de, 190

Saint-Simon, Comte de, 200

Salaberry, C. H. de, 379

Saurin, Mme, 138,

Savary, René, Duc de Rovigo, 379 f., 387 ff., 391, 397, 398, 419

Schelling, Caroline (*née* Michaelis, widowed Böhmer, divorced by A. W. Schlegel), 265–7, 270, 350

Schelling, F. W. J., 252, 264, 267, 270, 350

Schiller, Friedrich von, 255, 256, 257, 258, 259, 260, 265, 347, 355, 385; on Mme de Staël, 256, 258

Schlegel, August Wilhelm, 278, 288, 290, 320, 350, 359, 360, 361, 372, 375, 383, 384, 407, 424, 427, 432, 433, 434, 435, 445, 451, 460; Mme de Staël on, 265, 267–8, 294–6, 407; biographical sketch (up to 1804), 265–8; Heine on, 267, 296; and Mme de Staël, 267–8; journey to Coppet (1804), 268; and Sismondi, 290, 292; relationship with Mme de Staël, 267 ff., 293–6, 377–8, 382; in Italy, 300, 302, 303; at Auxerre, 321, 327; takes Albert on walking tour, 339; and Benjamin, at Dôle, 340–1; in Munich, 350; in Vienna (1808), 355–6; mystic tendencies, 360–1, 365; at Chaumont, 377–9; influence on *De l'Allemagne*, 382–5; ordered to leave

Coppet, 398; and Rocca, 405, 411; and Germaine's flight, 411 ff., 417; in Bernadotte's service, 420–2, 424; return to Coppet (1814), 441; in Germaine's will, 457

Schlegel, Caroline, *see* Schelling, Caroline

Schlegel, Dorothea, 266, 296, 355

Schlegel, Friedrich, 266, 294, 296–7

Sérilly, Anne-Marie de, 160 ff.

Shaftesbury, 3rd Earl of, 190

Shakespeare, 194, 202, 267, 296

Sheffield, Lord, 100, 122

Siéyès, abbé, 77, 101, 155, 179, 213, 216

Simiane, Mme de, 126

Simonde, Gédéon, 288–9

Sismondi, Jean-Charles-Léonard Simonde de, 295, 320, 327, 365, 377, 398, 400, 406, 445, 448, 455; on B. Constant, 240, 462; on Mme Necker de Saussure, 280; and Bonstetten, 287, 290, 293; biographic sketch, 288–93; *History of the Italian Republics*, 289, 291, 356; love for Mme de Staël, 292; criticizes Mme de Staël, 292; and Schlegel, 293–4, 295, 361; with Mme de Staël in Italy, 301, 303, 303 n., 304, 309; in Vienna, 356; on America, 375; supports Benjamin's Constitution, 448

Souza e Holstein, Pedro de, Duque de Palmella, 303–5, 318, 320, 326, 327

Spinoza, Benedict de, 208 n.

Staël, Albert de, 92, 124, 245, 265, 408; birth, 119; character, 220; at Auxerre, 321; Schlegel on, 339; in Vienna, 347, 352, 357, 359; backwardness of, 372; attempts to save *De l'Allemagne*, 389–90; joins mother in flight, 411 ff.; enters Swedish service, 420, 422; at Stockholm, 424; indiscipline and dissipations, 427–8; duel and death, 428; his mother, on his death, 428–9

Staël, Albertine de (Duchesse de Broglie), 220, 239, 245, 249, 263, 270, 340, 377, 411 f., 429, 445; birth, 170; in Germany, 251–3; slaps Prussian Crown Prince, 263, 424; acts in mother's plays, 278, 352; in Italy, 300, 302; at Auxerre, 321; in Vienna, 352–3; at Blois, 379; accompanies mother on flight, 411; in storm on Baltic, 420; at Stockholm, 423–4; obstacles to marriage, 440, 441, 449; marriage, 451; in mother's will, 456; birth of daughter, 459; later life, 462

Staël, Auguste de, 73, 88, 92, 93, 116, 124, 220, 245, 337, 340, 344, 379–80, 429, 452, 462; in Germany, 251; sent to Paris (1805), 317; pleads with Napoleon, 349, in love with Mme Récamier, 378–9, 408 n., 424; attempts to save *De l'Allemagne*, 387; and mother's flight, 411 f.; joins mother at Stockholm, 424; joins Bernadotte in Liége, 436; to Paris, 437; during Hundred Days, 445, 450–1; secures repayment of government debt, 451; inheritance, 456; death, 462

Staël, Baron de (Eric Magnus Staël von Holstein), 45, 47, 100, 230, 239; Mme de Staël on, 48; early career, 55–7; campaign for Mlle Necker's hand, 47, 57–9; appointed ambassador, 59; early years of marriage, 60; jealousy of, 72, 92, 130; paternity of his children, 73, 92, 116; 168, 168 n., 170; follows Necker on flight to Basel, 81–2, 92; and Mlle Clairon, 94, 128, 180, 181; occult practices, 94–5; pro-revolutionary policy, 105; first recall of (1792), 109; reappointed ambassador, 110; wife considers divorce, 116, 169; demands wife's return from England, 123; meets her at Berne, 124; wanderings, 127; resumes embassy (1795), 155; embarrassed by wife's politics, 151 ff., 165; relieved of post, 166; and birth of Albertine, 170; debts, 179–80, 246; reappointed minister (1797), 180; final dismissal, 180; misery of final years, 180–1; separation from wife, 181; death, 182, 226

Staël, Edwige-Gustavine de, 73–4

Staël, Germaine de (Anne Louise Germaine Necker, Baronne de Staël-Holstein), birth, 22–3; upbringing, 23–4, 27, 28–9; marriage projects, 47–9; at twenty: character and appearance, 52; marriage negotiations, 57–60; marriage, 60; beginning of social career, 65–8; as conversationalist, 69–70, 293; letters to King Gustavus of Sweden, late 1780's, 69; at Court (1786–7), 72; birth of first child, 73; at opening of States-General, 76–7; on June 23, 1789, 80; and events of July 14, 81–2; and events of October 4–5, 1789, 84–6; birth of Auguste, 88; at Coppet (1790–1), 99–101; in Paris (1791–2): role in political events, 101–9; on June 20, 1792, 110; effort to rescue royal family, 111–12; and September Massacres, 112–

113; at Coppet and Rolle (Sept.–Dec. 1792), 116–20; birth of Albert, 119; at Juniper Hall, 120–3; rescues victims of Terror, 126; at Coppet and Lausanne (1793–4), 126–7; at Zurich (1794), 128; at Mézery (1794–5), 129–31, 149–50; returns to Paris (1795), 152–5; political activities, 157–9; exiled, 164; in Switzerland (1796), 162–6; at Hérivaux (1797), 167; return to Paris, 167; birth of Albertine, 170; politics, 170 ff.; secures Talleyrand's appointment, 172; and 18 Fructidor, 173; meets Bonaparte, 174; and invasion of Switzerland (1798), 177; wanderings (1798–9), 179–80; 18 Brumaire, and return to Paris, 179; separates from husband, 181; death of husband, 182; as a thinker, 187–210; begins opposition to Napoleon, 216; ostracized, 217–18; returns to Coppet (May 1800), 219; learns German, 220, 250; back in Paris (1800–1), 223; in Coppet (1801), 224; returns to Paris, 224; threatened by Bonaparte, 225; and 'Generals' Plot', 226; returns to Coppet (May 1802), 226; defies Bonaparte, 227; reception of *Delphine*, 227; attempts to conciliate Bonaparte, 242; affairs with O'Brien and Dr. Robertson, 243–4; at Mafliers (Sept.–Oct. 1803), 245–9; exiled, leaves for Germany, 250; at Metz, with Villers, 252–3; Frankfurt, 253; impressions of Germany, 254, 255–8; Weimar, 256–60; Berlin, 251–5, 267–8; learns of father's death, 269; return to Coppet, 270 ff.; her grief, 271, 272–3; management of her fortune, 273–4; life at Coppet (general description), 275–9; dramatic performances, 258–9; guests at Coppet, 279–83, 286 ff.; leaves for Italy (Dec. 1804), 297; impressions of Italy, 299–303; friendship with Monti, 302; reception in Rome, 302; Naples, 304; return to Coppet (June 1805), 317; seeks end of exile and return of Necker's 2,000,000-franc deposit, 318; theatricals in Geneva (winter 1805–6), 320–1; at Auxerre (April–August 1806), 321–6; moves to Rouen, 326; moves to Acosta (Nov. 1806), 331; leads opposition to Napoleon, 334; sneaks into Paris, 335; leaves for Coppet (April 1807), 336; plans to visit U.S., 337; Coppet and Ouchy in 1807, 337–9; excursion to Mont Blanc, 339; in *Andromaque*, 343; great scene with Benjamin, 343–4; in Munich (Dec. 1807), 350; in Vienna, 350–7; meets Gentz at Teplitz, 357; Napoleon's reaction, 358; crosses Germany, 358; at Interlaken, 360, Coppet in 1808: mysticism, 360–2, 363–4; learns of Benjamin's marriage (May 1809), 368; at Lyons (June 1809), 369; Coppet in 1809, 369 ff.; Geneva (winter 1809–10), 373–4; plans trip to U.S., 375; Chaumont (April–August 1810), 376–9; *petite poste*, 378–9; moves to Fossé, 379; suppression of *De l'Allemagne*, 385–91; exiled, 390–1; return to Geneva (Oct. 1810), 391–2, 397; resistance to Napoleon, 398, 399; increasing persecution, 398–400; has child by Rocca, 407–8; flight (May 1812), 409 ff.; Vienna, 412–13; Poland, 413; Russia, 414–19; Moscow, 418; St. Petersburg, 418; sees Alexander I, 419; schemes on behalf of Bernadotte, 419 ff.; Stockholm (Sept. 1812–May 1813), 419–424; London, 427–37; death of Albert, 428–9; Byron's comments, 430, 463; role in Coalition politics, 433–4; makes peace with the Bourbons, 437, 439; returns to Paris (May 1814), 437; hostess to kings, 438; liberal politics, 440; money difficulties, 441; Coppet in 1814, 441–2; Paris 1814–15, 442–5; Hundred Days, 446, 448; Crawford letter, 449–50; correspondence with Duke of Orleans, 450; departure for Italy, 451; two million francs recovered, 451; Albertine's marriage, 451; Coppet in 1816, 453–5; and Byron, 453–4; secret marriage with Rocca, 465–6; last will, 456–7; return to Paris, 457; and Doctrinaires, 457; stroke and death, 458–60; burial, 460

—— and Albert de Staël, 124, 220, 359, 424, 427–9; and Albertine de Stael, 429, 441; and Auguste de Staël, 124, 220, 317, 424, 429; and Prosper de Barante, 319–21, 322–4, 325, 330 ff., 332, 338, 345, 370, 371, 377–8, 404, 406; and Benjamin Constant, 131, 148 ff., 162–3, 169–71; 180–1, 234–8, 239, 250–5, 260–1, 311 ff., 316 ff., 321, 326–35, 340–5, 346–9, 354–5, 368, 369, 372 ff., 391, 425–6, 441, 447–8, 453, 460, 462; and Goethe, 232, 256, 258–9, 359, 396; and Guibert, 51, 72–3; and Mathieu de Montmorency, 97, 98, 120–30 *passim*., 169, 387, 399, 440, 457,

459; and Napoleon, 156, 172 ff., 181, 188, 209–11, 212–15, 217–19, 223, 224, 241, 244–50, 282, 318, 335–6, 349–50, 386–7, 395, 396, 397, 419–22, 442, 448–451; and Narbonne, 91, 104–8, 112–13, 116–31, 428; and Necker, 3–4, 22, 36–9, 43–7, 63–4, 65, 116 ff., 162 ff., 169, 220, 245, 260 ff.; and Madame Necker, 9 ff., 19, 22–3, 24–5, 28–9, 30, 31, 33, 35, 44–7, 57–60, 116 ff., 129, 309; and O'Donnell, 353–60; and François de Pange, 149, 159–63, 165–6; and Madame Récamier, 229, 283–4, 326, 373–4, 399–400; and Ribbing, 130, 149, 155; and Rocca, 400–7, 426, 429, 431–3, 440 ff., 455, 459; and A. W. Schlegel, 265–8, 267 ff., 291–303, 321 ff., 405; and Sismondi, 228–93; and Souza, 303–5, 318 ff., 326; and M. de Staël, 45, 48, 58–62, 72, 92–4, 95, 96, 116–17, 119, 123, 127, 130, 155, 165, 167, 170, 179–83; and Talleyrand, 89–90, 120, 121, 124, 126, 127, 172, 213
—— Writings: diary (1785), 45, 46, 48; *Sophie* (1786–7), 63, 195; *Jane Grey* (1787), 195; *Letters on Rousseau* (1788), 67, 195; *Eulogy of Guibert* (1789), 72, 195; *Reflections on the Trial of the Queen* (1793), 86 n., 125, 148; *Zulma* (1794), 52, 155, 198; *Reflections on Peace* (1794/5), 149, 156, 196; *Adélaïde et Théodore* (1795), 192, 195; *Histoire de Pauline* (1795), 195; *Mirza* (1795), 195; *Essays on Fiction* (1795) 155, 232; *Reflections on Internal Peace* (1795), 161–2; *On the Influence of Passions* (1796), 121, 149, 167, 177, 197, 206; *Jan de Witt* (1797, unpublished), 175; *On the Present Circumstances Capable of Ending the French Revolution* (1799, published 1906), 177, 179; *De la littéra-ture* (1800), 160, 185, 188, 192, 199, 201–11, 219, 228, 230, 251, 289, 310, 381; *Delphine* (1803), 64–5, 66, 67 f., 70, 74, 90, 218, 222–3, 227–35, 241, 255, 309; *M. Necker's Character and Private Life* (1804), 82, 272; *Hagar in the Desert*, (1806), 278, 352; *Corinne* (1807), 53, 69, 70, 188, 191 n., 193, 229, 299–300, 301, 302, 303, 304, 305, 306, 307–10, 323–6, 331–3, 335, 336, 338; *Geneviève de Brabant* (1808), 278, 352; *La Sunamite* (1808), 278; *De l'Allemagne* (1810/13), 69, 188, 203, 254, 255, 261, 375, 376, 380–5, 386–91 (suppression of, by Napo-

leon), 397, 427; *Captain Kernadec* (1810), 403; *La Signora Fantastici* (1811), 403; *Sapho* (1811), 406; *Reflections on Suicide* (1813), 406; 'The Spirit of Translation' (1816), 463; *Richard Coeur de Lion* (un-published fragment), 417, 442; *Considera-tions on the . . . French Revolution* (1818), 76, 109, 110, 176, 205, 219, 381, 439, 442, 448, 453, 457; *Ten Years of Exile* (1821), 213, 219, 414–16, 442

Stein, Karl vom, 418, 420
Stendhal, 301
Suard, Jean Baptiste, 24, 26, 41, 136, 138, 155, 157, 167, 177, 213
Swedenborg, 94

Tacitus, 381
Talleyrand (Talleyrand-Périgord), Charles Maurice de, 51, 98, 99, 102, 124, 173, 175–6, 180, 213, 221, 231, 242, 281, 288, 323, 443; liaison with Mme de Staël, 89–90; as Mme de Vernon, in *Delphine*, 90, 222, 230–3; and Civil Constitution of Clergy, 104; mission to London (1792), 105; on Mme de Staël, 90, 111, 173; at Juniper Hall, 120 ff.; in America, 127; appointed foreign minister, 172; drops Mme de Staël, 217 f.; achieves Bourbon Restoration (1814), 436; under Restora-tion, 438, 443, 449
Tallien, J. L., 115, 151, 153, 155
Tallien, Mme, 231
Talma, François Joseph, 369
Talma, Julie, 238, 314–16, 333
Tambroni, Clotilda, 300
Taube, Baron, 57, 95
Terray, J. M., abbé, 7, 40
Thélusson, Pierre Germain, 7, 8
Thierry, Augustin, 205
Thomas, Antoine Léonard, 25 ff.
Thomson, James, 25, 194
Ticknor, George, 459
Tieck, Friedrich, 365
Tieck, Ludwig, 264, 266–7
Tieck, Sophie, see Bernhardi, Sophie
Tissot, Dr., 128
Tocqueville, Alexis de, 210, 380
Trevor, Mrs., 137, 149
Tronchin, Dr., 20, 31, 35
Tuffiakin, Prince, 281
Turgot, A. R. J., 27, 40–1, 199–200
Tuyll van Serooskerken, Isabelle van, see Charrière, Mme de

Uginet, Joseph, called Eugène, 279, 322, 340, 347, 386, 411, 426
Uginet, Olive, 400

Veit, Brendel, *see* Schlegel, Dorothea
Venet, secret police agent, 127 f., 129
Vergennes, Charles de, 42, 58
Vermenoux, Germaine de, 8, 9, 20
Vernet, Isaac, 6, 7
Vigée-Lebrun, Elisabeth, 281
Villers, Charles de, 251–3, 255
Voght, Caspar von, 281, 365, 371, 377
Voltaire, 5, 17–18, 68, 133, 187, 273, 278, 286, 321, 461; correspondence with Mme Necker, 25, 40; on Galiani, 40; influence on Mme de Staël, 194, 380

Walpole, Horace, 121
Washington, George, 91, 213
Wellington, Duke of, 68, 438, 439, 439 n., 445
Werner, Zacharias, 278, 362–5, 373, 383, 408
Wieland, C. M., 251, 257, 265
Wilberforce, William, 430
Wilde, John, 136

Young, Arthur, 75
Young, Edward, 25, 194

Zuylen, Belle van, *see* Charrière, Mme de